VENICE'S MEDITERRANEAN COLONIES: ARCHITECTURE AND URBANISM

This book examines the architecture and urbanism in the Venetian colonies of the Eastern Mediterranean and how their built environments express the close cultural ties with both Venice and Byzantium. Using the island of Crete and its capital city, Candia (modern Herakleion), as a case study, Maria Georgopoulou exposes the dynamic relationship that existed between colonizer and colony. She studies the administrative, ecclesiastical, and military monuments set up by the Venetian colonists, which served as bold statements of control over the local Greek population and the Jewish communities, who were ethnically, religiously, and linguistically distinct from them. Georgopoulou demonstrates how the Venetian colonists manipulated Crete's past history in order to support and legitimate colonial rule, particularly through the appropriation of older Byzantine traditions in civic and religious ceremonies. At the same time, Crete and the other Mediterranean colonies – and the material goods that they exported to Venice – offered the city the cultural prestige it needed in order to foster a new "imperial image" of the Venetian Republic after the Fourth Crusade of 1204.

Maria Georgopoulou is Associate Professor of Art History at Yale University. A scholar of Byzantine art and architecture and a Getty Postdoctoral Fellow, she has contributed to *The Art Bulletin, The Journal of Medieval and Early Modern Studies,* and *Medieval Encounters.*

VENICE'S MEDITERRANEAN COLONIES

Architecture and Urbanism

MARIA GEORGOPOULOU

Yale University

CAMBRIDGE
UNIVERSITY PRESS

PUBLISHED BY THE PRESS SYNDICATE OF THE UNIVERSITY OF CAMBRIDGE
The Pitt Building, Trumpington Street, Cambridge, United Kingdom

CAMBRIDGE UNIVERSITY PRESS
The Edinburgh Building, Cambridge CB2 2RU, UK
40 West 20th Street, New York, NY 10011-4211, USA
10 Stamford Road, Oakleigh, VIC 3166, Australia
Ruiz de Alarcón 13, 28014 Madrid, Spain
Dock House, The Waterfront, Cape Town 8001, South Africa

http://www.cambridge.org

First published 2001

Printed in the United Kingdom at the University Press, Cambridge

Typefaces Bembo 11.5/14 pt. and Opti Bauer Text-Initials *System* DeskTopPro$_{/UX}$ [BV]

A catalog record for this book is available from the British Library.

Library of Congress Cataloging in Publication Data
Georgopoulou, Maria, 1961–
Venice's Mediterranean colonies : architecture and urbanism / Maria Georgopoulou.
p. cm.
Includes bibliographical references and index.
ISBN 0–521–78235–X (HB)
1. Architecture – Greece – Herakleion – Venetian influences. 2. Architecture and state – Greece – Herakleion. 3. Architecture – Italy – Venice – Byzantine influences. 4. Crete (Greece) – History – Venetian rule, 1204-1669. 5. Byzantine Empire – Civilization – Influence. 6. Herakleion (Greece) – Buildings, structures, etc. I. Title
NA1101.H465 G46 2001
720'.9171'245310902 – dc21 00–046809

ISBN 0 521 78235 X hardback

CONTENTS

ILLUSTRATIONS

PREFACE

The seeds of this project were planted during my graduate studies at the Sorbonne by my adviser, Léon Pressouyre, who, in his unique insight, predicted my fascination with the artistic and cultural relationships among different ethnic groups on Venetian Crete and the Mediterranean at large. The project materialized into a doctoral thesis at UCLA, where its focus was redefined several times thanks to the constructive advice of Irene Bierman, Barisa Krekić, Carlo Pedretti, Speros Vryonis, Jr., and above all my adviser and mentor, Ioli Kalavrezou. I am truly indebted to all of them for their unwavering trust and support.

I am grateful to the Getty Foundation for granting me a Getty Post-Doctoral Fellowship that enabled me to complete a first draft of the manuscript and to my department for giving me leave during that year; to the YCIAS Faculty Research and Griswold Travel Grants of Yale University for awarding me funds for summer travel; and to the Hilles Publication Fund of Yale University for providing support for the index and the illustrations in this volume. Beverly Lett, Tony Oddo, and Sue Roberts of the Yale library have often gone beyond the call of duty to assist me with endless bibliographical issues. I thank them warmly. The stimulating environment of the Department of the History of Art at Yale has contributed a lot to the completion of this book. My colleagues have shared with me their expertise and wisdom to help me sharpen my thoughts and navigate through the world of publishing. I am thankful to them, especially to Walter Cahn, who followed the progress of this book closely. I am also grateful to my students at Yale, whose insightful inquiries played a major role in the crystallization of my thoughts.

A large part of the research for this book was conducted in Venice and Crete. I am indebted to the Istituto Ellenico di Studi Bizantini e Postbizantini in Venice, especially its Directors, Chryssa Maltezou and the late Nikos Panagiotakes, as well as the librarian, Despoina Vlassi, for offering me their hospitality, support, and access to their fine library. I am grateful to the Directors and the staff of the Archivio di Stato di Venezia under the direction of Dr. Maria Francesca Tiepolo and Professore Paolo Selmi; the Biblioteca Marciana and its Director, Marino Zorzi; the Museo Civico Correr under the directorship of Giandomenico Romanelli; and the Istituto Veneto di Scienze, Lettere, ed Arti and its Director, Professore Bruno Zanettin, for their assistance throughout my stay in Venice and their willingness to provide me with archival and photographic material central to my study. I would also like to thank the Ephor of Byzantine Antiquities in Herakleion, Manolis Borboudakis, and the Director of the Historical Museum of Crete, Alexis Kalokairinos, for their assistance with unpublished photographic and archaeological material from Herakleion. The library staff at the University of Crete in Rethymnon were of great help during the early stages of my research. The Gennadius Library in Athens under the direction of Haris Kalligas has proved an exquisite place to work and a wonderful resource for rare books and photographs.

I am greatly indebted to Madeleine Sorapure, who read the first draft of the manuscript a few years back. Her helpful suggestions and encouraging comments convinced me that it was indeed possible to produce a book. The invaluable advice and constructive comments of the readers of this manuscript for Cambridge University Press, Sharon Gerstel, Sally McKee, and Annemarie Weyl Carr, helped me clarify much of my writing and sharpen the focus of the manuscript. I also thank Benjamin Arbel, who read an earlier version of the manuscript for E. J. Brill, for his useful comments. I did my best to respond to the readers' suggestions, but of course I claim responsibility for all the remaining errors.

Over the course of the years I have profited greatly from the advice and support of so many colleagues and friends that it would be impossible to thank them all individually. I apologize if I omitted several persons who have stood by my side at various stages of this project; I am hopeful they will understand. For numerous fruitful discussions that helped shape my thoughts I am thankful to Tony Cutler, Esther da Costa Meyer, Charalambos Gasparis, David Jacoby, Angeliki Laiou, Katerina Mylopotamitaki, Rob Nelson, Bob Ousterhout, Roberta Panzanelli, Aspasia Papadaki, Debra Pincus, Jahan Ramazani, Caroline Rody, Sally Scully, Nancy Ševčenko, Liana Starida, Ioanna Steriotou, Panagiotes Vokotopoulos, and Annabel Wharton. The fellows of the Istituto Ellenico in Venice have been immensely generous with their time during my visits to Venice and eager to act as my delegates when I was away from the archives and monuments. For their warmth and selfless assistance I thank Photis Baroutsos, Rena Papadaki, and Giorgos Pileidis. I am mostly grateful to my extended family in Crete, the Petrakis, without the guidance of whom the mysteries of the island would have remained beyond reach for me.

My editor at Cambridge University Press, Beatrice Rehl, and production editor Holly Johnson, offered me advice and help at critical moments in the life of this project. I thank them for their continuous support. I am grateful to Susan Thornton for her thorough copy-editing and her joyful response to the manuscript. My deepest gratitude goes to my family for their continuing support and encouragement. I would have never been able to travel to Crete and Venice without the conviction that my daughter, Katerina, was happy in the company of her grandparents. I will be eternally grateful to them for cheerfully devoting most of their summers to baby-sitting. Above all I am indebted to my husband, Christos Cabolis, for his love, humor, encouragement, and helpful criticism that brought some mathematical logic into this study. I thank him for never getting tired of this project and, as usual, I will blame him for all the mistakes.

INTRODUCTION: VENICE'S EMPIRE

It has already been repeatedly stated, that the Gothic style had formed itself completely on the main land, while the Byzantines still retained their influence at Venice; and that the history of early Venetian Gothic is therefore not that of a school taking new forms independently of external influence, but the history of the struggle of the Byzantine manner with a contemporary style quite as perfectly organized as itself, and far more energetic. And this struggle is exhibited partly in the gradual change of the Byzantine architecture into other forms, and partly by isolated examples of genuine Gothic, taken prisoner, as it were, in the contest; or rather entangled among the enemy's forces, and maintaining their ground till their friends came up to sustain them.

John Ruskin[1]

From the fascination with the merging of cultural traditions in Venice to the true admiration of Byzantine elements in Venetian art of the Middle Ages, the writings of John Ruskin set the tone for much of what is still generally perceived as the cultural relationship between Venice and Byzantium. The architecture and decoration of the San Marco basilica have been admirably explored by Otto Demus and other art historians to offer excellent insights into the workings of Byzantine artistic currents in Venetian architecture, sculpture, and the art of mosaics.[2] When the subject of inquiry is Byzantium's legacy on public and domestic architecture, however, current scholarship still follows Ruskin's tracks.[3] When these "byzantinisms" are addressed, they come, one feels, directly from Ruskin's works and are presented as purely formal incrustations without any deeper cultural meaning. For instance, a page from the *Stones of Venice* entitled "The Orders of Venetian Arches" still stands as the normative visual aid for identifying and dating the Venetian palazzi (Fig. 1). Yet, we implicitly assume that the translation of Byzantine architectural or decorative forms into a Venetian vocabulary had a particular cultural and perhaps also political significance because within the sociohistorical framework of the Venetian maritime empire these formal elements pointed to the Byzantine empire and its cultural supremacy. By the same token, the presence of Venetian (read Gothic) architectonic and decorative forms on the soil of Venice's colonies would have the opposite effect, that is, to boast Venetian hegemony overseas. This overly simplified view of artistic encounters played out within the context of Venice and its empire may be enriched by an inclusive look at the colonies of Venice as agents that were shaped by Venetian rule and that in their turn molded the metropole herself.

From the legendary foundation of Venice in 421 to the Fourth Crusade of 1204 the status of Venice vis-à-vis Byzantium changed dramatically.[4] Originally a dependency of the exarchate of Ravenna, by 751 Venice was turned over to the Byzantines. Venice remained under their jurisdiction until the ninth century, when she sought her independence from Byzantium by proclaiming herself a *civitas*. To boost these claims of independence the Venetians forged a sacred history for their city by raising the cult of the relics of St. Mark, stolen from Alexandria in 828, to a state religion. The depository of these relics, the new eleventh-century basilica of San Marco, was modeled after the celebrated Constantinopolitan church of the Holy Apostles, and as the chapel of the doge it became a major symbol of the city of the lagoon (Fig. 2). At the same time Venice established its commercial authority in the Mediterranean by securing privileges and tax exemptions from the Byzantines in the form of imperial decrees (*chrysobulls*) and by building a formidable fleet.[5] The tables were turned in favor of Venice in 1204 when the Venetians urged the crusaders to attack Constantinople and to plunder the city for treasures.

The significance of the Fourth Crusade for Venice cannot be overstated. The Republic transformed herself from a small state into a superpower: she had multiplied her territorial holdings, was the leader in Mediterranean trade, and claimed hegemonic rights over Byzantium.[6] An overview of the artistic remains in the Venetian colonies along the Adriatic and the Aegean coastline reveals port cities, such as the Dalmatian cities of Zara/Zadar and Ragusa/Dubrovnik and the Greek cities of Modon/Methoni, Candia/Herakleion, Corfu/Kerkyra, and Negropone/Chalkis, endowed with Latin churches dedicated to the patron saint of Venice, as well as with impressive fortifications, palaces, and loggias adorned with effigies of the lion of St. Mark. A collective view of the architecture of these towns sends a clear message even today: these places belonged to Venice's empire as they partook in its architectural tradition. All these monuments seem to proclaim the submission of indigenous cultural traditions to the religious, political, and

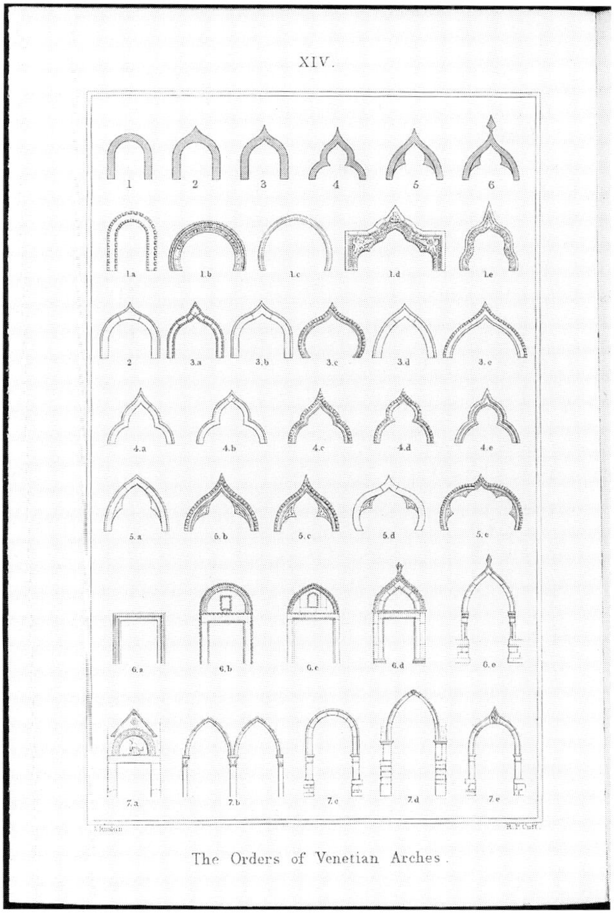

FIGURE 1. Orders of Venetian windows, John Ruskin, *Stones of Venice*, vol. 2 (1851), pl. XIV (Beinecke Rare Book and Manuscript Library, Yale University)

architectural heritage of the mother city. But this transformation was a gradual process, which was not completed until the sixteenth century, when many of the fortifications were erected. How did Venice set the foundations of its rule in the Eastern Mediterranean in the course of the thirteenth century? While in most instances of modern colonization there is a violent imposition of the "national" traditions of the metropole, which overtake the local heritage of each colony, the Venetian colonies exemplify a different pattern an exchange of cultural forms that allowed the colonizers to maintain a smooth transition from the former Byzantine to the new Venetian hegemony.

The term that the Venetians use to designate their maritime empire, the

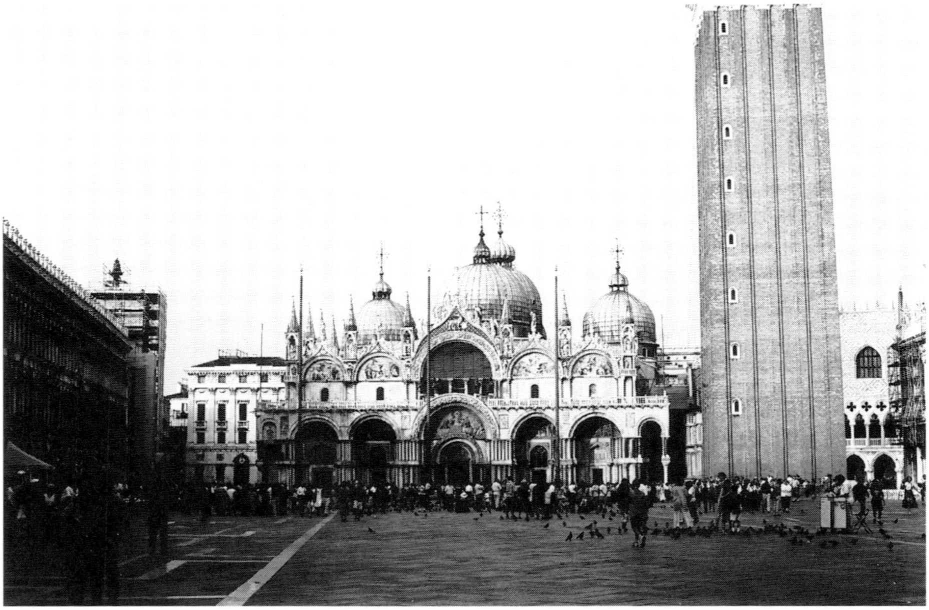

FIGURE 2. Venice, basilica of San Marco, western façade

Oltremare, stresses the distance between Venice and its colonies along the coast of the Adriatic, the Ionian, and the Aegean Seas. The strong mark that these colonies left on Venice, however, suggests that they functioned as extensions of Venice herself well beyond the economic sphere. The carefully arranged system of commercial maritime convoys constituted a well-trod communication path between Venice and its colonies in the Eastern Mediterranean and has been adequately explored by scholars.[7] Just as goods, merchants, and pilgrims traveled this path so did intellectual and artistic ideas. But this communication path was a two-way street. The complexity of this colonial reciprocity as it is exemplified in architecture has been already addressed by Ruskin, albeit obliquely: for him the hybridity of forms in the ducal palace made it "the 'central building of the world' offering an imperial model for architecture."[8] It comes as no surprise that an Englishman of the Victorian era would look to Venice for imperial models for Great Britain as the parallel that the maritime empire of Venice offered to that of the British is striking. What is surprising is the extent to which the study of the relations between Venetian and Byzantine culture is usually confined to Venice and Constantinople and neglects the rest of the Venetian and Byzantine commonwealth.[9] This study seeks to broaden this horizon by bringing to the fore the complex relationship between Venice and its colonies, focusing on the exchange and transfer of cultural forms from and to the metropole. The lasting traces of Greek/Byzantine heritage in Venice confirm the fact that her colonial expansion in earlier Byzantine territories offered the Venetians the necessary economic, ideological, and cultural capital to define themselves as an imperial entity.[10] As the buildings sponsored by Greeks, Armenians, Albanians, and Slavs in Venice indicate, the metropole was the destination of numerous immigrants (merchants, but also artists and scholars) from its former colonies.[11] These people were by no means outcasts, as was often the case in the modern colonial empires. The dominion of Venice cast its net widely: it incorporated customs, practices, and forms peculiar to the colonies directly into the heart of the metropole. Thus, the inquiry into the architectural styles in Venice and its colonies proves a slippery ground as it drifts between the familiar and the foreign: was Venice's Byzantine façade a result of the colonial experience? Was there in the minds of the people a clear, meaningful distinction between "Byzantine" (i.e. Eastern, Christian Orthodox, Greek) and "Gothic" (i.e. Western, Latin Catholic, Venetian) forms? Finally, how were the colonies constructed in the rhetoric of the Venetian regime and in the minds of the colonists living in the Oltremare?

Crete is a prime case study for these considerations because it was the first full-fledged colony of the Venetians. The island's geographic position at the crossroads of three continents provided a strategic base for the growing Venetian maritime empire, which was made up of a network of outposts. Crete was situated on the crossing of the major maritime routes that connected, on the one hand, Constantinople with Alexandria and, on the other hand, the Western Mediterranean Sea with Syria (Fig. 3).[12] The Venetians ruled Crete for four and a half centuries (1211–1669), a period during which the island became an important commercial center in the Eastern Mediterranean, with agricultural and artistic products renowned in the East and West.[13] Drawing on the works of political, economic, and social historians of the Venetian maritime empire as well as on archival material, my work centers on the buildings, architecture, and art that the Venetians set up in the colony's capital city, Candia (Byzantine Chandax/modern Herakleion), in relation to their urban setting and use. The issues of urban planning and civic practices revealed by the study of these buildings and their topographical relationships speak to the realities of colonization and address several points about which the governmental records are mute. Not only is the identity of the users of the built environment in a colonial setting by definition multicultural, but the very act of erecting buildings in a colonial territory is a process that problematizes notions of neatly organized categories according to ethnicity or cultural background: in many cases the patron was a Venetian colonist (or the state authorities) but the masons and architects were locals.[14] Moreover, the topographical arrangement of a colonial town by directing movement through streets or squares and by controlling access to civic resources prescribes specific perceptions of power relations within the urban space. By analyzing these issues this study seeks to bridge the distance between Venice and Candia and to understand better the impact of Venetian imperialism on the colonies and the metropole. Although the bulk of the archival material applies to the city of Candia, six other colonies in the area of the Aegean will also be surveyed here to flesh out more fully the outlook and meaning of architecture and urbanism within Venice's Mediterranean empire.

The focus is on the formative period of Venetian colonization, that is the first three centuries of Venetian rule in the Levant and on Crete in particular (roughly 1204 to 1500). Although it will often be necessary to look at documents, objects, and structures of the sixteenth and seventeenth centuries to supplement incomplete archaeological and archival information, the considerable change in the urban fabric of the city that occurs around the year 1500 offers a natural break point in the architectural and urban outlook of Candia and most of the Venetian colonies. The fall of Constantinople to the Ottoman Turks in 1453, the collapse of the Byzantine empire, and the increasing Ottoman threat in the Mediterranean modified the role of Crete in international politics. With the islands of Crete and Cyprus remaining the only strongholds of Christianity in the Levant, Venice could no longer afford the open display of hostility toward its subjects in the area that it could in the past.[15] The extensive archival material on Crete shows that the Republic made significant concessions to its non-Latin inhabitants that resulted in a new modus vivendi for the population of the island, a climate of creative coexistence between Latins and Greeks. Moreover, in the sixteenth century the medieval appearance of the cities was gradually transformed to accommodate technological developments in warfare as well as new architectural projects that followed the model of Renaissance Venice, using "state" architects and the lessons learned from the newly available architectural treatises.[15] My study tries to reconstruct and understand the appearance of the city that preceded this Renaissance homogenization of the urban centers. In this context the case of Negroponte/Chalkis, which fell to the Ottomans in 1460, is particularly instructive because it does not display the grand Venetian fortification schemes of the early modern period.

Thinking about all this in our postcolonial frame of mind it is easy to theorize about the architecture of empire and the overwhelming power that urbanistic and architectural associations with the metropole had on the fabric of the colony. Indeed, numerous examples of urbanistic and architectural choices of the Venetian colonial authorities confirm schemes that have been observed in modern imperial configurations.[17] As soon as the Venetians

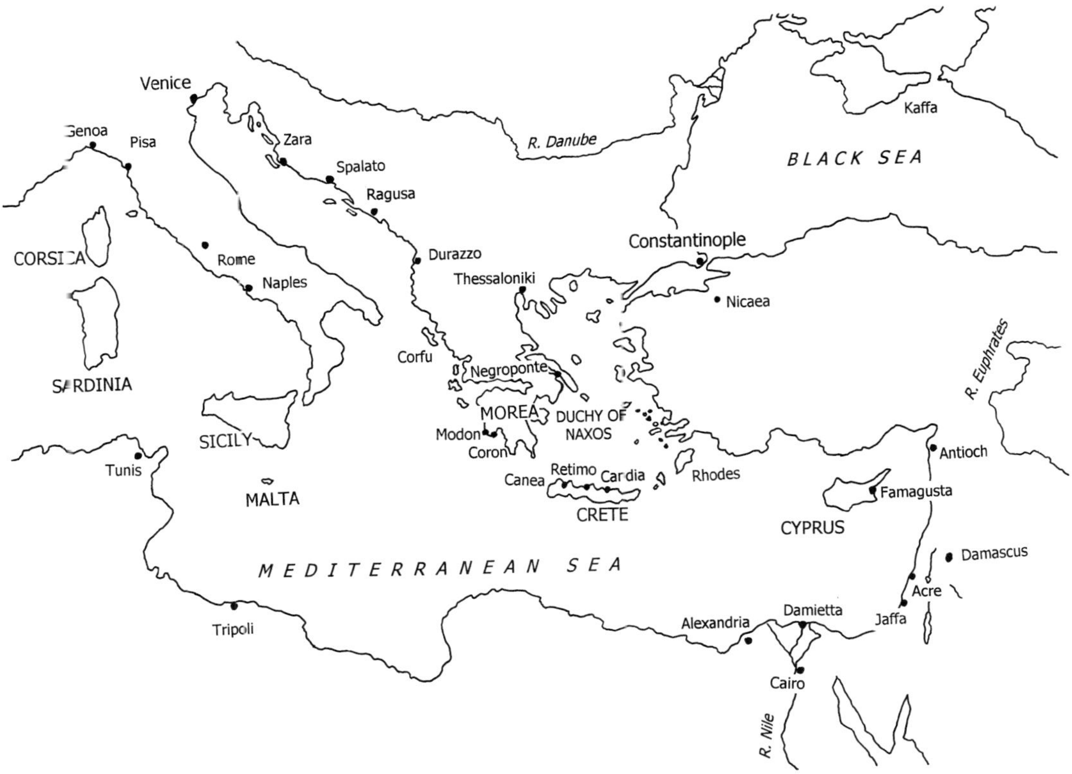

FIGURE 3. Map of the Eastern Mediterranean

settled Crete for instance, they reorganized the capital city, Candia, to satisfy the needs of the colonists. The other major centers of the island, Canea, Rethymnon, and Sitia, followed soon. In all colonies large administrative monuments housed the Venetian government and new large Western churches served the Latin population. Candia, Canea, and, to a lesser degree, Retimo/Rethymnon, Modon/Methoni, and Coron/Koroni had ports that could support the exigencies of international trade and the burden of maintaining or constructing a war fleet in their arsenals. As important centers for international and local trade these cities became poles of attraction for merchants and professionals of Venetian, Latin, or other origin. In line with that of all major harbors of the Mediterranean their population was multiethnic: Latins/Venetians, Greeks, Jews, and a few Armenians (immigrants of the midfourteenth century) figure prominently among the residents of Venetian Candia. While the hinterland was populated primarily by Greeks, in the urban centers the Venetians constituted a considerable part of the population, which, nonetheless, never outnumbered the locals.[18] Each colonized city with its political, economic, social, and religious institutions was essential in the construction of this empire, so it is paramount to identify the processes of cultural negotiation generated in these colonies, and the contention of this study is that much of this is borne out in the physical appearance of the cities.

As in other multicultural cities in the Mediterranean religious monuments occupy a unique position in this symbolic appropriation and colonization of urban space. The two dominant groups in the Venetian colonies, Venetians and Greeks, adhered to two competing Christian rites: Catholic Latin and Greek Orthodox. The differences between the two rites were especially acute in the wake of the Fourth Crusade and the sack of Constantinople by the crusaders. After all, the dissolution of the Byzantine empire and the formation of Venice's colonial empire were the prize for the Republic's involvement in the crusade. Even if the chroniclers of the Fourth Crusade accused the Venetians of having participated merely for economic and political purposes, Latin Christianity had been a significant component of the image of the Republic after the schism between the Eastern and Western churches in 1054.[19] For the Greek population Western Christianity was linked with the pope and insurmountable differences in doctrinal matters prevented a rapprochement between the Latin and Orthodox rites. For the Venetians, on the other hand, the Eastern rite embodied a dangerous tie with the Byzantine empire. Orthodoxy represented a spiritual cause for rebellion and a unifying force for local resistance against the Venetian lords. To prevent such revolts and contacts between the Greek clergy and the Orthodox patriarchate of Constantinople, the Republic banned the Byzantine metropolitan and the Orthodox bishops of Crete and replaced them with Latin prelates: the major ecclesiastical authority on Crete was the Latin archbishop of Candia.[20] Only Orthodox priests of a lower rank were allowed in the Venetian colonies and they had to endure a complicated ordination process.[21] Having officially proclaimed religious tolerance in the document that handed Crete over to the colonists in 1211 (the *Concessio Crete*), the Venetians placed the church of the island under the jurisdiction of the Latin patriarch of Constantinople, maintaining the framework of the preexisting ecclesiastical structure in the former Byzantine territories.[22]

Despite the concerted efforts of the authorities to establish a rigid administrative and political apparatus that controlled the locals, the colonial enterprise of the Venetians does not appear as a straightforward military campaign against the colonized peoples. An analysis of civic ceremonial, economic interaction, artistic production, and religious practices illustrates how the city was used by the various social and ethnic groups and suggests new ways of interpreting its meaning for both its designers and its users. In contrast to the binarism that characterizes earlier studies on Crete, this study attempts to uncover the instances of interaction and blurring of boundaries between the new settlers and the indigenous people. The issues that such an approach confronts are the formation of community identity before the advent of nationalism, the significance of a cultural/artistic style for defining a social or ethnic group, and the exchange/appropriation of cultural forms. As the studies of Sally McKee have shown, the first centuries of Venetian rule in Crete have to be looked at very carefully because they provide prime examples of multiethnic and polyglot societies that challenge our traditional understanding of two constantly competing cultures.[23] The illuminating cases that McKee explores in her work come from a deep knowledge of the notarial material and a commitment to understanding history from the bottom up, so to speak. The economic, civic, and social relations of Latins and Greeks in the fourteenth century show "diminishing distinctions between [the] communities."[24] For her, ethnic identity in Venetian Crete seems to be a purely practical matter of a legal stature. My own work differs in that although there is no doubt that to a certain extent the population experienced a common "material life," I believe that the physical world that the Venetians constructed in Candia embodied a colonial framework that promoted Venetian hegemony. A daily encounter with such a landscape presented an uneven environment for Greeks and Venetians in Candia even if in the testaments of the Latins, for instance, we detect a nexus of social relations, economic interactions, and emotional attachments to their Greek family members and servants.[25]

At this point I should clarify the usage of *Byzantine* and *Greek* in this study. I use the term *Byzantine* to refer to the population and institutions of the Byzantine empire, including the inhabitants of Crete before the arrival of the Venetians in 1211. In relation to buildings, the term *Byzantine* alludes to structures built before 1204, or to churches whose form followed the Byzantine artistic tradition. On the other hand, the term *Greek* is used to designate the Greek-speaking, Orthodox Christian community of the Venetian colonies after 1204. The parallel existence of the Latin and Greek communities in Crete created peculiar conditions for the cultural development in the late medieval and Renaissance period, observed primarily in language, literature, architecture, and art. To the degree that artistic products created at the same time in the same place are based on common grounds, the art of these ethnic groups inevitably shared many technical, iconographic, and stylistic features. There are indeed examples of unique artistic trends of Cretan origin, especially in painting, literature, and theater, which are known as the *Cretan school*.[26] The last centuries of Venetian rule on Crete witnessed an especially pronounced symbiosis between the two communities. Following 1453 religious and ethnic differences lost their importance in the urban societies of Crete, which were increasingly stratified by class.[27]

The architecture and urban planning of the Venetians in their colonies in relation to the architecture commissioned by non-Latins are seen here as a means to mitigate conflict among the diverse population groups of the city while still embodying Venetian colonial ideology. Examples of a cultural rapprochement between Greeks and Latins abound in the arts of Crete but are still not perfectly understood. For instance, Western architectural features and artistic styles of painting appear on many of the Orthodox churches of Crete from the second quarter of the fourteenth century.[28] And the image of a purely Western saint, Saint Francis, shows up at least four times in wall paintings of the fourteenth and fifteenth centuries in Byzantine rural churches of Crete.[29] Are we to follow Gerola's suggestion that the asceticism of St. Francis appealed to Orthodox monks?[30] Or should we imagine that the patrons of these churches were products of a mixed marriage of a Greek and a Latin or some other cross-ethnic relationship with another member of the household, to include an otherwise "foreign" saint in their church? Only multiple prosopographic studies, which surely can be generated from careful scrutiny of the extensive unpublished notarial material, may give us a clearer picture of the role that the colonized people played in this context.[31] In the absence of such collective information I have tried to reconstruct the physical and symbolic landscape of each colony by situating the different publics of the city – its designers, everyday users, and visitors – at a variety of positions so that we may see the topographical features and architecture of the city from multiple viewpoints. Buildings commissioned by Greeks and to a lesser extent by Jews, as well as one Armenian church in Candia, are placed vis-à-vis the Venetian urban monuments to establish their history, appearance, location, and function, as well as their symbolic presence in the city.

As in any colonial city, the architectural metamorphosis of Candia (which is taken here as the most sophisticated example of Venetian colonial rule) – apparent in the names, form, and placement of buildings and their linkage to, or exclusion from, official civic practices – made a strong hegemonic statement in favor of the rulers. What sets Candia apart from later colonialist enterprises is the systematic incorporation of local heritage into the colonial "language" of Venice. In Candia, enough Byzantine structures remained in place to suggest that the Venetians made a concerted effort to present their rule not as a mere military conquest over the Byzantines, but rather as a continuation of imperial Byzantine administration. The topographical characteristics of Candia and the legendary "hagiographies" that favored the settlement of the colonists on the island exemplify how the Venetian authorities incorporated preexisting structures (i.e. political symbols, cultural treasures, administrative and religious buildings) in their rule to forge a history of Crete that fitted their imperial aspirations. The special kinship between the Republic and Byzantine culture in the centuries prior to the Fourth Crusade served as a basis for the success of the colonial strategies of the Venetians. Unlike other colonizers in the period of the crusades, the Venetians knew and admired Byzantine culture; in order to undermine Byzantine presence, they assimilated it into their own rhetoric in an attempt to present themselves as the lawful successors of Byzantium on Crete. The colonial ideology of the Venetians entailed a carefully orchestrated equilibrium between the demonstration of absolute power by the colonists and the display of gracious concessions to the colonized. Although manifest in other facets of colonial presence as well (political, religious, ethnic, social, mercantile, and linguistic), this ideological construction is observable above all in the urban layout of Candia.

Throughout the book the architectural and urban profile of the colony takes center stage in its historical, civic, social, religious, professional, cultural, and artistic dimensions. Architectural designs and spatial patterns or the use of buildings and urban sites by resident communities of various ethnic backgrounds evoke and explicate patterns of social and historical behavior. All these suggest that the Venetian period was a time of interaction, rather than constant clash, among the different ethnic communities. I argue that the medieval heritage of polyvalent, multiethnic cities like Candia as exploited and outfitted by the Venetian colonists offers us a glimpse into the workings of the first systematic colonialist effort of the early modern period: to portray their major colonies as extensions of the Most Serene Republic of Venice. In Crete, this successful colonial experiment not only lasted for a long period, but also set the basis for and bolstered a unique phenomenon in the art, literature, and theatre of early modern Greece, the *Cretan Renaissance*, in the sixteenth and seventeenth centuries.[32] After all, the most famous of Crete's sons in the sixteenth century was Domenico Theotokopoulos, a painter born and trained in Candia who traveled to Italy (Venice and Rome) and finally immigrated to Spain, where he became famous as The Greek (El Greco).[33]

PART ONE

CONSTRUCTING AN EMPIRE

ONE

THE CITY AS LOCUS OF COLONIAL RULE

I believe that one of the major tasks (of a ruler) is to know how to maintain the loyalty of the people and the subjugated cities, how to avoid and resist all the evils that can sometimes incite rebellion. Such vices are peculiar to every city and nation, but happen primarily and more frequently in newly conquered cities and nations whose native language is different from that of the ruler. Because people obey more easily a fellow countryman than a foreigner. . . . So, even the slightest opportunity is enough to instigate a fight to shake off the yoke.

The princes have thought of diverse strategies to deal with this evil. But I would think that nothing is more secure than what the Romans have already done: as soon as a city came under their jurisdiction, they elected a number of their own people that seemed sufficient, and they sent them to inhabit [the city]. And these were called colonies. This practice produced an infinite number of good results, and was the reason why the cities became populous, why damaged buildings were restored and why in some cases other new cities were founded; empty spaces were filled with laborers, and uncultivated land was rendered fertile; the arts flourished, trade increased, the new inhabitants became wealthy, the locals were loyal, and thus the people could live securely without fear of being disturbed by foreign or domestic enemies.

Antonio Calergi[1]

In the words of the sixteenth-century chronicler Antonio Calergi the Venetian colonization of Crete is projected as a continuation of antique practices as if the strategies of the Romans were current in the late Middle Ages. In fact this rhetoric does not reflect the realities of the thirteenth century, when the Venetians struggled to invent a system to sustain their newly amplified maritime enterprise. This is apparent above all in the physical appearance of the colonies and the monuments that adorned them. The first concrete reference to monuments in the colonies dates to 1252: a unique text containing prescriptions from the doge for rebuilding the city of Canea instructs the colonists to found public squares, administrative buildings, a main street (*ruga magistra*), one or more (Latin rite) churches, and city walls:

> Cum itaque a nobus ordinatum sit, quod civitas fieri *debeat* in dicta terra Puncte de Spata, et dicto capitaneo et consciliariis iniunxerimus et comiserimus, quod civitatem Chanee rehedificare. . . . Et sciendum est, quod, sicut comisimus dicto capitaneo et eius consciliariis, debet idem cum suis consciliariis vel altero eorum accipere ante partem in civitate pro comuni plateas pro domo et domibus comunis et ruga magistra et ecclesia seu ecclesiis et municionibus hedificandis, sicut eidem capitaneo et eius consciliariis vel ipsi capitaneo et uni ex ipsius consciliariis bonum videbitur; et muros dicte civitatis facient capitaneus et consciliariii hedificari, et pro ipsis hedificandis et foveis civitatis seu aliis munitionibus faciendis rusticos dictarum partium habere et angarizare debent, scilicet unum rusticum pro qualibet militia, sicut idem capitaneus et sui consciliarii vel ipse capitaneus eu unus illorum voluerint.[2]

Forty years after the establishment of the first Venetian colony on Crete (Candia), the doge Marino Morosini defined a new Venetian colonial city as an ensemble of public official structures and Latin churches that were closely related to the state. A comparison of this detailed enumeration of specific architectural elements with the first charter of colonization composed in 1211 for the settling of the western and central part of Crete, the so-called *Concessio insulae Cretensis*, reveals tons about the sophistication in Venice's colonial approach as the thirteenth century progressed.[3] In 1211 there is no mention of urban features and monuments; the colonial city was still not a realized focus of Venetian rhetoric for the first colonists who were sent to Crete. The 1252 document represents a mature understanding of the essential components of the Venetian colonial city, which now consists of distinct urban spaces that presumably work for the success of the colony.

Moreover, this document emphasizes the crucial role that the city played in the imperial strategy of the Venetians. Cities had formed the core of Venice's mercantile involvement with the Levant from the twelfth century. Not only did the Venetians have emporia on many coastal cities on the shore of Palestine, but they also had especially designated quarters in Constantinople and Acre that took advantage of the tax exempt status that was accorded them by the Byzantine emperors in 1082 and 1147.[4] These quarters provided the Venetian merchants and their families with places to gather as a community, including a church typically dedicated to St. Mark, a palace for the leader of the community (*podestà* or *bailo*), as well as mercantile facilities such as loading docks and warehouses. These localities were highly important to the establishment and betterment of Venetian commercial activities overseas, but they also offered the citizens of the Republic a haven away from home. The original quarter of the Venetians in the region of Perama in Constantinople (created in 1082) was expanded in 1147 to accommodate the growing population of Venetians in the capital of the Byzantine empire.[5] Until the third quarter of the twelfth century this quarter sealed the monopoly of the Venetian merchants in Constantinopolitan trade. By the year 1200 they were in possession of two churches, St. Mark de Embulo (of the market) and St. Akindynos.[6] Nevertheless, these quarters within the cities of the Byzantine empire were not real colonies of Venice, as many of their inhabitants seemed to be transient and the very existence of the colony itself depended on the flow of international politics. For instance, in the year 1171 the emperor Manuel Komnenos reportedly arrested twenty thousand Venetians throughout the Byzantine empire in response to Venice's alliance with Hungary for the recapture of Dalmatia.[7]

In the wake of the Fourth Crusade Venice followed similar settlement patterns in her new colonies and outposts along the coast of the Adriatic, the Ionian, and the Aegean Seas. On the one hand, the port cities of the territories left to the Byzantines continued to serve as entrepots where Venetian merchants had special trading posts. The treaty between the ruler of the Byzantine despotate of Epirus, Michael Komnenos, and the Venetians in 1210 is indicative of the kinds of services the Venetians expected to find in such an entrepot: "habere ecclesiam et curiam et fondicum et omnes alias honorificentias tam in spiritualibus, quam in temporalibus, quas habebant tempore domini Emanuelis Imperatoris."[8] On the other hand, the majority of the coastal territories were nominally colonies of the Venetians: Zara (Zadar), Ragusa (Dubrovnik), Corfu (Kerkyra, which was originally under Angevin control and was finally taken by the Venetians in 1386), Cephallonia, Zante (Zakynthos), Modon (Methoni), Coron (Koroni), Cerigo (Kythera), Crete, Negroponte (Euboea), many of the Aegean islands (Cyclades), and eventually Cyprus. The position of each locality within the trade system of the Mediterranean and the degree of involvement that the Republic intended to have with the colony's hinterland determined the adoption of varied governing solutions for each place (Fig. 3). The Aegean Cycladic islands (known also as the *Archipelago*), for instance, formed the Duchy of Naxos, a political entity where each of the islands was governed by a different Venetian overlord.[9] The island of Negroponte, which was perceived as a buffer zone between the Byzantines and the regions of central Greece and the Peloponnesos, was nominally a Venetian colony, which until the end of the fourteenth century was the fiefdom of three Veronese barons, the *Terzieri*, who were vassals of the doge.[10] The towns of Modon and Coron, which were vital lookouts for the navigation of the waters in the southern

Ionian and Aegean Seas, remained in Venetian hands much longer than any other of their colonies in Romania. They were referred to as the "eyes" of the Republic because of their strategic position in the southern tip of the Peloponnesos at the point of convergence of the maritime routes to Syria and to the Black Sea. The Venetian convoys stopped there to get supplies and information and to repair the ships in the arsenals on their way to the Eastern Mediterranean. Crete with its hinterland rich in agricultural resources and wood was fully colonized.

THE ACQUISITION OF CRETE

Crete had been given to the leader of the Fourth Crusade, the marquis Boniface of Montferrat, by the Byzantine emperor Alexios Angelos as a token for his help in establishing the Byzantine emperor Isaak II on the throne before the crusaders captured Constantinople.[11] In 1204 Boniface sold the island to the Venetians for 1,000 marks of silver in order to assure the support of the Republic in his dispute with the Latin emperor, Baldwin of Flanders.[12] The Venetians had already been assigned the islands of the Archipelago, so the acquisition of Crete was critical for the establishment of their maritime hegemony in the Aegean. The Republic, being engaged in establishing her rule in her new possessions in Byzantium, did not send armed forces to Crete immediately after 1204.[13] The imposition of Venetian rule on the island was not easy, however, because the Genoese, who, like the Venetians, must have also used the port of Chandax (the Byzantine name of Candia) as a stopover on the way to Constantinople in the second half of the twelfth century, were also keen on taking control of Crete.[14] In 1206 a pirate assault led by Enrico Pescatore, count of Malta, and supported by the Genoese succeeded in occupying Crete. No Venetian presence is recorded in the sources – mostly chronicles – which state that the only opposition Pescatore encountered in Crete came from the local population. Profiting from the absence of a Venetian army, the Genoese of Pescatore established their presence on the island by reinforcing or building fourteen castles: Mirabello, Monforte, Bonifacio, Castelnuovo, Belriparo, Milopotamo, Pediada, Priotissa, Belvedere, Malvesin, Gerapetra, Chissamo, Bicorna, and Temene (or S. Niccolò).[15] The Venetian reaction was not slow in coming this time. In the summer of 1206 the Republic sent a fleet of thirty-one galleys to Crete under the command of Ranieri Dandolo and Ruggiero Premarino. After an unsuccessful attempt to reconquer the island, the two commanders were sent back to Crete in 1207 and occupied its capital city, Chandax, after a fierce fight.[16] Pescatore managed to hold his territory on the island against the Venetians until the Venetian fleet and army under the leadership of the new duke of Crete, Jacopo Tiepolo, arrived in 1209. Trying to boost Pescatore's efforts against the Venetians, in 1210 the Genoese offered him privileges, but the count was forced to concede the island to the Venetians at the beginning of 1211.[17]

After five years of fighting for Crete and cognizant of its strategic importance, the Venetians realized that it was not enough to oversee the ports and to establish emporia in the cities: they had to impose their direct political and economic control over the whole island. The consolidation of Venetian rule proved particularly difficult, however, because the local population resisted it fiercely. This presented a major problem for the Venetians, who, in addition to the wars against Genoa and the Byzantines, had to man a skillful navy to safeguard the Mediterranean voyages of their commercial fleet.[18] The Republic could not afford the additional cost of maintaining a regular army stationed on Crete, so she opted for the solution of a landed aristocracy of colonizers who were to defend the island militarily.

VENETIAN COLONIALISM

Crete stands as a unique case in the maritime possessions of the Venetians, but the extent and longevity of the Venetian empire indicate that the Venetians found effective ways to "package" their authority in territories away from the metropole, first in the Levant (Oltremare) and later on the Italian peninsula (Terraferma).[19] In general, relatively few Venetians moved to the colonies (roughly up to ten percent of the whole population) and when they did so they lived almost exclusively within the limits of the towns.[20] A Venetian was placed at the head of the colony and the colonists spoke their own language and lived according to the customs and laws of the metropole, observing the same feast days as in Venice and recognizing St. Mark as their patron saint. Only occasionally did the Venetian settlers form close ties with the locals.[21] In many ways, therefore, this system may be compared to the modern colonialist empires of the French and the British.

Nevertheless, the discourse of modern imperialism seems to have little resonance for earlier periods.[22] The application of its models to a precapitalist society questions the validity of certain definitions and theoretical paradigms used in the context of modern colonialism. A crucial question needs to be raised at the onset: can we speak of colonialism in the thirteenth century?[23] First and foremost, the absence of a racially informed agenda against the colonized peoples makes Venetian imperialism less systematic than its modern counterparts about invalidating local culture.[24] Furthermore, in contrast to most colonial situations, the Byzantine empire was not a completely foreign territory for the Venetians. Indeed, the cultural kinship between Venetians and Byzantines/Greeks makes Venetian colonies stand apart from later colonial enterprises. Yet, the administration, politics, and ideology of the Venetian imperial enterprise were similar to modern colonialism. A cogent administrative apparatus of governors and their associates that was closely overseen by the metropole duplicated the organizational and linguistic schemes of the metropole and stressed the coherence of the Venetian empire. Moreover, layers of symbolism embedded in religious associations or calendrical choices (e.g. the decision not to adopt the Gregorian calendar in the colonies in 1582)[25] transformed economic transactions and political choices into significant symbolic expressions meant to subdue the indigenous population to colonial authority.

Along the same lines distinct public spaces and certain architectural symbols defined a city as part of the Venetian maritime empire. The built environment of a colonial settlement works by definition as an agent that mediates social strife. The allocation of space and the prescription of architectural norms are in the hands of a foreign ruling elite, but the built environment addresses two audiences at the same time: the colonists and the colonized. The masters of a new colony usually take their own artistic style with them (often along with architects and artists) in order to recreate individual elements and whole spatial units of the metropole in their newly acquired territory. In this way, the settlers feel at home, and, perhaps more importantly, the locals are constantly reminded of who is in charge. It is usually only after many years of successful colonial rule, when the supremacy and confidence of the colonizers have been established, that a hybrid style allowing for the intrusion of local elements may occur in the monuments of the colony.

By creating a framework within which the city dwellers function, the urban environment plays a major role in defining the parameters of life within the city. If the intentions of a city's architect shape its built environment, they also affect the way its inhabitants view and use the city space. Along with its designer, the inhabitants of a given city create their own meanings by taking possession of and by changing the urban environment according to their needs and aspirations. Thus, the creation of meaning is a question of personalizing the built environment, a question of power and control, a latent (or open) clash between the various publics of the city. Consequently, no city is neutral in terms of meaning. Meaning for whom, however? A city has a different meaning for its designers and for its users, on the one hand, and it has multiple meanings for its inhabitants, depending on their political, social, and economic status, on the other.[26] Matters become even more complicated when the population consists of different ethnic groups that do not equally share the control of city resources, as in the case of a colonial society. The less homogeneous a society is, the more meanings the cityscape has for its users.

Obviously, there are parts of the urban environment where the designers' meaning is more permanent; this is the case of the public official spaces, be they military, administrative, or religious structures. The institutional character of these establishments and their close association with the authorities – who in the Middle Ages were usually identified with the designers of the urban environment – prevent the users of the city from modifying the already established meanings of these structures for the different publics. Only a change in the sociocultural conditions would bring about a modification in the meaning of these structures. On the other hand, the meaning of private dwellings is less easily controllable by the designer of the city and thus cannot be imposed from above. Here it would be beneficial to bring to mind Michel de Certeau's brilliant distinction between strategies and tactics: those in power can have a concrete, long-term plan, i.e. a strategy, while the weak can only act through small-scale, short-term, isolated actions, i.e. tactics (or trickeries). It follows that strategies are related to place, they have a definite *locus*, and they are more or less "independent with respect to the variability of the circumstances," whereas tactics are connected with time (or circumstances), they take place in "the space of the other," and they "are organized by the law of a foreign power."[27]

ARCHAEOLOGICAL CONSIDERATIONS

When we think about the archaeological record in the context of de Certeau's analysis we are struck by the disparities in the material at hand. In the core of this study stand grand defensive, administrative, and religious structures not only because they commanded a significant urban space but also because they are showcased nowadays by local authorities as major tourist attractions. The outlook of a city, however, may depend to a large degree on unpretentious domestic structures that make up the bulk of the urban fabric. As in most medieval towns that have outlasted the Middle Ages, few remains of domestic architecture can still be detected in the cities of Crete and even fewer in other colonies in the Aegean. Since many of the humbler medieval structures in the towns have fallen victim to twentieth-century urban developments, I have made extensive use of the invaluable photographs taken by Giuseppe Gerola in the years 1902–3 and published in his monumental oeuvre *I monumenti veneti nell'isola di Creta*, because until the beginning of the twentieth century the towns of Crete had conserved more of their medieval appearance.[28] Fortunately, recent projects of preservation and restoration of the medieval monuments of Herakleion, Rethymnon, and Chania in Crete have once again made these structures visible and "user-friendly." Moreover, as more attention is paid to the material culture extracted from salvage excavations, we may soon be able to answer pressing questions of chronology and everyday life by placing the pottery and other finds within a more coherent archaeological context. Indeed, the newly established wing of the Historical Museum of Herakleion focuses on the topography and archaeology of medieval Candia and invites a fresh, comprehensive look at this material.

In contrast to this largely uncharted material, the prolonged rule of Venice over most of its colonies in the Oltremare and the Terraferma (mainland Italy) has resulted in impressive sixteenth-century fortifications that overshadow all other parts of the city and figure prominently in surveys of fortifications and Mediterranean urbanism. In 1538 the famous architect Michele Sanmicheli redesigned the fortifications of Candia, Canea, and Retimo as well as other places in Dalmatia according to the demands of the military inventions of the sixteenth century: the new line of walls enclosed a much larger space that was strengthened by heart-shaped bastions. The wall circuit of Canea was rectangular in form and had four heart-shaped bastions (Fig. 4).[29] Retimo's new walls consisted of a rampart wall that followed an east-west direction connecting the two coasts on either side of the acropolis (Fig. 5). One of the three gates that pierced this wall, the Porta Guora, still marks the entrance to the old city of Retimo/Rethymnon from the south (Fig. 6). Its decorated gable (preserved in a photograph taken by Gerola) and the rustic masonry around the opening of the gate confirm its Renaissance date.

The few topographical drawings that predate these grand fortification campaigns suggest that the appearance of the medieval colonies of Venice was quite uniform until the end of the fifteenth century and did not differ much from that of other Mediterranean cities. In fact, the woodcuts of Erward Reuwich in Bernhard von Breydenbach's *Transmarina Peregrinatio*, a best-seller of the second half of the fifteenth century, provide unique testimonies to the urban history of the Mediterranean port cities that were located on the main trade and pilgrimage routes (see Fig. 7 and following section). These images offer concise if rather generic urban portraits confirming the fact that the urbanistic and architectonic outlook of the port cities of the Eastern Mediterranean gave out an air of familiarity, displaying a common Mediterranean vernacular architecture with the notable exception of Venice itself.

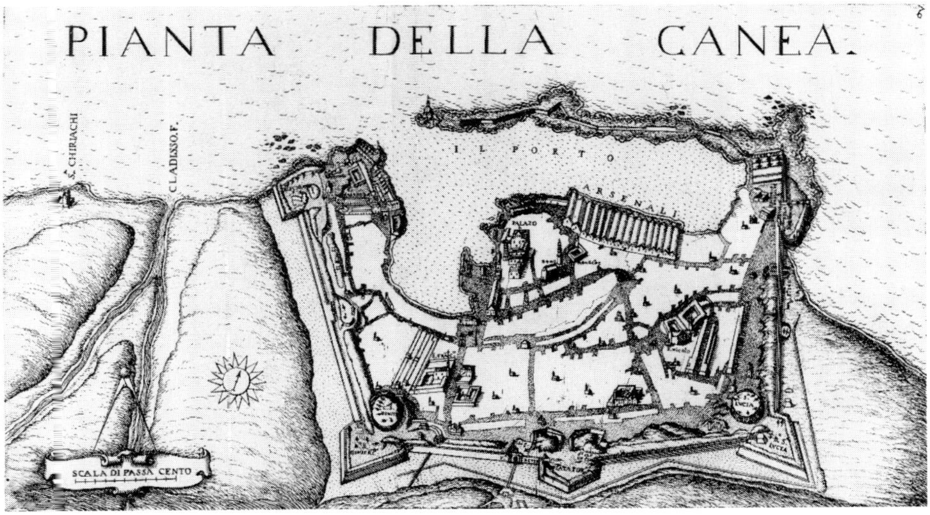

FIGURE 4. M. Boschini, "Pianta della città di Canea," *Il Regno tutto di Candia* (Venice, 1651) (The Gennadius Library, American School of Classical Studies)

The city walls were quite low and were fortified with square or round towers. The cityscape was primarily individualized by the silhouettes of churches, their lofty bell towers, and a few governmental buildings. The apparent absence of famed architects moving along the Aegean, Adriatic, and Dalmatian coastlines to supervise the construction of civic or religious monuments in the Venetian colonies makes one wonder what distinct features if any would identify a city as Venetian, Latin, or Byzantine other than the Gothic spires of churches broadcasting their connection with the Roman church and their break with the Byzantine empire. Even for these features, however, we do not possess enough material to know with certainty what they demarcated in the eyes of the medieval inhabitants and visitors of the cities.

The lack of significant Venetian trademarks on these city views should not lead us to the immediate conclusion that there were no unifying urban or architectural themes in the colonies, however. To a large extent, we expect to discern "signature buildings" in these cities because of our own experience of modern cityscapes. Urban spaces are not exclusively spatial or architectonic: urban monuments and other spaces also exist within a linguistic nexus and make their mark on the city by inscribing their presence in verbal utterances and by extension in the oral history of a site and in the memory of its users. This is particularly true of medieval cities, which were much smaller in size than their twentieth-century counterparts. What is sometimes invisible to the remote observer or to the cartographer who intends to capture a wholistic, bird's-eye view of a place may be immediately

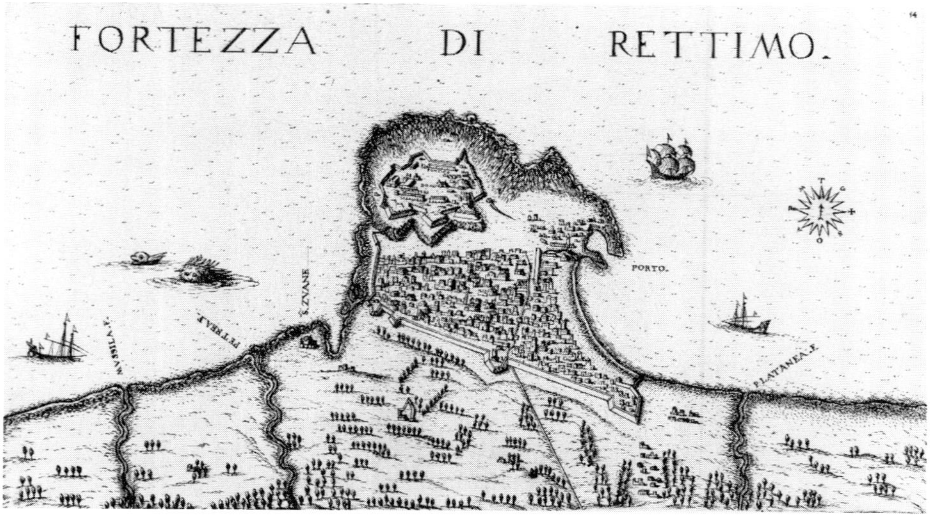

FIGURE 5. M. Boschini, "Fortezza di Rettimo," *Il Regno tutto di Candia* (Venice, 1651) (The Gennadius Library, American School of Classical Studies)

discernible by the person who walks the streets of the city. Compare, for instance, the neatly orchestrated view of Manhattan that one gets from the top of the Empire State Building and the infinitely more chaotic impression that a pedestrian has of the city.[30] So, the existence of an imperial master plan or lack thereof in the Venetian colonies at large depends on the extensive survey of the archaeological remains, the careful reading of accounts of life in the city, and the understanding of economic and social relations.

Obviously, the available material is conditioned by the archaeological remains and the degree of their integration within the modern landscape. A visit to the cities of Chania and Rethymnon (the two provincial capitals of Venetian Crete) nowadays, for instance, reveals picturesque "old towns" that seem to retain a lot of their Renaissance splendor even if their rehabilitation dates to the 1980s and 1990s. Conforming to present aesthetic values, this impression informs a distinct mental image of a Venetian colonial city confirmed by its resemblance to the city of Venice itself. Since the remains of elite houses are scant before the sixteenth century, it is hard to establish whether they possessed distinct architectural or decorative features that stood out, as in the case of the Venetian palazzi on the Canal Grande.[31] The lack of historical documentation does not allow a neat understanding of the various layers of rebuilding or restoration and precludes secure dating of the available architectural and decorative material. Furthermore, the disparity between the limited archaeological remains of Candia/Herakleion – which, as the modern capital of Crete, is highly urbanized – and the more out of

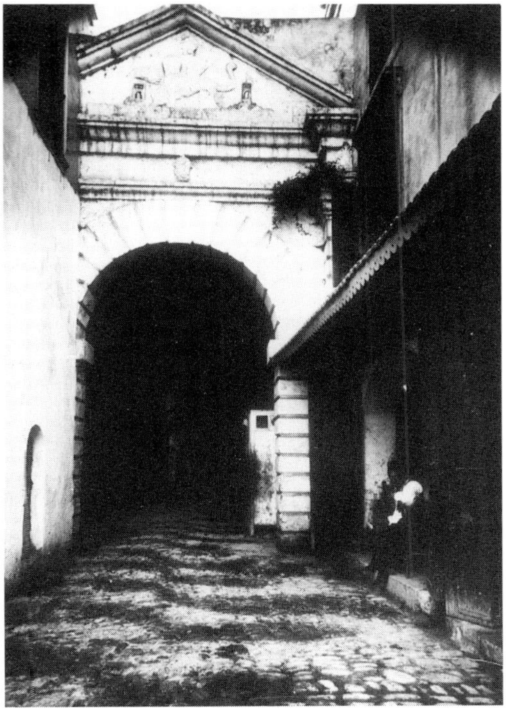

FIGURE 6. Rethymnon, Porta Guora (Istituto Veneto di Scienze, Lettere ed Arti. Venezia. Archivio fotografico della Missione in Creta di Giuseppe Gerola)

the way, tourist oriented Venetian colonies along the coast of Dalmatia, Crete, and the Aegean makes any comparison between them quite tenuous. The twenty-five-year-long Ottoman siege that Candia sustained from 1645 to 1669 added to the destruction of certain parts of the Venetian town, whereas the other cities of Crete fell into the hands of the Ottomans without major resistance. The buildings and fortifications of Canea and Retimo suffered only minor damage and a large number of them were reused by the Ottomans. The most impressive religious or administrative structures of the Venetians were also reused and remodeled by the Ottomans to become mosques or palaces. It is mostly the churches/mosques that have survived: e.g. the church of St. Mark in Negroponte became the Friday mosque of the city, and the cathedrals of Canea and Candia were also turned into mosques, just to name a few examples. How, then, are we to picture medieval Candia? As a more lavish version of Renaissance Chania? Or as a modest provincial city with a few significant public monuments that accentuated its importance as an outpost of Venice?

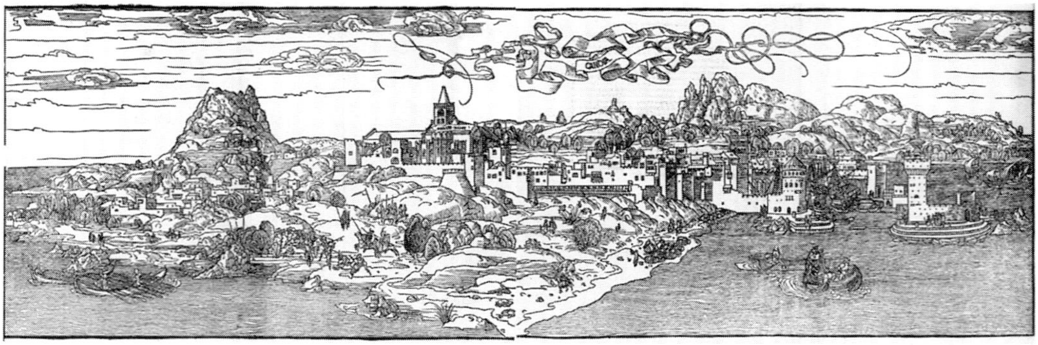

FIGURE 7. View of Candia, etching of Edward Reuwich, in B. Breydenbach, *Transmarina Peregrinatio ad Terram Sanctam* (Mainz, 1486) (Beinecke Rare Book and Manuscript Library, Yale University)

A look at the urban planning of the main cities of Venetian Crete and the other Venetian colonies in the Aegean offers a better sense of the broader parameters of the Venetian colonial world. The replication of specific monuments in the colonies and their unique spatial interrelations signal the existence of parallel urban strategies across the Venetian empire. Similarities in urban choices, naming of buildings and spaces, appearance of military forts, and repetition of symbols of the Republic are all elements that marked a town as part of Venice's empire. By locating sites that seem indispensable for forging colonial presence and authority we can understand the centrality of certain monuments in the urban context; the multiplication of such sites would broadcast the existence of an empire.[32] In this study I have surveyed six Levantine colonies of Venice whose function and administration closely resembled the Cretan pattern: the main cities of Crete (Canea/Chania, Retimo/Rethymnon, and Sitia), Modon/Methoni and Coron/Koroni in the Peloponnesos, and the colony of Negroponte/Chalkis, where a large Venetian community settled and lived for centuries. The geographical relationship and the political correspondences of these colonies had made them a group apart already by the middle of the fourteenth century as the new monetary policy of Venice suggests. On July 29, 1353, it was decided that a special coin, known as the Venetian tornesello, would be minted in Venice for use only in the colonies of Crete, Negroponte, Coron, and Modon. Displaying the lion of St. Mark holding a book and inscribed as the standard bearer of Venice on the reverse, and a cross and the name of the ruling doge on the obverse, this low-denomination coinage with tremendous circulation in Greece clearly identified Venice's colonial dominion.[33] In addition to these tightly knit colonies, a few references to the town of Corfu/Kerkyra are also included here despite the fact that the island presents a variant in colonial

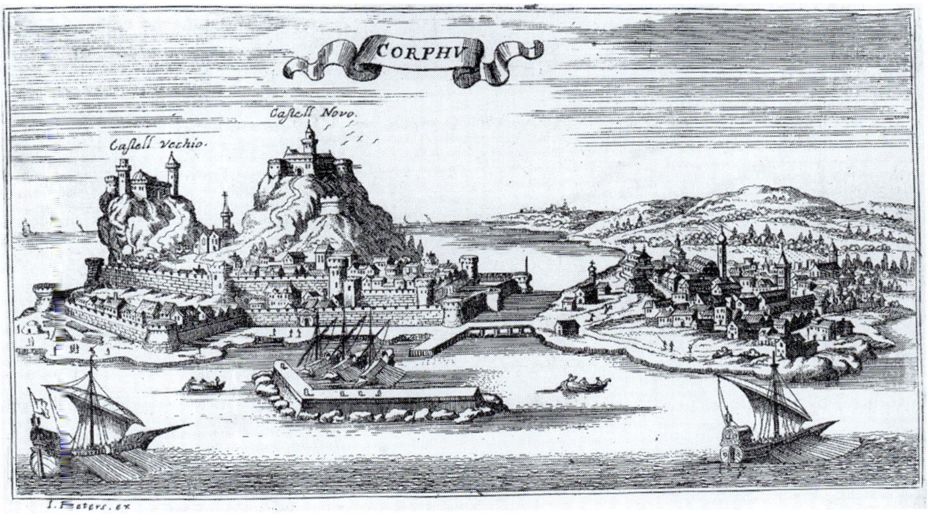

FIGURE 8. Jacques Peeters, *Corphu*, in *Description des principales villes . . .* (Anvers, 1690) (Civico Museo Correr, M. 43851)

practice, as it was colonized in 1386 (Fig. 8). The particular interest of Corfu lies in the fact that as it was a later addition to the Venetian empire, the formation of its monuments offers a glimpse at a mature stage in Venetian colonial discourse. As former parts of the Byzantine empire all these towns shared certain characteristics: they all had fortifications and ports of varying importance and possibly had in the recent past hosted a high Byzantine official and his chancellery (except in the case of Canea and Retimo, both cities that were administratively dependent on Chandax).

THE SOURCES

The extensive archival material originating at the seat of government of Crete (Candia) provides unique insights into the appearance, function, and use of parts of the city as well as individual buildings or objects. Unfortunately, extensive archival documents are lacking for the other colonies, so to complement their extant monuments we have to rely on information contained in the accounts of travelers or in church and monastic records – in a very few instances there are notarial books preserved from the fifteenth or sixteenth century. Like public structures, governmental records, which to a large degree form the basis of our understanding of Venetian colonial rule, appear rigid and stable: they portray an idealized and biased version of the colony from the top down. The information on the nonelite and ethnically different groups is necessarily filtered through the eyes of the Venetian elite on the island and the government in Venice. Preserved in the State Archives in Venice the archival material drafted by or addressed to the Venetian authorities of Crete consists of three groups: (1) the general series of the governmental bodies in Venice, i.e. the Senate, Maggior Consiglio, Council of Ten, Collegio, and Avogaria di Comun; (2) the Archives of the duke of Crete, or *Archivio del Duca di Candia* (hereafter DdC), comprising ninety-seven folders (*buste*) in all;[34] and (3) the acts of the notaries of Candia, which contain a vast amount of information about private, everyday life, including information on private property and churches.[35] These extensive records contain abundant information on patronage, function, use, and repairs of buildings, as well as on important religious matters, movement of population groups into Candia, supervision of the local authorities, military questions, revolts, and other matters. Apart from the technical documentation of building projects how can we see through the prejudices of this material to find the stories of the nonelite groups, the colonized peoples? I believe that a careful consideration of the archaeological remains in conjunction with the documents tells us more than the sources want to elicit about specific urban patterns. They test the official rhetoric of the authorities and provide information on topographical relationships and the behavior of the population.

The vast majority of the documentary evidence is written in Latin (or in Italian after the sixteenth century), but there are some documents written in the language of the colonized peoples, like notarial documents of the sixteenth and seventeenth centuries, which are written in the Greek language transliterated into Latin characters, or the much earlier statutes of the Jewish community of Candia, the *Takkanoth Kandiya*, dating from 1228 with additions throughout the Venetian period to the sixteenth century.[36] These communal statutes regulated the self-government of the Jews, the internal institutions of their community, and their relationship with the other ethnic groups of Candia. These rich documents provide information on the topography of the Jewish quarter, i.e. the synagogues, the ritual bath, the meat market, and other institutions of the Jewish community of Candia.

Although architectural treatises and theoretical writings on art are lacking, descriptions of the cities and their buildings in accounts of travelers of the late medieval and early modern period (up to the nineteenth century) contain helpful and sometimes entertaining details about parts of the city that are absent from all other records. In addition to the invaluable illustrations that are sometimes included in travel books (see for example Figs. 7 and 8), the written accounts of travelers, who typically were pilgrims to the Holy Land, usually record details selected because they seem extraordinary or different from common practices in their places of origin. They describe monuments, religious litanies, or malfunctions in the organization of everyday life (i.e. lack of inns, garbage odors) or discuss the morality of the inhabitants. Thus, although the late medieval travelers recorded mostly what looked strange to them and never included an all-encompassing account of the places they visited, the curious mind of these early modern tourists captured details that can only be found in the travel literature genre. Even the chronicles written about Crete as a colonial territory do not contain details as distinct as in these accounts.[37]

As far as possible, I have looked into the original placement and function of a representative number of military, administrative, and domestic buildings as well as a number of Latin religious institutions that played a key role in the sociopolitical life of the Venetians, in their urban setting and their relationship to each other and to the city as a whole. Working from the archival material I suggest how the buildings, the town squares, and the major arteries of the city were likely to be used and by whom: who were the patrons of the most prominent structures and what was the meaning of the structures for the Venetians and the locals? As expected, the available material privileges the elite of Candia and provides information on the meaning that the city had for the government rather than for its users. Yet, no city is an immutable entity. Venetian Candia continued to function for more than four and a half centuries and its built environment was modified over time. These changes mainly occurred because of the realities of everyday life, which also affected the sociopolitical circumstances in the colony. The strict policy that the Venetians adopted toward the Byzantine aristocracy in the early thirteenth century was gradually replaced by a milder attitude that encouraged cohabitation between the Venetian and Greek communities. By the beginning of the fourteenth century the Greek-speaking middle class had acquired a stronger position in the social hierarchy of the colony; many Greek professionals are recorded doing business and owning large property in Candia. The topography of the city supports this evidence.

CARTOGRAPHY AND TOPOGRAPHY

To set the stage for the study of Candia let us explore the cartographical renditions that allow us a glimpse into its medieval fabric.[38] Despite the claim that maps are objective, scientific representations of a region, they offer a view of the world that reflects the concerns of the cartographer and/or the preoccupations of the patron. Maps construct the world because they are selective.[39] As the famous Venetian cartographer Fra Mauro says in his memoirs: "My map . . . was only one version of reality. The likelihood of being of any use to anybody remained entirely dependent upon its effectiveness as a tool of the imagination. It dawned on me then that the world had to be considered as an elaborate artifice, as the inimitable expression of a will without end."[40] This distortion is even more pronounced in cases of territories dominated by a foreign ruling elite where arguably maps were used not simply to record but also to forge a territorial reality that reinforced the claims of the rulers. The six late medieval and early modern maps (or rather city views) of Candia that have come down to us indeed present variable configurations of the urban space. Although the features shared by these maps, i.e. the few prominent Gothic churches with bell towers, the governor's palace, the city walls, and the harbor, strive to affirm scientific (perhaps firsthand) observation, the lack of reference to the local, Greek population that outnumbered the Venetians is suspect. The omissions and "mistakes" in the late medieval maps of Venetian Crete seem to offer a view of the world that conforms to the imagination of the Venetian colonizers as they present selective features of the urban space. By exploring the contents of the maps in relation to the ideological preoccupations of the cartographers and their patrons, we can understand the purpose of each map (informative, encyclopedic, or propagandistic) and infer its impact on the consolidation of Venetian colonial ideology. If we could also determine the patterns of circulation and audience we would have a clearer view of the situation.

In the topographical representations of Candia, a city whose most prominent monuments seem to have been ecclesiastical, it is the presence or absence of churches of the Latin or Greek rite that manipulates the realities of the urban space to create an image that conforms with the intentions of the cartographers and their patrons. The monuments that each cartographer chose to include in his map in conjunction with the orientation of the city views crystallize on paper an imagined view of the colonized space. Thus, these cartographic exercises become an instrument of control by the governing elite and a valuable tool of its "imagined community" – a community devoid of problems and obedient to the demands of the Most Serene Republic of Venice. Because of the nature of the evidence, the reconstruction of certain sections of the city is hypothetical. To facilitate the conceptualization of the city space, I placed all the buildings that are known from the sources onto a plan that captures the appearance of the urban space at given historical moments. This plan is based on the most accurate representation of the urban space of Candia in the seventeenth-century map of General Werdmüller (Fig. 17). One of the difficulties in this reconstruction was the irregular distribution of data over time, especially concerning the churches,

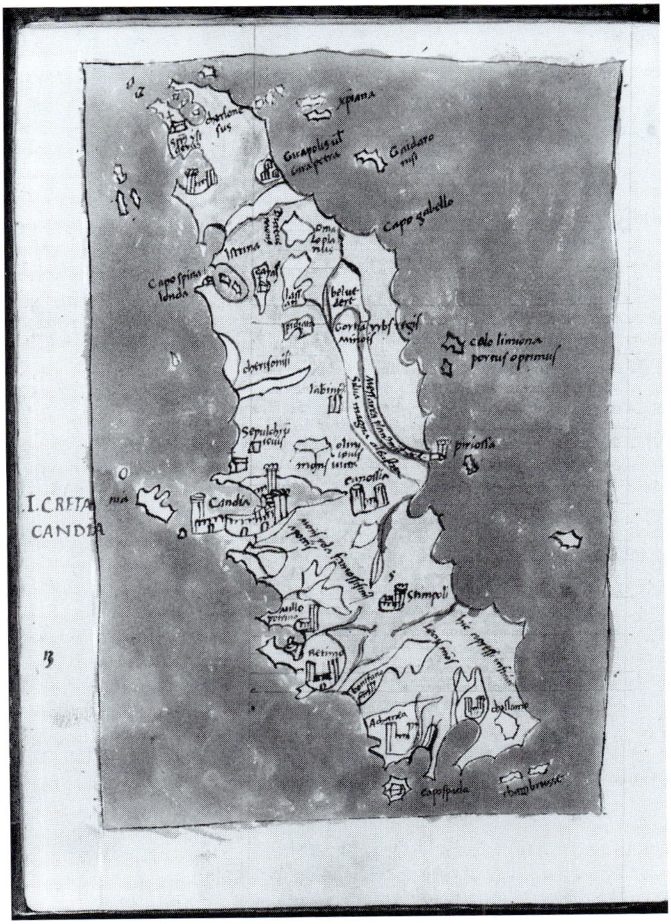

FIGURE 9. Cristoforo Buondelmonti, *Creta – Candia*, in Liber insularum Archipelagi, c. 9v (The Gennadius Library, American School of Classical Studies)

which were not all built at the same time. I tried to overcome this difficulty by arranging the available material in chronological sections, which were primarily defined by textual evidence, so four maps of the city were created (Figs. 21, 103, 118, 119). In the case of buildings that are not well documented, I assembled as much information as possible about the neighboring structures and tried to establish their relations in space. Thus, moving slowly from known to unknown, the texture of the city slowly appears in front of our eyes.

The first two topographical renderings of the city were not initiated by Venice: the *isolario* of the Florentine geographer Cristoforo Buondelmonti made c. 1419 (Fig. 9) and Erward Reuwich's view of Candia in the famous

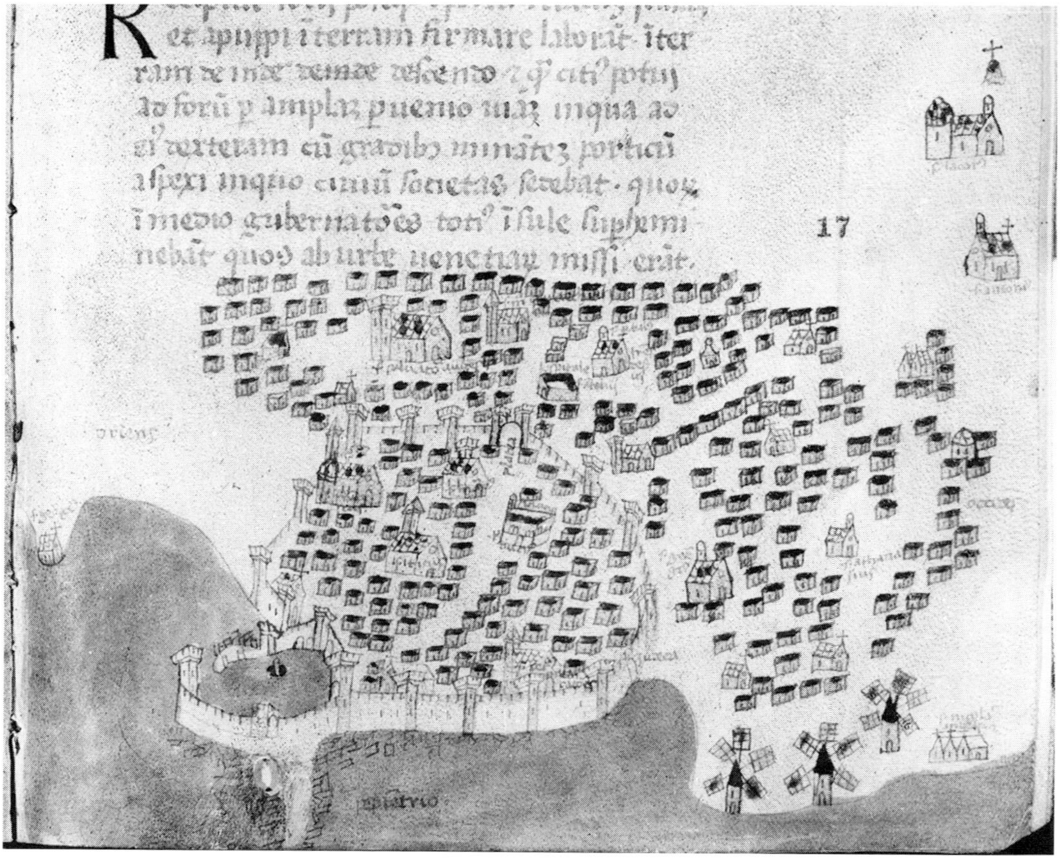

FIGURE 10. Cristoforo Buondelmonti, "View of Candia," in Descriptio insulae Candiae, 1419. (Firenze, Biblioteca Medicea Laurenziana, ms. Plut. 29.42, c. 17 [1429]) Su concessione del Ministero per i Beni e le Attività Culturali. Èvietata ogni ulteriore riproduzione con qualsiasi mezzo

Transmarina Peregrinatio of Bernhard von Breydenbach of 1486 (Fig. 7). Both works were intended to present to their audience snapshots of Mediterranean harbors along with textual descriptions. The degree of accuracy in the depiction of details is not always very high, but in the case of Candia, we can be sure that both cartographers had a good command of its urban space. In fact, Buondelmonti's *isolario* (a common way to represent the islands of the Aegean or Archipelago) is accompanied by another work, the *Descriptio insule cretensis* of 1419/20.[41] The manuscript in the Biblioteca Laurenziana in Florence contains a bird's-eye view of Candia that accompanies the description of the city (Fig. 10). In this careful attempt at recording the urban space Buondelmonti paints the view of Candia as a visitor. The map defies the conventional northward orientation of maps to align the viewer with some-

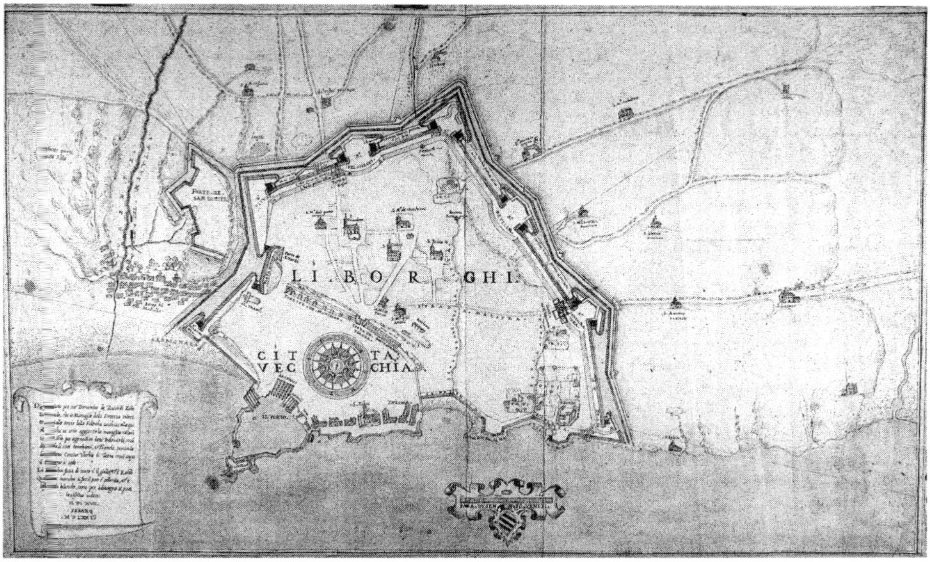

FIGURE 11. Domenico Rossi da Este, Città vecchia di Candia, August 17, 1573. (Biblioteca Marciana, Ms. It. VI, 188 [10039])

one approaching from the sea: thus the town is presented not from the point of view of its inhabitants but rather from that of the visitor/traveler. This sets the tone for the majority of later views of Candia. Even when the whole island is represented with a northward orientation in atlases, the close-up view of the city is given in an inverted way. Thus the city of Candia and its harbor are placed not only under the gaze but also in the service of outsiders traveling to the island and its capital. Buondelmonti's sketch indicates the city walls strengthened by towers; the city gate; the central square (in its Greek name *platea*); the harbor; the ducal palace; the churches of St. Titus, St. Mark, St. Francis, and St. Peter the Martyr within the city walls; and those of the Savior, St. Mary of the Crusaders, St. Anthony with its hospital, St. Paul, St. George, St. Athanasius, St. Nicolaus, St. Anthony, and St. Lazarus in the suburbs. A number of other churches are also shown but without specific labeling. These must be the most important Greek churches of the city, all relegated to the suburbs outside the walled city. Their nondescript presentation renounces their full ecclesiastical power and sanctity within the city. The Orthodox churches are almost equated with the nameless houses and mills that function almost as fillers in the map to indicate the growing suburbs of the city. At the same time, the Jewish quarter is clearly labeled as *Judeca*.

The second earliest surviving view of Candia is the well known etching by Reuwich in the *Transmarina Peregrinatio ad Terram Sanctam* (Fig. 7), the

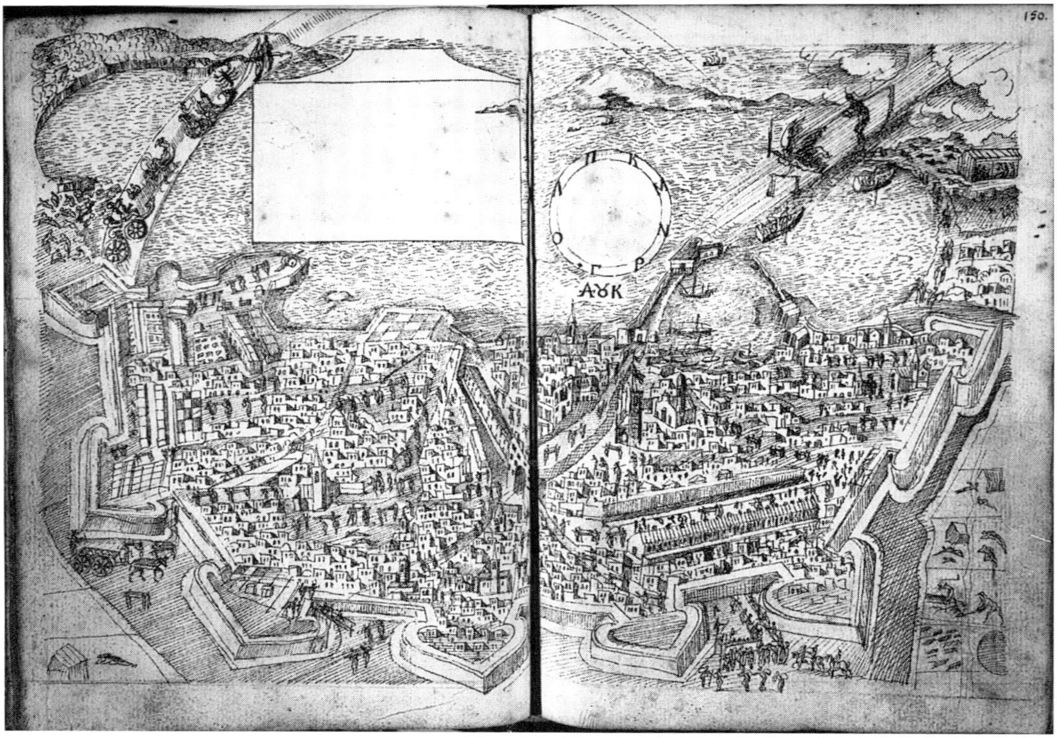

FIGURE 12. George Clontzas, view of Candia during the time of the plague, Istoria ab origine mundi. (Biblioteca Marciana, Ms. Graec. VII, 22 [1466], fols. 149v-150r)

first book where the topographical elements are quite accurate.[42] Here, too, the city was conceived from the point of view of a seafarer, in this case a pilgrim traveling to the Holy Land. The same tall buildings are singled out in the cityscape of Candia: the Franciscan monastery of St. Francis, the ducal chapel of St. Mark with its bell tower flying the flag of the Republic, the fort in the entrance of the harbor and the high walls. Among the rest of the buildings little is discernible as the point of view is on the same level with the sea more or less.

This placement of Crete on the receiving end of the traveler, colonizer, or pilgrim is concurrent with the political developments on the island and its colonial, i.e. subordinate, position to the maritime power of the Venetians. When in the sixteenth century Crete's role as a bastion of Christianity was accentuated by impressive fortifications that encompassed the extensive suburbs of its capital city, the attention of the cartographers also focused on these defenses, which demanded a lot of money, materials, skilled architects, and masons and took more than half a century to complete. These walls were the pride of the city and its Venetian masters, and the majority of the

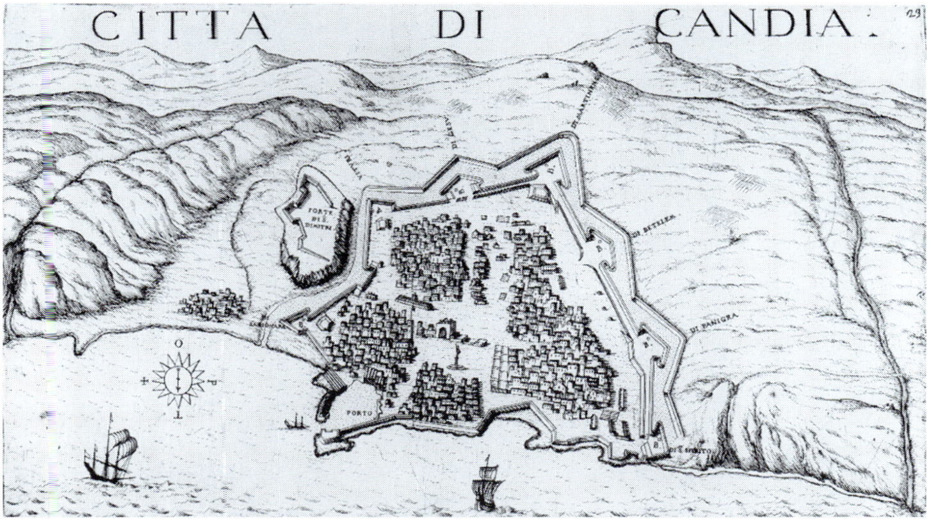

FIGURE 13. Marco Boschini, "Città di Candia," *Il Regno tutto di Candia*, (Venice, 1651), c. 23 (The Gennadius Library, American School of Classical Studies)

cartographers who surveyed Candia following 1550 were engineers and technicians employed by the Venetian Senate.[43] As such, their primary role was to elevate and celebrate the achievements of the military architects who worked on Crete: Michele Sanmicheli, Savargnola, Basilicata, and so on. Thus, it is accuracy in measurement and recording of specific features as well as attention to detail that these maps advertise.

Domenico da Este (Rossi) made in 1567 and 1573 two maps of Candia during the first campaigns of the fortifications that intended to envelop the suburbs (Fig. 11).[44] As an engineer employed to make a record of the new walls of Candia, he created plans that show the wall circuit, the bastions and new gates, as well as some of the Latin churches within the walls, all of them labeled. The suburbs are clearly marked as such so as to emphasize the new section of the town that was fortified from 1540 onward. Interestingly, very few of the more than a hundred Greek churches figure in this map of 1573. In the captions of the map we read Maria delle Quattro Campane (SW), S. Salvatore, S. Zuane, S. Maria de Croseschieri, La Madonna de Piazza, S. Maria delli Anzoli, S. Paulo in the west of the borgo, and S. Dimitri, that is to say, most of the Latin churches, even those that were not significant in terms of size and importance. The Jewish quarter is also prominently shown, in contrast to the real political and social situation: whereas the Orthodox Greeks had enough freedom to participate in the political and economic life of the city, the position of the Jewish community had deteriorated dramatically in the sixteenth century. This highly selective treatment of the urban

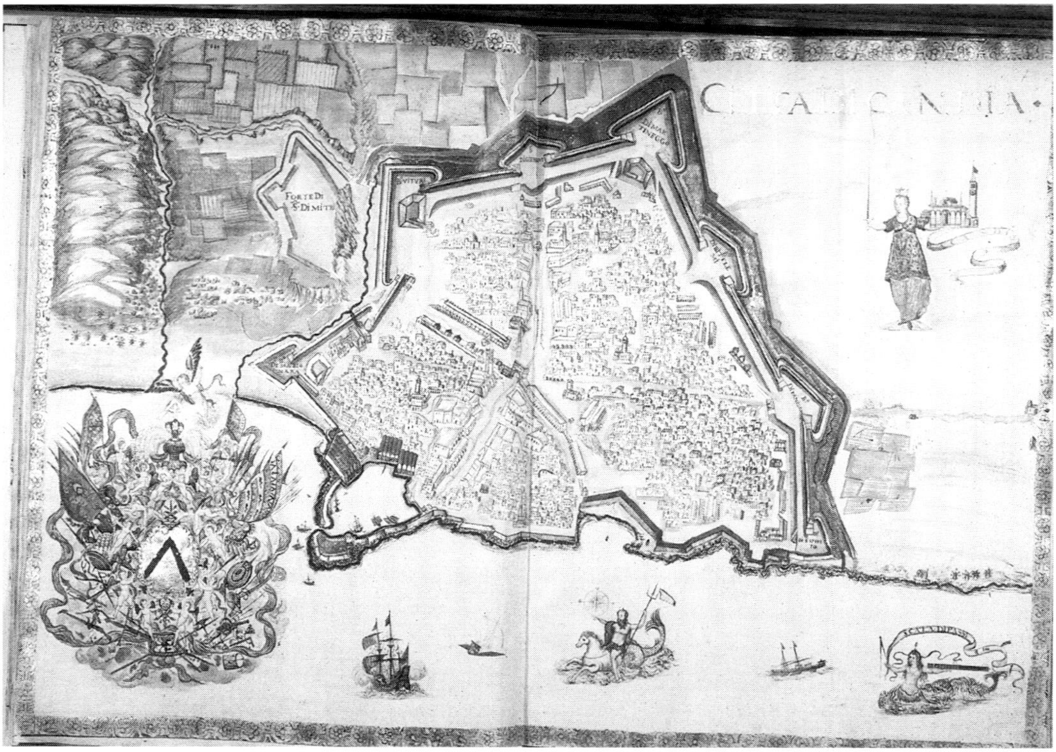

FIGURE 14. Zorzi Corner, Città di Candia (1625). (Biblioteca Marciana, Ms. It. VI, 75 [8303])

space announces without any doubt the ideological manipulations of the cartographer and his commissioners.

This synoptic treatment of the urban space, which erases so to speak the presence of the Greek community, is apparent in many more views made in the seventeenth century. Against these we should examine a view of Candia made by a Greek artist, George Clontzas, at the end of the sixteenth century (Fig. 12). This "map" is included in Clontzas's unpublished codex *Istoria ab origine mundi*.[45] In fos. 149v–150r an image of Candia shows the city at the time of the plague. Not only does the cartographer use a northward orientation with the harbor in the upper part of the page, but he has made every effort to record an all-inclusive view of his native town. Even if the function of this miniature that shows Candia at the time of the plague is different from that of a map, the contrast between this representation and earlier views of Candia is vast. This is a town that is lived in, a real place for the people to occupy. We can see the Latin cathedral of St. Titus, St. Mark, St. Francis, St. Peter the Martyr, and many Greek churches, although they are not labeled. Another view of the city dated to 1628–45

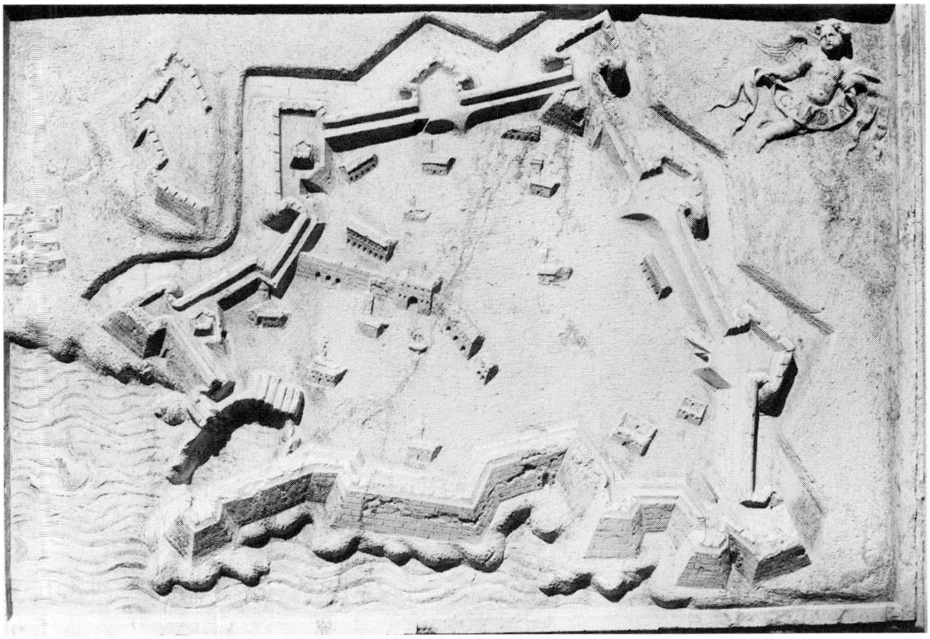

FIGURE 15. Venice, Santa Maria del Giglio, façade

was made by the son of George Clontzas, Maneas. This is now in a private collection of Burhnard Traeger in Germany and was recently published by Ioanna Steriotou.[46]

The most informative views of the cityscape of Candia are the maps of the seventeenth century, most of which were made by engineers dispatched to Crete for the construction of new fortifications on the island.[47] Francesco Basilicata was an engineer who remained in Crete for many years (1612–38) and his works were chiefly concerned with the state of the defenses of the island: he produced descriptive texts, general maps of the island, detailed landscape drawings, plans and elevations of individual buildings, and plans of fortresses, harbors, cities, and coastal plains.[48] His maps show landscape as seen and experienced from the ground and have a high level of detail and accuracy. Interestingly, when it comes to the treatment of urban space his observations are not as accurate as in the rendition of topographical details. Basilicata's maps and views had a significant impact in the history of the cartography of Candia because they served as sources for later printed maps of the island, especially Marco Boschini's album titled *Il Regno tutto di Candia* (Fig. 13). Published in Venice in 1651 at the time of the war of Candia, the last stronghold of Christianity in the Levant, when the whole of Christendom was focused on Crete, this album had the purpose of advertising Venice's greatness in her struggle against *la potenza vastissima ottomana*.[49] The

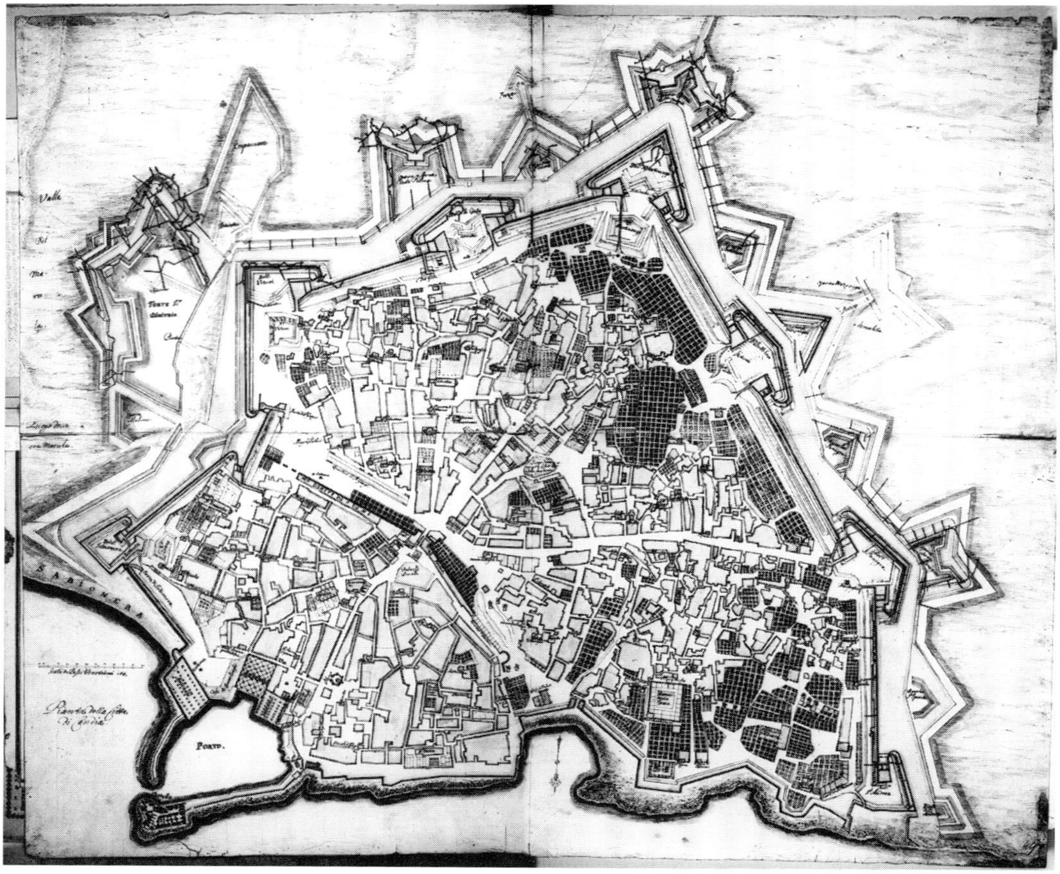

FIGURE 16. Werdmüller, Pianta della città di Candia, 1666–68. (Zürich Zentralbibliothek, T 76, act. 28)

view of Candia in addition to the landmarks of the city (the land gate, the old and new circuit of walls, and the vaults of the arsenals) also fills the space with houses and emphasizes the public fountain on the main square.

In 1625 Zorzi Corner, possibly a native of Candia, produced a luxurious album of maps similar to that of Basilicata but with more attention paid to the specifics of urban space (Fig. 14). The collection of these manuscript maps, now in the Biblioteca Marciana in Venice, was never destined to be printed and displays a lavishness of material that is not found in any other cartographic representation of the city.[50] The album contains a frontispiece, where the author offers it to an unnamed high official belonging most probably to the Trevisan family, whose coat of arms appears on every page with words that emphasize the artist's deep appreciation. One senses that this

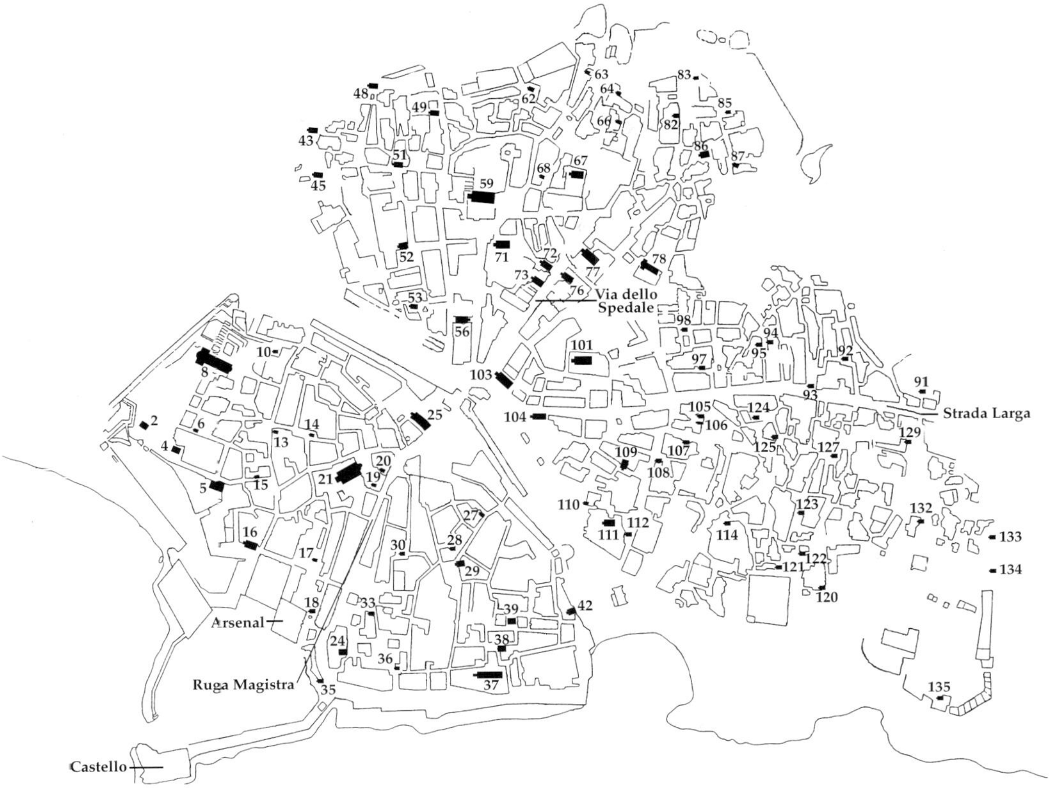

FIGURE 17. Map of Candia, after Werdmüller

is a product meant to flatter the recipient. The urban space is shown in every detail with emphasis placed on its main streets, squares, public monuments, and Latin churches, albeit with no captions – as if to say that both author and recipient knew the town well. This is a space dear to the cartographer, well constructed to emphasize the order and decorum of the city, even adorned with a personification of the city holding its most significant colonial symbol, the church of St. Mark. Although we cannot be certain that Zorzi Corner came from Candia, a comparison of this detailed view of the city with the summary treatment of the other major cities of Canea/Chania and Retimo/Rethymnon points to a person who was very familiar with Candia and drew a view that conveyed his special relationship with it. We may have here the Venetian counterpart of the Greek Clontzas.

The twenty-five-year-long siege of Candia by the Ottomans that ended with the surrender of the city by Francesco Morosini was a catalyst for the production of maps that in essence showed the effectiveness of the bastions

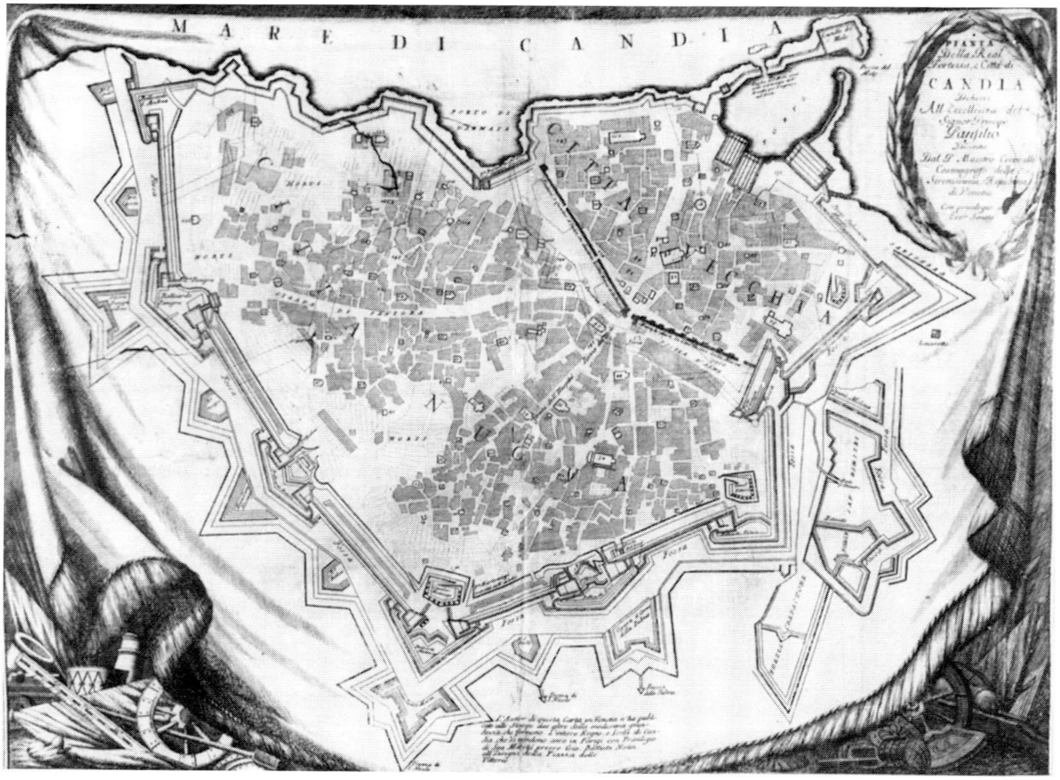

FIGURE 18. Vincenzo Coronelli, Pianta della real fortezza e città di Candia, in *Città, Fortezze, Isole e Porti principali d'Europa* (Venice, 1689) (Civico Museo Correr, M. 32484)

and city walls. The vast majority display the attacking forces with their siege machines and the trajectories of the artillery toward the walls. On the commemorative façade of the church of Santa Maria del Giglio in Venice we see in stone the ideology that developed in the cartographic tradition on Crete and the colonial territories of Venice (Fig. 15). The church was sponsored by Antonio Barbaro, who had served as a high official in the Venetian maritime empire. The façade displays topographic reliefs of Rome, Padua, Corfu, Candia, Zara, and Spalato. In contrast to Rome and Padua, where the sculptor has reproduced houses and other buildings to fill in the space, Candia is shown in a synoptic manner. As this church was decorated during the siege of Candia by the Turks the fortifications of the city take center stage. In addition, the few Latin churches that are included announce to the viewer the identity of those who are in control of the city: these monuments are directly related to the Latin church and the pope in Rome, who at the time was the only hope for the Christian defenders of Candia. In the imagination of the Venetians in the midseventeenth century the long-lasting colonial control of Crete is exemplified once more by the omission of monuments foreign to the Venetians.

After the end of the siege two extremely detailed city views follow the new cartographic principles of the time and announce a new era in the cartography of Crete. A map made by the Swiss general Werdmüller who was personally involved in the defense of Candia in 1667–69 (Fig. 16 and Fig. 17), and a later map that is included in the works of the cosmographer Vincenzo Coronelli's *Atlante veneto* and *Theatro della città* of the end of the seventeenth century (Fig. 18).[51] Here the maps are inclusive and extremely informative: we read the names of more than one hundred churches (Greek and Latin) with correct toponymic references. Once again, however, despite their scientific look the maps are totally imaginative. Although they represent a Venetian city, at the time they were made Candia had fallen to the hands of the Turks and its portrayal as a city full of Latin and Greek churches was no longer the reality. Most of the major churches had been converted to mosques, and many of the buildings must have been in disrepair. In the twilight of the Venetian colonial empire, the metropole could only envision its past glories by encapsulating them within an image of empire long gone. The nostalgic, idealistic view of the lost empire where sanctity was shared between Latin and Orthodox churches made Candia once again a city with a Byzantine past and a hundred Orthodox churches. In the face of the progression of the Ottomans this was a sacred territory, which was only possible in the imagination of the Republic's cosmographer.

The informative map of General Werdmüller constitutes the perfect springboard for entering the city of Candia to examine its urban fabric. Postdating the foundation of Venetian Candia by four and a half centuries, the map offers a clear view of a heavily urbanized city with its most distinct monuments. It comes as no surprise that the monuments labeled on Werdmüller's map are the ones about which we have the most archival information. We sense that the backbone of the colonial city was made up of the administrative palaces (of the duke, his counselors, and the admiral), military installations (city walls, army barracks, and arsenals), main squares and markets, and numerous churches and monasteries. The following chapters will explore these monuments and their interrelationships within the city space: reused sites and objects will be contrasted to newly founded structures with the intent to grasp the workings of the colony vis-à-vis its different publics. Obviously, since the Venetians held Crete for four and a half centuries, a variety of hybrid cultural formations can also be attested on the island. If the juxtaposition of Latin and Orthodox churches speaks to the points of contact and the mechanisms of self-definition between the cultures of the colonizers and colonized as seen in the maps of Candia, the appropriation and reuse of ancient structures by the colonizers may be explored in the context of Venice's imperialist aspirations. Let us now look into the beginnings of Venice's colonial expansion in the thirteenth century.

TWO

SIGNS OF POWER

> It is said that the Venetians in all these places that they are recovering are painting a lion of St. Mark which has in its hand a sword rather than a book, from which it seems that they have learnt to their cost that study and books are not sufficient to defend states.
>
> N. Machiavelli, December 7, 1509.[1]

By the thirteenth century Crete was hardly unknown territory for the Venetian merchants who are recorded doing business on the island as early as 1111, making use of the tax exempt status that was accorded them by the Byzantine emperors in 1082 and 1147.[2] Whether or not many Venetian merchants were aware of the political and social organization of Byzantine Crete, as colonizers the Venetians did not drastically change any mechanism that had proved adequate for the administration of Byzantine Crete but had incorporated them into their feudal system. For instance, the mode of agricultural production was not modified drastically after 1211. The agricultural lands were redistributed to Latin settlers, who were brought from Venice (the *feudatarii* or *feudati*) according to the following scheme: the whole territory was divided into six parts following the older military and administrative subdivisions of the Byzantine theme of Crete, the *turmae*.[3] Every sixth was broken into 33⅓ lots, the *cavallerie*, which went to the *milites* (knights), and each *cavalleria* was subdivided into 6 *sergenterie*, which went to the *pedites*, i.e. sergeants or foot soldiers. In return for these fiefs and for residences in the capital city, probably suggested to the doge by the first Venetian governor of Crete, Jacopo Tiepolo, the colonists were responsible for the military defense of the island.[4] Thus only the higher echelon of the pyramid changed: i.e. the landlords were now Venetians, instead of Byzantines. The cultivators of the land, who were assigned to specific fiefs, remained the same, with similar responsibilities and privileges under the new regime.[5] In other words, the so-called feudal system instituted by the Venetians was not a totally foreign concept in the administration of Byzantine Crete. Nonetheless, the arrival of the new Venetian feudatories had a significant impact on the local *archontes*, the old Byzantine aristocracy, who lost their landed property, their urban residences, and their political clout. Throughout the thirteenth century the local aristocracy mounted revolts against the Venetian regime to have their property rights recognized and to regain some of their economic and political privileges.

The feudatories were expected to assist the Venetians in wars outside Crete, a fact that they resented.[6] In other words, the Latin colonists of Crete formed a "national" army, following the example of the administrative system of the Byzantine theme of Crete, where the duca-katepano was in charge of large army units made up of people who lived permanently on the island.[7] This system had definite benefits for the Venetians as it boosted their ideological constructs: the absence of a stationed army of mercenaries symbolically portrayed the Republic as a nonbelligerent, generous overseer on Crete. At the same time, the decision to rely militarily on the colonists presented a potential risk for the Venetian authorities: the feudatories and their offspring born on Crete could potentially form ties of friendship and camaraderie with the locals. In the long run this army would be unsuited to police Crete against internal enemies, as the rebellion of 1363 showed.[8]

In administrative and political terms Crete was organized as a provincial version of Venice. The government of the island was modeled on that of the Republic and few initiatives were left to her representatives on Crete: issues of security and the choice of high officials were decided in Venice, and all the decisions taken in Candia needed the approval of the Senate in the mother city. The head of the island, the *duca*, whose term of office was two years, had to be a real agent of the Republic without any attachments with the island.[9] Similar status was expected of his closest associates, the *consiliarii*. The Venetian settlers could be elected to the Senate (Consilium Rogatorum Candide) or the Maggior Consiglio of Candia, two bodies that dealt with diplomatic and administrative matters, as well as embassies to Venice.[10] The juridical system was based on the Venetian legal system, with special judges, called *presopi* or *prosopi*, settling cases involving Greeks or Jews, but Byzantine law was also applied in some cases involving Greeks.[11] The highest court of the colony consisted of the duke and his two counselors; their decisions were final and could only be appealed in Venice.[12] As with the mode of agricultural production, in fiscal matters the Venetians maintained the Byzantine policies that they found on Crete, because their objective was to cover the expenses of the colony from local income, that is, taxation and rents from state property.[13] The fiefholders were responsible for a collective property tax of five hundred hyperpera that was to be paid by each *sestiere*

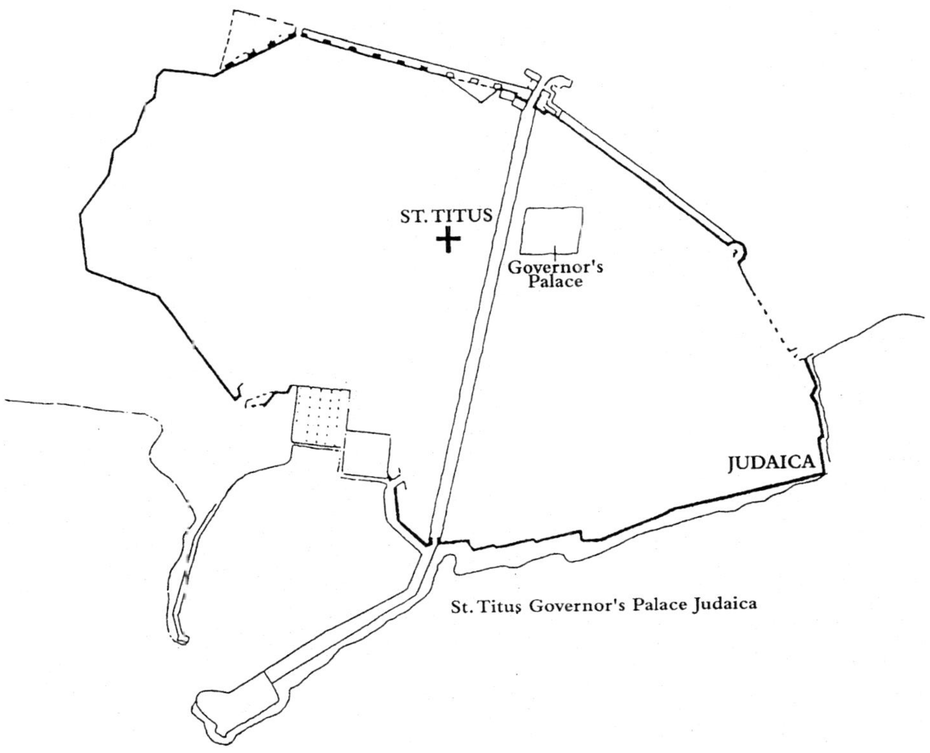

FIGURE 19. Map of Byzantine Chandax, after Nikolaos Platon

annually;[14] all inhabitants of Candia including Latin and Greek priests were responsible for a tax called *pedagium porte*, or *datium porte;* special taxes were paid by the professionals and non-Venetians; finally, one of the heaviest burdens of the local population was the *angarie* (corvées), the forced labor that the state demanded in times of war or during major construction campaigns.[15]

THE CITIES OF CRETE

What did the city of Candia look like upon the arrival of the Venetians in the thirteenth century? Originally a harbor serving the Roman town of Knossos, the site developed into a significant urban center when the Muslim conquerors of Crete made it their capital from 826 to 961.[16] The Byzantine name of modern Herakleion was *Chandax*, based on the Arabic name *al-Khandaq* (the ditch).[17] Once reconquered by the Byzantines in 961, Crete was turned into a *theme* governed by a *strategos*, who was responsible for the

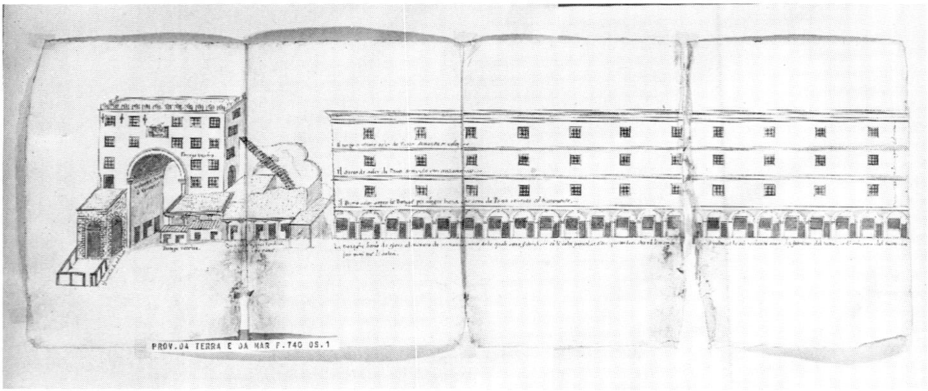

FIGURE 20. Plan of the Voltone area, 1577 (Archivio di Stato di Venezia, Provveditori da Terra e da Mar, f. 740 DS. 1)

land military resources.[18] The limited Byzantine monetary and ceramic finds that have been excavated on the island have revealed Chandax to be the only urban center that prospered from 961 to 1204: most international economic activities must have centered around this harbor (Fig. 19).[19] The seat of the metropolitan was also transferred by the early twelfth century from the early Christian church of St. Titus in Gortys to the new cathedral of Chandax dedicated to Ἅγιοι Πάντες (All Saints).[20]

Using the foundations of the Muslim walls, the Byzantines must have refortified the city soon after 961 and extended the city walls onto the north side, toward the harbor.[21] The thickness of the walls was 7.20 meters,[22] with square towers, set at 21-meter intervals, abutting the exterior of the wall toward the moat.[23] The main gate was located at the intersection of the actual streets Kalokairinou and 25th of August, below the Venetian monumental gate of Candia known as *Voltone* (Fig. 20). Of the numerous Orthodox churches that prospered in the Venetian period, only eleven can be proved to have originated in the Byzantine period and another seven may have also been erected before 1204 (Fig. 21).[24]

Because of the terrain, the winds, and the sea currents all major cities of Crete were located on the north coast. Like Candia, Canea/Chania, Retimo/Rethymnon, and Sitia already existed in the Byzantine period and were refurbished by the Venetian colonists in the thirteenth and fourteenth centuries in order to meet the needs of the new ruling class.[25] The aforementioned treaty between Genoa and count Pescatore in 1210 offers valuable information about the topography of these towns. In return for monetary support Pescatore promised Genoa, among other things, commercial privileges and a quarter in every Cretan city (Candia, Retimo, and Canea?) and

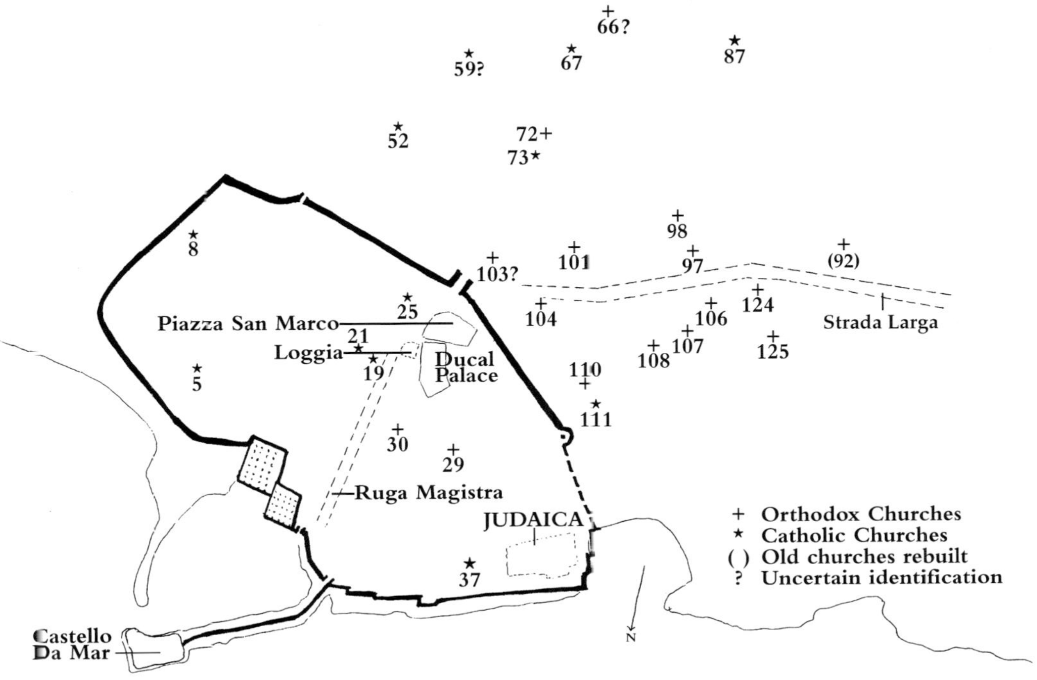

FIGURE 21. Map of Candia in the thirteenth century

in four other localities of the island: each quarter was to have a church, a street, a public bath, a warehouse (*fondaco*), and an oven.[26] These specific arrangements of the urban quarters suggest that there was more than one city on the island and that the existing cities of Crete had been well equipped before the arrival of the Venetians. A Venetian rector who was elected by the Senate in Venice and served under the duke in Candia governed each city and its territory assisted by two counselors.

The increasingly important role of the urban centers for the dominion of the Venetians is apparent in the new administrative division of Crete in the fourteenth century. In 1211 the Venetians divided the island into sixths (*sestieri*), a system that reproduced the political partition of the city of Venice and followed the older Byzantine division of Crete into *turmae*. In the fourteenth century, however, the new historical realities overshadowed the symbolic importance of the division of Crete in *sestieri*: the agricultural economy of the thirteenth century had shifted to a trade oriented community centering on the urban marketplaces.[27] Thus, four regions, named after their capital cities, the territories of Candia, Canea, Retimo, and Sitia, were created. The regions were further divided into nineteen *castellanie*, which were headed by special officials, the *castellani*. These officials supervised the rural lands located around their place of residence, the *castelli* (castles or, rather, forts).

Although it is difficult to estimate the population of each city, the figures contained in a census at the end of the sixteenth century give us some indications for the earlier centuries as well. In the sixteenth century Candia had approximately sixteen thousand inhabitants with the Venetian nobility (964 people) representing 5.7 percent of the total population.[28] The highest estimate given for the population of Candia in the thirteenth century is thirty thousand; this is undoubtedly an inflated figure, given in a document of 1224 that the Greeks of Candia sent to the Venetian government to request better treatment from the authorities.[29] On the other hand, it is not likely that there were more than one thousand Latins in Candia at any given time, although originally Venice had decided to send about twenty-five hundred Venetian settlers to the colony.[30] The figures of the census suggest the following numbers for the other Cretan cities: Canea had eight thousand, Retimo seven thousand, and Sitia barely fifteen hundred inhabitants.[31] The authorities made concerted efforts to boost the significance of these four Cretan cities and their other colonial possessions. The main colonies of the Venetians continued to be or were elevated to bishoprics, an act that underscored their ecclesiastical and consequently their political significance as well. For instance, in 1336 the town of Canea became the seat of the bishop of Agia, a Byzantine episcocal seat earlier located in the hinterland. The Latin cathedral of Retimo became the seat of the bishop of Calamon during Venetian rule, but we do not know precisely when this happened; it was recorded as a bishopric by 1358.

CANDIA: A SPACE DEFINED BY WALLS

How was Venetian Candia organized? The area that the Venetians thought of as "Candia" was delineated by city walls that enclosed the former Byzantine city. City walls were a significant part of the urban tissue as their purpose was to defend the city and to protect its population; they also provided psychological reassurance for the city dwellers by dividing, enclosing, and rendering space exclusive.[32] These demarcations acquire particular poignancy in colonial societies with a multiethnic population like Candia, as the walls also declared the superiority of the (foreign) ruling regime, which had full control over the space therein. The historical records from Candia show that the division between the *civitas*,[33] the city, and the *borgo*, the area outside the walls, persisted even after the walls of the Byzantine city had been made obsolete by the new fortifications that included the area of the suburbs. Until the sixteenth century the residents of Candia seem to have been divided in two broad categories, *habitator Candide* and *habitator burgi Candide*, already established in the earliest notarial acts surviving from Venetian Candia, those of the notary Pietro Scardon (1271). This distinction would remain in use throughout the Venetian rule in Crete even after the new fortification walls of the sixteenth century incorporated the suburbs into the city of Candia.[34] Note the peculiar labeling on the 1567 map of Domenico Rossi (Fig. 11), which still clearly marks the outline of the walls of the old city of Candia and labels the burgs as such. In order to be faithful to the language used in the historical documents, here I understand as urban space the inner core of the medieval city, which had been enclosed by city walls at least from the Byzantine period until the sixteenth century; the area outside these walls will be called the suburbs, or the burg.

No archival material of the thirteenth century addresses the city walls directly, but the fourteenth-century chronicler Lorenzo de Monacis asserts that the city was surrounded by walls during the rebellion of Marco Sanudo in 1213. In order to escape from the forces of the rebels in Candia, the first Venetian governor of Crete, duke Jacobus Theupulo (Jacopo Tiepolo), had to climb the city walls.[35] On the basis of the usual accuracy of de Monacis's reports, we are led to believe that two years after the first Venetian colonists were sent to Crete, Candia was already surrounded by a fortified enclosure. Hence, we can assume that these fortifications predated the arrival of the Venetians and were of Byzantine origin. The archaeological data corroborate this hypothesis.

The fortification walls that are preserved today in the south part of Herakleion belong primarily to the construction campaign of the sixteenth century, but the views of Candia by Buondelmonti (Fig. 10) and Erward Reuwich (Fig. 7) depict the walls that surrounded the city until the late fifteenth century: the enceinte ended in crenellations and was reinforced by seventeen square towers.[36] Fortunately, large sections of the medieval walls are still visible in the old city. In fact, the sea walls, photographs of which have been published by Gerola, survived almost intact until the beginning of the twentieth century (Fig. 22).

A large 28-meter section of the walls that was uncovered in salvage excavations in 1952 demonstrates how the Venetians strengthened the pre-existing Byzantine walls: they erected new flanking towers and a limestone sloping wall to the exterior of the existing enceinte that incorporated inside them the older Byzantine fortifications.[37] This glacis strengthened the original base of the Byzantine curtain walls, which now reached a width of 16 meters, while the upper section of the walls retained its original width of 11

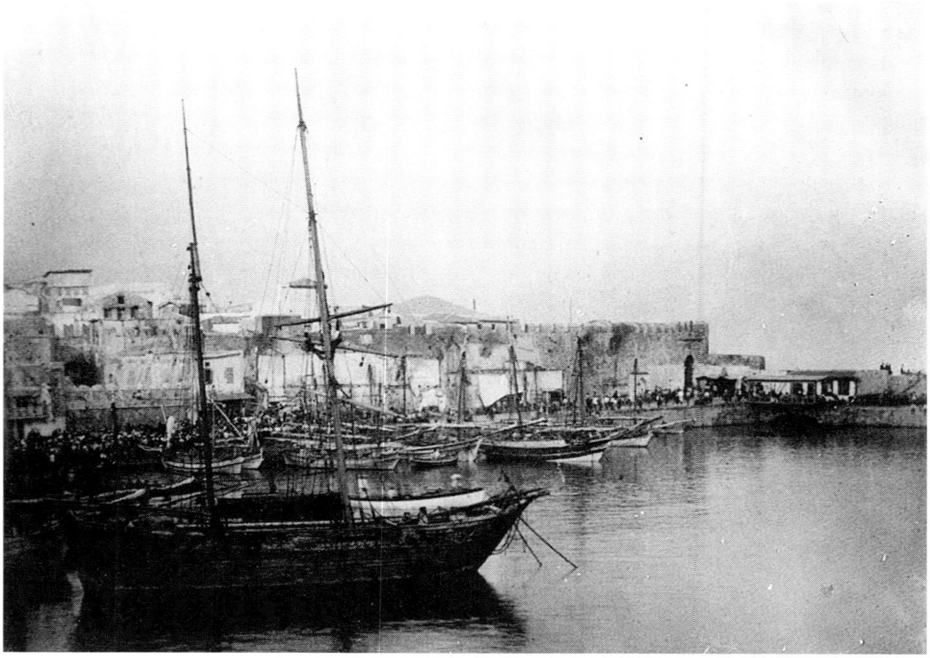

FIGURE 22. Herakleion, the high walls in the area of the harbor (Istituto Veneto di Scienze, Lettere ed Arti. Venezia. Archivio fotografico della Missione in Creta di Giuseppe Gerola)

meters. The height of the walls was also 11 meters. Stone buttresses that formed relieving arches supported the tension of the wall internally. Two rampart walks were created above the sloping revetment: the lower one was 3.50 meters wide and the higher one only 50 centimeters wide. A deep moat filled with sea water extended along the land walls.[38] The Byzantine towers seem to have been reused for a period after the walls had been widened by the Venetians, because there exist traces of a rampart walk along the curtain wall and a staircase leading to the towers. The Venetians raised the towers by adding a projecting rim at the top and opened a new casemate at a position higher than that of the old one. In times of peace it seems that the state leased these towers, which are referred to in the documents as *turres comunis*, to private individuals, who were required to preserve them in good condition.[39]

In 1585, when the suburbs to the south were fortified, the southern part of the old medieval fortifications between the land gate and the Porta Aurea was transformed into an ammunition warehouse and the quarters of the cavalry (Fig. 23).[40] The cavalry quarters alone had a hundred rooms on the ground floor that were probably located in the spaces created by the but-

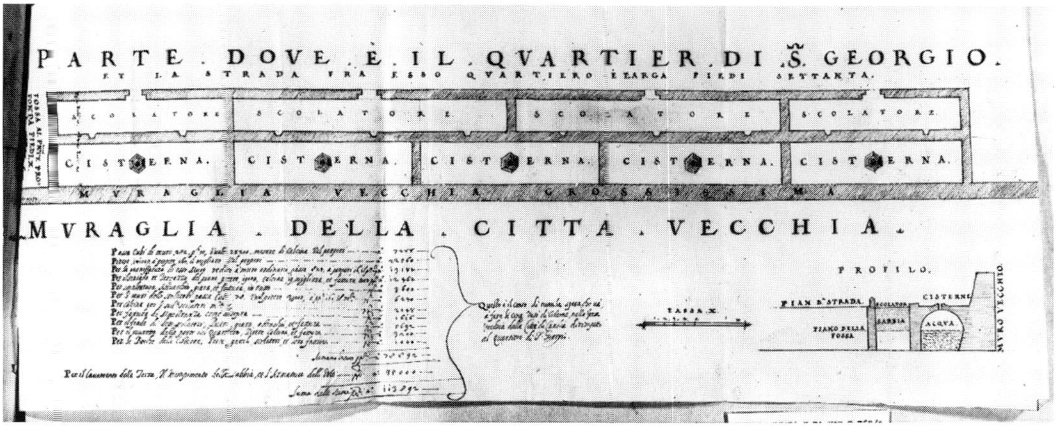

FIGURE 23. Francesco Basilicata, Cavalry quarters restoration project, 1625 (Archivio di Stato di Venezia, Provveditori di Terra e da Mar, F. 786/3)

tresses and the relieving arches in the interior of the walls. The walls to the east have not produced any vestiges until they approach the sea. From there the sea walls followed the natural trace of the coast and stood on a street that today runs parallel to the water; some vestiges of the rampart wall were unearthed on the actual Beaufort street in 1994.[41] In all probability the old arsenals abutted onto the fortification walls with two small gates opening into the harbor facilities. To the outside the sea walls were approximately 10 meters high, whereas toward the city (south side) the soil was elevated and formed a large platform, with the walls standing only 90 centimeters above ground. The lower courses were made of large ashlar blocks (Fig. 22). The sea walls were surmounted by crenellations and were fortified by defensive towers. According to an official report, written when these walls were repaired in 1560, they were 120 paces (208.68 meters) long and 6 meters high.[42]

The harbor was reinforced by two breakwaters. The western breakwater was crowned by a fort, the *castello*, at its north end. A tower also stood next to the arsenals, probably at the spot where the mole started.[43] The wall circuit continued to the west until the southwest corner of the city, at the bay of Dermata, where it was interrupted by the gate of the harbor, or Porta del Molo. In the late sixteenth century the western section of the old walls was transformed into quarters for the Italian soldiers in the area, which is still called in Greek *karteria*.[44] The walls to the southwest bordered the marketplace of Candia and were transformed in 1577 into a public warehouse (*fontico*) for the storage of grain, a building still standing when Gerola visited Candia. The detailed architectural drawing recording the conversion

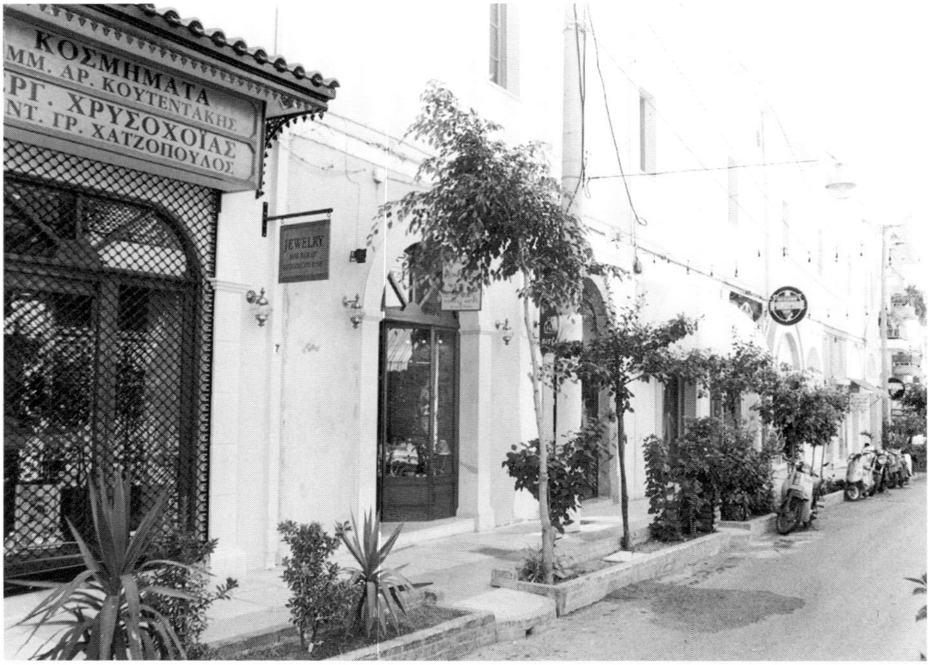

FIGURE 24. Herakleion, Chandakos street, relieving arches under city walls

of the walls allows us to conclude that the infrastructure of the curtain walls formed the basis for most of the twenty-nine vaulted shops at the ground floor of the warehouse (Fig. 20).[45] Only six of the shops had been made de novo in 1577. In fact, the function of these spaces has not changed as some of the rounded arches are still visible inside stores on the actual Chandakos street; these arched spaces must have been the original relieving arches of the city walls (Figs. 24 and 25). Additional documents assert that there were thirty-two stores on the ground level, each one of which measured 6.50 by 3 meters.[46] Their southern and northern walls, that is to say the exterior and interior face of the city walls, were 1 meter wide.

The maintenance of the fortifications was a large public expense that was met by fiscal revenues, especially the *comerclum,* which was the principal toll tax.[47] Any major restoration had to be authorized by the Senate in Venice and required additional state subsidies. The first such recorded instance occurred after the earthquake of 1303, which caused considerable damage in many parts of Candia, including large portions of the city's fortifications. Extensive restorations were undertaken from 1303 to 1309: workmen were sent from Venice,[48] and the chronicle of Lorenzo de Monacis records that the total cost of the repairs reached the enormous sum of thirty thousand gold ducats.[49] The capital necessary for the reconstruction of the city walls

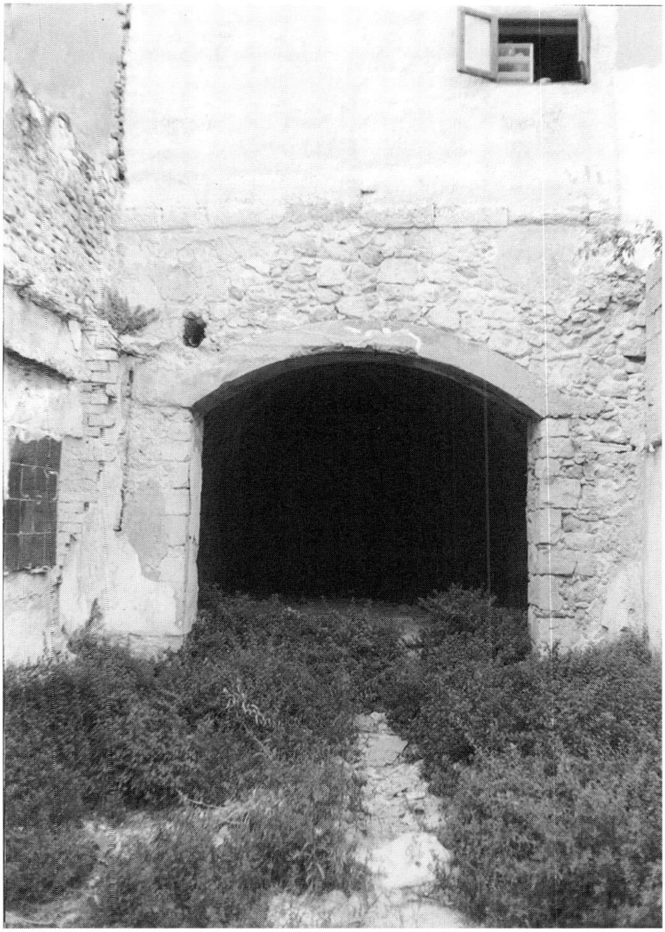

FIGURE 25. Herakleion, Chandakos street, relieving arch

in 1303 came in part from fiscal revenues, especially that of the *dacium porte civitatis* Candide, i.e. the import customs,[50] and in part from levies on the population and the clergy.[51]

The thirty thousand ducats that was spent on the fortifications following the earthquake of 1303 represents the largest documented amount ever spent on the city walls of Candia by the Venetians. We can assume, therefore, that the extensive damages inflicted on the wall circuit by the earthquake led the Venetians to approve a major reconstruction campaign: the curtain walls were to be reinforced by a glacis, probably the sloping wall that the archaeological excavations have revealed. Of course, this hypothesis can only be verified or refuted by archaeological excavations along the entire course of the walls, a project that is not likely to be undertaken very soon considering the urban growth of modern Herakleion and the prime location of the old

Venetian walls within the urban fabric. Yet, the admiration of the traveler Symeon Simeonis for the city's fortifications in 1322 corroborates the assumption that a major restoration had taken place just before his visit.[52]

In addition to the earthquakes that are an endemic risk in Crete, the Venetians had to battle the devastating waves of the Aegean Sea that eroded the northern section of the city walls. Major repairs were undertaken in 1403, 1451, and 1506.[53] In 1403 a thirty-five-meter-long section of the walls that bordered the Jewish quarter of Candia was reconstructed. The Jewish community had to contribute half of the expenses, since the Jews whose quarter abutted the walls at this point were those who benefited the most from this repair.[54] A special clause was included in the decree: private residences should not abut the new section of the wall as had been the practice in the thirteenth and fourteenth centuries.

People entered and left the city of Candia through two main gates, the land and sea gates. They were located on the same axis, marking the northern and southern edges of the main artery of the city, the *ruga magistra*. Both gates were guarded by Venetian officials so that access was regulated according to governmental prescriptions. The gates also regulated the flow of commodities into Candia: they opened to the agricultural hinterland and to the internationally oriented commercial harbor. The city walls, along with these gates, were the major architectural element that controlled population distribution, admission to the civic center, and accessibility to its administrative and commercial resources.

The principal gate, which was destroyed by an earthquake in 1856, was known as *Porta di Piazza* or simply as the *Voltone* (large vault), a name that recalls the monumental vaulted gateway that opened to the suburbs (Fig. 20).[55] A plaque decorated with the lion of St. Mark surmounted the arched opening and a similar plaque must have existed on the outer side of the gate, facing the burg.[56] The gate was closed at night and opened in the morning following the sounding of a bell, probably that of the bell tower of St. Mark.[57] In 1475 the gateway was strengthened with a portcullis meant to defend the city against an imminent Ottoman attack.[58] It is likely that the entire layout of the gate was reconfigured and strengthened during the same construction campaign, since the two towers that are visible in Fig. 19 contained coats of arms dating to 1472 (west tower) and to the early 1480s (east tower).[59] By the seventeenth century, but possibly from an earlier date, a guard was stationed at the land gate.[60] Vestiges of the gate's foundations, namely, parts of arched structures, were uncovered in 1952 and 1992.[61]

The Porta del Molo was the major gate that opened from the port to the city; it is through this gate that most foreigners entered the city of

Candia.[62] This gate was still standing when Gerola visited Candia (Fig. 26), but it was destroyed at the beginning of the twentieth century by the English troops that were in control of Crete at the time. Despite plans to enlarge this gateway in the sixteenth century, it remained a simple round arched opening with no traces of a monumental vaulted space behind it.[63] Approximately fifty meters to the west of the Porta del Molo there existed a smaller gate known as the gate of the arsenals.[64] It provided access from the interior of the city to the arsenals, which were located outside the city walls at a lower level, and it was probably a service entrance not used by the population. The gate was still standing at the beginning of the twentieth century (Fig. 27) but had been walled in before Gerola arrived in Crete. It was surmounted by three large merlons and was restored in 1552–54, as the surviving coats of arms indicate.[65]

FORTIFIED PORTS

Fortifications were a major concern throughout the Venetian colonies, their primary purpose being to stand as firm strongholds against enemy attacks. The extant governmental documents demonstrate that the authorities spent large sums for the repair and refurbishment of city walls, in the form of subsidies either from the metropole or from the local fisc. At times special contributions were demanded from the local communities, as in the case of the Jewish community of Candia, who were asked to subsidize the fortifications closest to their quarter. No information on the fortification of the cities of Crete is available until the year 1300; after the earthquake of 1303, which damaged many buildings in Crete and the Aegean, the archival information abounds. Rather than assume that the towns of Crete were perceived as well equipped militarily, I would suggest that it was the fierce indigenous rebellion led by the Greek aristocrat Alexios Calergi that did not allow the Venetians to mount construction campaigns for the walls of the Cretan cities. A year after a treaty was signed with the Greek lord (1299) the state channeled the income from the fisc for the consolidation of Canea's defenses. In the 1320s the rector was granted three hundred hyperpera for the construction of city gates.[66]

By the second quarter of the fourteenth century the growth of the population of the cities of Crete obliged the authorities of Canea and Retimo to expand the city walls to incorporate the suburbs. The decision to fortify the suburbs of Canea was taken in 1336,[67] but the completion of the project

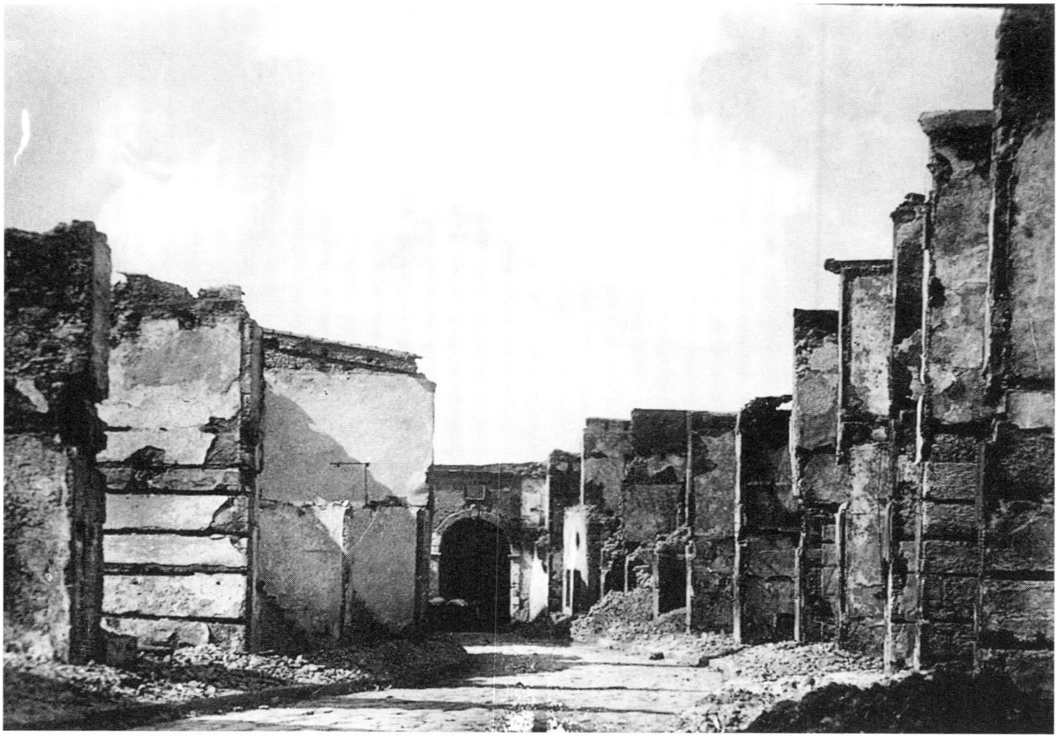

FIGURE 26. Herakleion, sea gate before demolition (Istituto Veneto di Scienze, Lettere ed Arti. Venezia. Archivio fotografico della Missione in Creta di Giuseppe Gerola)

took more than twenty years.[68] In 1383 the rectors were authorized to increase the height of the rampart from 1.74 to 2 meters for a distance of 260 meters. These walls incorporated the southern burg, forming an irregular pentagon, and were reinforced by square towers and bastions in the corners (Fig. 28).[69] The suburbs of Sitia that were located to the west of the fort were never enclosed by a circuit of fortification walls. The suburb of Negroponte was not fortified and during the incursions of Turks in the early fourteenth century the Jewish community that used to reside at the south-eastern section of the suburbs moved inside the walled city while their synagogue remained *extra muros* (1359).[70]

Indeed, the document of the colonization of Canea in 1252 (see Chapter 1, n. 2) ordered the rectors and the other officials to supervise the construction of city walls and moats in Canea – the enceinte, which was erected by the villagers who worked in the fiefs, was already in place by 1255.[71] In order to minimize the cost, earlier fortifications were reused and strengthened throughout the thirteenth and fourteenth centuries. In Canea the large quantities of spoils of antique columns that were used as building material

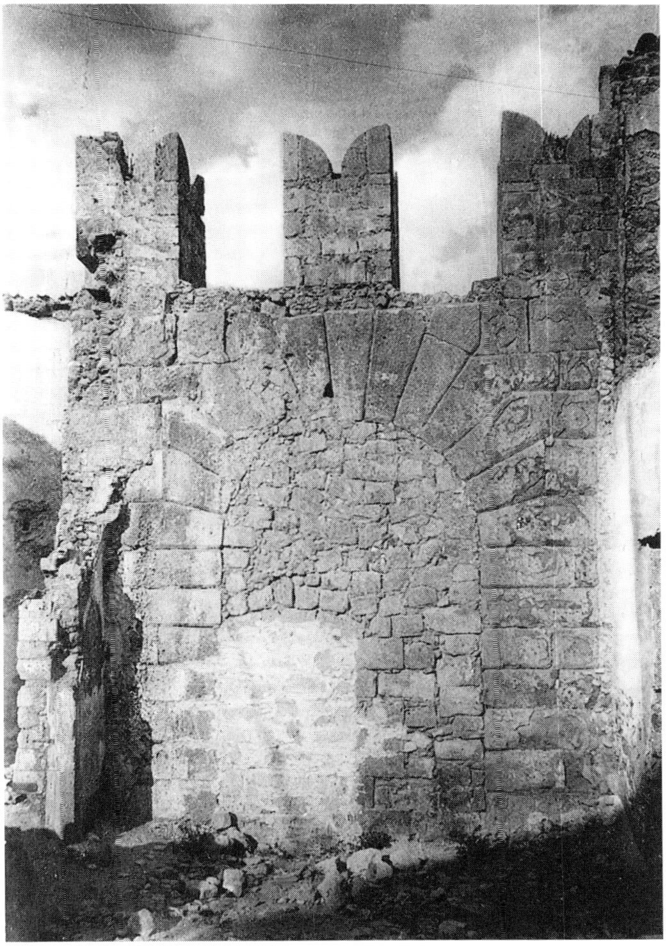

FIGURE 27. Herakleion, gate of the arsenals before demolition (Istituto Veneto di Scienze, Lettere ed Arti. Venezia. Archivio fotografico della Missione in Creta di Giuseppe Gerola)

suggest that the medieval walls followed the trace of the enceinte of the ancient acropolis (Fig. 29).[72] The walls that envelop the upper town of Chania are well preserved and two of the gates are still visible; a third was photographed by Gerola (Figs. 30, 31, and 32). In Negroponte, the "new walls" of the city are mentioned in a 1216 document, but similarly to the situation in Candia we must assume that this refers to a refurbishment of the Byzantine walls when the Venetians took over the island.[73] It is unknown whether the walls of Negroponte were dismantled in 1262 as the treaty between the *Tercieri* and William II Villehardouin of Achaia demanded. This

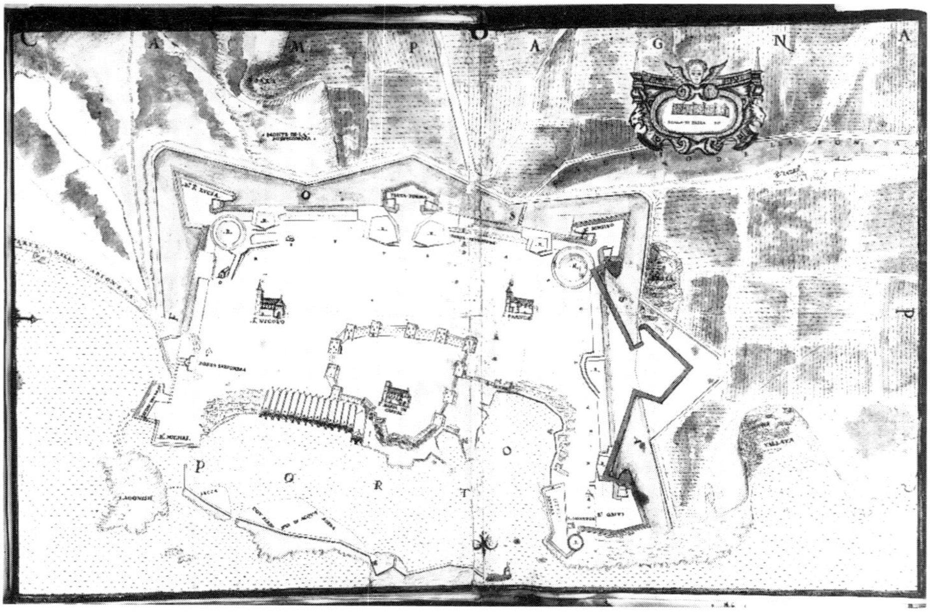

FIGURE 28. View of Canea in the sixteenth century, Pianta delle fortificazioni con la città, il porto di S. Lazzaro (Archivio di Stato di Venezia, Altante Mormori, c. 66, foto # 18, neg. DG 141/18)

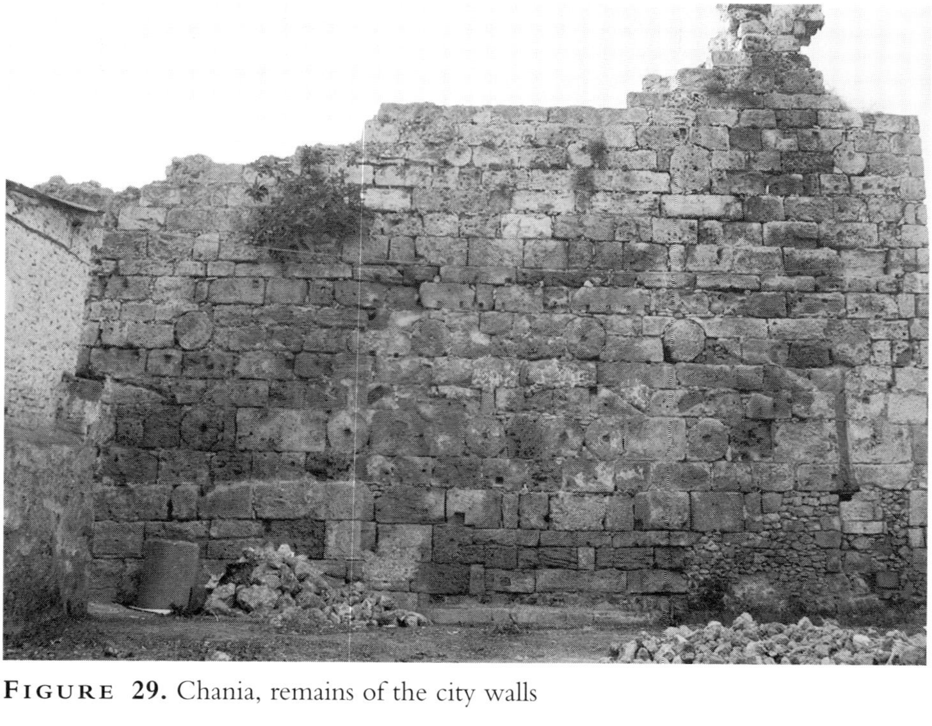

FIGURE 29. Chania, remains of the city walls

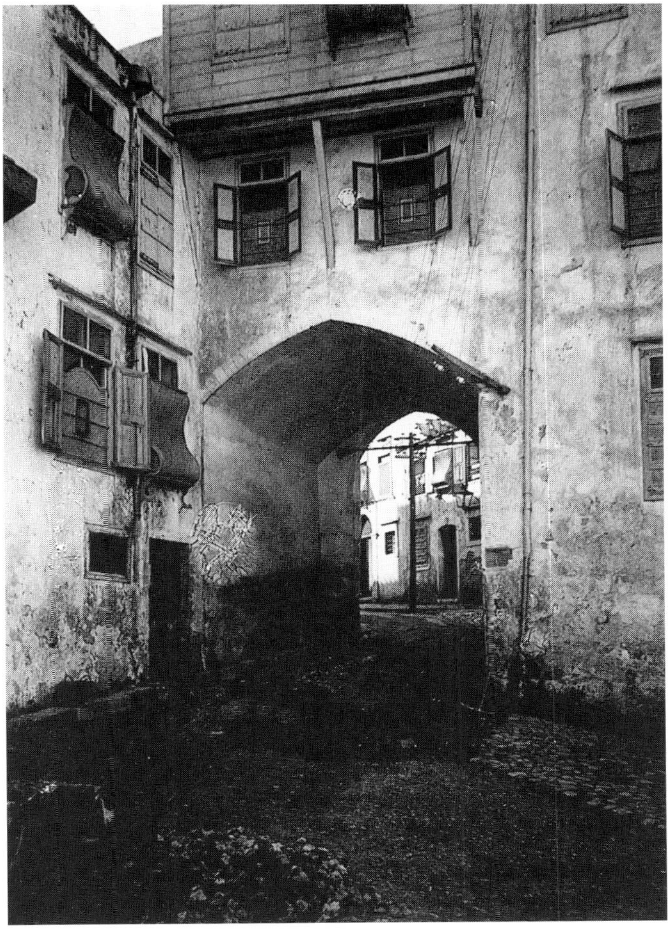

FIGURE 30. Chania, western gate of the castello (Istituto Veneto di Scienze, Lettere ed Arti. Venezia. Archivio fotografico della Missione in Creta di Giuseppe Gerola)

clause must have been just a rhetorical exhortation as the walls, towers, and moat of the city figure prominently in the records of the Venetian Senate throughout this period until 1470 when Negroponte fell to the Ottomans.[74] It is often difficult to discern the extent of repairs undertaken on the basis of the language of the documents, which for self-aggrandizing reasons often exaggerate the contribution of the official who supervised a given job. A careful consideration of the time allotted to the refurbishment or of the monies spent usually gives us some better sense of the situation. In fact, major fortification campaigns are recorded in the last quarter of the thirteenth century, probably anticipating attacks of pirates or even a war between Venice and Byzantium. After the Byzantine recovery of Constantinople it

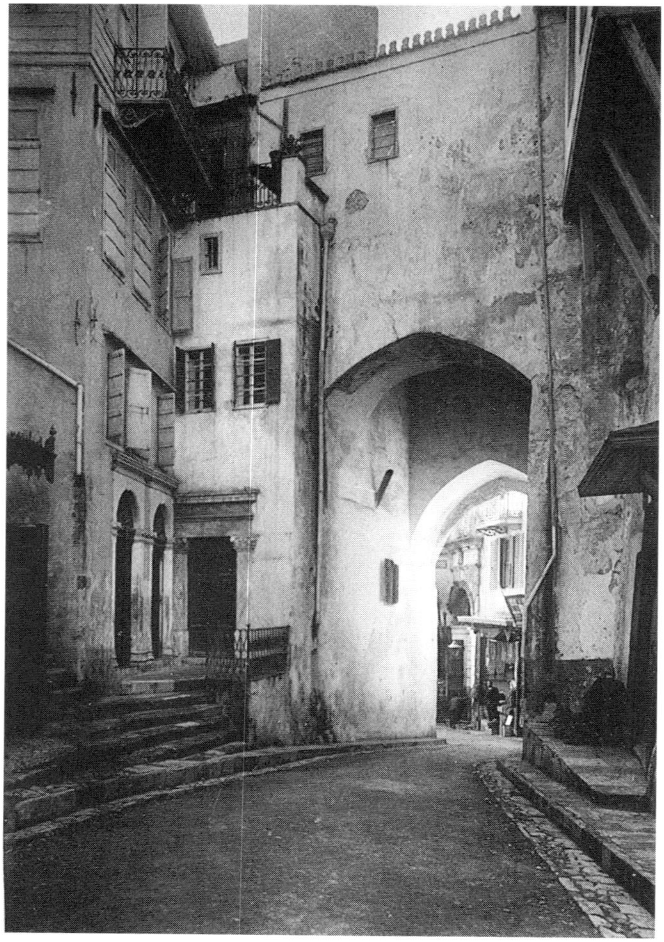

FIGURE 31. Chania, eastern gate of the castello (Istituto Veneto di Scienze, Lettere ed Arti. Venezia. Archivio fotografico della Missione in Creta di Giuseppe Gerola)

was clear that the Byzantine emperor Michael VIII Palaiologos mistrusted the Venetians and, in the face of the threat of Charles of Anjou, who was trying to reinstall his son on the throne of the Latin empire of Constantinople, wavered in his preferences between them and the Genoese.[75] Negroponte received large subventions from the Senate in Venice for its fortifications: in 1283 and 1285 the *bailo* was granted a loan of five thousand hyperpera to be used for the fortification of the island against the army of the Byzantines,[76] and in the early fourteenth century, when the city of Negroponte fought to resist the siege of the Catalans (1311), the large amount of ten thousand hyperpera was devoted to the walls (Figs. 33 and 34).[77]

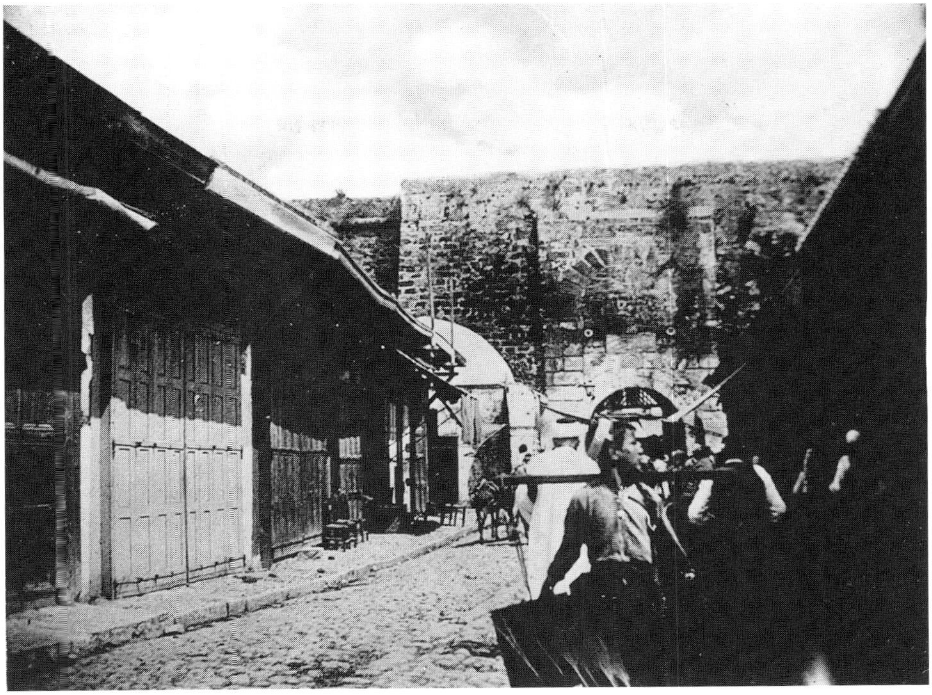

FIGURE 32. Chania, gate of Rethymnon, now destroyed (Istituto Veneto di Scienze, Lettere ed Arti. Venezia. Archivio fotografico della Missione in Creta di Giuseppe Gerola)

The impressive remains of the fortifications of Modon/Methoni date to the sixteenth century and later. We possess minimal documentation on the fortifications of the town before the fifteenth century, but we know that from the early days of the empire it was a highly fortified stronghold. The strategic position of this town made it an essential outpost for the maritime hegemony of Venice in the waters between southern Greece and Crete/Africa. In 1293 the Maggior Consiglio in Venice loaned two thousand hyperpera to the governors of Modon to rebuild the city. Unfortunately, the sources are silent about the reason for this expenditure, which must have been translated into extensive works: there is no record of any major catastrophe in the area or of an enemy attack destroying the city (Figs. 35 and 36).[78] The suburbs were encircled by a wall in the early fifteenth century: a large shipment of torneselli was sent to Coron and Modon for repairs to the walls in 1407, and in 1415 it was decided that two thousand hyperpera from taxes should be put aside annually until the completion of the fortification.[79] The sister city of Modon, Coron, never acquired the same prominence, but its fortifications were also strengthened in the last quarter of the thirteenth

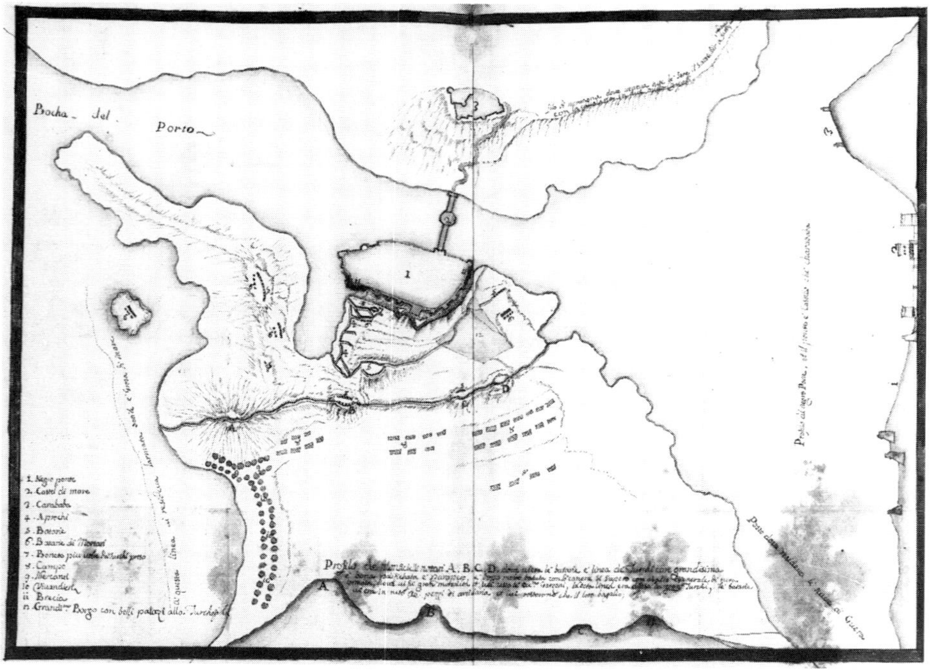

FIGURE 33. Negroponte. Pianta delle fortificazioni, con il porto e lo schieramento delle forze turche. (Archivio di Stato di Venezia, Archivio Grimani F. 57/172, Fasc. D/d, Neg. DS 139/5; positiva 59)

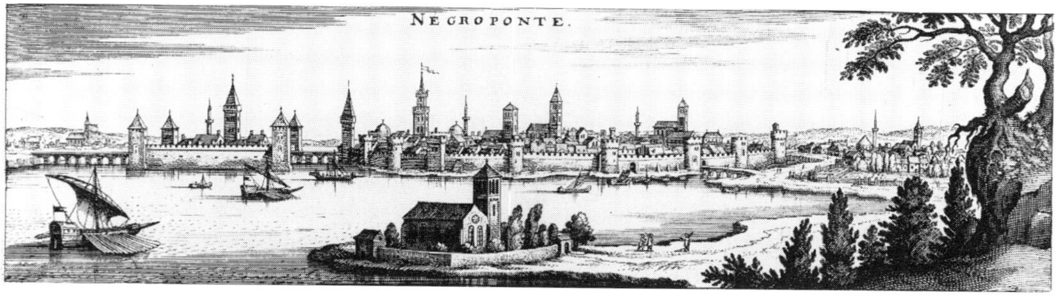

FIGURE 34. View of the city of Negroponte/Chalkis, sixteenth century (The Gennadius Library, American School of Classical Studies)

century (Fig. 37). In order to handle the large expenses for the maintenance of the city's fortifications in the 1280s the three governors (*castellani*) got authorization to proceed gradually: they could only have thirty-five meters per year erected. This project stalled at least twice: in 1283 the Maggior Consiglio in Venice instructed the governor of Coron to construct an arsenal and towers instead of the usual extent of the city walls, and in 1288 the governors had to restore the arsenals and the palaces instead.[80]

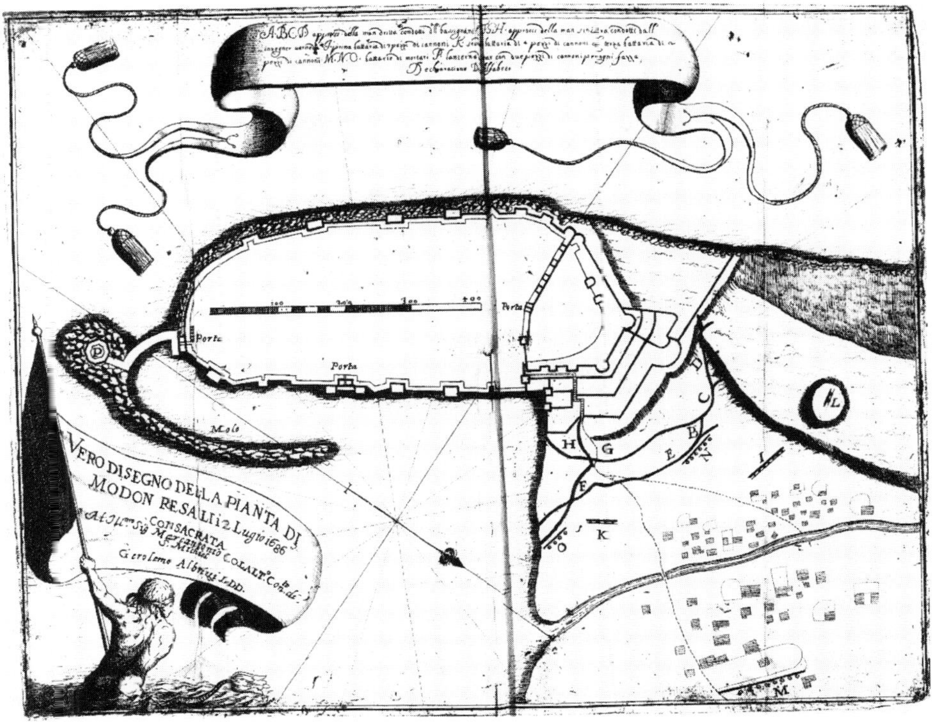

FIGURE 35. Gerolamo Albrizzi, Modone. Pianta della città e delle fortificazioni, 1686 (Archivio di Stato di Venezia, Archivio Grimani, F. 57/172, Fasc. B/c, Neg. 138/4, positiva 40)

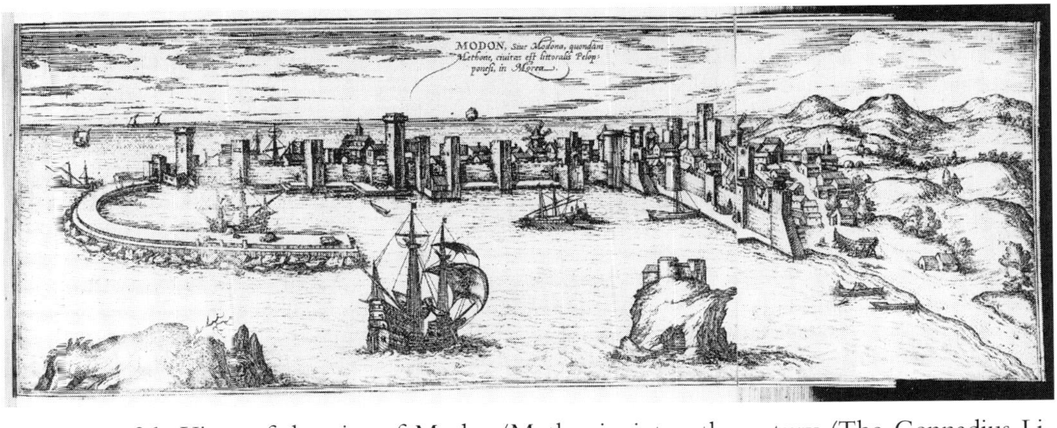

FIGURE 36. View of the city of Modon/Methoni, sixteenth century (The Gennadius Library, American School of Classical Studies)

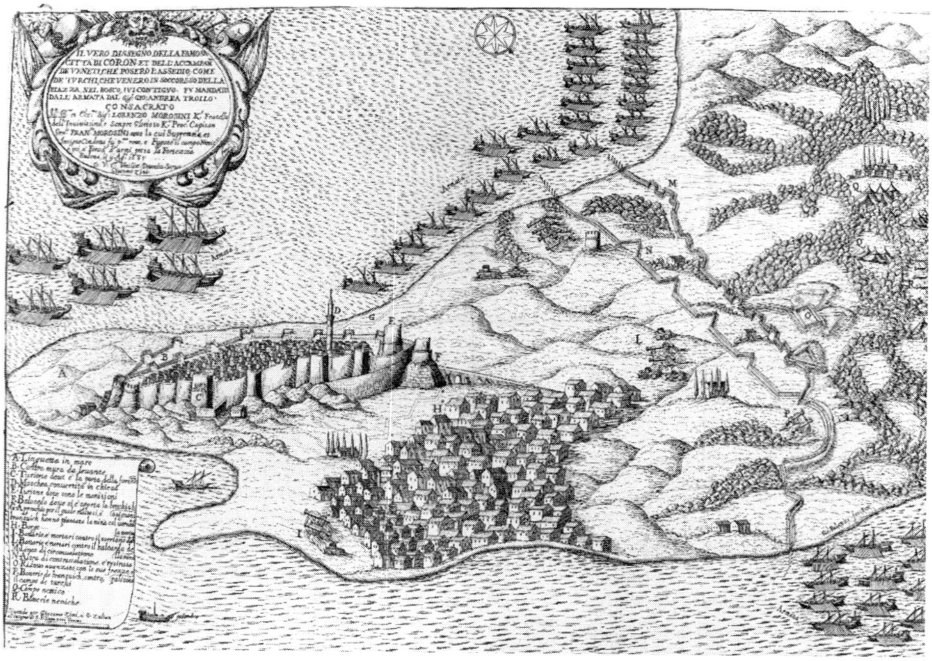

FIGURE 37. Città e fortezza di Coron (Civico Museo Correr, M 39665)

In the thirteenth century the city walls appear to have encircled relatively small territories, which, as we can tell, coincided with the Byzantine confines of the towns. The appearance of the walls seems to have been uniform: as we can see in the walls of Canea the rampart stood on large ashlar blocks more than two meters wide, with the upper faces displaying similarly ordered stones and the interior filled in with diverse materials (Fig. 38). Square or round towers were placed at intervals to provide additional reinforcement. Vestiges of eight circular towers and three bastions are still visible in Canea, where there were originally eleven or thirteen towers in all (Fig. 28).[81] A circular tower defended the harbor to the west.[82]

The gates that pierced the city walls ranged from two to four in number and usually defined the major urban arteries. They were decorated with coats of arms of Venetian officials (in the sixteenth century these are usually the *provveditori)* and the conspicuous lion of St. Mark; examples can still be seen on the sea gate of Negroponte (the Porta di Marina), and in Zara, Ragusa, Naupaktos/Lepanto, Napoli di Romania/Nauplion, and numerous islands in the Aegean, including Crete of course (Fig. 20).[83] Within these fortified enclosures the major administrative buildings and Latin churches of the Venetians acquired privileged status.

Topographical considerations often determined the appearance of the

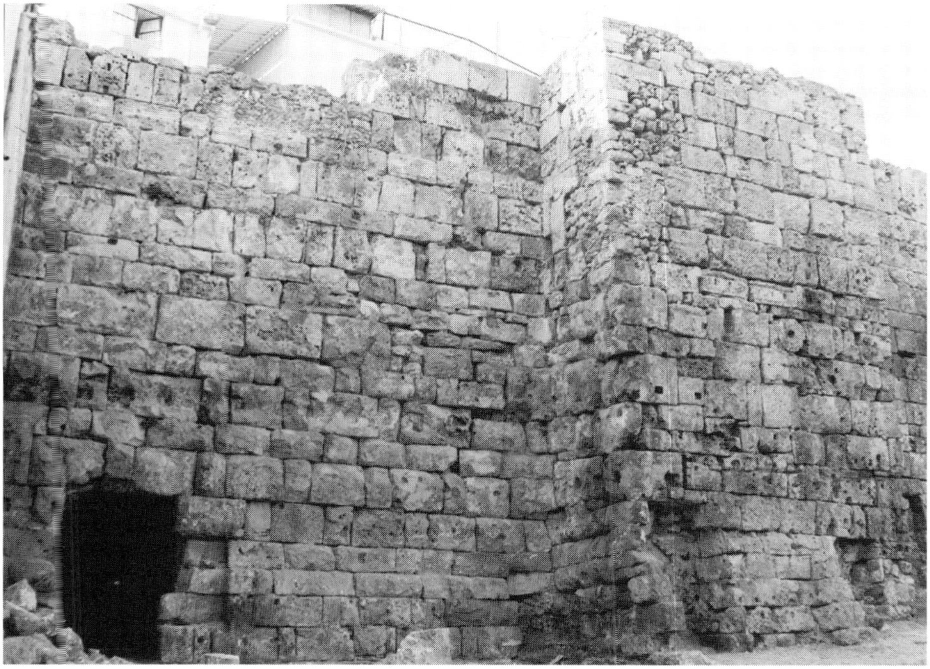

FIGURE 38. Chania, remains of the city walls

cities. Whereas the core of the city of Candia was enveloped by the city walls, in the case of the uneven terrain of Canea and Retimo there was a separate *castrum*. In Canea and Retimo the administrative structures were in the acropolis, and in this way they were separated from the main practical spaces of the city (the loggia, the public fountain, and the market square) that lay in the lower town. In these cases, questions of direct access to the primary economic urban resources by a larger segment of the population seem to have dictated the topographical arrangement. The lower city of Retimo must have been protected by city walls running along an east-west axis to the southern part of the city because Andrea Dandolo refers to the city as a *castrum* in 1229; few archaeological vestiges suggest that walls also fortified the northern side of the city toward the sea.[84] In 1316 the rector of Sitia, Marco Justinian, was granted two thousand hyperpera for the construction of his residence and the fortification of the town, which most probably was only then surrounded by walls.[85] However, concrete reference to the form of these fortifications is available only in the midfifteenth century, when we learn that the inner city was enclosed by walls and towers.[86] The fort had a triangular form and it comprised the residence of the rector and the Latin cathedral (Fig. 39).

Among the most significant functional spaces of the Venetian colonies

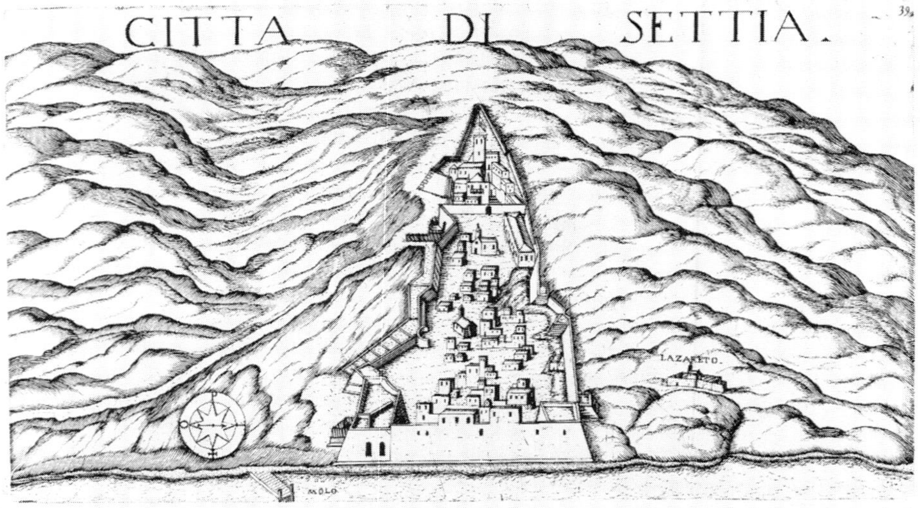

FIGURE 39. M. Boschini, "Città di Settia," in *Il Regno tutto di Candia* (Venice, 1651) (The Gennadius Library, American School of Classical Studies)

were the port and the arsenals, which were vaulted spaces meant to build or house Venetian galleys through the winter. The grandeur of the Venetian arsenal with its imposing entrance and its immense dimensions is not duplicated anywhere in the empire.[87] Nevertheless, it seems that whereas in the thirteenth century the colonies offered spaces merely for the protection of the galleys, in the fourteenth century new arsenals were built in the colonies (like the one in Ragusa/Dubrovnik in 1329) specifically for shipbuilding. The remains of the arsenals in Candia and Canea are still impressive. Candia's arsenal facilities are first mentioned in 1281, when the *duca* and his counselors were authorized to spend fifteen hundred hyperpera for the construction of a covered arsenal able to house one ship.[88] This must have stood near the southern entrance of the harbor and may have been an elongated vaulted space covered with a wooden roof, as fire was considered a hazard in 1361.[89] Between 1362 and 1366 two more vaulted spaces were constructed in Candia and in the 1370s the direction of the arsenal was transferred to the authority of the admiral of the port of Candia, highlighting the increased significance of the port and its facilities.[90] Three more vaults were added in 1412–30.[91] A devastating fire in the 1440s caused severe damage to the arsenals: the wall toward St. Daniel had collapsed, along with the roof of the new arsenal and the columns supporting it.[92] Rather than repairing the existing thirteenth-century arsenals, workers constructed five new elongated spaces covered with cross vaults by 1451, with explicit orders to produce a light galley every two years.[93] Each space measured 28 paces by 26 feet, i.e. 48.69 by 9 meters. Two smaller spaces 24 feet (8.35 meters) wide were going to be added next to the older arsenals. The archaeological vestiges of the western and southern walls allow us to reconstruct the original appearance of these fifteenth-century structures. The soil of the arsenals was at a slope, so that the piers ranged in height from 8 to 2.60 meters. Here the topography of the area served the practical application of forming a ramp, which made the dragging of the galleys easier. The western wall, on which the newer arsenals abutted, was built with irregular blocks and was strengthened with five piers, which were located at 9-meter intervals and supported side arches and the cross vaults (Figs. 40 and 41). The piers that marked the northwest and southeast corners that still survive were 4.30 meters and 3 meters large, respectively, and were constructed more carefully than the masonry of the wall, with well-cut stones (Fig. 42). The second and fourth piers that survive in the western side were smaller, measuring 1.60 meters, as does the fourth pillar on the southern side. There are still traces of the western arch and ribs for the cross vaults. Ten more vaulted spaces were added to the west and then to the east of the existing arsenals in the second half of the sixteenth century (1552, 1582, and 1608).[94] So, the nineteen vaulted spaces that could be observed in 1630 made a clear statement of the increasing significance of the arsenal and military importance of Candia (Figs. 41 and 43).

The arsenal of Canea was probably Byzantine in origin as it was mentioned in the first Venetian documents that deal with the city in 1252 and by 1255 it was referred to as the *arsena vetus*.[95] It was repaired in the first quarter of the fourteenth century, but the fragmentary documents of the Senate that have survived are not explicit about its architectural appearance.[96] Starting in 1467 the vaulted spaces of the arsenals were expanded to the south of the port: to the original two vaulted spaces another fifteen vaults were added by 1599.[97] Curiously, they had not been incorporated within the circuit of the city walls until the sixteenth century. Of the original seventeen vaults of the arsenals of Canea seven are still visible; they were used as a customs house until recently (Fig. 44). The main body of the arsenals was covered with barrel vaults, and the northern facade ended in a series of gable roofs. In Negroponte there are no remains of the arsenal, which may have been a twelfth-century construction of the Byzantine administration, but it is mentioned in the sources in 1319 and throughout the fourteenth and fifteenth centuries. It must have been located in the southern section of the walls near the Porta del Arsenal and was primarily a place for repairs and refuge of Venetian galleys as well as for storing of ammunitions.[98]

Of similar importance to the walls and the arsenals were the harbors, the raison d'être of the colonies.[99] The port accommodated the commercial ships

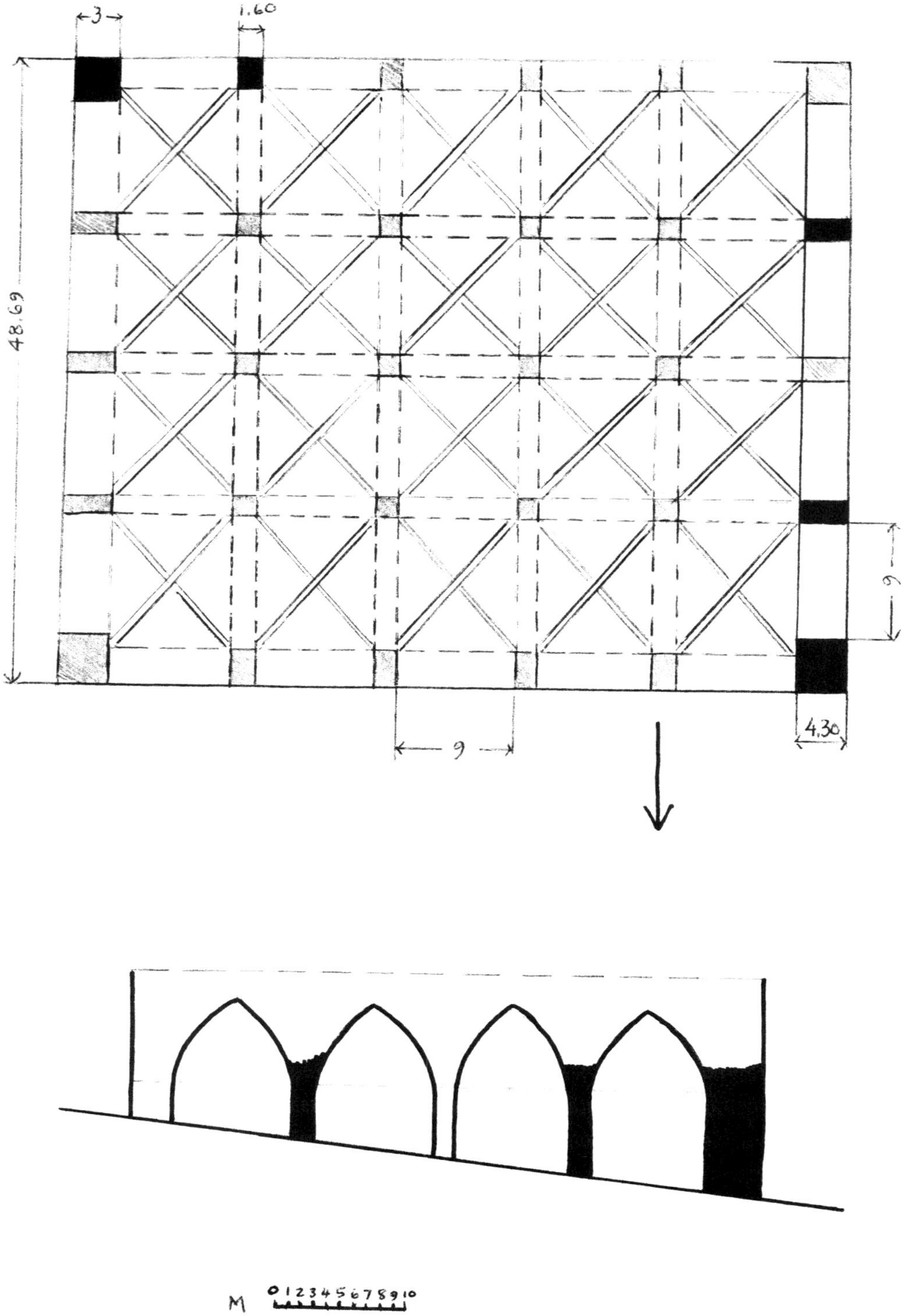

FIGURE 40. Herakleion, schematic plan of the arsenals in 1451

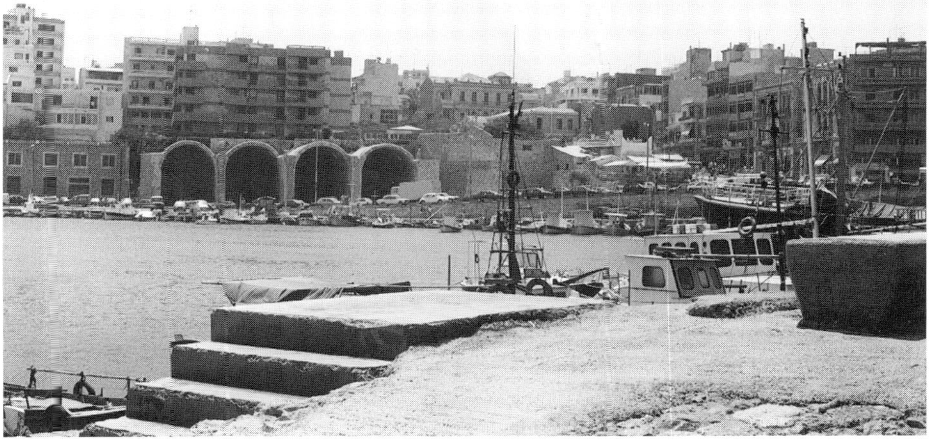

FIGURE 41. Herakleion, view of arsenals of the midfifteenth century

and the war galleys that protected the convoys of Venice in the Eastern Mediterranean. The commodities that arrived at the port were transported into the central marketplace of the cities, and in the case of Crete its agricultural products from the hinterland followed the same route before they were loaded onto the ships to be taken to Venice and the Levant. The port of Candia seems to have been the only harbor on the north side of the island when the Venetians took control of Crete, but a recent reevaluation of the sources has suggested that the artificial harbor was not well kept before 1204.[100] By the fourteenth century Candia attracted international trade and was a place where commercial ships anchored, were loaded, and departed for the Levant and Venice. Thus, its maintenance was a major concern for the Venetian authorities. Today the late medieval port is used as a marina for small sailing and fishing boats (Fig. 41); a larger commercial harbor has been constructed to the east of the city for the accommodation of the modern ships that transport passengers and merchandise to the island. Thus, the old port has kept to a large degree its original appearance, with the exception of the sea walls, which do not block the northward entrance to the city anymore.

The port of Candia was relatively small in size: it covered a surface of fourteen hundred square Venetian paces and could accommodate approximately fifty galleys when it was in excellent condition.[101] Whereas the eastern

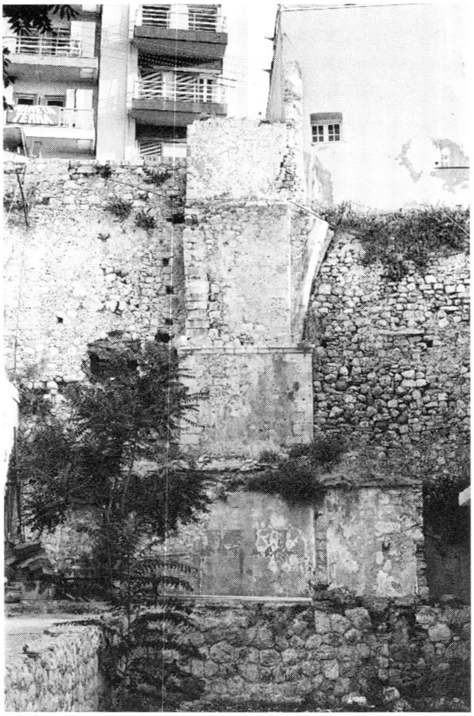

FIGURE 42. Herakleion, pier of the arsenals

side of the port was naturally protected, the Muslims had erected a 270-meter-long breakwater to protect the western and northern sides from enemy attacks and from the sea waves. The entrance to the port was defended by a castle that was built before 1269 at the end of this breakwater and will be discussed in more detail in the next chapter. The port faced two kinds of problems that were never fully resolved: on the one hand, the gusty north and northwest winds of the Aegean made the approach and anchorage of large ships difficult, and, on the other hand, sand brought in by the sea waves and the two small rivers of Dermata (to the west) and Cacinava (to the east of the city) silted the port.[102] Sea currents were also responsible for the silting of the moats; the documents use the word *amonite*, which is based on the Greek word for sand (ἄμμος).[103] In 1333 the Senate in Venice sent the engineer Francesco delle Barche in Crete to solve the problems of the port and granted considerable sums to the authorities to fund the campaign. By 1341 the existing breakwater had been extended by 26.10 meters to the northeast and another 139.20-meter-long (80-paces-long) breakwater was built on a northwest axis.[104] The entrance of the harbor was quite small (21

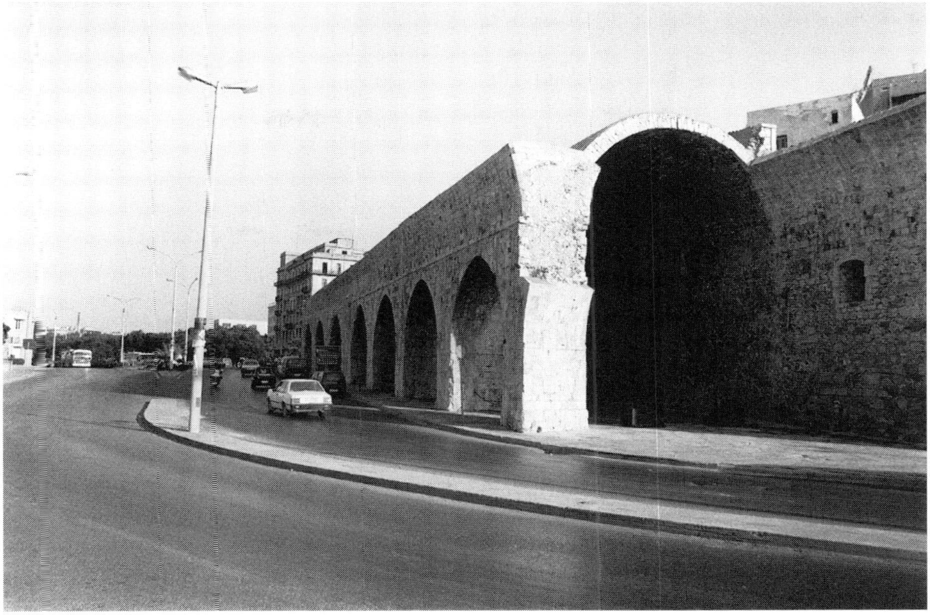

FIGURE 43. Herakleion, vault of the *arsenali nuovissimi*

paces), and it was closed at night by a chain so that no boat or ship could exit without the permission of the authorities.[105]

Despite the holes that were opened in the body of the new breakwater, its mass stopped the opposing current that drove the sand away so the harbor silted up.[106] By the middle of the fourteenth century the depth of the water had decreased from 4.86 meters to 2.43 meters, not allowing heavily loaded commercial galleys to anchor.[107] Piling of garbage into the port made the situation even worse.[108] Although large allocations were made for excavating the harbor in the second half of the fourteenth and throughout the fifteenth century,[109] more often than not it seems that the galleys would anchor at the island of Standea across from Herakleion or in the port of Paleocastro to the west and merchandise would reach Candia on smaller boats. In the late fifteenth century the best port for the Venetian fleet seems to have been that of Suda in the area of Chania.

In spite of its ultimate ineffectiveness as anchorage for the fleet, the port of Candia was equipped with all the necessary monuments that proclaimed it as a bastion of Venetian presence in the Mediterranean: arsenals, breakwater, and fort with effigies of the lion of St. Mark. The increasing importance of the port in the trade system of the Venetians is also reflected in decisions of the authorities to regulate private usage of the port. Private boats and

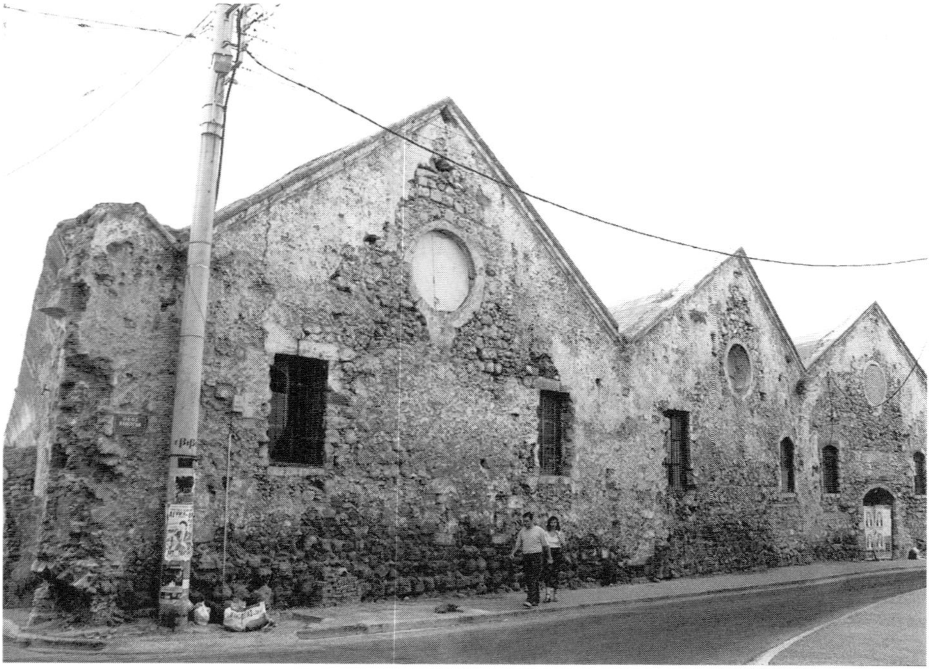

FIGURE 44. Chania, arsenals seen from the north

ships were ousted from the harbor in 1314, and in the following years (1316 and 1319) the ships were asked to obtain special permission from the state in order to load and unload merchandise in the harbor and the bay of Dermata.[110] The sources do not specify the reason for these decisions, but we can assume that the aforementioned decrees attempted to regulate the use of the port in favor of the large ships. This more public profile of the port was definitely promoted by the new public warehouse, which was built by midfourteenth century.[111]

In contrast, in Canea no warehouses stood in the area of the harbor until the end of the fourteenth century: in 1394 mules were used to transport the grain to the public storehouse, which was located four miles away.[112] The problems of the sea currents caused similar concerns of silting in the harbor, where a long breakwater was built and monies were spent annually on maintenance works.[113] However, the most frequent short-term remedy was the sinking of a ship toward the entrance of the harbor to close its opening.[114] The small port of Retimo, which still preserves its medieval outlook almost unchanged, had similar problems: in 1300 the authorities decided to spend the income of the fisc on the improvement of its breakwater, in 1383 an old galley was sunk in the harbor in order to prevent its silting, and in 1386 the state raised eight hundred hyperpera from the Jewish community in order to restore the port.[115] The town of Negroponte had two fortified harbors on each side of the Euripos bridge, where the sea gate, the Porta di Marina, stood.[116] In 1402 the Venetians erected a tower by the southern port, near the church of Saint Mark, to control the passage of ships, the so-called point of San Marco a Cazonelis or Ponte di San Marco. As in the case of the sea fort in Candia, which was built far out in the sea, the Venetians erected a conspicuous tower on the bridge that connected Euboea with the mainland, a visible landmark of their dominion on Negroponte. Only the base of this tower is still visible.[117]

This brief survey of the military structures set up in the colonies makes apparent that city walls, forts, and arsenals were prominent parts of the urban space that announced the significance of the Venetian empire and its military power to seafarers on a grand scale. The next chapter looks at the next stage of colonization. Once the cities were fortified and manned militarily, how did the Venetian colonists establish their rule? What did the urban space of the colonies look like? How many older structures did the colonists reuse? What were the new monuments that they erected? Was there a coherent plan in laying out the foundations of their colonial rule in the urban space?

THREE

VENICE, THE HEIR OF BYZANTIUM

Candida alias civitas Venetiarum apud Levantem.

Venetian senator, fifteenth century

Chief among the buildings promoting Venice's presence and political organization in the colonies were structures central to the exercise of colonial control: piazzas, markets, and governmental palaces, as well as the new Latin rite churches (which will be discussed in the following chapter), military structures, and obviously the new residences built for the colonists. On the basis of practices in the modern period, one right away assumes that the new monuments would be made in a style foreign to the region to proclaim the imperial political affiliations of the authorities. Matters seem to have been more complicated than that in the Venetian colonies. The spaces of Byzantine Chandax that were preserved in Venetian Candia take center stage in this investigation because they seem to deny the fact that there was a radical change in the architectural profile of Candia under the new Venetian regime. In fact, the reuse of fortifications and preexisting monuments betrays a disinterest in modifying the architectural appearance of the city. Given the usual sophistication and thoughtfulness in every aspect of the Venetians' political establishment in the Levant, such an act must signal a deliberate choice with a definite meaning.

By the middle of the fifteenth century the official position of the Republic was to portray Crete as a projection of the self-image of Venice. In 1455 the senators called Candia an *alias civitas Venetiarum apud Levantem.*[1] What exactly does such a proclamation mean? In order to view Candia as a second Venice in the Eastern Mediterranean, these senators must have had a distinct image of Venice in mind, presumably one that encapsulated a political and perhaps also a cultural portrait of the Republic. Did the architectural and artistic profile of the metropole play any role in this constructed image? Direct evidence on this point may be scant, but the striking replication of urban configurations of Venice in Candia as well as other colonies like Negroponte points to a conscious symbolic and possibly physical manipulation of the urban space. One can assume, therefore, that imitation of architectural patterns of the metropole was significant in creating the colonial space of Candia. This point is problematized, however, by the lack of a uniform architectural front in Venice itself and by the peculiar relationship between Venetian and Byzantine art in the thirteenth and fourteenth centuries. Not only was the basilica of San Marco modeled after the celebrated church of the Holy Apostles in Constantinople, but small cross-in-square churches like the original church of San Giacomo at the Rialto must have served as a model for most parish churches in Venice not only in the twelfth but well into the thirteenth century.[2]

To the extent that we can take the piazza San Marco as paradigmatic of Venice's own vision of herself, it is worth noting that before the sixteenth-century remodelings of Jacopo Sansovino the appearance of the Piazza and the Piazzetta was less ordered than it is today: nongovernmental buildings like hostelries, market stalls, and granaries occupied the spots of the actual Biblioteca Marciana, Loggetta, and Procuratie Nuove.[3] In fact, the variety of architectonic styles discernible in the byzantinizing church of San Marco, the Venetian-Byzantine colonnades of the palace of the procurators to the north of the piazza, and the Gothic forms of the ducal palace should be taken as cautionary signs when we think of Venice's architectural profile in the middle of the fifteenth century (Fig. 2).[4] A similar juxtaposition of Byzantine and Gothic forms can also be observed on the façades of the private residences (palazzi) on the canals of Venice.[5] Evidently, Venice shared many of the architectural features of Byzantine cities. The blend of Venetian and Byzantine forms was so intricate by the thirteenth century that the task of separating the Venetian from the Byzantine architectural elements is almost impossible.

In the capital of Venetian Crete as in Negroponte the most significant urban space was named after its famous counterpart in Venice: piazza San Marco. The sole usage of Latin or Italian terms to designate the different markets, *beccaria* or *pescaria*, or the main street of the city, the *ruga magistra*, must have also resonated as originating from the metropole. In Candia, however, these terms denote just a linguistic modification as the layout of Byzantine Chandax did not change drastically under the Venetians. The basic street pattern of the Byzantine city remained, and many old Byzantine structures were reused to house Venetian officials as in the case of the *castellum* in the port. Urban practices and the architecture of Candia, like the agricultural, political, and social organization of the island, also wavered between two worlds.

Two important Byzantine landmarks, the ducal palace and the cathedral, were also reused without major modifications. Obviously, economic considerations may have been the primary reason that prompted the Venetian regime to preserve these buildings in the capital of Crete; it was simply cheaper not to build something anew. More important, it was an effective statement of control over the civic resources, like the use of spoils as a sign of supremacy over the enemy. I would like to suggest an alternative reading of this decision, however. It goes without saying that the central location of these monuments and their new owners/primary users made them immediate, everyday reminders of the new colonial dominion on Crete. Their loaded symbolic significance presented to the Venetian authorities a fertile ground on which to found the myths of Venice's colonial heritage. To dissociate the buildings from their Byzantine past, the authorities invested them with a Venetian front – in their appearance, architectural details, function, or name. Then, an appropriate mythology was invented around them. This ingenious twofold strategy linked the physical and historical revision of the buildings and the institutions they reflected. Like other political structures of the Byzantines, the reuse of these buildings by the new masters of Crete manifested that Venice had lawfully inherited the imperial status of Byzantium in the Levant. This strategy presented the Venetians not as villains but rather as the noble successors of the Byzantine empire.

THE WORKINGS OF THE CITY

The authorities made vague references to the overall good appearance of the city, which seem to have been rhetorical more than anything else as no public monies were spent on private housing. On a local level, there existed complex rules for the cleaning of the streets (most of which were unpaved) and the disposal of garbage.[6] For instance, in Candia the inhabitants and shopkeepers on the *ruga magistra* from the land gate to the sea gate had to sweep the street in front of their houses every Friday morning; the refuse would be picked up by a special communal cart every Saturday.[7] In Modon we have only numerous decrees condemning the disposal of garbage on the streets, over the city walls to the sea, or in the port but no particular service for picking up trash.[8] No strict communal ordinances on the appearance of private houses seem to have existed throughout the empire. The fact that such decrees came directly from Venice confirms the hypothesis that there existed no communal regulations in Candia in regard to private houses. Such regulations were enforced only upon the most important parts of town, e.g.

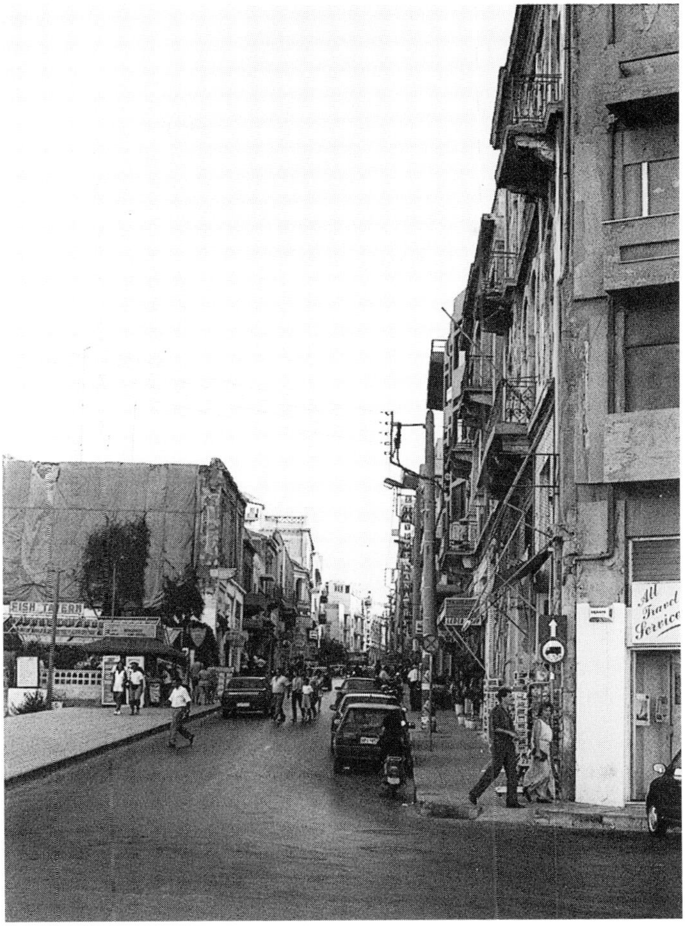

FIGURE 45. Herakleion, *ruga magistra* looking south

the façades of the houses overlooking the two main streets of Candia (Fig. 45).

In 1282 the Maggior Consiglio in Venice decided that the state properties that were located on the ruga magistra near the port and on the street intersecting it at the piazza could be leased to private individuals for twenty-nine years provided that the façades of the houses would be constructed in stone and mortar.[9] In 1297 the houses on the ruga were offered again for a twenty-nine-year lease period preferably to those who were planning to build anew.[10] Hence, the buildings that flanked the main street in its entire length now conformed with the prescriptions of the government: the public official structures standing on the south side (ducal palace, loggia, church of St. Mark, city gate) were directly related to the authorities, whereas the northern side was lined by a row of important palaces as attested by their façades. Thus, the first impression of the city for a visitor approaching from the harbor was one of decorum, wealth, and homogeneity in the organization of the urban space. In 1293 the Maggior Consiglio in Venice decreed that the revenues from a major state tax, the *comerclum*, had to be spent for the repair of the port, the mole, and the houses on the main street of Candia, suggesting that these houses were considered on par with the public monuments of the city.[11]

One has to take into account, however, that even if state directives did not control construction techniques, there existed trends that, along with local tradition, played a significant role in the formation of building styles specific to the island and its historical realities. The fact that Candia was a port city with fifteen hundred or two thousand Venetian residents and these people conducted business and had relatives back in the mother city determined to some extent the appearance of the individual *palazzi* – even their name recalled Venetian practices. People – both merchants and pilgrims – traveled extensively; through them stylistic motifs and patterns were transmitted all over the Mediterranean.[12] The "vernacular" architecture of Venice must have been a constant point of reference.[13] Interestingly, the "fashion" in thirteenth-century Venice was Byzantine, as can be seen in the Ca' Loredan and the Ca' Farsetti on the Grand Canal (Fig. 46). Following the formal typology of John Ruskin, Paolo Maretto has labeled this architectural phase "Romanesque-Byzantine."[14] The main façade of the Venetian *palazzi* had a series of semicircular arches opening to the canal and a second-story loggia that extended to almost the entire width of the façade. The same type of semicircular windows opened in the two upper stories. Domestic architecture in Byzantium from the thirteenth century onward displays a similar kind of façade articulation and follows a rectangular plan. The thirteenth-century architecture of Tekfur Sarayi in Constantinople, for instance, is that of a palatial or aristocratic structure with the ground floor supported by columns, topped by two stories with series of semicircular windows decorated with ornate brickwork (Fig. 47).[15] Similar patterns are discerned in the palaces and houses of Mistra in Peloponnesos dating from the thirteenth to the fifteenth century. Whereas the choice of an undecorated façade versus an arcaded or window-pierced one seems to respond to issues of security or the terrain, as in the hilltown of Mistra, in every case the main reception hall was located on the upper story, as was the case in the Venetian *piano nobile*.[16] Although no substantial remains of Byzantine houses have survived in Candia and the other colonies, we can assume that domestic architecture must have followed general trends. Thus, it was perfectly logical that upon their arrival on Crete the Venetian colonizers would reuse the residences of the Byzantine aristocracy in Candia without major modifications. These would be trendy by thirteenth-century Venetian standards! In the fourteenth century pointed-arch windows and a more symmetrical arrangement of the main façade gave a Gothic flair to the *palazzi* in Venice, but similar pointed, decorated arches are also known from fourteenth- and fifteenth-century Mistra. The layout of Venetian houses was still based on thirteenth-century principles, but the houses had acquired larger areas around them.[17]

As the visual renditions of Candia indicate, the façades of private dwellings played a major role in the overall impression that the built environment of Candia gave to the viewer. This is also evident in travelers' accounts, which are full of interesting details about the appearance of the city.[18] A feature that puzzled most northern European visitors was the absence of sloping roofs on the buildings, a feature present in some Venetian houses as seen in the 1500 map of Venice made by Jacopo de Barbari, and also on many Byzantine structures.[19] Instead, the houses in Crete were covered with flat terraces that were paved with a layer of crushed horns or shells up to thirty centimeters thick. The inhabitants often slept in the open air on these flat roofs during the hot summer months as is still the case in Greece during heat waves.[20]

CREATING A VENETIAN CIVIC CENTER

The terrain and topography of the colonies dictated, it seems, the urban layout and the placement of the most significant urban monuments. Candia, Negroponte, and Modon were built on flat terrain, whereas the towns of Canea, Retimo, and Coron incorporated rocky hills that were fortified by the Venetians. Depending on the topography of each city, either the civic center was identified with the economic heart of the city (as in Candia, Negroponte, Modon, and Retimo until the sixteenth century), or the two were divided between two areas. For instance, in Canea the oldest part of the city that formed the core of the Venetian settlement occupied the roughly circular space of the ancient acropolis of Kydonia that was elevated a few feet above the suburbs that surrounded the city (Fig. 48). The raised terrain that was enclosed by the city walls formed a real citadel that contained the palace of the rector, the Latin cathedral, the residences of the Venetian feudatories, and that of the renowned Greek aristocratic family of Calergis. The main public spaces of the city (the main square, the loggia, and the public fountain) were located in the lower part of town outside the city walls possibly for greater accessibility. However, a document of 1302 suggests that a market, shops, and taverns existed inside the fortified city as well, but

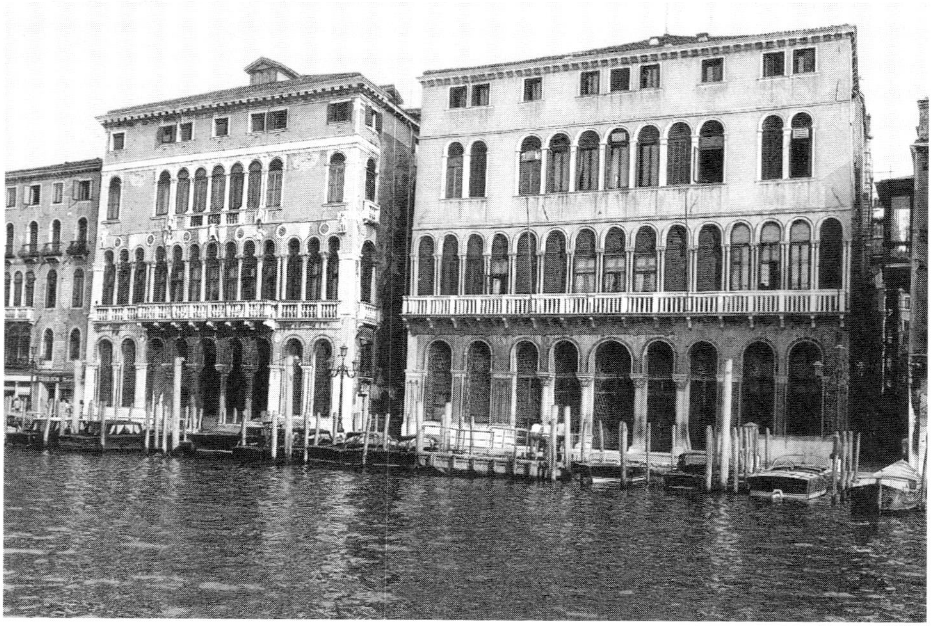

FIGURE 46. Venice, Ca' Loredan or Ca' Farsetti

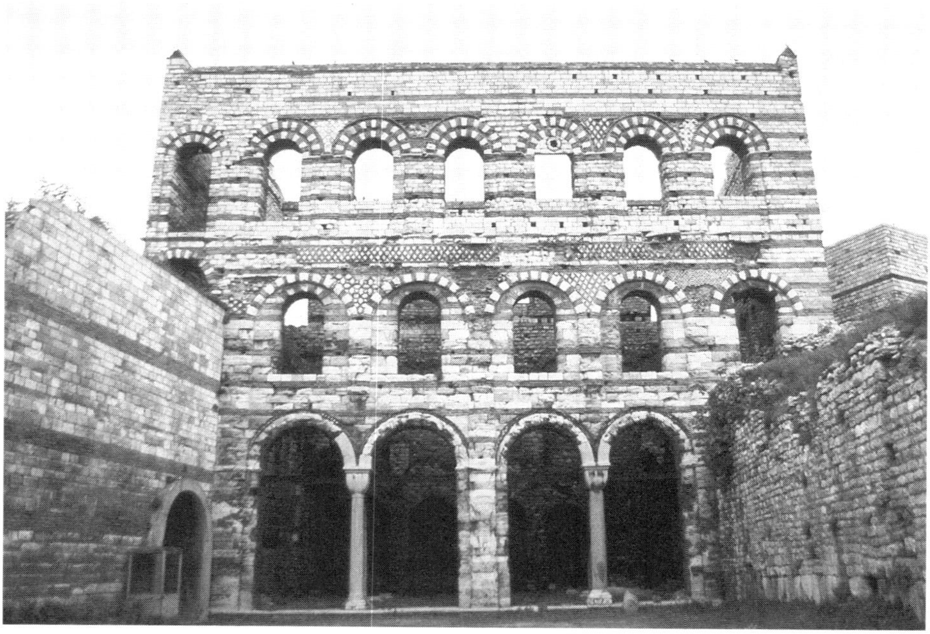

FIGURE 47. Istanbul, Tekfur Sarayi (Photo: Robert Ousterhout)

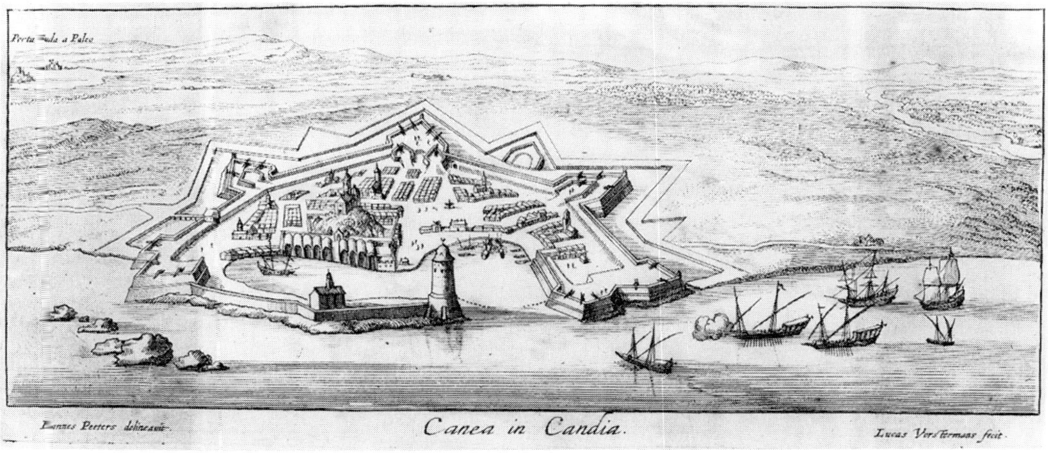

FIGURE 48. Jacques Peeters, Canea in Candia, in *Description des principales villes* . . . (Anvers, 1690) (The Gennadius Library, American School of Classical Studies)

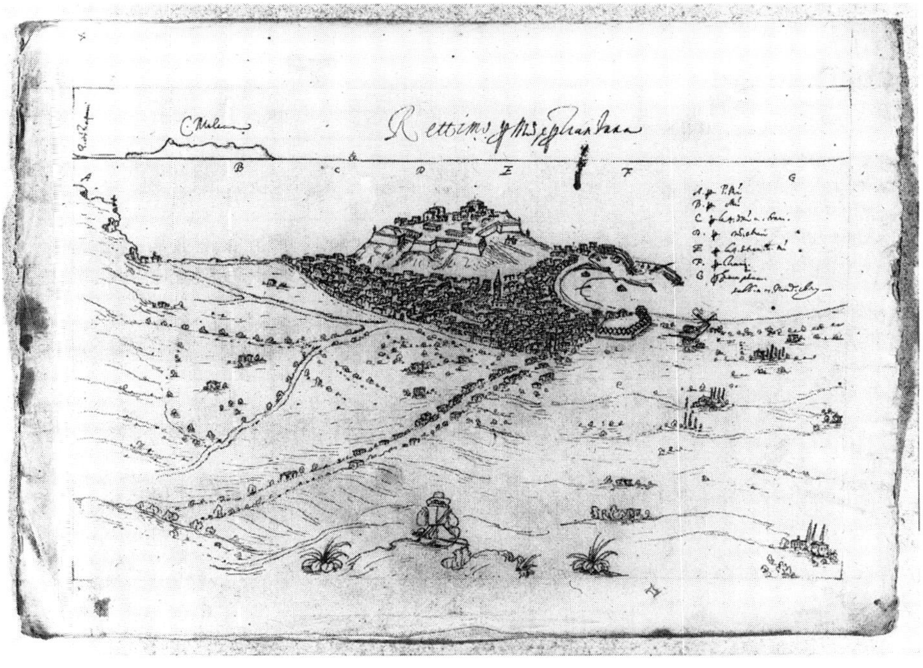

FIGURE 49. Retimo, Prospetto della città e della fortezza, first half of the seventeenth century (Archivio di Stato di Venezia, Provveditori alle Fortezze, B. 43, dis. 153)

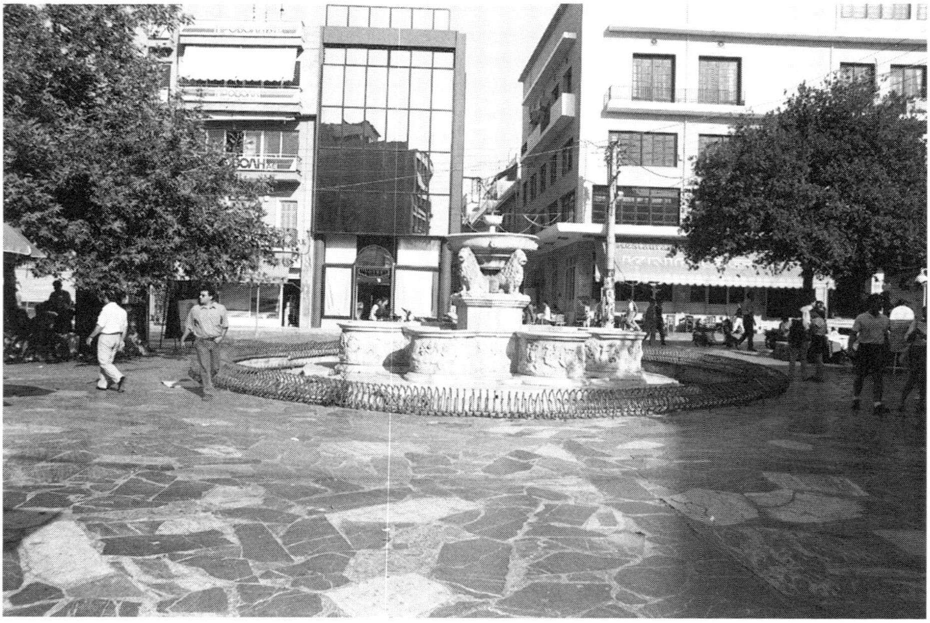

FIGURE 50. Herakleion, piazza San Marco (Liontaria)

this must refer to a secondary marketplace.[21] In Retimo the old Venetian town developed at the feet of a dramatically situated rock that is now crowned by the imposing Fortezza, which was set up after the Ottoman raids of the late sixteenth century (Fig. 49).[22] Even in cases where the topographical layout was similar, the differing functions of the Venetian colonies demanded varied solutions in their urban planning.

In Candia the Venetians placed their administrative buildings, their churches, and their marketplace inside the city walls. The most striking similarities between Venice and Candia are to be found in Candia's piazza San Marco, which in its name and organization replicated Venice's main square. The same topographical pattern is also observed in Negroponte, where the loggia was also located across from the palace and the church of St. Mark. Similar arrangements must have existed in the old city of Modon, for which there is an intriguing reference to S. Marco in 1479;[23] the piazza was lined by the palace and residence of the counselor, shops (*botege*) selling foodstuffs, a large loggia, and several public loggias, which may refer to particular buildings or to arcaded spaces around the square.[24]

Opening in front of the land gate and the ducal chapel of St. Mark, the piazza of Candia had probably been the primary marketplace of the city of Chandax since Byzantine times (Figs. 50 and 13). Despite its Byzantine origins, it was the piazza San Marco that, as the prime business sector of the

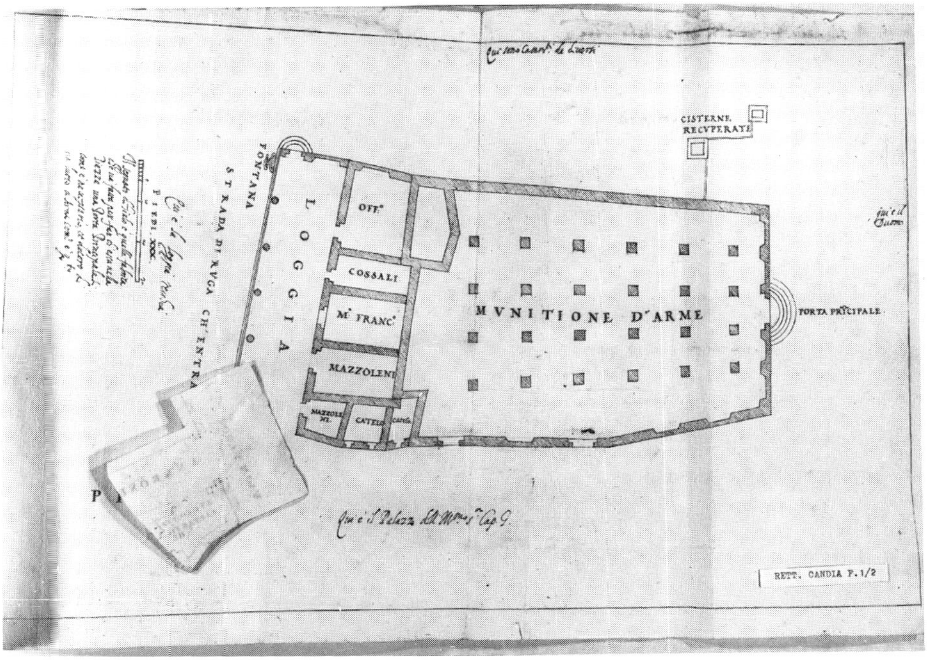

FIGURE 51. "Pianta della salla d'arme del palazzo del capitano con loggia e zona circonvicina e modifiche ai locali attigui": plan of the loggia and the armeria (Archivio di Stato di Venezia, Senato, Dispacci, Rettori di Candia F. 1, disegno 2)

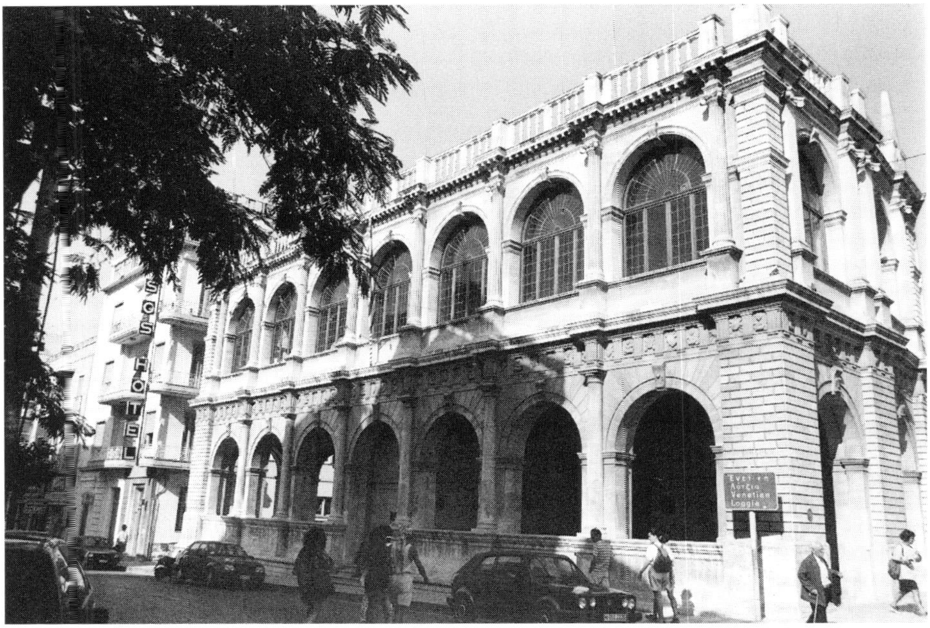

FIGURE 52. Herakleion, loggia of the sixteenth century

city, became an emblem of the new economic status of Crete after the arrival of the Venetians and justified their presence in Candia from a pragmatic point of view. Whether or not the physical arrangement of the piazza maintained its Byzantine forms, the commodities that were now displayed in the marketplace appealed to a much larger audience of an international stature. By the fourteenth century numerous artisans and vendors of foodstuffs were based in the piazza, either doing business in their own workshops and boutiques or selling their merchandise on public benches rented to them by the state. The well-being of all these businesses was so vital to the colony that all important public official monuments (the basilica of St. Mark, the Latin cathedral, the ducal palace, the loggia, the palace of the general, the public warehouse, the land gate) were placed at the boundaries of the piazza, sanctioning the commercial and economic transactions taking place therein.[25] Representing the government and the official faith of the Venetians, these religious and administrative buildings, in conjunction with the major stately rituals that culminated in this area, stood as a visual symbol of Venetian supremacy in every level of colonial life.

Public usage of the piazza further emphasized its central position in the life of the city as it did in the other colonies of the Venetian empire. Most administrative structures of the colonies were spatially related to the market. The utilitarian monuments that were closely related to the civic landscape and to the well-being of the citizens, such as the loggia, the tower of the clock, the public warehouse, and the public fountain, were all structures that meant to accommodate and serve the members of the elite and the higher middle class (merchants and professionals). As the foremost symbols of the commune, these public edifices promoted the democratic nature of the Venetian state. In Candia one of the primary monuments linked with Venice was the *lobium* (loggia), a place used for public announcements, for meetings, and for gambling. Originally located on the waterfront, it was moved in 1325 to a more salubrious and prestigious location across from the church of St. Mark on the piazza (Fig. 51 and Fig. 52).[26] The public auctions of state property were only allowed here, at three o'clock in the afternoon after Sunday Mass.[27] During these occasions the piazza became a theatrical stage for the higher Venetian officials: the duke, his counselors, and one of the *camerarii* supervised the event from the loggia of the church of St. Mark.[28] Their personal involvement in the distribution of state lands offers a concrete example of state authority, one that can be paralleled with the nearby pillory (*berlina*) intended to punish crime publicly.[29]

The *lobium* (loggia) of Canea, a public building used by the colonists as a meeting place, is recorded in archival documents of the early fourteenth century without a precise mention of its location in the city; it was at a ruinous state in 1334.[30] As we can see in the view of the city made by Zorzi Corner and according to the governmental records in the sixteenth century the loggia was relocated closer to the piazza – to the west of the gate of Colombo near the street that connected the piazza to the breakwater in the harbor – possibly to accommodate the needs of its users better (Fig. 53).[31] The loggia was a large two-story building preceded by a series of arcades (possibly shops); a smaller one-story edifice serving as the residence of the general (*capitaneus*) was connected with it.[32] A fountain with a basin decorated with lions stood in the middle of the main square of the city until 1914, replicating the most impressive fountain that the duke Morosini erected in Candia at the same time (Fig. 50).[33]

Following similar topographical arrangements with Canea, in Retimo, the main practical public spaces of the city (e.g. the loggia, the principal fountain of the city, the market square) were located outside the acropolis near the port. At the beginning of the fifteenth century a large empty space outside the *castrum* served as a *platea*. It had been decided that this area should be left open without any buildings on it.[34] As the old plans of Retimo indicate, the impressive loggia that serves as the Archaeological Museum of Rethymnon still stands at the spot of the original medieval building, but we possess no specific documentary information on the earlier architectural history of the structure (Fig. 54).[35] The highly ornate Rimondi fountain that still dominates the northern side of the piazza of the lower city of Retimo was remodeled in 1625–26 (Fig. 55), but an older fountain was located in the center of the piazza at least since 1588.[36] Although the subsequent use of the city changed its urban layout, it is clear that the area of the Rimondi fountain defined a prime public space since the clock of the town was placed in its vicinity.

Clock towers broadcasted another aspect of state control as we see in the examples in Venice and its colonies. In Candia the duke Giacomo Barbadigo in 1463 set up a clock on the western side of the bell tower of the church of St. Mark, as can be seen in the plan of Zorzi Corner (Figs. 14 and 56).[37] Rather than being installed on a new tower as with the piazza San Marco in Venice, the clock of Candia was placed on the bell tower of the ducal church, which bore many symbolic associations. In addition to its housing the bells that sounded the beginning and end of the work day, the flag of the Republic that flew above it indicated that the Venetian government was in control of this valuable public good that displayed time, and thus also had power over all activities in the marketplace. As only the foundations of this bell tower exist today, we have no way of knowing what the actual clock

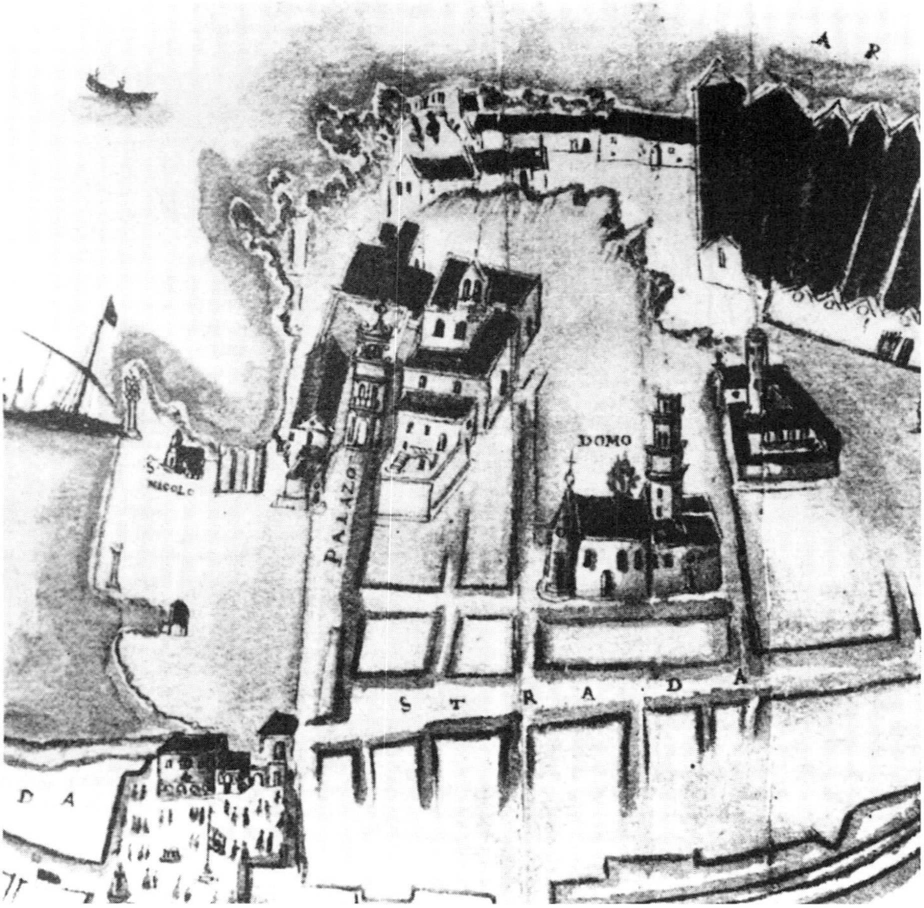

FIGURE 53. Zorzi Corner, Città di Canea, 1625, detail (Biblioteca Marciana, Ms. It. VI, 75 [8303], fol. 4)

looked like. The vestiges of the free-standing square clock tower that are still preserved in Rethymnon may give us some clues as to the appearance of the one in Candia. The town clock of Retimo was located on a monumental square tower overlooking the piazza. A large section of the tower survived during Gerola's visit; the tower had possibly been repaired in 1601 (indicated by an inscription) after its cupola was damaged in 1596 (Figs. 57 and 58). Although we do not possess detailed information on the exact date of construction of this tower, its rusticated masonry, the decoration of the entrance, the entablature of the reliefs, and the inscription suggest a date in the late sixteenth century.[38] It had a monumental entrance door and was decorated with reliefs representing the lion of St. Mark and coats of arms whose state of preservation does not allow a secure identification or dating.

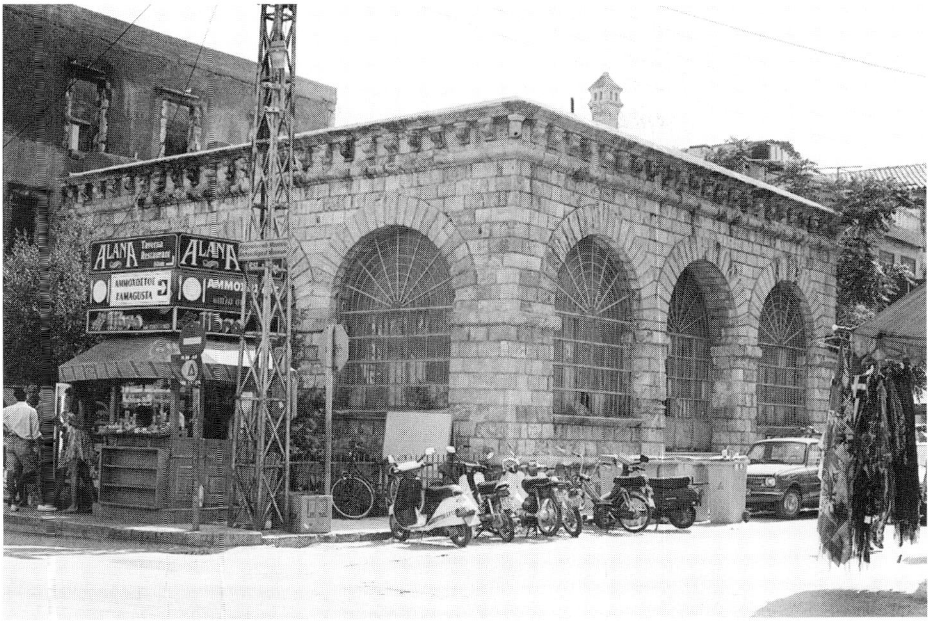

FIGURE 54. Rethymnon, loggia

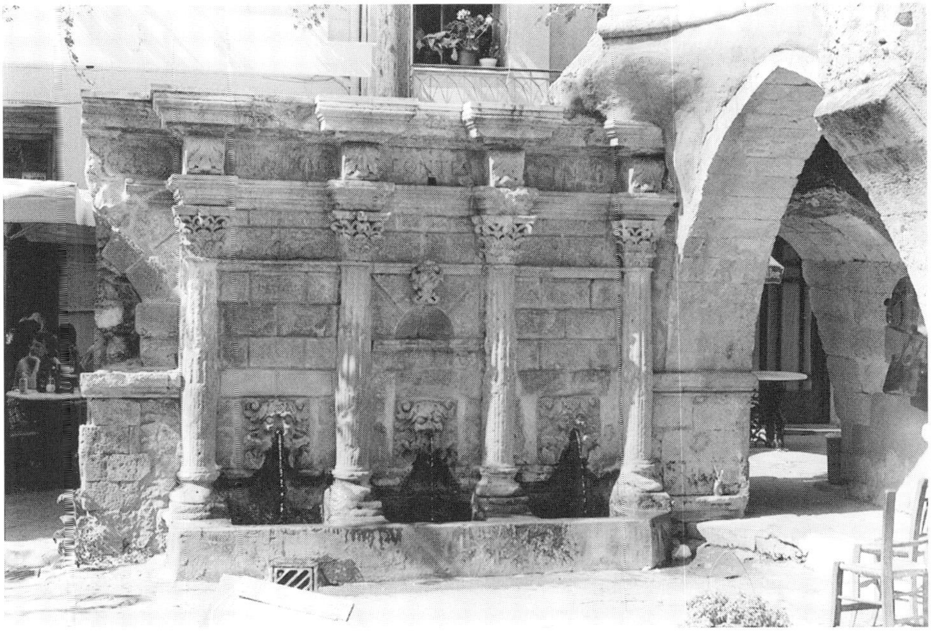

FIGURE 55. Rethymnon, Rimondi fountain today

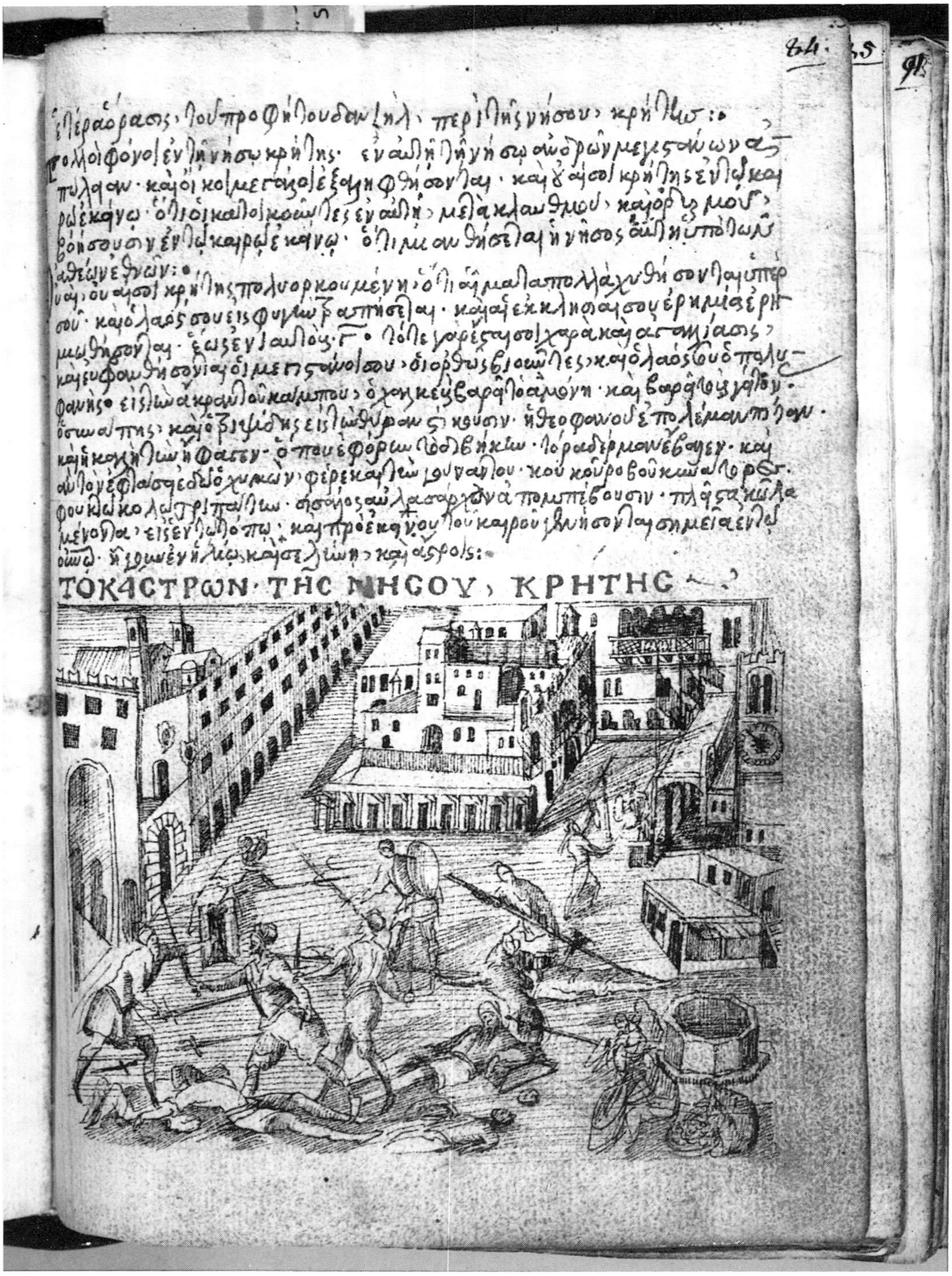

FIGURE 56. George Clontzas, view of the ducal palace in Candia, in Istoria ab origine mundi (Biblioteca Marciana, Ms. Graec. VII, 22 [1466], fol. 84r)

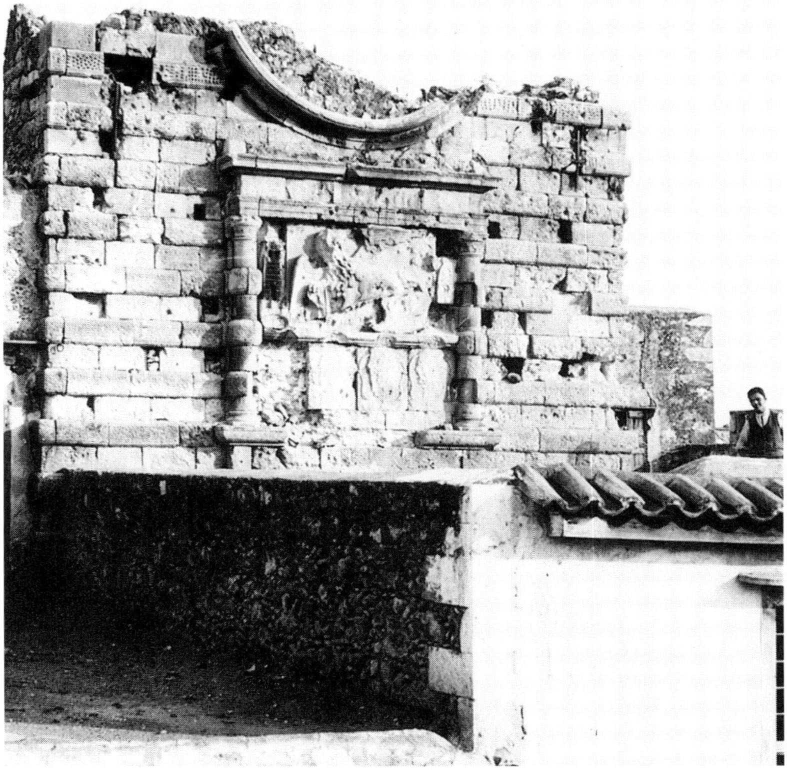

FIGURE 57. Rethymnon, remains of the clock tower (Istituto Veneto di Scienze, Lettere ed Arti. Venezia. Archivio fotografico della Missione in Creta di Giuseppe Gerola)

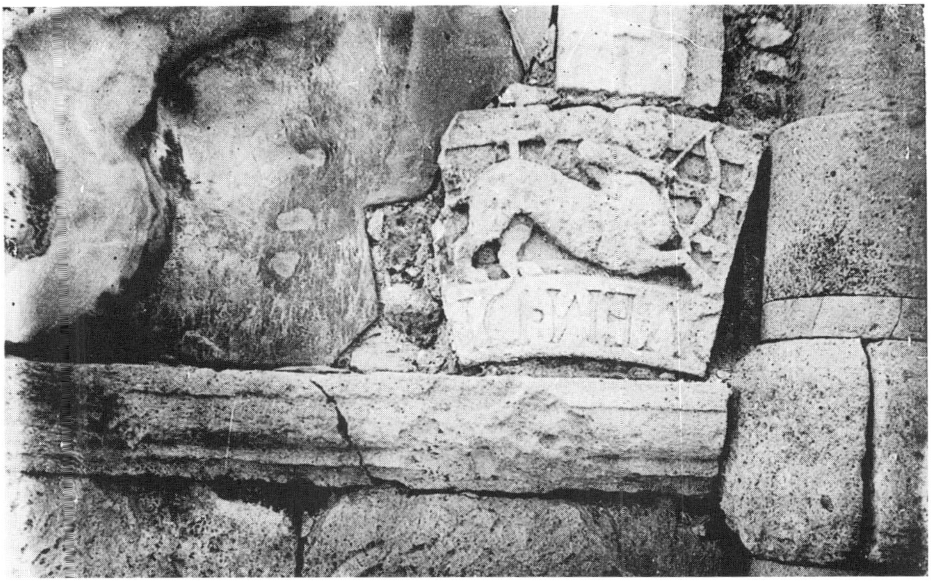

FIGURE 58. Rethymnon, clock tower (Istituto Veneto di Scienze, Lettere ed Arti. Venezia. Archivio fotografico della Missione in Creta di Giuseppe Gerola)

Above these reliefs the clock was adorned with the signs of the zodiac, as a fragment of the sign of Sagittarius indicates.

Venetian control over the economic resources of Candia was not entrusted to symbolic sanctioning alone, of course. A special administrative apparatus with the sole purpose of regulating business was also concentrated on the piazza. The *camera pesarie comunis*, more commonly known as the *statera comunis*, housed the weights and measures of the state. All wholesale commodities had to be weighed by the *ponderatores comunis* in the weighing chamber, and the retail vendors had to weigh their merchandise using the official weights and measures; this service produced a tax for the state, called *messetaria*.[39]

Three special officers, the *justiciarii*, were responsible for the smooth functioning of the market and for supervision of all economic transactions.[40] For instance, bread was mainly sold by the bakers or their employees in the piazza, but in 1366 it was announced that bread should be sold in baskets in the main street and in the squares around it.[41] The case of smiths, who in 1321 were relocated from the suburbs inside the city, illustrates the significance of concentration of workshops in the center of town, an area that could be easily monitored by the authorities.[42] In 1351 the state decreed that nails and horseshoes had to be sold exclusively in the piazza. Similarly, all goldsmiths were ordered to move into workshops located on the piazza in 1336.[43]

All these professionals worked in separate shops lining the piazza. A horseshoe shop,[44] a barber shop,[45] and a two-story *speciaria*, i.e. a pharmacy or grocery store, are singled out in the documents.[46] One of the shops is described in detail: in 1319 Johannes Quirino rented one of his shops located on the south side of the piazza ("in platea posita") to Madalena, widow of Marcus de Bonhomo. The façade of the shop toward the piazza was 1.30 meters wide (4 feet minus 3 *digites*), whereas its back side toward the city walls was only 1 meter wide (3 feet minus 3 *digites*). The shop also included a second story (*solarium*), possibly used for storage. Of particular interest is the specific reference to the "courtyard" (*curia*) that pertained to it; this must refer to the open area of the piazza in front of the store.[47] It is unclear whether this "courtyard" was used for displaying merchandise or was intended as an open space that would allow the buyers to browse the commodities displayed at the store. Fortunately, the architectural drawing that shows the conversion of the old city walls into a new public warehouse in 1577 gives us concrete visual cues for the appearance of these shops. The stores at ground level were preceded by a portico made of wooden posts and covered by an awning or a wooden sloping roof (Fig. 20). Indeed, the area defined by the awning may correspond to the aforementioned "courtyard."

Additional decrees monitoring the professional life of artisans and shopkeepers, demanding rent or sales taxes, and regulating prices were announced by the public crier at the piazza. These lively documents provide valuable information on the workings of the marketplace and the topography of the piazza. For instance, we learn that most of the merchandise was placed on permanent benches, which were probably simple tables covered with an awning. Apparently, in 1343 vendors without a permit brought movable benches (or kiosks) for displaying grain or vegetables in the piazza, an act that was condemned by the authorities.[48] The benches were arranged according to trade. As in the case of the smiths, the commodities that the state wished to regulate most had to be sold at the piazza, near the market officers.[49] For instance, vegetables and fruit could only be sold on designated benches in the piazza;[50] oranges, olives, and nuts should only be displayed from the corner of the moat to the west until the public benches; the vendors of asparagus, *fenogles* (fennel?), and other vegetables had to sell their merchandise exclusively between the two columns that demarcated the beginning of the meat market.[51] Finally, game animals were to be sold exclusively in the piazza.[52] Thus, it seems that by 1360, when the shopping area of the piazza was enlarged toward the area of the meat market, the authorities had devised a rigid blueprint for the display of goods in the piazza. One may surmise that similar control was exercised over the professionals and the administrators who supervised the market. It is tempting to propose that these two columns had a significance similar to that of the columns set up in the *piazzetta* in Venice. Unfortunately, I have found no evidence that such a parallel may have existed. The fact that the pillory of Candia must have been located nearby indeed points to a parallel function. Is it possible to identify the columns as marking the area where the state executed the punishment of its subjects, as did the two columns in Venice?

The only significant administrative building that was not placed on the piazza San Marco was the residence of the counselors, the officials who were second in command after the duke. They resided inside the *castellum*, a fort of strategic significance situated at the entrance of the harbor.[53] The *castellum* was located outside the city precinct but was connected to the city walls by an extension of the sea wall at the mole. In all probability, this tower predated the arrival of the Venetians since it formed an integral part of the city's fortifications. This fort, which in 1333 was recorded as the "tower of the *castello*,"[54] was one of the buildings that suffered terribly in the devastating earthquake of 1303.[55] The impressive fort that today dominates the old port of Herakleion is a sixteenth-century remodeling of the original thirteenth-century structure (Figs. 59–61).[56] Reuwich's view of Candia portrays the original fort as a large circular tower similar in appearance to the other towers that reinforced the city walls (Fig. 7). This schematic representation of the castle,

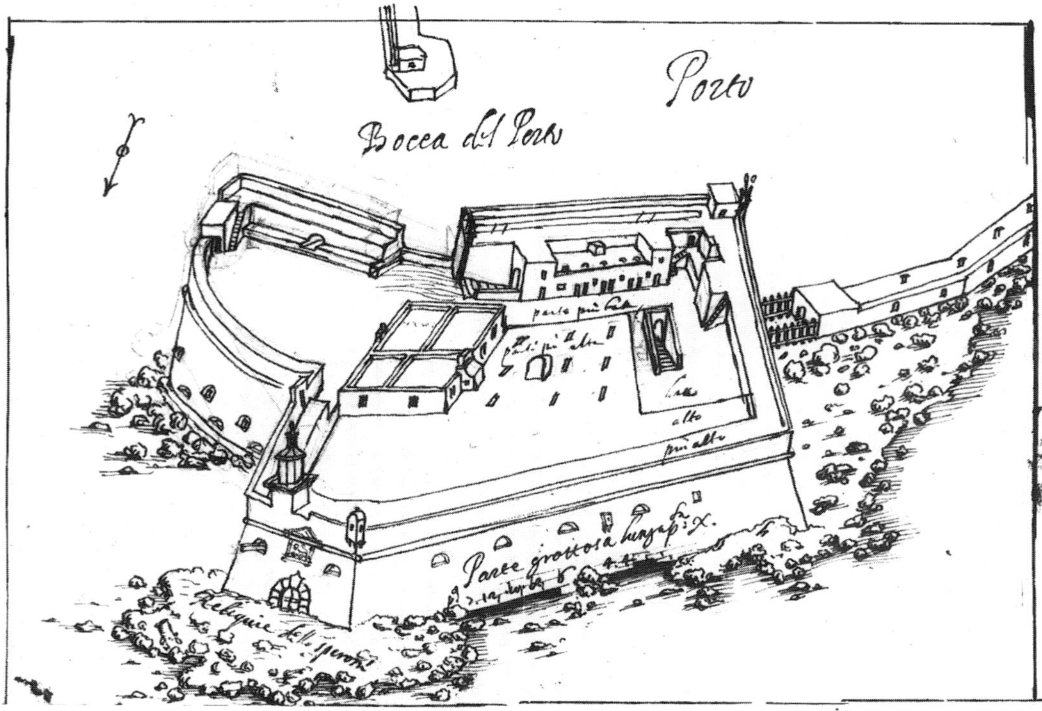

FIGURE 59. Provveditori alle Fortezze, B. 43, dis. 160: Candia. Castello di Candia, seventeenth century (Archivio di Stato di Venezia)

however, does not demonstrate the complex structure that must have served as the basis for its sixteenth-century rebuilding. The Byzantine/Venetian fort was a multifunctional building with tall walls five to six feet thick;[57] it housed – apart from the residence of the counselors – a state prison[58] and chambers for the guard, which during the rebellion of 1363 amounted to fifty persons.[59] Its prominent position at the entrance of the harbor displayed it as the first urban structure that the visitors from the sea would see. It seems that the counselors were relegated to the Byzantine castle at the harbor to supervise the sea approach to the city. Hence, their palace and the ducal palace were set on antithetical parts of the city, on the projection of the same north-south axis defined by the *ruga magistra.* Thus, the counselors became the guards of the Venetian colony, overlooking its growth into the Mediterranean. The *camerarii* also lived in the area of the port, next to the arsenals (Fig. 62). The appearance, function, and names of all administrative structures bore the signature of the colonists. Venetian symbols, e.g. the flag of the Republic on the bell tower of the church of St. Mark, the lion of St. Mark on the fort and the city gates, and Latin inscriptions on the cathedral of St. Titus, marked the new buildings as Venetian and altered the façades of the former Byzantine

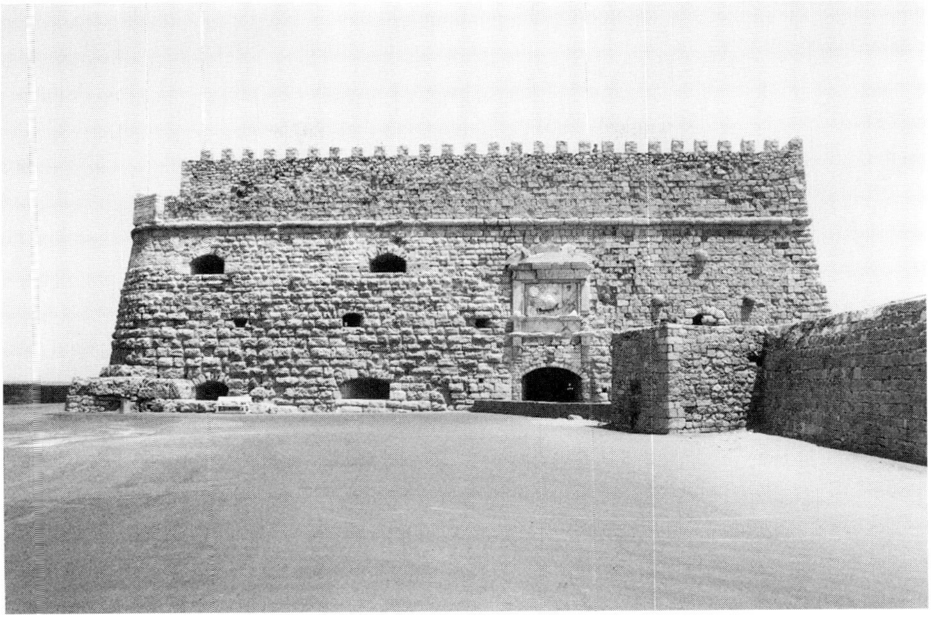

FIGURE 60. Herakleion, Castello da Mar, view

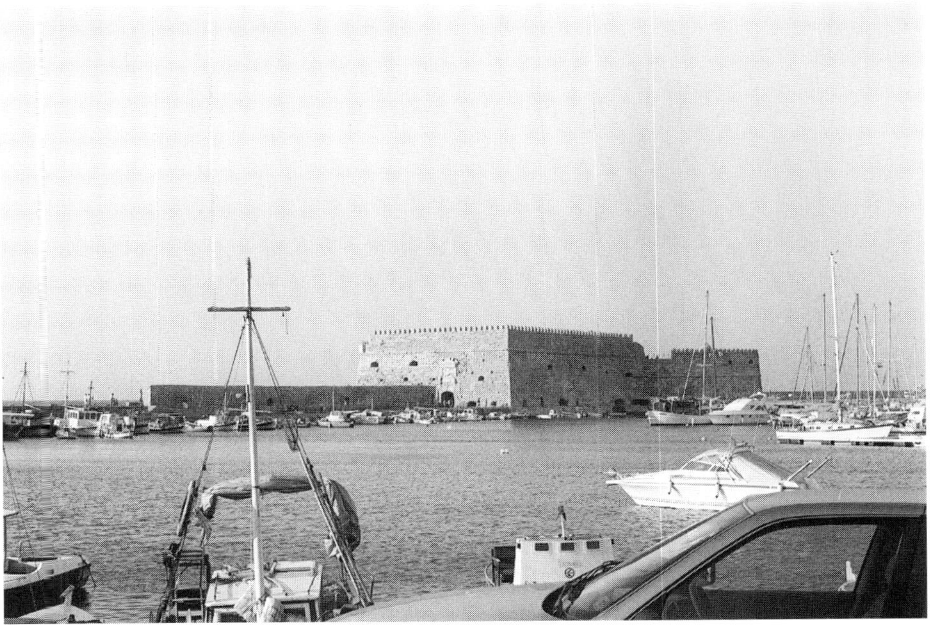

FIGURE 61. Herakleion, view to harbor with Castello da Mar

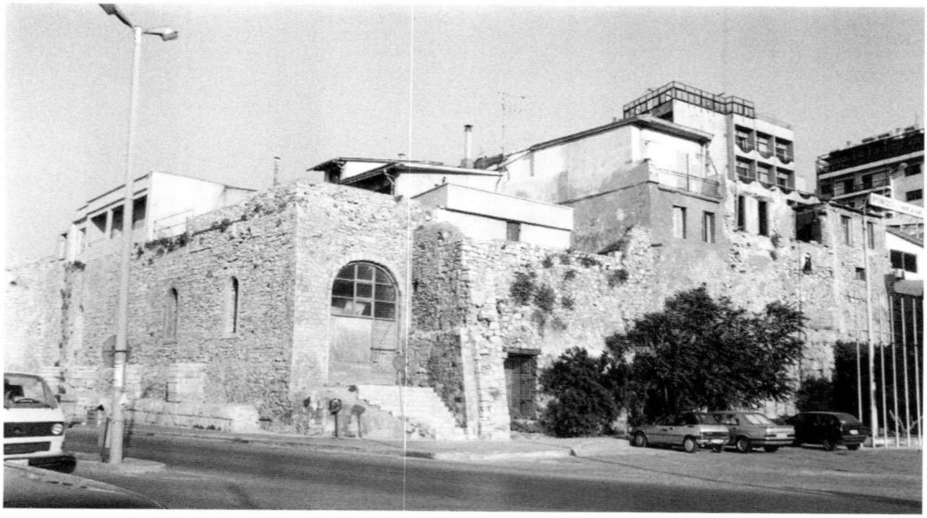

FIGURE 62. Herakleion, residence of the *camerarii*

structures. For example, the entrance gate of the sea fort, which faced the city, is still surmounted by an effigy of the lion of St. Mark (Fig. 63). Two additional marble lions in relief decorated the northern and eastern façades, which overlooked the open sea and the entrance to the harbor.[60] The conspicuous placement of these symbols of the Republic marked the castle as a Venetian structure, which, by virtue of its placement, acted as a billboard announcing to the newcomers on the island that the city of Candia was part of the Venetian maritime empire. Similar lionine emblems are blazoned above the city gates of Modon and Negroponte.

REUSED MONUMENTS

The most striking example of a reused Byzantine structure is the residence of the *duca* in Candia, which stood on the north side of the piazza San Marco. Unfortunately, in the central square of modern Herakleion very little reminds us of the palace that housed the Venetian governor for four and a half centuries. A series of arcades still visible in the small shops that occupy the area of the palace probably represent the stores that abutted the south side of the palace facing the town square (Figs. 64–66).[61] These shops may also incorporate the foundations and remains of the palace, but excavations will probably not be undertaken as this section of town represents a prime commercial sector in Herakleion. A combination of documentary evidence

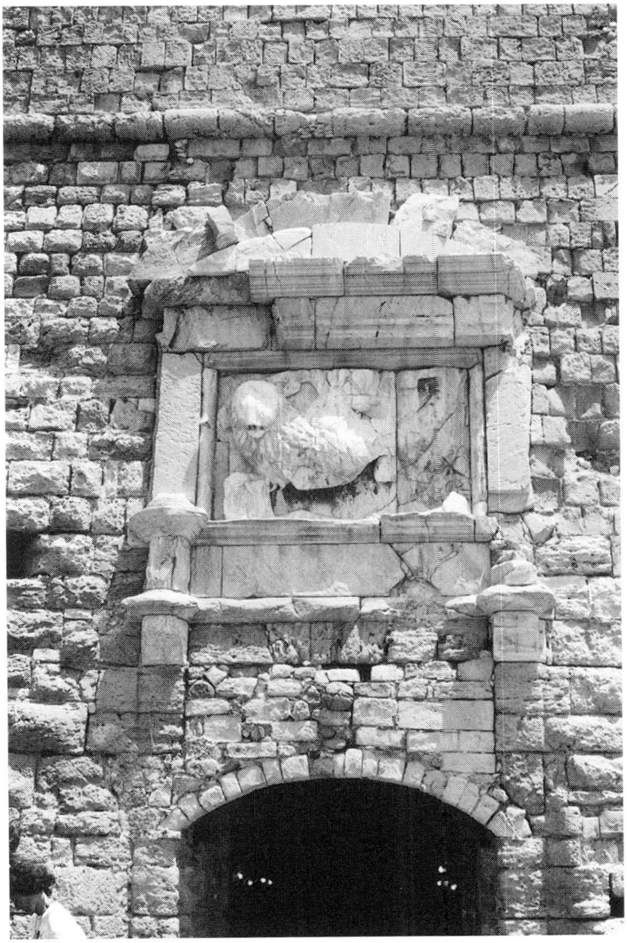

FIGURE 63. Herakleion, Castello da Mar, sculpture above southern entrance

and information gleaned from topographic renderings of Candia demonstrates that the palace was a complex structure surmounted with crenellations. An Ottoman document of 1670 recorded the layout of the structure during the last years of Venetian rule.[62] Its upper floor, which must have comprised the apartments of the duke, consisted of two halls, nine rooms, a kitchen, and three terraces. The ground floor probably comprised the service areas: it had twenty-two rooms, a large stable, a large storage room, a prison, and three cisterns. Next to the main building an auxiliary structure with nineteen rooms, a loggia (portico or gallery), two fountains, four courtyards, three wells, sixteen shops, and a warehouse must have been used for additional official functions.[63]

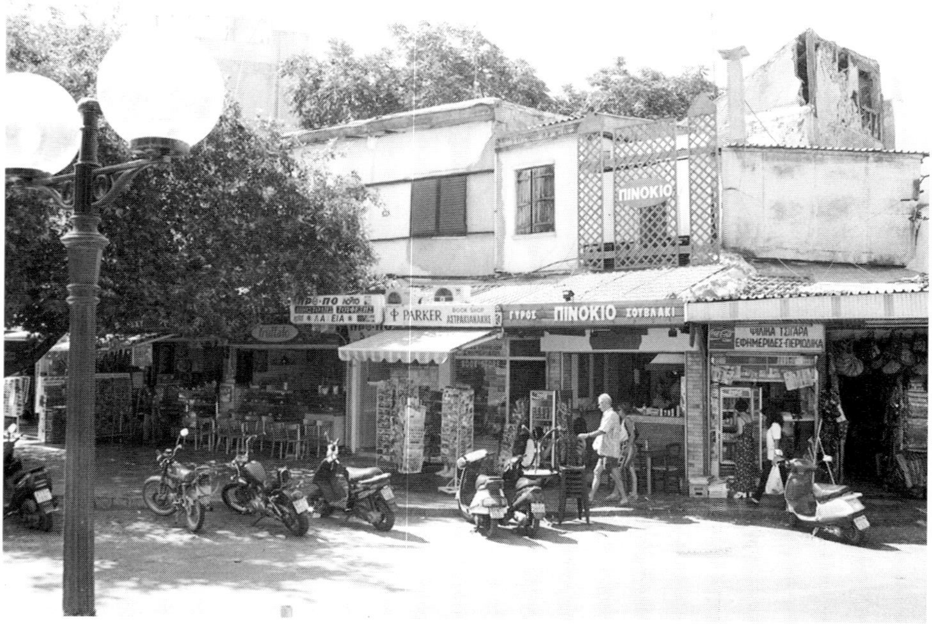

FIGURE 64. Herakleion, view of the shops in the area of the ducal palace

Fortunately the medieval "cartographers" Buondelmonti (Fig. 10) and George Clontzas (Figs. 12, 53, 67) have reserved a special place for the ducal palace of Candia in their views of the city.[64] Even though almost 150 years separates the two manuscripts, the similarities of the general features that they represent lead us to believe that both Buondelmonti and Clontzas were illustrating the same building, which by the end of the sixteenth century had undergone a series of remodelings (Fig. 68). The palace was a two-story structure surmounted by M-shaped crenellations and a tower, probably reserved for the guard, on the northeast corner.[65] The main entrance was situated across from the church of St. Mark, on the southern side of the palace. The central portal was surmounted by an arch and a projecting exedra and was flanked by windows and two minor doorways. This Renaissance façade probably represents the additions that the *provveditor* Giacomo Foscarini made to the palace in 1575. In line with the antiquarian considerations of sixteenth-century architectural styles, Foscarini was given permission to transport marble pieces from the ruins of Gortys (the first Byzantine capital of Crete) to decorate the ducal palace.[66] At the same time he was proclaiming the continuity between the older Roman/Byzantine heritage of the building and in this way legitimated its glorious provenance. On the second story of the structure we can distinguish a large tripartite lancet window and two

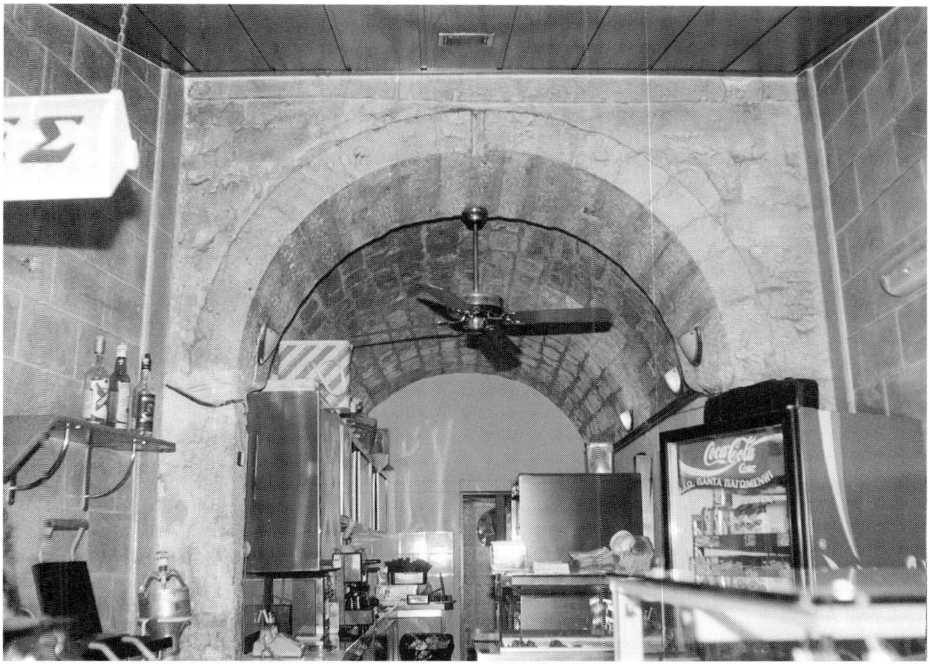

FIGURE 65. Herakleion, arcade shops at the area of the ducal palace

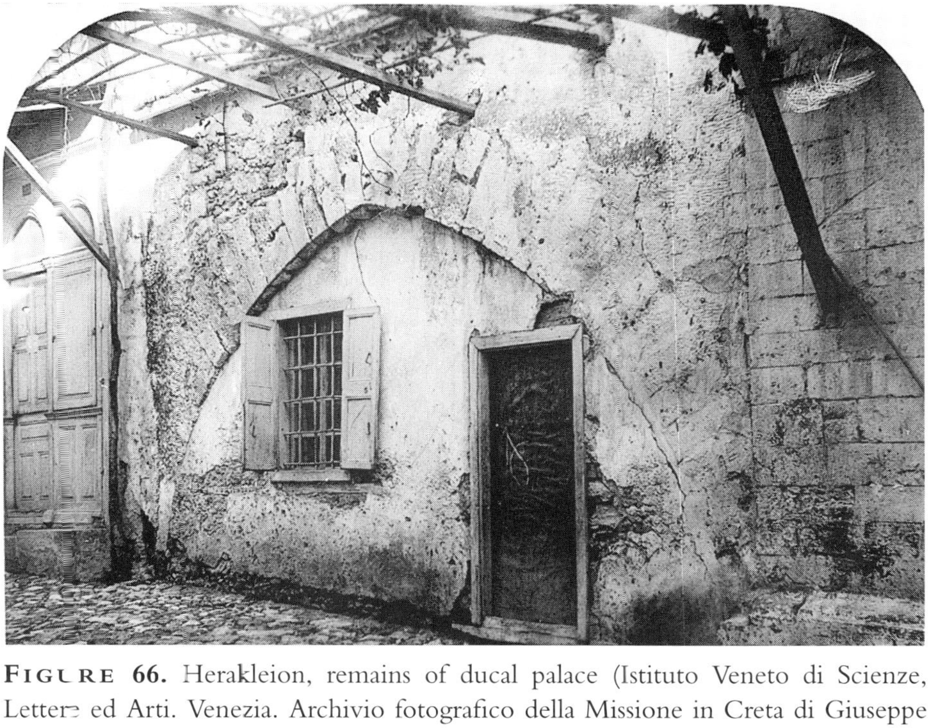

FIGURE 66. Herakleion, remains of ducal palace (Istituto Veneto di Scienze, Lettere ed Arti. Venezia. Archivio fotografico della Missione in Creta di Giuseppe Gerola)

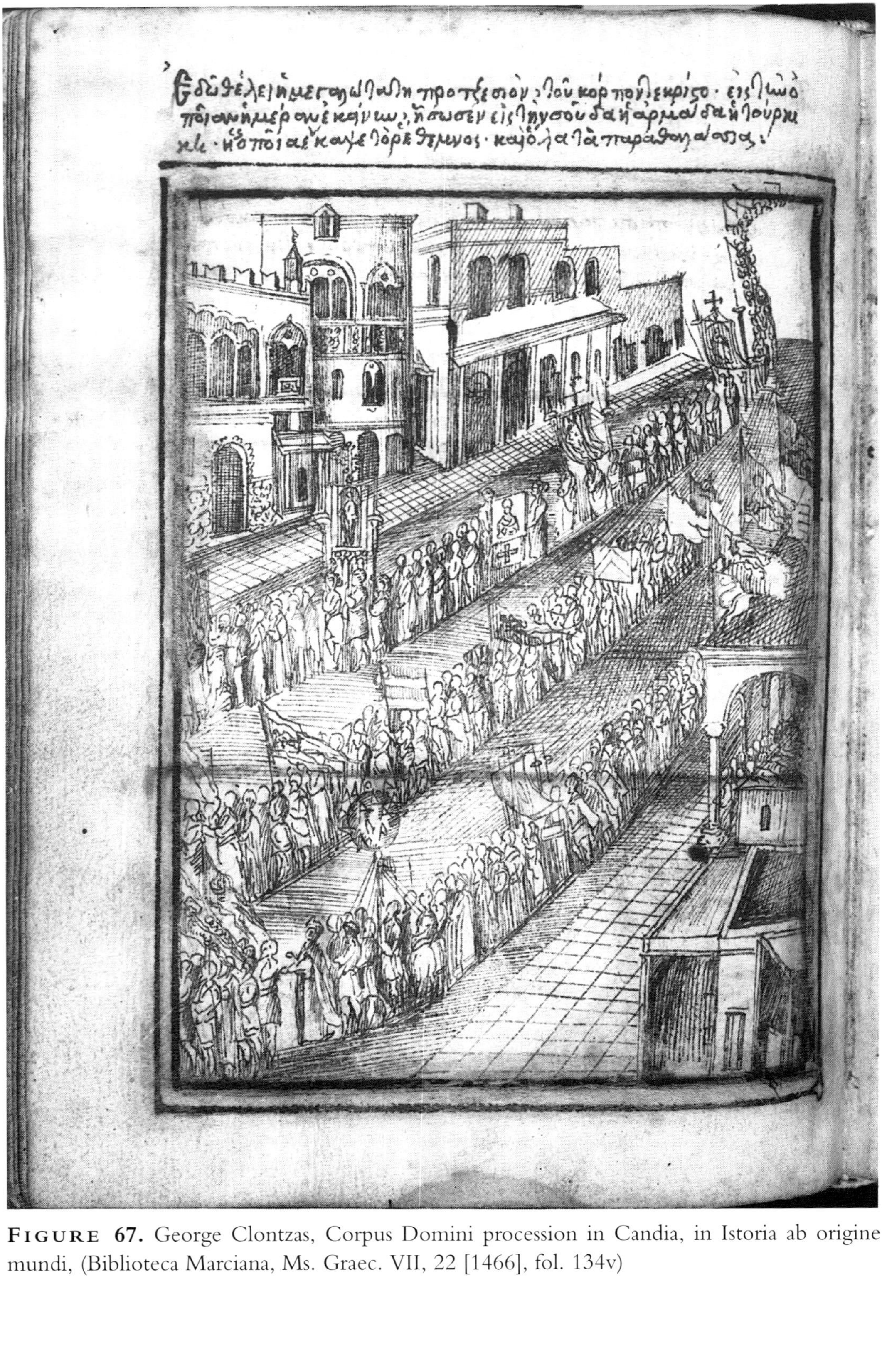

FIGURE 67. George Clontzas, Corpus Domini procession in Candia, in Istoria ab origine mundi, (Biblioteca Marciana, Ms. Graec. VII, 22 [1466], fol. 134v)

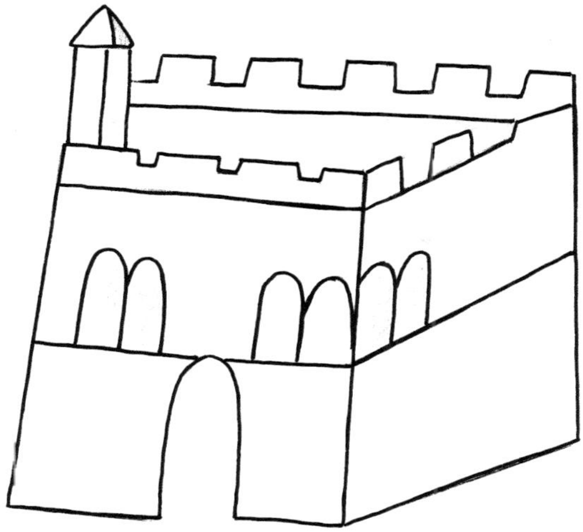

FIGURE 68. Drawing of the ducal palace based on Buondelmonti's view, after Stylianos Alexiou

smaller double openings. The south side of the building toward the square of San Marco was covered on the lower level by a continuous sloping roof, creating a portico with eight arched openings. These doorways can probably be identified with the shops that abutted the palace, which are mentioned by fourteenth-century chroniclers.[67] The same sloping roof seems to continue onto the west façade of the palace. In the center of the structure we can distinguish a square area covered with tiles, which must indicate the roof of a large room on the second floor.[68]

The second floor must have served as the private quarters of the duke and chambers for guests. Apart from being the residence of the duke, the palace also had administrative functions centering around the two large halls on the upper level: the audience hall and the tribunal. The oldest part of the palace, its north wing, housed the audience hall, where the duke received ambassadors and met with his council.[69] This hall was probably also used as the meeting place for the Maggior Consiglio of Candia.[70] The opposite side of the palace contained a second hall, which was the seat of the Avogaria and must have had direct access to the central courtyard so that its users would not have to go through the palace proper.[71] A document of 1636 mentions other juridical offices that were housed inside the ducal palace: the judici del Proprio, those of the Prosopi and the Signori di Notte, and offices dealing with commercial and criminal law.[72] As in the Venetian ducal palace, there was a chapel inside the palace in Candia, which was dedicated to St. Bernard.[73] A cistern providing water for the house and the family of the duke also served the needs of other residents of the city because it was the only cistern in the neighborhood.[74]

The ducal palace existed already in 1213, two years after the arrival of the Venetians, but no records have survived that mention construction or financing of a new palace by the colonial authorities.[75] Thus, it is safe to assume that the residence of the Venetian *duca* was housed in the palace of the former Byzantine governor of Chandax. Why did the Venetians decide to place the most important symbol of Venetian administration on Crete inside the Byzantine palace? This act must have been a conscious political choice: the Venetian governor of Crete resided in the most prominent structure in the city, the only building associated directly with the imperial authority of Constantinople. Thus, rather than weakening the position of the Venetian duke of Crete, the Byzantine origin of the palace enhanced his prestige. He had succeeded the lawful Byzantine *duca-katepano*, the governor of the Byzantine "theme" of Crete, appointed directly by the emperor. In fact, it has been suggested that the Venetians assigned the Greek title *duca* and not the Latin *dux* to their representative on Crete in order to continue Byzantine practices.[76] In doing so, they uprooted – and at the same time reproduced – the Byzantine administration of the empire. The reuse of the Byzantine ducal palace corroborates this hypothesis. The Byzantine origin of the palace legitimized the position of authority of the Venetian duke on the island and enabled the Venetians to proclaim a smooth transition from Byzantine to Venetian dominion.

In every colony the Venetian governor's palace was located on a prominent spot either on high ground or in the center of town, but the vestiges of these palaces are insignificant for any cogent art historical analysis. The palace of the rector of Canea is first mentioned in 1333, when the rector Bartuccio Grimani was authorized to expropriate the property of a private citizen, which blocked the entrance of the palace to the south and the gate of the church of St. Mark to the north. Thus, although there are no remains of this early structure, we can surmise that it was connected or communicated with the ducal church of St. Mark. The Canea palace is clearly shown inside the old fortified city in the detailed city view drafted by Zorzi Corner in 1625 (Fig. 53): a tower with the flag of the Republic marks this building as the foremost symbol of Venetian presence in Canea.[77] No archaeological remains of the palace in the lower city of Retimo survive. After the new *fortezza* was built in the sixteenth century, the palace of the Retimo rector was moved onto the hill, but the counselors continued to occupy the residence of the rector in the lower city, thus allowing for a close supervision of the population and the marketplace down below.[78]

In Negroponte, a colony that has produced both archaeological remains

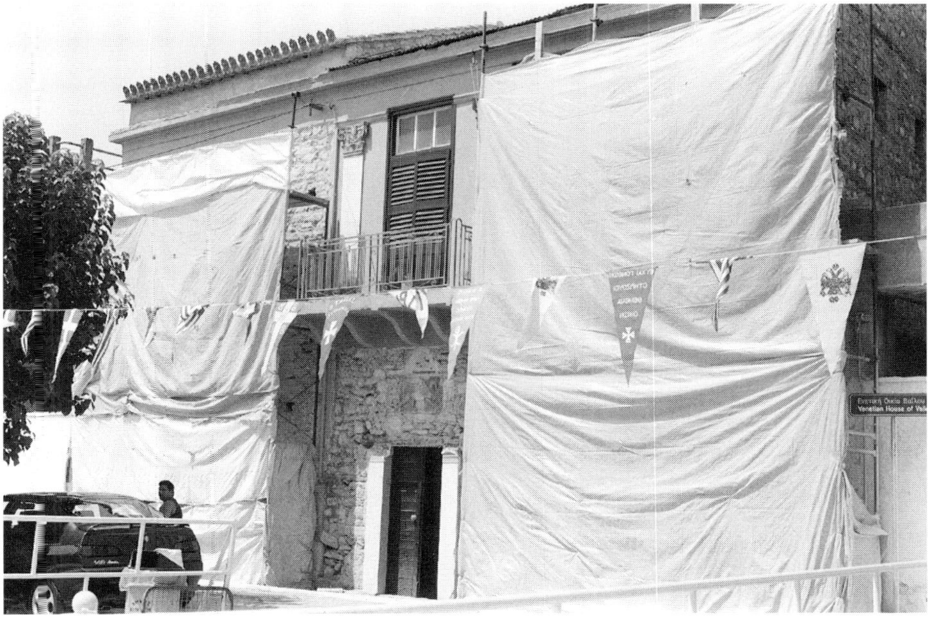

FIGURE 69. Chalkis, "House of *bailo*"

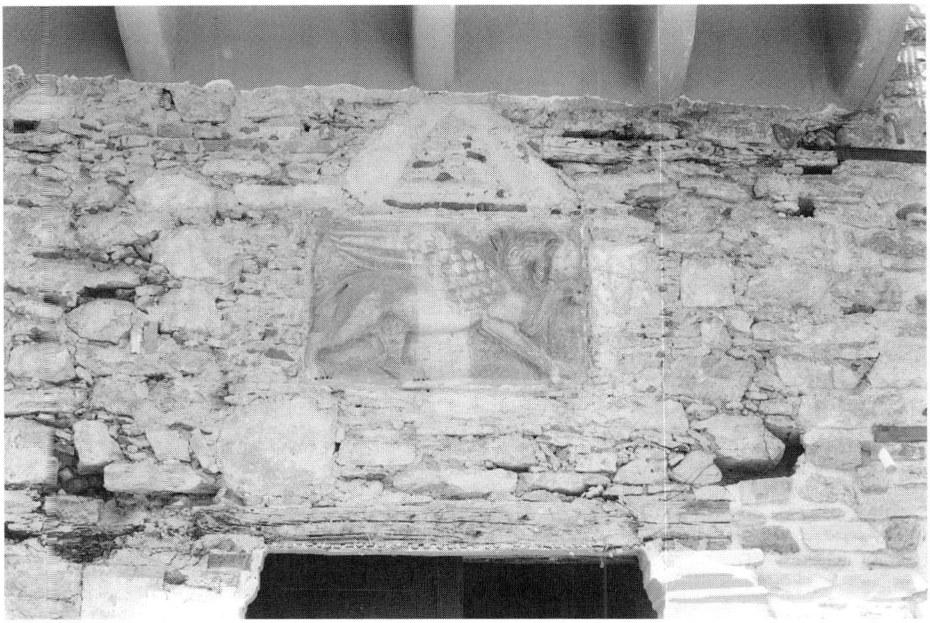

FIGURE 70. Chalkis, lion above the entrance to the "house of *bailo*"

and early archival documents, the Venetians possessed only a quarter inside the capital city with their own church dedicated to St. Mark, a palace for their governor (*bailo*), and a loggia. In 1216 this concentrated area included certain churches, houses, and a piazza for the Venetian settlers, as we learn from the document that ratified the transfer of the colony to the brothers Merino and Riçardo de Carcere:

> Retinuit quoque in se ecclesias et domos Venetorum, quas in Nigroponte habet, et domum positam retro ecclesiam sancti Marci, in qua habitat Jeremias Gisi, et duas alias similiter domos; una quarum quondam fuit Ottonelli de Erro, altera vero Morandi, cum campo, in quo venduntur magaze de vino, et in pectore sui loci et ecclesie sancti Marci ex alia parte platee.
>
> Retinuit in se similiter illas domos et terras et ecclesias, quantum murus novus civitatis extenditur, hoc est ab ipso longe pedes sexaginta usque mare, excepta domo, in qua habitat Ugolinus, Comes de Callippi.[79]

The piazza that still forms the core of the old city of Chalkis, the square of the Unknown Soldier, must have been the backbone of the Venetian settlement with houses for the settlers and merchants lying nearby. Located across from the church of Saint Mark (now a mosque), the residence of the *bailo* delimited this central square, which coincided with the wine market of the city.[80] In the fifteenth century this palace was preceded by a colonnade, probably a covered portico.[81] Traditionally a large structure across from the church of Hagia Paraskeve has been known as the "house of the *bailo*" (Fig. 69). This structure rests on an early Christian foundation, possibly the baptistery of the church, and displays a Venetian lion above its door (Fig. 70). The other public structure on the piazza was also a central part of Venetian presence in Negroponte: the loggia. First mentioned in 1281 in relation to a Venetian house, the loggia also housed the government chancellery.

The ducal palace in conjunction with the piazza San Marco created a symbolic framework that ingeniously manipulated history and the appearance of the cities of Candia and Negroponte to generate a collective memory of Venetian presence in the minds of the city dwellers. In order to counteract the violent imposition of Venetian rule in Crete, the makeup of the city of Candia showed a smooth transition from Byzantine to Venetian control, which favored a new blend of the two traditions. As with the public monuments that framed the piazza San Marco in Candia, certain policies of the Venetian colonizers took over older Byzantine traditions. In addition to the reuse of the title *duca,* the Venetians also manipulated another significant Byzantine tradition for their own benefit: the famous legend of the Twelve Archontopoula. A legend originally meant to provide a legal justification for the possessions of twelve powerful Byzantine families in Crete, it was by the seventeenth century explicitly modified to link these families not with the Byzantine emperor in Constantinople but with the doge in Venice.[82] Antonio Calergi, a descendant of one of the most important of these families, in his chronicle written in the sixteenth century stresses the continuity between the precolonial past of the island and the advent of the Venetian colonists in the thirteenth century: ten of the fourteen books of the chronicle refer to the period before 1204 and the remaining four books present Venetian rule as a continuation of the Byzantine history of Crete.[83]

All of these later developments are the result of concrete political steps that the Venetians took to link the island once and for all with its new masters. This is already obvious in the *Concessio Crete*, which was intended as the definitive official document setting the stage for the Venetian settlement of Crete: it underlined the fact that the Republic conceded the *whole* island of Crete to the colonists.[84] Probably the 1211 partition of the island was not enforced as rigorously as the *Concessio Crete* implies nor did it cover the whole territory of Crete, since more colonists were sent from Venice in 1222, 1233, and 1252.[85] However, insisting that the whole island submitted to the Venetians and dividing it in sixths that were named after the Venetian *sestieri* indicated the theoretical framework for the partition of Crete. It was part of the post-1204 rhetoric of the Republic, that is to say, an attempt to present the situation on Crete as a perfectly uniform, clear-cut case of transplantation of Venetian practices to the colony. The official cadastres of the colony, recording the possessions of the feudatories and organized in a similar manner, further emphasize the intended similarities between Venice and Crete.[86]

The symbols that linked the buildings to the Venetian authorities and the important role that these structures played in the religious life and the administration of the Venetians gradually dissociated these buildings from their Byzantine roots and made them symbolic of Venetian rule on Crete. This change in the meaning of the old Byzantine structures, along with the prominence of the new Venetian palaces, fostered the new political image that the Venetians wanted to establish following the Fourth Crusade and eventually transformed the city into a Venetian colony. Once the basic landmarks of the Venetians were set in Candia, Latin churches seem to have been used to ratify the establishment of colonial rule on Crete. These new buildings and the carefully orchestrated ceremonial of the colony enlivened the cityscape to make it work for the Venetians, as we will see in the next chapter.

PART TWO

MAPPING THE COLONIAL TERRITORY

FOUR

PATRON SAINTS, RELICS, AND MARTYRIA

> To Titus, mine own son after the common faith: Grace, mercy, and peace, from God the Father and the Lord Jesus Christ our Saviour. For this cause left I thee in Crete, that you should set in order the things that are wanting, and ordain elders in every city, as I had appointed you.
>
> St. Paul (Tit. 1:4–5)

The peacefulness of the transition from the Byzantine to the Venetian rule was jeopardized by religious differences between the Latin faith of the colonizers and the religious convictions of the colonized, who in their majority followed the Eastern Orthodox rite. One of the first acts of the Venetian colonists was to seize the old Byzantine cathedral of Candia from the Orthodox Greeks and offer it to the Latin archbishop so as to sanction the new Western religious authority on Crete.[1] Next to this important Byzantine structure, a new church was dedicated to the patron saint of Venice, St. Mark. On the edges of the urban space impressive new Latin establishments sponsored by the Mendicant orders demarcated large portions of the city. The prominence of these Latin churches and monasteries in medieval views and in accounts of travelers exemplifies the significance of these structures for defining Candia as a Western city. Which buildings besides the church of St. Mark turned Candia into a Venetian city? What did they look like? How were they incorporated within the city? How was space appropriated? Were the architects Venetians or locals? Who were the patrons? To suggest answers to these questions this chapter analyzes newly constructed churches and monasteries that were sponsored by the Venetian authorities or by patrons who were closely linked to the authorities and often had similar agendas. Certain establishments of the Latin faith became extremely important for identifying parts of Candia as Venetian, for spurring population growth into specific parts of town, and ultimately for sanctifying urban (and suburban) space.

Ubiquitous features in every city and easily recognizable as building types, temples, churches, and mosques have had a standardized function and a consistent purpose since ancient times. Their role was even more pronounced during the Middle Ages, when no state could be effective without the sanctioning of the highest religious authority. This was especially true in the period of the crusades. Conforming with the Western church in colonies distant from Venice was an important component of the colonists' political allegiance. Latin settlers in Venetian Crete followed the same rite as their compatriots living in Venice and other parts of Italy, and their faith became one of the primary symbols of Venetian dominion in Romania. Thus, Venice's political establishment in the Eastern Mediterranean largely depended on the success of the Latin church in the region.

In addition to the cathedral of St. Titus and the ducal chapel of St. Mark, several churches and monasteries were erected in the city and the suburbs to serve the Venetian community and to proclaim the official creed of the colonists. It was crucial, it seems, that the Latin settlers could find in the colonies the same establishments that existed in Venice itself. Churches and monasteries were significant constituents of the urban environment. Not only were they places where the population would gather on regular occasions during the year, but each Latin church was preceded by an open space, the *campo*, following the building practices observed in the city of Venice. Moreover, the distinct architectural features of these structures accentuated their Venetian character. As a result, in the colonial context of Crete, the Western churches were symbols not only of the Latin church, but also of the political power that commissioned them. As we saw in the first chapter, in a number of plans of Candia the Latin churches seem to stand for the ruling power, being the only Venetian buildings indicated in the city. Even if we imagine that these plans were made for a Venetian audience, the prominence of churches over military or administrative monuments is striking. The imagery of a church of Western rite seems to encompass more than the religious identity of the Venetian overlords: it also embodies the political identity of their state. Furthermore, the spatial arrangement of the Latin churches in the cities of Crete speaks to an attempt to "westernize" the urban space by creating landmarks associated with the presence of Venice on the island.

The Venetian character of the Western churches and monasteries was also stressed by religious rituals that duplicated customs of the mother city. Fusing these practices with earlier Byzantine traditions, the major Western churches were connected through religious processions in which both Greeks and Latins participated. In this section I argue that the siting of the Latin churches and their linkage through processions represented a deliberate attempt of the colonial authorities to manipulate the city space; the ritual layout of the city "dictated" the use of the urban space in order to promulgate the impression of a harmonious coexistence of the clashing ethnic communities of the colony under the sage governance of the Venetians.

THE LOCAL PATRON SAINT

Being the seat of the Orthodox metropolitan in the second Byzantine period, the site of the cathedral of the city had acquired a primary importance in Byzantine Chandax and was certainly recognized as the most sacred spot of the city by both Venetians and Greeks in the early thirteenth century.[2] The cathedral was located on the main artery of the city, the *ruga magistra*, to the north of the piazza (no. 21 on the map, Fig. 17). Originally, it was preceded by a large open space that opened to the street. The cathedral was thus the first large Latin church that one saw when walking on the main street from the harbor. It was only in the seventeenth century that the construction of the new loggia and the *armeria* obstructed the view to the church (Figs. 52 and 71). All sources maintain that by 1211 the relics of St. Titus, the patron saint of Crete, were located in the Byzantine metropolitan church of Chandax. Despite the fact that later Venetian records emphasized the Greek Orthodox origin of the cathedral of Candia and its dedication to St. Titus since its inception,[3] it seems that until the arrival of the Venetians and even later the cathedral of Chandax continued to be dedicated to All Saints as in earlier Byzantine times. In fact, two documents of 1312 that record the construction of the churches of the Madonna Catafigiani and the Madonna Eleousa were signed in the church of All Saints ("actum est hoc in ecclesia Omnium Sanctorum civitatis Candide"), which cannot be other than the cathedral.[4] It is possible that the church had two dedications: to All Saints and to St. Titus. Be that as it may, the close association of the cathedral with St. Titus personalized the connection of the church with the unique sacred history of Crete and it is this dedication that was emphasized by the Venetians

After 1211, the Venetians appropriated the Byzantine church. We have no record of a major modification of the church, but we can surmise that the liturgical layout of its interior was changed to conform with the Western rite, presumably by creating new chapels and multiple altars. As the actual church of St. Titus is a modern building (Fig. 72), we have to rely on documentary and liturgical evidence to reconstruct the appearance of the medieval cathedral. The actual building was damaged in the devastating

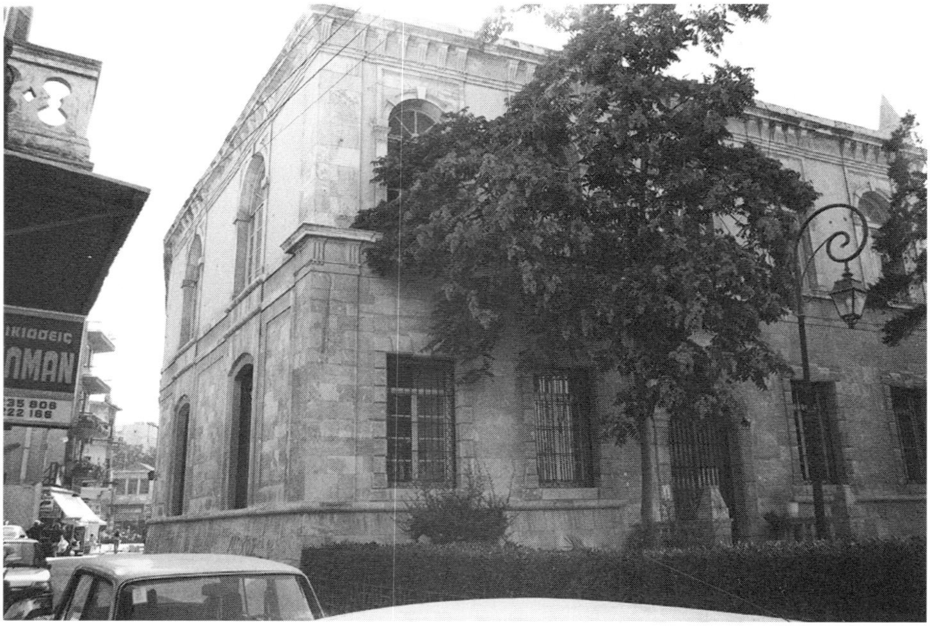

FIGURE 71. Herakleion, armeria

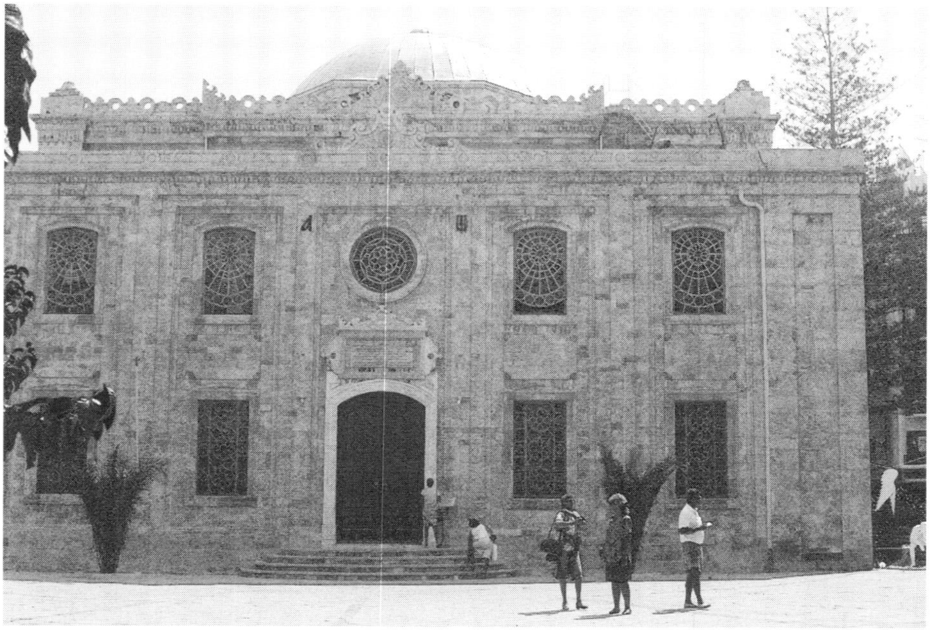

FIGURE 72. Herakleion, view of Hagios Titos

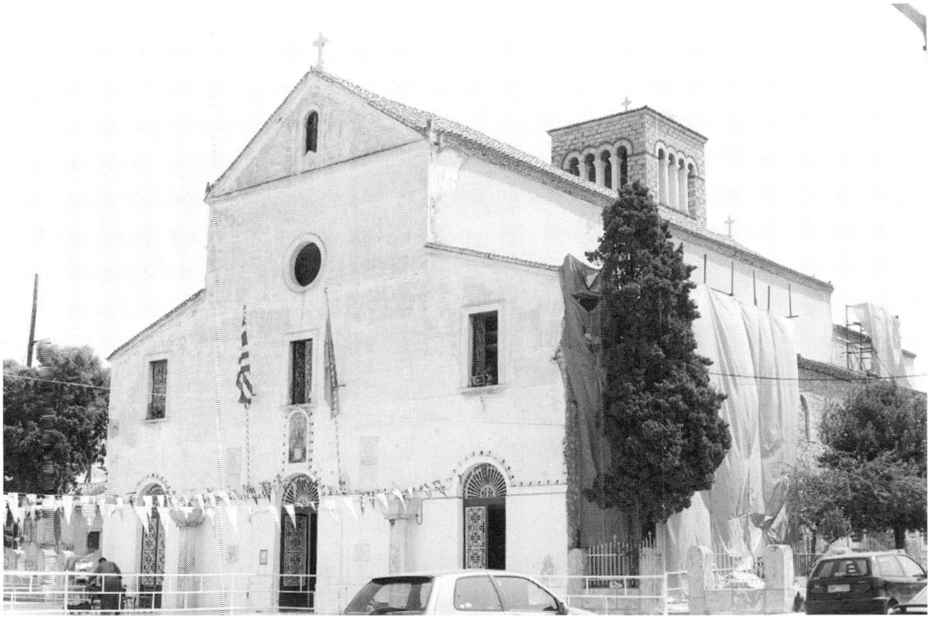

FIGURE 73. Chalkis, church of Hagia Paraskeve, exterior view from west

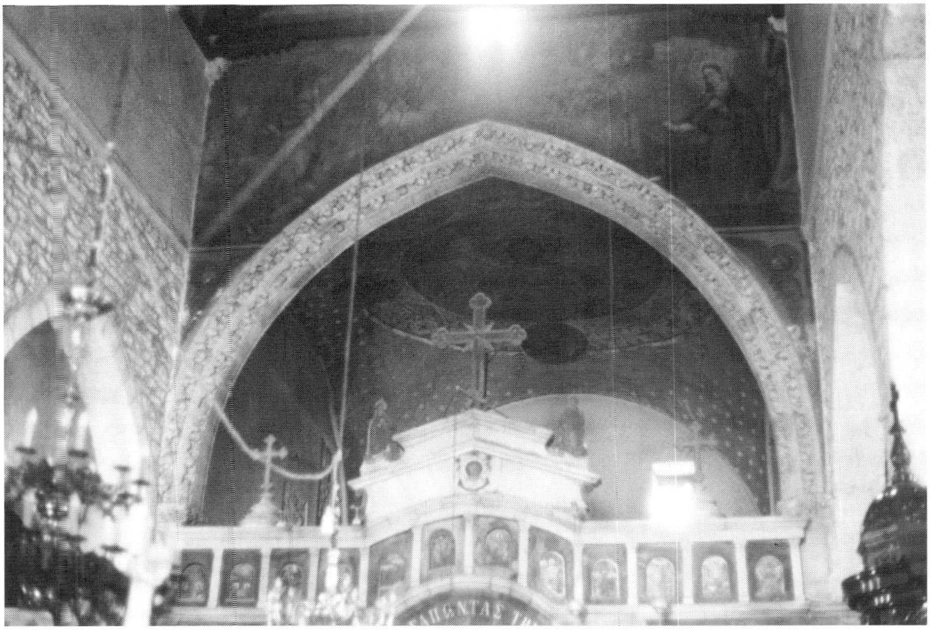

FIGURE 74. Chalkis, church of Hagia Paraskeve, view to choir

earthquake of 1856, was rebuilt as a mosque in 1878, and was eventually restored as a church in 1925. There are no records of an extensive reconstruction of the church during Venetian rule except for the addition of ornamental details in the exterior of the building and changes in its liturgical furnishings.[5] Since there are relatively few instances in Byzantium where we have more than one altar within a church, we can also safely assume that the church ended in an apse to the east, which was probably vaulted. It is unclear whether there were side chapels (pastophoria) flanking the central apse.

The cathedral of Negroponte, a reused Byzantine church that is still standing, offers a good indication as to how the transformation of the church of St. Titus may have been achieved (Fig. 73). The Euboean church in fact parallels that of Candia in importance as the older Orthodox church of Negroponte became the seat of the Latin patriarch of Constantinople when the Byzantines recovered that city in 1261. The cathedral of Negroponte, the church now dedicated to St. Paraskeve, was probably dedicated to the Virgin Peribleptos during the Byzantine period.[6] This impressive, whitewashed church, which now is celebrated for holding the miracle-working hand of St. Paraskeve and an icon representing a full-length portrait of the saint and scenes from her life, was an early Christian church of the sixth century. The Latins added a ribbed vaulted Gothic choir and possibly a bell tower in the thirteenth and fourteenth centuries (Fig. 74). The apse is flanked by two chapels, that of the Holy Trinity to the south with elegantly carved foliage capitals and consoles, and that of St. Eleutherios with traces of frescoes to the north next to the bell tower. There are, however, enough discrepancies in the elevation of the church to indicate, first, that the original church was longer (the two columns that flank the main western entrance are identical to those of the nave), and, second, that the Latins remodeled only parts of the nave.[7] Not only are many of its older columns still visible, but the nave arcade shows a combination of rounded and pointed arches indicating a different construction campaign. In fact, the different articulation of the elevation of the nave in the two most eastern bays before the choir suggests that this area and the chevet date to the thirteenth century. The nave arcades are surmounted by foliage capitals, seemingly made up of ancient and Byzantine spoils (Figs. 75, 76, and 77). A marble figure of a woman with her head covered now in the Archaeological Museum of Chalkis possibly comes from the pediment covering the western entrance to the church.[8]

To return to the cathedral of St. Titus, it seems that the transformation of the naos from a more or less uniform space divided in two by the templon into a series of private chapels surrounding the stalls of the choir happened gradually. In the fifteenth century three large chapels were probably set around the choir (*capellae primae*), with four smaller ones adorning the southern and northern sides of the church.[9] However, as more wealthy patrons were buried inside the cathedral, new, elaborately decorated private chapels were added.[10] We know, for instance, that when the tomb of archbishop Fantinus Valaresso was placed under the floor of the axial chapel, the whole chapel had to be remodeled and a new altar was reconsecrated there by his successor, Fantinus Dandolus, on the feast day of St. Titus, January 4, 1446.[11] The altar contained relics of St. Titus, St. Martin, St. Lucy, and St. Stephen, the last housed in an elaborate Byzantine reliquary made in silver and decorated with enamel.[12] The cathedral prided itself on possessing other significant relics as well: a crystal reliquary containing some blood of Christ,[13] the head of St. Barbara,[14] and the tibia of St. Saba.[15]

Further details of the exterior of the church can be obtained from a careful consideration of written sources. The central doorway of the west façade was surmounted by a circular arch, probably designed in the sixteenth century: lateral colonnettes supported an arch, which was topped by inscriptions. In the early sixteenth century the church was described as "a large, tall structure with innumerable columns of various styles made of rare marble; it was adorned with the tombs and coats of arms of famous noblemen and with precious altars and chapels decorated in such a way that all these were an eternal ornament to the city."[16] Most probably the marble columns were reused spoils from ancient monuments, but we have no further information on these spoils. The emphasis on the numerous columns gives the impression that the church was a basilical building, whereas other documentary evidence shows the cathedral to have been covered with a dome. In 1350 Heregina Asoleis intended to build a church that should be surmounted by a dome "made exactly like the dome of St. Titus."[17] Thus, we must assume that the church was a domed basilica.

Similar impressions are conveyed about the building in two seventeenth-century accounts of the mosque of the grand vizier in which the church was converted in 1670. The whole space including the narthex was an eighty-by eighty-foot square, that is, approximately thirty by thirty meters.[18] A twelve-bay-deep nave was flanked by double side aisles opening through semicircular arched arcades;[19] the space was covered by a roof made of cypress wood beams and was reinforced with lead, as was the roof of the narthex. According to Evliya Çelebi, "the eastern side of the nave resembled a garden," probably as a result of the colorful decoration and of the light that came in through the numerous windows. A vault or cupola (the Turkish document reads *toloz* from the Greek word θόλος) supported by four columns soared over the mihrab, which would have been located at the same spot as the apse of the Christian building (the *qibla* in Crete would be due east).[20] From

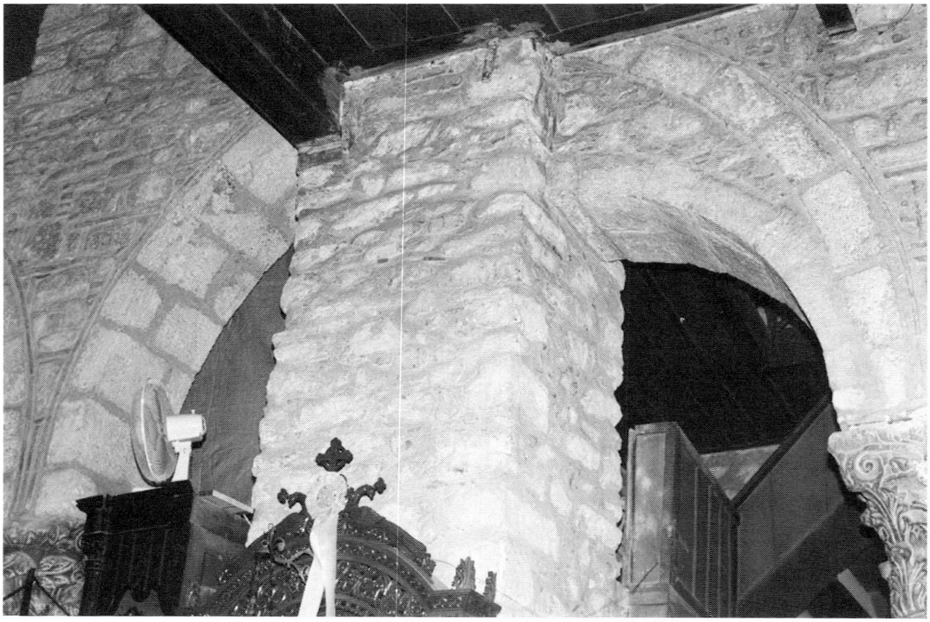

FIGURE 75. Chalkis, church of Hagia Paraskeve, arches

Evliya's account it seems that there were four new arches of vaults toward the *qibla*, to expand the area in front of the mihrab perhaps. In this way the shape of the building changed from a rectangular basilica into a square structure, and a central aisle leading to the mihrab also created between the two colonnades led to the sanctuary of the older church.[21] The mosque had two doors: the main western entrance, which was a very large, tripartite opening, and a smaller door on the north side. In medieval times this door must have served as an entrance to the corridor that connected the cathedral with the residence of the archbishop.[22]

The plans of Zorzi Corner (Fig. 14), George Clontzas (Fig. 12), Werdmüller (Fig. 16), and Manea Cloza confirm the description of Evliya Çelebi and suggest that the Ottomans did not alter the overall architecture of the building: the structure was almost square in plan without projecting apses. Although no dome is indicated in the plans of the city, the fourteenth-century dome of the Venetian document must be identified with the *toloz* referred to in Evliya's account. Perhaps the bell tower of the Venetians, which is prominent in all views of Candia, obstructed the depiction of the dome behind it. In fact, since the minaret stood on the same spot at which we see the bell tower of the church in the Venetian plans, it is possible that the Ottomans reused the existing bell tower as a minaret. Silihdar's description strengthens this argument as the forms he describes do not evoke a

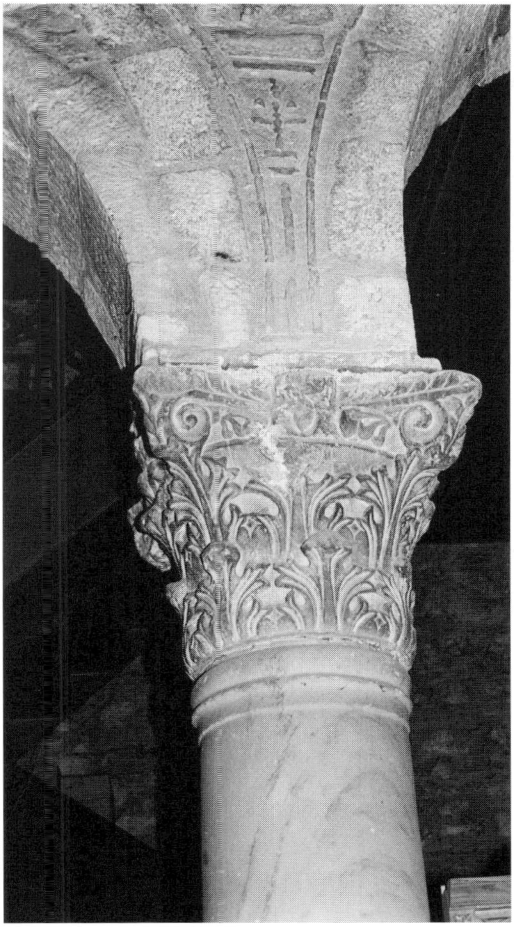

FIGURE 76. Chalkis, church of Hagia Paraskeve, capital

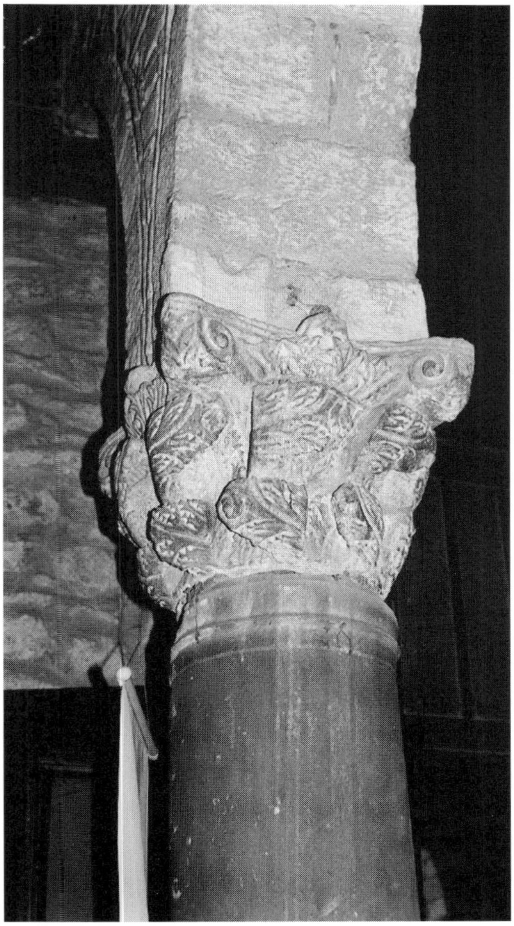

FIGURE 77. Chalkis, church of Hagia Paraskeve, capital

typical Ottoman minaret, which would be a slender, tall tower.[23] We can, therefore, assume that the bell tower of St. Titus was square in form with five stories and by the sixteenth century was covered with a cupola.

Like the church of San Marco in Venice, the Latin cathedral of Candia had a Byzantine ancestry, but was Western in practice. Unlike the ducal basilica of San Marco, however, as the cathedral of Candia the church of St. Titus was placed under the jurisdiction of the Latin archbishop and not of the state. Nevertheless, the cathedral was an important public monument because the duke attended Mass in it and several dukes of Crete were buried therein.[24] Under extraordinary circumstances state funds were channeled to the church with the understanding that maintaining its appearance was a primary concern of state authorities. For instance, in 1320 the toll tax (*pedagium porte*), one of the most important income sources of the city, was offered for two years to the archbishop for repairs to the cathedral.[25]

The cathedral of St. Titus was one of the most significant landmarks of Venetian Candia as it attracted Christians of the Greek and Latin rites who venerated the holy relics inside the church. It was, thus, the best spot to publicize the patron saint of Venetian Candia. Three factors enhanced the value of St. Titus's cult and consequently influenced the Venetian decision to adopt this relatively unimportant saint, who until then had not figured among the ecclesiastical calendar of Venice, as the primary religious cult figure of their colony: the early Christian origin of the saint, the presence of his relics in Chandax, and the civic connotations of the continuing Byzantine tradition of his cult. Titus, a pagan converted to Christianity by the teachings of Peter, followed the Apostle Paul to Crete in 66 A.D. He was believed to have been ordained the first bishop of Crete by Paul, and after Paul's departure he remained there to organize the church on the island (Tit. 1:5); the *Life* of Saint Titus reports that he appointed eight bishops on Crete.[26] Indeed, to stress the formative role that Titus played in the region, the famous metropolitan of Crete, Andrew (712–40), had called St. Titus the "father of the country" (πατήρ πατρίδος).[27] Early Christian accounts identify his place of origin with Corinth or Antioch, whereas later hagiographical sources maintain that he came from Crete and even claim a Minoan ancestry for his family. Interestingly, the saint's *Life* insists that Titus had received a fine classical education that included Homer and the philosophers, which a divine vision told him to reject in favor of the Bible:

> The family of the most holy Titus is descended from Minos, the king of Crete. Desirous of the poems and dramas of Homer and the rest of the philosophers, when he turned twenty years of age he heard a voice telling him: "Titus, you have to leave this place and save your soul; because this education will not be useful."[28]

These same sources placed him in Jerusalem at the time of Christ and made him a witness of Christ's passion and a recipient of the Holy Spirit during the Pentecost.[29] A survey of the painted Byzantine churches of Crete shows that the saint appears in at least four rural churches: in the eleventh-century church of St. Euthymios, near Chromonastiri in Rethymnon; that of St. Michael the Archangel at Kouneni (in the region of Chania); in the late fourteenth-century frescoed apse of the church of St. Photeini in the south of Crete, near the monastery of Preveli; and in the church of Panagia Gouverniotissa in Potamies Pediados.[30] Following standard Byzantine iconographic patterns, St. Titus is depicted as an Orthodox bishop.

When the Venetians colonized Crete the saint was the most important figure in the saintly hierarchy of the island, recognized by everybody as the patron saint of Crete. The fact that he is depicted on the walls of an eleventh-century church demonstrates that his cult was already flourishing on the island before the arrival of the Venetians, as does the late date of the compilation of his *Life*. Titus's tomb, originally preserved in the cathedral of Gortyna, was the site for significant posthumous miracles according to the hagiographical accounts: "There is an altar on his true tomb with handcuffs where those possessed by evil spirits are chained to; in there all those who are deemed worthy to embrace the tomb of the saint are healed."[31] Despite the accounts of Cristoforo Buondelmonti and Flaminio Corner, the early Christian cathedral of Gortyna containing the saint's tomb was not destroyed by the Arabs in the ninth century.[32] Both the archaeological evidence and the fact that the *Life* of St. Nikon, who visited Crete after the Byzantine reconquest of Crete, mentions Gortyna provide ample evidence of the well-being of Gortyna in the second Byzantine period.[33] However, the only relic of the saint that was later displayed in Candia was his head. This must have been transported to Chandax when the city was elevated to the seat of the metropolitan, thus turning the Byzantine cathedral of the city into a virtual martyrium. One wonders whether this partial translation of relics indicates a compromise between Gortyna and Chandax, the two largest cities of Crete in the second Byzantine period. In any event, the Venetians upon their arrival on the island found an already formed cult to a local patron saint centering around his miracle-working relics. St. Titus's personal experience of the Passion of Christ and his special ties with Crete made him a perfect symbol for the newly established Latin church on the island.[34] Already in 1209 pope Innocent III had promised the pilgrims who would visit Crete (presumably the primary church of the island, that is to say, the cathedral of the capital city) the same indulgences as the crusaders who went to Jerusalem, thus elevating the position of the saint and his church within the hierarchy of the Latin church.[35] The road was now open for the Venetians to incorporate this cult into their state rhetoric. The local appeal of the saint's relics had the power, if used correctly, to work as a catalyst for the success of the Venetian dominion on Crete and to provide a divine sanctioning for its actions.[36] The one icon of St. Titus that has survived attests to the effectiveness of the Venetian strategies of assimilation. The icon, now in the Vatican, reveals Western patronage: it was painted by the Candiote painter George Clontzas at the end of the sixteenth century and depicts the saint as a Latin bishop.[37] In all probability the icon was commissioned by a Latin who had known (or experienced) the unique qualities of the patron saint of Crete. Let us see how this worked.

To appropriate the particular civic qualities of Saint Titus, the Venetian authorities evoked his support in their governing of the island.[38] Continuing a Byzantine custom, the Latin archbishop invited the duke and his entourage to the metropolitan's palace on the feast day of Saint Titus.[39] In the mid-fifteenth century, the hymns sung during the civic celebrations of Candia provide eloquent testimony as to how St. Titus's alliance with the new authorities of Crete was underscored in the official ceremonial of the colony. St. Titus parallels St. Mark, the patron of Venice. On Crete the Lauds service began with the evocation of the victorious Christ ("Christus vincit"), praising God and his representatives on Earth, the doge, and the wise government of Venice. Then St. Titus's help was solicited ("Sancte Tite tu nos adjuva"), especially for the duke of Crete.[40] By the end of the sixteenth century the cathedral was a focal point in most civic ceremonies, which either started or ended in front of the church.[41] St. Titus had become the patron saint of the colonial authorities.

The unique role that the cult of St. Titus played in forging the identity of Venetian Crete is further highlighted in 1363 when the Venetian feudal lords formed an alliance with the local Byzantines and revolted against the colonial government in response to excessive taxation placed on them by the metropole. Their banner proclaimed the independent Republic of St. Titus on Crete and the figure of the saint was to appear on the flags of all ships registered in Crete.[42] After the effective suppression of the rebellion, the Venetian authorities instituted an annual solemn procession and a horse race (*palium*) to commemorate their victory against the rebels: the procession started at the cathedral of St. Titus, who was once again on the side of the Venetians.[43] In fact the cult of St. Titus had become such an integral part of the Venetian heritage of Crete that when the Venetians were forced out of Candia by the Ottomans in 1669, the relics of the saint migrated to Venice with them. They were displayed on the high altar of the basilica of San Marco on his feast day (January 3).[44]

Likewise in the other Venetian colonies that had been seats of Orthodox bishops, the thirteenth-century Latin cathedrals were housed in the older Byzantine churches and took over the cult of local patron saints. In addition to providing an already existing building this move emblazoned the new Latin ecclesiastical hierarchy onto the former Byzantine Orthodox towns. For instance, the Latin cathedral of Modon was dedicated to St. John and contained among its sacred relics the head of St. Athanasius, an important saint for the Orthodox church.[45] Similarly in Corfu the Latin cathedral was set until the seventeenth century inside the old Byzantine metropolitan church of Peter and Paul that housed the relics of St. Arsenios, a tenth-century bishop of Kerkyra, as well as those of Saints Jason and Sossipatros.[46]

Although the cathedral of St. Arsenios was destroyed by fire, old views of the city show that it was a basilica, which according to tradition had been built in the thirteenth century.[47]

The cathedrals of Canea, Retimo, and Sitia seem to have been built anew as the cities were elevated to bishoprics after the Venetian conquest of Crete. A Gothic basilica of modest size (circa twenty-eight by twenty-one meters), the Latin cathedral of Canea was dedicated to the Virgin and was located close to the main street on the summit of the citadel, as we can see in the detailed plan of Zorzi Corner (Fig. 53, clearly labeled the *Domo*) and in the view of the city that Peeters drew in the seventeenth century, when the church had been turned into a mosque after 1645 (Fig. 78).[48] This pointed-barrel vaulted basilica had a façade constructed in the fourteenth century, and we may assume that it was erected shortly after the city was elevated into a bishopric in 1336 (Figs. 79 and 80).[49] The choir in front of the axial chapel contained sacred relics (a finger of St. Luke and sacred oil) the throne of the bishop, and seats for the ten canons of the church made in cypress wood. To the south an altar was dedicated to the Virgin Agiocastrini, possibly a reference to the icon of the Virgin that stood in it; the icon was endowed by the state and carried in procession every Tuesday. In this central chapel there were also a large painting of the Deposition above the altar and to the right a Byzantine icon of St. Titus, a clear reference to the subordination of the cathedral of Canea to the metropolitan church of Candia. Another very old wooden icon depicting St. Peter, St. Paul, St. George, and St. Francis adorned the first chapel to the north. What we see on the view of Peeters shows a much later façade in a classicizing style as well as a choir with a soaring dome reminiscent of High Renaissance buildings in Italy.

The Latin cathedral of Retimo became the seat of the bishop of Calamon sometime during Venetian rule, but no remains of this church in the lower town have survived. The first documentary information on this church, a decree of the Senate in Venice, suggests that in 1358 the cathedral was housed in the church of St. Mark which is described as an old structure.[50] In 1583–85 the cathedral was moved inside the *fortezza* to a new church dedicated to St. Nicholas, the patron saint of the city, but the location of the Latin cathedral away from the old civic center of Retimo displeased the city dwellers, who found it inconvenient to attend services far from their homes.[51] Apparently, for some unspecified reason the church of St. Mark was no longer available for this purpose. To remedy the situation, in 1588 construction of another Latin church inside the city was authorized – a project that never materialized. The population attended Mass in the small church of St. Catherine, no archaeological remains of which are preserved.

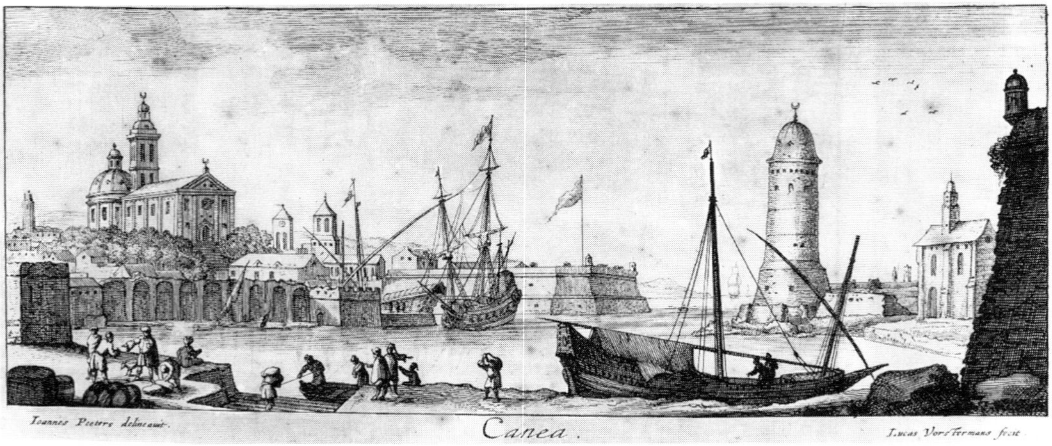

FIGURE 78. Jacques Peeters, Canea, in *Description des principales villes . . .* (Anvers, 1690) (The Gennadius Library, American School of Classical Studies)

The identification of the Latin cathedral of Sitia is even more problematic: the church of St. Mark, which was located in the center of the city from early on, would be a good candidate but it only became the official seat of the bishop of Sitia in 1566.[52] Furthermore, as Gerola has already observed, this small, undecorated church of St. Mark was not suitable for a cathedral. Obviously, this was a relatively poor foundation, which must have been endowed in the fifteenth century by two Latin noblemen whose coats of arms appeared on the church.[53] Finally, in 1645 the church was abandoned.[54] The earliest mention of the Latin churches of Sitia is preserved in the 1475 testament of a Ragusan merchant, Antonius Benchi Bratossalich, who died in Sitia. In his testament he made donations to all the major Latin churches of the city: the cathedral of St. Mark; the monastery of Santa Caterina, where he wanted to be buried; the church and hospital of Santa Maria; and the churches of St. John and St. Nicholas in the suburbs.[55] Unfortunately there are no remains of the cathedrals of Modon and Coron, which were both bishoprics when the Venetians acquired them in 1209.[56]

THE PATRON SAINT OF THE EMPIRE: SAINT MARK

To emphasize the special colonial position of Crete, the Venetian colonists in addition to honoring the Byzantine patron of the island revered the patron saint of Venice by erecting a church in his honor. Just as the cathedral of St.

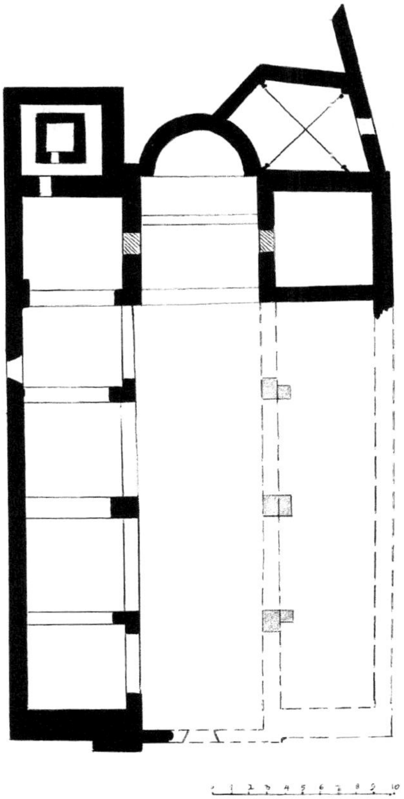

FIGURE 79. Chania, Latin cathedral, ground plan after Gerola

Titus was a landmark of Byzantine Crete that proclaimed the lawful inheritance of Byzantine sacred traditions by the Venetians, the church of St. Mark that was built nearby to the south stood as a ubiquitous symbol of Venice. St. Mark had a close, almost personal association with the doge that was brilliantly expressed in the ducal chapel in Venice: in the metropole the basilica of San Marco was connected to the ducal palace and the ceremonial of the church centered on the appearances of the doge and his retinue.[57] By the beginning of the thirteenth century the ducal chapel of San Marco had become a symbol of the magnificence of the Republic. The Venetians attempted to reproduce this successful scheme on Crete, where the office of the *duca* of Candia emulated that of the Venetian doge and the colonial government of Crete attempted to reenact – in a provincial way – the situation in Venice. At the time of the first Venetian settlement in 1211, St. Mark's feast day was introduced as one of the four most important feasts of the liturgical calendar of Crete.[58] Perhaps an altar or chapel dedicated to the

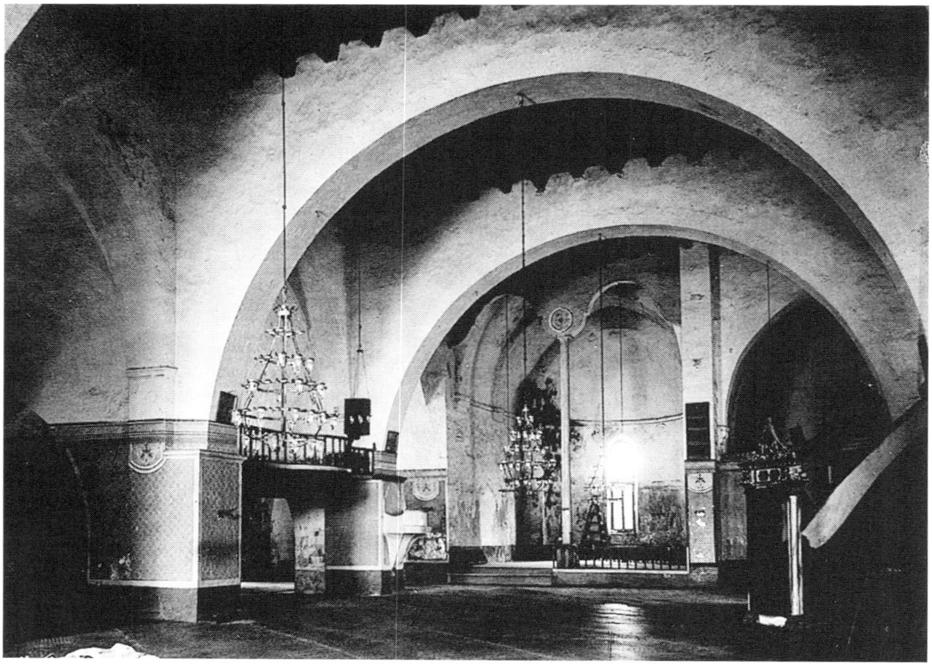

FIGURE 80. Chania, remains of the Latin cathedral in the upper town (Istituto Veneto di Scienze, Lettere ed Arti. Venezia. Archivio fotografico della Missione in Creta di Giuseppe Gerola)

saint was erected at that time either in the cathedral or in the ducal palace. The first record of a church dedicated to the Evangelist in Candia dates to 1228,[59] and one of the first dukes who died in Candia, Bartolomeo Gradonigo, was buried therein in 1236.[60] This early church must have been either a small chapel inside the ducal palace or an older Byzantine church that had been temporarily converted to the Latin rite, because in 1239 the Venetian feudatories were granted papal permission to lay the foundations for a new church using building material from the Cretan town of Ierapetra.[61] This new ducal chapel was placed directly under the jurisdiction of Rome, and, like the church of San Marco in Venice, it was not subject to the local archbishop,[62] but rather was administered by a state official called *primicerius*, who elected and ruled over the sacristans, the undersacristans, and the canons of the church.[63]

The actual church of St. Mark in Candia was completed before 1244, when a bell tower was constructed to the south of the church following the model of the piazza San Marco in Venice. For the construction of this bell tower, which is clearly visible in Clontzas's view of Candia (Fig. 12), and an adjacent cemetery the church of Crete exchanged one of its land possessions close to the city walls for a lot that was located between the church of St. Mark and the city walls.[64] The church stood close to the land gate on the main square, which was named after it. A detailed depiction of the church has survived in the seventeenth-century plan of the city made by Zorzi Corner (Fig. 14), and this representation served as a guide for the 1950s restoration of the basilica to its medieval shape. A personification of Candia stands on the right side of the plan holding a model of the basilica of St. Mark in her hand. The church is clearly shown with its prominent bell tower, on which the flag of the Venetian Republic is waving.[65] The church has been singled out as the only Venetian monument held by the figure of Candia, demonstrating its symbolic significance for the Venetian colonial government.

The church, which immediately after the Ottoman conquest of Candia was converted into the mosque of the Defterdar Pasa, is still standing; it is now used as an exhibition space and lecture hall. Two rows of five columns made of local grayish granite divide the interior of the basilica into six equal bays (see plan and elevation, Fig. 81).[66] The capitals of the nave have a simple cubical profile and show traces of gold paint (Figs. 82 and 83). The same simplicity in form is detected in the bases of the columns, which imitate simple Romanesque base profiles with stylized corner leaves. Elegant Gothic crochet capitals adorned the triumphal arch, suggesting a later date for the apse. The height of the columns was not the same throughout the nave; the restorers believe that the difference in height suggests not reuse of the architectural members, but rather different construction phases. They attribute half of the columns to the extensive consolidation campaign of 1552–57, which reinforced the northern part of the church with four buttresses.[67] The pavement of the church was made of local stone that was cut in rectangular pieces set at an angle to the east-west axis, forming a diamond pattern throughout the church; two tombstones are still preserved in the area of the choir but there is no inscription identifying the persons buried in them. During the restoration, traces of wall paintings were also discovered, but their state of conservation did not allow an identification of the patterns depicted. Five of the original lancet windows survived in the south aisle. The sacristy of the church must have been situated at the north side of the building and was reached by the side door midway down the nave.[68] The residence of the *primicerius* was probably located on the south side of the church.[69]

The church was preceded by a portico that was elevated on several marble steps and is referred to as *loggia*.[70] The portico measured 17.60 by 6.15 meters and was covered by a sloping timber roof. It opened to the main square through a five-partite arcade that was supported by cylindrical columns; the central arch was wider than the side arches (Fig. 84). Three of the original pillars still survive and were incorporated in the restoration of the 1950s. They are surmounted by simple crochet capitals, a standard feature of Gothic monuments. The actual central door, which is crowned by a simple lintel, also belongs to the original Venetian church. There is documentary evidence that a painting decorated the lintel, depicting the Virgin Mary.[71] Despite the existence of a religious image over the doorway, the portico did not have a strictly religious function: merchants sold their merchandise on benches and the public announcements were read from this spot, reproducing practices in Venice.[72] So, as its prominent location on the piazza announces, the church played an important role in civic life.

The bell tower that no longer survives was a separate structure to the southwest of the church and was severely damaged during the earthquake of 1508.[73] Today, only the square stone base of the Turkish minaret remains near the southwestern corner of the church; it measures 4.20 meters in height, but its width cannot be calculated because it has been incorporated in the adjacent structures (Fig. 85). A close study of the representation of the campanile in the plans of Zorzi Corner (Fig. 14) and George Clontzas (Fig. 12) indicates that it was the tallest structure in the city. The tower had three stories, was covered by a flat roof, and had a parapet with crenellated battlements. A clock was set on the west wall of the campanile in 1463 to serve the needs of the market and the population, following the example of Venice.[74] The upper part of the tower was pierced by biforal windows.

The maintenance of the ducal chapel and the house of the *primicerius* of St. Mark was the responsibility of the duke, who had to raise the necessary capital from the treasury in Candia, not an easy task. For instance, after the devastating earthquake of 1303 that seriously affected the church, the duke faced great difficulties raising funds for the repair of St. Mark and the necessary restorations were not undertaken for a number of years. Although by 1309 wood had been sent from Venice for the repair of the church, no major works were undertaken until 1315.[75] In 1336 the Senate in Venice finally took action on the matter and sent 1,000 ducats for the restoration of the ducal chapel, because they thought that "the bad condition of the church of St. Mark was harmful to the honor of the Republic and did not satisfy the devotional needs of the people."[76] The association of the good appearance of the church with the honor of the dominion demonstrates that – in theory at least – the Senate thought of the church of St. Mark as a symbol of Venetian rule on Crete. Belying these declarations about the significance of the church, though, the basilica had been left in a desolate condition for thirty years. This may suggest that at the beginning of the fourteenth century the ducal chapel in Candia had not acquired a role comparable to that of

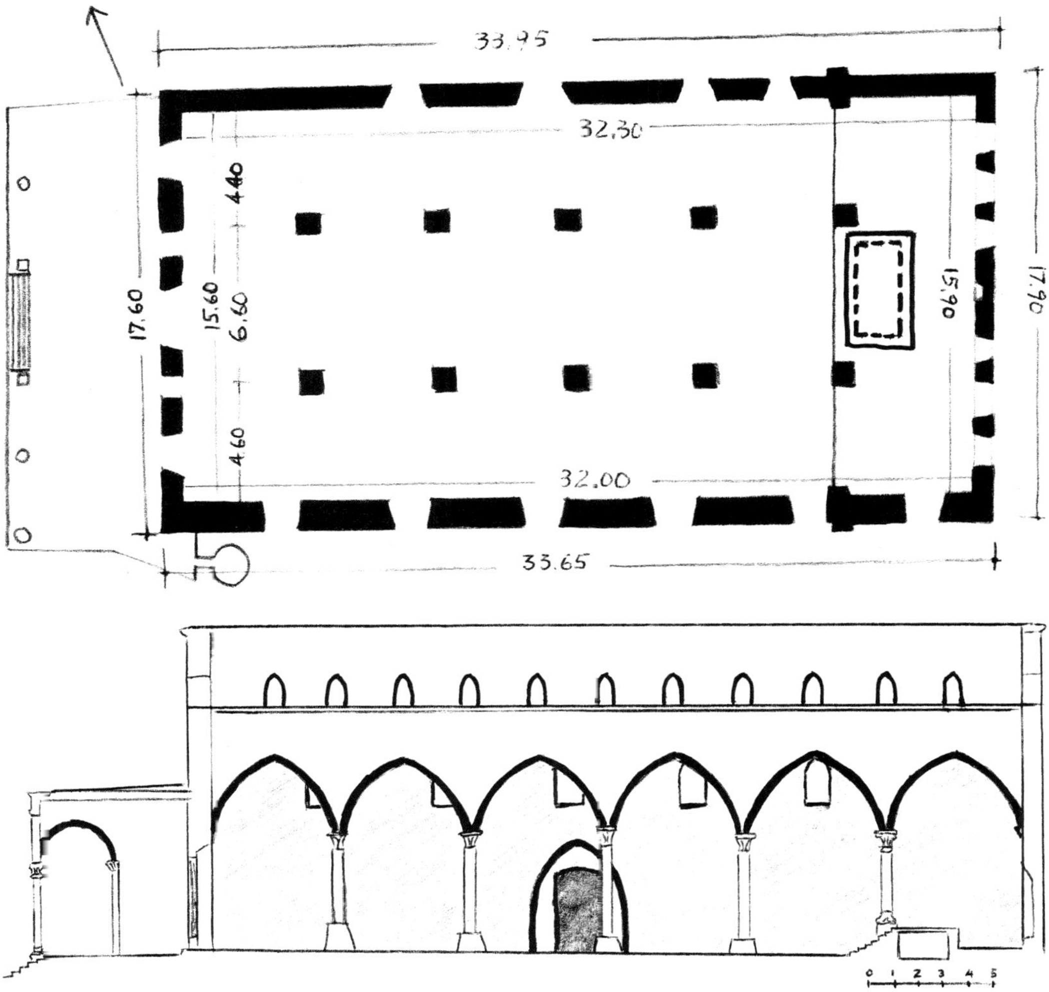

FIGURE 81. Plan and elevation of the church of St. Mark in Herakleion after the restorers S. Alexiou and K. Lassithiotakis

San Marco in Venice. At the time that the basilica of San Marco in Venice was adorned with new chapels and a baptistery,[77] state financiers did not pay much attention to its counterpart on Crete. The reliance of St. Mark's church on local funds almost guaranteed its poor condition. A century later (1442) the Senate in Venice had to intervene again on behalf of the church of St. Mark in Candia: the government of Crete was ordered to use the revenues from the sale of the state possessions at Lembari to provide for ornaments (*paramenti*) for the processions and ceremonies.[78]

The absence of documentary evidence for any other Latin church prior to 1239 suggests that St. Mark was the first new Latin church that the

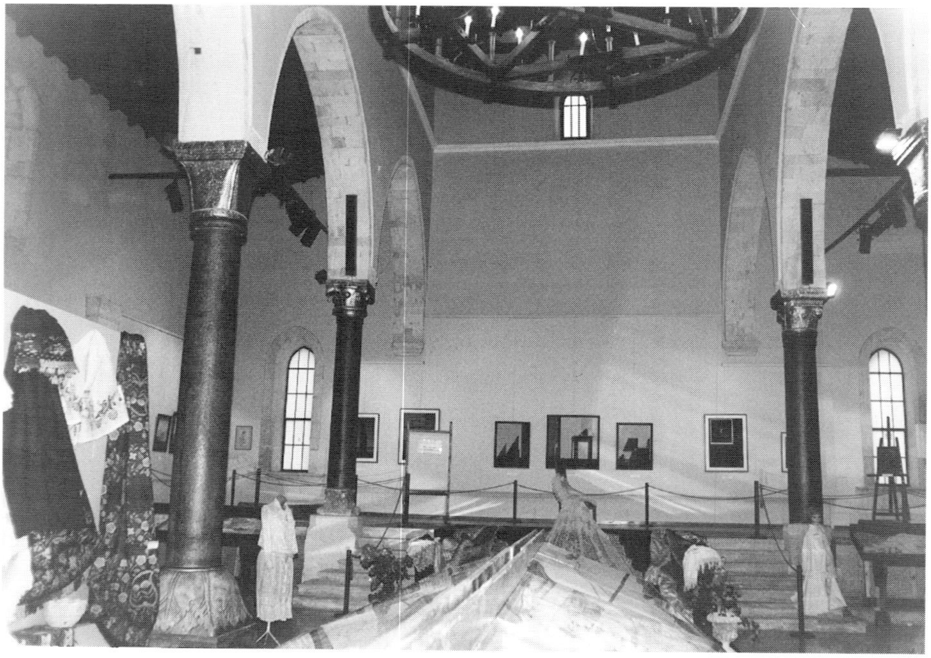

FIGURE 82. Herakleion, church of St. Mark, interior, view east

Venetian authorities sponsored in Candia. Therefore, its appearance must have made a strong statement of Latin/Venetian presence in the city. Like San Marco in Venice, it functioned as the private chapel of the duke and served as the burial place of high officials. A juxtaposition of the church of St. Mark and the cathedral of St. Titus provokes interesting observations. In contrast to the emphatically byzantinizing form of the church of San Marco in Venice, its counterpart in Candia was an elongated basilica conforming to the latest artistic style in Western Europe. In both Venice and Candia, the church that contained the relics of the patron of the city was the one built according to the Byzantine style. San Marco in Venice and the cathedral of St. Titus in Candia were presented as martyria. As such they had to look old, and for the Venetians this meant that the churches had to be built according to the style of centuries past, that of Byzantium. Within this frame of mind, the ducal chapel of St. Mark in Candia had no reason to resemble a Byzantine structure. On the contrary, as a symbol of the newcomers it stood in the center of Candia to advertise their alterity and the particular strand in their artistic heritage that was different from that of the local Byzantines. The basilica of St. Mark was there to show the new blood that had arrived in the colony. So despite the fact that in the early fourteenth century the colonial government seems to have faced difficulties in maintain-

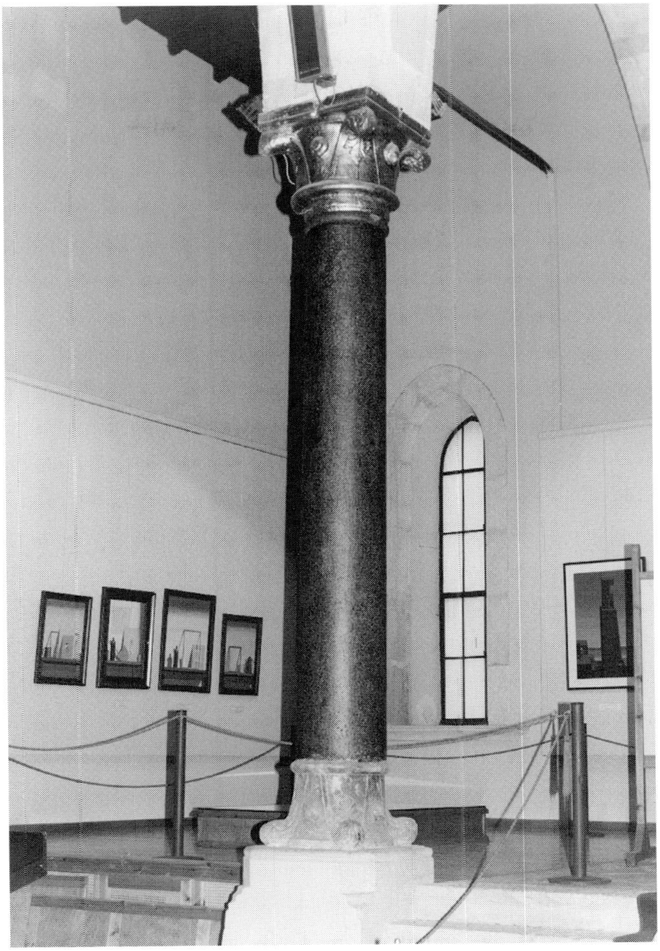

FIGURE 83. Herakleion, church of St. Mark, interior, column

ing the proper appearance of the church, by the seventeenth century the church of St. Mark in Candia was regarded as one of the primary symbols of Venetian rule on the island, because its name, placement, and function reproduced the schemes of the famous San Marco basilica in the mother city.

In fact, intriguing questions are raised by the role of the church of St. Mark in the Venetian colonies at large. To what extent was it a vital monument for the identification of a city as Venetian? Indubitably, the church of St. Mark was the most obvious sign of Venetian presence in cities like Constantinople, Acre, Beirut, or Tyre, where the Venetians owned only one quarter, rather than in the colonies where they were the sovereign rulers.[79] Similarly in Negroponte where the Venetians possessed only a quarter inside

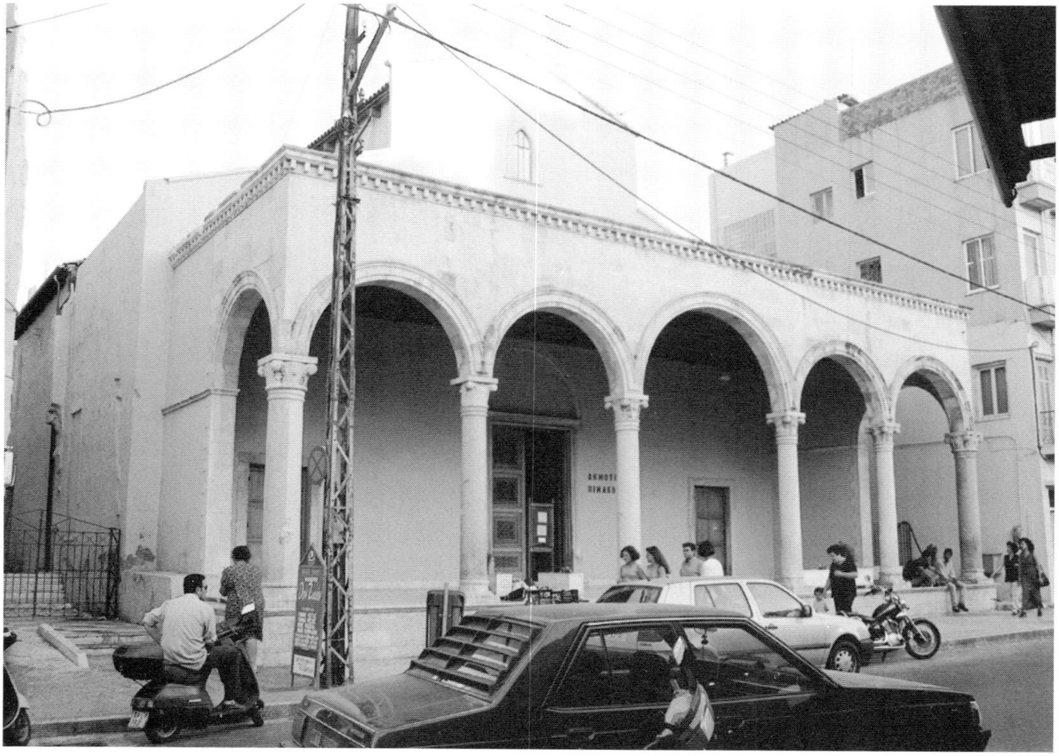

FIGURE 84. Herakleion, church of St. Mark, exterior, the loggia

the capital city, the church of St. Mark played a vital role in defining the area and its public monuments (a palace for the Venetian *bailo* and a loggia where the government chancellery was housed) as Venetian.[80] The topographical relations in this square are closely connected to those in Candia. The church of St. Mark in Negroponte predates that in Crete as it is mentioned in the will of Pietro da Famo of 1215.[81] As the location of the church within the town is debated between the spot of the church of Hagia Paraskeve mentioned earlier and that of the mosque (alternatively shown to have been the monastery of St. Francis), it is difficult to make definitive statements about it. The piazza delimited by the church must have been the backbone of the Venetian settlement, with houses for the settlers and merchants lying near the wine market of the city and several other unspecified churches. I have already mentioned the slight possibility that there was a church of St. Mark also in Modon.[82]

The same arrangement was not preserved in the other cities of Crete, especially Canea and Retimo, where the public structures of the colonists were split in two parts: the palace of the governor and the church of St.

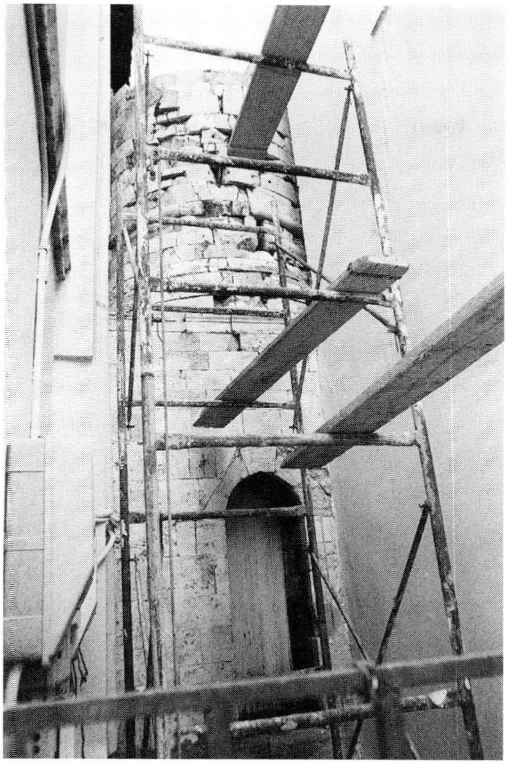

FIGURE 85. Herakleion, church of St. Mark, remains of the belltower

Mark stood in the fortified enclosure, whereas the main practical spaces of the city (the loggia, the public fountain, and the market square) lay in the lower town outside the acropolis. Almost nothing is known about the church of St. Mark in Canea except that it was in some way connected to the governor's palace. As we have already mentioned, in Retimo the cathedral was probably housed in the church of St. Mark, which is described in 1358 as an old structure.[83] Despite the fact that the document does not explicitly refer to the church as the cathedral, it mentions that the lauds should be celebrated there according to the prescription to the first colonists of Crete, that is, in the seat of the bishop. This point emphasizes the significance that the cathedral had in the community as a focal point in urban space.

In Canea and Retimo the ducal chapel of St. Mark seems to have a relatively unimportant position in the life of the city, possibly because the role of the Venetian governor was different in the towns outside the capital of the island. In contrast, the Latin cathedral of each city played a much more vital role in urban life. Except in Sitia and maybe also in Retimo, the cathedrals were associated either in their dedication or in the relics that they contained with the patron saint of the city, whose cult obviously predated the arrival of the Venetians. By appropriating part of the saintly heritage of each city, the new Latin cathedrals conditioned the sacred topography and the sacred history of the colonies. Although it is not clear whether the Latin cathedrals in Canea and Retimo were situated on the foundations of or in reused Byzantine churches as was the church of St. Titus in Candia, the ideological concerns of their patrons can be clearly seen in the liturgical furnishing and the special function of these churches. They seem to have mediated between the two rites either by possessing relics of local saints and sacred Byzantine icons as in Canea, or because of the building's historical connection with the city as in the case of the Virgin Peribleptos/Hagia Paraskeve in Negroponte. Thus, the inclusion of Byzantine sacred objects inside the Latin cathedrals or the reuse of older Byzantine churches charged the newly established Latin churches with prestige and was meant to persuade the Greek Orthodox population to accept the official doctrine of the colonists, since their sacred icons and relics were now housed in Latin churches.

Contrary to the situation in Venice, where the church of San Marco had usurped the rights of the cathedral, the most significant church in the Cretan cities (including Candia) was the Latin cathedral, which was under the direct jurisdiction of the pope. Obviously, the tension between the Greek and Latin rites demanded different solutions in the realm of ecclesiastical authority in the colonies. Whereas in Venice the ducal chapel of San Marco commanded the formal religious demeanor of the Republic through its clergy, its ceremonial, and its unique sanctity, the chapels/churches that were dedicated to St. Mark were far less important in the religious life of the colonies. Despite their titles, which resonated the direct sanctioning of the metropole, they functioned as small state chapels, their maintenance being left to the discretion of the local government. Whether or not they followed the ceremonial of San Marco in Venice, or they ever functioned as parish churches, the various churches of St. Mark must have come to life primarily during special state ceremonies including the inauguration or funeral of Venetian officers. Their imposing silhouette, which emulated Venetian Gothic architecture of the thirteenth and fourteenth centuries, made them monuments of a foreign power to the eyes of the locals. Consequently, they had minimal impact on the formation of the urban fabric except in a highly symbolic manner.

The pairing of Titus, the local saint, and Mark, Venice's protector, exemplifies the ambiguities of the Venetian colony. As part of the Venetian empire Crete had to be made into a replica of Venice, which had started out as a colony and imitator of Byzantium in the sixth century. At the same time, in order to establish their successful colonial authority the Venetians showed special reverence to the sacred heritage of Crete.

Here, I believe, lies the key to understanding the significance of using a Byzantine or a Western-looking building in the Venetian colonial empire: for the Venetians, Byzantine architectural style signaled not the patrons but rather the antiquity of a structure.[84] The ability to waver between two artistic styles and to exploit the formal qualities of a building in order to indicate its age was a subtle way to repackage the past of the island in order to foster the new colonial practices of the Venetians. By denoting antiquity, the Byzantine appearance of a structure implied authenticity (in the case of the cathedral of St. Titus) or imperial connections with the Byzantine – and by extension with the Roman – empire (in the case of the palace). Both attributes were auspicious for consolidating Venetian colonial rule and for presenting the Venetian colony as a continuation of the Byzantine province of Crete.

The architecture of the church of St. Mark must have made the opposite impression on the viewer. The famous San Marco basilica in Venice was a centrally planned edifice modeled after the church of the Holy Apostles in Constantinople; it was, for all intents and purposes, a Byzantine church.[85] The church that the state authorities sponsored in Candia was totally different in appearance: it was an elongated basilica, preceded by a simple arcaded portico, reminiscent of Western rather than Byzantine churches. As a church dedicated to the patron saint of the Republic, it was the foremost symbol of Venetian presence in the former Byzantine soil and the one structure that in the eyes of the colonists linked the colony with the metropole. In fact, the choice of a Western architectural style for this church was a decision that extended beyond the limits of Venetian Candia. Every Venetian colony had a similar Latin basilica dedicated to St. Mark. The question then is, Why not duplicate the appearance of the Venetian church of San Marco in the colonies? Apparently in the Venetian empire it was important that such a building be perceived as an imported edifice, foreign to the indigenous, Byzantine tradition of the colonies. As a symbol of Venetian rule, the colonial churches of St. Mark had to be built according to the current stylistic trends in Venice. Age was, once again, the important consideration for selecting the style of the basilica. In the colonies the Western-looking church of St. Mark indicated that, following the Fourth Crusade, the city of Venice had come of age. The Republic was no longer looking to Byzantium for artistic and cultural inspiration; as the head of an empire Venice could dictate its own new artistic forms. In the metropole, the Venetians claimed the antique origin of the church of San Marco, and in Candia, the Byzantine ducal palace showed the ancient roots of their rule. Thus, they could appropriate the past and impose the present at will.

FIVE

THE BLESSINGS OF THE FRIARS

Latin Christian faith, as it had been professed by the pope, was the primary reason for launching the crusades, and the Mendicant friars were the best agents of the Latin church in spreading its doctrines to the East and in promoting the union of the Eastern and Western churches under the universal jurisdiction of the pope.[1] Not only did the Franciscans and Dominicans have the right to preach, hear confessions, and bury laymen in their own churches, but their monasteries were autonomous establishments, exempt from the jurisdiction of local bishops and independent of the civic authorities.[2] The philanthropic activities of the friars enhanced popular belief in the sanctity of the monastic garb and intensified lay donations to their establishments, consisting primarily of funds to perform commemorative Masses on behalf of the deceased. Several wealthy Latins also left funds to endow private chapels (or altars therein) and family tombs (*archa* or *arca*) inside the churches of the Mendicant friars. As depositories of gifts of rich Latin patrons, these institutions played a major role in the life of the city because they became poles of attraction for city dwellers and visitors alike. Consequently they represented significant public spaces in the city of Candia. The major orders established their presence on Crete from the first years of Venetian rule; by the sixteenth century eleven conventual churches stood in Candia, some of which still stand today.

CONSECRATING THE URBAN SPACE

Each convent was assigned a specific section of the city in which the friars paid visits to people to solicit alms. The dependence of the friars on financial resources from the urban population must have been the primary reason why the pope regulated the distance between the Mendicant monasteries within the same city.[3] The surviving documents from Crete do not indicate an open antagonism between the Franciscans and the Dominicans of the island, but it is likely that similar concerns played a role in the location of their convents. In Candia, the monasteries of the Franciscans and the Dominicans were built on the extremities of a street intersecting the *ruga magistra,* as far apart as possible within the limits of the city. Thus, whether by accident or by design, the two convents stood at the edges of the urban landscape of Candia, as we can see in Cristoforo Buondelmonti's bird's-eye view of the city (Fig. 10).

The Franciscan monastery of St. Francis was situated at the southeast corner of Candia, on the highest hill in the city, thus being immediately visible to anyone approaching from sea or land (no. 8 on the map, Fig. 17). The site is presently occupied by the Archaeological Museum and only remnants of large arches that were probably part of the conventual buildings to the north of the museum are now extant. The large church was already standing in 1242 and was possibly constructed on a lot that was given to the Franciscans by the state.[4] Later sixteenth-century accounts maintain that St. Francis himself was the founder of the monastery in Candia; presumably the saint stayed in Crete on his way to the Holy Land in 1219.[5] Very few direct references to the church survive in the governmental archives of Venetian Crete, which tell us that the significant sum of 1,000 hyperpera was used in major works in the church in 1390.[6] Only a photograph and two architectural drawings remain of the Franciscan convent, which was demolished after it suffered severe damage in the earthquake of 1856 (Figs. 86 and 87).[7]

Fortunately reports, inventories, and topographical renderings of Candia allow us to reconstruct the original appearance of the church. Being one of the tallest buildings in the city, the church figures in every view of Candia. Its most detailed medieval representations are the 1486 etching of Candia by Reuwich (Fig. 7) and the depiction of the monastery by Marco Boschini (Fig. 13). In both, the church is shown with three round arch openings topped by Gothic spires, as described in accounts of medieval travelers. The three-aisled basilica (104.30 by 38.25 meters) had a projecting transept and ended to the east in a tripartite apse or a chevet. In the early fifteenth century the three axial chapels were dedicated to the Holy Sacrament of the Corpus Christi, to St. Francis, and to St. John the Baptist.[8] Six or eight additional chapels and a sacristy opened along the side walls.[9] Following the prescriptions of the statutes of the order, a timber roof covered the main church and only the presbytery was vaulted.[10] Its two-story elevation may have been partly due to the relatively limited space available for construction. A crypt that housed a number of tombs extended under the choir.[11] At the end of the fifteenth century the pilgrim Pietro Casola praised the church for having the most beautiful choir in the city, with three rows of stalls (two hundred seats) masterfully carved in walnut wood. In later centuries an organ with gilded decoration stood above the choir in the middle of the nave. The architecture and liturgical setting of the church may have followed Western practices, but intriguing reports of the existence of an icon and Greek frescoes (?) therein suggest that its interior must have looked different from that in the churches of the Franciscans in Venice.[12] As no trace of paintings has survived, it is unclear what the traveler meant: was it the particular style or subject matter of the paintings that seemed unfamiliar to visitors from Europe? Was he referring to wall paintings or to panel paintings? A later report favors the latter solution as the decoration of the church seems to have reflected the particularities of art appreciation in the sixteenth century: the church was adorned with works of the best artists in Crete and Venice – including religious paintings by Giovanni Bellini and Palma Vecchio, a sculpture by Sansovino, and presumably Greek/Cretan icons.

An elaborately decorated portico adorned the west façade of the church, preceded by a staircase, semicircular in plan. Today the entrance doorway of the church is still used in the courthouse of modern Herakleion; three marble colonnettes formed the jambs of the portal, which was surmounted by an architrave. Two fragments of the decoration of its façade (a bust of Christ and that of an angel) are exhibited in the Historical Museum of Herakleion (Fig. 88). Busts of the apostles completed the decoration of the archivolt. A bell tower stood on the south side of the church. Among the conventual structures we only hear of the dormitory with a large portico (*magna loggia dormitorii*) and an infirmary that was paid for in 1417 by Johannes Greco.[13]

Nowhere else are the significance and the wealth of the convent better illustrated than in its impressive collection of relics and reliquaries, many of which were commissioned by noblemen or friars of high status and at least one dated to the Byzantine period. In fact, the numerous donations of the faithful made this church the richest and most ornate religious establishment in Candia according to travelers' accounts.[14] The most famous donor to the convent was Pope Alexander V (1409–10), a Franciscan friar from Candia, who endowed the monastery with precious relics, sacred vessels, a private chapel adorned with a tomb bearing his coat of arms, and elaborate marble doors that were crafted in Rome.[15] The most significant of the relics he gave the church was a large fragment of the column of the Flagellation. This relic was showcased in a large elaborate silver reliquary with enamels of the Crucifixion on one side and Saints Anthony, Christopher, and Andrew on the other.[16] The monastery also owned the arm of St. Symeon,[17] a fragment of the True Cross, the head of St. Stephen,[18] fragments of the golden doors of Jerusalem, some blood of St. Bernard, and a piece of the habit of St.

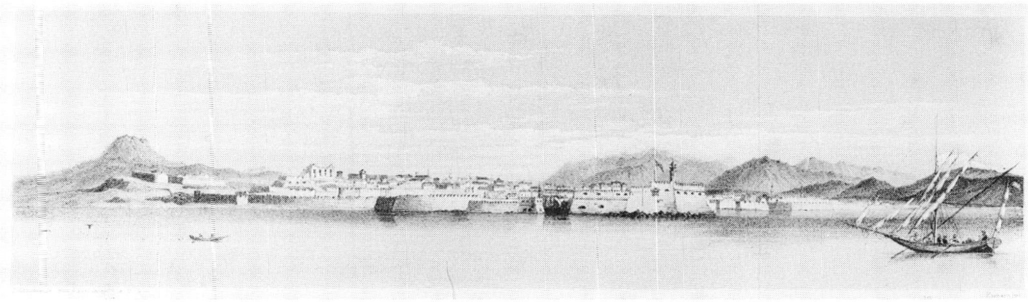

FIGURE 86. T.A.B. Spratt, "The Town of Candia," *Travels and Researches in Crete* (London, 1865) (The Gennadius Library, American School of Classical Studies)

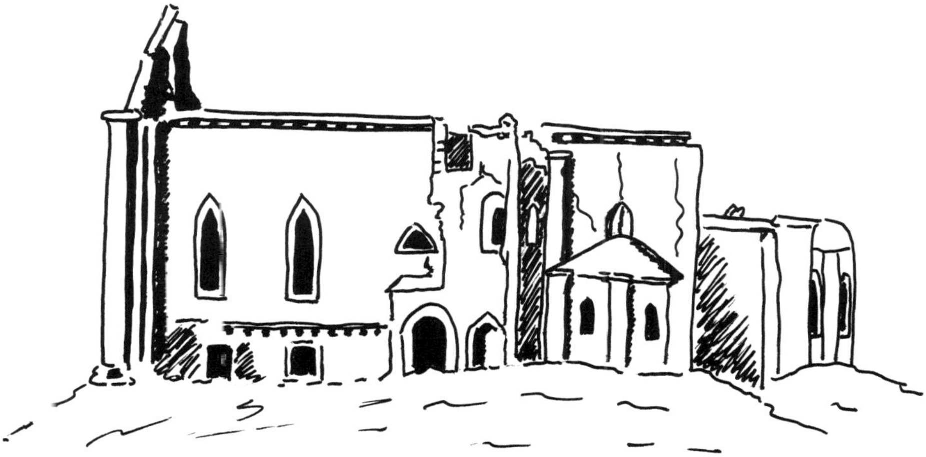

FIGURE 87. Drawing of the remains of the monastery of St. Francis following the earthquake of 1856, after Alexandrides (Istituto Veneto di Scienze, Lettere ed Arti. Venezia. Archivio fotografico della Missione in Creta di Giuseppe Gerola)

Francis, which was exhibited in a silver reliquary adorned with precious stones and a large crystal.[19] The receptacle within which the Holy Sacrament was displayed is also described as a remarkable crystal reliquary mounted in silver. Many of the treasures of the church were destroyed in the earthquake of 1508, when the bell tower on the east side collapsed and destroyed part of the convent.[20] Despite these misfortunes, however, if we compare the possessions of the church in 1417 with the contents of a list of objects that were shipped to Venice in 1669, we see that the relics bestowed on the monastery were multiplied in the last 250 years of Venetian presence on the island, pointing to an increased devotional importance of the Franciscan monastery for the population of Candia.[21]

The major monastery of the Dominicans, St. Peter the Martyr (Hagios Petros), was located in the northwestern section of the city near the sea walls (no. 37 on the map, Fig. 17); to the west its possessions touched the boundaries of the Jewish quarter of Candia. Although direct evidence for the foundation date of St. Peter the Martyr is lacking, the documentary material suggests that the monastery was established in midthirteenth century at the time when the archbishop of Crete was a Dominican, Giovanni Querini (1247–52).[22] In 1248 the Dominican friars were granted a large urban estate covering an area of more than 850 square meters, which had been given earlier to the feudatory Thomas Fradello in 1224.[23] This lot probably formed the core of the monastery of St. Peter the Martyr. Further concessions of feudal lands enriched the Dominican foundation in the second half of the thirteenth century. In 1257 Petrus Sanudo was given an empty lot in the city as compensation for property of his that had been granted to the Dominicans, in 1275 a lot pertaining to the fief of Valasio Pascaligo was sold to the friars for sixty-five hyperpera, and in 1301 the other half of this lot was also sold to the friars.[24] The fact that the Dominicans founded their monastery on urban land that had previously belonged to the state suggests that the placement of the convent inside the city walls was a conscious choice by the state authorities who controlled this land. On the one hand, such a concession to the friars underlined the special relationship between the state and the order. This relationship was further stressed by the customary donation of twenty-five hyperpera that was granted in the fourteenth century by the Maggior Consiglio of Candia to the friars to convene their provincial chapter.[25] On the other hand, the selection of this lot for the Dominican convent introduced a significant urbanistic pattern in Candia: the monastery of St. Peter the Martyr was meant to echo the Franciscan monastery, which was located on the opposite side of town. Both buildings marked the extremities of a street perpendicular to the *ruga magistra* and framed the old town of Candia with their silhouettes.

The siting of the Dominican church on the waterfront made it highly visible to anyone approaching from the sea. The surviving archaeological remains attest to the grandeur of the monastery, which must date to the latter part of the thirteenth century with later additions.[26] Its size (circa forty-one by fifteen meters), which is less than half of that of the Franciscan church, and the lack of sculptural decoration point to a foundation poorer than that of the Franciscans. This simplicity in plan and decoration may be due to the existing statutes of the order that insisted on regulating height, vaulting, and sculptural ornament in an attempt to show churches consistent with a vow of poverty.[27] Nevertheless, by local standards this was a quite grand structure. A long, once timber-roofed nave ends in a rib-vaulted square choir flanked by two semicircular chapels (Fig. 89). Two square piers without capitals support the triumphal arch. Large rounded arches give access to the side

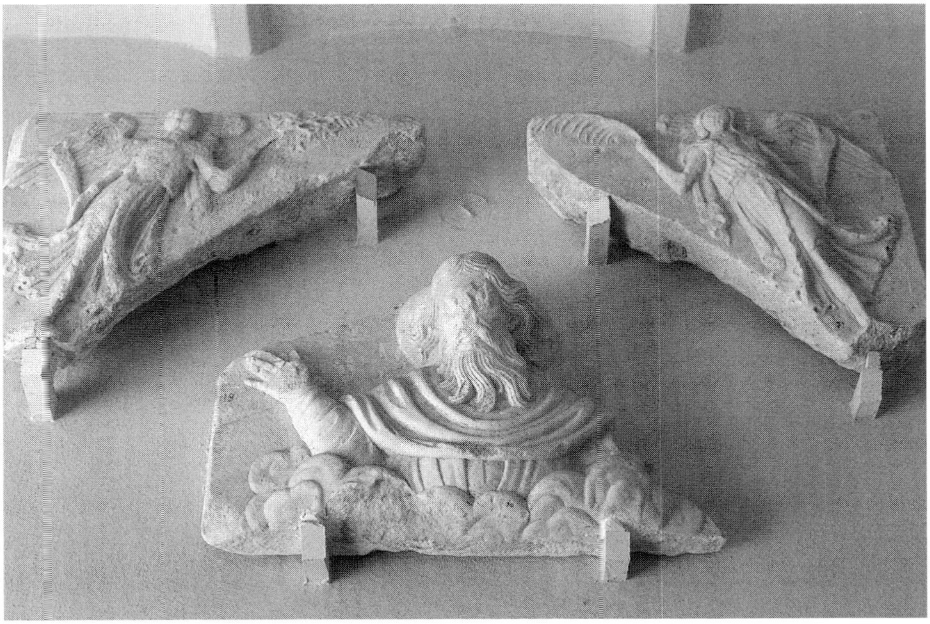

FIGURE 88. Herakleion, Historical Museum, fragments of the sculptural decoration of St. Francis

chapels. Two buttresses cut through the original wall of the thirteenth-century church to strengthen the structure; they must be of a fourteenth-century date but are surely later than the original building.[28] A smaller vaulted chamber stood at the north angle of the choir and was probably used as a treasury (see plan, Fig. 90). Two elongated side chapels (forming a sort of truncated side aisle) were added along the south wall at a later date, as the difference in vaulting technique indicates. In one of them there are traces of wall paintings depicting female saints, but their poor state of preservation does not allow for an identification of the subjects. Four pointed-arch doors in the lower story of the southern wall led to these lateral chapels and possibly to the other monastic structures (Fig. 91). Two construction phases are also apparent in the exterior walls of the nave: they were extended to the entrances of the side chapels in the sixteenth or seventeenth century. These restorations, probably performed after the earthquake of 1508, extended to other parts of the church as well.[29] The ribbed vault of the choir was replaced by a semicircular barrel vault made of evenly cut limestone blocks (Fig. 92). The west wall window was cut into a circular shape and the entrance door at the west was surmounted by a flat entablature. The north wall was redone and two rows of pointed arched windows were opened. The interior of the church was lit by numerous windows pierced in the exterior walls. The

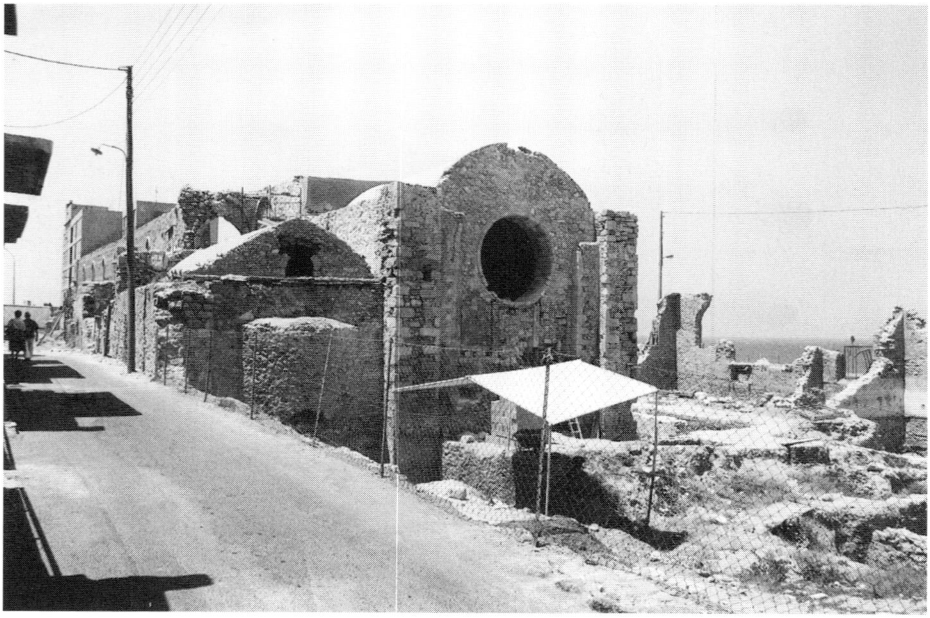

FIGURE 89. Herakleion, church of St. Peter the Martyr, exterior view from southeast

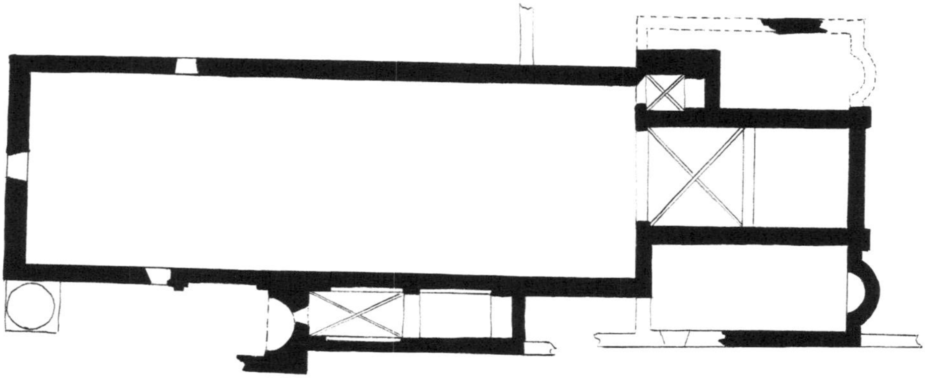

FIGURE 90. Herakleion, church of St. Peter the Martyr, ground plan after Gerola

southern wall had eight windows, six of which were topped by circular arches; the two first windows to the east were pointed arch windows, much taller and thinner than the rest.[30]

If the vestiges of the church cannot tell us much about its original appearance a report of the archbishop Luca Stella in 1625 informs us that there were eleven altars in the church and a chapel dedicated to St. Vincent in the courtyard. In addition, the wills of wealthy patrons partly indicate the interior arrangement of the Dominican church, sections of which were

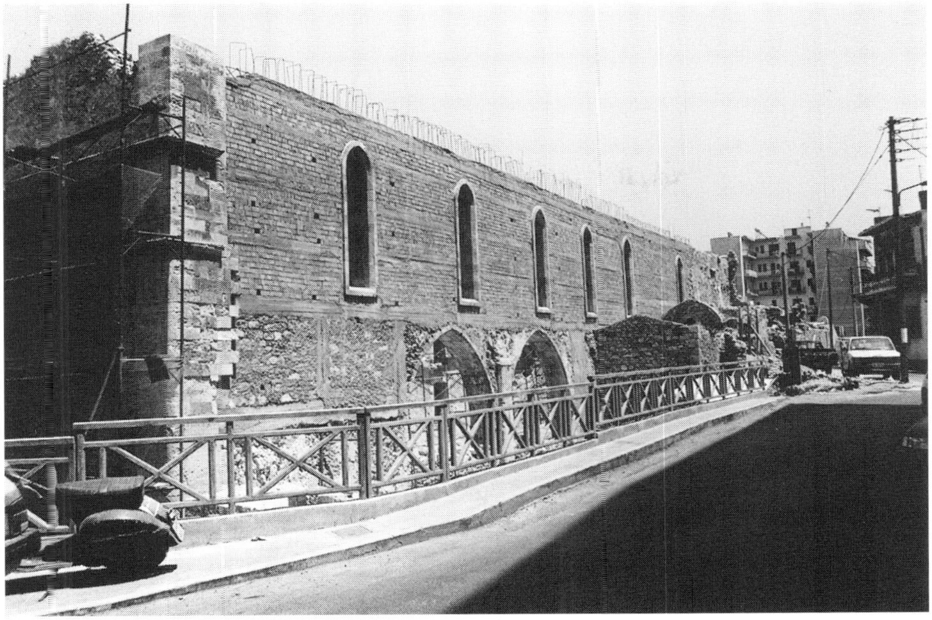

FIGURE 91. Herakleion, church of St. Peter the Martyr, south wall of the nave

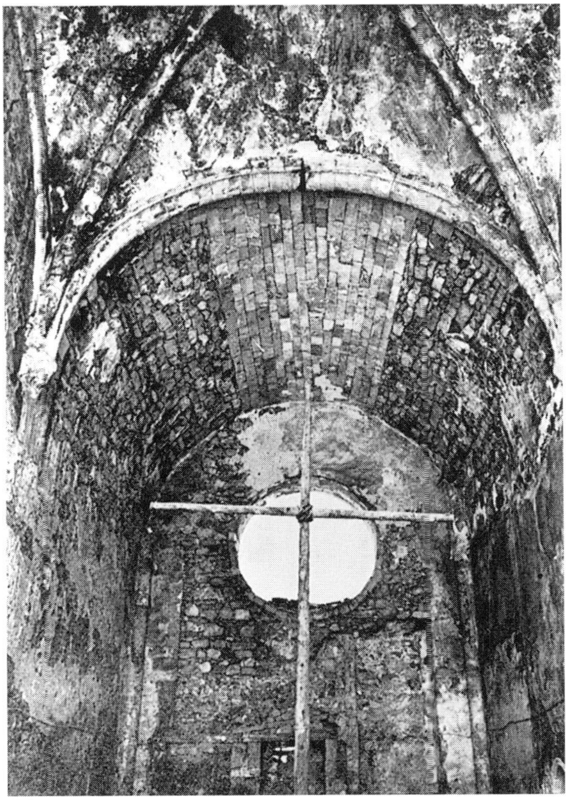

FIGURE 92. Herakleion, church of St. Peter the Martyr, vault of the choir

sponsored by prominent families of Venetian Candia: the chapel of St. John the Baptist belonged to the Grimaldo family, another chapel belonged to the Pasqualigo family, an altar was dedicated to St. Paul, another stone altar that was consecrated in 1496 on the south side of the church belonged to the Lulino (or Tulino) family, and another chapel housed the sepulchral monument of the Bon[o] family.[31] Significantly, the statutes of the order in the midthirteenth century had banished carved tombs from prominent parts of the church. In this case we can assume either that the Bon family tomb was not sculpturally ornate or that it stood in a remote part of the building or finally that this statute was no longer observed by the midfourteenth century.[32] An organ was installed in the church in the sixteenth century. Its case was gilded and was located above a vaulted chamber and its door opened opposite the chapel dedicated to Christ.[33] From an archival document of 1634 we learn that a new altar, which was to be erected in the Dominican church of St. Peter the Martyr, would have as a model the altar of St. Mark that was situated in the sacristy of the Latin cathedral of St. Titus. The altar was decorated in turquoise, enamel, and gold.[34] As in the church of St. Francis, the sacristy of St. Peter the Martyr was decorated with a painting depicting St. Francis embracing St. Dominic, which according to the seventeenth-century document existed since the beginning of the monastery, that is, since June 28, 1097![35] In this context it would be important to flesh out what this painting may have looked like. In fact, the absurd early date of this painting probably indicates that it was executed in the Byzantine or rather Cretan icon style. A late fifteenth-century triptych in the Pushkin Museum (no. 266) shows the Dormition of the Virgin in the central panel flanked by standing images of Francis and Dominic.[36] Although the two saints are not shown embracing, their parallel existence in the triptych offers a concrete example of the iconographic possibilities available to the painters of the period. Embracing saints are known from representations of Saints Peter and Paul in triptychs of the middle and second half of the fifteenth century that have been attributed to the famous artists Angelos Acotanto and Nikolaos Ritzos.[37]

Four fourteenth-century dukes of Candia were buried inside the church: Marco Gradenigo (1331), Giovanni Morosini (1327), Filippo Dorio (1357), and Marino Grimani (1360).[38] Members of the aristocracy either were buried in the church or had endowed private chapels therein. For instance, Johannes Albi had erected a family tomb inside the church before 1335, according to the testament of his son, and Maria, wife of the Venetian lord Marco Faletro, had requested to be buried in the church next to her father.[39] A unique document of 1370 even informs us how much was the cost of a monumental tomb erected in the church: Petrus Quirino spent two hundred ducats for *laborerio arche* in St. Peter the Martyr.[40]

The tombs of less distinguished individuals were relegated to the courtyard/cemetery of the monastery in the open space in front of the main entrance of the church.[41] This is one of the best known archaeological areas of Herakleion. Excavations have shown that the area in front of the church was used as a cemetery until the fifteenth century at least. The space in front of the west façade was shown to have been paved with slabs and traces of steps were found; ceramics, coins, and a few metal fibulae date this level to the eleventh or twelfth century.[42] A series of unidentified rectangular tombs were dug in the ground with their sides set in limestone. The findings inside the graves were Venetian jewelry and furnishings, which according to the glazed pottery found within the same stratum can be dated to the twelfth and thirteenth centuries. Thus, this cemetery must have coincided with the first occupation of the area by the Dominican monastery. More pottery in other strata has been identified as imported from Italy (Umbria or Faenza) or manufactured locally and dated to the years 1450 to 1530.[43] In addition, the excavations uncovered the beginning of a passageway, which Miles identified as leading to a crypt beneath the floor of the Dominican church. This proposal has not yet been evaluated; there is no documentary evidence for the existence of a crypt, and further excavations inside the church have not been undertaken.[44]

The conventual buildings, i.e. a dormitory, a refectory, and offices, were located to the north of the church as the plans of the city (Fig. 93) and the account of the fifteenth-century traveler Felix Fabri indicate.[45] Gerola recorded the remains of a small cross-vaulted absidal room to the northeast of the church and a few vestiges of another structure next to the choir.[46] These remains no longer exist, however. The whole monastery was surrounded by a wall that in all probability was constructed in 1450 in order to prevent the neighboring Jews from looking inside the church, the courtyard, the cemetery and the other conventual structures (see Fig. 11 and Chapter 7). A bell tower is also visible in all the medieval representations of the city (see for instance the plan of Clontzas, Fig. 12). The church of St. Peter the Martyr was converted into the mosque of sultan Ibrahim Han after the Ottoman conquest of Candia.[47]

The prominence and visibility of the four principal Venetian churches, the Latin cathedral, the ducal chapel of St. Mark, and the Mendicant monasteries of St. Francis and St. Peter the Martyr, confirmed the dominant position of the Latin rite in the colony and the close spiritual relationship of these Western churches with Venetian authorities. These four churches

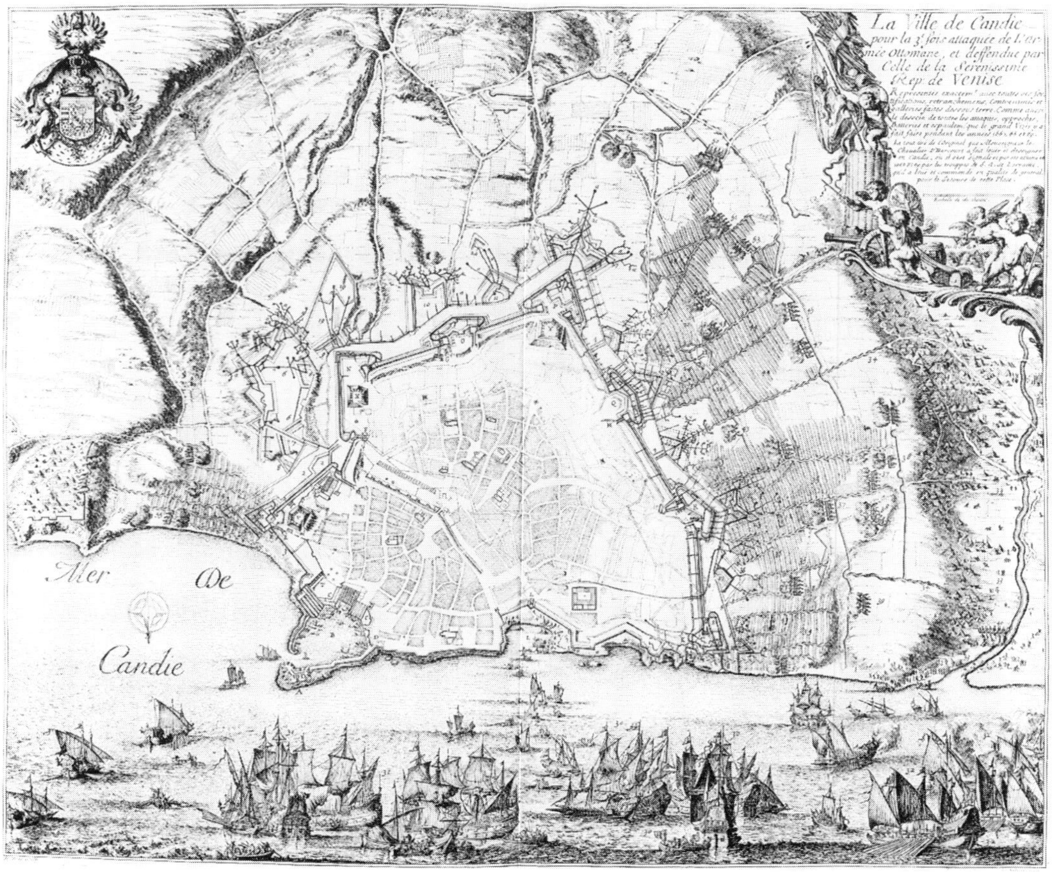

FIGURE 93. Chevalier d'Harcourt, La ville de Candie attaquée pour la troisième fois de l'armée Ottomane . . . , 1669 (Gennadius Library, American School of Classical Studies)

framed the city with their imposing silhouettes and defined Candia as a Latin town. Moreover, when seen in relation to the other prominent public buildings of the city, these Western churches sanctified the colonial enterprise of the Venetians on behalf of the Latin church. In architectural terms, the fortified city of Candia in the later thirteenth and fourteenth centuries recalled the circumstances of the acquisition of Crete by the Venetians: the defeat of the Byzantine empire in the course of the Fourth Crusade and the victory of the Western church vis-à-vis Orthodox Christianity. The public image of Venetian Crete as one of the first colonies of the Venetians in the Levant was double-faced: it was portrayed as a bastion of Latin Christianity in the Levant and as a continuation of imperial Byzantium under the aegis of the Republic.

CREATING POLES OF ATTRACTION IN THE SUBURBS

Additional monasteries were constructed in the southern burg of Candia in the thirteenth and early fourteenth centuries. The most significant among them were the Franciscan monastery of St. John the Baptist, the Augustinian monastery of the Savior, and St. Mary of the Crusaders, which also supported a hospital. The archaeological remains and the documentary records attest to the fact that in the early fourteenth century these monastic institutions were impressive in size, occupied extensive open spaces, and were richly endowed by the Latin population of the city.

The Franciscan monastery of St. John the Baptist was a foundation more modest than St. Francis, yet it must have acquired a significant status among the churches of the city as four dukes used it as their resting place. No specific account of its construction has survived, but we know that it was already in use by 1271, when duke Pietro Badoer was buried in it.[48] Located on what is today 1821 street, known as *via della spedale* in Venetian times, the monastery became a possession of the Observants by 1431 when it served as a hospice for pilgrims going to and from Jerusalem (no. 73 on the map, Fig. 17).[49]

In 1625 the church had five altars: the high altar was dedicated to the Madonna Santissima. In the monastery, converted into the mosque of Mahmut Aga by the Ottomans in 1669, parts of the masonry, a few pieces of marble, and a tomb with an illegible Venetian escutcheon were visible in the early twentieth century.[50] The church was a small timber-roofed basilica with two naves separated by a series of pilasters creating four bays (Fig. 94). The two eastern bays of the south aisle were replaced by Turkish cupolas. The cloister was situated on the northern side and the bell tower was at the southeast corner of the nave. In the 1668 map of Werdmüller (Fig. 16) the monastery is shown as bordering a large open green space to the south, possibly a garden.

The monastery of the Augustinians centered around an impressive basilica dedicated to the Savior (the church of San Salvatore), which was one of the largest churches in Candia (Figs. 95 and 96).[51] The conventual buildings stood to the south of the church, as archaeological vestiges indicated at the beginning of the twentieth century.[52] The whole complex was located at the southern end of the market street (now known as 1866 street) and was one of the best preserved Venetian structures in Candia until 1970, when it was demolished. In 1669 the Ottomans converted this church to a mosque endowed by the mother of the sultan, the Valide sultan Cami. The only modifications that they brought to the church were the construction of a mihrab and a minbar in the choir, and the addition of a minaret outside the church. The original structure was a timber-roofed three-aisled basilica of dimensions similar to those of St. Peter the Martyr with a projecting apse probably of a fourteenth-century date (Fig. 97).[53] The choir was covered by two ribbed vaults and thick buttresses (nine on each side), which strengthened the side walls, which were originally pierced with pointed-arch windows (Fig. 98). The minaret on the northeast of the structure must have replaced the original bell tower, which was struck by lightning in April of 1601.[54] It was a three-story stone structure attached to the basilica, with which it communicated through a small door.[55] The west façade of the church originally had three doors surmounted by a gable that was pierced by a window, obviously a Renaissance design. An inscription set above the central doorway of the southern wall of the church commemorated the opening of this door when the choir was moved from the center of the church behind the high altar in 1616.[56]

In the absence of specific information indicating the exact date of the construction of the monastery, we can assume that it was built sometime before 1330, when its name first appears in testaments of Latin patrons. Their wills often include bequests to San Salvatore among the other popular Latin churches of the city. For instance, ten hyperpera was provided for the repair of the church in 1332,[57] another thirty hyperpera was donated for works in the church in 1348,[58] and finally two years later, thirty hyperpera was given for paintings in the church.[59] A fifteenth-century account describes the paintings that decorated the cypress wood stalls of the choir: they were adorned with the figures of Christ, the Virgin Mary, the apostles, St. Augustine, and the (lay?) patrons of the church.[60] Further bequests to the Augustinian friars consisted of land property and endowments for chapels and family tombs inside the church. All these records show that the maintenance and embellishment of the church depended to a large extent on donations from wealthy lay individuals. In one instance the state authorities provided twenty-five hyperpera to subsidize the convocation of the provincial chapter of the Augustinians in Candia, an occasion to bring together in Crete friars from other parts of the world.[61] At the end of the sixteenth century the monastery of the Augustinians seems to have acquired a higher status in the political hierarchy of Venetian Crete, because two dukes of Candia were buried in the church of the Savior: Daniele Venier (shortly after 1594) and Pellegrino Bragadin (1598).[62] Medieval travelers recorded the sacred objects that enriched the church. An otherwise unknown icon of the Virgin originating from the island of Rhodes was apparently used in litanies in the

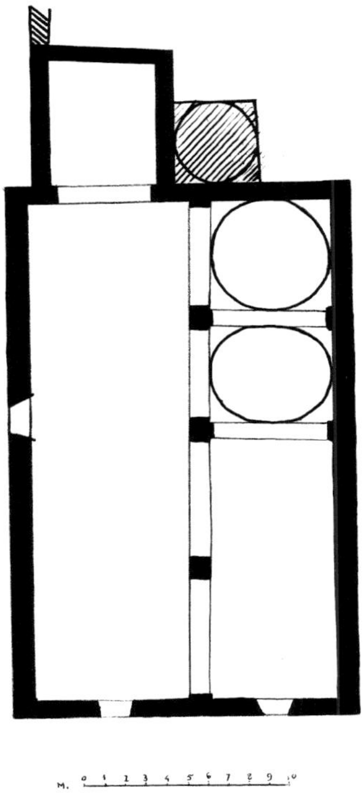

FIGURE 94. Herakleion, Franciscan monastery of St. John the Baptist, ground plan after Gerola

suburbs.[63] The bronze lectern of the choir was transported to the church of St. Stephen in Venice in 1669, but it no longer survives. The high altar, which was dedicated to St. Augustine, was covered with gold and bore the arms of the Piovene family; there were ten altars in total in the church in 1625.[64] In 1546 a painting of the Passion of Christ was done for the church by the Candiote artist Zuan Gripioti.[65]

The church of St. Mary of the Crusaders (Santa Maria Cruciferorum) is recorded for the first time in 1232 as the seat of the Italian order of the Cruciferi or Cruciati (crusaders), but it was probably functioning even before this date.[66] The Cruciferi were a community of regular canons founded in Bologna by the former crusader Cletus; they followed the rule of St. Augustine.[67] By 1357 they had also established a confraternity (Scuola) of St. Mary of the Crusaders in Candia.[68] The monastery was located on a street that came to be known as *via dello spedale* from the hospital that stood at its southern end (no. 67 on map, Fig. 17). The church is one of the best preserved examples of Venetian religious architecture in Candia. During the

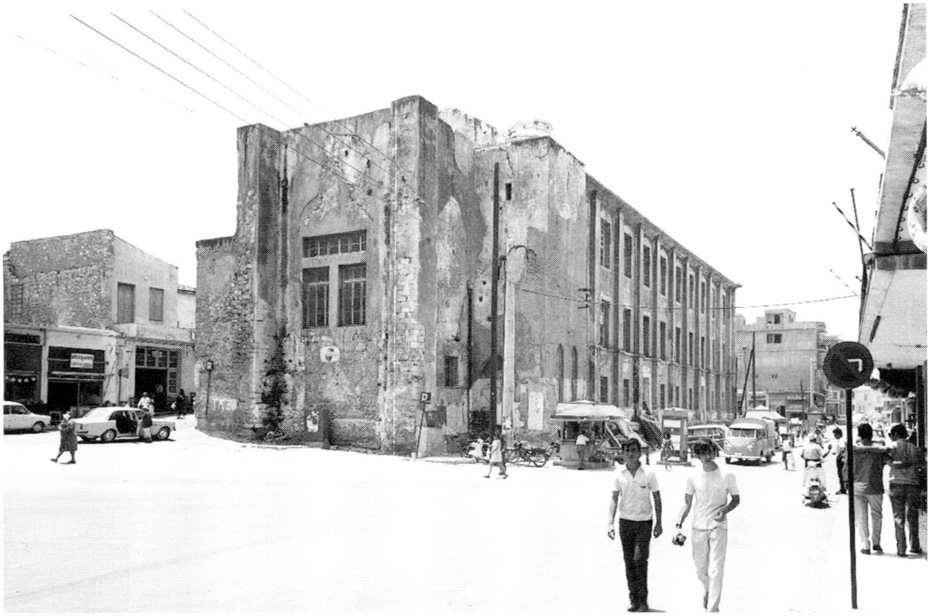

FIGURE 95. Herakleion, church of the Savior, exterior view from northeast

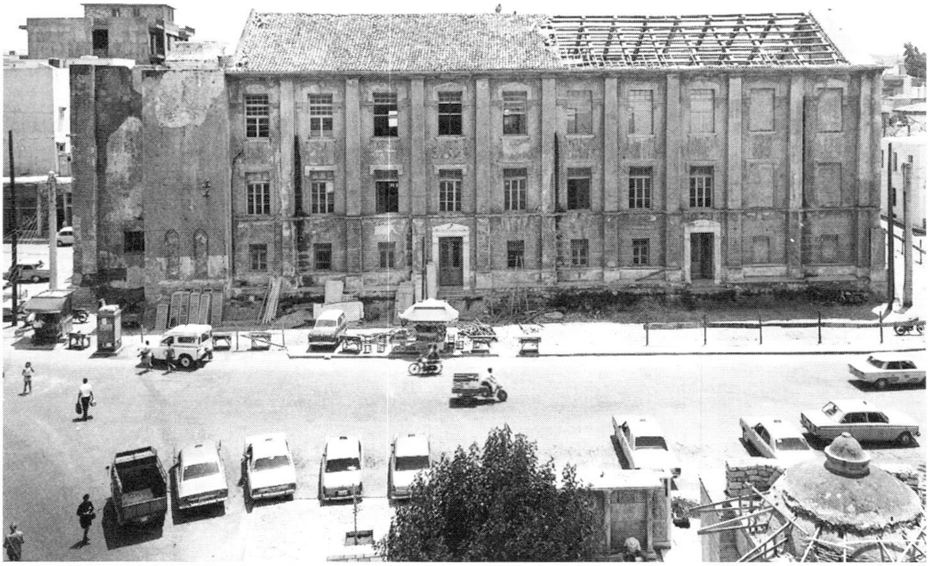

FIGURE 96. Herakleion, church of the Savior, exterior view, north wall

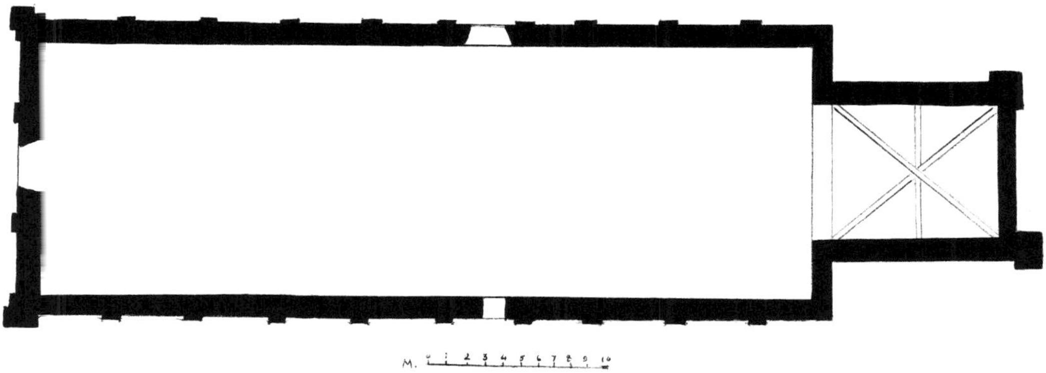

FIGURE 97. Herakleion, church of the Savior, groundplan after Gerola

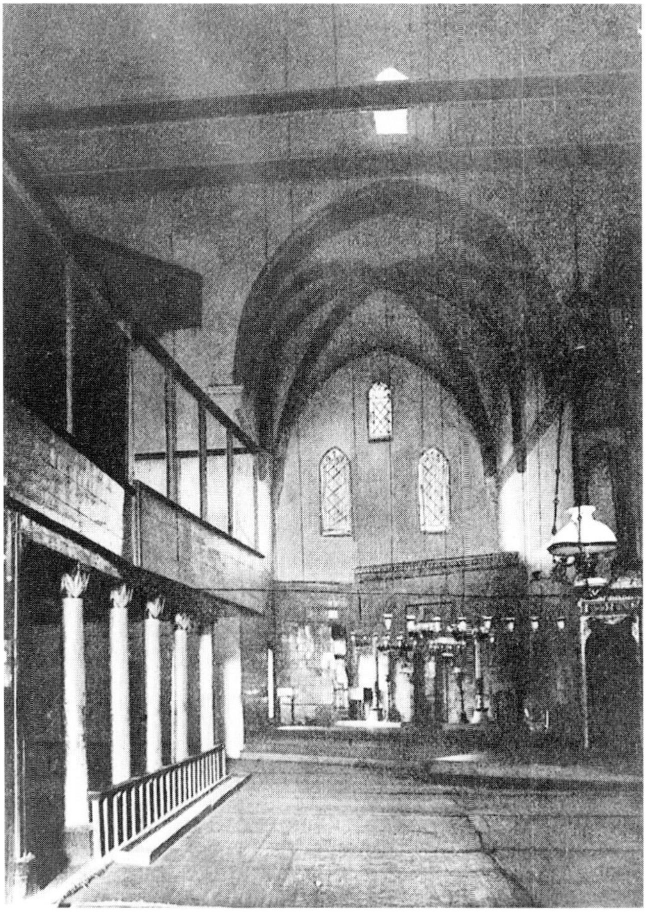

FIGURE 98. Herakleion, church of the Savior, interior view in Gerola's time (Istituto Veneto di Scienze, Lettere ed Arti. Venezia. Archivio fotografico della Missione in Creta di Giuseppe Gerola)

Ottoman rule it was converted to the mosque of Agebut Ahmet Pasa or Chusciakli and it is presently used as a Greek Orthodox church.

The church of St. Mary was a three-aisled timber-roofed basilica ending in a rectangular apse (Fig. 99).[69] The pointed-arch arcades in the nave were supported by two series of octagonal piers crowned by simple cubical capitals (Fig. 100). The supports of the triumphal arch were copies of Corinthian columns and were topped by Corinthian capitals. A clerestory was pierced by five windows to let light into the church. Traces of four doors that are now blocked appear on the north wall (Fig. 101). The one closest to the narthex is surmounted by a simple pointed arch. The south wall contains traces of three large doorways, which probably led to the conventual (Fig. 102). The western end of the church was preceded by a narthex, covered by a timber roof and opening to the inner church by a large round arch. Two large windows flanked the central entrance door on the west façade. The simple architecture of the basilica does not allow for a safe dating of the structure on stylistic grounds, but it allows us to assume that the building existed in its actual form since the thirteenth century. In the extensive restorations that were undertaken from 1955 to 1963, the north wall, apse, side chapels, and portico were consolidated, the clerestory was redone, the piers of the nave were strengthened, and a new wooden roof with tiles was added.[70] In 1960 while cleaning the pavement of the church, archaeologists uncovered a large portion of the medieval pavement, and in 1968 tombs were found in the courtyard of the monastery.[71]

The three altars of the church were decorated with wall paintings, very few traces of which were preserved at the time of the restoration of the church. The most precious objects in the church were three silver chalices with patens, a no longer surviving icon of St. Anthony,[72] and an icon of the Virgin Mary that was displayed on the altar closest to the door leading to the cloister, possibly on the south side of the church.[73] Although the church was the recipient of generous bequests by the aristocracy of Candia, its fame never paralleled that of the Franciscan and the Dominican establishments within the city.

Another monastery located in the vicinity was St. Paul of the Servites (no. 78 on the map, Fig. 103), which was founded according to the sources by the *nobili cretesi*.[74] The Mendicant order of the Servites, or Servants of Mary, was founded in 1240 and was primarily concerned with propagating the devotion to the Virgin Mary, with special reference to her sorrows. Early in the fourteenth century it possessed more than a hundred monasteries and supported missions to Crete and Cyprus.[75] The monastery of St. Paul in Candia centered around a modest basilica 3.55 meters wide. Part of a tall barrel-vaulted is now incorporated into a private home, and few archaeological remains of the conventual buildings were still visible to the east of the church when Gerola visited Crete.[76] According to the 1625 report of the archbishop Luca Stella the church had two altars and an icon of the Virgin called *Agiopaulitissa*.[77] Although the church does not appear to have played a significant role in the public life of the city, it was endowed by wealthy patrons throughout the fifteenth century. For instance, in 1445 Georgius de Chanali, the son of the city herald, owned a private chapel in the church, and in 1416 a monumental tomb of the Dandolo family was erected in the church.[78] This last point suggests a special relationship between the Dandolo family and the church (or order) of the Servites. So, the church could be identified with that founded by Andrea Dandolo, son of Nicolaus, in 1346. Andrea's testament provided that a church dedicated to St. Paul should be erected in the burg and be decorated with paintings. The church was completed by 1400, but as it was much larger than what Andrea had had in mind (it measured 29.56 by 8.69 meters), its painted decoration turned out to cost more than what he had intended to spend. Thus, the case went to trial and the court decided that only the main chapel, probably the apse (or the apse and nave), measuring 8.69 by 5.21 meters, would be painted.[79] Unfortunately, we are not told why the church was larger than was originally planned. It is possible that Andrea Dandolo cosponsored the construction of St. Paul along with other patrons and that he was solely responsible for the frescoes.

The Augustinian monastery of the Savior and St. Mary of the Crusaders were erected on two streets that were extensions of the *ruga magistra* to the south (see map, Fig. 103). These thoroughfares eventually became significant marketplaces in the suburbs and created two north-south axes that converged in front of the land gate of the city. Although on the basis of the surviving material it is difficult to prove that the Latin churches were built before the southern area of the suburbs was fully inhabited, the large size of these monasteries suggests that they were built in parts of the suburbs that were not yet heavily populated. Additional evidence corroborates this view: in 1280 the prior of the monastery of St. Mary of the Crusaders leased some lands near the cemetery of the monastery to Iohannes de Albrigo. The lots included a garden that was adjacent to a vineyard, a point suggesting that the area around the monastery was still agricultural land in 1280.[80] It seems, therefore, that in the thirteenth century the hospital of St. Mary of the Crusaders had been set well outside the limits of Candia, much farther than the inhabited part of the suburbs.

I would argue that these monasteries became poles of attraction for population growth in this part of the suburbs, as happened in Italian and French cities of the same period.[81] In the 1320s houses and churches were

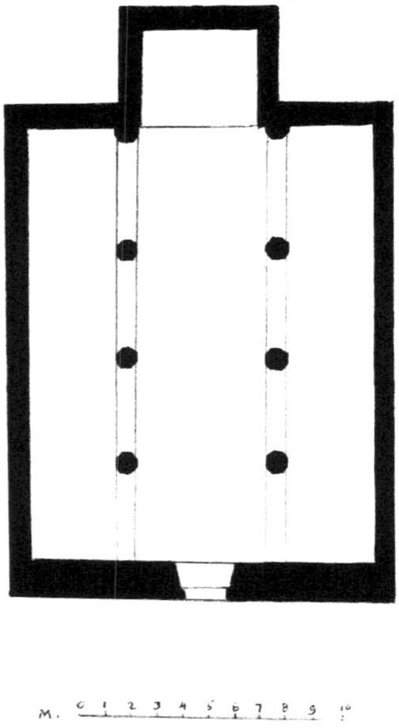

FIGURE 99. Herakleion, church of St. Mary of the Crusaders, ground plan after Gerola

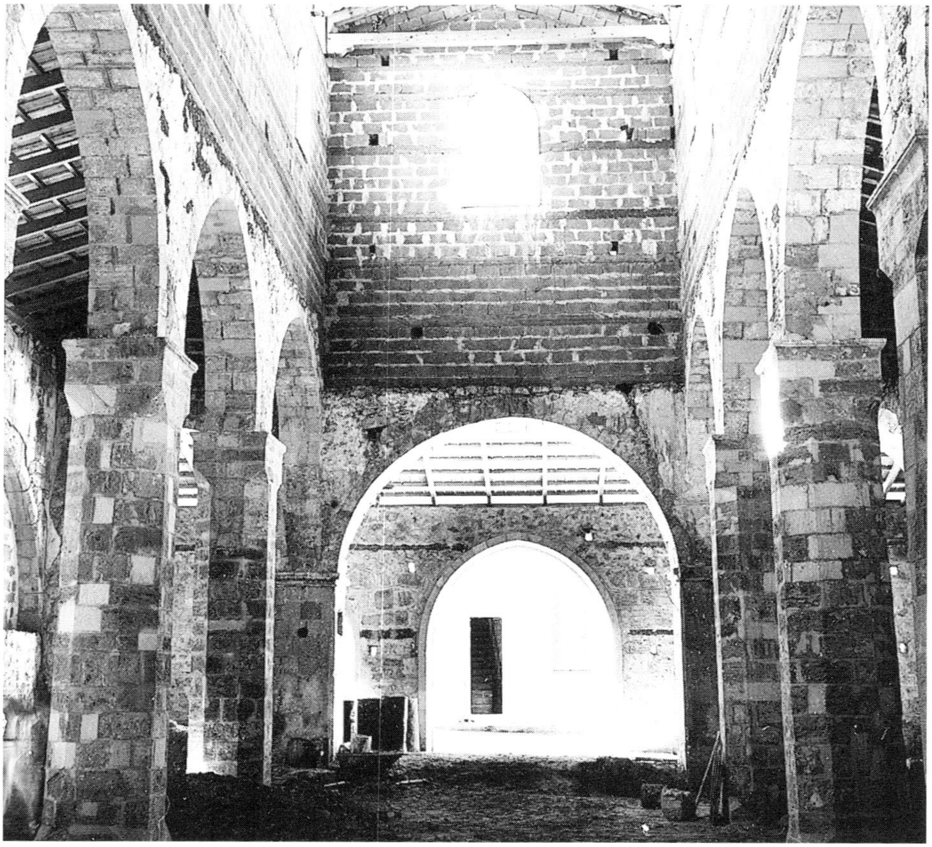

FIGURE 100. Herakleion, church of St. Mary of the Crusaders, interior, looking west

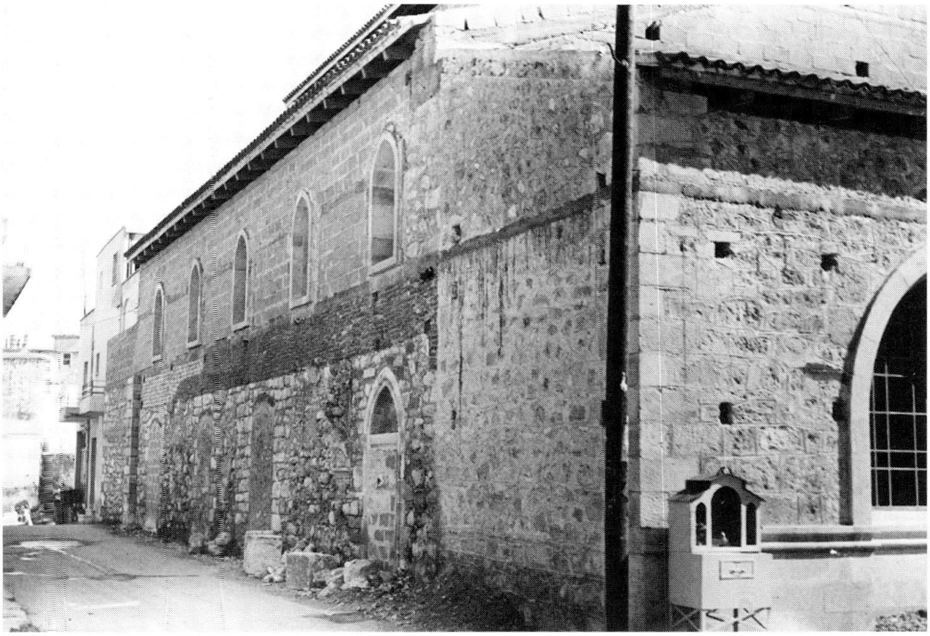

FIGURE 101. Herakleion, church of St. Mary of the Crusaders, north wall

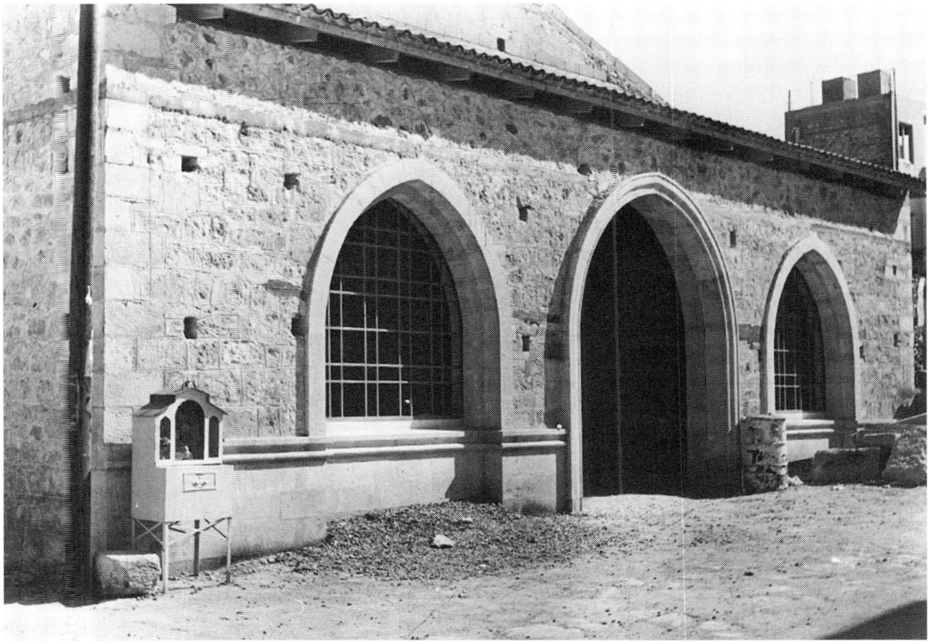

FIGURE 102. Herakleion, church of St. Mary of the Crusaders, south wall

built not only around the two monasteries but even beyond the church of the Savior to the south. The construction of the two monasteries seems to have "dictated" the growth of the suburbs toward the south. The new streets that the two Latin monasteries defined in the southern suburbs met the major suburban artery from the west *(strada larga)* at an almost right angle in front of the land gate. Their intersection emphasized the centrality and importance of this gate as a passageway to the city. Furthermore, this act "readjusted" the expansion of the suburban area toward a different direction from the westward one followed by the Byzantine population during the second half of the thirteenth century (see following chapter). Thus, the old city, i.e. the core of the Venetian official space, was kept central to the growing fourteenth-century urban settlement and was not displaced to the farthest edge of the city. The success of this urban planning design is demonstrated by the fact that after the 1320s construction in the suburbs boomed. More Latin churches of modest dimensions were built to the south of the city in the late thirteenth century and in the fourteenth century, such as the Franciscan monastery of St. John the Baptist and St. Paul of the Servites. With this strategy the built environment of both the city and the suburbs created symbolic landmarks of Venetian presence in a city whose central core was exclusively Venetian and whose suburbs were primarily populated by Greeks. Moreover, by overseeing the construction and use of religious buildings the Venetian authorities also secured control over the composition of the suburbs.

MENDICANT ESTABLISHMENTS IN THE VENETIAN EMPIRE

The churches and monasteries that the Mendicant friars established in the other colonies are worth surveying here as they confirm practices already observed in Candia. Most of them were situated outside the old city walls but eventually became parts of the city when new fortifications were set up to incorporate the suburbs. Fortunately, some of the Mendicant churches and monasteries outside Herakleion are better preserved archaeologically and can give us a better sense of what the establishments in the capital of Crete may have looked like.

The best preserved of these foundations is the church of St. Francis in Canea/Chania, which now houses the Archaeological Museum of the city. It was the major Franciscan monastery of Canea and it lay outside the fortified citadel in a prominent spot of the main street of the burg. We do not

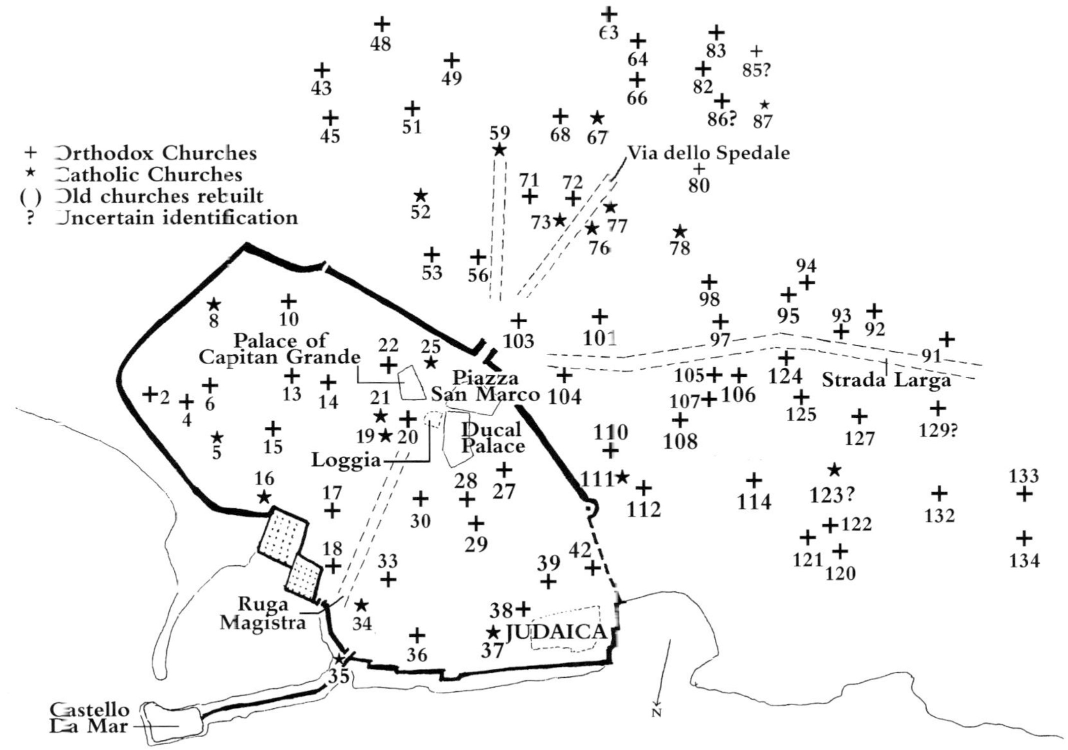

FIGURE 103. Map of Candia in the fifteenth century

possess a foundation charter, but the monastery appears in the records of the Franciscan order before 1343 so it must have been erected in the first half of the fourteenth century. Today the Archaeological Museum of Chania is entered from the east (Figs. 104 and 105).[82] The conventual church was a basilica with a large nave flanked by considerably narrower side aisles and a choir with three chapels (see ground plan, Fig. 106). The cloister lay to the south. Square, heavy pillars divided the interior into five bays that were covered by a pointed-barrel vault; the bay divisions were accentuated by transverse arches resting on corbels (Fig. 107). The side aisles were surmounted by half-barrel vaults, decorated with similar transverse arches. Three ribbed-vaulted side chapels stood to the north of the main church; their composite columns and elegant vegetal capitals indicate a different construction campaign later in the fourteenth century (Fig. 108).[83] A fourth chapel to the west was considerably smaller and was covered by a barrel vault. A three-story bell tower was located at the southeast corner of the church, displaying a tripartite window with Gothic tracery in the upper story.

Interestingly, the second major foundation of the Franciscans in Canea must have been built on a lot that belonged to St. Francis, as its convent

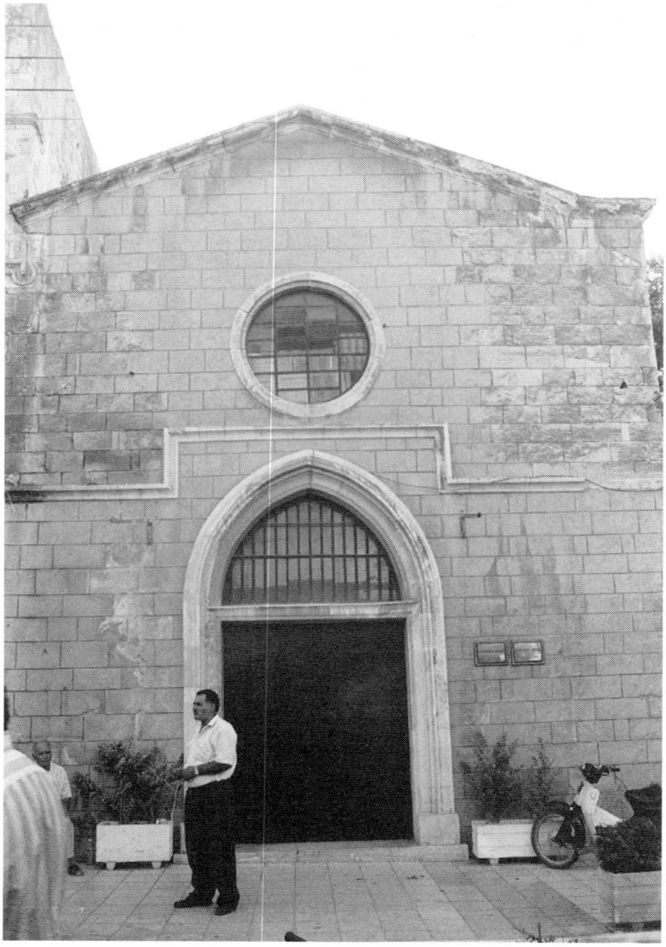

FIGURE 104. Chania, church of St. Francis, exterior view from the east

formed a cluster with the nunnery of the Clares, which was located across from it on the main street of the suburbs (Fig. 109).[84] Sponsored by a noblewoman in 1402, this small single-nave church measuring 17.40 by 9.50 meters was dedicated to the Virgin Mary.[85] The side walls of the church had seats and benches for the nuns and were adorned with a large painting of the Virgin to the south and with a relief depicting St. Clare to the north. A belfry surmounted the choir and a small door led to a square cloister surrounding a fruit garden to the south. Six cells for the nuns were located to the north, a fact showing that the Clares never had a large following in Canea; in fact, between 1633 and 1638 the convent was transformed into a seminary because the last nun had died.[86]

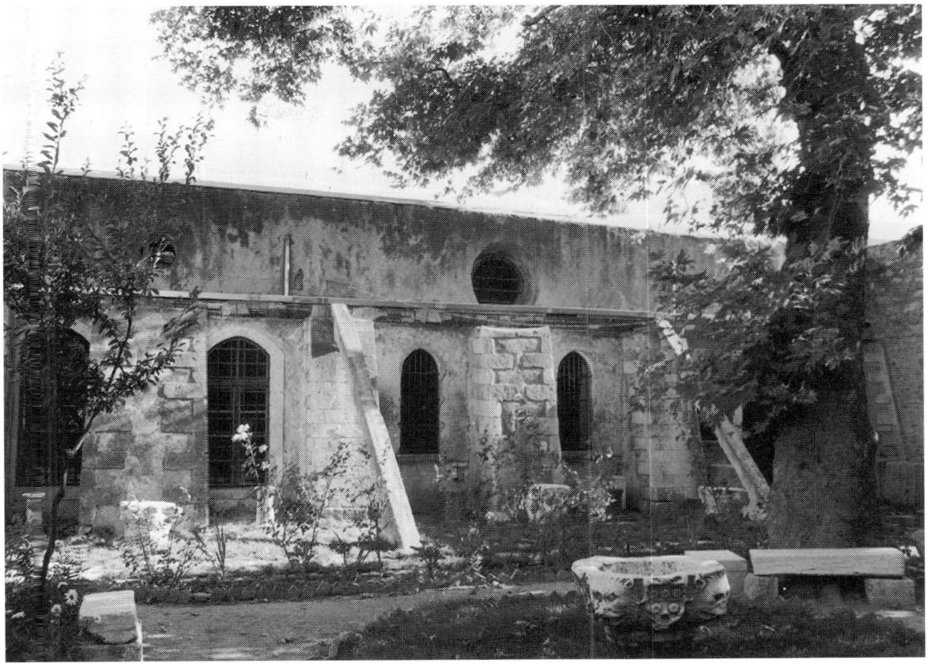

FIGURE 105. Chania, church of St. Francis, exterior view from the south

The Dominicans established their first monastery in Canea between 1306 and 1320; it was dedicated to St. Nicholas (indicated in Fig. 110).[87] It was a single-nave basilica with a slightly projecting transept and a choir consisting of three rectangular chapels: the central one was covered with two six-partite ribbed vaults and the side ones with barrel vaults. A monumental Renaissance portal adorned the western façade. A cloister to the north and a small oratory dedicated to Christ on the south completed the remains of the convent.[88] A Dominican nunnery dedicated to Santa Maria dei Miracoli was restored or built anew in 1606 by Marussa Mengano. The church measured 17.40 by 10.50 meters and had three altars, a sacristy, a bell tower, and a small portable organ located on the south side of the church on a terrace.[89] The nuns had a special choir located on the second story of the church that was closed by a heavy door and was accessed directly from their dormitory via a special passageway.[90] Only a few sections of its southern wall with traces of four blind pointed arches and the beginning of a barrel vault were visible in the 1900s.[91] It is worth comparing the dimensions of this church to that of the Clares – the closeness in size possibly suggests an antagonism between the two and the relatively few resources available to nunneries. The Dominican convent must have been much larger than that of the Clares because there were thirty cells in the dormitory.

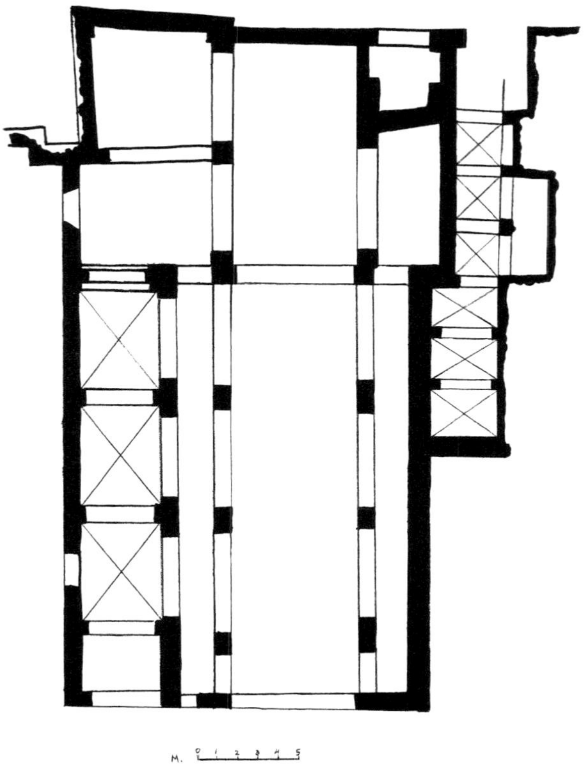

FIGURE 106. Chania, church of St. Francis, ground plan after Gerola

The Augustinians also possessed a monastery in the city of Canea; it was demolished when the new fortification walls of Canea were built in 1583 and must have been immediately replaced by the church of Santa Maria della Misericordia, which is mentioned in documents of 1585 in connection with the new loggia of the town. The new monastery was situated in the southern part of the suburbs, close to the sixteenth-century city walls. A barrel vault covered the nave of the church, which measured 15.20 by 8.90 meters. The south wall, which was 1.20 meters wide, was reinforced with three buttresses. An oculus opened to the west, probably above the portal. The bishop George Perpignano also recorded the altar of the Holy Sacrament and a sacristy inside the church.[92]

The principal church of the Franciscans of Retimo/Rethymnon was dedicated to St. Francis. This impressive structure was erected around 1530 and transformed into a mosque by the Ottomans (Figs. 111 and 112).[93] The Franciscans possessed a second church dedicated to St. Athanasius, which was located in the suburbs of the city not far from the walls.[94] A third

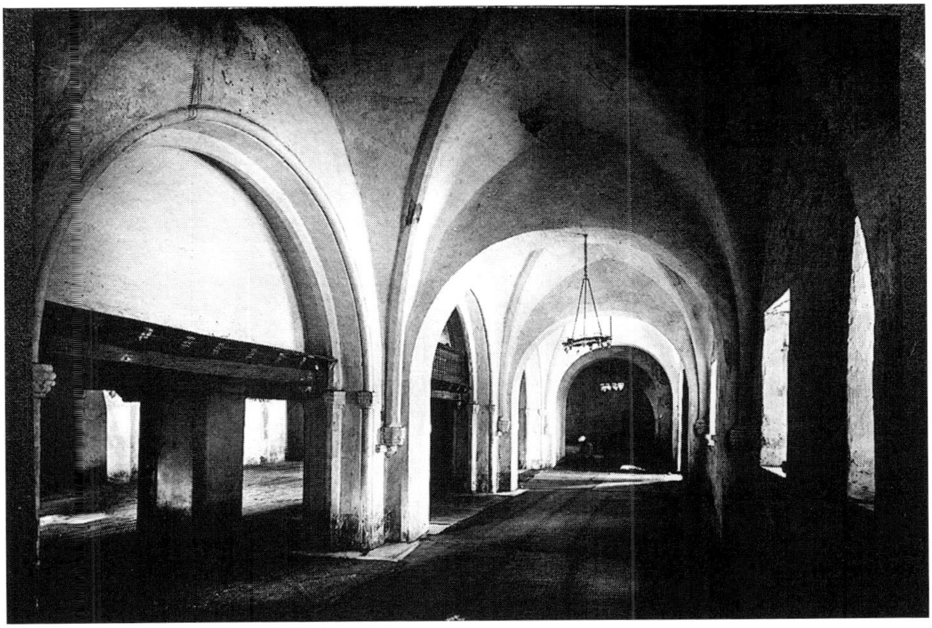

FIGURE 107. Chania, church of St. Francis, nave looking west, transverse arches in the barrel vault (Istituto Veneto di Scienze, Lettere ed Arti. Venezia. Archivio fotografico della Missione in Creta di Giuseppe Gerola)

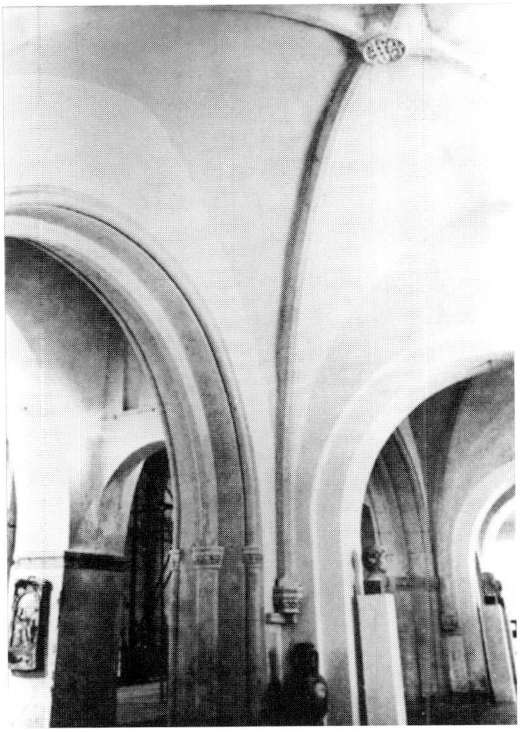

FIGURE 108. Chania, church of St. Francis, ribbed vault in the choir, north chapel

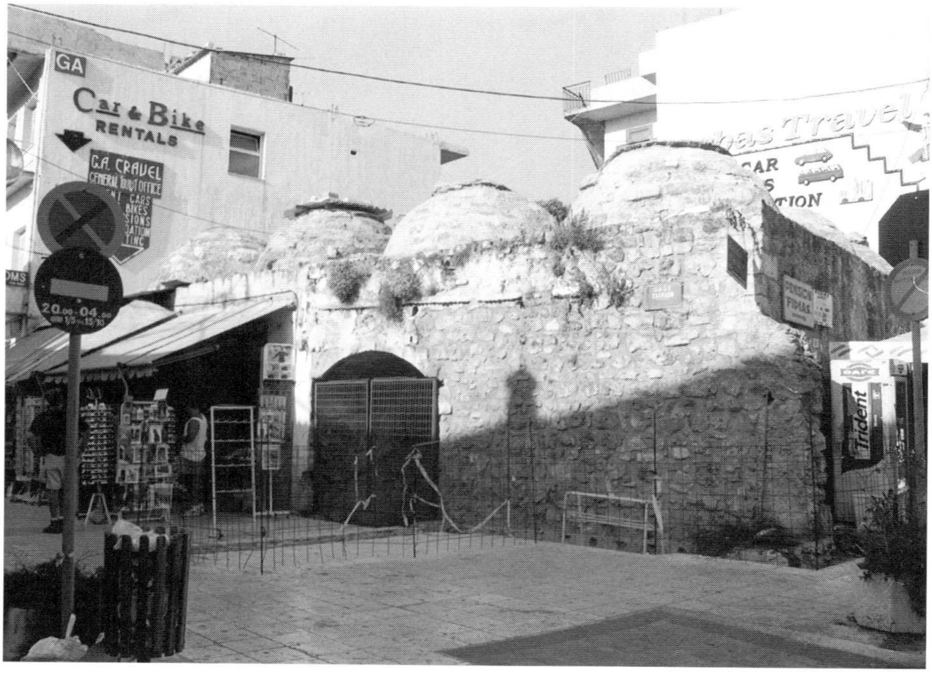

FIGURE 109. Chania, possible location of the nunnery of the Clares

Franciscan monastery, dedicated to St. Barbara, was located close to the eastern bastion of the fortifications.[95] The Dominican friars of Retimo were housed in a church dedicated to St. Mary Magdalene, a structure turned into the mosque of Anghebut by the Ottomans. The church was a barrel-vaulted basilica with three naves of equal width ending in three circular apses.[96] The Augustinians possessed a church dedicated to St. Mary, which was converted by the Ottomans into the mosque of Ghazi Hussein Pasa, or Nerantza, with the addition of three cupolas and a freestanding minaret. Today the building serves as a music conservatory (Fig. 113). The first documentary evidence that we possess for this church comes from a notarial act in 1340.[97] According to further documentary evidence the church had a special area for women, probably following the architectural prototypes of Byzantine churches. The church had a single nave and at the time of Gerola only the northern and part of the eastern wall survived.[98] The northwest portal, which is now used as the main entrance to the church, was remodeled during the Renaissance, probably shortly after 1619, as it has been shown to follow decorative patterns published in the architectural treatise of Sebastiano Serlio.[99]

Sitia possessed a Franciscan monastery dedicated to St. Lucy/Santa Lucia, a church dedicated to St. Mary that might have been a Franciscan foundation, and the Augustinian church of St. Catherine in the suburbs.[100] A

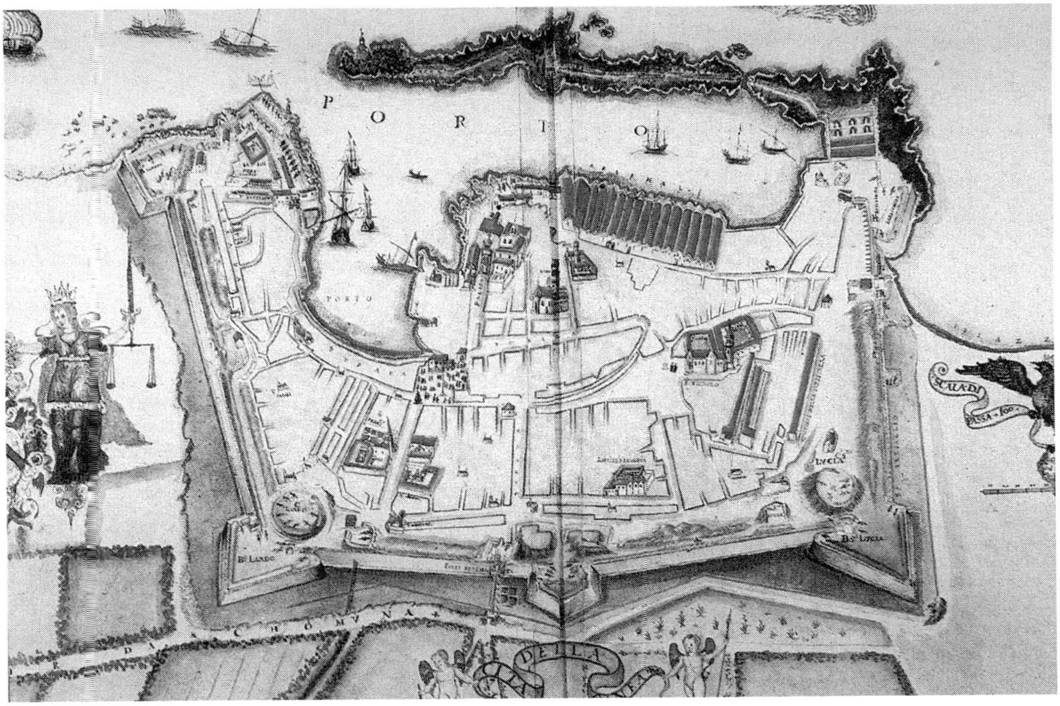

FIGURE 110. Zorzi Corner, Città di Canea, 1625 (Biblioteca Marciana, Ms. It. VI, 75 [8303], fol. 4)

Franciscan monastery existed in Modon before 1446, but in 1482 it was in a bad financial state, housing only two friars.[101]

The ecclesiastical significance of the city of Negroponte/modern Chalkis in Euboea, which became the seat of the displaced Latin patriarch of Constantinople after the Byzantines recovered their capital in 1261,[102] already attracted Mendicant monasteries in the city by the thirteenth century. All of them were probably located in the burg but their remains have not been securely identified. A small Franciscan monastery (San Francesco) with two friars and a nunnery of the Clares were established in Negroponte before 1318.[103] The Dominican friars had founded their monastery in the burg by 1262, whereas the Latin monastery of the Crusaders, dedicated to Santa Maria, and the hospital it supported are mentioned in a papal letter of 1223.[104] Two additional suburban churches were dedicated to Saint Nicholas and Saint Margaret, but there is also mention of other churches.[105] Negroponte and Candia, as important ecclesiastical centers, commanded the presence of numerous Mendicant establishments from the beginning of Venetian presence in the Aegean. The other colonies were somewhat slower, it seems, in attracting friars and monies for convents. Not only do the monasteries

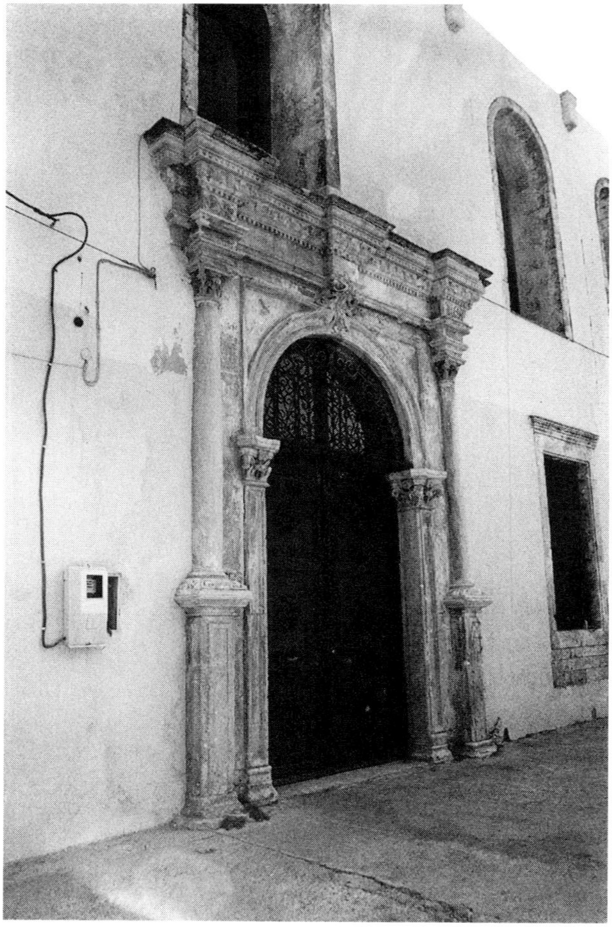

FIGURE 111. Rethymnon, church of St. Francis, exterior view from the south

appear relatively late in the sources (midfourteenth century and later) but they were also founded outside the old core of the cities, indicating that the friars had not been around early on in the life of the colonies.

The new Mendicant monasteries, built in the Gothic style, rose high above the walls of the city and were highly visible and immediately recognizable as symbols of the Latin rite. The Franciscan church of Santa Maria Gloriosa dei Frari and SS. Giovanni e Paolo of the Dominicans had broken with the older architectural tradition of Venice and stood as major monuments of the new Gothic architectural style of Western Europe.[106] Similarly, the remains of the Mendicant churches in the cities of Crete attest to their popularity, their wealth, and their prominence in shaping the visual identity of the colonies. They were characterized by lofty elongated basilicas with

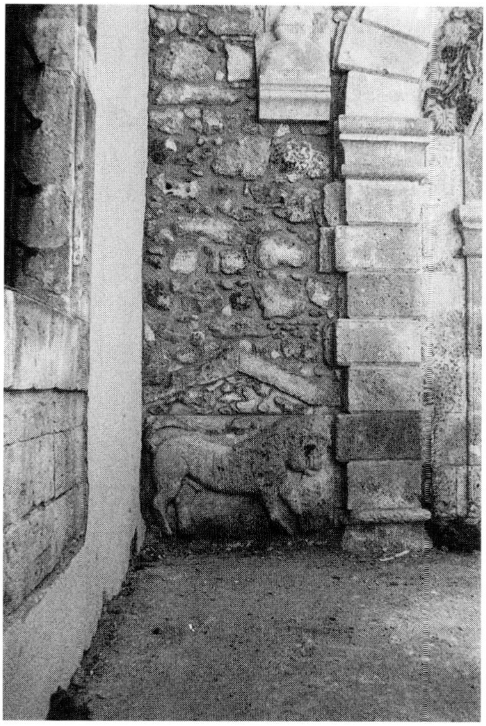

FIGURE 112. Rethymnon, church of St. Francis, sculpture of lion

crochet capitals and much more sculptural ornament than the Orthodox churches of the region, ribbed vaults over the choir as the statutes of the orders allowed, and numerous chapels endowed by private persons; the loss of their painted decoration makes these deconsecrated buildings sad heirs to a most brilliant religious history. Although it would be pointless to insist that their interior would have evoked the Frari or Zanipolo in Venice, it must be kept in mind that in the eyes of the colonists and numerous travelers to Crete these conventual churches did reflect the spiritual wealth of the Mendicants in the metropole.

WESTERNIZING CANDIA

Within the urban space the religious foundations of the Venetians broadcasted the superiority of their Latin faith and accentuated its difference from the Orthodox rite. Although the Mendicant monasteries did not support

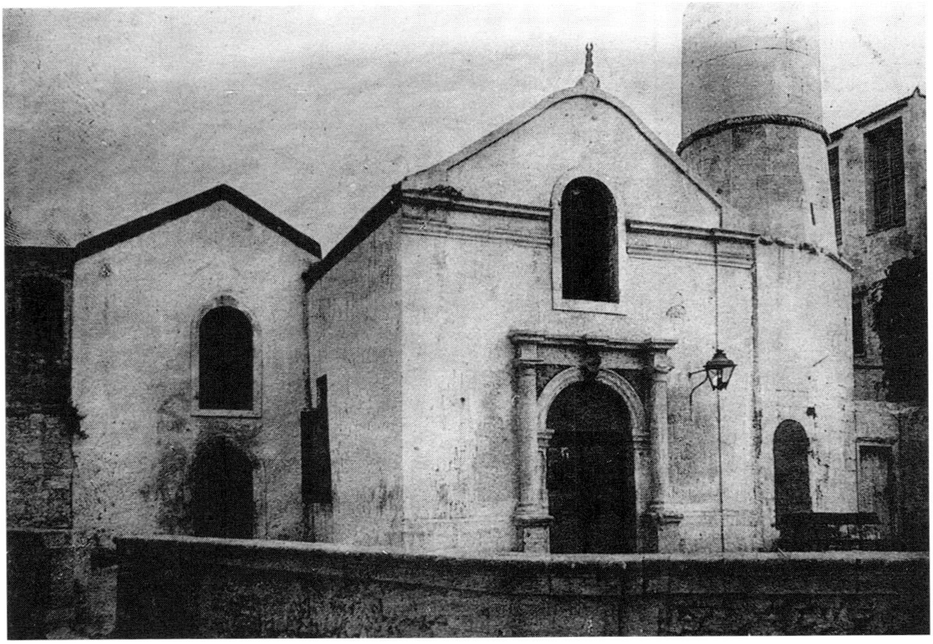

FIGURE 113. Rethymnon, Augustinian church of St. Mary, exterior (Istituto Venteto di Scienze, Lettere ed Arti. Venezia. Archivio fotografico della Missione in Creta di Giuseppe Gerola)

Venetian rule directly, their mere presence in a Levantine port city denoted the Western religious identity of its rulers since these were structures sanctioned by papal authority. If we take into account all the monuments connected with the Venetian overlords of the colonies, we soon realize that the Mendicant orders represented an immensely important component in broadcasting and sustaining a Catholic presence in the colonies both as builders and as spiritual leaders. Every colony appears to have been furnished with at least one Franciscan and one Dominican monastery, not to mention nunneries of the Clares and convents of the Augustinians or the Crusaders. Depending on the wealthy patrons among the Latin aristocracy and the Venetian state officials that each monastery attracted, the buildings and their decoration were more or less lavish.

Following the standard architectural form of the Gothic timber-roofed basilica with a soaring vault over the choir and a high bell tower, the churches of the friars along with the Latin cathedral and the church of St. Mark dominated the cityscape of Candia. Indeed, the presence of the bell tower is one of the most pronounced elements indicated in the late medieval maps of city (see for example Reuwich's view, Fig. 7). These towers, although present in some twelfth-century Byzantine churches, were for the most part foreign to the local tradition, yet under colonial rule became the most salient features of the skyline of the city.[107] It is unfortunate that very few of the Byzantine churches survive in the cities to give us precise information on their formal relationship with the Latin churches (see Chapter 7).

The one disparity that we can be certain about by looking at the most detailed views of Candia is that, in stark contrast to the impressive Western churches of Candia, the Byzantine churches were small and did not command a large space around them. Thus, the formal arrangement of the Latin churches made them powerful indexes of the dominance of the official rite of the Venetians. In addition, the placement of the Latin churches at the extremities of the main arteries of the city created a network of routes that encompassed the major public structures of the Venetians. Inside the old city the Western churches were built on the main street and on the confines of the sea wall, so as to frame the Venetian city with their imposing silhouettes. In the suburbs, the Latin convents were erected on the extensions of the main artery of the city, the *ruga magistra,* creating two major axes that met at the inland gate of the city. In fact, the Mendicants with their significant monetary and spiritual resources were vital contributors to forging an alternative sacred history to the religious Byzantine traditions by inscribing their establishments into the ceremonial profile of the colonies. Although the surviving evidence does not allow us to specify whether any non-Catholics endowed such places, the prominence of these structures in the cityscape and in the spiritual life of the elite might have induced the Orthodox to follow some of their prerogatives.

Whether or not the Orthodox churches of the towns incorporated any Gothic features in their layout and decoration, the Latin churches modified the appearance of Byzantine Chandax and constituted an architectural framework that identified the new city of Candia as Latin. This message was directed to the city dwellers, to the people who visited the city from the hinterland, and to those who arrived from abroad by sea.[108] Indeed, the spatial arrangement of the major Latin religious foundations speaks of an attempt to "westernize" the urban space by creating landmarks that the city dwellers would associate with the Venetians' presence on the island. In the suburbs, on the other hand, the placement of the Latin institutions indicated the boundaries of the Venetian urban settlement to people approaching from the hinterland and at the same time incited further expansion of the city. The spatial interrelationships between these structures and their non-Venetian counterparts (Orthodox Christian and Jewish) account for the Latin buildings' becoming signifiers of Venetian presence and dominance. By obstructing the visibility and by usurping the "rights" of the Greek churches, the new Latin churches minimized the impact of the Greek religious structures on the life of the city. The patrons and faithful of the Orthodox rite were made to seem unimportant and powerless.

SIX

THE GREEKS AND THE CITY

> We understand that in your cities and dioceses there are mixed races with different languages, namely Latins and Greeks, who in one faith have different rites and customs, and that, whereas the Latins under the obedience of the Roman Church follow in everything the rites of that Church and are wisely ruled by your government and that of your suffragans, the Greeks have been and are without a Catholic Greek prelate to minister the sacraments to them and to instruct them both by word and example according to the customs of the Roman Church.
>
> Letter of Pope John XXII to the archbishop of Crete (April 1, 1326)[1]

The Venetian colonists constituted only a minority within the multiethnic and polyglot society of late medieval Candia.[2] Yet, this minority controlled most of the economic and civic resources of the city and shaped the history of the colony. At the beginning of the thirteenth century the majority of the population was Greek. A significant Jewish community also resided inside the city. Although non-Latins did not have access to the highest posts in the colonial administration, daily life, professional encounters, and economic transactions required interaction among Latins/Venetians, Greeks, and Jews. The settlement of the Venetians in Candia was followed by commercial growth that resulted in an increased urban population, a process that seems to have been only partially delayed by the Black Death in the middle of the fourteenth century. Soon a trade-oriented middle class was formed, the *burgenses*. A large number of people, mostly local merchants and peasants, circulated in the city of Candia, where the major commercial spaces were situated. Among these people language barriers were bridged by Greek and the Venetian vernacular in everyday life, whereas official documents were drafted in Latin.[3] When matters vital to the colony had to be communicated to non-Latin speakers the official decrees were announced in Greek, especially in places frequented by Greeks, like the market or close to their place of residence.[4] Interestingly, in the town of Modon, where the Venetian population was smaller, the announcements were uniformly made in both Latin and Greek, whereas this was not always deemed necessary in Candia. In addition to heralds, other officers of the government like judges and notaries had to know Greek. In fact, when in the early fifteenth century the Venetian authorities of Negroponte made the compilation of the *Assizes de Romanie*, which were based on local law and for which knowledge of Greek was essential, the notaries who worked on the project did not use interpreters.[5]

In contrast to the relatively innocuous amalgamation of languages, ethnic and religious differences between the colonists and the locals were thorny matters that more than once caused revolts on the island. Ethnicity and religious creed were inextricably woven together to the extent that religious affiliation is often the only indication of one's ethnic origin in the surviving documents. The text of the *Concessio Crete* professed religious freedom for all inhabitants of the island.[6] As a result, the religious allegiance of the Latin Christians, the Greek Orthodox Christians, and the Jews remained unaltered throughout the period of Venetian rule.[7] In fact, the Greek and Jewish communities constructed their proper group identity by maintaining their specific rite and religious practices under the close supervision of the Latin ecclesiastics.

The sense of belonging to a distinct, named ethnic community – constituted by common ancestry and kinship, common cultural characteristics such as language or religion, and a common living space (homeland) – created separate "imagined communities" within Venetian Candia.[8] Different strategies were used to bind these communities together and to foster a sense of collective identity. For instance, as Sally McKee has ably shown, "Latin" was not so much an ethnic attribute as an ideologically charged concept that embodied a legal distinction between Latins and Greeks with the objective to create a sense of group identity among the colonizers; it was "a legal and ontological fiction" created by the authorities.[9] In practical terms to be Latin meant to be free, to be able to own property. Most important, however, to be Latin meant to be different from the locals. Additional governmental policies, such as special levies targeting a distinct community, accentuated the particularities of each ethnic group.[10]

These administrative measures were reinforced by the layout of the city as it was ordered by the colonial authorities. Since religious expression was a primary component in defining the identity of an ethnic group, the placement of the religious structures of the Latins, Greeks, and Jews within the urban space denoted the parts of the city that were available to each group. Similarly, the appearance and usage of public monuments signaled to their audience accessibility to civic resources and/or exclusion from administrative control. Thus, the accessibility and visibility of Latin and Orthodox churches on the one hand, and of synagogues on the other, set the boundaries of interaction between the ethnic-religious groups and each group's potential for development within the limits of Candia. Where were the public buildings of Venetian Candia placed vis-à-vis their users? Were the Orthodox churches and Jewish synagogues located within the walled city or in the burg? What were the spatial interrelationships among the most significant public structures? Theories of liminality emphasizing the significance of boundaries in marking status will be helpful in understanding the importance that the allocation of space and the regulation of access to civic resources had for the successful establishment and sustaining of the Venetian colony of Crete.

PROPERTY RIGHTS

The wall circuit of Venetian Candia shielded an area to which access was monitored by the state authorities. Although some of the side gates of the city seem to have allowed free access, the entry to the city through its principal gates was patrolled by special guards. Moreover, building activity was regulated by the state, which owned most of the urban territory and the surroundings of Candia.[11] Thus, in legal terms the walled city of Candia was the property of the colonial authorities. The state not only raised taxes on these lands, but also set rules for any transaction regarding the properties given to the Venetian feudatories. For instance, in 1292 the Maggior Consiglio in Venice prohibited the duke and the counselors of Candia from selling any land or house pertaining to a fief.[12] A century later the Senate prohibited the feudal lords from bequeathing their fiefs to monasteries, hospitals, or the poor, because these patrons did not maintain the estates in a good condition. Instead the state urged the lords to sell their fiefs at a good price and then distribute the money at will.[13]

This attempt to control the urban landholdings at large provides the basis for understanding the Venetian actions in the wake of the colonization of Crete. The evidence implies that in 1211 the Venetian authorities wanted to present Candia as a city dotted with urban estates belonging to the new Venetian/Latin aristocracy and allowed only smaller houses to be given to private persons, both Latin and Greek. The 152 settlers who were sent from Venice to Crete in 1211 were explicitly ordered to maintain residences inside the cities, and upon their arrival on Crete they were granted urban estates in

Candia (*burgesie*).[14] Whether this requirement was instituted with the intent to supervise the feudal lords or simply to have them available in the capital city as political representatives of the Republic, by midfourteenth century it was clear that the feudatories looked forward to the chance to enjoy urban life among their compatriots, who were scarce in the countryside.[15] Whom did they take these estates from? A document of 1224–25 suggests that upon the arrival of the Venetians the members of the Greek aristocracy of Candia were expelled from the city so that their residences be given to the colonizers, but there is no explicit reference to such an action.[16]

Other observations point in the same direction. There exists no documentary information on the construction of these urban residences immediately after the Venetians arrived on Crete, whereas such references abound in the beginning of the fourteenth century, especially because in an attempt to have residences that resembled those in Venice the *burgenses* who built houses in Candia often obtained building material from the metropole. For example, in 1312 Johannes de Regio was authorized to receive one hundred *miliaria* of stone, which was to be used in his house, and Pietro Borgognani twenty *miliaria* of bricks.[17] It would be hard to imagine that in 1211 the Republic spent an extremely large amount of money to sponsor the construction of new houses for the feudal lords. In fact, since the authorities tried to lure Latins to Crete with a four-year property tax exemption, it is logical to assume that the settlers did not have to worry about erecting their own houses in the city. Indeed, an entry in the cadastre demonstrates that the lords expected that a house would be included among the urban possessions that they were granted: when Fruçerius de Toaldo realized that the property granted to him did not include a house, he complained to the authorities. The state tried to appease him by awarding him a larger piece of land.[18] Since there is no record that Candia was destroyed during the war between the Genoese and the Venetians, therefore, we can assume that the Venetian fiefholders moved into households that had originally belonged to the Byzantine population of the city. A clear message of Venetian supremacy was thus proclaimed by the privileged positioning of the Venetian patricians vis-à-vis the Greek nobility.

One further proof of this process of ostracizing the Greek nobility from Candia are the multiple rebellions against the Venetian authorities. The Byzantine landowners, who according to the legend of the *Twelve Archontopoula* had been prominent figures in the aristocracy of Crete before 1204, assembled the Greek rural population under their leadership and instigated nine uprisings during the thirteenth century in order to have their property rights recognized by the Venetian authorities.[19] The Orthodox clergy joined the insurrections for the maintenance of their faith and the populace fought for the preservation of the traditional social structure.[20] Soon the Venetian authorities had to revise their strict segregational policy and to concede privileges to the rebellious local population. Land concessions were made to members of the Byzantine aristocracy as early as 1219. In the treaty signed by Konstantinos Scordilis and Theodore Melissenos, on the one hand, and Duca Domenico Delfino on the other, the rebels were accorded 67½ *cavallerie* that had been previously granted to Latin feudatories.[21] These lands represented one whole sestiere; in other words, by 1219 (only eight years after the Venetians arrived on Crete) one sixth of the agricultural lands of the island was legally owned by Greeks. Probably these agricultural lands had been offered to absentee Latin settlers and it was easy to turn them over to the Byzantines.

Unlike the Venetian settlers, however, the Greek lords who were awarded these lands did not get their urban properties back. It took a few more decades of fighting by the Greeks to obtain the privilege to reside and own property within the walled city of Candia. In the treaty that the Venetians signed with the inhabitants of Apano and Kato Syvritos (1234), Greeks were granted the privilege to enter and leave the city of Candia and the fortresses of the island freely, a point indicating that they had to fight for this privilege.[22] Clearly, the admission of Greek lords into the capital city carried more symbolic weight than their inevitable presence in the countryside. The chronicle of Antonio Trivan implies that in the second half of the thirteenth century Alexios Calergis, a member of the most powerful aristocratic Byzantine family on Crete, claiming descent from the emperor Nikephoros Phokas, could choose to reside inside the city of Candia if he pleased.[23] The land mentioned in Trivan's chronicle probably appears in a 1258 entry in the *Catasticum of SS. Apostoli* which records a land division by Agathe widow of the Venetian lord Marcus Faletro, and Alexios Calergis.[24] The urban landholdings of Marcus Faletro were large in size and occupied a central position in the city, near the ducal palace.[25] Assuming that the division cut the lot in half (as was usually the case), we can conclude that the lot that was given to Alexios Calergis in 1258 covered an area of approximately 670 square meters. Thus, the state granted a significant piece of urban land – both in size and in location – to Alexios Calergis. The Byzantine lord was not only considered equal to the Venetian lords, he was also assigned a special symbolic status in the feudal hierarchy of the island.

Thus, it is not clear why a few years later the Byzantine aristocrat led a successful sixteen-year-long revolt against the Venetians. Perhaps the earlier privileges had gone to another branch of the family. The text of the treaty that the Venetians signed with the rebel Alexios Calergis in 1299 is a crucial document that reveals the points of contention between Latins and locals in the first century of Venetian colonization: property rights, freedom of movement, mixed marriages, and the presence of Orthodox bishops on the island.[26] The treaty recognized Alexios's feudal possessions and granted him an urban estate (*burgesia*); he was thus equated with the Venetian nobility.[27] In 1299, after a century of cohabitation the Venetians came to an understanding of local conditions: the key to a peaceful coexistence with the Greek population of Crete was a pact with the *archontes*. In order to govern the polyglot and multiethnic society of medieval Candia effectively, the Venetians modified their original policy of segregation of the Greek lords by admitting the local Byzantine aristocracy into the ranks of the higher class of feudatories. The new generations of Venetian citizens born on Crete were more eager to interact with their neighbors, putting aside their ethnic differences.[28] Nevertheless, a clear distinction was maintained between the Venetian and the Byzantine elite. The Venetian feudal lords belonged to the highest social class, the *nobili Veneti*, who enjoyed complete political privileges and owned the largest estates in town. Although their title was hereditary, Venice demanded proof that the heir of each feudal lord could fulfill the requirements of his title.[29] The local aristocracy could become part of a lower elite class, that of the *nobili Cretensi*, a title that was granted to the old Byzantine nobility by ducal decree in return for special services to the state.

In the course of the fourteenth century there were a few exceptions to this rule. Certain Greek families of a slightly lower social status than Calergis were offered a privileged status in the social hierarchy of Crete. For instance, the great grandfather (or grandfather) of the poet Stephanus Saclichi, Zanachi, was admitted into the class of feudatories before 1317. Later on (1345–48) Zanachi became a member of the Senate of Candia and his son, Stephanus, was elected to the Maggior Consiglio of Candia in December of 1356.[30] The Saclichis, a Greek family who in the thirteenth century had produced three Orthodox priests, by the midfourteenth century were intermarried with Venetian noble families, and Stephanus's sister must have been of Latin confession, because her will contains bequests to Western monasteries.[31]

It goes without saying that the acceptance of Greek lords into the political life of the colony must have changed the makeup of the population of Candia. After 1258 and surely following the treaty of 1299, gradually more and more members of the old Byzantine aristocracy were allowed to possess a residence inside the city, since property rights were now recognized for non-Latins as well. In fact, a 1319 decision of the Senate in Venice prohibiting the Greeks from exchanging the feudal property that they possessed in Candia with the Latins confirms that by that time more Greeks had been awarded urban estates.[32] It is worth noting, nevertheless, that from this point on it is often difficult to establish with certainty the ethnic background of the city dwellers, because their names may be italianized or do not express their place of origin. Furthermore, the degree of intermarriage between Latins and Greeks also complicates matters. These restrictions were lifted in 1395 when the state decreed that all territories could be sold to Greeks or Latins freely, except for the fortified estates that were reserved for the Latin feudal lords.[33] This official welcome of the Greek community into the city lies in sharp contrast to the gradual deterioration of the position of the Jewish community. There is no concrete evidence of feudal possessions or of residences granted as *burgesie* to the Jews of Candia. However, at least until 1495 the Jewish community had the right to own property in the urban areas, that is, houses inside the designated Jewish quarters.

OUTSIDE THE CITY WALLS: SPATIAL EXCLUSION

Given the considerable concern of the state about the identity of the urban landholders, we can safely assume that the ethnic, political, or religious affiliation of the patrons of the buildings that stood in the city had to be approved by the colonial authorities. Thus, to a large extent the spatial relationship between the buildings and the core or the boundaries of the city defined the degree to which certain structures were politically and topographically privileged. In a similar way, the clustering of structures, and the placement of buildings in antithetical parts of the cityscape, constituted a framework that identified sections of the city ethnically (as Venetian, Greek, Jewish, or other), religiously (Catholic, Orthodox, Jewish), and politically. Furthermore, the buildings' location within the city denoted the status of their patrons. The placement of Venetian administrative buildings and Latin rite churches in prominent parts of the city rendered them highly visible. Thus, the Venetian buildings gained importance in the life of the city. In contrast, the siting of Greek Orthodox churches and Jewish synagogues in less advantageous areas of the city and in the suburbs made them invisible, inaccessible, and unimportant. By virtue of the placement of their structures the Venetians were seen as the political ruling elite, whereas the Greek and Jewish communities were discerned as physically and/or symbolically excluded from the Venetian core of Candia and the administrative apparatus of the colony. However, one cannot attribute hierarchical importance to space itself without taking into consideration who used it and how accessible it was. The question, then, is whether the location of these administrative structures and places of worship within the cityscape indicates the position of each group in the social, religious, and political hierarchy of the island.

Venice employed a "divide and conquer" strategy that did not foster any real alliance between Latins and Greeks, who followed the Greek Orthodox rite and recognized the Greek patriarch of Constantinople as the spiritual head of the church of Crete. The new Latin church took over the possessions of the Orthodox church, and the property of the Byzantine patriarch on Crete was appropriated by the Latin patriarch of Constantinople.[34] Very few rural Orthodox churches were allowed to keep their landed property. An exception was made for the Cretan dependencies of two major Orthodox monasteries, which because of their antiquity maintained excellent relationships with Rome and Venice: the monastery of St. Catherine on Mount Sinai and that of St. John on Patmos, both exempted from the fisc.[35]

Local church policy was determined by the Latin archbishop of Crete, who also regulated the function of all ecclesiastical institutions regardless of rite.[36] He or the state owned the Orthodox churches that continued to exist in Candia and the new ones that were built during the Venetian dominion.[37] They were usually leased to Latin feudatories or to Greek priests; in most cases the Orthodox churches were given to canons of the Latin church as *prebende*, a term indicating that although these churches belonged to Greek priests the income that their possessions generated went to the Latin canons.[38] The owners of the Orthodox churches, or those who rented them from the state, had the obligation to pay the *exenium* (an annual contribution of six grossi) and to offer the Latin archbishop two pounds of candle wax every year.[39] In an attempt to monitor the treatment of the non-Latin population of Candia, the Venetians did everything in their power to appoint Venetian patricians as archbishops. Even if the chosen archbishop was not Venetian in origin, all Latin archbishops and bishops of Crete had to give an oath of loyalty to Venice before they could occupy their seat.[40]

With only lower-rank priests (*papades*) forming the Orthodox clergy from 1211 on, the Greek Orthodox church was essentially left acephalous with the number of priests strictly regulated.[41] Despite all these blows leveled against the Orthodox church, priesthood was a desirable career for the Greeks: they enjoyed several privileges and had prestige in the Byzantine community because they constituted its only officially recognized authority of the Greeks.[42] The Greek priests of the large cities (Candia, Retimo, Canea, and Sitia) elected with the approval of the state the *protopapas*, the head priest, who had administrative authority over the papades in his district and held his office for life.[43] He was assisted in his duties by the *protopsaltes*, the first cantor, who was also chosen by the Greek clergy. Both of these religious officials had to recognize the primacy of the pope, participate in the civic ceremonies, and prove their loyalty to Venice. One of their most important duties was the education of the new clergymen.[44] They became a special class of citizens as they were independent of the Greek patriarch of Constantinople and the Latin archbishop of Candia but were under the jurisdiction of the duke of Candia or the rectors in the other cities of Crete. These priests were subject to civil law and not to ecclesiastical courts. One hundred and thirty of the remaining Orthodox priests from the archbishoprics of Candia and St. Myron were placed under the jurisdiction of the Latin archbishop of Candia, to whom they had to pay an annual tribute of six grossi.[45]

In a period when the Orthodox church represented the only officially approved form of self-determination for the Greek community, religious affiliation was not only a spiritual privilege but a political one as well. The recognition of the *protopapas* as the head of the Greek community was the sole political concession that the Venetian colonial authorities made to the locals, a fact that in the eyes of non-Latins reinforced the significance of maintaining their faith in order to safeguard their unique ethnic identities. Religious ceremonies played a crucial role in creating a sense of communal conformity by preserving the distinct language, customs, and rituals of each ethnic group. At the same time, by demarcating the individual traits of each community, weekly Mass or prayer gatherings, special festivities, weddings, and funerals became identifying mechanisms of the various population groups of Candia. Moreover, the Orthodox churches and Jewish prayer-houses were the only public official buildings reserved exclusively for these non-Latin communities. Like the leaders of the two peoples, these buildings provided an institutionalized framework for their respective communities, a point of reference visible to everyone in the city. In such a situation, the Latin Christian, Greek Orthodox, and Jewish sanctuaries necessarily became the symbols of each community's very existence. Within the urban landscape of Candia, therefore, ethnic identity was primarily delineated by religious practices.

As few of the urban Orthodox churches have produced extensive archaeological vestiges it is important to dwell on the appearance of these churches and their position on the map (Fig. 17): St. Mary of the Angels (no. 104), St. Mary Manolitissa/Hagia Paraskeve (no. 97), St. George Doriano (no. 125), St. Mary Trimartyri (no. 56), and Madonnina/Panagia tou Forou/Santa Maria de Miraculis (no. 103). All remaining churches were basilicas of modest size, some employing piers and others circular columns with elegant capitals. Pointed-arched windows survive in a few instances and

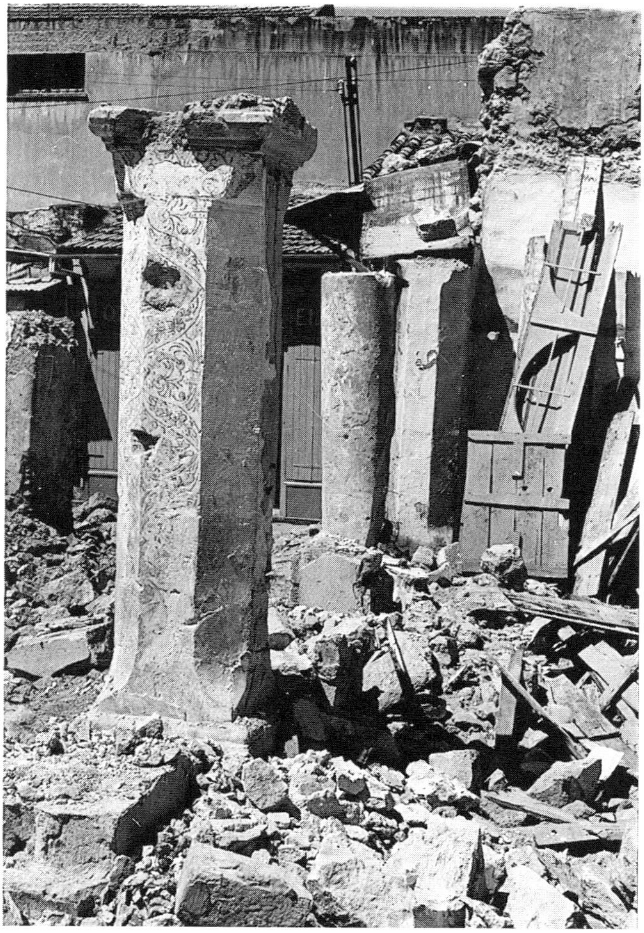

FIGURE 114. Herakleion, church of the Madonnina, colonnettes of the sanctuary

the few remains of the superstructure of the church of St. Mary of the Angels hint to the presence of a pointed-barrel vault over the nave. However, no Orthodox church with a Western (or westernizing) façade remains.

Originally a Byzantine church with an inscription in one of the columns, the archaeological remains of the Madonnina were photographed by the Archaeological Service before its demolition (Fig. 114). The central nave of the church was more elevated than the side aisles, creating a clerestory pierced with five pointed-arch windows. Heavy square piers formed two colonnades that supported round arches that separated the nave from the aisles. Some of the arches were replaced by modern doors when the site was reused. There were also pointed-arch windows in the eastern side that are not visible in the photographs but were recorded by Gerola as original

Venetian windows. The area of the choir/apse was more ornate than the rest of the church as the decorated colonnettes that survived suggest. The whole was covered by a sloping timber roof. Although this building could never be taken for a Gothic construction, the absence of a dome and its basilical form meant that overall it did not look very different from a Western church of the time, except in scale, height, and building material. In order to acquire a mental image of what the Orthodox churches of thirteenth- and fourteenth-century Candia may have looked like, we may bring to mind the provincial town of Kastoria in northern Greece with its six minuscule basilical churches (some of them domed) dating from the tenth to the twelfth centuries that all display the typical Byzantine cloisonné brickwork on their exterior walls.[46] One assumes that the use of marble or local limestone and the addition of sculptural decoration on the exterior of Latin churches may have stood as a trademark of the Gothic style vis-à-vis the Byzantine buildings of the city.

The fact that eighteen Orthodox parish churches existed within the fortified city in the fourteenth century implies that the Orthodox population had a strong presence in the life of the city.[47] Interestingly, the European travelers chose not to comment on these churches, a point that suggests their inconspicuous appearance or their conformity with ecclesiastical architecture in Europe. These churches represent a significant number and assert that the fortified city accommodated a considerable Greek population. Nevertheless, the documentary evidence and the size of the churches as it is indicated in Werdmüller's map, which has been drawn to scale (Figs. 16 and 17), suggest that these Byzantine foundations were quite small. Most probably they were also surrounded by private residences that obstructed their visibility especially if they are viewed in relation to the large foundations of the Mendicant friars. Following the appropriation of the cathedral of Chandax/Candia by the Venetians, the main church where the Greeks were allowed to worship according to their rite was moved outside the city walls; inside the fortified city only the smaller, less important Greek Orthodox churches were allowed to function. The available archaeological evidence and the surveyed documentary material are not explicit as to the construction dates of the Greek churches located within the city walls, with the exception of the church of St. Anthony, which – we are told – was erected in 1385–91. It is logical to assume that most of the other eighteen Greek Orthodox churches that existed in fourteenth-century Candia had stood in Chandax before the arrival of the Venetians. This assumption should hold true at least for the six churches that are mentioned in documentary sources of the beginning of the fourteenth century, namely, St. Barbara,[48] St. Lucy,[49] St. Demetrius,[50] Christo Chefala,[51] Chera Pisiotissa,[52] and St. Constantine.[53] There is no reason to believe that there were any restrictions on the construction of Orthodox churches in the core of the Venetian city in the fourteenth and fifteenth centuries, as the Greeks had the freedom to observe the Eastern rite. In any event, Greek parishioners must have frequented these eighteen churches. So, the fortified city was open to a considerable Greek community, even if the old Byzantine aristocracy was excluded from it.

Of all the Orthodox establishments in Candia, the most significant was the monastery of St. Catherine, a dependency of the famous Sinai monastery (no. 101, Fig. 17). Not only did the Venetians preserve this Byzantine foundation, but the possessions of the Sinai monastery were emphatically placed under the protection of the doge in 1212 and of the pope in 1217.[54] This monastery, now a Baroque structure that houses a significant collection of icons of the Cretan School, was located outside the city walls close to the area of the modern Greek Orthodox cathedral of Herakleion, and it was preceded to the west by a cemetery (Fig. 115).[55] The monastery must have been one of the most important Greek churches in the city because the Byzantine lord Alexios Calergis possessed a private chapel therein, which served as his burial place in the early fourteenth century.[56] The church was the recipient of many donations by the Greek population of Candia, including a *rondo* depicting St. Catherine, which was painted and bequeathed by the famous Cretan painter Angelos Acotanto in the fourteenth century.[57] Following the important status that the monastery on Mount Sinai also held among Latin Christians from early on, the Sinaite dependency in Candia acquired prominence among the Latin population, who either chose to be buried therein or donated funds for its upkeep. In numerous testaments of Latin donors the monastery is the only Orthodox establishment that figures in a long list of Latin churches, certainly because of its fame as an early Christian foundation and pilgrimage site. Although more often than not it is hard to establish the genealogy of the wives of Latin feudatories, one senses that women like Maria (wife of Frangullus Catalano) or Challi (wife of Philippus Orso) who chose to be buried in the Sinai church may have been Orthodox by conviction and Greek by origin. This must be true at least of Challi, who specifies in her testament that the services should be celebrated according to the Greek rite.[58] The church of St. Catherine's so prominently located outside the land gate must have stood as a unique locus of interaction between the Greek and Latin communities of Candia. Along with the cathedral of St. Titus, it must have figured prominently in the minds of the city dwellers as one of the two most important ancient religious landmarks of the town. As a surrogate of the famous holy place on Sinai, the dependency in Crete could retain its Byzantine liturgy and Orthodox outlook and yet appeal to the Latins who came to it as pilgrims. As such it could be taken

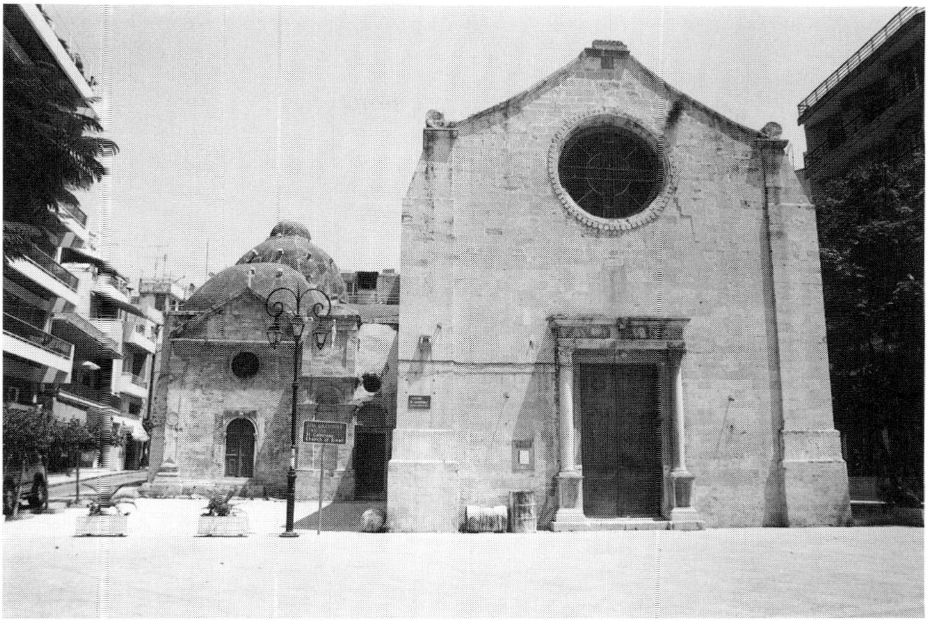

FIGURE 115. Herakleion, church of St. Catherine of Sinai

as a metaphor for the colony as a whole: here was a sacred structure that physically and liturgically embodied the past of Crete.

In the sixteenth century the monastery supported a Greek school, where most of the famous Cretan intellectuals and artists studied, including the famous painter Domenico Theotokopoulos (El Greco). After the Ottomans converted the church of St. Catherine into a mosque, the monks of Sinai moved into the nearby church of St. Matthew. In Candia the monastery of Sinai also possessed the monastery of St. Symeon, one of the few Greek Orthodox churches that have been documented as existing in the suburbs of the city before the arrival of the Venetians. It can be identified with Werdmüller's no. 72 (Fig. 17), where it is erroneously labeled St. Andrea.

Despite the significant place that the monastery of St. Catherine had, as a monastic foundation it could not take over the role of the Byzantine metropolitan church, whence the Orthodox had been ostracized. In response to this exile from the old Byzantine cathedral of St. Titus in the urban center, the Greeks chose for their new cathedral the most conspicuous spot in the suburbs. This church was the seat of the *protopapas* and was dedicated to St. Mary of the Angels. It belonged to the archbishop of Candia, who in 1320 rented it to presbyter Marco, a painter.[59] The church, a few vestiges of which exist (Fig. 116), was located diagonally across from St. Catherine's at

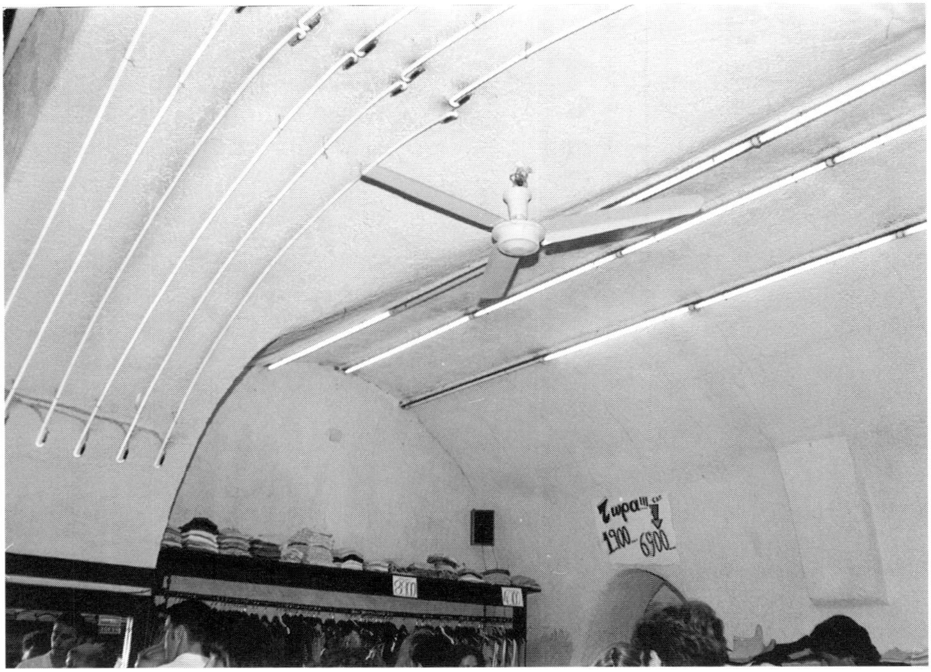

FIGURE 116. Herakleion, remains of the church of St. Mary of the Angels

the eastern end of the major street of the suburbs, the *strada larga*, just outside the land gate (no. 104, Fig. 17). It was preceded to the west by an open space 5 paces and 3½ feet wide (9.91 m), possibly a square.[60] A cemetery occupied the area behind the eastern apse of the church.[61]

As we learn from a series of documents in 1410, the church had been almost in ruins at the end of the fourteenth century.[62] Marco Paulopulo, the Greek priest who had leased it for twenty-nine years, rebuilt it in stone and added a bell tower next to it before 1410. This fifteenth-century church can be identified with the basilical church and bell tower that are shown outside the city walls in the codex of George Clontzas (Fig. 56). In 1421 Marco Paulopulo commissioned the famous icon painter Angelus Apocafco to paint the Last Judgment on the upper part of the (western?) wall of the church, as was the tradition in the Byzantine churches of Crete in this period.[63] Manoussakas believes that this church became the Greek Orthodox cathedral as late as 1452, when Marco Paulopulo held the office of *protopapas*, but the available evidence is not conclusive on this point. In the first half of the fifteenth century (1423 and 1434) the *protopapas* is recorded officiating in the church of Cheragosti inside the city, but we cannot be sure that he could not officiate in more than one church.

If we account for the considerable cemetery that lay to the east of the church, toward the city walls and the land gate, we realize that this church occupied a conspicuous spot in the suburbs; not only did it mark the beginning of the street that led to the hinterland, it also announced the disparity between the Greek and Latin rites. The cathedral of the Orthodox was the last structure that visitors from the hinterland saw before entering the Venetian city, and the first public building that travelers saw when leaving Candia. This unique position of the Orthodox church outside the city walls underscored the removal of the Greek population from civic life and emphasized the supremacy of the Latin rite vis-à-vis the Eastern rite. On the other hand, the high visibility of the new Orthodox cathedral accentuated the strength of the Orthodox rite in the suburbs. Hence, it marked the difference between Latins and Greeks and it demarcated the suburbs as a primarily Greek space.

The large number of Orthodox churches in the suburbs confirms this reasoning and suggests that the economic possibilities offered by the markets of Candia attracted a large Greek Orthodox community. A unique document for the religious topography of suburban Candia, the *Catasticum ecclesiarum et monasteriorum*, generated to settle a dispute between church and state, certifies the existence of thirty-seven Orthodox churches in the suburbs by 1320 and contains information on their history, size, and possessions. Most of the churches were of modest size, as is the extant church of St. Anastasia (Fig. 117), and owned a dozen houses, which they rented to private individuals.[64] On the basis of the principle that each congregation lived near its parish church, the presence of Orthodox and Latin foundations points to the religious (and therefore also the ethnic) composition of the suburbs. Furthermore, the extent of the territory owned by each of the churches may be used as an indicator of the density and the size of the population in a specific area.[65]

By the first half of the thirteenth century, the suburbs had grown outside the main land gate of the city, following a southwest direction (Fig. 21). However, the oldest part of the suburbs had already been shaped by at least 1266, when the dispute about church property arose.[66] Twelve churches are recorded in the area along the *strada larga* or *strada imperiale*, the main road used to approach the city from the hinterland, and the western section of the city walls; eight of them had an adjacent cemetery. Except for the Benedictine nunnery of St. George, situated near the city walls (close to the major meat market of the city), all other churches were Greek Orthodox foundations. Five churches flanked the *strada larga*. The rest were built close to the city walls: five were monasteries, and the other six were parish churches owned by the Venetian state and leased to Greeks (mostly to priests who officiated in them). All of the churches were considered old in 1266 and three of them were explicitly attributed to the Byzantine period: the imperial monastery of Panagia, which cannot be securely identified with any known church; the monastery of St. Mary Manolitissa (no. 97, Fig. 17); and finally the church of St. Michael Asomatos (no. 98, Fig. 17). Thus, the southwestern burg had probably been formed before 1204. Indeed, on topographical grounds this was the most logical direction for the development of the city: the tall hill that defined the northeastern limit of the city prevented urban growth beyond the confines of the medieval city and the rocky ground to the south was also prohibitive.[67] From 1266 until 1303, when a major earthquake destroyed many buildings in Candia, the construction of churches indicates further expansion of the suburbs to the west (Fig. 118). The eleven religious structures built during this period were all located to the north and south of the *strada larga*, the primary focus of life outside the city walls. The function of this street was vital to the commercial development of the city, since most of the people and commodities approaching the city from the hinterland entered Candia through this route. With the possible exception of one, all churches seem to have been Greek Orthodox foundations, probably indicating that this area was primarily inhabited by Greeks, who must have been the beneficiaries of mercantile activities in the area.

After the earthquake of 1303 construction in the burg boomed, to the extent that by 1319 the size of Candia and its suburbs had tripled (Fig. 119). This period coincides with an era of security and tranquility for the Venetians in Crete. The rebellions of the locals had come to an end with the treaty of 1299 (see Chapter 6, n. 27). These privileges must have attracted new Greek settlers, who moved to the city and its suburbs, creating a new middle class. Despite the lack of documented censuses for this period, the large number of Greek Orthodox churches indicates an increase of the Greek population in the suburbs that could likely have been linked to the commercial expansion of Candia. Candia had become a pole of attraction for all those interested in trade. The involvement of the population with international trade would suggest a newly acquired wealth for those taking part in it, but the majority of the religious structures built during this period seem to have been much smaller foundations than before. The small size of the churches may indicate lack of resources or patrons belonging to a lower financial stratum, but it can also point to a shortage of large open spaces in the suburbs, which were already densely populated. It is worth keeping in mind that, in contrast to the limited space allotted to the Greek Orthodox churches, the major monastic foundations of Latin rite that were constructed in the suburbs in the thirteenth and fourteenth centuries were large-scale foundations.

What does all this tell us about the ability of the Greek community to

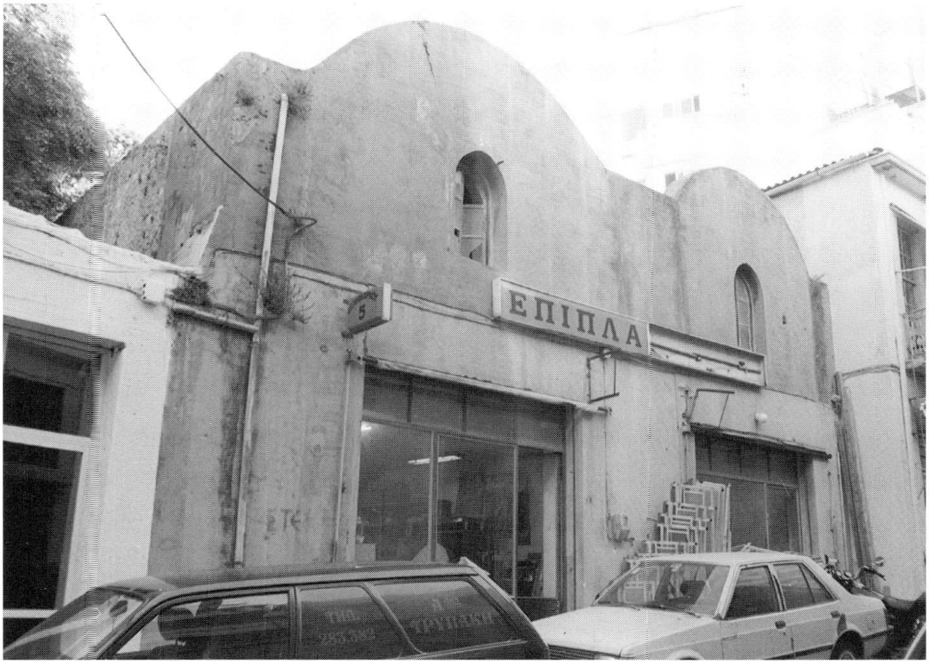

FIGURE 117. Herakleion, church of St. Anastasia

assert its presence in the city? Evidently, until the midfourteenth century the state had been quite lax in regard to the foundation of new churches. A decree regulating the erection of new churches that was publicly announced by the city crier in 1360 leaves no doubt about this: "because many churches have been constructed anew in the suburbs without a permit to the [financial?] detriment of already existing churches, . . . the duke and the *regimen* decided that from now on no one should erect a church without a state license under penalty of 200 hyperpera."[68] Although Orthodox churches are not singled out in the document, it goes without saying that this was the focus of the decree since there were at least thirty-six Greek churches that sprang up in large numbers in the burgs, whereas the Latin churches amount to fewer than a dozen. The huge penalty imposed suggests that although Orthodoxy was not promoted by the authorities, the possession of a Greek church was a profitable enterprise and a highly desirable way to channel one's wealth.[69] Of particular significance is the notion of competition among neighboring churches; obviously, if a church could not attract enough parishioners its income would decline.[70] More important for evaluating the financial situation of the patrons, the promulgation of such a decree also implies that many Greeks had the means to erect Orthodox churches, more than were needed for worship in the greater area of Candia. The erection of even

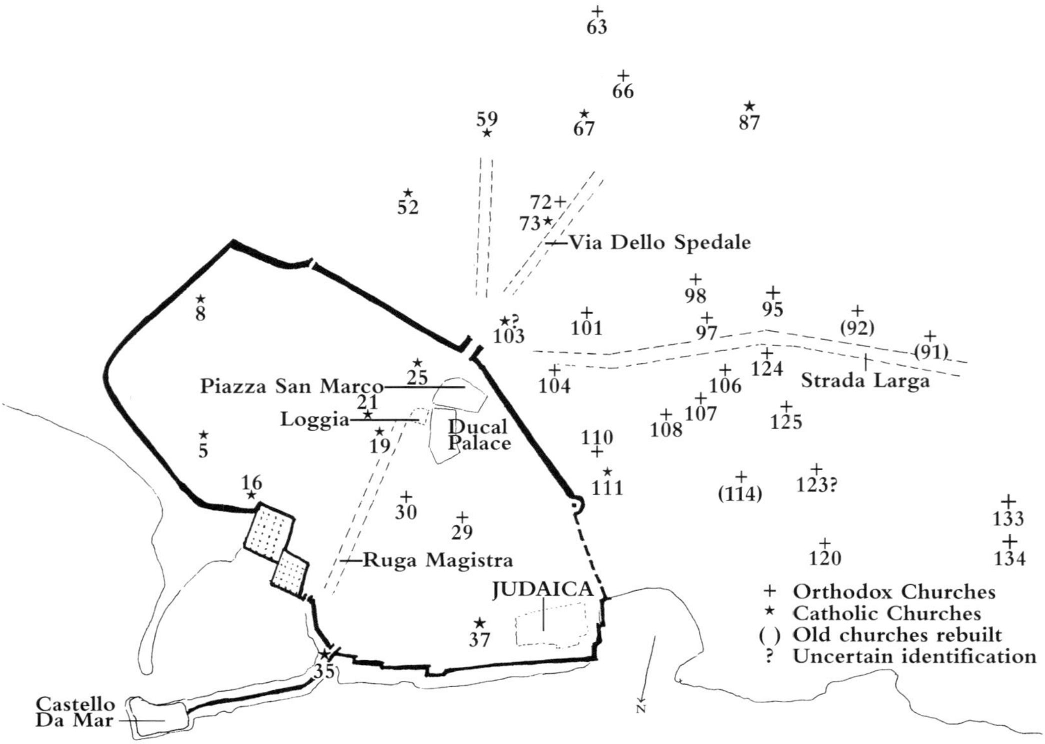

FIGURE 118. Map of Candia in 1303

a small chapel certainly represented a quite expensive undertaking, which demanded a patron with an income at least above average.

The thousand Orthodox churches that have been attested in the hinterland of Crete offer a more nuanced understanding of patronage.[71] The humble exterior of these remote churches (either small single-nave halls or centrally planned edifices) usually does not announce their extensive wall paintings. The overwhelming majority of these small, but often lavishly decorated Byzantine churches attests to the existence of important painting ateliers available to the wealthy patrons of these churches (presumably the Greek nobility). Even a cursory survey of the hundreds of churches that the Orthodox population sponsored in the countryside from the thirteenth through the midsixteenth century shows that there was only a superficial influence of Western architectural or decorative details on these churches: untiled barrel vaults, pointed-arched windows and doorways, or limited use of architectural sculpture.[72] This minimal relationship between the Gothic and the local Byzantine style may be explained by the limited number of Venetians who lived in the countryside. Consequently we have to assume that the masons working on the Orthodox churches were Greek.

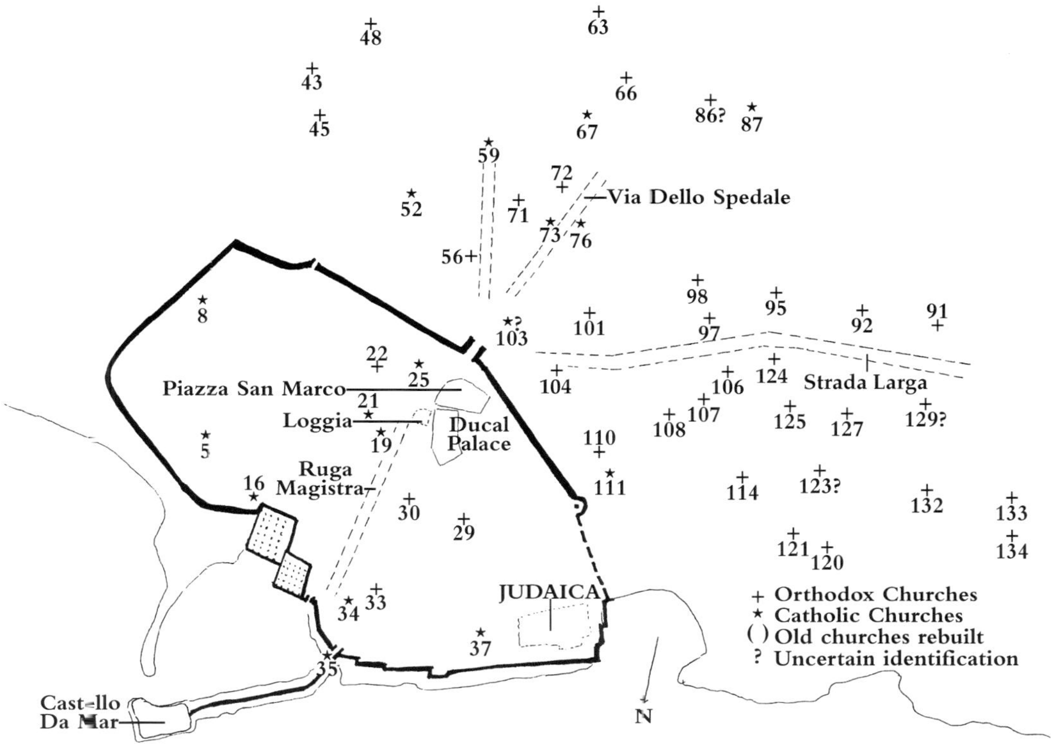

FIGURE 119. Map of Candia in 1323

Similar observations can be made concerning the frescoes of these monuments. Often located in areas with only itinerant Orthodox priests, these remote Greek churches played a vital role in strengthening the Orthodox religious feeling and in fostering the ethnic identity of the Greek rural population by offering them a place of gathering and worship. The obvious connections of the style of the Cretan frescoes with traditional Byzantine art but also with the art of Constantinople and Thessaloniki at the beginning of the fourteenth century point to the close ties that existed between religious circles and artists across the Aegean. After a period of isolation in the thirteenth century in which its art appears tentative and conservative, Crete plays a vital role in the development of late Byzantine art in the fourteenth century. This has to be related to the new improved conditions for the Greeks of Crete after the treaty of 1299. The appearance of innovations of the Palaiologan Renaissance, such as the heavy bodies or the fantastic architecture in a variety of churches of the fourteenth century, demonstrates the successful movement of communication that existed between the Byzantine empire and its lost provinces. The revival of the older cycle of the life of Constantine the Great and the inclusion of dedicatory inscriptions that commemorate the name of the reigning Byzantine emperors make a strong case for the political significance of these churches as bastions of Byzantine consciousness.[73] Three examples are from the reign of the emperor Andronikos II Palaiologos (1282–1328), a period coinciding with the rebellion of the Greek aristocrat Alexios Calergis. It seems logical to assume that during the time of the rebellion the notion of a reconquest of Crete by the Byzantines would have been promoted on many Greek fronts – aristocracy, clergy, and the populace. The patrons of these churches, possibly members of the Greek upper class (*archontes*) but definitely individuals of certain means, established close ties with the Byzantine church and its monks, who exercised great influence on the people. Consequently, the importance, prestige, and influential status of the Byzantine aristocracy who paid for these churches among the Greek population increased, along with their revenue. It is worth mentioning that there are at least fifteen rural churches sponsored by the Calergis family, mainly located in the fiefs of the family in western Crete, in the end of the fourteenth and early fifteenth centuries.[74] Indeed, the Byzantine character of these frescoes is accentuated by the small degree of cross-fertilization by Western painting until late in the fifteenth century. The majority of the churches that have been published suggest that Latin elements are confined to iconographic peculiarities like the intrusion of Western saints like St. Francis or particular Venetian vessels in scenes of the Last Supper.[75] St. Francis appears on four Orthodox churches: the church of St. Michael at Kato Astraki Pediados (a wall painting that was recorded at the beginning of the twentieth century and is now damaged), at the northwest pillar in the nave of the church of Panagia Kera at Kritsa (dating to the first half of the fourteenth century),[76] on the north wall of the church of the Presentation of the Virgin at Sklaverochori Pediados (fifteenth century), and at the church of Zoodochos Pege at Sambas Pediados (end of the fourteenth or beginning of the fifteenth century).[77]

The situation may have been quite different in the urban centers. The few churches that have survived in the cities from this period are almost uniform in their appearance: small, single- or double-aisled halls with unpretentious piers or columns surmounted by simple capitals and supporting tall semicircular arches (Fig. 116, St. Mary of the Angels, Herakleion; Fig. 117, St. Anastasia, Herakleion; Fig. 120, St. Catherine's church in Chania). With their interior decoration and original furnishings gone, one has to rely on the hundreds of Greek churches in the countryside to reconstruct their internal appearance. It is possible that the urban churches of the Orthodox, which were built in a space where Western workmen, styles, and tastes were readily available, exhibited many more Gothic elements. After all, in the second half of the sixteenth century with the advent of European architec-

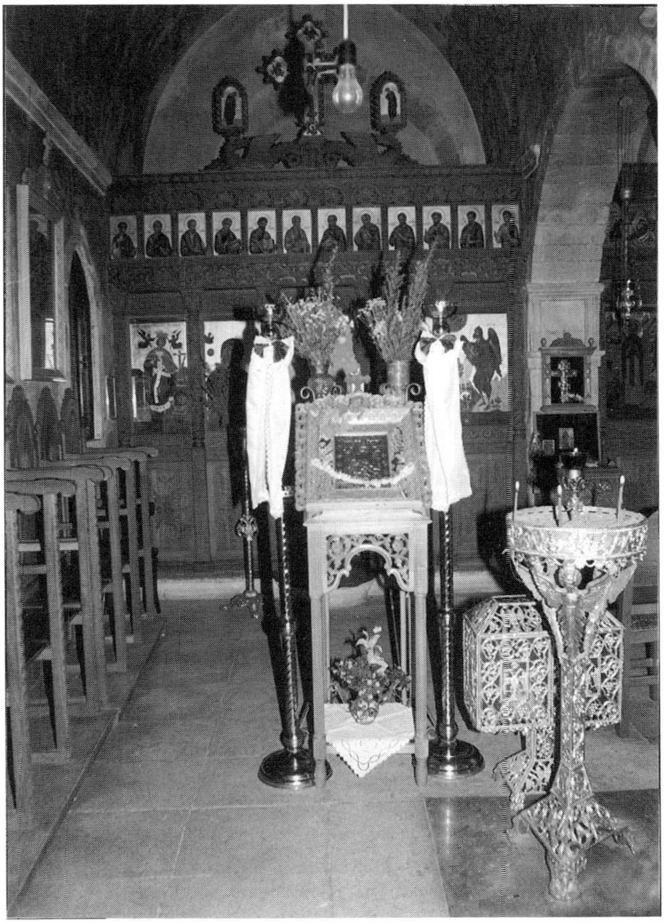

FIGURE 120. Chania, St. Catherine's, Greek church, interior

tural treatises on Crete the new Orthodox churches and monasteries seem to follow Western Renaissance patterns.[78] These influences could be minimal, such as the use of particular sculptural styles in the capitals, or may reflect more significant changes in the liturgical planning of the churches, especially those following the uniate rite after the Synod of Ferrara/Florence in 1439.

The prominent role of the patron of a church in the community at large is also attested in Candia, where at least six churches (two inside the city and four in the burg) came to be known by the family names of their original donors or benefactors. Obviously the people who erected churches or bequeathed money to ecclesiastical institutions, either Orthodox priests or members of well-to-do families, played a leading role in the Greek community of Candia as their generosity to the church was remembered through the centuries. Near the harbor the monastery of St. Nicolaus Vergici must have belonged to the Vergici family, although no explicit evidence tying the family to the church is available at this point (no. 36, Fig. 17).[79] In the sixteenth century (1568) this church belonged to the Scuola dei Calegheri, possibly an indication that the Vergicis had special connections to the guild of the shoemakers. Inside the walled city the church known as Christo tu Sculudi, is first mentioned in a document of 1496 and in the testament of Constantine Sculudi indicating that it belonged to the Sculudi family.[80] In the suburbs the church of Christo Casturi (no. 87, Fig. 17) was a possession of the monastery of St. Catherine at Mt. Sinai, but it was known until the seventeenth century by the name of its owner/renter in 1320, *papa* Thomas Casturi.[81] This Greek priest must have left a lasting impression on the church – either by endowing it or by being buried there. The church of St. John Prodromos (no. 48 on the map) was built by Michael Xafilino (probably Xiphilino) around 1303 on a territory belonging to the state, rented to Nicolaus Pothigna.[82] The Xiphilinos were an important family in Constantinople, a branch of which had evidently been attracted to Candia presumably because of international trade.[83]

In addition to parish churches, private chapels sprang up in the estates of the feudatories: a governmental license explicitly stating that the chapel was not going to usurp the function of a parish church was necessary for this purpose, possibly to appease the church of Crete. Clearly, since these churches were built on land belonging to the state, the government made sure that the Latin archbishop had no say in their construction, nor any monetary benefits from them. In 1418 Johannes Sotiriachi was accorded a permit to build a small private chapel dedicated to St. Nicholas in his estate next to his house in the parish of the Savior (of the Augustinians) in the suburbs.[84] This chapel can be identified with the Orthodox church dedicated to St. Nicolaus Sotiriachi that is recorded in 1548 – it is labeled S. Nicolo Stirgliachi on Werdmüller's plan (no. 68, Fig. 17). The few archaeological remains of the church were photographed by the Archaeological Service before it was demolished: it had a single nave that was covered by a large barrel vault. Traces of a circular arch opening to the east, probably the entrance to the sanctuary, are barely visible in the photographs. However humble this chapel may have been, it shows that a Greek patron had enough resources to erect a private chapel, an act unusual for the Orthodox, which probably tried to emulate Latin prototypes. Another private church dedicated to St. John was built by Nicolaus Costomiri in the courtyard of his house in 1445.[85]

The evidence thus far asserts that although the Greek community had lost some of its most significant sacred spaces, it had the freedom to erect numerous churches within the fortified city but especially in the burg, where the newcomers must have established their households following 1211. If the absence of references to Orthodox churches in the accounts of travelers and pilgrims who passed through Candia accounts for their inconspicuous position within the city, their fascination with other facets of religious life that were connected with the Orthodox proves the remarkable position that Greek culture played in Candia. In fact, the accounts of late medieval travelers attest to the diverse composition of the population of the city. Such reports illustrate the fact that until the end of the fifteenth century, and maybe later, Candia remained to a large extent a Byzantine/Levantine city open to Orthodox customs foreign to the Westerners, such as icon veneration.[86] Less dramatic habits also impressed visitors: in 1439–40 Gilles de Bouvier was struck by the bizarre attire of the Greeks, wearing jackets and pantaloons;[87] in 1470 Gaudenz von Kirchberg recorded the peculiar religious feasts of the Orthodox and their fasting practices;[88] finally, in 1494 the pilgrim Pietro da Casola was overwhelmed by a procession following an earthquake. His description mentions certain features that would be deemed typical by a Byzantine but must have seemed extraordinary to a Westerner:

> I happened to see the beginning of the procession made in consequence of the earthquake. It was a very pitiful thing to see and hear. For in front of the great company of Greek boys without any order, who cried with a loud voice "Kyrie Elieson" [*sic*], and nothing else, those Greeks carried in the said procession many very large figures, painted on wood. There were crucifixes, and figures of Our Lady and other saints. There was a great display of handsome vestments on the part of the Greek priests. They all wear on their heads certain hats, of which some are white, some are black. Those who have their wives living wear a white hat, the widowers wear a black one. The cords hang down like those of the cardinals' hats. The higher in rank the priests are the more beautiful is the hat. I was greatly astonished at the chanting of the said Greeks, because it appeared to me that they chanted with great discords. Nevertheless I think this was due to the motive of the said procession, which was the general sadness.

Evidently, the custom of carrying icons, the distinct vestments of the Orthodox priests, and Byzantine isotonal chanting differed greatly from Italian practices in the fifteenth century.[89]

There are other instances where Orthodox and Latins shared religious customs. Apparently, Greeks and Latins occasionally used the cathedral of St. Titus at the same time. During Lent the sermon was delivered in the cathedral of Candia in both Greek and Latin for the benefit of those who did not know Italian.[90] Although the document is not explicit, it seems that it refers to Catholics who did not know Italian, that is, probably the wives of the nobility. There is, however, further indication that the Orthodox also had their own space inside the cathedral of St. Titus: in 1583 the traveler Nicholas Christophe Radzivil observed the Greeks holding offices at a Greek altar, located next to the Latin altar of the cathedral.[91] In the sixteenth century we have further evidence that the cathedral of St. Titus was used by both Greek and Latin priests three times a year: on Epiphany, All Saints Day, and the feast of St. Titus, the Latin and Greek clergy celebrated Mass together inside the cathedral in the presence of the government officials, the nobility, and the people.[92] With the exclusion of Epiphany, a major feast day for both Greeks and Latins, the other two days recall the two dedications of the cathedral in Byzantine and Venetian times: All Saints and St. Titus, respectively.[93] Both clergies chanted hymns to the pope, the Latin archbishop, the doge, and the duke of Candia. At this point it is impossible to establish with certainty whether the Greek priests who performed these services belonged to the Unionist clergy or were simply part of the 120 priests associated with the Latin archbishopric of Candia.

There are additional occasions that attracted Latins and Orthodox into the same church. For example, in addition to the monastery of St. Catherine which attracted donors of both Greek and Latin confessions because of its antique history and the special connection that Latin pilgrims had with Sinai since at least the period of the crusades, for three churches of Candia (St. Nicholas at the wharf, Madonnina, and the monastery of St. Jacob) there exist testimonies affirming an affiliation with both rites. Each one of them had a different function and history. The church of St. Nicholas was a private chapel erected by ser Michael Gradonigo in 1448 on the edge of the wharf next to the warehouse (no. 35, Fig. 103). Built over the portico of a preexisting structure, the chapel could be reached via a staircase.[94] Although it seems that the church served the Latins, in the seventeenth century it is recorded as a Greek rite church; yet, we have no information as to whether the chapel was ever converted from a Latin into an Orthodox building. The church of the Madonnina (known also as Santa Maria de Miraculis or Panagia tou forou) was located in the suburbs near the land gate of the city at the piazza (no. 103, Fig. 103) and was first mentioned in the will of Donatus Grioni in 1482.[95] It stood on the foundations of an earlier Byzantine church. Although Venetian noblemen acted as procurators of the church in 1499, it is recorded as a Greek Orthodox sanctuary the alms of which subsidized the salary of the Greek *protopapas* in 1492.[96] Most probably the church belonged to the Latin archbishopric of Candia but functioned primarily as a Greek Orthodox foundation; in 1625 the Latin archbishop reported that it had two altars, one "alla latina, poiche l'altro é alla greca."[97] It

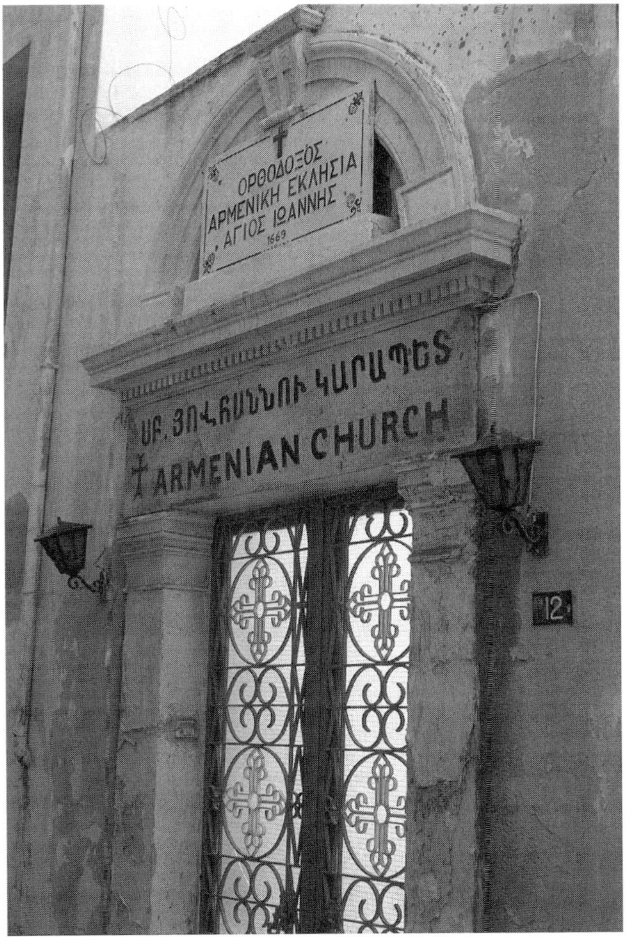

FIGURE 121. Herakleion, St. George Doriano, now Armenian church of St. John, entrance

was converted into the mosque of Reishub Kuttab Hazi Hussein Efendi by the Ottomans and was demolished in 1961.[98] The structure was a relatively small timber-roofed basilica, with two rows of square piers creating a round-arched arcade and separating a central nave from single side aisles.[99] A clerestory pierced with five pointed-arch windows let light into the church. Since this basilical space could have served both Latin and Orthodox rites, it must have been the particular furnishings and decoration that signaled the specific rite of the church and its clergy. Finally, the suburban monastery of St. Jacob (no. 52, Fig. 17), which was a possession of the bishop of Kalamon, often figured in the testaments of Latin faithful, as in the will of Thomasina Sclença of 1328, who wished to be buried in the monastery.[100] There is, however, some indication that it once was a Greek church.[101] The original church was an old structure of small scale, which was enlarged around 1290; this enlargement possibly entailed the construction of a gallery, recorded in 1373.[102] Does this indicate a conversion of the building from the Latin to the Orthodox rite, or a simultaneous use of the church by both Latins and Orthodox?

THE ARMENIAN MINORITY

The Orthodox population of Crete can hardly be thought of as a minority within the space of the city. Before we turn to the treatment of the Jewish community we should dwell briefly on another Christian community that settled on Crete in the middle of the fourteenth century: the Armenians. Following the war between the Venetians and the Genoese a relatively large number of Armenians and their families (two thousand) from the Black Sea were given permission to settle on Crete. As in the case of the leadership of the Greek community of Candia, it was an Armenian priest who negotiated the arrangement with the duke of Crete and then with the Senate in Venice.[103]

In 1363 Armenians originating from the Black Sea obtained permission from the Venetian Senate to settle on the island of Crete. Two documents from the Venetian Archives (Senato Misti) of June 8 and July 1 of that year record the terms for the transportation and settlement of the group. The second document was published by Theotokis. These people were accepted in Candia and were given a church, which had already been known as the Armenian church. This is the first documentary indication that I know of that surmises the presence of Armenians on Crete. What is more interesting is that this church, which is still owned by the small Armenian community of Herakleion, had been located in the earlier Jewish quarter. The church of St. George Doriano is located in the western suburbs of Candia near the *strada imperiale* (Fig. 121, and no. 125, Fig. 17). The Armenian settlers were promised an empty stretch of land in the vicinity of the church to build the houses of their community. They were also awarded the privilege to live in already existing houses in the vicinity with the understanding that the persons who were displaced would be compensated. Finally, since this was an arrangement before the arrival of the immigrants, the Armenians had also negotiated for a reasonably priced transport from the Black Sea to Candia on Venetian vessels. Furthermore, the immigrants were promised that they would attain Venetian citizenship in four years. We don't know for a fact whether this sizable group of Armenian refugees reached Crete or another colony. Maybe the outbreak of the revolt of St Titus in August 1363 delayed the group or prevented them from reaching Candia. Another flow of Armenians from the southern coast of the Black Sea this time applied for residency in Candia in 1414. The Senate was again favorable to their request but it is not clear whether they moved to Candia or Negroponte.[104]

SEVEN

SEGREGATION WITHIN THE WALLS: THE JUDAICA

THE JEWRY OF CANDIA

As many Byzantine cities of Greece with a strong mercantile bent, the port cities that became parts of the Venetian empire had significant Jewish communities. The twelfth-century Jewish traveler Benjamin of Tudela recorded many of these communities in the Byzantine empire, but unfortunately he did not visit Crete.[1] Following administrative tactics similar to those used in the case of the Greek community, the elders of the Jewish community of Candia were responsible for electing the *contestabile/condestabulo*, a figure who was not necessarily a religious personage but was considered the head of the synagogue and of the community at large.[2] Despite this similarity in organization, however, the position of the Jewish community of Candia lies in great contrast to that of the Greek community in the allocation of urban space.[3] The Judaica,[4] as the Jewish quarter was called by the Venetians, occupied the northwestern part of the city, a neighborhood vulnerable to attacks from sea and land and located near the tanneries, which were a source of undesirable odor and waste.[5] The Jews had thus been forced to settle in a bad neighborhood that had no appeal to the Venetians or to their predecessors.

Strong evidence suggests that a Jewish quarter existed already in Byzantine Chandax and that the Venetians did not change it considerably until the end of the thirteenth century.[6] Apparently, there existed in Byzantium a law confining the Jews (and other ethnic groups) to one area of the city (quarter), as Benjamin of Tudela asserted in 1165. However, this law was not strictly enforced in Constantinople since the twelfth-century patriarch Eustathios of Thessaloniki (c. 1175–85) complained that Jews lived everywhere in the city, even inside Christian houses adorned with sacred images.[7] We may therefore assume that enforcement was lax in other localities as well. These customs were in agreement with the prescriptions of the Latin church on the subject: the Third Lateran Council of 1179 forbade Jews and Christians to dwell together, but this decision was not followed to the letter.[8] It is not until the end of the thirteenth century that charges of host desecration and permanent expulsions of Jews indicate that the position of the Jews of Europe deteriorates.[9] Not surprisingly the position of Venice toward the Jewry of Candia responded to international trends against the Jews or to a particular situation in the metropole.

The Jewish community of Crete appears in the Latin and Greek versions of the treaty signed between Venice and the Byzantine rebel *archon* Alexios Calergis (1299): the treaty provided that Jews could live wherever they wished and could own landed property.[10] We should regard this measure not as an innovation related to the situation of the Jews by Venice and its colonial authorities, but rather as a confirmation of earlier Byzantine practices, like other points of the treaty of 1299, which were concessions that the Republic made to the victorious rebel. Earlier references to Jewish inhabitants of Candia suggest that until the midthirteenth century the Jewish population was not confined to a particular area. Jews seem to have inhabited two distinct spots, one of which was the Judaica inside the city, the other the area around the suburban church of St. George Doriano (no. 125 in Werdmüller's plan, Fig. 17), which was located close to the *strada larga*. This was the church that in 1363 was given to the Armenian settlers from the Black Sea (see the discussion in Chapter 6). Furthermore, the *burgesie* of the Venetian feudatories included lands in the Judaica, which clearly was considered an integral part of the city.[11]

The situation changed in the fourteenth century, when the limits of the Judaica were emphatically delineated in a decree of the Maggior Consiglio in Venice (1334): no Jews could own or rent property outside the limits of their quarter; special state permission was needed to rent houses located outside the formal limits of the Judaica.[12] What provoked the Venetians to impose the physical segregation of the Jewish community from the Christian population in the early fourteenth century? Could it have been prompted by issues of security related to the situation in the Venetian quarter in Constantinople? It seems that in 1324 the Venetians of Constantinople were worried about the safety of their settlement and asked the Byzantine emperor for a new, safer quarter in Constantinople enclosed with walls (*locus conclusus*), possibly modeled after the area that the Byzantines had awarded to the Genoese in Pera across from the Golden Horn following their reestablishment in the city in 1261.[13] Whether or not similar concerns affected the actions of the Venetians in Crete, the policy of ethnic separation of the Jews of Candia was not absolute until the fifteenth century.

It is clear that by 1390, when a new arch (decorated with the lion of St. Mark and coats of arms) was put up as a marker of the southeastern limit of the Jewish quarter, the Judaica had become a separate entity within the city. The arch spanned the street to the south of the Judaica: the houses on the south side of the street could only be inhabited by Christians, whereas those on the north side belonged to the Judaica. The Jewish households had to block the doors and windows that had previously opened onto that street.[14] It is likely that this act restricted the size of the Judaica somewhat. Was this related to events in the metropole? Indeed, at the same time the authorities in Venice had to deal with the question of Jewish settlement in their city and a similar segregational policy was instituted in the mother city and the colonies. In 1385 the Senate had lured Jewish moneylenders into Venice because the state was in need of cash after the Black Death and especially during the war of Chioggia: the state offered the Jews a special quarter for their establishment in the city and a vineyard on Lido to use as a cemetery.[15] However, in 1388, when the war was over and moneylending was no longer essential to the state, the authorities modified the prior agreement by demanding that the Jews reside together in a quarter separate from the Christian population of the city. Finally, in 1394 the Senate decided to expel Jews from Venice altogether: after the expiration of the ten-year charter of 1387 no Jew was to reside in Venice for more than fifteen days, during which he had to display a yellow badge on his exterior clothing.[16] This eviction encouraged many Jews to move from Venice to Candia.[17] Whether this decision was an outcome of internal problems caused by the behavior of the Jewish moneylenders or a reflection of Venice's fear of a large Jewish settlement in the city when the services of moneylenders were no longer needed, it seems that its repercussions were felt on Crete as well.

In the fifteenth century the Candiote Jewish quarter was almost completely surrounded by walls. The eastern border of the quarter had been delimited by the Dominican monastery of St. Peter the Martyr since the thirteenth century. Since the early fifteenth century the Jews living across from the monastery had been accused of peeping into the interior of the church. In 1450 the Jews were ordered to block their windows and balconies facing the monastery and to build a wall high enough to block any visual contact between the monastery and the Judaica.[18] As a result, in 1450 the third side of the Jewish quarter was separated from the Christian city by a wall. These segregational walls were justified as pious means to "protect" the Christians from sacrilegious looks from the Judaica. This act against the Jewish community is likely to have been prompted by the powerful campaign against the moneylending activities of the Jews mounted by the Franciscans in the midfifteenth century. The friars were in favor of the newly instituted *monti di pietà,* the new philanthropic moneylending institutions connected to the church.[19]

The segregation of the Jewish community was further highlighted in 1430 when the Jews of Candia were compelled, like the Jews of Venice, to display a yellow badge on their outer garments. The purpose of this badge was to distinguish them from the Christians when they circulated inside the city presumably in order to protect them against violence from the Christians.[20] At this time there is also evidence that the Jewish population was expected to keep Christian holidays and apparently to work on the Sabbath. In 1407 a document from the statutes of Modon spells out the feast days that the Jews ought to observe: in addition to every Sunday, Christmas, Epiphany, Presentation, Circumcision, Annunciation, Easter, Corpus Christi, Pentecost, Dormition of the Virgin, Nativity of the Virgin (September 8; this was probably a holiday particular to Modon), St. Mark's feast day in April, St. Peter and Paul in June, St. John the Baptist, St. Jacob the Major, St. Laurence, St. Luke, St. Matthew, St. Andrew, St. Philip, and St. Jacob.[21] Some years later (1465) the *justiciarii* in Candia were ordered not to burst into Jewish houses at any hour just to check whether the people worked on feast days; it was decided that whereas Jews working outside the home during Christian holidays were to be convicted, they were allowed to work at home.[22]

At approximately the same time (1423) the government of Venice promulgated a radical decree that forbade Jews in all Venetian territories to buy or possess land outside the limits of the Jewish quarters.[23] Interestingly, the same decree had been promulgated in the island of Corfu in 1406: the Jewish community had to give up all animals and landed possessions that they owned in the city and the countryside except within the limits of the Jewish quarter. The decision was modified two years later when it was calculated that Jews could keep property worth up to four thousand gold ducats but could not have *villani* attached to their land.[24] In 1496 a previously unnoticed series of notarial acts implies that the Council of Forty in Venice decreed against the property rights of the Jews even inside the Judaica of Candia.[25] The available data do not allow us to determine whether this was a decision against all Jewish property, or whether it was geared toward a special group of individuals who had offended the state. The names that are mentioned in the notarial acts, e.g. Casan, Ballaça, Vergioti, and Balbo, indicate wealthy Jewish families who owned large estates in the Judaica. Thus, although the situation in the colonies was much better than that in Venice, the legal status of the Jews had worsened considerably since Byzantine times.

Despite the deteriorating position of the Jewish settlement of Candia, there is no evidence of a guarded gate regulating the movement of Jews about the city. On the contrary, the gate of the Judaica that opened in the northwestern section of the city walls was meant to facilitate business traffic for Jewish and other merchants: it was the Jewish community who had to pay for the enlargement of the gate in 1464 because the authorities felt that it was they who were going to benefit most from it.[26] Not only was the Jewish community free to enter or exit the city through this gate, but the Jews of Crete were free to migrate to other Venetian territories, such as Constantinople or Padua, and other Western European cities to attend foreign jeshivas.[27] According to Foscarini's account on the Jews of Candia in 1577, there were also Jews who lived outside the Judaica of Candia, in the Dermata bay area and in the area adjoining the "Jews' Gate."[28] This freedom of passage is corroborated by the special permits granted in the late fourteenth century to Jewish merchants for renting stores outside their quarter; clearly, the Judaica and its merchants must have played a significant commercial role in Candia.

Of the four synagogues that served the community in the fifteenth century only one existed until World War II (Fig. 122).[29] Already by 1228 there must have been two synagogues in the city, one of which is specifically named: that of the prophet Elijah, which was the oldest synagogue on Crete.[30] The second synagogue may be the one included in the *Takkanoth* of 1363: its Greek name was *Kretiko*, i.e. that of Crete.[31] Could this be identified with the synagogue with a portico built after 1260 on the territory offered to Eleazar and to other Jews by Petrus Quirino?[32] An alternative name for one of these synagogues may be the *Chochanim* synagogue (the synagogue of the *cohen*/priest), or its hellenized form *Chochanitico*.[33]

By 1363 a third synagogue stood in the Judaica of Candia: like that of Kretiko, it had both a Hebrew and a Greek name, the latter being *Siviliatiko*.[34] The name probably refers to the Spanish city of Seville, indicating that Jews had immigrated from Spain as early as the middle of the fourteenth century.[35] The synagogue had been commissioned by the ancestors of Cagus, who was the legal owner in 1373 and had paid the large expenses for the upkeep of the building;[36] in 1415 his son, Jaco, offered the synagogue to the community under the condition that he would have a say in its administration and management.[37] The Jewish statutes also mention the Great Synagogue in 1530, which may be a different name for the *Siviliatico* synagogue that was administered by the community.[38]

A fourth prayerhouse was erected in 1432 on the main street of the Judaica. It was situated on the third floor of four contiguous houses belonging to the widow Elea Nomico. In her testament, Elea made provisions for the construction of an elegant entrance giving access to the prayerhouse.[39] On the basis of the loftiness of this synagogue, David Jacoby proposed the

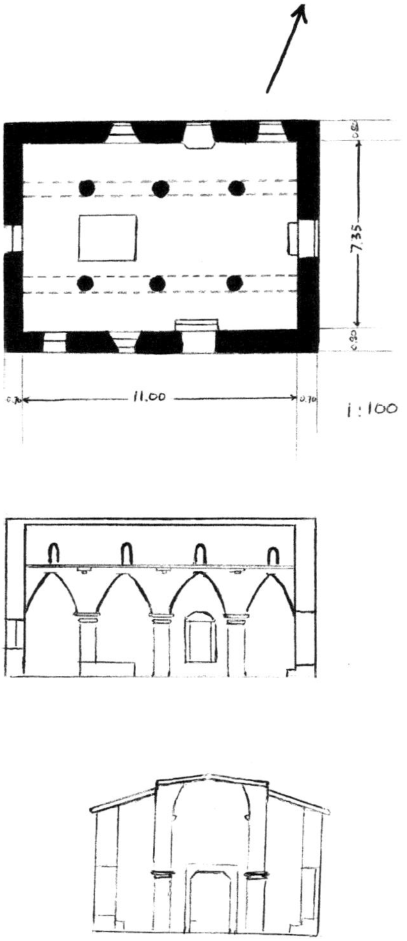

FIGURE 122. Herakleion, plan of the Lower Synagogue, 1942, after Stergios Spanakis

identification of Elea's synagogue with the High Synagogue (*Beth ha-Knesseth ha-Gavoah*) mentioned in the communal statutes of the Jewish community in 1529 and in later Ottoman documents.[40] In 1496 there is mention of yet another synagogue name, that of *Alamanico*, indicating a German/Ashkenazic origin; constructed around 1400, this synagogue commemorated the German origin of the father of the donor, Abba b. Judah Delmedigo.[41]

Although what remains from the residences of the Jewish quarter is minimal, archival sources tell us a lot about the special status and form of the houses in the Judaica. Property in the Judaica was owned by the Venetian feudal lords and a few wealthy Jewish families, so that the nonelite people lived in rental housing.[42] Internal mechanisms of the community attempted to protect the tenants from injustices committed against them by their landlords: one of the communal statutes prescribed that if a landlord had evicted a Jew from his residence (presumably in the Judaica), all Jews had to boycott this house and not rent it for a whole year.[43]

One of the immediate effects of the enclosed nature of the quarter was the density of the population therein. Not only were the rents in the Judaica almost as high as those for the houses in the *ruga magistra* in the midfourteenth century, but the houses rose higher and higher to comprise three or four stories.[44] A similar situation with multiple-story houses was also present in the ghetto of Venice in later times (Fig. 133). Apart from height, the houses of the Judaica must have looked like the other houses of the city. This seems especially true for the elite houses. When Gerola visited Herakleion in the early twentieth century a complex of three houses was still standing in the Judaica; one photograph of these remains was published (Fig. 123). The difference in their building technique led Gerola to think that these houses were made in different periods but constituted a typical example of elite residences in the city.[45] The first one was built with fine ashlar masonry. In the ground floor there were traces of two circular arcades and a door surmounted by an architrave, which would indicate a date in the fifteenth century. The upper story had a balcony, as the three surviving corbels indicated, and a window that was marked by a simple circular molding. The family coat of arms was imprinted in a decorated cornerstone, but its poor state of preservation did not allow an identification with any known escutcheon. The second house had a highly decorated doorway that betrayed a date in the sixteenth century. Few sculptural vestiges remained in the third house.

In addition to these scanty archaeological remains, the general appearance of private residences can be inferred from the accounts in notarial acts stipulating contracts for work undertaken in residences. One such early account dates from 1300 and comes from the books of the notary Pietro Pizolo. The mason Petrus Gracianus signed a contract with the Jew Anastasus, son of Tefilactus (Theophylaktos), for the construction of a house inside the Jewish quarter. The walls on three sides of the house (north, south, and a transverse wall) had to be made of limestone measuring 1½ feet (52 centimeters); this information probably indicates that the wall should be built with regularly cut blocks of limestone. It also shows that the building techniques used in the Judaica were similar to those used in the city proper. The house had to be as high as that of Anastasus Arinco and have good foundations. In addition, the mason had to pierce three doors and a window. Two of the doors (on the south side and on the transverse wall) and the window should be framed with wide, fine blocks of stone. The other door on the

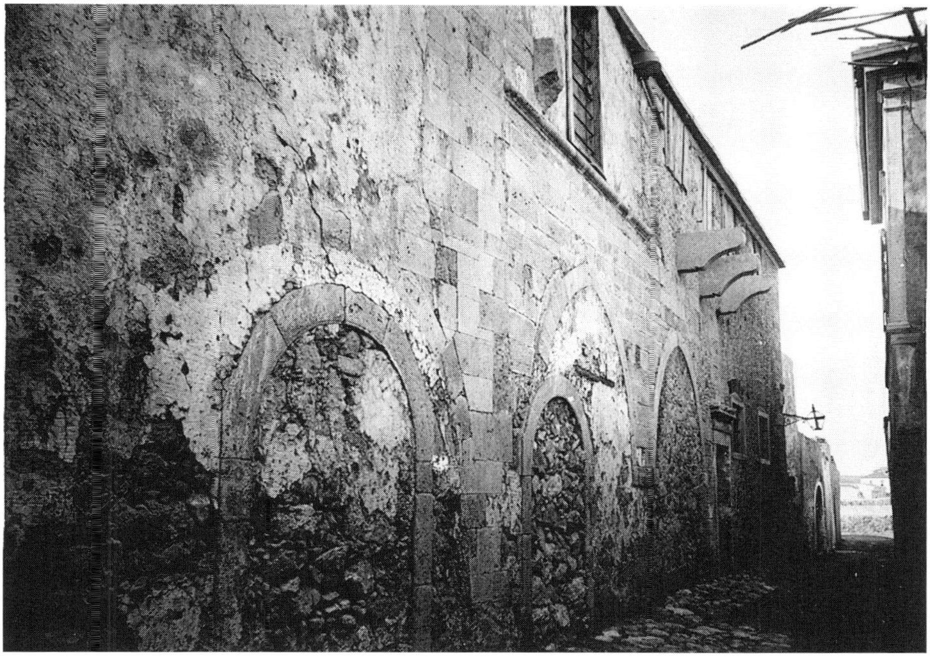

FIGURE 123. Herakleion, remains of houses in the Judaica (Istituto Veneto di Scienze, Lettere ed Arti. Venezia. Archivio fotografico della Missione in Creta di Giuseppe Gerola)

transverse wall (*tresa*) in the upper story should be made of blocks of medium size (*maçachanis*). Finally, the whole should be covered with a roof, made of wood and shrubs.[46] Additional information on the Jewish households can be gleaned from court cases judged by the Venetian authorities. For example, in 1405 the rabbi Çadoch asked that his neighbor, Michael de David, should demolish the oven that he abutted on the wall of the rabbi's house.[47]

The waterfront at the Jewish quarter was occupied by a series of imposing mansions that have occasionally impressed the travelers of the period. For example, in 1571 a Venetian official, Lorenzo da Mula, described the Jewish quarter as being full of handsome houses and mansions located in the most elegant and beautiful part of town.[48] Z. Ankori has argued that these mansions belonged to the few wealthy italianized Jews, who never constituted more than 20 percent of the Jewish population of the city.[49] Few of these structures have yielded any remains. Between the actual Xenia hotel and the Historical Museum of Crete, on the southern edge of the *stenon*, the façade and the walls of a fine Venetian-Jewish mansion stood until the 1960s, but unfortunately no photographs of this structure were available to me.[50] A coat of arms with Hebrew characters of the sixteenth century, which probably decorated the façade of one of these mansions, is preserved in the Historical Museum of Crete in Herakleion. A true landmark of the Judaica were the houses of Sabbatai Casani, later known as the houses of Judah Casani. This estate belonged to one of the most important Jewish families in Crete and was located close to the High Synagogue. The majority of the Jewish residences, however, were small houses lacking the open areas that the other city dwellers enjoyed. In the words of Evliya Çelebi efendi in the seventeenth century all the Jews of Candia "have small as well as large decrepit houses, 300 hopeless dwellings." And he goes on: "Altogether there were 300 fenced-in vegetable gardens, ponds, rose gardens, and in each of them one or two wells of water of life."[51]

There is one domain where the Jews seem to have enjoyed more freedom: their work space. The decrees defining the limits of Jewish presence in the city differentiated between residential and work space. So, when at the end of the fourteenth century the Jews were categorically forbidden to reside outside the Judaica, they could still rent shops located near their quarter with special permission from the authorities. For example, in 1391 the Christian Johannes Basilio was allowed to rent three shops that he owned to Jews. The conditions of the lease were very strict: the renters were not allowed to live or sleep in these shops at night; they were only permitted to keep their merchandise therein.[52] Clearly, in contrast to Jewish households, Jewish businesses did not necessarily contaminate the Christian image of the city. This conforms with the typical makeup of the marketplace in most medieval cities of the Levant, where artisans and merchants were grouped by trade and not by ethnicity. In this context it is interesting to point out that from the fourteenth century on, Candiote Jewry asked its members to follow the sounding of the vesper bells in the Dominican church St. Peter the Martyr in timing their cessation of work on Fridays.[53] This may indicate that the members of the Jewish community were really more integrated in the life of the city than the documentation might suggest.

JEWISH QUARTERS IN THE VENETIAN EMPIRE

The city of Negroponte in Euboea also had a significant Jewish community that antedated the arrival of the Venetians. Benjamin of Tudela mentions the Jewish community of the city in his twelfth-century travel account. The first time that the Jewish merchants of Negroponte figure in Venetian sources is in 1290, when a new tax regulation was instituted: they had to pay 5 percent whenever they traveled.[54] In the thirteenth century the Negroponte Jewry was located in the southern suburb of the city outside the city wall but originally seems to have shared the space with new immigrants to the area. Their quarter was the first among all Jewish quarters in Venetian colonies to be segregated from the rest of the city. In 1304 the Senate in Venice decided that the Jewish quarter of Chalkis be enclosed by walls probably for reasons of security. However, this measure was not enough to secure the lives and possessions of the Jews of Negroponte outside the city walls during the period of Turkish incursions and other enemy attacks in the fourteenth century, so the Jewish population moved inside the fortified city. In 1355 the Senate in Venice recognized this status quo and the Jews of Negroponte were awarded a small quarter therein. It was clear, however, that once admitted within the city walls, the Jewish population had to reside in this quarter which was separated from the rest of the city (i.e. its Christian inhabitants) by a wall.[55] This new Jewish quarter was located between the cathedral church (now Hagia Paraskeve) and the part of the city walls that were adjacent to the old Zudecha in the suburbs, that is, to the southeast section of the church. Unlike the situation in most Jewish quarters throughout the Mediterranean region, this new Jewish settlement did not possess a temple. By law the Jews were not allowed to perform their rites inside the city, so in 1359 they were given permission to leave the city in order to get to the synagogue. They were also exempted from guarding the walls on Fridays.[56] Thus, one may assume that the gate of the Zudecha in the city walls was precisely the point in the walls through which the Jewish community reached the synagogue in their old quarter. The surviving synagogue is a nineteenth-century temple that replaced the older synagogue, which was destroyed by a fire in 1847; it is located on 27 Kotsou street.[57]

Until this moment in the fourteenth century it seems that the measures regarding the Jewish settlement were not instigated by strong anti-Jewish sentiments. But by the beginning of the fifteenth century the climate had changed and we attest a different tone in the treatment of the Jewish inhabitants of Negroponte. In 1402 the former *bailo* of Negroponte warned the Senate in Venice that unless measures were taken, the Jewish community was soon going to own all possessions of the Christians. As a result, the Senate decreed that in the future all acquisition of land by Jews inside or outside the city would be considered illegal, except inside their quarter. Furthermore, all Jewish landed property had to be sold promptly. Moreover, the Senate ordered that the gates leading to the Jewish quarter should be closed permanently, except for the three main gates, which would serve the coming and going of the Jews into their quarter.[58] After 1423, even the privilege of owning land inside their quarter was taken away from them. In

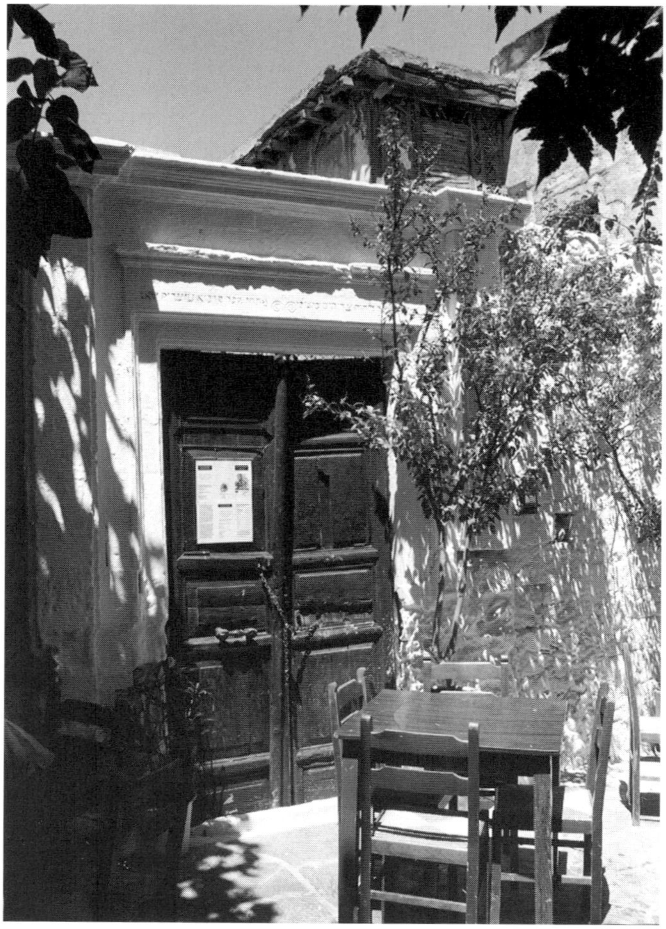

FIGURE 124. Chania, synagogue, east façade

1425 the Jews got permission to erect a wall along two streets of their quarter that led to the Christian section of town.[59] In 1440 the Jewish quarter was enlarged to encompass the settlement of new Jewish immigrants from Euboea and mainland Greece in Negroponte, who were allowed to buy houses outside the boundaries of their old quarter.[60] The community was responsible for constructing another wall to encircle their expanded quarter. The Jewish cemetery of Negroponte was located near the hill of Velibaba, to the southeast.[61]

Canea/Chania had a large Jewish community that continued to exist well into the twentieth century; in the second half of the sixteenth century its population was reportedly three hundred souls.[62] This community must have been formed after the arrival of the Venetians on the island, because we first hear of it in 1325, when the Senate in Venice authorized the rector

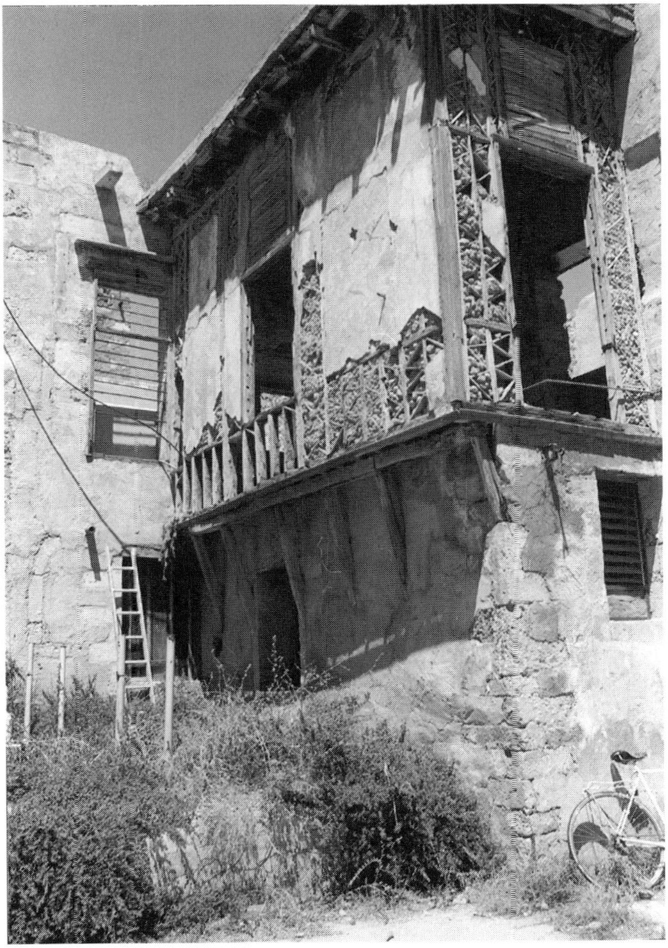

FIGURE 125. Chania, synagogue, remains of the interior

to place the Jewish community in any part of the suburbs he thought convenient.[63] Nine years later this quarter was a fact: it was relegated to the northwestern portion of the suburbs.[64] Located outside the city walls, the Jewish quarter of Canea was served by two synagogues that were recorded and described by Zvi Ankori in 1970. The medieval synagogue, called *Kehal Hayyim* (Old Synagogue), was on Kondylaki street behind the church of St. Francis.[65] The building, originally a fifteenth-century Venetian church, was turned into a synagogue in the seventeenth century. Until the mid-1990s, when the ceiling collapsed, it survived almost intact as a private residence (Figs. 124–126). It is currently being restored by the World Monuments Fund. In form it resembles the single-nave churches of the island, but the remaining reliefs around the door and its windows indicate a rather lavish

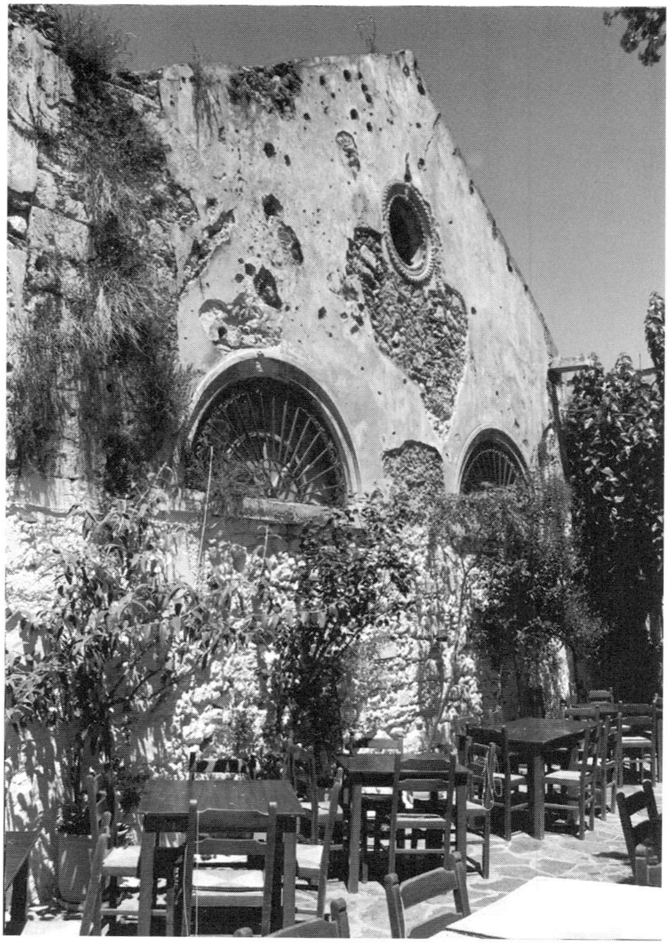

FIGURE 126. Chania, synagogue, decorative details

structure with a second-story section for women (*mehitza*). The dedicatory inscription on the lintel bears the date 1521 and features the name of Michael Geni[a]ti, but the outer gate of the courtyard contains an older undecipherable inscription.[66]

The second synagogue was located on a parallel street, which was one of the two main streets of the Canea Judaica. Its name, *Kehal Shalom* (New Synagogue), was given to the building in the late nineteenth century when it was inaugurated. However, Ankori maintains that the actual building replaced an older prayerhouse dating back to 1487, because the popular name of the area refers to a synagogue and the remains of an inscription attest to the existence of a Jewish prayerhouse there since the fifteenth century.

A Jewish quarter was also part of the suburbs of Retimo/Rethymnon: it was located close to the old fortifications of the city as we learn from Jewish petitions to open windows in the city walls and to abut their residences against these walls.[67] In 1386 the Senate in Venice ordered the reopening of an old synagogue that had been closed by Pietro Grimani in return for the Jewish monetary contribution that allowed the refurbishing of the harbor.[68] No traces of an enclosed Jewish quarter exist in Retimo, and two documents of the fifteenth century suggest that the Jews of Retimo enjoyed greater freedom than in the other cities of the island. In 1412 a Senate decree maintained that the Jews occupied almost all the shops in the area on and around the *platea* of the city.[69] More compelling evidence for the absence of walls limiting the Judaica of Retimo is provided by a document of 1448 that suggests that the boundaries of the Judaica were indicated by crosses.[70]

In 1391 certain Jews are recorded living in the suburbs of Modon.[71] This is corroborated by a travel account of 1442, which reported that only Venetians could live inside the fortified city of Modon in the Peloponnesos, whereas the other ethnic groups lived in the suburbs. Bernhardt von Breydenbach's *Peregrinatio ad Terram Sanctam* (1486) also maintains that the large Jewish community of Modon was relegated to the suburbs near the quarter of the gypsies. However, in 1481 Meshullam b. Menahem reported that three hundred Jewish families of merchants and artisans lived inside the city walls, probably indicating that by that point new walls had enveloped the suburbs of the city.[72] Among the main occupations of the Jewish inhabitants of Modon was the silk industry and leather production, already attested in 1389.[73] Latins and Greeks were also involved in the leather business, which must have been highly controlled by the state as leather goods had to be sold exclusively in the public square and not privately.[74]

A significant Jewish community lived in Corfu/Kerkyra until the Second World War. The community must have been formed at some point between the twelfth century, when the traveler Benjamin of Tudela recorded only one Jew in Corfu, and the early fourteenth century, when the Angevin kings confirm certain privileges of the Jewish community (1317, 1324, 1365, and 1370). From all these decrees it is obvious that there was a significant Jewish presence in the city of Corfu before the arrival of the Venetians in 1387. Specific charters of the Angevin rulers of the island provided a safe haven for immigrant Levantine and Italian Jews in the next years; their synagogue was in the Campiello district. A particular event demonstrates the importance of the community in the Angevin period: one of the six representatives of Corfu who went to Venice in 1386 to seek the protection of the Republic was the Jewish David Semo. Until the large immigration of Sephardic and Apulian Jews (following 1492 and 1540, respectively) to Corfu, the main language of the community was Greek, indicating an Oriental origin.[75] Numerical data of the seventeenth and eighteenth centuries indicate the growing importance of the community following the expulsion of the Jews from Granada. The Venetian *bailo* Antonio Foscari reported that the four hundred Jews of the city of Corfu lived among the Christians – presumably without a distinct quarter of their own. The historian Marmora, who wrote an extensive history of Corfu, recorded five hundred Jewish houses in town in 1665, and in 1760 the *provveditore* Grimani reported that the Jewish community numbered 1,171 people of 44,333, the total population of the town.[76] Multiple decrees of the Venetian Senate show that on the one hand the Jewish community was harassed and obstructed from performing even basic everyday functions (like buying bread, vegetables, and foodstuffs or getting water from the public well), and on the other that the Venetian authorities tried to restrain the ire of the people against the Jewish community.[77]

In the early fifteenth century the community was divided in separate quarters inside and outside the city walls, in the burg. At the time when new walls encircled the town and its suburbs (1524) the Jewish population had to move among the Christian population, until, in response to several petitions of the residents, a separate quarter was given to the Jews, located in the lowest part of town beyond the church of the Virgin Hodegetria. High walls enclosed their quarter by 1562 or 1592 at the latest.[78] The three major streets of the Jewish quarter (now called Velissariou, Haghias Sophias, and Palaiologou streets) ran perpendicular to the two main thoroughfares of the city, the *cale dei mercatanti* (Nikephorou Theotoki street) and the *cale delle Acque* or *strada Reale* (Eugeniou Boulgareos street).[79] Of the three main synagogues of the city only the Suola Greca survives: it is a seventeenth-century basilical building with the temple functioning in the upper story and the ground floor used for community services.[80]

THE POLITICS OF SEGREGATION

Was there a grand strategy that the Venetians employed in their treatment of the Jewish community in their colonies? Even if we account for the fact that Candia had a significant Jewish community, the incorporation of the Judaica within the small space enveloped by the city walls demands some explanation as it is different from what we see throughout Venice's empire. In the previous chapter I argued that the relegation to the suburbs of the new Orthodox cathedral, the symbol of the Greek community of Candia, signified an attempt to restrain the power of this community. Following the same reasoning, in observing the Jewish settlement we can assume that the existence of at least four synagogues within the city of Candia does not suggest that the Venetian colonists saw the Jewish community as threatening to their power. To be sure, conversion of Latin Christians to Judaism must not have been an issue, whereas Orthodoxy was a viable alternative for the colonists, especially those married to locals. It is also true that the synagogues were less accessible than the Orthodox churches of the suburbs since the Jewish temples were located not only outside the civic center of the city but also within the limits of the Jewish quarter. The Jewish community was spatially incorporated in the fortified city but was excluded from every official manifestation of colonial life.

To be sure the most important members of the community must have been quite well off and were we to look only at them we would have a biased view of the position of the Jewish community in the Venetian colonies. We know for instance that Elijah Capsali, son of the *condestabulo* of the Jewish community of Candia, was able at the end of the fifteenth century to travel to Italy to study the Talmud and to be trained as a rabbi; he was also a historian. In fact, his chronicle records an instance when a nun accused the Jewish community of Candia of desecrating the host: as a result of the accusation nine members of the community were arrested and were taken in front of the Avogaria di Comun in Venice, where two of them died. Having insufficient evidence to convict them, the Maggior Consiglio had to acquit them in 1452 and again in 1454.[81] Evidently, such a false accusation was extremely disruptive, if not fatal, for the Jewish community, who had little means to pressure the authorities. The one individual who managed to influence the authorities is David Maurogonato of Candia, who made his living as a secret agent for the Republic in the 1460s: he was allowed not to wear the yellow sign and to settle anywhere he wanted on the island of Crete, as well as to own state property.[82] Part of the reward for his services was to obtain assurances that the overzealous behavior of the authorities would be regulated so that the everyday life of the Jewish community of Candia would improve. The content of the surviving decrees shows the vast distance between the Venetian rhetoric of tolerance and the actual situation of its subjects as denounced by David: the *justiciarii* would apparently burst into the houses of the Judaica at any time day or night to check whether people worked on a feast day; the Jews could be fined for keeping their doors open at night or for walking in their quarter without carrying a torch; they were prohibited to buy food before the third hour of the day; or they had to work as executioners even on the Sabbath.[83]

The precarious position of the Jewish community observed in the shifting fortunes of the quarters throughout the colonies is also reflected in the participation of the community in public events and festivities. The civic ceremonial of Venetian Candia, with its strong religious connotations, prescribed once and for all the role of the Jewish community in the official civic life of the colony. Unlike the desired participation of the Greek Orthodox community, Jewish presence was inappropriate or even dangerous to the civic image of Venetian Candia. Following a much earlier practice the Fourth Lateran Council of 1215 decreed that during the three days before Easter the Jews were to be confined inside their quarter so as not to scandalize the Christians.[84] When there were public processions centering on the Holy Sacrament, the cross, or religious icons Jews had to leave or show their reverence by kneeling on the ground until the end of the procession.[85] All Christians formed one corporation and Jews had no part in this society.[86] There are few documented instances when the Jewish community was required to participate in public events. Elijah Capsali in his chronicle reports that during the festivals that celebrated the treaty of Venice, Pope Julius II, and Spain in 1511, forty Jews performed war dances in the court of the ducal palace in Candia.[87] In addition to this unique occasion, another more regular occurrence must have had a longer tradition. In the seventeenth century the Jewish community was required to participate in the public reception of a new Latin archbishop in the towns of Candia and Corfu.[88] The compulsory presence of the Jewish community at this ceremony promoted the authority of the head of the Latin church as the spiritual leader of the whole population on the island. The Jews were allowed to be present only to show their submission to the Christian religious authorities and to hear a sermon about their erroneous faith. This religious antagonism, most forcefully carried out by the Mendicant friars, seems to have played a major role in forming popular opinion against the Jews of Candia. It comes as no surprise, therefore, that at the very moment when the Monti di Pietà tried to take over the economic power of the Jewish moneylenders, the Dominicans of Candia accused the Jewish community of sacrilegious acts. The proximity of the Jewish quarter to the civic authorities and to their religious partners allowed the colonial authorities to confine and sometimes suffocate the Jewish establishment within the walls of Candia.

Hence, the acceptance of the Jews within the boundaries of the city did not reflect a privileged position in the social hierarchy of the colony. On the contrary, the proximity of the Judaica to the central government offices placed it under immediate surveillance of the state; this was the most effective means to regulate their presence and economic activity in the city. Professional Jews – tanners, local merchants, moneylenders, and physicians – may have become indispensable to the Venetian government of Candia for their trade expertise. This Jewish minority was also important to the Venetian authorities for its monetary contributions to the state while not constituting a political threat to the existing government. In contrast, the numerous Greek merchants, artisans, landowners, and aristocrats were instrumental in the creation of a homogeneous civic image of Venetian Crete. Like that of the Byzantine cathedral of St. Titus, the presence of the Greek Orthodox was necessary for the well-being of the colony. Thus, they had access to most economic resources of the city and were allowed to conduct business in the old city. The Orthodox community was even permitted to attend Mass inside Venetian churches.

The notarial records of the fourteenth century that have been recently explored as well as the information that we possess on the social structure of Venetian Crete in the fifteenth, sixteenth, and seventeenth centuries lead us to assume that the Greeks and Jews of Venetian Candia gradually stretched their sphere of action and influence well beyond the limits that the Venetians had originally intended for the non-Venetian nobility in the thirteenth century. We know that by the middle of the fifteenth century the Greek population had fairly good economic and social standing: Greeks were successful merchants, painters, and professionals, and many of them were regarded by the Venetians as significant members of the cultural elite of the island.[89] Careful scrutiny of the documentary material also allows glimpses into the social and financial position of the Jews in Candia. For example, in the fourteenth century the state demanded an increasingly higher annual contribution from the Jewish community (from 980 hyperpera in the period 1310–20 the amount rose gradually to 4,000 hyperpera in 1395), claiming that Jewish fortunes had multiplied.[90] The authorities go as far as to describe the Jews as "rich and powerful" by 1439.[91] However inconclusive and one-sided, this analysis suggests that the situation of the Candiote Jewry resembled that of the Greeks: individual members of the Jewish community were successful merchants, moneylenders, doctors, and literary figures, who could afford luxurious houses and who could occasionally influence the political scene, as in the case of David Maurogonato (discussed earlier).[92] How were these new social relationships among Venetians, Greeks, and Jews first generated in the thirteenth and fourteenth centuries?[93]

In certain ways the Venetians were "trapped" in their own grandiose plans to create and head a magnificent empire in the Levant. The tacit acquiescence – if not the support – of the local population was crucial for the preservation of peace on Crete. The consent of the Greek and the Jewish populations of Crete was indispensable for the welfare of the island in pragmatic terms as well: the locals worked the land or acted as agents between the producers and the merchants. By the end of the thirteenth century the state was forced to accept the participation of the locals in the public life of Crete – at least in the professional sphere – and consequently had to condone their particular religious practices.

The presence of the Greek community within the walled city is closely related to the role that the physical boundaries of Candia played in the life of the city. Were the locals cut off from the city resources by the Venetian authorities, or was this access obstructed only symbolically? State regulations regarding the city walls are telling in this respect. For instance, the fact that in the fourteenth century Greeks and Jews were responsible for guarding portions of the city's ramparts indicates that the non-Latin inhabitants of Candia were deemed trustworthy and could participate in the defense of the city.[94] It seems, therefore, that the walls functioned primarily as a barrier for the outside enemies of the colony and not for the locals. The same is true of the city gates, which stood primarily as symbolic barriers in regard to accessibility to the city; one need only remember the Judaica gate, which was open to everyone (as discussed previously). At the same time, admittance inside the fortified city did not guarantee access to every part of the urban space. One assumes that the Venetian citizens of Candia would be privileged with access to public official structures reserved for the feudatories, such as the loggia.

As seen, the proximity of the various religious buildings to the urban core does not relate directly to the social and political status of the different groups. Simply viewing the map of Candia, we notice that the Jews are closer to the urban core than the Greeks, but this does not mean that the Jewish community was in a better position than the Greek community. As different from the Venetian elite, both Greeks and Jews were symbolically displaced from the Venetian core of the city. For the Greek population the fortifications of Candia constituted a barrier that denied access to the highest administrative posts of the colony but did not exclude religious structures. The Greeks played a major role in shaping the colonial image of Venetian Candia and were allowed to function and expand freely in the suburban area. On the other hand, the city walls obstructed the growth of the Jewish settlement beyond the confines of the Judaica. The activities of the Jews, who were spatially included in Candia, albeit in the worst section of town, were highly regulated and were never instrumental to the ritual life of Crete. In fact, although they were not entirely confined to their quarter, its mere existence set them apart from the Christian population of Candia; when in the Judaica, they became invisible to the rest of the city and to the outside world.

PART
THREE

SYMBOLS OF COLONIAL CONTROL

EIGHT

RITUALIZING COLONIAL PRACTICES

The administrative and religious topography of Candia constituted the stage on which the colonists and their subjects interacted according to – or in opposition – the prescriptions of the Venetian administration. The social relationships and interdependence of the different ethnic and social groups were mainly determined by their participation in urban life. The stately ritual instituted by the Venetians offers the most detailed evidence on how the Venetian authorities attempted to structure and present the interaction between the different population groups and their cultures. I strongly believe that it is in the careful consideration of these ceremonies that the symbolic capital of such endeavors may be seen with a certain clarity. These formally orchestrated ceremonies enlivened the city space, preserved the symbolic order of the colony, and created a concrete official image of the society.[1]

In addition to these events, which were closely associated with the civic government, less formal occurrences like fairs centering around local churches and cults or older urban traditions such as religious litanies and processions must have continued to happen or were newly instituted after the arrival of the Venetians in the colonies. The supposed grass roots origin of local happenings guaranteed the participation of the indigenous population and enriched the interaction between colonizers and colonized. One such case was the fair of the Nativity of the Virgin celebrated on September 8 around the church of the Virgin on the beach of the town of Modon. Interestingly, it is the castellan of Modon and his counselors who announced the institution of this fair by including it in the statutes and chapters of the city in 1453 – there is, however, no way of knowing whether this was a newly established event. The fair lasted for three days, during which commercial transactions were tax-free.[2] Clearly, this must have attracted people to the festival. Blurring differences between religious and civic customs was an ingenious way to dress politics (and money matters) in a sacred mantle.

NORMALIZING RITUAL

For the Venetians communal feasts constituted an essential part of urban life. According to the *Corpus juris civilis*, in 1321 the doge defined a permanent resident as someone who had moved to a place with his family and his belongings and who celebrated the official feasts of his new residence.[3] Thus, the normative nature of civic ritual provides a window into the concerns of the ruling elite and this elite's ideal vision of a place. Meant to illustrate the role of the city dwellers in the colonial society according to the power relationships determined by the elite, the official ceremonial was to be understood by any observer as the ultimate embodiment of social order.[4] This rigidity and conservatism allow us to assume that an official ritual recorded at a certain period is likely to reflect much more archaic practices.

Following the practices in the mother city, the stately ceremonial of the Venetian colonies and Candia in particular had a strong religious character.[5] Not only did such ritual coincide with the major religious holidays, but its basic form, the liturgical acclamation of the doge, was for all intents and purposes a religious performance that had been inspired by Byzantine civic and religious ceremonies. On the other hand, the church also tried to explore its potential for temporal power and to present itself as a crucial player in the political scene. For instance, in Candia the arrival of the Magi in Bethlehem was apparently reenacted during the "feast of the Star" on Theophany, January 6.[6] The Latin priests disguised themselves as the three wise kings for this festival and presumably posed as royal figures in the reenactment of the event, thus reinforcing the temporal power of the highest echelon of the church. Unfortunately we do not have concrete information about the origins of this festival as we only hear about its intended abolition in 1467 because the priests in disguise were misbehaving.[7] This festival was not an invention of the Latin church of Crete, however, and we can understand more about its motivation and ultimate meaning from comparing it to other similar occurrences like the festival of the Magi, which was first observed in Florence in the 1390s. It has been interpreted as an ingenious way to make up for the lack of princes and high nobility of Florence in order to provide a forum where the people dressed up as courtiers and followed "phony kings."[8]

If the study of Venetian colonial architecture and its topographical arrangement sometimes seemingly fails to comply with a definite blueprint, the organization of stately ritual gives the impression of a well conceived plan from the very conception of the Venetian empire. The documents that seal the colonization of the territories of Zara (1204), Corfu (1207), Negroponte (1209), Durazzo (1210), Candia (1211), and Ragusa (1232) are accompanied by a clause that carried a heavy symbolic weight: on Christmas, Easter, and the feast of St. Mark, all major religious holidays for Venice, the colonists were asked to remember and honor the metropole by singing the Lauds service in honor of the duke.[9] The consistency in the wording of these documents reveals the concerted effort of the Venetians to create a carefully planned colonizing expedition to the East: the clergy had to take part in the performance of the Lauds service in honor of the doge, the patriarch, and the archbishop in the cathedral of the colony. In Crete and in Durazzo, two more holidays were added to the calendar: Epiphany and the feast of the patron saint of each city, St. Titus in the case of Candia and St. Ysarius in Durazzo.[10] In these two cases the cult of the local patron saint was incorporated in the hierarchy of the colony. The instructions of the doge Petrus Ziani to the first Venetian settlers of Crete in 1211, contained in the *Concessio insulae Cretensis*, are worth recording:

> Laudes nobis et successoribus nostris in archiepiscopatu et episcopatibus decantari facietis quater in anno: in natiuitate Domini, in pascha Resurrectionis, in festo sancti Marci et in festo maioris ecclesie Cretensis.[11]

From these documents we are led to believe that in the case where there was an important cult of a local saint, the Venetian authorities were eager to place it under the aegis of their colonial government. As we have already seen in the case of St. Titus (Chapter 4), this practice must have borne fruit as it was repeated in later times. When the Venetians took over the island of Corfu in 1387 they incorporated into their ceremonial the cult of the local saint, St. Arsenios, a metropolitan of the island in the tenth century (died 953), who had been already co-opted by the Angevins in the thirteenth century.[12] In this way, the official religious calendar of the colonizers merged Venetian and local cults. Curiously, in Ragusa the feast of the local saint, Blasius, displaced that of St. Mark, which is not even mentioned in the document of concession of the city to the Venetians in 1232. This is probably due to the fact that Ragusa was only a dependency and not a real colony of Venice.[13] In fact, there is no church of St. Mark recorded in Ragusa.

The aforementioned thirteenth-century texts stress above all the subordination of the local Latin clergy of each colony to the Venetian authorities, but they also regulate stately ceremonies as they prescribe the solemnities for the possible visit of a doge or for the inauguration of a new Venetian governor in the colonies. In Durazzo, the text of 1210 explicitly mentions a solemn procession from the port of the city to the cathedral in the case of a doge's visit: "et quod ad recipiendum vos et successores vestros cum clero, cruse precedente, veniemus ad ripam, usque ad ecclesiam vobiscum euntes sollempni cantico."[14] The highest religious authority (archbishop or bishop) along with the clergy greet the doge at the port and march to the church. For the installation of a governor the document mentions a solemn greeting and benediction in front of the cathedral: "Duces vero . . . et capitaneos vestros et successorum vestrorum qui aplicuerint ibi [Durazzo], a clericis maioris ecclesie recipi faciemus ad eiusdem ecclesie portam cum aqua sancta et incenso."[15] The statutes of Ragusa (1272), whose different political relationship with Venice make it a special case, offer additional details as to the reception of a new Venetian governor into the commune: after swearing an oath to the commune of Ragusa, presumably at the port, the Venetian lord would proceed to the central square of the city, where he would be given the banner of St. Blasius and be installed in office. Then he would proceed to the cathedral to receive holy water, incense, and a Bible, on which he renewed his oath in the presence of the cathedral chapter. Back to the square the banner of St. Mark is raised, and the people pay homage and vow to be loyal to Venice.[16] Although not elaborate, the text for Crete informs us that the new *duca* was to be received by the clergy standing behind the cross, thus possibly also referring to a solemn march.[17] By the sixteenth century this occasion had received all the trappings of a formal reception for a high official: the new *duca* of Candia was greeted at the gate of the port (whence the *duca* entered the city after disembarking the ship that brought him from Venice). A procession started at the harbor and moved toward the basilica of St. Mark and the ducal palace through the *ruga magistra*.[18] The similarities in these accounts suggest that in essence the ritual did not change much from the thirteenth to the sixteenth century. This is not to say that the pageantry of the later period did not bring a change but rather to suggest that the kernel of these ceremonies was set early on in the Venetian dominion.

Obviously the parts of the city that are singled out in these documents must have occupied a unique position within the ritual space of the colonies. The periodic occurrence of these events, especially the biannual inauguration of each colonial governor, must have conferred particular significance on the port as a gateway to the city but also as a space that looked directly out to the sea and was confidently linked to Venice. After all, it was a Venetian galley that carried the new official to the colony. The city gate at the port became a symbolic threshold past which the governor would first experience the colonial territory. The greeting party at the harbor, the solemn march through the main thoroughfare of the town to the cathedral, and the culmination of the ceremony in the application of holy water and incense on the newly installed Venetian official further highlighted this symbolic nexus. The short distance between the sea gate, the cathedral, and the main square with the governor's palace became a ceremonial pathway that announced the ties between the Republic and its devoutly Latin Christian community on the colony.

Although these prescriptions were primarily addressed to the Venetian colonists, strong evidence suggests that the official civic ritual was intended to include the local population as well – in this way the Greeks would show their reverence to the colonial authorities. In fourteenth-century Candia, the religious festivities called specifically for the involvement of Latin and Orthodox priests. For instance, for the commemoration of the suppression of the rebellion of 1363 all the clergy of Candia, including the Greek priests, had to participate in the litany and in the solemn procession. Moreover, the entire population was ordered to take part in the celebrations under penalty of law (see also Chapter 4, n. 43).[19]

THE VIRGIN MESOPANDITISSA

The available archival documents may not be forthcoming with detailed information on the participation of the Orthodox population in these ceremonies in Candia, but the sacred objects that formed the centerpieces of the religious ceremonies provide eloquent testimonies to the intended intermingling of cultures in these rituals. It seems that Byzantine religious symbols were incorporated within a Venetian setting and framework to serve the needs of the Venetians on Crete. The most conspicuous of these cases involves a miracle-working icon of the Virgin that now adorns the high altar of the church of Santa Maria della Salute in Venice. The investigation of this icon's history and cult provides unique insights into the careful planning of the official ceremonial in Candia. As we will see in the following chapter it also seems to have had a lasting impact on the religious profile of the metropole herself.

As the most venerated object in Candia, this icon resided in the cathedral of St. Titus. The Madonna of St. Titus or the Virgin Mesopanditissa was an icon of the Virgin in the type of the Hodegetria flanked by two angels (1.45 by 0.95 meters, Fig. 127). Despite the fact that icons did not play an important role in the ecclesiastical practices of Venice in the twelfth century, the cult of this icon was incorporated in the Venetians' religious customs soon after their arrival on Crete. Only an extremely powerful sacred object would deserve such an honor. Indeed, the icon of Candia had a glorious history: reportedly it was a portrait of the Virgin painted by St. Luke, like the famous Hodegetria icon in Constantinople.[20] The chronicle of Andrea

Cornaro maintains that it was taken to Candia from Constantinople during Iconoclasm along with other icons of the Virgin, stressing the antiquity and sacredness of the image, as do all other Venetian accounts on the icon.[21] Unfortunately, the image has been overpainted numerous times and it is impossible to establish its date on the basis of stylistic analysis, but it appears to be a product of a Byzantine atelier of the twelfth or thirteenth century. On regular days the icon resided inside the cathedral, where it was probably set in its own chapel.[22]

Such a powerful symbol of Byzantine Chandax had to be reactivated so to speak to fit the exigencies of Venetian Candia and its new overlords. Indeed, the icon took an active role in promoting friendship between the two communities of Crete: its miraculous intervention brought peace between the Venetians and the Greek rebels in 1264. The chronicler Antonio Trivan gives a detailed account of the procession of Greeks and Latins that was staged around the icon of the Virgin to celebrate the treaty:

> A sincere and honorable peace, and obedience to the most serene republic of Venice were sworn . . . in front of the icon of the Glorious Virgin Mary, which in Greek is called *Mesopanditissa*, that is "mediator of peace between the two parties"; and as a token of this, the sacred icon was carried in procession throughout the city, followed by all the people of both rites, Greeks and Latins, monks and laity, blessing and thanking Divine Providence for inspiring this heavenly peace.[23]

Trivan translates the special Greek title of the image, *Mesopanditissa*, as "mediator of peace between the two parties." Thus, the icon is invested with conciliatory power: it secured a meeting of the two communities midway and laid the basis for their peaceful coexistence. This ingenious justification of the icon's epithet does not represent its Greek meaning, which probably indicated the original location of the image.[24] It seems, therefore, that the emphasis on the mediation qualities of the icon was a Venetian invention that appropriated its charisma for the purposes of promoting the colonial cause.

The reference to the procession is intriguing. By 1368 the icon was carried by eight persons in public procession every Tuesday from the cathedral of St. Titus to the Greek and Latin churches in honor of the Virgin Mary and in praise of the Venetian dominion.[25] Their family names indicate that some of the people involved in the procession were Latins and Greeks of a high status. For their service to the community these eight bearers of the icon were exempted from guard duty (*vaita*) in the suburbs and from the corvées, indicating that at least some of them were Greeks who lived in the burg as the corvées was reserved for the colonized population. By the sixteenth century the bearers of the icon were elected by the duke for life; their appointment was almost hereditary – in fact, from 1539 on they were exclusively chosen among the inhabitants of the village of Ambrousa.[26]

The whole arrangement recalls the weekly *lite* of the icon of the Virgin Hodegetria in Constantinople, an event recorded from the eleventh century onward. The similarities are striking: the Constantinopolitan litany was a Tuesday procession that stopped at various churches in the city; ca.1390 the bearers of the Constantinopolitan icon were eight in number, the same number recorded in Candia twenty some years earlier. Also similarly to the situation in Candia in later centuries, the same family had the privilege of carrying the icon for generations. Furthermore, the Hodegetria icon of Constantinople also paid visits to other icons in the city, which later joined it in the litany.[27] A seventeenth-century traveler to Candia, Wolfgang Stockman, marveled at the fact that the "Madonna of St. Titus" was taken to the Augustinian church of the Savior, where another icon of the Virgin originating from Rhodes was kept.[28] Are these similarities enough to posit a Byzantine origin for the litany, however?[29]

There is strong evidence to suggest that the Tuesday procession in Candia reproduced an older Byzantine custom. First, the Venetians had direct knowledge of the Constantinopolitan practice from their presence in that city in 1204 since the Hodegetria icon had come into the possession of the Latin patriarch of Constantinople, the Venetian Thomas Morosini.[30] Second, regular litanies are recorded in at least two other localities in mainland Greece in the twelfth century: the area of Thebes and Thessaloniki.[31] Finally, the contrast between the numerous accounts of the *lite* of Constantinople and Candia written by foreign visitors and the almost complete absence of Greek allusions to them suggests that these events formed such an integral part of public devotional life that they were almost invisible to the city dwellers. Thus, it is tempting to propose that weekly processions were more extensive than the sources lead us to believe.

Let us turn to the *lite* of Candia again. The early accounts of the Tuesday procession simply refer to the "image of the Virgin" without specifying its title; this is probably a clue that the procession honored the most venerable icon of Candia. It is only in the fifteenth century that we have an explicit reference to its title in the minutes of the church councils of the archbishop Gerolamo Lando: the icon was taken to the front of the church of St. Mark, where the Lauds service to the Republic was sung (the document reads, "il laudo di S. Serenita").[32] It was then taken to various Greek churches, where Mass was celebrated in honor of private persons and donations were collected. Many people followed the litany, including women, who oftentimes

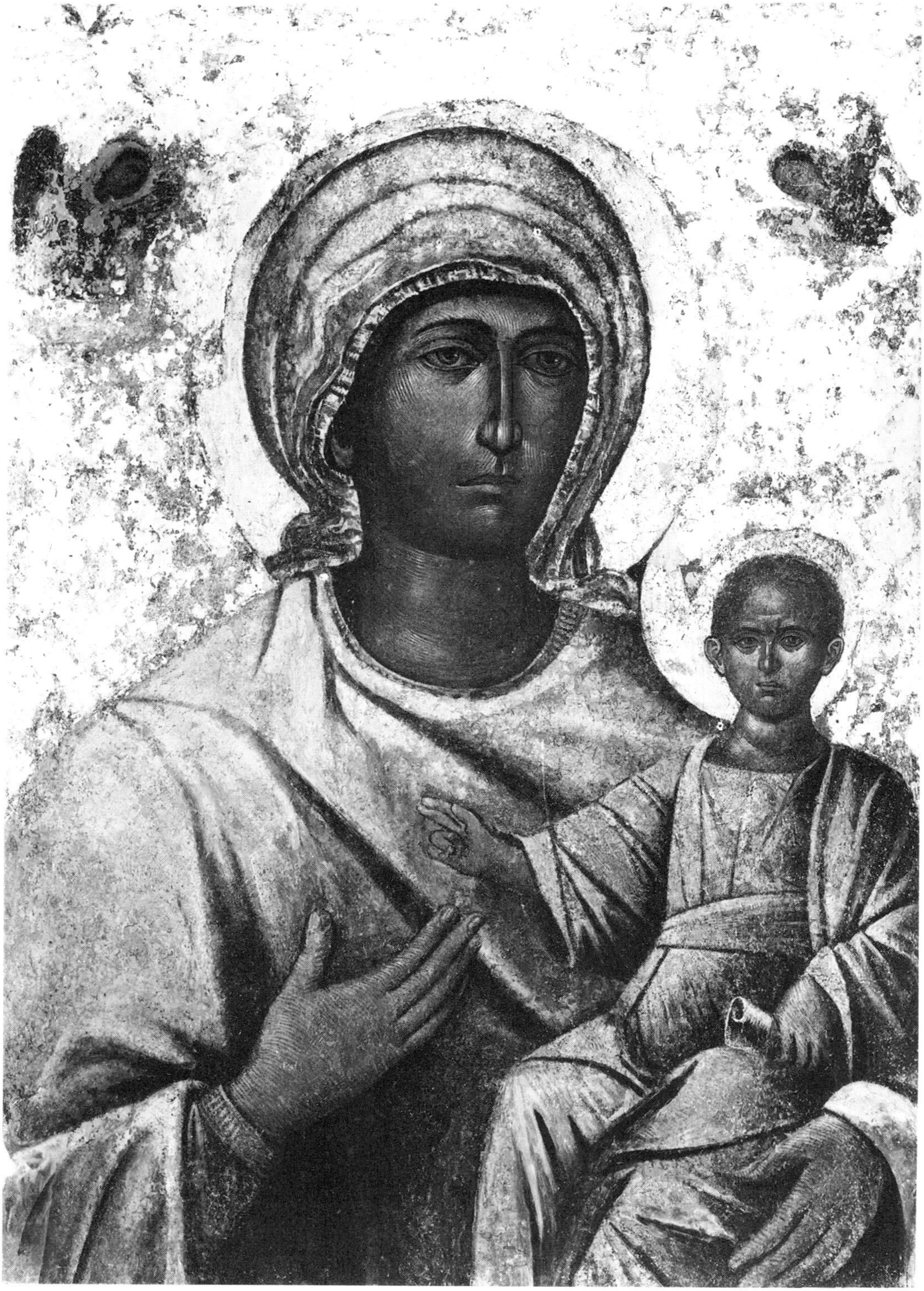

FIGURE 127. Venice, church of Santa Maria della Salute, icon of the Virgin Mesopanditissa (Foto Böhm-Venezia)

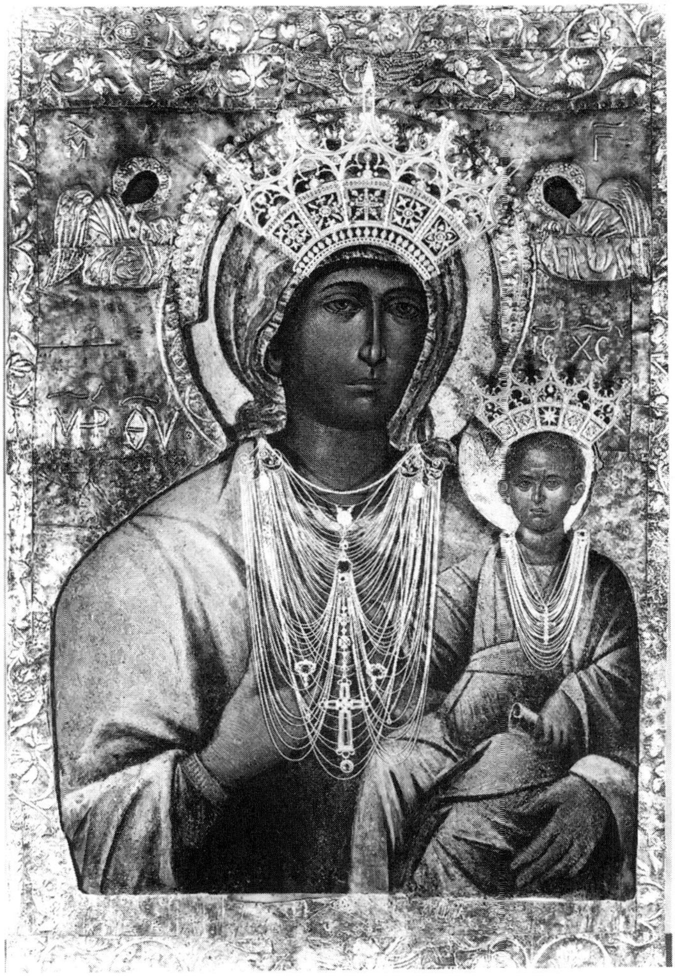

FIGURE 128. Venice, church of Santa Maria della Salute, icon of the Virgin Mesopanditissa covered with silver revetment and jewels (Foto Böhm-Venezia)

were barefoot to fulfill a vow to the Virgin. Upon the icon's return to the Latin cathedral, the Lauds were sung for the archbishop. In the seventeenth century Angelo Venier reports that in the exact same procession the *protopapas* and the *protopsaltis*, the leaders of the Greek Orthodox religious community, carried the icon of the Virgin Mesopanditissa in procession ("levar processionalmente") in the name of all Greeks.[33] Whether this custom had a Byzantine origin or not, by midfourteenth century the procession required the participation of both the Latin and Greek clergy. Rather than viewing their inclusion in the litany as a sign of the goodwill of the authorities, however, the Greek clergy was often unwilling to participate.[34] Apparently, the litany included acclamations to the duke and the Venetian Republic, and its bearers had to accept the authority of the pope and the wishes of the *protopapas*, who was elected by the Latin archbishop. By 1515 the Greek and Latin priests were threatened with a fine of four hyperpera if they did not take part in the Tuesday procession, which clearly had become a major event in city life.[35] The involvement of Greek priests in the litany of Candia further supports the hypothesis that the Tuesday procession predated the arrival of the Venetians. Another such weekly procession occurred in Venetian Crete. One of the Byzantine icons of the cathedral church of Canea, an icon of the Virgin that has not survived, was paraded in the streets of the city every Tuesday.[36] May we assume that a similar custom was observed in Retimo and Sitia?

The old Byzantine roots of the Candiote procession provided the firm ground on which to base further elaborations of the ritual. Its Byzantine origins enhanced the authenticity and miraculous power of the icon, a power that, for the Venetians and Greeks alike, was traced back to St. Luke. Its antiquity emphasized the unique status of the icon in the city. Its thirteenth-century Venetian interpretation, that is, the stress on the new mediating role of the Mesopanditissa in the rebellion of 1264, modified the meaning of the old Byzantine procession by changing the recipients of the sacred grace of the icon. The weekly litany of the Mesopanditissa now underlined the icon's miraculous role in the establishment and perpetuation of colonial concord. The Lauds sung to the Venetian duke and the Latin archbishop of Crete proclaimed the new bonds among the Byzantine icon, the Latin church, and the Venetian authorities. This weekly association of the icon with the leaders of the colony soon turned it into a palladium of Candia and the foremost symbol of harmonious colonial life. Marco Molino, a *provveditor general* of Candia in the seventeenth century, mentioned the Tuesday procession of the icon to the Greek churches as a means of satisfying the devotion of the Christians, presumably of both rites.[37]

The same devotion was shown to the icon during other civic ceremonies, e.g. supplication for rain or deliverance from an earthquake.[38] Special Sunday litanies were performed in preparation for the feast of the Assumption of the Virgin in August.[39] The most magnificent procession of all, the Corpus Christi celebration, focused on the Holy Sacrament but reserved a unique position for the icon of the Mesopanditissa in the procession through the streets of the city.[40] As we can see in George Clontzas's codex, the icon had an elaborate frame and was elevated on a complex baldachinlike structure, which displayed it as the most precious relic in the procession (Fig. 67). Three or four people bore the baldachin on their shoulders. Another possible reference to this procession may be an icon in Copenhagen recently attributed to Clontzas.[41] The icon depicts the Council of Nicaea but in the foreground it represents a procession of clerical and imperial figures carrying two icons: one of the Virgin Hodegetria and the other of Peter and Paul. Although this icon shows similarities with an engraving at Trent and thus does not seem to reproduce scenes from real life, the inclusion of the icon of the Virgin in such a prominent position points to a wish of the painter to glorify the palladium of his native town. Although we do not know the exact location of the icon inside the church it seems logical to assume that this famous, miracle-working icon adorned one of the most important (i.e. central or visible) chapels in the church. It was worshipped with donations and ex votos (Fig. 128), as well as with gathering of people around the icon in expectation of a miracle.[42] In later centuries the whole icon was covered with a silver revetment and other offerings that were given in the last days of Venetian rule on Crete, possibly as the last resource to save Candia from the Turks.[43] The icon was an integral part of the colonial heritage of the Venetians, so much so that when Candia was lost to the Ottomans in 1669, the Mesopanditissa was among the sacred objects that were shipped to Venice, where it was displayed on the high altar of Longhena's church dedicated to Santa Maria della Salute.[44]

Undoubtedly, the cathedral of St. Titus that housed the icon of the Mesopanditissa and the saint's relics represented the most important sacred heritage of the Byzantine city of Chandax. The preservation of these Byzantine customs demonstrates that the Venetians found in Crete a powerful, sacred heritage worthy of respect and admiration. Despite the minimal changes that were made to the original setting of these religious treasures, the relationship of the Venetians to these customs was not merely receptive, but was actively dialectic. Although still preserved in their Byzantine place of worship, the new staging of these loca sancta in the civic ceremonial of Venetian Candia neutralized their special ties with the native Greeks and forged a new history for these sites of sanctity. Now, their powers were reserved for the safeguard of the new colonial regime, a regime that was Catholic in faith but depended on the coexistence of the Orthodox and Latin communities.[45]

LINKING CHURCHES THROUGH RITUAL

How was this played out in civic ceremonies? Whether or not it was the norm to force the population to participate in these rituals, a careful look into the kind of events that formed the core of public festivals can inform us about the preoccupations and aspirations of the authorities. A seventeenth-century copy of a manuscript, which was originally written in 1595 and is now preserved in the Museo Correr in Venice, contains a list of the annual festivities that were observed in Candia:[46] Christmas, Epiphany, Giovedi Grasso (literally "Fat Thursday," a day marking the end of Carnival and the beginning of Lent), Palm Sunday, Holy Week, Good Friday, Good Saturday, Easter, St. Mark's feast day (April 25), the commemoration of the rebellion of 1363 (May 10), the Ascension, the feast of the Corpus Domini, that of St. Titus (October 2), the commemoration of the battle of Lepanto (October 7),[47] the feast of St. Theodosia (May 29) commemorating the deliverance from the earthquake of 1508 but also the fall of Constantinople to the Turks, and a festival for the *capitaneus;* to these we should add extraordinary events like the arrival of a new *duca*, the funeral of Venetian noblemen, and the funeral of a *duca*. Twelve of these nineteen observances commemorated religious holidays. Nonetheless, even the festivals that had a purely stately character were celebrated either inside the Latin churches of Candia or with processions and acclamations that venerated religious objects.

As was the case with the festive solemnities observed in Venice, the most common way of celebrating these occasions was a solemn procession through the streets of the city. Similarly, the statutes of Modon also indicate that processions of the Holy Sacrament, the cross, or church icons were usual occurrences in the fifteenth century.[48] In addition to the inauguration of a colonial governor, on Christmas the *duca* went from the courthouse located in the ducal palace to the church of St. Mark for Mass, then to the cathedral of St. Titus, which stood nearby. At the end of the solemnities, the high officials accompanied the *duca* back to his palace (f. 3r). Processions on the streets of Candia were also a means to display the city's devotion to God in cases of natural catastrophes, such as earthquakes.[49] The traveler Pietro Casola provides a vivid description of such a spontaneous event in Candia in 1494:

> A procession was at once formed to go through the city. It was joined by the priests, both Greek and Latin, and also by the friars of every kind, though there were only a few of them. Behind them went many men and women, who beat their breasts with their fists most miserably. . . . At the end of the procession walked the priests of the cathedral, with the archbishop's vicar.[50]

The participants in this spontaneous event followed the planned arrangement of a solemn procession. Obviously, the strict protocol enforced by the state or established by long tradition transformed these rituals into definitive representations of the social order and consequently gave them the authority to present the history of the colony. Thus, these rituals served to structure the past and condition the present of the colonial society.

Nowhere is this more evident than in the planning of the religious processions. At different times of the year all major Latin rite churches took an active role in a solemn procession: the cathedral of St. Titus, the ducal chapel of St. Mark, the Augustinian church of the Savior (on St. Mark's feast day and on the Ascension), the Franciscan church of St. Francis (Ascension), and the Dominican church of St. Peter the Martyr (Ascension). No matter what the starting point of the procession, all processional paths converged at the ducal palace. Hence, the siting and processional linkage of the Western churches pointed to the civic center of the city and its Venetian qualities. Thus, we can view the religious ceremonial of Candia as a primary factor in construing the religious and civic identity of Venetian Candia. By linking the most significant Latin churches and monasteries, the ritual framework of sacred routes animated the city space according to the prescriptions of the Venetians.

The place that the Orthodox churches, clergy, and treasures occupy in these processions is indicative of the official rhetoric of the Venetians. The determined route of the processions was punctuated by the major Latin establishments. Only one religious ceremony in Candia incorporated the main church of the Orthodox in the official ritual: the solemn procession on Good Friday centering around the Greek *epitaphios*, the decorated baldachin containing the embroidered textile with the body of Christ. Here is what occurred in the late sixteenth century:

> Il venere santo si va a San Tito per sentir l'officio et poi doppo il disinar passando la procession drento della chesia, li signori accompagnano il santissimo sacramento et li loro camerieri con le torze davanti. Et finita che sarà la pertetione *[sic]*, cominciando la processione greca accompagnano li eccelentissimi signori per ordenario insieme con l'illustrissimo arcivescovo, che sarà in quel tempo overo il suo vicario, il santissimo sacramento fino alla Madonna di Anzoli et poi tolendo la perdonanza si partino de lì accompagnando l'illustrissimo arcivescovo fino a San Tito.[51]

While the Latins followed Mass in the church of St. Titus, the Greek clergy assembled at the church of the *protopapas*, St. Mary of the Angels. The Greek priests paraded the *epitaphios* toward the Latin cathedral to meet with the Latin archbishop and his clergy, then they headed back to the Orthodox cathedral together. Finally the Orthodox accompanied the archbishop back to St. Titus, when he displayed the reliquary with the blood of Christ.

Although we do not know the specifics of the Greek procession in Candia, we may surmise that it followed traditional Orthodox practices performed by the Byzantine clergy for centuries – thus, the presence of an *epitaphios* should be taken as a given. The liturgical procession is recorded visually in church frescoes and icons of the fourteenth and fifteenth centuries. A wall painting dated to the first third of the fourteenth century from the church of St. Anthony in the area of the Vrondissi monastery in Crete shows an angel holding two large candles leading three persons who have an *epitaphios* cloth over their shoulders like a canopy. The cloth contains a figure of the dead body of Christ wearing a loincloth. The first of the three figures carrying the cloth must stand for a clergyman as he holds a censor.[52] A similar scene is depicted in a sixteenth-century icon of the Angelic Liturgy by Michael Damaskinos in the Museum of Icons in the church of St. Catherine of Sinai in Herakleion. This depiction of the Angelic Liturgy must portray a current ecclesiastical ritual and thus offers a visualization of the Good Friday ceremony. In fact, only such a peculiar ceremony, including a replica of the tomb of Christ, would explain the unique homage paid to the Orthodox cathedral of Candia by the Latin ecclesiastics of Crete.

At the same time, the most precious relics and icons of the Byzantine church (the relics of St. Titus and the icon of the Mesopanditissa) took a central part in these processions and became foci of veneration for the entire Christian community, regardless of their creed. Both clergies – with the Latin priests preceding the Greeks – were called to participate in religious processions, especially on the feast of Good Friday, on that of St. Mark, and at the funeral of a *duca*.[53] The placement of the ecclesiastics of the Orthodox church at the very end of the dignitaries, not only after the Latin clergy but also behind the secular confraternities, underlines the inferior status to which the Greeks were relegated in these formal occurrences.[54] These sacred ceremonies construed the new social order of the colony, in which the old Byzantine sacred objects became symbols of colonial authority. All these ritual occasions were meant to show how eventually, through the annual or weekly repetition of such solemnities, the two religious creeds came into direct contact and (possibly) modified their initial antithetical positions. There are recorded instances when this was achieved. An interesting outcome of this cultural rapprochement is apparent in a 1455 decision of the Senate in Venice. The document states explicitly that the *Regimen* had compelled Latins and Greeks to observe Western feasts that were more numerous than those observed in Venice. This must refer to local feasts that were directly connected with Crete, e.g. the commemoration of the rebellion of St. Titus. In addition, the Greeks celebrated their own religious holidays. The authorities of Crete complained that with so many holidays there was not much time left for work and asked the Senate to make sure that the population of Crete observe only the feasts that were commemorated in Venice and that all other feasts be treated as normal work days. The decision of the Senate explicitly specified that from then on the population of Crete should observe only the feasts of the Roman Catholic saints; the celebration of any additional feasts should be their personal business.[55] In view of this evidence, we can assume that until the midfifteenth century the Greek Orthodox population was free to celebrate religious feasts according to the Byzantine ecclesiastical calendar. The Venetian authorities reacted to this custom not because of religious fervor but for practical reasons: there were too many public holidays in Candia. One might also assume that in addition to the Greeks some Venetians also observed such holidays, to the detriment of official business.

In the end it is the public, civic function of these occasions that sanctioned and advocated the official image of Venetian Candia. The ritual processions and the major Latin churches that outlined them in space created a network of routes that defined the sacred space of Venetian Candia as that of a Latin city. Similarly, the former Byzantine structures – the city walls, the ducal palace, and the cathedral – also changed meaning as they now became focal points in the ritual of Venetian Candia. The walls, which were marked with emblems of the Venetian Republic, enclosed the significant ritual space of the city. Within the city walls the state buildings marked the route and the stopping points of the processions. Their Byzantine origin validated the claims of Venice on Crete and constituted a bond with the past of the island. Only the most sacred icon of the Virgin Mesopanditissa could transcend the boundaries of the city and retain its miraculous power beyond the walls, in the burg. Thus, the cult of the Mesopanditissa constituted a symbolic link between city and suburbs, just as it had acted as a mediator between colonists and colonized. In short, in order to subvert Byzantine power, the Venetians assimilated it in their own rhetoric, presenting the colony as a continuation of imperial Byzantium under the government of Venice. At first sight, this sacred ceremonial would seem to lessen the apparent hostility between the settlers and the locals because it was largely based on Byzantine traditions and allowed Greeks to participate in the celebrations. On closer inspection, however, the Orthodox Greeks were not fully welcome into the Venetian commonwealth.

The intended show of harmony between Greeks and Latins was sometimes threatened by Catholic newcomers, especially in the period of the counterreformation. For instance, in 1576 the Orthodox population of Canea was "violently forced to kneel when the Holy Sacrament passed" through the streets of the city.[56] The authorities tried to appease the Greek population by attributing such violence to the zeal of the Catholics, who were unaware of the Eastern custom of "showing reverence to the lord standing on foot" and who acted in this way because of ignorance and not because of "hatred towards the Greek nation." The purpose of such processions was stated once again: "our intention is not to hinder the Greek rite." Along the same lines, in order to prevent a clash between the two communities the Venetian authorities decided not to institute the Gregorian reform of the calendar in their colonies in the Oltremare in 1582.[57]

The recurrence of public ceremonies further accentuated the symbolic messages broadcasted by the architecture of the civic center of Candia, where the spatial relationship between Venetian and Byzantine structures proclaimed the superiority of the new rulers. The fortified city housed the Venetian political and religious authorities. The buildings where these authorities were housed were hallmarks of Venetian presence, making the Republic's authority tangible and publicizing Candia's submission to Venice's empire. The city walls marked the Venetian character of Candia by allowing or preventing access to urban resources. This accessibility also defined the symbolic participation of the non-Latin ethnic groups in city life, albeit on different levels for each group. Both the Greek and Jewish communities were excluded from the highest political offices, but as we saw this was translated differently in the allocation of urban space and in the public official life of the colony.

NINE

COLONIALISM AND THE METROPOLE

> And round the walls of the porches there are set pillars of variegated stones, jasper and porphyry, and deep green serpentine spotted with flakes of snow, and marbles, that half refuse and half yield to the sunshine, Cleopatra-like, the "bluest veins to kiss" . . . ; and above these, another range of glittering pinnacles, mixed with white arches edged with scarlet flowers, – a confusion of delight, amidst which the breasts of the Greek horses are seen blazing in their breadth of golden strength, and the St. Mark's lion, lifted on a blue field covered with stars.
>
> John Ruskin[1]

No study of colonialism is complete without a look at the metropole, because the pure existence of an empire implies that the metropole got things in return. This is especially true in the case of Venice, which, within a few decades after 1204, was transformed from a small city-state to an imperial power that commanded the respect of its neighbors. Until the early fifteenth century, when Venice acquired territories in the Italian mainland, her power and wealth largely depended on her colonies beyond the sea, the Oltremare. Having investigated how the Venetians dealt with Byzantine culture in Candia, I will examine in this chapter the impact that their presence in Crete and the colonies in general had on the formation of the new political and cultural identity of Venice itself. Studies of modern colonies have recently shown that colonial territories were often used by the metropole as proving grounds for experiments that would be difficult to conduct at home – this is the line of reasoning that I follow in this chapter.[2]

It has been often argued that Venetian culture owes a lot to Byzantium, but at the conclusion of this study on Venice's empire it would be significant to review the evidence and to put forth some concrete examples of how this may have worked. In contrast to the usual tendency to attribute all things

Byzantine to Constantinople, I will be particularly concerned here with the legacy of the colonies (i.e. the former periphery of Byzantium) to Venice. The evidence used to support my argument is chronologically dispersed among governmental documents, notarial registers of the colony of Crete, and records that deal with the basilica of San Marco and the ecclesiastical history of Venice. These records date more often than not from the fifteenth and sixteenth centuries, when all this material was archived. As such, my conclusions are not based on a complete analysis of Venetian practices that may have been informed by the colonies. It is my hope that what this chapter proposes will prompt others to investigate the material they have at hand to expose similar situations. For no metropoleis of the magnitude of Venice do flourish without active borrowings from other cultures with which they come in contact; when this encounter involves direct colonization the results can be quite extraordinary.

No matter how much Venice admired Byzantine culture prior to the Fourth Crusade, the direct contact of Venetian officials and colonists with the realities of the Byzantine world that the settlement of Crete demanded must have opened new channels for appreciating Byzantine culture. This firsthand experience with old Byzantine customs had a beneficial spillover effect for the Venetians: it widened their cultural horizon, offering them novel ideas on how to deal with situations at home. This process is most obvious in three practices that, I believe, share a common ancestry in Venetian Crete: the cult of the patron saint of Crete/Venice, the rituals centering on icons of the Virgin, and the establishment of a segregated Jewish quarter.[3] Similar reasoning informs Deborah Howard's argument that the fifteenth-century cathedral of Sibenik in Croatia (1430), a work of the local architect Giorgio da Sebenigo, functioned as a model for the church of San Michele in Isola in Venice (1468).[4]

These borrowings from Crete represent the flip side of the strategies of appropriation that the Venetians used on Cretan soil; like the reuse of Byzantine traditions in Candia, the transference of Cretan customs to Venice explores the potential of cultural symbols to foster new power relationships when reused in different political situations. To what degree can the symbolic value of these cultural "implants" be transferred from one culture to another? How are such objects or traditions incorporated in a new setting? Why are certain cultural treasures deemed worthy of preservation in a new political context?

IMAGING VENICE AS HEAD OF AN EMPIRE

The success of the Venetian colonial enterprise has been attributed to a large degree to the close cultural relationship between Venice and Byzantium. By the eleventh century Venice was a politically independent state, but she never forgot her cultural ties with Byzantium, which dated back to the foundation of the city in the sixth century. The basilica of San Marco demonstrates that well into the twelfth century Venice turned to Byzantium for cultural inspiration.[5] In the early thirteenth century, when the Republic of Venice transformed itself from a small state into an imperial power at the expense of the Byzantines, a change can be observed in the reception of the Byzantine heritage in Venice.

The civic center of Venice, with its grand monuments, spoils of war, and ordered layout, is a visual statement of Venetian supremacy – a statement engaging primarily the Byzantines but also speaking to the maritime arch-enemies of Venetians, the Genoese. Later additions to the piazza San Marco and the Piazzetta (the Procuratie, the Loggetta, and the Library of Bessarion) enrich the byzantinizing appearance of the space with somber classicizing façades. At the same time, Venice offers the most significant testimony to the brilliance of Byzantine culture in the Middle Ages, because she tried to emulate it in her most powerful moment. Most of the Byzantine treasures that were used by the Venetians have been studied extensively as they represent some of the most famous tourist attractions in the world. In the absence of archival documents, however, the chronology of the decoration of the façades of San Marco has not been established with absolute certainty, nor is the mastermind behind these changes known. I believe that specific cultural, political, and social events that shaped the emerging role of Venice in the Eastern Mediterranean may offer a more nuanced understanding of its meaning and a cogent hypothesis for dating it.

The refurbishment of the civic center of Venice highlighted several imperial treasures and Christian relics that the Venetians had acquired at the sack of Constantinople in 1204. The incorporation of these objects into the civic center of Venice played a major role in shaping her political identity, as they were used by the Republic to demonstrate her supremacy over Byzantium and to support her claims in the Mediterranean.[6] The relics, icons, and liturgical vessels were preserved in the treasury of the basilica of S. Marco, enhancing the sacred character of the state church and legitimizing Venice's involvement in the crusade.[7] Famous sculptural treasures from Constantinople were set up outside the basilica to proclaim Venice's military success against the Byzantines. As Michael Jacoff has amply demonstrated for the Bronze Horses, the spoils were displayed in innovative ways that did not simply duplicate earlier practices of exhibiting antiquities in other Italian cities.[8] Without forgetting the source of these Byzantine treasures, the Venetians assimilated them into their ceremonials and succeeded in transforming them into symbols of the Republic.[9]

Following the success of the Fourth Crusade the new title of the Venetian doge, "quartae partis et dimidiae totius imperii Romaniae Dominator" (master of one fourth and a half of the whole empire of Romania), advertised the imperial ambitions of the republic.[10] In fact, in the years immediately following 1204 this title reflected Venice's imperial dreams and not the actual situation, as the Venetians possessed three eighths of the Byzantine empire only on paper.[11] There is no doubt that the establishment of a maritime empire affected the self-image of Venice and her worldview. As we have already seen, instead of imposing their hegemony in the colonies violently, the Venetians appropriated certain Byzantine traditions to secure a smooth transition from Byzantine to Venetian rule. The outcome was a blend of Venetian and Byzantine cultures that served the needs of Venice as a new world power.

Arguably, the hardships and difficulties that the Venetian settlers encountered in the Levant and more specifically in Crete motivated them to develop an imperial rhetoric at home in order to consolidate their authority in the territories beyond the sea. Places such as Crete may be seen as areas where the Venetians experimented with their newly acquired imperial power. In fact, it seems that the appropriation of the religious traditions of Byzantine Crete preceded the incorporation of the Fourth Crusade treasures in Venice. The state ceremonial of the colonial authorities assimilated the cult of Saint Titus from the first year (if not the first day) of Venetian rule on Crete. In Venice the area of the piazza S. Marco was not restructured to accommodate the booty from the Fourth Crusade until after the middle of the thirteenth century: the western façade of S. Marco was remodeled in the 1260s, the piazza was repaved in 1266 or 1267, and the palace of the procurators of S. Marco was restored in 1269.[12] Within this setting the Byzantine treasures adorned the major public space of Venice, proclaiming the special relationship between Venice and Constantinople and projecting Venice as the lawful heir to imperial Byzantium.[13]

The effective display of the Byzantine spoils implies the existence of a sophisticated plan to exploit the symbolic value of these artifacts so as to further the political ambitions of the Venetians. Direct documentation on the placement of the Byzantine treasures in the civic center of Venice is lacking, but this undertaking must have occupied the Venetians for a large part of the thirteenth century. The parallels in the appropriation of Byzantine objects and traditions that can be detected between Venetian Candia and midthirteenth-century Venice point to an active exchange of ideas between the colony and the mother city. To what extent did the colonial experience of the Venetians on Crete suggest the possibilities presented by the constantinopolitan booty for molding the political image of the new Venetian empire?

A figure pivotal for Crete and Venice, Jacopo Tiepolo, stands as the obvious architect of such a cultural exchange. Tiepolo started his illustrious career as the first duke of Crete in 1208–16 to conclude it as doge from 1229 to 1249. His administrative measures changed the political profile of Venice. There he was responsible for a new, enlarged version of the *promissio ducale*, a text that detailed the duties of the doge, many of which had not been specified before his time, and also for the first codification of Venetian law, the *Statuta Venetorum*.[14] Furthermore, Tiepolo's firm rule in Crete was crucial for the establishment of the Venetian colony on the island after the first revolt of the Byzantine aristocracy. He realized that the viability of the colony depended not on military confrontation but on an alliance with prominent local people. Soon, he made land concessions to the leaders of the rebellion, the Melissinoi brothers.[15] It is unclear whether the duke himself was responsible for the concessions made to Greek religious practices by the Venetian authorities. Be that as it may, when he was elected to the highest office in Venice Tiepolo was aware of the subtleties of Byzantine religious traditions, because he had experienced the sacred treasures of Byzantine Crete. It is quite likely that the project of the embellishment of S. Marco was laid out during his time in office. Even if it cannot be shown conclusively that Tiepolo was directly involved with the transformation of the civic center of Venice, his rule seems to have coincided with the establishment of two major components of the so-called myth of Venice: the cult of St. Mark and that of the Virgin.[16] In both instances we can detect the influence of the sacred heritage of Byzantine Crete on Venice.

THE LEGACY OF VENETIAN CRETE

The cult of Saint Titus may have played an instrumental role in the renewed interest in Saint Mark that the Venetians showed in the thirteenth century. In addition to being the sanctified leader of the religious community, the patron saint of any medieval city also held a privileged position in fostering civic pride and supporting communal claims.[17] In Byzantine Crete, for instance, the hagiography of Saint Titus went so far as to claim that he was a descendant of the mythical king of Crete, Minos, in order to link the saint with the celebrated mythology of the island.[18] Byzantine art, on the other hand, emphasizes his sacerdotal role and by extension the authority that Titus received from Saint Paul to found the church of Crete.[19] The obverse of a lead seal at Dumbarton Oaks, dating to the early eighth century, contains a portrait of St. Titus: the saint is depicted as a youthful bishop, blessing with his right hand and holding the gospels in his left hand according to the traditional Byzantine iconography (Fig. 129).[20] The dual identity attributed to Titus highlighted his role in the uninterrupted history of ancient and Byzantine Crete. The situation was not as neat when it came to the relics of the saint. Titus's tomb, as noted earlier, had been uprooted by the Arab invaders of Crete in the ninth century. After the ousting of the Muslims, however, only the saint's head was recovered, and it was subsequently transferred from Gortyna to the city of Chandax for protection.

This ingenious plot paralleled the special association of the relics of Saint Mark with Venice. Saint Mark was considered the real founder of the patriarchate of Venetia, the seat of which was contested by Aquileia and Grado/Venice: the relics of the saint played a crucial role in this dispute. The Venetian hagiography of Saint Mark insisted that Saint Peter had sent Mark to christianize the region of the northern Adriatic before Mark established the patriarchate of Alexandria. On the basis of this precedence the Venetians claimed that they were the legitimate owners of the saint's relics despite the fact that he had been martyred in Alexandria.[21] In fact, in 828 two Venetian merchants stole Mark's bodily remains from Alexandria to support Venice's primacy over the see of Aquileia.[22]

Thus when the Venetians settled in Crete they encountered a familiar situation: the mother city owned the relics of the Evangelist, a disciple of Peter, and the colony on Crete those of a disciple of Paul.[23] The Venetian and Cretan churches sought to enhance their prestige by claiming an apostolic foundation. Furthermore, the former Byzantine and now Latin cathedral of Candia duplicated in function the basilica of S. Marco in Venice: each contained the relics of the saint associated with the establishment of Christianity in the local community.[24] Thus, in honoring their Christian traditions S. Marco in Venice and St. Titus's in Candia were emblems of their respective patrimonies.

One point in the history of Saint Titus was specifically relevant to the situation in Venice in the early thirteenth century. The translation of Titus's relics to Chandax/Candia hinged upon the presence of Muslims in Crete and the danger that the relics would have faced had they stayed in their old

FIGURE 129. Lead seal with a portrait of St. Titus on the obverse. Dumbarton Oaks 58.106.5521 (Byzantine Collection, Dumbarton Oaks, Washington, D.C.)

location, Gortyna. This event may have provided the grounds for the reformulation of the hagiographical legend of St. Mark in the thirteenth century when the *praedestinatio* story was elaborated: it contained the prophecy – revealed to Saint Mark in a dream while he was in Venice – that his body was going to be rescued from the infidels (that is, from Muslim Alexandria) and find a resting place in Venice.[25] The insistence on the Muslim threat to justify the translation of the relics of both saints is instructive.

If we are to view the mosaics that were put up in the basilica of San Marco in the thirteenth century as reflecting the newly founded concerns and aspirations of the Venetians, we realize the primary role that the *praedestinatio* legend played in formulating a coherent rhetoric that linked Saint Mark to the city of Venice firmly. A full narrative cycle of the life of the saint (including the first representation of the saint's dream) embellished the south vestibule of the basilica (the Capella Zen) in the 1270s.[26] The divine dream message to Saint Mark that he would be buried in Venice gave the Venetian state direct power from Christ to protect the relics of the saint. The rescue of his relics justified Venetian expansion to the East as a crusade. Saint Mark evolved into the personification of this crusading/imperial ideal, being venerated as the sacred representative of the Venetian state.[27]

This is not all, however, for the effects that the inclusion of the *praedestinatio* had in St. Mark's life are also seen on the mosaics of the western façade of the basilica. Set up in the 1260s, these mosaics repeated the story of the translation of his relics, which had already been twice illustrated in the interior.[28] The façade mosaics broadcasted a new message: the relics were now associated with the state and not with the clergy as in earlier representations. The only surviving mosaic of this cycle – at the Porta di S. Alipio – serves as a perfect example: the saint's body is received by the doge and his retinue in a solemn procession in front of the basilica (Fig. 130) with only two clerics present. The story was reworked to depict a historical truth and to stress the relics' contact with the doge.[29] The original inscription, recorded in the seventeenth century, is revealing: COLLOCAT HUNC DIGNIS PLEBS LAUDIBUS ET COLIT HYMNIS UT VENETOS SERVET TERRAQUE MARIQUE GUBERNET (The people place him [here] with worthy praises and reverence him with hymns in order that he guard the Venetians and rule over land and sea).[30] Here the presence of Saint Mark's relics in Venice is explicitly associated with the Republic's claims of supremacy on land and sea, extending the implications of the *praedestinatio* legend beyond the religious sphere. By saving the relics of the saint from the Muslims, Venice became a guarantor of the Christian empire she led.

The accurate iconographical rendering of San Marco's façade on the mosaic proclaims the exclusive connection that the Venetians secured with Mark in this period. In this respect they may have been prompted by the concentration of the cult of Saint Titus almost exclusively on Crete; this had made Titus the national saint of the island. Saint Titus did not figure in Venetian religious practices before the thirteenth century. Outside Crete, Titus was venerated in Dalmatia, where he was sent after organizing the church in Crete (2 Tim. 4:10).[31] Titus's special relationship with Crete might indeed have offered the Venetians the foundation upon which to base the legend of Saint Mark as it was reinterpreted in this period.

In fact, the traces that the cult of St. Titus has left in Venice may be instructive. The feast of the apostle St. Titus appears only in one of the two missals of San Marco, but its inclusion is significant as a sign of the promulgation of the saint's cult in the metropole. The later missal (Biblioteca Marciana, lat. III 47 [= 2100]) is an illustrated copy datable to the years 1327 and 1344 and should not be taken as a totally reliable copy as it omits a few saints. The earlier missal (Biblioteca Marciana, lat. III 45 [= 2444]), probably made in Padua in the first half of the fifteenth century, contains a date of 1456 in the marginal additions and records the feast of St. Titus on January 4.[32] In Western iconography Titus appears relatively rarely, in decorated initials to the epistles of Paul and in the scene of Paul's preaching. An interesting example of the thirteenth century is the Epistolary of Gaibana, written in 1259 and now preserved in the cathedral of Padua. The painting style of the missal shows that the miniaturist either was a Venetian or at least had been trained in the Venetian school of painting, thus pointing to a familiarity with the saint's figure a few decades after the colonization of Crete.[33] It is evident that St. Titus acquired a more prominent role in Venetian art after the conquest of Crete in 1211; it is quite probable that his little known history offered a valuable exemplum to the Venetian ecclesiastics and politicians.

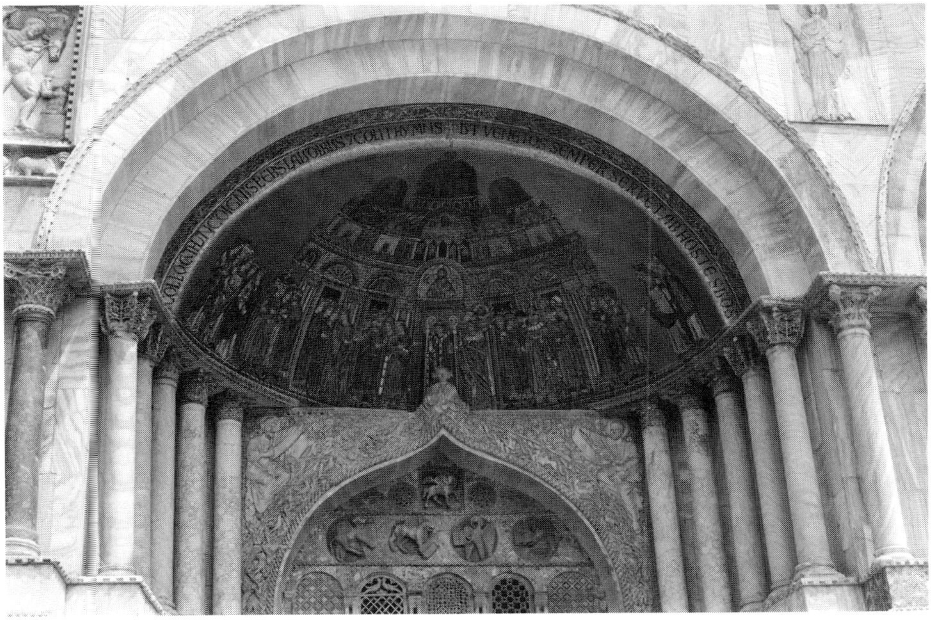

FIGURE 130. Venice, basilica of San Marco, mosaic over the door of S. Alipio

ICONS IN VENICE

Another vital contribution of Crete lies in the religious sphere: the incorporation of miracle-working icons in civic ceremonies. There is no doubt that the most successful manipulation of a Byzantine religious symbol to serve the needs of the Venetians on Crete was the incorporation of the miracle-working icon of the Virgin Mesopanditissa into civic ritual and its central role in official processions (see Chapter 8). Did these Candiote practices affect religious life in Venice?

The acceptance of Byzantine icons within Venetian piety must have required some theological justification as icons did not constitute an integral part of the Latin liturgy. As far as I have been able to establish, there are no records of processions centering on icons in Venice prior to 1204, although an annual procession of icons is recorded in Rome from the last decades of the seventh century.[34] In Venice, the feast of the Twelve Marys, celebrated on February 2, involved a procession centering around twelve wooden statues of the Virgin Mary, but there is no mention of panel paintings.[35] In fact, there is no record of any such icon's being present in Venice prior to the Fourth Crusade, when sacred images arrived in the treasury of San Marco.

It would be beneficial to review the evidence that we possess on religious processions in the church of San Marco in Venice, which was a depository of Byzantine icons at least after the Fourth Crusade. The best sources for such information are the ceremonials of San Marco, which record the comings and goings of the doge and his entourage from and to the ducal church. Within the earliest surviving texts of the sort, the ceremonial book of 1546, written by Bartolomeo Bonifacio, there are intriguing, if vague references to processions.[36] The index of Bonifacio's *cerimoniale* (f. 55v) records the following eight occasions for a solemn procession, presumably regular annual processions in the piazza San Marco: the feasts of St. Isidore (April 26), Corpus Christi, St. Anthony of Padua (June 13), St. Vido (June 15), apparition of St. Mark (June 25), Redentore (third Sunday in July), St. Marina (July 17), St. Justina (October 7), and the Presentation of the Virgin (November 21).[37]

Fortunately, the processional route used on the feast of the translation of St. Isidore is clearly indicated in the manuscript (c. 25v): the confraternities entered the church from the main door, passed in front of the chapel of St. Isidore and through the chapel of St. Peter to the choir in front of the high altar, then to the chapel of St. Clement. They left the church through the middle door and the golden gate of the palace and circled the whole piazza along with the clergy and the canons, singing the hymn *Deus tuorum militum*. The chapter of San Marco emerged from the door of the choir and joined the end of the procession as they did on Wednesdays; they sang litanies in two voices. The procession reentered the church through the door of St. Bassus and through the middle door of the palace.

If we read the Cerimoniale carefully, we realize that this ritual was repeated many more times than these eight most solemn occasions. Three entries from the period of Lent are especially interesting in this regard: "Hodie [de feria quarta cinerorum] facta processione di hora solita . . . [f. 4]," or "In diebus mercurii fiebat processio hora solita [f. 5v]," or "Et si occurrat in hac domenica [quarta in quadragesima] fieri processionem ut fit in prima domenica singulorum mensium . . . [f. 5v]." It seems that two different processions took place on a regular basis: one on the first Sunday of every month and a weekly procession on Wednesdays. The silence of the *cerimoniali* of San Marco on the specifics of these two processions makes one wonder whether they were liturgically insignificant, or whether they did not interest the master of ceremonies in San Marco because they did not involve the various choirs of the basilica.[38]

The Wednesday procession is indirectly mentioned in the passage on the procession of St. Isidore, which when outside the church followed a clearly delineated route: "per viam processionis diei mercurii." In fact, the silence of the sources on these two regular occurrences (one monthly and the other weekly) most probably means that this was an old custom that was embedded within the most basic ceremonial of the city and did not have to be repeated yet another time.[39] An intriguing account written by a keeper of the bell tower of San Marco, Giovanni Romanesco (1563–70), confirms the old custom of a weekly procession of the canons and clergy of the basilica on Wednesday mornings around (or within) the church. From the same account we also learn more about the procession that took place on the first Sunday of every month: the procurators accompanied the Holy Sacrament to the prisoners, while the clergy was involved in its customary procession around the church.[40] Unfortunately since the point of the account is to record the responsibilities of the carilloneur there is no mention of an icon's taking part in the procession.

If we can more or less figure out the routes of the processions and those participating in them it seems more difficult to ascertain whether icons were paraded outside the church. Let us review the evidence for the icons in San Marco. Of the numerous sacred objects that reached Venice after the Fourth Crusade the most venerated was the icon of the Virgin Nikopoios, presumably the panel that was carried in battle by the Byzantine emperors (Fig. 131). The legends about its acquisition from Emperor Alexios V Mourtzouflos during the siege of Constantinople in 1203 emphasized the power of the icon in military matters.[41] It is possible, however, that the icon did not reach Venice until 1234, when an icon of the Virgin (not explicitly the Nikopoios) is first recorded in San Marco.[42] Like many miracle-working icons the Virgin Nikopoios was attributed to the hand of Saint Luke, but it was probably made in Constantinople in the late eleventh century.[43] The Venetians tried to prove that the icon was made during the lifetime of the Virgin in Jerusalem, and that subsequently it was taken to Constantinople by the Byzantine empress Eudoxia to the monastery of the "Hodegoi."[44] Such legends trying to establish an uninterrupted continuity were used to justify the sanctity and authenticity of an icon that took on the role of a relic; as such it would be suitable to become the centerpiece in Marian devotion.[45]

Eventually, the Virgin Nikopoios was adopted as a city patron who conferred victory on the Venetian state. It must have taken the Venetians some work to incorporate the cult of the icon of the Virgin into city life. The main events that centered around the icon were public processions, as in Candia. The icon was carried in an annual procession in the piazza S. Marco on the feast of the Assumption on August 15, while the patriarch said Mass.[46] However, the accounts of Ramusio and Giustiniano, which are based on the antique *cerimoniale* of San Marco, maintain that the icon was taken on procession on more than one of the Marian feasts from the fourteenth century onward.[47] Indeed, a document in the Collegio Cerimoniale font in the State Archives of Venice records a procession on the feast of the Annunciation, which was not normally celebrated with a procession. In the year 1581, the festivities for the day of the Annunciation, which fell on Holy Saturday, had to be moved to another day. At this new date there was a solemn procession:

> La processione e stata fatta con la immagine miracolosa della beata Vergine attorno la piazza, et si stando anco in chiesa con essa di S. Filippo e Giacomo, et passando per la sacrestia di detta chiesia si entro nella casa del Seminario et si usci poi per la porta principale di esso seminario di dove ol serenissimo Principe torno in Palazzo . . . ma essendo aperto questo giorno il seminario di S. Marco nominato Gregoriano per questa causa e stata fatta una solenne processione, nella quale si sone andati tutti li preti, fratti e scole grandi di questa città, et il serenissimo Principe ancora con l'eccellentissimo Senato.[48]

Thus, in this extraordinary instance the icon was paraded in the piazza. The casual way in which the author mentions the presence of the icon in the procession suggests that this was a common enough occurrence that it did not surprise either the author of the *cerimoniale* or the onlookers. Is this enough to indicate that the icon of the Virgin Nikopoios left its chapel in the basilica more often than a few times a year? We know that it was also paraded throughout the city in times of need and became the focal point of special Masses in San Marco.[49] In 1822 the following processions are recorded in conjunction with the piazza S. Marco: Corpus Christi, on the third day of the year; that of the Rogazioni; St. Mark; Palm Sunday; the Purification; and the Presentation of Mary.[50] Whether the Nikopoios icon took part in these regular litanies or not, its role was parallel to that of the Virgin Mesopanditissa in Candia: the icon embodied the essence of Mary for the Venetian state as the Virgin Mesopanditissa did for Crete.

The special position of the icon of the Virgin Nikopoios within the church of San Marco further highlighted this role. First of all, the doge honored the Virgin Nikopoios, the most significant cult object related to the Virgin that resided in the ducal chapel, by attending all of Mary's feast days in the basilica of San Marco.[51] Second, the icon was singled out among the religious treasures that were taken from Constantinople. Rather than residing in the treasury along with the other treasures from Constantinople in 1204, the icon of the Nikopoios was housed in the sacristy, a more public sector of the church.[52] Although the documents are not explicit about the accessibility of the sacristy to the general public, later practices suggest that this placement increased the visibility and usability of the icon. In fact, in the sixteenth century during Christmas and the feasts of Annunciation (March

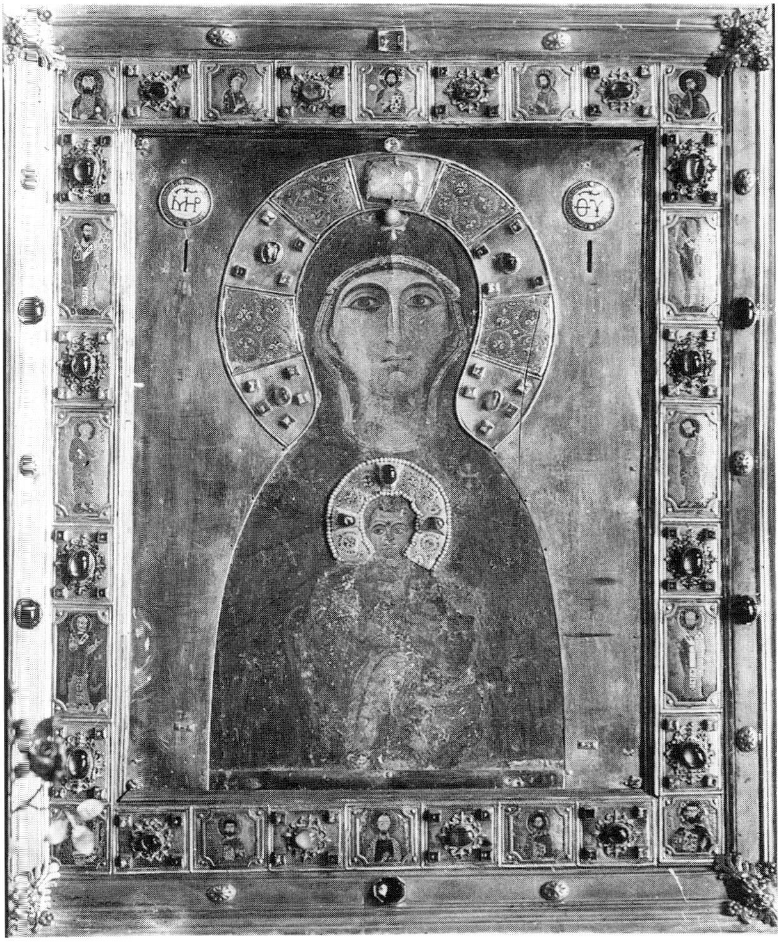

FIGURE 131. Venice, basilica of San Marco, icon of the Virgin Nikopoios (Foto Böhm-Venezia)

25), Purification (February 2), and Assumption of the Virgin (August 15) the image was displayed on the high altar of the church.[53] The prominent display of the icon during these major holidays advertised its unique role inside the basilica and increased its charisma. Moreover, the sixteenth-century *Ritum Cerimoniale* of the basilica of San Marco in Venice records weekly Sunday processions after Vespers from the high altar to the icon of the Virgin in the sacristy in the period between Pentecost and the feast of the Assumption (c. 18r).[54] Thus, the devotion to the Nikopoios icon and its appropriation by the Venetian church paralleled the newly established Venetian cult of the icon of the Virgin Mesopanditissa in Candia, which must have been in full bloom by 1264. The cult in the colony might also have fueled the special association of the Venetian state with the Virgin by offering the Republic a fully elaborated civic (and religious) ritual to build on.

On a liturgical level the surviving evidence does not allow us to make secure claims about the influence of the ecclesiastical rituals of Crete on Venice. Despite the assertions of Sansovino that the liturgy of San Marco followed the practices of Constantinople, the rite of San Marco is now believed to be closer to the Roman rite than to the Constantinopolitan one. Suffice it to say, however, that both the origins of the liturgy of San Marco from Grado and Aquileia and its development in the late thirteenth century are intriguing: the liturgy and ritualistic practices of San Marco were reformed in 1287–91, when the primicerius was Simeono Moro, who in 1291 became bishop of Castello.[55] Once more the timing of the reforms and the reconceptualization of the space of San Marco converge with a date in the third quarter of the century, at least sixty years after the colonization of Crete, and a period close to the refurbishment of the western façade of the basilica. In the absence of indisputable proof only a hypothesis can be forwarded that religious rituals that the Venetians experienced on Crete formed the basis for the changes in Venice.

Another indication of a Byzantine ceremony influencing the ritual of San Marco provides a more solid basis for the hypothesis stated. It is quite possible that the elaborate ceremonies in the evening of Good Friday in San Marco were also a result of direct influence of Cretan/Byzantine customs. As we have seen, the procession of the Epitaphios on Good Friday was the only ceremony when the Latins of Crete went to the Orthodox church of St. Mary of the Angels in Candia (see Chapter 8, n. 51). The complex ritual of Good Friday and Holy Saturday morning in San Marco, which reportedly was more splendid than that of Easter morning, was unusual in the context of the Latin rite. Bonifacio's Cerimoniale informs us that the consecrated host was put inside the sepulchre, which was sealed using the doge's ring. On Easter Sunday morning it was the doge who, after checking the empty sepulchre, announced to the procurator the resurrection of Christ. Susan Rankin has suggested that the ritualized singing of "Surrexit Christus" and the response "Deo gratias" among the celebrants and clergy throughout the church are modeled on the Byzantine Easter greeting Χριστός ἀνέστη.[56] Such a close correspondence naturally suggests that the acts in Venice emulated Byzantine practices as they were performed, among other places, in the colony of Crete. The exchange of these Easter greetings would take place inside and outside the church, as they assume the role of a joyful announcement of the resurrection and at the same time a profession of faith. In all probability these were the words exchanged by the Greek and Latin clergy outside the church of St. Mary of the Angels in Candia as well. In the church of San Marco the announcement had an additional purpose: as initiator of this ceremony, the doge mimicked the Byzantine emperor and took on his imperial role. The evidence points to the traditional Byzantine ceremony as being the basis of the elaborate procession toward the temporary sepulchre of Christ set up against the wall of the chapel of St. Isidore in San Marco.

To return to the Nikopoios icon, on a civic level its effectiveness was paired with the sacred origins of the city of Venice itself. By 1275 the Venetians claimed that their city had been founded on the feast of the Annunciation to the Virgin and considered her a patron of the republic.[57] The icon of the Nikopoios was there to assist and sustain these claims. Its most celebrated intervention is recorded during the devastating plague of 1630. In order to avert the deathly danger of the plague the icon of the Nikopoios was carried in procession on the piazza San Marco for fifteen consecutive Saturdays while litanies were sung. When the state decided to erect the church of Santa Maria della Salute in supplication for the cessation of the plague, it was the Nikopoios icon that was taken to the site of the new church when the first stone was set; Mass was celebrated, then the procession returned to San Marco (Fig. 132). Eventually a procession was instituted on the feast of the Presentation of the Virgin from San Marco to Santa Maria della Salute centering around the Nikopoios icon.[58] It is telling that when the Venetians lost Candia to the Ottomans and acquired the icon of the Mesopanditissa as a relic of their colony, the Cretan icon was placed on the high altar of the church of Santa Maria della Salute, where it remains today. Once the icon of the Mesopanditissa arrived there in 1670 it was no longer deemed necessary to carry the Nikopoios in procession.[59] At this point the two icons seem to have been interchangeable; after all, because of their connection with St. Luke, these were the most venerated icons in Venice and its colonial dominion. It is indeed telling that the Venetians went out of their way to procure other Byzantine icons, which were subsequently displayed in the churches of their city.[60]

Other images of the Virgin, which had been in Crete or in other Greek territories for some time, also made their way to Venice either at the end of Venetian rule (1669) or on some other occasion through miraculous intervention. One of the most venerated of those was another Hodegetria panel reportedly from Constantinople known as the *Madonna della Pace*. According to tradition this icon had been taken to the church of San Giovanni e Paolo in Venice by Paolo Morosini in 1349, but it figures prominently in the history of the Dominican church in 1503, when a new chapel was built to showcase the painting. Subsequently the icon was also venerated by the Greek community of Venice, suggesting, as Ennio Concina has demonstrated, a complex matrix of associations with Venice's outlook about its

Levantine colonies.[61] An elaborate legend surrounded the *Madonna di Spagna*, a marble statuette of the Virgin, located in the stables of the feudatory Andrea Muazzo in Candia. After the statue was transported to the cathedral of St. Titus, it miraculously returned to the stable, where a chapel was built in its honor. Later some Spanish merchants, recognizing the Spanish origin of the statue, tried to take it back home with them, but the statue escaped the ship and returned to Candia. Finally, after the fall of Candia to the Ottomans the statue was given to the nunnery of St. Justina, then to the monastery of St. Francesco della Vigna in Venice.[62] Obviously, this legend seeks to prove the special relationship that existed between the statue of the Virgin and the Venetians, since it decided to stay in Venice when Crete was no longer a Venetian colony. Another miracle-working icon, known as *Mater del Perpetuo Succurso*, is of a rare type produced in Crete, possibly by Andrea Rizo. Presumably this icon was painted by St. Luke with the collaboration of St. Lazarus. The icon was stolen from Candia in 1498 and was taken to Rome, where it currently adorns the church of S. Alfonso all'Esquilino.[63]

The affinity of the processions and legends surrounding the Hodegetria of Constantinople, the Mesopanditissa of Candia, and the Nikopoios of Venice suggests a conscious effort by the Venetians to emulate a powerful sacred tradition. In all three cases it was the hand of Saint Luke that authenticated the icon; the Virgin took an active role in military and political matters; and finally, the regular processions (in the streets of the city or within the church) prescribed definite roles to the urban landscape (Constantinople or Candia) or to the state landscape, in the case of the ducal chapel of San Marco. It was the experience of the Venetians in their colonies, I have argued, that allowed them to appropriate these traditions for their own benefit.

Even if it cannot be shown conclusively that the cultic practices centering around the icon of the Nikopoios in Venice were directly influenced by the cult of the Mesopanditissa in Crete, the role of Crete in stimulating the cult of icons in Venice can be ascertained on a different level. After the end of the Dugento, which witnessed a resurgence of numerous "byzantinisms" in Italian panel painting, Venice remained the only beacon of byzantinism in Italy.[64] As recent archival research has shown, this must be partly due to the presence of Cretan icon painters throughout the Venetian empire.[65] Sergio Bettini has gone so far as to argue that 95 percent of the artists working in Venice or in areas under her influence were Cretans.[66] Because of the peculiar multiethnic and multireligious mixture of the population of Venetian Crete, Cretan painters were able to produce two kinds of panel paintings, presumably to satisfy their diverse clientele. Their (religious) paintings are characterized as being made "a la greca" and "a la latina," a term used for

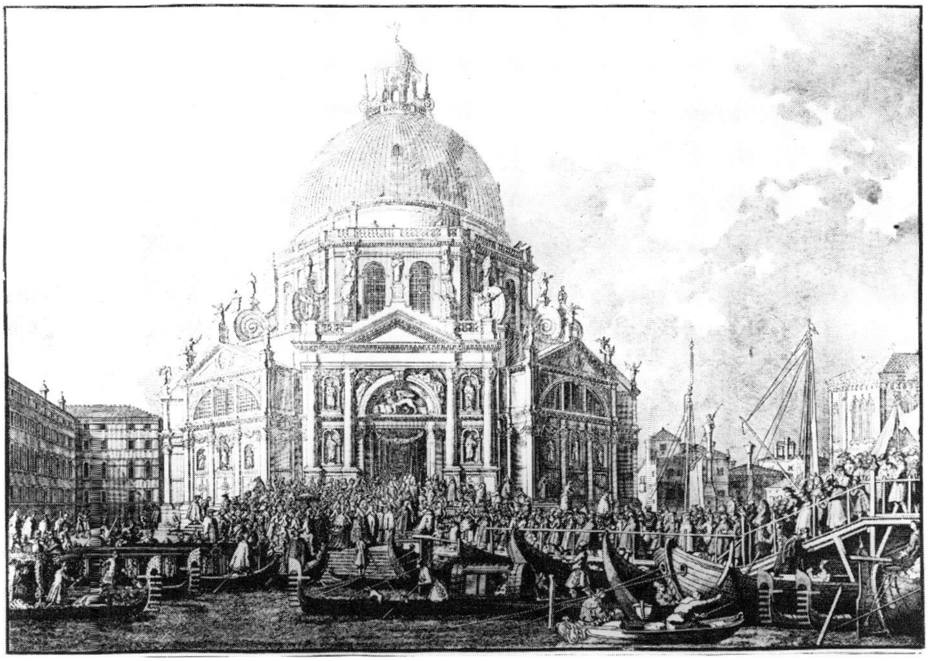

FIGURE 132. Engraving of the church of Santa Maria della Salute in the time of the procession (Archivio di Stato di Venezia, Misc. Mappe, Dis. 1433/i)

the first time in a document of 1499 published by Mario Cattapan.[67] Whether these distinctions referred to style, language, or iconography is often unclear.[68] Presumably a panel painting made in the "Greek manner" would imply a traditional Byzantine-looking icon, whereas the icons painted "a la latina" belong to a peculiar painting style that originated in Crete. These were sacred images of a Byzantine style interpreted in a Western way; made by Greek painters, they were exported in large quantities.[69] They were probably geared to a Catholic clientele with a conservative taste or attached to the cult of icons.[70] It is worth mentioning just one of them: the icon of the Virgin in the Western type of the Madre di Consolazione flanked by Saint Francis with the stigmata in the Byzantine Museum in Athens. This icon of the second half of the fifteenth century provides a dual signal that it was made for a Latin patron in Crete, where it still resided until 1897. It has been suggested that it may have decorated a Franciscan monastery or a private home and that it was produced in the atelier of the famous icon painter Nikolaos Tzafouris in Candia, thus taking center stage in the production of icons for a variety of audiences in Crete.[71] Among the most significant types produced at this period were the *madonne nere*, icons of the Virgin painted by Saint Luke and thought to be miracle-working. These dark-skinned Madonnas signaled an Eastern origin, which implied antiquity and authenticity.[72]

These panel paintings from Crete that in the fifteenth and sixteenth centuries were sold in Venice by the hundreds kept alive a Byzantine tradition and transferred it to the West, where a market was growing steadily in the fifteenth and sixteenth centuries. In fact, Robin Cormack has recently argued that the Cretan painters revitalized Byzantine icon painting.[73] The survival of an extraordinary contract of two icon dealers, one in Venice and the other in the Peloponnesos, placing an order for seven hundred paintings with three Cretan painters, tells it all: the icons had to be delivered in forty-five days. Obviously, in 1499 the production of icons was the most important industry in Crete – and its clientele was enormous.[74] When we consider that the majority of these icons depicted the Virgin and that the most famous icon in Candia was the Mesopanditissa, we may understand the vital role that she may have played in informing religious customs in Venice and beyond. The large quantities of Cretan icons surviving in museums throughout the world should also remind us that these panel paintings from Crete represent what is commonly understood as an icon in the West. It is therefore only fair to suggest that in late medieval and Renaissance Venice the notion of the sacred icon was also coming from Crete. Of course, among these hundreds of icons very few were *acheiropoieitoi* (made by nonhuman hands); Venice can only claim to possess two: the Nikopoios and the Mesopanditissa icons. It would be logical to imagine parallel lives for these two sacred icons, lives that were ultimately based on the prototype of the Hodegetria in Constantinople, the *acheiropoieitos* par excellence.

THE JEWISH GHETTO

The experience that the Venetian colonial authorities had with immigrant and indigenous Jewish groups in their colonies surely gave them ample expertise to govern the Jewish community in the metropole. The suggestion that the roots of the Jewish ghetto in Venice can be traced to the old Jewish quarters of the Venetian Oltremare views the colonies as a laboratory where experiments were carried out that would ultimately benefit Venice herself. Prior to 1516, when the Jewish ghetto was established in Venice, there was no settlement of Jews in that city. Occasionally, some Jewish persons would settle in Venice for specific reasons, usually having to do with financial assistance to the Republic or moneylending.[75] Apparently they stayed in Christian houses most often located close to the piazza San Marco.[76]

To be sure, the Byzantine port cities that constituted the Venetian empire were not unique in incorporating special territories for the Jewish population. In the eleventh and twelfth centuries, especially in the cities of France and the Provence, in the territories of Germany and Spain, there were special quarters for the Jews, called *Giudecca* in Italian, *Juderia* in Spanish, *Juiverie* in French, *Judengasse* in German, *Jewry* in English, *Ulica Zydowska* in Polish. These were not compulsory or segregated quarters and the Jews continued to have direct contacts with the Christians.[77] So, the situation of the Jewish quarters in Crete, Negroponte, or Corfu was not unique. Nevertheless, there can be little doubt that settlement patterns in the colonies confronted the Venetian authorities with the issue of confining the Jewish population in an enclosed, segregated quarter. Jewish communities had existed in almost every town of the Byzantine empire so when the Venetians colonized its port cities they found full-fledged Jewish establishments in these areas.[78] Thus, the patterns of settlement and property rights of Byzantine Jewries seem to have informed – to some extent at least – practices in the Venetian colonies.

Although the Byzantine state was not uniformly anti-Jewish, Jews were treated as a group apart; at the turn of the ninth century they were not allowed to hold high office in the administration of the empire, to own a Christian slave, or to ride on a horse in Constantinople;[79] intermarriage between Jews and Christians was legally treated as adultery,[80] and Benjamin of Tudela reports in the twelfth century instances when hatred was demonstrated by the tanners, who threw their slops on the streets in front of the houses of the Judaica.[81] At the same time, there were laws that safeguarded the well-being of synagogues and no Byzantine law prohibited Jews from owning urban or rural property, except in the case of a plot where a church stood (*Basilics*, c. 890).[82] In most Byzantine (and Muslim) cities ethnic groups lived in separate quarters although they were not compelled to do so. Benjamin of Tudela reports that Alexandria, Antioch, Constantinople, and Thebes in Greece had significant Jewish quarters in the twelfth century: their inhabitants were involved with the silk industry or the tanning business.[83]

Interestingly, the Jewish quarter of Constantinople was moved from the suburb of Pera within the limits of the walled city (in an area called Vlanga) in the later thirteenth century.[84] Was this an attempt to secure the peaceful existence of the Jewish community? In fact, the Arab historian al-Gazari reports in 1293 that the Jewish and Muslim quarters of Constantinople were enveloped by walls and had gates that were closed at night.[85] Of particular significance is the special status that Jews connected to Venice had by the early fourteenth century. After 1324 there was a special Jewish section within the Venetian quarter of Constantinople; the Jews who lived therein were placed under the protection of the Venetians. The Jews of Constantinople had their own landing dock in the city, along with the Venetian merchants.[86] Thus, for the Byzantines these Jews presented a legal entity comparable to the Venetians.

In Candia, where the Jewish quarter is attested inside the city walls, it seems that the settlement of the Jewish community predated the arrival of the Venetians as it did in Corfu. In Negroponte the Jews were allowed to move inside the fortified city for protection only. In Rethymnon and Chania, on the other hand, the Jewish quarter was relegated to the suburbs, not very far from the city walls, but definitely outside the civic core of the Venetian city. These were presumably quarters newly configured by the Venetians in the latter part of the thirteenth century. If this assumption is correct it follows that already by the midthirteenth century a stricter segregational attitude can be detected vis-à-vis the urban settlement of Jews, suggesting that the Venetians decided not to follow to the letter the blueprint of earlier Byzantine cities. This goes hand in hand with the views of the church at the time. In fact, the thirteenth century has been seen as a crucial period when Christian states put in place elaborate mechanisms against the Jewish population of their cities. The Fourth Lateran Council of 1215 codified the regulations against the Jews: they had to distinguish themselves in their dress and were prohibited from holding public office.[87] Nevertheless, these regulations seem to have had no immediate effect on Venetian policies. Similarly, the Inquisition, which acted against the Jews in France (burning of the book of Maimonides in Paris and Montpellier in 1234, and of the Talmud in Paris in 1240), was ineffective in territories under Venetian control, where from 1249 it had to obtain the approval of the government before acting.[88]

We can evoke economic reasons for the different attitudes in the Venetian colonies. The Jews made substantial contributions to the state and the Venetian authorities must have been eager to have large, flourishing Jewish communities in the colonies, which did not exist in Venice itself. Be that as it may, the Jews along with the Greeks of Crete were excluded from the universal award of Venetian citizenship to the immigrants to Venice in 1340 and again in 1352.[89] In fact, there was a clear-cut distinction between Venice and the colonies in regard to the Jewish community. In the fourteenth century the juridical status of the Jewish communities in the Venetian territories of Italy was set by the *condotta*, an agreement that made of each Jewish community a collective entity, but this type of legal document was not used in the Mediterranean colonies.[90] In Venice more attention was paid, it seems, to a symbolic ban of Jews from the city. More pragmatic considerations, such as monetary contributions and the relatively small number of Latins in the colonies, informed the treatment of Jewries in the Oltremare.[91] For instance,

Jews were prohibited from possessing real estate in Venice but could own property within the limits of the Jewish quarters in the colonies at least until the end of the fifteenth century.[92] The results of this different policy surface in 1423, when the Senate complained that soon the Jews in the colonies would have more houses and possessions (*domos et possessiones*) than the Christians.[93] This is not to say that financial considerations were not at stake in Venice: Jewish moneylenders were offered a special quarter in Venice where they could reside in peace and a vineyard on the island of Lido to use as a cemetery during the war of Chioggia (1382–94).[94] However, when their moneylending activities were no longer needed after the end of the war the Jews were expelled from Venice:[95] they could stay in Venice for a maximum of two weeks and could not return to the city before four months had passed.[96] In addition, Jewish men of more than thirteen years of age were compelled to display a yellow badge on their outer garments when they were in Venice.[97] As in Candia, the realities of everyday life made Venice more lenient toward Jewish professionals in the fifteenth century: merchants and doctors were welcome in the city, where they lived in houses belonging to Christians that they used as synagogues.[98]

By the beginning of the sixteenth century, possibly responding to the influx of Jewish settlers to the city following the expulsions from Spain in 1492 and to a moneylending necessity after the failure of three great Venetian banks in 1499, Venice instituted a new form of Jewish settlement, the ghetto, which was an area of compulsory residence for the Jewish community (Fig. 133 and 134).[99] The ghetto was located far from the center of town in the region of San Geremia in Cannaregio, in a spot undesirable to the Jewish population.[100] After the initial establishment of the Ghetto Nuovo in 1516, a locality known as Ghetto Vecchio was attached to it in 1541 solely for the Levantine Jewish merchants, whose presence in the city was thus recognized formally.[101] Within the walls of the ghetto the Jewish community was free to exercise its religious rituals and to be involved in business. Permanent synagogues were established a few years later: the first was known under the title *Scuola Grande Tedesca* and was established in 1529.[102] By 1580 there were at least four prayerhouses in the ghetto each serving a different nation.[103] I propose that the strategies employed by the Venetians when the ghetto was established in 1516 were a direct result of specific events that had happened in the colonies in the Levant. In fact, it can be argued that the ability of Venice to contain foreign heterodox groups or infidels without infecting, so to speak, the host population is due to the situation in its colonies.[104]

Although the form of the ghetto in Venice had a somewhat different character from that of the Jewish quarters in the colonies in that it was enclosed by walls on all sides and had guards posted at the gates, its inception

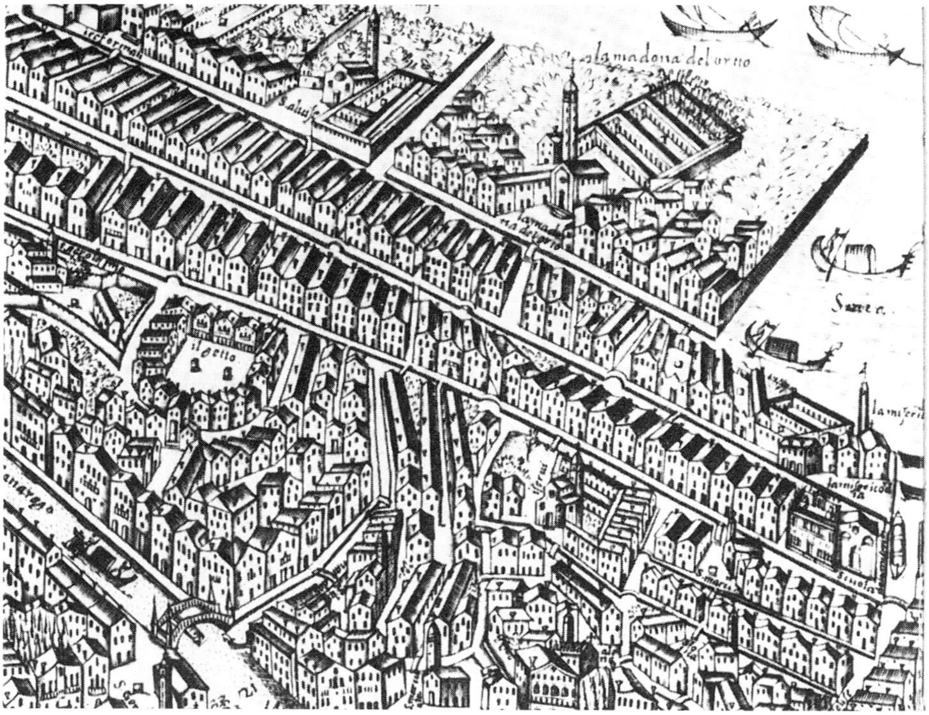

FIGURE 133. Scolari, view of the ghetto of Venice, detail, Pianta di Venezia, c. 1700 (Civico Museo Correr, M. 20868)

and realization must have been related to the colonies. The feature of blocking the doors and windows of Jewish houses (promulgated as a decree in Candia in 1390) was repeated in the ghetto of Venice 150 years later (1541). Along the walls of the ghetto starting at Cannaregio there should be no balconies, except for the traditional *luce ferrati*, so that the part of the ghetto that remained Christian would have no contact with the Jews.[105] Also, there existed in Venice a wall separating the Jewish settlement from the Christian part of town (similar to the wall separating the Judaica of Candia from the Dominican church of St. Peter the Martyr). The two gates of the ghetto in Venice were guarded by Christians, opened each morning at the sound of the large bell of the campanile of San Marco, and closed in the evenings at nightfall.[106] Similarly, the Jews of Candia had since the fourteenth century followed the bell of St. Peter the Martyr as a marker of the beginning and end of their work day. Not only are there specific features of the colonies replicated in the ghetto in Venice, but the imposition of such a bold idea of a completely segregated quarter for the first time appears to be the culmination of the experiments that the Venetians had tested in the colonies. The ghetto in Venice surfaces from its inception as a fully thought out

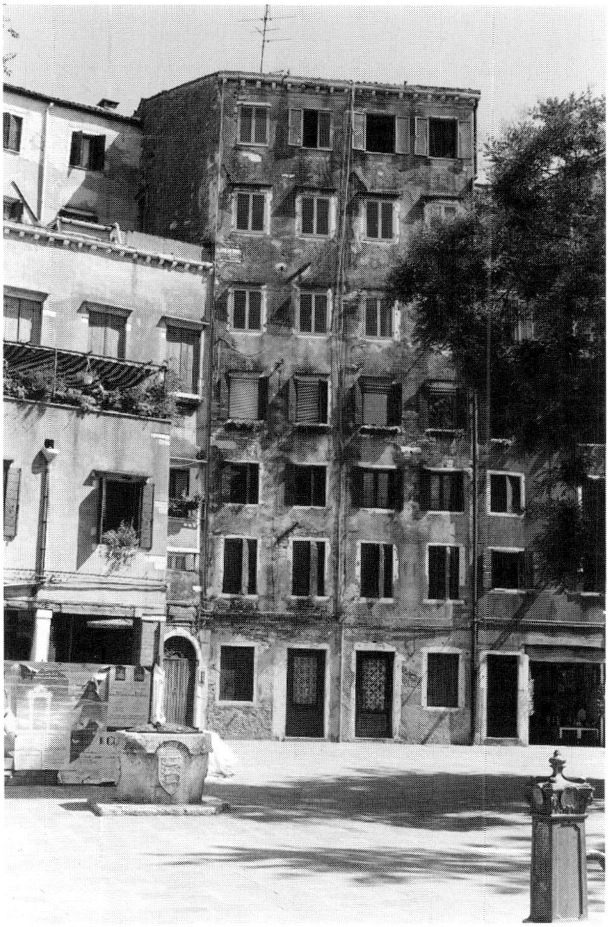

FIGURE 134. Venice, view of the ghetto

working mechanism. In fact, it worked so well that within a few years it was enlarged without any major changes recorded in its operation.

This successful implantation of colonial practices in the heart of Venice opens the large issue of the cultural relationship between center and periphery. Obviously, the subsequent turn of events and later history confirmed what was evident in the wake of the Fourth Crusade: the primacy of Venetian culture over that of its colonies. It would be worth, however, examining the cases in which this relationship between metropole and colonies was not always predestined or transparent. In fact, as one could argue that the makeup of modern metropoleis is due to some degree to the immigration of ethnically varied people from postcolonial territories, one may also maintain that for Venice the profits of empire went beyond the economic and political ramifications of its elaborate mercantile system, for the success of such a complex undertaking needs more than political speeches and money in the bank: for the Republic of Venice the indispensable symbolic capital was provided by the cultural richness of a Byzantine/Levantine culture found in its colonies.

THE LEGACY OF BYZANTIUM

Just as the Venetians of Crete recognized the value of the sacred traditions of the island, the conspicuous display of riches in the piazza S. Marco exemplified the reception of the Byzantine treasures in Venice as the legacy of an unrivaled culture shared by Byzantines and Venetians. Thus, the constantinopolitan booty played a catalytic role in the formation of the new image of Venice in the thirteenth century. The successful manipulation of Byzantine traditions and artifacts to serve the political ends of the Republic transformed Venice from a "privileged daughter of Byzantium" to an heir of its imperial status.[107] This status was soon to be challenged. In 1261 the Byzantine emperor Michael VIII Palaiologos conquered the capital and dissolved the short-lived Latin empire established by the crusaders in Constantinople. The official Byzantine policy favored the Genoese, who had helped Michael VIII regain Constantinople from the Venetians, and the Genoese had been at war with Venice since 1257.[108] Thus, in the 1260s the Venetians found themselves in greater need of publicizing their leading position in the Mediterranean. We do know, of course, that mosaicists were busy in the basilica of San Marco as early as 1258,[109] but the dramatic changes in the political scene surely affected the outcome of the program – at least in certain details. Despite the blows that the Byzantine emperor and his alliance with the Genoese leveled against Venice, the Republic had managed to establish her colonies on safe ground; Venetian and Byzantine heritage continued to blend there and in the mother city. The Byzantine treasures exhibited in Venice became more than symbols of Venetian victory over the Byzantines: they represented the very essence of the Republic and were seen, by Venetians and foreigners alike, as the foremost symbols of the Venetian empire. The Bronze Horses, for instance, became the most salient feature of the newly redecorated façade of S. Marco, overlooking and glorifying the piazza (Fig. 2).[110]

The first few decades of Venetian presence on Crete seem to have been particularly constructive in this encounter between Venice and Byzantium. The colonial experience of the Venetians in Crete was doubly successful: it provided them with material rewards in the form of territories to be exploited commercially, and, most important, it offered them new cultural treasures. This armature taught the Venetians how to advertise their empire in the piazza S. Marco and by extension to the world at large. By the 1260s (but perhaps from as early as the rule of doge Jacopo Tiepolo, 1229–49) the stage was set for the successful incorporation of the constantinopolitan booty in Venice. The Venetians had acquired the ability to exploit to its fullest the power of the Byzantine spoils at home.

The experience of the Venetians in the colonies was fruitful in various respects. The exercise of power in the distant colonies demanded novel solutions of an administrative, social, and political nature. The longevity of the Venetian overseas empire secured agricultural resources and a convenient network of outposts for the international trade of the Venetians. In addition, the tangible manifestation of Venetian colonialism through its officers, monuments, ceremonies, and pomp offered Venice invaluable opportunities to sustain its imperial claims and its dominion. I have tried to trace the backbone of this development in the artistic and architectural urban projects of the Venetians in Candia and the other colonies, following certain lines of inquiry that attempt to modify a strict dualistic concept of clash between Greeks and Latins. Any such model fails to grasp the symbiotic relationships that arise between communities that share the same territory. As I have argued, this would have been impossible in the case of Venetian Crete as Byzantine culture was such a large part of Venetian heritage.

CONCLUSION: CRETE AND VENICE

> Vicini enim cesi capti et fugati hostes, cives vinculis eruti, urbes ad obsequium reverse, reimpositum Crete iugum, posita arma victricia, pactum denique sine cede bellum et pax parta cum gloria.
>
> Petrarch (1364)[1]

> The land of Cyprus, which is inhabited by Greeks, and the island of Crete, and all the other lands and islands, which belong to the principality of Morea and the duchy of Athens, all are inhabited by Greeks, and although they are obedient in words, they are none the less hardly obedient in their hearts, although temporal and spiritual authority is in Latin hands.
>
> Marino Sanuto Torsello (April 10, 1330)[2]

A land of ancient ruins and impressive early Christian basilicas, the home of King Minos and Saint Titus, the island of Crete gained a new, significant position in the Mediterranean trade system when it was colonized by the Venetians in the thirteenth century. Although exceptional in many respects, the Venetian colony of Crete (the Regno di Candia) was not a unique or isolated phenomenon. It is an exemplary part of the Venetian maritime empire, arguably its most successful experiment.

It is never an easy task to assess the role that a foreign, colonial rule played in a region, even in the case of modern European colonialism, which can be more readily accused of exploiting the colonized population or having a clear, racially informed agenda. Although the overwhelming majority of archival documents are written about and not by the non-Latins of Crete, Venetian rule was by no means a constant struggle between the Latin elite and the local communities, many of whose members prospered. Despite the fact that the figures of per capita income are not known, the increasing material prosperity of the island during the Venetian period appears to have offered a variety of new opportunities to its inhabitants. The success of

Crete's agricultural products (wine, oil, and cheese) in the international trade scene, the wide circulation of Cretan religious icons, and the wealth of the island's intellectual and artistic life in the sixteenth century demonstrate that both Venetians and locals molded the economic and cultural life of the island.[3] From the perspective of the sixteenth century the long symbiosis of Greeks and Latins on Cretan soil reveals the Venetian colonial enterprise on Crete as being flexible in its policies and willing to make concessions to the locals. The urbanistic choices in Candia in conjunction with the governmental and notarial records further highlight these strategies for the duration of the Venetian presence on Crete.

Only rarely does the archival material offer specific information that would associate particular members of the middle and lower classes with public monuments, but the plethora of notarial records account for their active role in the city, endowing churches, setting up shops in the marketplace, forming joint commercial ventures, selling and buying products, building houses, making their living fishing or toiling the land. Urban residences of the lower classes have not produced significant archaeological vestiges but there is enough information on court records and work contracts to suggest that Greeks could have comfortable if not palatial dwellings in the city and its suburbs, often containing gardens (Fig. 135).[4] The earliest surviving notarial books from Candia, those of Pietro Scardon (1271), suggest that the local population had already acquired a significant role in various crafts and regional trade by the third quarter of the thirteenth century: Christian (including Greeks) and Jewish inhabitants of Candia were involved in the production and distribution of agricultural goods as well as in artisanal production.[5] With the financing of international commercial expeditions in the hands of Latin partnerships possibly from the metropole itself, only local commerce seems to have been an option for adventurous Greeks in the thirteenth century.[6] By the end of the century, however, the Greeks seem to have acquired more capital and in the first years of the fourteenth century all lenders are inhabitants of Candia, many of whom have Greek names, as seen in the notarial acts of Leonardo Marcello (1278–81) and Benvenuto di Brixano (1301–2). Thus, it seems that after a cohabitation of about a century Greek (and Jewish?) merchants and investors were widely accepted in the Venetian trade system. From the available documentary material one gets the impression that the Venetian merchants welcomed the local population of Crete among their ranks as soon as they realized that the involvement of Greeks and Jews in trade would not harm Venetian interests.

The sources dealing with the beginning of Venetian rule on Crete, therefore, suggest that by the midthirteenth century the Venetian authorities had generated a thoughtful plan of Candia that in conjunction with govern-

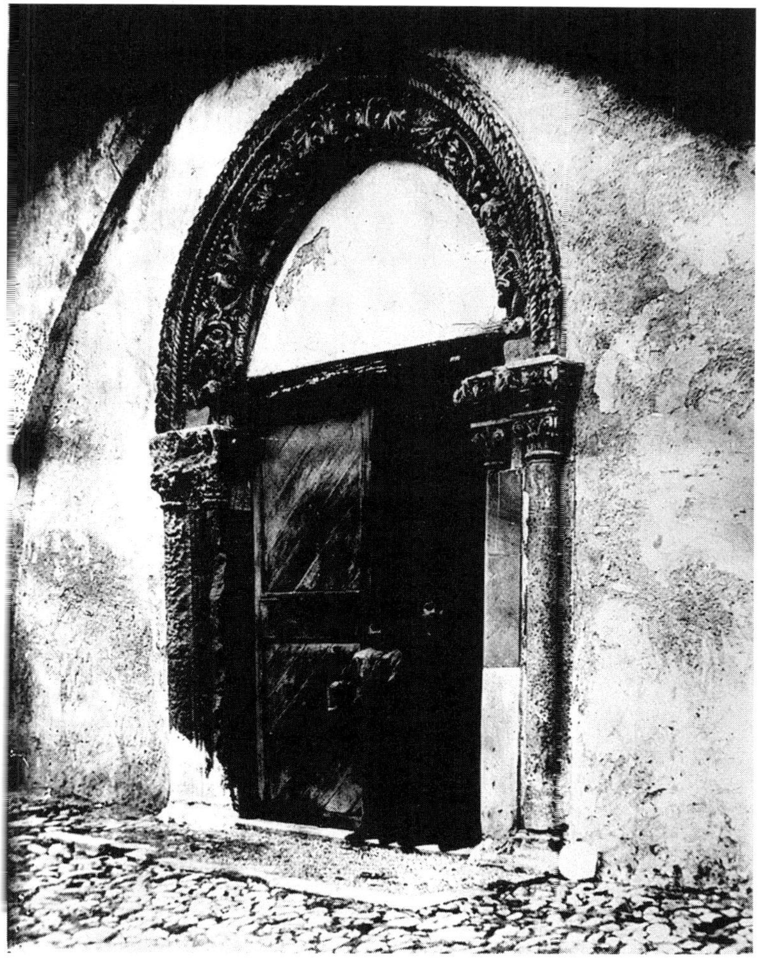

FIGURE 135. Herakleion, portal of the Palazzo Ittar (Istituto Veneto di Scienze, Lettere ed Arti. Venezia. Archivio fotografico della Missione in Creta di Giuseppe Gerola)

mental decrees regulated the movement, the behavior, the religious practices, and the legal rights of the population. Nevertheless, the changes that the Venetians introduced to the city in the first three centuries of their presence on Crete were not dramatic enough to disrupt urban life. Like the exclusion of non-Latins from the highest posts of the government, the most drastic urban modifications were aimed at the highest echelon of the population of Chandax/Candia: the Byzantine patricians. Denying full political rights to the nonprivileged population groups was probably considered an act strengthening the position of the colonial state, but soon the realities of colonization showed otherwise. In the fourteenth century the colonial regime had to revise this policy: Greek families appear as prominent persons within the hierarchy of the colony, holding offices and posts in the council of the feudatories and the Senate of Candia. The Calergis had in fact acquired urban properties prominently located in the old city.

Other members of the Byzantine aristocracy married into the Venetian elite and thus we often encounter cases of ethnically and religiously mixed households in the fourteenth century.[7] In fact, intermarriage between Latins and Greeks has been attested from early on in Venetian Crete.[8] One wonders whether the fact that Greek clerics (priests and monks) were emphatically prohibited from giving communion to the wives or heirs of Latin men in Modon does not reflect the realities of such mixed marriages and the concern of the authorities that the Latin rite would dwindle.[9] In any case, these intracultural marriages produced households that represented a microcosm of the society of Venetian Candia: a symbiotic environment between the different Christian peoples of the city. Interestingly, Latins who were married to Greek women ended up speaking Greek at work and at home, where they were surrounded by Greek servants as well as Greek-speaking children; being buried in Orthodox monasteries; and making bequests to both Latin and Orthodox churches.[10] By the midfourteenth century the realities of such a world demanded knowledge of both Latin and Greek in order to take full advantage of the possibilities offered by local and international trade, with Greek taking the upper hand.[11] Indeed, by the second quarter of the fourteenth century concrete evidence points to the function of schools in Candia, where Frankish (it is not stated whether this meant Italian or medieval Latin) and Greek were taught.[12] Apparently Greek became even more widely used in the following centuries. Interestingly, toward the end of Venetian rule even a Greek religious text such as the Apocalypse of the Virgin, which was copied in Crete, was transliterated in Latin characters, apparently for an Orthodox (?) population who understood Greek but could not read it.[13] Despite the fact that the Venetians tolerated mixed marriages and the instruction of the Greek language, they never promoted such practices: one wonders whether this reluctance was due to the ever-prominent role that the Greek language, the Orthodox faith, and the Cretan customs played in the life of the city to the detriment of the Latin/Venetian culture. Nevertheless, the prominence of the culture of the metropole, whose brilliance as a cosmopolitan center was obviously well known on Crete, is apparent in a variety of customs, including the clothing *a la forestiera*, that is to say, according to Venetian practices. The case of the young Quirina Calergis, great-great-granddaughter of the famous Alexios and wife of Antonio Mudacio, who authorizes her uncle to buy her clothes in Venice in 1444 in order to be dressed according to her social status is instructive in this respect.[14] The reverse seems to have happened in Modon in 1341: many of the Venetian soldiers were scolded for wearing a beard as they were indistinguishable from the Greeks; they were ordered to shave immediately.[15]

These borrowings of customs and fashions indicate a cross-fertilization between the two dominant communities on the island and in the colonies at large. It is harder to establish how deeply was this rapprochement felt by the two cultures. For instance, the intrusion of Venetian household objects in scenes of the Last Supper or the banquet of Herod in Greek churches not only seems to be devoid of any ideological weight but reinforces the common material culture available to the typical Cretan household of the period. If, then, on this basic level of everyday life we are led to imagine a community where ethnic and religious boundaries dissolved, in other words a community of perfect colonial concord, there are just as many indications of insurmountable obstacles between Greeks and Latins, manifested primarily in the religious sphere. Just as the authorities centered their attention on the Byzantine sacred traditions in order to neutralize the power of Orthodoxy, in the eyes of the locals it was the Latin faith and its representatives that were singled out as the enemy. This is particularly evident in the promulgation of the Unionist doctrine following 1439: according to the decisions of the Synod of Florence the Orthodox priests could celebrate the liturgy in their own language but had to include the name of the pope. Contrary to this assertion of the synod, the pope attempted to regulate services in the few Unionist churches by translating the Greek liturgy into Latin.[16] Furthermore, in 1467 the pope ordered the *protopapas* to read the Unionist decision in the church of St. Mark in Candia twice a year, and once a month he and the other Catholic (read Unionist) priests in the Orthodox churches of Candia.[17] Despite the attempts of the most fervent architect of the Union on the Greek side, cardinal Bessarion, to institute a college for Unionist priests in Candia, only twelve or thirteen priests became members of this college.[18]

The hundreds of Greek churches in the countryside of Crete are only partially known, but we can use them as indicators of the degree to which the Western rite had an impact on the Orthodox faith of the Cretans. The appearance of Saint Francis on the walls of a Greek church may be taken as a sign of rapprochement and an indication that the Franciscan friars were looked upon by Greeks and Latins alike as uniquely qualified to serve God (see Introduction, nn. 28 and 29), but for each figure of St. Francis that appears on the walls of a Greek church just as many "Franciscans and cardinals" are shown "among the sinful in the Last Judgment," indicating "the Orthodox hostile attitude toward the Roman Catholic church and its representatives."[19] A similar attitude of suspicion toward the Latin (and this time also the Greek) clergy is attested in the satirical verses of Stephanus

Saclichi drafted in the second half of the fourteenth century: among the clients of the prostitutes in Candia Saclichi includes a bishop (presumably Catholic, since there were only Latin bishops on Cretan soil), the prior of a monastery, friars, and a Greek priest.[20] These apparently contradictory attitudes vis-à-vis the most important among Western friars signal the complexities in the origin and patronage of particular monuments as well as the specific historical moments in which such projects originated. It may well be that the inclusion of a figure of Saint Francis suggests that the patron was a product of an intermarriage between a Latin and a Greek of the upper social strata. The flow of international politics and the particularities of events internal to the colony, such as rebellions, may indeed have generated specific trends in certain monuments, thus making the task of generalizing extremely difficult.

Moreover, the phrasing of the governmental documents and the formulaic descriptions of historical events by the clergy or travelers often disguise the true historical circumstances. These records are so successful in masking reality that one still wonders whether the apparent "cruelties" of the authorities were due to minor misunderstandings of local customs or to a major clash between the different communities of Candia as the case of the refusal of the Greeks to kneel during the litany of the Holy Sacrament in Canea shows (see Chapter 8, n.56). These examples indicate that despite the signs of coexistence between the two communities, at some level there existed a voice of dissent among the Greek population. This voice was articulated more vigorously when international or local developments warranted a unified Byzantine (Greek or Orthodox) consciousness against Venice. To the distress of the Venetian authorities, such an occurrence in 1363 had even broader implications for the colony. In response to a new heavy taxation for the maintenance of the port of Candia, the Latin and Greek population of Candia joined forces under the leadership of the Gradonigo, the Venier, and the Calergis families and rebelled against the central government of Venice.[21] This dramatic reaction to Venetian rule confirms that after 150 years of cohabitation some Venetian settlers of Crete under pressure to act against the metropole felt closer to their Greek compatriots than to the central government in Venice.[22] The history of the Venetian colonies seems to be full of such particularities. It is understandable that when the news of the fall of Constantinople to the Ottoman Turks reached Crete in late June 1453 the Greek community would be shocked, as the marginal note in a British Library manuscript tells us.[23] Wholly unexpected, on the other hand, is a Hebrew lament produced in Candia. Why would the Jewry of Candia feel so distraught by the fall of Constantinople, identified in that lament as the new Rome or Edom, which in the Bible is portrayed as the enemy of world Jewry?[24]

The affinities among the Greek, Latin/Venetian, and Jewish cultures in the context of the Mediterranean offered fertile ground for a symbiotic relationship among them, a setting in which the locals undermined Venetian authority gradually and quite inconspicuously. The non-Latin inhabitants of Candia acted – by definition – in a place that was not their own anymore, "the place of the other."[25] However, because this place had belonged to them in the past, it was relatively easy for the locals to find ways to accommodate their needs and to adjust their lives within the framework of the new Venetian city of Candia. Their similar mind-set guaranteed the success of their subversive tactics in the long run. It is quite telling that the Greeks (and to a lesser degree the Jews) of Candia used their religious convictions and their professional activities to challenge the "benevolent rulers" ideology of the Venetians. By cooperating with the authorities in agricultural production and the distribution of goods the locals championed their active involvement in agriculture, manufacture, and trade as a critical means to further Venetian interests. In fact, as we have already seen, the Greek and Jewish population groups were vital players in the production process on Venetian Crete. Their increasing success was translated into greater autonomy and easier access to the resources of the colony – this, in turn, meant that they acquired more power to adjust the rules of the game to their benefit. The already mentioned studies of Sally McKee, based on the vast notarial material in the State Archives of Venice, have shown the extensive degree of interaction between Latins and Greeks but have also demonstrated how overwhelmingly Greek the culture of Candia was already by the fourteenth century.

In the end, the long symbiosis of the Eastern and Western rites accomplished what the decrees of the Synod of Florence had not in 1439: apparently, in the late sixteenth century it was not rare to hear Mass in Greek and in Latin in altars built especially for such dual use.[26] Unfortunately for the Venetians, this rapprochement of the two rites was cultivated in favor of Orthodoxy. Furthermore, practical reasons determined the fate of Catholicism in Crete. Latin had almost become a foreign tongue on Venetian Crete; Greek, on the other hand, was spoken extensively, especially by the female population of the island.[27] In 1637 the archbishop Luigi Mocenigo complained that none of the Dominican nuns of Candia understood Latin or Italian; they only spoke Greek.[28] These seventeenth-century Dominican nuns are paradigmatic of the peculiarities of the colonial society of Candia. In fact by the seventeenth century many notarial documents were written in Greek using the Latin alphabet. Evidently, the "inhabitants of the city knew Greek, but very few had learnt the language systematically at school."[29]

Obviously, the physical arrangement of Candia – that is, the administrative and religious public buildings, the military structures, and the street pattern – in conjunction with the official ceremonial demonstrate how the designers of the colony thought that the city ought to be. By clustering the most significant public monuments of the colony in the center of Candia and by inventing a civic ceremonial profile that enlivened the space according to the rhetoric of the Venetian authorities, the civic core of Candia was turned into an exclusively Venetian space that meant to project and reinforce two diverging and yet complementary policies: on the one hand, the segregation of the Latins from the indigenous elite population groups and, on the other hand, the seemingly harmonious cohabitation of the different ethnic groups within Candia. This double-faceted strategy, which crystallized at some time in the early fourteenth century, was vital for the preservation of Venetian rule.

The urban landscape of Venetian Candia has been analyzed from three perspectives seeking to understand its complex personality up to the sixteenth century: within the context of imperialism, religion and ritual, and colonial policies. The larger framework of empire, the Oltremare experience of the Venetians, appeared to defer to the glorious legacy of Byzantium, as seen in reused monuments and in the maintenance of older traditions. The new regime of the city was sacralized by appropriating older cult objects within a new framework sanctioned by the fervent Mendicant friars. The politics of segregation and acceptance of the Greek and Jewish cultures and peoples in the colony and in the metropole promoted Candia as a site of converging and diverging communities that produced a unique, hybrid culture on Crete. I hope to have shown that it is the precautious balance between concessions to local customs and rigid display of colonial power observed in the civic images of the colony and the metropole that provides the foundation for the success of the Venetian empire. Although the horizon of all Venetian colonies on the Mediterranean coastline is dominated by an undisputable emblem of Venice, the lion of St. Mark, these colonies worked because the colonized population was convinced peacefully to bow to the Venetian authorities. The fact that the Greeks continued to use the same relics and sacred objects in worship but prayed that these offer their miracle-working powers to a new overlord shows the subtle workings of the Venetians over local traditions.

The official standard of the last Venetian governor of Crete, Francesco Morosini, epitomizes the sacred ties that the Venetians had established with Byzantine tradition on the island by the seventeenth century. As Panagiotes

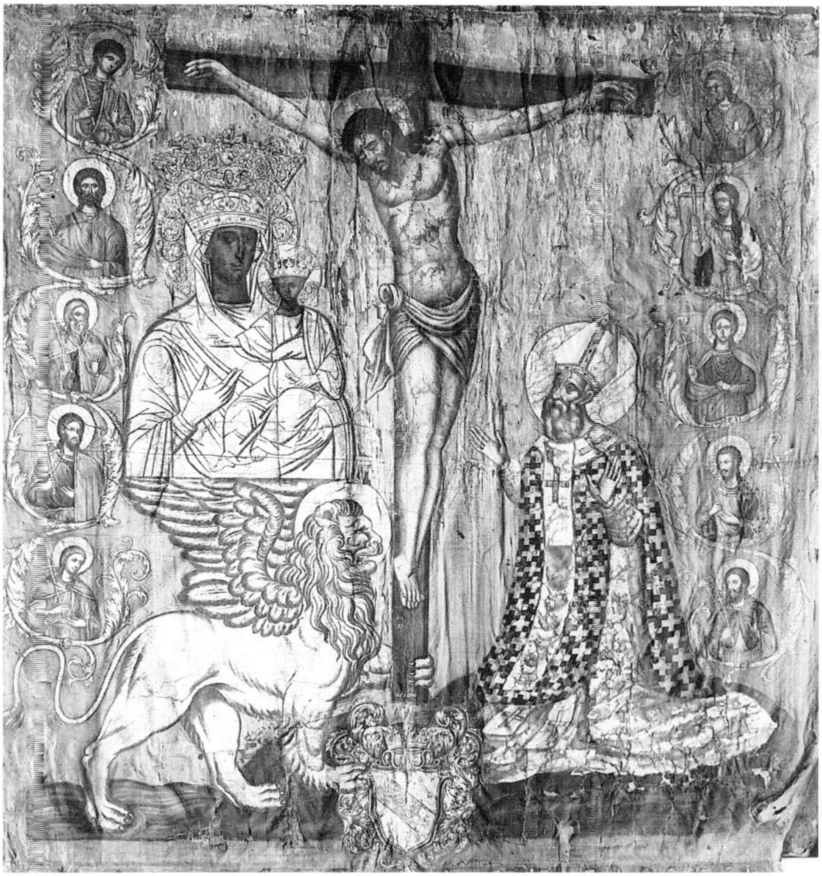

FIGURE 136. Victor, standard of Francesco Morosini, made in Candia in 1667–69 (Civico Museo Correr)

Vocotopoulos has convincingly argued, the standard was made in Crete by the painter Victor between 1667 and 1669, during the final years of the siege of Candia by the Ottoman Turks (Fig. 136).[30] The banner displays a curiously assembled image of Christ on the Cross, with the religious symbols of the now well-established Latin church in Crete. On the left the Virgin Mesopanditissa is portrayed above the lion, the symbol of Saint Mark; on the right Saint Titus, in Latin episcopal garments, adores Christ. Medallions of ten additional Cretan saints flank the whole.[31] The placement of the lion of Saint Mark at the same level as Saint Titus and below the Virgin demonstrates the Republic's acceptance of the Cretan relics: Saint Mark does not assume a place above the local patron saint and a Cretan cult object. As in the Corpus Christi procession in Candia (Fig. 67), the Virgin Mesopanditissa occupies the highest position in the hierarchy of saints in Venetian Crete. If we recall the acclamations sung during the civic ceremonies of Candia, we can substitute the state authorities for the two saints: the doge of Venice for Saint Mark's lion and the duke of Crete for Saint Titus. In this display of humility they both bow to the sacred authority of the icon and the crucified Christ. The standard reiterates the role of the icon as a mediator. According to the official ideology of the Venetians in Crete, it was thanks to the miraculous presence of the Byzantine icon of the Virgin Mesopanditissa that Venetians and Greeks coexisted for four and a half centuries on the soil of Crete. When the Mesopanditissa icon was taken to Venice in 1669 it was covered with precious stones and a golden revetment that leave visible only the faces of Christ and the Virgin (Fig. 128). It is in this relic of the colony that the story of the Venetian empire is still embedded. Within it, the glorious history of Byzantium, its artistic practices, and its institutions also resonate in the heart of one of the grandest churches of Venice, the "privileged daughter of Byzantium."[32]

APPENDIX: THE LIST OF CHURCHES ON WERDMÜLLER'S PLAN OF CANDIA

(FIGURES 16 AND 17)

This list is reproduced here from Gerola, "Topografia delle chiese della città di Candia," *Bessarione* 22 no. 1–4 (1918), 99–119 and 239–81. The original plan of Candia, as it was drawn by General Werdmüller in 1668–69, did not include numbers; it only contained the names of the Latin and Orthodox churches of Candia. The names of the churches are not translated into English but are preserved as they appear on the original map so that any discrepancies may be evident to the reader.

Following the title of each church I provide the date of construction of the church if available, or its first mention in the documents, and alternate names associated with it. Some of the churches were built in later centuries, but a large number of them must have existed during the period of the thirteenth to the fifteenth century. However, I have not been able to gather enough documentary and topographical information to identify these churches with buildings mentioned by Werdmüller, with any degree of certainty.

Churches Inside the City

1 [without name]
2 S. Michel (mentioned in 1376)
3 S. Zuanne Eremita
4 S. Nicolò (mentioned in 1376)
5 S. Catarina de Monache (mentioned in 1325 and earlier)
6 La Madonna = Cheragosti? (mentioned in 1344)
7 S. Zuan da Mascro
8 S. Francesco (mentioned in 1242)
9 [without name]
10 Chera Pisiotissa (mentioned in 1330)
11 S. Nicolò Maluzi

12 [without name]
13 S. Costantino (mentioned in 1330)
14 S. Zorzi Cavura (mentioned in 1356)
15 S. Antonio Castro (mentioned in 1436)
16 Madonna Spanopuliotissa (mentioned in thirteenth century)
17 S. Anna Cipuro (mentioned in 1346)
18 S. Pantaleone (mentioned in 1406)
19 La Madona
20 S. Nicolò (mentioned in 1335)
21 S. Tito (Byzantine church)
22 Christo Chi = Chefala (1323)
23 Chesola
24 S. Bastian
25 S. Marco (built in 1239)
26 [without name]
27 S. Chiriachi = Santa Domenica (mentioned in 1332)
28 Madonna Barozani
29 S. Fotini = Santa Lucia (mentioned in 1331)
30 S. Michel (mentioned in 1320)
31 S. Rocco (mentioned in sixteenth and seventeenth centuries)
32 [without name]
33 S. Dimitri (mentioned in 1319)
34 S. Zorzi Venetico (mentioned in 1319)
35 S. Nicolò (mentioned in 1448)
36 S. Nicolò dei Caligieri = Vergici? (mentioned in 1356)
37 S. Pietro (built in midthirteenth century)
38 S. Anna (mentioned in 1375/1360?)
39 Christo Sculudi C. Vertmiller (mentioned in 1496)
40 La Madona
41 S. Marina
42 S. Zuane Crisostomo (mentioned in 1333)

Churches in the Suburbs

43 S. Maria Vituri = Ascepastos? (1310)
44 [without name]
45 S. Maria Periblecto (built c. 1303)
46 S. Zorzi Varda
47 S. Giorgi Casomati
48 S. Zuanne Cristofilina (built c. 1303)
49 S. Giorgi di Volta (1330)
50 S. Zorzi di Volta
51 S. Maria Odistria = Hodegetria (1368)
52 S. Giacomo (1290)
53 Chera Psigosostra
54 S. Spirito

55 S. Theodosia (beginning of fifteenth century)
56 S. Trimartira (?)
57 S. Onofrio (sixteenth and seventeenth centuries)
58 S. Zuanne di Merceri
59 S. Salvator (early fourteenth century)
60 S. Anargiri
61 S. Todoro
62 S. Panaia (1360)
63 Gnia Mognì (1323)
64 S. Nicolò Casmaleuri (1348)
65 S. Atanasia
66 S. Veneranda
67 S. Maria de' Capucini (1232)
68 S. Niclo Stirgliachi (built in 1418)
69 S. Ollia
70 S. Michel
71 S. Maria Faneromeni (built in 1319)
72 S. Andrea = St. Symeon of the Sinaites? (mentioned before 1204)
73 S. Giovanni (mentioned in 1271)
74 S. Giorgio Vertmiller
75 S. Chiara
76 S. Antonio
77 S. Gierolimo (mentioned in the fifteenth century)
78 S. Paolo (possibly mentioned in 1346)
79 S. Spiridion
80 S. Marco (mentioned in 1391)
81 S. Matio
82 S. Giorgi Vlicocaridi (mentioned in 1355)
83 Ss. Apostoli
84 S. Maria Faneromeni
85 S. Veneranda
86 S. Giorgi Surgiano
87 Cristo Casturi (mentioned in 1320)
88 S. Illia Candeloro
89 Madonna Catafiana (mentioned in 1362)
90 S. Zorzi Taoloto
91 Chera Thalasoma (mentioned in 1320)
92 Chera Leusa = Panagia Eleousa (rebuilt in 1305)
93 S. Croce
94 Chera Politissa (mentioned in 1368)
95 S. Zuane Theologo (mentioned in 1320)
96 S. Basilio
97 Chera Manolitissa (built c. 1000)
98 S. Michel (mentioned in 1320)
99 S. Nicol. Murgutaria
100 S. Maria Pandonasa
101 S. Caterina (Byzantine)

102 Dieci Martiri Cretensi
103 La Madonina (Byzantine?/1482)
104 S. Maria de Angoli (mentioned in 1320)
105 S. Anastasia (mentioned in 1375)
106 S. Erini (mentioned in 1320)
107 [without name] = St. George Muglino? (mentioned in 1320)
108 [without name] = St. Mary Vrachiotissa? (mentioned in 1320)
109 Ss. Apostoli (mentioned in 1378)
110 S. Zuanne Stamacheolia (mentioned in 1320)
111 S. Giorgio di Moneghe (mentioned in 1303)
112 S. Cirillo (built before 1373)
113 [without name]
114 Chera Luviani = Luludiani (built in 1312)
115 S. Spirito
116 S. Gioan Armacri
117 Madonna Acrotiriani
118 S. Croce
119 S. Zorzi di Remeri
120 S. Marina (mentioned in 1320)
121 S. Zorzi Mosco
122 S. Atanasio (built c. 1348)
123 S. Zuane Geraca (built before 1280)
124 S. Dimitri (considered old in 1320)
125 S. Zorzi D'orciano (considered old in 1320)
126 [without name]
127 [without name] = Santa Chiara? (built in 1316)
128 S. Zuane
129 S. Zorzi Doxara (mentioned in 1313)
130 Cristo Colona
131 Pandocratora
132 S. Trinita (built c. 1310)
133 La Madona = Gorgopacussa? (mentioned in 1320)
134 S. Nicola (mentioned in 1320)
135 S. Dimitri Perati (mentioned in 1461)

NOTES

Introduction

1 John Ruskin, *Stones of Venice* (London, 1867) 2: 249.

2 Otto Demus, *The Church of San Marco in Venice History, Architecture, Sculpture*, Dumbarton Oaks Studies 6 (Washington, D.C., 1960); idem, *The Mosaics of San Marco in Venice* (Chicago, 1984); and F. W. Deichmann *Corpus der Kapitelle der Kirche von San Marco zu Venedig* (Wiesbaden, 1981).

3 Paolo Maretto, *La casa veneziana nella storia della città dalle origini all'Ottocento* (Venice, 1986).

4 For an account of this period see Donald M. Nicol, *Venice and Byzantium. A Study in Diplomatic and Cultural Relations* (Cambridge and New York, 1988), 1–123, with further bibliography, and Frederic C. Lane, *Venice. A Maritime Republic* (Baltimore, 1973), 1–43.

5 David Jacoby, "Italian Privileges and Trade in Byzantium before the Fourth Crusade. A Reconsideration," *Annuario de estudios medievales* 24 (1994): 51–54.

6 See Nicol, *Venice and Byzantium*, 149–50; Robert De Clari, *La Conquête de Constantinope*, ed. Ph. Lauer (Paris, 1924); J. Gordon, "The Novgorod Account of the Fourth Crusade," *Byzantion*, 43 (1973): 297–311; A. Carile, "Partitio terrarum imperii Romaniae," *Studi veneziani*, 7 (1965): 125–305; eidem, *Per una storia dell'impero Latino di Costantinopoli (1204–1261)*, 2nd ed. (Bologna, 1978), 265–68; and F. Frances, "Sur la conquête de Constantinople par les Latins," *Byzantinoslavica* 13, (1952–53): 68–92, and 15 (1954): 21–26.

7 Lane, *Venice. A Maritime Republic*, 67–85, and Doris Stöckly, *Le Système de l'incanto des gallées du marché à Venise (fin XIIIe siècle–milieu XVe siècle)* (Leiden and New York, 1995).

8 Mark Crinson, *Empire Building. Orientalism and Victorian Architecture* (London and New York, 1996), 53.

9 See for example the preface to Nicol, *Venice and Byzantium*, viii, who admits that a book on diplomatic and cultural relations cannot make extensive use of documents concerning trade and commercial interests. Nicol writes: "The book might have been entitled *Constantinople and Venice*. But this would have obscured the fact that Constantinople was the hub of the wheel of a wider world which the Venetians half admired and half despised, and which in the end they sought to appropriate, to exploit it for their own profit and honour."

10 Compare in this respect the seminal work, *Orientalism* (New York, 1978), of Edward Said who set the foundations for this kind of reasoning, more specifically his point of view that "the Orient has helped to define the West as its contrasting image, idea, personality, experience," pp. 1–2.

11 The district of the Greek community centered around the church of San Giorgio dei Greci (1539–61) occupied the present spot on the rio dei Greci since 1526. The Albanians were based around San Severo and then San Maurizio. The Dalmatians (or Schiavoni) established a devotional *scuola* in 1451 close to the Greek parish. Both Albanians and Dalmatians commissioned paintings by Carpaccio for their religious edifices. See Richard Goy, *Venice. The City and Its Architecture* (London, 1997), 234–35; and Brünehilde Imhaus, *Le minoranze orientali a Venezia. 1300–1510* (Rome, 1997).

12 For a discussion of the economic importance of Crete see Angeliki Laiou, "The Byzantine Economy in the Mediterranean Trade System, 13th–15th Centuries," *Dumbarton Oaks Papers* 34–35 (1980): 177–222, and Angeliki Laiou-Thomakis, "Quelques observations sur l'économie et la société de la Crète vénitienne (ca. 1270–ca. 1305)," in *Bizanzio e l'Italia. Raccolta di studi in memoria di Agostino Pertusi* (Milano, 1982), 177–98.

13 The island was particularly famous for its grain, wine, cheese, and oil and was rich in wood, which was necessary for the construction of a fleet. See Dimitris Tsougarakis, *Byzantine Crete. From the 5th Century to the Venetian Conquest*, Historical Monographs 5 (Athens, 1988), 278–83. The production of all these commodities seems to have sufficed for local consumption and also for export trade.

14 In the early fourteenth century there is evidence for such patronage in the rural holdings of the Venetian landowners of Crete. In the villages of Steriano and Agio Silla, the local lords sponsored the rebuilding of churches that were actually built by the villagers; see Chryssa A. Maltezou, "Byzantine 'Consuetudines' in Venetian Crete," *Dumbarton Oaks Papers* 49 (1995): 277. Similar arrangements abound in work contracts in Candia.

15 Chryssa Maltezou, " Ἡ Κρήτη στή διάρκεια τῆς περιόδου τῆς Βενετοκρατίας (1211–1669) (Crete during the period of Venetian rule [1211–1669])," in N. Panagiotakes, ed., *Κρήτη. Ἱστορία καί πολιτισμός* (Crete. History and civilization) 2 (Herakleion, 1988), 142–47. On the reevaluation of the situation in the colony of Negroponte/Chalkis in the early fifteenth century (1421) and the preeminence of local customs over Venetian law see Alain Major, "L'Administration vénitienne à Négrepont (fin XIVe–XVE siècle)," in Michel Balard and Alain Ducellier, eds., *Coloniser au Moyen Age* (Paris, 1995), 252.

16 See in this respect the works of Ioanna Steriotou, "Le fortezze del regno di Candia. L'organizzazione, i progetti, la costruzione," in *Venezia e Creta. Atti del Convegno Internazionale di Studi. Iraklion-Chania, 30 settembre–5 ottobre 1997* (Venezia, 1998), 283–302; eadem, " Ἀρχές χαράξεων καί κατασκευῆς τῶν ὀχυρώσεων τοῦ 16ου ἰώνα καί ἡ ἐφαρμογή τους στίς ὀχυρώσεις τοῦ Χάνδακα (Principles of design and building fortifications in the sixteenth century and their application in the fortifications of Candia)," in *Pepragmena tou D′ Diethnous Kretologikou Synedriou. Herakleion, 29 August–3 September 1976* (Athens, 1981), 2: 449–75; and Jordan Dimakopoulos, " Ἡ 'Lozza' τοῦ Ρεθέμνου. Ἕνα ἀξιόλογο ἔργο τῆς ἀρχιτεκτονικῆς τοῦ Michele Sanmicheli στή Κρήτη," in *Pepragmena tou G′ Kretologikou Synedriou 1971*, vol. 3 (1974): 64–83; idem, "Italian Renaissance in Crete," *Architectural Review* 960 (1977): 129ff.

17 Among the ever-growing literature on the topic see indicatively Zeynep Celik, *Urban Forms and Colonial Confrontations. Algiers under French Rule* (Berkeley and Los Angeles, 1997); Mark Crinson, *Empire Building. Orientalism and Victorian Architecture* (London and New York, 1996); Thomas R. Metcalf, *An Imperial*

Vision. Indian Architecture and Britain's Raj (Berkeley, 1989); Timothy Mitchell, *Colonising Egypt* (Cambridge and New York, 1988); David Prochaska, *Making Algeria French* (Cambridge, 1990); and Gwendolyn Wright, *The Politics of Design in French Colonial Urbanism* (Chicago, 1991).

18 The first colonists were required to reside in the city despite the fact that they owned extensive landholdings in the interior of the island. G. A. Sefakas, *Παραχώρησις ἀπό τῆς Ἑνετικῆς Συγκλήτου τοῦ διαμερίσματος τῶν Χανίων ὡς φεούδου εἰς Ἑνετούς εὐγενεῖς ἐν ἔτει 1252* (The Concession by the Venetian Senate of the department of Chanea as a feudum to Venetian nobles in the year 1252) (Athens, 1940), 96, attributes this requirement to three reasons: first, the protection of the Venetian citizens; second, the preservation of their language and ethnic character; and third, the creation of a Venetian environment in which the state authorities would exercise their rule.

19 On the anti-Venetian bias of the chroniclers e.g. the anonymous of Halberstadt, Gunther, and Robert de Clari, see Roberto Cessi, "Venezia e la quarta crociata," *Archivio Veneto* 48–49 (1951): 24, note 1.

Brian Pullan, *The Jews in Europe and the Inquisition of Venice, 1550–1670* (Totowa, N.J., 1983), 313, highlights the significance of the Latin church in the history of the Venetian state. He argues that Venice might have been

> a lay state excluding clerics from public office and from formal influence on policy, but it was never a secular state, in the sense of one frankly devoted to worldly and material ends, or one which saw itself as a man-made growth, without divine consecration and protection. It needed formulae to reconcile religious duty with political independence and economic interest.

For a detailed history of the church in Venice see G. Cappelletti, *Storia della chiesa di Venezia*, 3 vols. (Venice, 1849–53).

20 The highest figure of the Byzantine church of Crete, the metropolitan Nicholas II, left the island in 1204 and took refuge in the court of Theodore Lascaris in Nicaea; cf. Silvano Borsari, Il *dominio veneziano a Creta nel XIII secolo* (Naples, 1963), 105. On a few occasions Greek bishops' short visits to the island. Despite the attempts of the Venetians to prevent contact of the Greeks of Crete with Nicaea or with Constantinople, vicars (*epitropoi*) of the Greek patriarch managed to visit Crete every year. See Fedalto, *Chiesa latina*, 3: 181, no. 466.

21 The treaty between Venice and the Greek aristocrat Alexius Kalergis (1299) provided for a Greek bishop in the bishopric of Ario, where indeed a certain bishop Nikephoros is mentioned in 1303. See Nikolaos Tomadakis, "Οἱ Ὀρθόδοξοι παππάδες ἐπί Ἑνετοκρατίας καί ἡ χειροτονία αὐτῶν" (The Orthodox priests on Venetian Crete and their ordination), *Kretika Chronika* 13 (1959): 47, and Stephanos Xanthoudides, "Οἱ Ἕλληνες ἐπίσκοποι ἐν Κρήτῃ ἐπί Ἑνετοκρατίας" (The Greek bishops of Crete during Venetian rule), in *Christianike Krete* 2 (1913): 301–6.

22 Fedalto, *Chiesa latina in Oriente*, 1: 252, 254, 412. Interestingly, the new Venetian churches in the empire were placed under the jurisdiction of the patriarch of Grado. See also Bertold Spuler, "Les Chrétiens orientaux et leurs relations avec les vénitiens en général pendant la domination latine dans le Levant," in *Venezia e il Levante fino al secolo XV*, 1/2 (Florence, 1973), 679–86, and R. L. Wolff, "The Organization of the Latin Patriarchate of Constantinople, 1204–1261. Social and Administrative Consequences of the Latin Conquest," *Traditio* 6 (1948): 44–60.

23 Sally McKee, *Uncommon Dominion. Venetian Crete and the Myth of Ethnic Purity* (Philadelphia, 2000). This book appeared after my book was already in production so references are to the author's dissertation; and eadem, "The Revolt of St. Tito in Fourteenth-Century Venetian Crete. A Reassessment," *Mediterranean Historical Review* 9 (1994): 203–4.

24 Sally McKee, "Households in Fourteenth-Century Venetian Crete," *Speculum* 70 (1995): 27–67, esp. 66.

25 McKee, "Households," 41–56, and eadem, "The Revolt of St. Tito," 190–96.

26 Manolis Chatzidakis, "Essai sur une école dite 'Italogrecque' précédée d'une note sur les rapports de l'art vénitien avec l'art crétois jusqu'à 1500," *Venezia e il Levante fino al secolo XV*, 2 (Florence, 1973), 69–125. To take just one example from art history, the fascinating topic of numerous Cretan artists working for a variety of patrons in Crete and Venice has generated interesting scholarly work in the last decades. See Mario Cattapan, "Nuovi elenchi e documenti dei pittori in Creta dal 1300 al 1500," *Thesaurismata* 9 (1972): 202–35, Maria Constantoudaki-Kitromilidou, "Οἱ ζωγράφοι τοῦ Χάνδακος τό πρῶτον ἥμισυ τοῦ 16ου αἰ. μαρτυρούμενοι ἐκ τῶν νοταριακῶν ἀρχείων (The painters of Candia in the first half of the sixteenth century witnessed in the notarial archives)," *Thesaurismata* 10 (1973): 291–380; eadem, "Μαρτυρίες ζωγραφικῶν ἔργων στό Χάνδακα σέ ἔγγραφα τοῦ 16ου καί 17ου αἰώνα (Evidence on paintings in Candia in documents of the sixteenth and seventeenth centuries)," *Thesaurismata* 12 (1975): 35–36; and Maria Vassilakis, " Ὁ ζωγράφος Ἄγγελος Ἀκοτάντος. Τό ἔργο του καί ἡ διαθήκη του (1436) (The artist Angelos Acotanto. His oeuvre and his will [1436])," *Thesaurismata* 18 (1981): 47–80.

27 Maltezou, "Crete during the period of Venetian rule," 150–56; Nikolaos Panagiotakes, *Ἡ κρητική περίοδος τῆς ζωῆς τοῦ Δομηνίκου Θεοτοκοπούλου* (The Cretan period of the life of Domenico Theotokopoulos) (Athens, 1987), esp. 19–27, 58–76, and passim. Nikolaos Panagiotakes, " Ὁ ποιητής τοῦ Ἐρωτόκριτου (The poet of Erotokritos)," in *Pepragmena tou D′ Diethnous Kretologikou Synedriou* (Athens, 1981), 2: 332–38, went as far as to propose that in the sixteenth century the society of Candia resembled not a colony of Venice but a confederation.

28 Maria Vassilaki-Maurakakis, "The Church of the Virgin Gouverniotissa at Potamies, Crete," Doctoral Thesis. (Courtauld Institute of Art, University of London, 1986).

29 K. Lassithiotakes, " Ὁ Ἅγιος Φραγκίσκος καί ἡ Κρήτη (St. Francis and Crete)," in *Pepragmena tou D′ Diethnous Kretologikou Synedriou* 2 (Athens, 1981), 146–54.

30 G. Gerola, "I Francescani in Creta al tempo del dominio veneziano," *Collectanea Francescana* 2, no. 3 (1932): 301–25; no. 4 (1932): 445–61.

31 Nikos Karapidakis, " Ἡ προσωπογραφία ὡς προϋπόθεση γιά τή διευρεύνηση τῆς διαμόρφωσης τῶν κοινωνικῶν ὁμάδων τῆς Ἑλληνοϊταλικῆς Ἀνατολῆς (Prosopography as condition for the investigation of the formation of social groups in the Greco-Latin East)," in Chryssa Maltezou, ed., *Πλούσιοι καί φτωχοί στήν κοινωνία τῆς Ἑλληνολατινικῆς Ἀνατολῆς/Richi e poveri nella società dell'Oriente Grecolatino* (Venice, 1998), 73–90; Reinhold Müller, "Greeks in Venice and 'Venetians' in Greece. Notes on Citizenship and Immigration in the Late Middle Ages," in the same volume, 167–80. Angeliki E. Laiou, "On Individuals, Aggregates and Mute Social Groups. Some Questions of Methodology," in *Symmeikta* 9 (1994). *Μνήμη Δ. Α. Ζακυθηνοῦ*, vol. 1, 386–96.

32 See most recently, Nikolaos Panagiotakes, "The Italian Background of Early Cretan Literature," *Dumbarton Oaks Papers* 49 (1995): 281–323, and Stella Papadaki-

Oekland, "El Greco's 'Byzantinism.' A Re-Evaluation," in *El Greco of Crete. Proceedings of the International Symposium Held on the Occasion of the 450th Anniversary of the Artist's Birth. Iraklion, Crete, 1–5 September 1990* (Herakleion, 1995), 409–24.

33 Chryssanthi Baltoyanni, "The Place of Domenicos Theotocopoulos in 16th-Century Cretan Painting, and the Icon of Christ from Patmos," in *El Greco of Crete*, 75–95, explores the artistic milieu of Candia at the time of El Greco's youth and his artistic connections with the Cretan painters George Clontzas and Michael Damaskenos. See also in the same volume Kanto Fatourou-Hesychakis, "Philosophical and Sculptural Interests of Domenicos Theotocopoulos in Crete," 45–68, and Maria Constantoudaki-Kitromilides, "Italian Influences in El Greco's Early Work," 97–118, with further bibliography. For a general overview of the artist's life in Crete see Panagiotakes, *The Cretan period of the life of Domenico Theotokopoulos.*

1: The City as Locus of Colonial Rule

1 Venice, Bibl. Marciana, Ital. VI, 155 (5801), Antonio Calergi, "Commentari delle cose fatte dentro et fuori del regno e isola di Candia d' Antonio Calergi Gentilhuomo veneziano," 699–702. The still unpublished chronicle of Antonio Calergi was written in the sixteenth century. The text reads:

> Tra queste io stimo esser una della maggiori, et forse la principale il saper mantener in fede i popoli, et le città soggiogate, crevedendo et ormiando a tutti quei mali, da i quali potesse in tempo alcuno sascitarsi ribellioni. Il qual uitio, come che ad ogni città et natione sia peculiare non di meno in quella [*sic*] principalmente et molto più spesso suol cascare, le quali sono di linguagio diverso dal signore, et sono da nuovo conquistate. Conci[o]ssiaque, et molto più facilmente ubbidiscono i popoli ad uno della loro patria natione, che ad un stranno. . . . Per il che ogni minima occasione è attissima à metter lori in animo di fare ogni sforzo per sotrarsi il collo dal nuovo giogo.
>
> À questo male i prencipi si sono diversi rimedi imaginati. Mà io crederei niuno esser vene più isfridito, ò sicuro, di quello, che già osservano i Romani, i quali subbito che Cittade alcuna era nella loro potesta venuta illetto quel numero de' suoi, che pareva loro bassevole, ne gli mandavano ad habitare. Et questi erano chiamati colonie. La qual cosa produceva infiniti effetti buoni, et era raggione che le cittadi devenivano popolose, et ruinate edifici si rifacevano, et alcuna volte altri cittadi da nuovo vi edificavano. Compievansi i luoghi votti di lavoratori, et i campi steveli erano à buona coltura ridotti. Crescevano le arti, aumentavasi la mercantia, i nuovi habitatori s'arrichivano, et gli antichi erano confermati in fede, et cosi potevano gli huomini siccuramente vivere senza tema di esser ò da stranieri, ò da domestici nemici perturbati . . .

2 G. L. Fr. Tafel and G. M. Thomas, *Urkunden zur älteren Handels und Staatengeschichte der Republik Venedig mit besonderen Beziehungen auf Byzanz und die Levante*, Fontes Rerum austriacum 2, (Vienna, 1856), 2, no. 322, pp. 471–72; Sefakas, *Concession by the Venetian Senate*, 15–17.

3 Tafel and Thomas, *Urkunden*, 2: 130–36.

4 For the Venetian quarter of Constantinople see Chryssa Maltezou, "Il quartiere veneziano di Costantinopoli (Scali marittimi)," in *Actes du XV Congrès International d'Études Byzantines. Athènes – Septembre 1976, IV Histoire* (Athens, 1980), 208–39; H. F. Brown, "The Venetians and the Venetian Quarter in Constantinople to the Close of

the 12th Century", *The Journal of Hellenic Studies* 40 (1929): 68–88; and M. E. Martin, "The Chrysobull of Alexius I Comnenus to the Venetians and the Early Venetian Quarter of Constantinople," *Byzantinoslavica* 39 (1978): 19–23. For Acre David Jacoby, "Crusader Acre, in the Thirteenth Century. Urban Layout and Topography," *Studi Medievali* ser. 3, 20 (Spoleto, 1979): 1–45. Reprinted in *Studies in the Crusader States and on Venetian Expansion* (Northampton, England: Variorum Reprints, 1989).

5 Tafel and Thomas, *Urkunden*, 1: 51–54 and 113–24.

6 Raymond Janin, "Les sanctuaires de Byzance sous la domination latine (1204–1261)," *Etudes byzantines* 2 (1944): 174–75.

7 Nicol, *Byzantium and Venice. A Study in Diplomatic and Cultural Relations* (Cambridge, 1981), 95–98.

8 Tafel and Thomas, *Urkunden*, 2: 121.

9 William Miller, *Essays on the Latin Orient* (Cambridge, 1921, repr. Amsterdam, 1964), 161–77. The nephew of doge Dandolo, Marco Sanudo, was the architect of this duchy, which survived for three centuries and whose descendants still form a distinct Catholic community in the islands.

10 Alvise Zorzi, *Venice, The Golden Age* 697–1797. (New York, 1983), 108, and more detailed information in Johannes Koder, *Negroponte. Untersuchungen zur Topographie und Siedlungsgeschichte der Insel Euboia während der Zeit der Venezianerherrschaft*, Österreichische Akademie der Wissenschaften. Philosophish-Historiche Klasse. Denkschriften 112 Band (Vienna, 1973), 45–62. The three fiefs or baronies were Oreus in the north, Carystus in the south, and Chalcis or Egripus in the center. The text of the concession of the island to Ravano delle Carceri and his *promissio*, both dating to 1209, were published by Tafel and Thomas, *Urkunden*, 2: 89–96. He paid an annual tribute of 2,100 gold hyperpera to the doge. The pertinent passage on the Venetian possessions in the cities reads (p. 91):

> Homines Venecie in ipsa insula salvos et securos habebit ubique in personis et rebus, et sine datione; similiter etiam et in omnibus partibus, que sunt vel erunt eius ditioni subiecte. Et erit eis libera potestas mercandi, ubicunque voluerint in ipsa insula, et extrahendi exinde, quecunque voluerint, sine contrarietate eiusquam. Habebit quosque gens vestra ecclesiam et fondicum in Negrepo et omnibus ipsius insule civitatibus, in quibus et ubi volueritis, quod quidem in vos retinuistis.

11 Tafel and Thomas, *Urkunden*, 1: 452, and discussion in A. Carile, "Partitio terrarum imperii Romaniae," *Studi veneziani* 7 (1965): 125–305. Romania was the name that the Latins gave to the Byzantine empire under their rule.

12 The treaty between Boniface of Montferrat and the Venetian representatives, doge Enrico Dandolo, Marco Sanudo, and Ravano delle Carceri, is called *Refutatio Cretae* and was signed in Andrianople on August 12. For the original text of the treaty see Tafel and Thomas, *Urkunden,* 1: 513–15. For a brief discussion of the terms of the treaty see Silvano Borsari, *Dominio veneziano a Creta nel XIII secolo* (Naples, 1966), 12–13 with further bibliography.

13 Only the chronicle of Antonio Calergi states that a Venetian admiral went from Corfu to Crete in order to establish Venetian presence on the island, presumably sometime between 1204 and 1206. According to Calergi the Greeks fought bravely, but Candia fell into the hands of the Venetians. When after a few days events calmed down, the Venetian admiral (and fleet) departed, leaving only a small garrison in the city. See Antonio Calergi, "Commentari," 710–11:

> Poi per commissione del Senato partito il Capitano dell'Armata da Corfù, se n'andò in Candia per siglarne il pos-

seso, il quale essendoli vietato da Greci, che con le armi in mano arditamente li s'opposero, egli si dispose voler per forza quello, che per amore haver non poteva, et fatte smontare la gente in terra, et ordinatele alla battaglia appixerentò [?] l'assalto alla città di Candia, la quale havendo finalmente dopo vari accidenti et difficoltà expugnata concesse le robbe di quella, come cose aquistate per raggioni di guerra in preda all'essercito. Et poi che per alquanti giorni vi fu dimorato acdendo [?] le cose tutte pacifiche, et in stato tranquillo, lasciatavi dentro per guardia una buona banda de'suoi soldati et fornitala di tutte le cose bisognevoli per potersi diffendere et mantenere contra gli assalti di chiunque havesse voluto molestarla, carico d'honore et di riche spoglie se ne ritornò à Venetia, ove con grandissimo honore fù dal Senato ricevuto, et comendato.

14 David Jacoby, "Byzantine Crete in the Navigation and Trade Networks of Venice and Genoa," in Laura Balletto, ed., *Oriente e Occidente tra Medioevo ed età moderna. Studi in onore di Geo Pistarino* (Genoa, 1997), 533–34. The surname of a merchant active in Genoa in 1157 and 1158, Guglielmo de Dandida/Candea, suggests that this person had resided in Chandax for a considerable period.

15 According to the chronicle of Antonio Calergi, "Commentari," 714, the Genoese built fourteen castles in all. Of these only five are mentioned: Mirabello, Monferato, Castelnuovo, Castel Bonifacio and Bel Riparo. Calergi informs us that these forts were constructed by the people, refugeés, and outlaws. The text reads: "Per queste fabriche, oltra le soverchie angherie imposte al popolo, furono rimessi di ogni maniera ribaldi, et fuorusciti, i quali havevano obligatione di lavorar continuo in rincompensa et satisfatione dei deliti commessi." The concentration of these fortresses in the central and eastern part of Crete indicates that the Genoese had only this area under their control.

The best overview of this obscure period of Genoese rule is an article by G. Gerola, "L'occupazione genovese in Creta," *Atti della Reale Accademia degli Agiati in Rovereto*, ser. 3, 8 (1902): 134–75. In the absence of diplomatic records, Gerola studied the chronicles that have been preserved in the Marciana Library of Venice. Further investigation in the Archives of Genoa may yield fruitful results for understanding this seven-year period. See also Georges Jehel, "The Struggle for Hegemony in the Eastern Mediterranean. An Episode in the Relations between Venice and Genoa According to the Chronicles of Ogerio Pane (1197–1219)," *Mediterranean Historical Review* 11, 2 (1996): 206.

16 Venice, Bibl. Marciana, Lat. X 36 (3326), "Chronica Venetiarum," fourteenth century, p. lxxxviii: "Eodem anno, videlicet MCCVII galee L et naves VII . . . de Venetiis exierunt de quibus domini Raynerus Dandulo et Rugerius Premarino . . . fuerunt capitanei generales. . . . civitatem Candide et alia loca insule Crete . . ." See also Martino da Canal, *Les Estoires de Venise*, ed. Limentani (1972) 346–48, 350:

> Quant Mesire Renier Dandle et Mesire Rogier Promarin, li Chevetains, orent pris Corone, il la mistrent en bone garde, et se partirent d'ileuc a tote lor compagnie, et s'en alerent a Candie: c'est une vile de l'isle de Crit. Si fu erraument comenciee la bataille grant et mervilleuse; et bien se defendoient ciaus de Crit, et les Venisiens lor donoient mult grant assaut. Mult font s'armes andeus les Chevetains; et li Venisiens s'efforecerent tant, que ciaus de la vile ne les porent endurer. Si l'en tornent fuiant, et Venisiens les enchaucent apres. Si font tant por lor proesces, que li pristrent Candie: c'est la maistre vile de Crit; et de lors en avant fu

Monseignor li Dus Piere Zians sire de l'ysle de Crit. Si la dona a maint Venisiens, que de lors en avant furent chevalier, et tienent lor chevalerie por Monseignor li Dus de Venise.

See also Giorgio Ravegnani, "La conquista veneziana di Creta e la prima organizzazione militare dell'isola," in Gherardo Ortalli, ed., *Venezia e Creta. Atti del convegno internazionale di Studi. Iraklion-Chania, 30 settembre–5 ottobre 1997* (Venice, 1998), 33–42.

17 Borsari, *Dominio veneziano a Creta*, 24–25.

18 For an analysis of the vital role that the merchant marine played in securing Venice's position in the Mediterranean in conjunction with the establishment of convoys protected by warships see Frederick C. Lane, *Venice. A Maritime Republic* (Baltimore and London, 1973), 67–73, 124–31.

19 For an introduction to the Venetian empire see D. S. Chambers, *The Imperial Age of Venice 1380–1580* (London, 1970), 33–72. On the perception of Venetian imperialism see Nicolai Rubinstein, "Italian Reactions to Terraferma Expansion in the Fifteenth Century," in J. R. Hale, ed., *Renaissance Venice* (London, 1973), 197–217.

20 On the different patterns of settlement and colonization in the Eastern Mediterranean after 1204 see David Jacoby, "The Encounter of Two Societies. Western Conquerors and Byzantines in the Peloponnesos after the Fourth Crusade," *American Historical Review* 78 (1973): 873–906, esp. 874. Jacoby argues convincingly that "the very nature of the ruling class as well as the structure of the local society determined to a large extent the character of their encounter."

21 W. Heyd, *Le colonie commerciali degli Italiani in Oriente*, 2 (Venice, 1868); J. K. Fotheringham, *Marco Sanudo, Conqueror of the Archipelago* (Oxford, 1915); Miller, *Essays on the Latin Orient*, 162–68, 199, 202, 206–8; and Peter Lock, *The Franks in the Aegean, 1204–1500* (London and New York, 1995), 144–51.

22 Two issues explored in Edward Said's *Culture and Imperialism* (New York, 1994), 52, however, are especially helpful: the formation of an imperial ethos among the colonizers and the mechanisms that make a culture the dominant one in the context of empire. In his own words, Said looks for the "distinctive cultural topography of empire." See also Ferro, *Colonization. A Global History* (London and New York, 1997), 1–23.

23 In regard to the colonies of Venice the question has been raised by Charles Verlinden, *The Beginnings of Modern Colonialism. Eleven Essays with an Introduction* (Ithaca and London, 1970), xii–xxi, who argues that the term *colonization* as we use it today, i.e. conquest followed by exploitation, started with the crusades in the late eleventh century, although these early colonialist enterprises were not capitalist ventures. Verlinden places weight on the technological superiority of the conquering people over those conquered and the accelerated technological development effected by the colonizing enterprise in an overseas territory. On the crusader states of the twelfth and thirteenth century in the Holy Land see Joshua Prawer, *The Crusader Kingdom. European Colonialism in the Middle Ages* (New York, 1972). On the other hand, in regard to the presence of Venice in the Levant (excluding its island colonies such as Crete), Eliyahu Ashtor, in "The Venetian Supremacy in Levantine Trade. Monopoly or Pre-Colonialism?" *The Journal of European Economic History* 3, no. 1 (1974): 5–53, has argued that despite her tremendous economic supremacy Venice did not exercise the necessary political hegemony to be called a precolonial or neo-colonial state.

24 According to Homi Bhabha, *The Location of Culture* (London and New York, 1994), 70, "The objective of colonial discourse is to construe the colonized as a popula-

tion of degenerate types on the basis of racial origin, in order to justify conquest and to establish systems of administration and instruction."

25 Aliki Nikeforou, *Δημόσιες τελετές στην Κέρκυρα κατά την περίοδο της Βενετικής κυριαρχίας 14ος–18ος αι.* (Public ceremonies in Corfu at the time of Venetian rule, 14th–18th centuries) (Athens, 1999), 131.

26 Amos Rapoport, *The Meaning of the Built Environment. A Non-Verbal Communication Approach* (Tucson, 1990), 19–22. Rapoport distinguishes perceptual from associational meaning. He relates perceptual meaning to the designers and associational meaning to the users. For Venetian Crete this very issue of economic inequality was the theme of a conference whose proceedings were edited by Chryssa Maltezou, *Πλούσιοι και φτωχοί στήν κοινωνία τῆς Ἑλληνολατινικῆς Ἀνατολῆς/Ricchi e poveri nella società dell'Oriente Grecolatino,* Biblioteca dell'Instituto Ellenico di Studi Bizantini e Postbizatini di Venezia no. 19 (Venice, 1998).

27 According to Michel de Certeau, *The Practice of Everyday Life* (Berkeley, 1984), 29–42, esp. 34–39, a *strategy* is "the calculation (or manipulation) of power relationships that becomes possible as soon as a subject with will and power [in our case the architects of a city] can be isolated," whereas "a *tactic* is a calculated action determined by the absence of a proper locus."

28 Giuseppe Gerola was sent to Crete by the Reale Istituto Veneto di Scienze, Lettere ed Arti of Venice to record the Venetian archaeological remains on the island in 1902–3. The results of his research and photographs of the most important monuments were published in four volumes (in five parts) under the title *Monumenti veneti nell'isola di Creta* (Venice, 1905–32). Gerola's art historical method is descriptive and comparative, and this is the weak point of his work. Most of the medieval monuments of Crete are not of the highest quality, so Gerola's attempt to compare them to their Venetian counterparts and the resulting dating that he proposes can often be questioned.

29 On the Renaissance fortifications of Canea see Gerola, *Monumenti veneti*, 1/2: 416–72. Most sections of the new city walls were constructed from 1538 to 1566, but the entire project was completed only in the early seventeenth century.

30 Michel de Certeau, "Practices of Space," in Marshall Blonsky, ed., *On Signs* (Baltimore, 1985), 122–23.

31 For an overview of the remaining Venetian houses in Crete see Jordan Dimakopoulos, *Ἡ κατοικία στὴν Κρήτη κατά τὴν τελευταία περίοδο τῆς Βενετοκρατίας* (The residences in Crete during the last period of Venetian rule) (Athens, 1997), and idem, *Τά σπίτια τοῦ Ρεθέμνου. Συμβολή στή μελέτη τῆς Ἀναγεννησιακῆς ἀρχιτεκτονικῆς τῆς Κρήτης τοῦ 16ου καί 17ου αἰώνα* (The houses of Rethymnon. Contribution to the study of the Renaissance architecture of Crete in the 16th and 17th centuries) (Athens, 1977).

32 Irene Bierman, "The Message of Urban Space: The Case of Crete," *Espaces et sociétés* 47 (1985): 377–88, has argued that similar concerns drove urbanistic choices of the Ottomans in Crete.

33 Alan M. Stahl, *The Venetian Tornesello. A Medieval Colonial Coinage,* Numismatic Notes and Monographs no. 163 (New York, 1985), 7, 14, and 29. Different towns in mainland Greece had different accounting systems based on the hyperperon but defined in actual terms according to the Venetian tornesello; ibid., 59.

34 The most important material for this study is contained in the following folders: *Ducali e Lettere Ricevute* (buste 1–3, covering the period from 1368 to 1502), i.e. the letters that the duke of Crete received from the central government in Venice. These records include informa-

tion on building activities that were approved by Venice, e.g. the restoration of administrative palaces, fortifications, or the harbor; *Missive e Risponsive* (busta 8, covering the period 1417–1550), i.e. the responses that the duke sent to Venice. Many problems that were raised in the administration of the island are revealed in these documents; *Atti Antichi* (buste 10 and 11, dating to 1225–1474), i.e. various decisions of the local authorities on ecclesiastical and private property; *Quaternus Consiliorum* (busta 12, dating to 1344–63), which consists of the deliberations of the Maggior Consiglio in Candia. These records deal with problems that arose in the city and the embassies that were sent to Venice; *Bandi* (buste 14 and 15, dating to 1313–1543) containing the proclamations that the city crier announced in Candia. This series of documents is of extreme value for understanding the everyday life of the city. The announcements of the city crier could be compared with a daily newspaper, because they refer to every aspect of civic life, ranging from serious cases of murder to simple warnings about throwing garbage in the streets of the city; *Catastici* (buste 18–20, dating from the thirteenth to the sixteenth century), i.e. the official cadastres of the colony, where all the urban possessions of the feudatories are recorded. This section of the archives is of particular interest for the history of Candia because it includes the earliest surviving documents from Venetian Crete, which allow us to reconstruct part of the topography of the city; *Sentenze* (busta 26, dating to 1364–1496) containing court decisions of civil and criminal law. These court cases often deal with disputes over private property rights that reveal the social structure of the city; *Memoriali Antichi* (buste 29–32, dating to 1319–1505) containing the minutes of similar court cases to those of the *Sentenze*. This category of documents is extremely valuable because it is the only complete series for the period of the fourteenth and fifteenth centuries and the recorded testimonies include lively information on the appearance of the city; *Registri di Leggi statutarie* (busta 50, dating to 1207–1669) containing a collection of various laws that were in power on Crete; and *Miscellanea di Carte sciolte e Frammenti* (busta 51) containing various copies of important laws and decrees.

35 I have surveyed only a small part of the notarial records, but the ongoing investigation of the extensive notarial archives (100 folders) by a number of scholars has yielded significant results. Three recent publications underscore the importance of this material for the thirteenth and fourteenth centuries and address the significance of these records for capturing unique glimpses of the life of the elite and the subjects of the colony: Sally McKee, ed., *Wills from Late Medieval Crete* (Washington, D.C., 1997), Charalambos Gasparis, *Η γη και οι αγρότες στη Μεσαιωνική Κρήτη, 13ος–14ος αι.* Land and Peasants in Medieval Crete, 13th–14th Centuries, National Hellenic Research Foundation Monographs 4 (Athens, 1997), and idem, *Franciscus de Cruce. Νοτάριος στον Χάνδακα,* 1338–1339/Franciscus de Cruce. Notaio in Candia, 1338–1339, Istituto Ellenico di Studi Bizantini e Postbizantini di Venezia, Graecolatinitas Nostra Fonti 1 (Venice, 1999).

36 E. S. Artom and M. D. Cassuto, eds., *Taqqanot Qandya we-Zikhronoteha* (Statuta Judaeorum Candiae eorumque memorabilia), I (Jerusalem, 1943). The second volume never appeared.

37 Most of the chronicles of the period are preserved in the Marciana Library of Venice. They are the following: (1) Monumenta historica quae ad Cretam insulam se referunt o Monumenta historica Insulae Cretensis a Saec. XIII ad saec. XVI; (2) Chronicon Venetum ad 1360; (3) Chronica Venetiarum, fourteenth century; (4) Antonio Calergi, Commentari

delle cose fatte dentro e fuori del Regno di Candia, scritti da Antonio Callergi, gentilhuomo veneziano; (5) Andrea Corner, Historia Candiana; (6) G. A. Muazzo, Cronica delle famiglie nobili venete che abitarono il regno di Candia; (7) Antonio Muazzo, Chronica di Candia de 1204–1363, written in the sixteenth century; (8) Antonio Trivan, Racconto di varie cose occorse nel Regno di Candia dall'anno 1182 sino al 1669 di Antonio Trivan notaro ducale in Venezia; (9) Nicolò Trevisan, Cronaca veneta, composed c. 1585. In addition to these chronicles, there is a series of manuscripts under the general title *Description of Candia*, which contain geographical, topographical, and historical information on the island from the ancient period to the late Middle Age . The most important for our purposes are (1) Castrofilaca, Descrizione del regno di Candia, copy of 1583, which contains a detailed statistical account of the population of Venetian Crete in the late sixteenth century specifying occupation, gender, and ethnic origin; (2) Andrea Cornaro, Descrizione di Candia; (3) Benetto Gatto, Descrizione dell'isola di Candia; (4) an anonymous, Descrizione del territorio di Canea & Descrizione dell isola di Candia; and (5) another anonymous, Descrizione dell'isola di Candia. These chronicles were written by Venetian noblemen in Venice and Crete. They contain information on specific families, on revolts, and on incidents of the Venetian rule on Crete. All chroniclers were members of the elite and wrote their version of the history of Crete to serve a specific goal. For instance, Antonio Muazzo's chronicle tries to promote the interests of his family. One has to be careful in evaluating the information contained in these chronicles, since it often contradicts or embellishes historical events as we know them from other sources. Thus, each chronicle deserves a thorough study of its own in order to establish the reasons for its compilation and the ideological concerns of its author.

38 For an overview of these maps see Antonio Ratti, ed., *Le immagini dell'isola di Creta nella cartografia storica* (Venezia, 1997); idem, "I cartografi di Creta nati o residenti nell'isola," in *Pepragmena tou E′ Diethnous Kretologikou Synedriou* (Herakleion, 1985), 2: 330–37. On the maps of Candia see also Ioanna Steriotou, *Τά βενετικά τείχη τοῦ Χάνδακα (τόν 16ο καί 17ο αἰ.). Τό ἱστορικό τῆς κατασκευῆς τους σύμφωνα μέ βενετικές ἀρχειακές πηγές* (The Venetian walls of Candia in the sixteenth and seventeenth centuries. The history of their construction according to the Venetian archival sources) (Herakleion, 1998), 4–8.

39 Denis Wood, *The Power of Maps* (New York and London, 1992), 47: "The map's effectiveness is a consequence of the selectivity with which it brings this past to bear on the present. This selectivity, this focus, this particular attention, this interest is what frees the map to be a representation of the past. Maps work by serving interests . . . as embodied in the map as presences and absences" (p. 1). For a concise overview of the history of medieval maps and city views as well as a discussion of their meaning see Jürgen Schultz, "Jacopo Barbari's View of Venice. Map Making, City Views, and Moralized Cartography before the Year 1500," *Art Bulletin* 60 (1978): 441–72.

40 James Cowan, *A Mapmaker's Dream. The Meditations of Fra Mauro, Cartographer to the Court of Venice* (Boston and London, 1996), 41. Fra Mauro (1459) is considered to have reached the apogee of medieval cartography; cf. J. B. Harley and David Woodward, eds., *The History of Cartography*, Vol. 1, *Cartography in Prehistoric, Ancient, and Medieval Europe and the Mediterranean* (Chicago and London, 1987), 315.

41 Cristoforo Buondelmonti, *Descriptio Insule*

Crete et liber insularum, Cap. XI: Creta, ed. Marie-Anne Van Spitael (Herakleion, 1981).

42 James Elliott, *The City in Maps. Urban Mapping to 1900* (London, 1987), 21.

43 In this context we should note that at this time the main audience hall of the ducal palace in Venice was also decorated with a series of maps representing the world (by the geographer Giovan Battista Ramusio in 1540, and in 1762 by Francesco Grisellini), recording especially the discoveries of the Venetians Marco Polo, Giovanno Caboto, and Alvise da Mosto to glorify Venice by showing that her sons had their share in the world of discovery. Interestingly, it is in periods of crisis that the Venetians commissioned their most important works on geography. This fact alone argues for the ideological use of these maps for the political concerns of the Republic. See R. Gallo, "Le mappe geografiche del Palazzo ducale di Venezia," *Archivio Veneto*, 5th ser., vol. 32–33, no. 63–66 (1943): 1–67.

44 The 1567 view of Candia shows only the military structures of the city.

45 Venice, Biblioteca Marciana, Graec. VII, 22 (1466).

46 Ioanna Steriotou, "῾Ο Χάνδακας πρὶν ἀπὸ τὴ μεγάλη πολιορκία σέ σχέδιο τοῦ Μανέα Κλόντζα (Candia before the Great Siege in a drawing of Maneas Clontzas)," *Thesaurismata* 26 (1996): 225–40.

47 Heleni Porfyriou, "La Cartografia veneziana dell'isola di Creta," in *Venezia e Creta*, 386–413, and Elisabeth Clutton, "Some Seventeenth Century Images of Crete. A Comparative Analysis of the Manuscript Maps of Francesco Basilicata and the Printed Maps by Marco Boschini," *Imago Mundi* 34 (1982): 48–65.

48 E. Clutton, "Political Conflict and Military Strategy. The Case of Crete as Exemplified by Basilicata's Relazione of 1630," *Transactions of the Institute of British Geographers*, n.s., 3 (1978): 274–84. The maps were recently published by V. Danezi-Lambrinou, ed., *Τό Βασίλειον τῆς Κρήτης. Cretae Regnum, Francesco Basilicata 1618* (Herakleion, 1994).

49 It contains two maps of Crete and sixty plates of landscapes and plans of the main fortresses and cities. See also Porfyriou, "Cartografia," 410.

50 Venice, Biblioteca Marciana, Cod. It. VI, 75 (8303): Giorgio Corner, *Il Regno di Candia*, dated November 10, 1625; cf. P. Zorzanello, ed., *Venezia – Marciana. Mss. Italiani – Classe VI*, Vol. LXXVII, *Inventari dei manoscritti delle Biblioteche d'Italia*, Serie iniziata da Giuseppe Mazzantini e già continuata da A. Sorbelli a L. Ferrari (Florence, 1950), 21–22.

51 For a detailed explication of the contents and labels in Werdmüller's view see Appendix and Fig. 17. For Coronelli's map of Candia see Steriotou, *Venetian Walls*, 182–84.

2: Signs of Power

1 Cited in M. E. Mallet and J. R. Hale, *The Military Organization of a Renaissance State. Venice c. 1400 to 1617* (Cambridge, 1984), 1. Machiavelli in this letter from Verona reports the changing in Venetian military policy after the League of Cambrai.

2 An act signed in Constantinople by two brothers, Giovanni and Frederico Orio, refers to the liquidation of a company that had been formed by their brother Pietro and Michele Titino in Crete. See Borsari, *Dominio veneziano a Creta*, 9. The document reads: "quando insimul ambulastis in Creti." Jacoby, "Byzantine Crete in the Navigation and Trade Networks," 524, interprets the absence of any reference to Crete in the chrysobulls of 1082 and 1126 that gave trading privileges to the Venetians as a sign that the island was not a prominent part of the Mediterranean

navigational and trade system before 1147

3 Tsougarakis, *Byzantine Crete*, 186. Fortunately for the Venetians, this six-part division also duplicated the partition of the city of Venice in *sestieri*.

4 Freddy Thiriet, *La Romanie vénitienne au Moyen Age. Le développement et l'exploitation du domaine colonial vénitien (XII–XV siècles)* (Paris, 1975), 106. The text that regulated the first Venetian settlement of Crete in 1211 has come down to us as the *Concessio Crete*, a set of prescriptions of the Venetian doge Petrus Ziani to the 121 colonists who moved to Crete; see Tafel and Thomas, *Urkunden*, 2: 129–36. Elisabeth Santschi, *La Notion du "feudum" en Crète vénitienne (XIIIe–XVe siècles)* (Montreux, 1976), bases her interpretation of the "feudal" system of Crete on an analysis of the *Concessio Crete*. See also David Jacoby, "La Colonisation militaire vénitienne de la Crète au XIIIe siècle. Une nouvelle approche," in Michel Balard and Alain Ducellier, eds., *Le Partage du monde: Échanges et colonisation dans la Méditerranée médievale*, Byzantina Sorbonnensia 17 (Paris, 1998), 301–7, 312 and Chryssa Maltezou, "*Concessio Crete*. Παρατηρήσεις στά ἔγγραφα διανομῆς φεούδων στούς πρώτους Βενετούς ἀποίκους τῆς Κρήτης (*Concession Crete*. Remarks on the documents of distribution of fiefs to the first Venetian colons of Crete)," in *Λοιβή. Εἰς μνήμην Ἀνδρέα Γ. Καλοκαιρινοῦ* (Herakleion, 1994), 107–31.

5 Gasparis, *The land and the peasants in medieval Crete, 13th–14th centuries*. On the interesting problem of the transplantation of "feudal" practices in the colonies of Romania see also David Jacoby, *La Féodalité en Grèce medievale. Les "Assises de Romanie." Sources, application et diffusion* (Paris-La Haye, 1971).

6 McKee, "Uncommon Dominion. The Latins and Greeks of Fourteenth Century Venetian Crete," unpublished Ph.D.Diss. (University of Toronto, 1992), 27.

7 H. Ahrweiler, "L'Administration militaire de la Crète byzantine," *Byzantion* 31 (1961): 223.

8 Sally McKee, "The Revolt of St. Tito in Fourteenth-Century Venetian Crete. A Reassessment," *Mediterranean Historical Review* 9 (1994), 180–81. It is indicative that the army dispatched from Venice against the Latin rebels who had joined forces with the local Greeks was composed of foreigners, Lombard and German mercenaries as well as Turkish soldiers. See also A. F. Gemert, "Ὁ Στέφανος Σαχλίκης καὶ ἡ ἐποχή του (Stephanus Saclichi and his era)," *Thesaurismata* 17 (1980): 47–48.

9 Spyridon M. Theotokes, *Ἀποφάσεις τοῦ Μείζονος Συμβουλίου τῆς Βενετίας* (Decisions of the Maggior Consiglio in Venice), in *Μνημεῖα τῆς Ἑλληνικῆς Ἱστορίας* (Monuments of Greek history) 1/2 (Athens, 1933), 9–11, and Hippolyte Noiret, *Documents inédits pour servir à l'histoire de la domination vénitienne en Crète de 1380 à 1485, tirés des archives de Venise* (Paris, 1892), 48–49. For an overview of the administration of Venetian Crete see Maltezou, "Crete during the period of venetian rule," 112–15.

10 Thiriet, *Romanie*, 206, 208, and a more detailed analysis in his article "Recherches sur le nombre des 'Latins' immigrés en Romanie gréco-vénitienne," in *Mélanges Ivan Dujcev* (Paris, 1979): 432–33.

11 Thiriet, *Romanie*, 241; Zacharias N. Tsirpanlis, *"Κατάστιχο Ἐκκλησιῶν καί Μοναστηρίων τοῦ κοινοῦ" (1248–1548). Συμβολή στὴ μελέτη τῶν σχέσεων Πολιτείας καὶ Ἐκκλησίας στή βενετοκρατούμενη Κρήτη* (Catasticum of the churches and the monasteries of the commune (1248–1548). Contribution to the study of the relations between church and state in Venetian Crete). (Ioannina, 1985), 35, and the two editions of the capitolari of Candia: Emiliano Barbaro, *Legislazione Veneta. I capitolari di Candia* (Venice, 1940), 94–99, and Spyridon M. Theo-

tokes, "Τά καπιτουλάρια τῆς βενετοκρατούμενης Κρήτης 1298–1500 (The capitolari of Venetian Crete 1298–1500)," *Epeteris Hetaireias Kretikon Spoudon* 4 (1941): 146–49. See also Chryssa Maltezou, "Byzantine 'Consuetudines' in Venetian Crete," *Dumbarton Oaks Papers* 49 (1995): 269–80.

12 E. Santschi, "L'Apparition des considérants du droit dans la jurisprudence vénéto-crétoise du XIVe siècle," *Thesaurismata* 12 (1975): 17, and Tsirpanlis, *Catasticum*, 36.

13 Thiriet, *Romanie*, 219 and 221.

14 Tafel and Thomas, *Urkunden*, 2: 133, and Santschi, *La Notion du "feudum,"* 34.

15 This was required by the lower strata of the indigenous population, excluding the Byzantine lords and the Orthodox clergy; see Thiriet, *Romanie*, 231, and David Jacoby, "Les États latins en Romanie. Phénomènes sociaux et économiques (1204–1350 environ)," in *Recherches sur la Méditerranée orientale du XIIe au XVe siècle. Peuples, sociétés, économies* (London, 1979), 13.

16 Herakleion is mentioned in the first Byzantine period, when it appeared once as the seat of a bishop; cf. Tsougarakis, *Byzantine Crete*, 391.

On the Muslim rule on Crete see E. W. Brooks, "The Arab Occupation of Crete," *English Historical Review* 28 (1913): 431–43; I. Papadopoulos, *Ἡ Κρήτη ὑπό τούς Σαρακηνούς* (Crete under the Saracens). Texte und Forschungen zur byzantinische-neugriechischen Philologie no. 43 (Athens, 1948); S. M. Imamudin, "Cordovan Muslim Rule in Iqritish (Crete)," *Journal of the Pakistan Historical Study* 8 (1960): 297–312; Vassilios Christides, *The Conquest of Crete by the Arabs (ca. 824). A Turning Point in the Struggle between Byzantium and Islam*, Academy of Athens (Athens, 1984); and the studies of George Miles, "Byzantium and the Arabs. Relations in Crete and the Aegean Area," *Dumbarton Oaks Papers* 18 (1964): 3–32; eidem, *The Coinage of the Arab Emirs of Crete*, American Numismatics Society, Numismatic Notes and Monographs n. 160 (New York, 1970); eidem, "Test Excavations for Arab Remains in Herakleion, Crete," *Yearbook of the American Philosophical Society* (1968): 643–45.

17 During the Muslim occupation of Crete al-Khandaq had mosques and other buildings that the Byzantine emperor Nikephoros Phokas destroyed when he captured the city, and the suburbs of the city had villas surrounded by gardens, which belonged to the amira of Crete and other Arab nobles of the city. See Nikolaos Panagiotakes, *Θεοδόσιος ὁ Διάκονος καί τό ποίημα αὐτοῦ "Ἅλωσις τῆς Κρήτης"* (Theodosios the Deacon and his poem "The Fall of Crete") (Herakleion, 1960), 54, and Christides, *The Arab Conquest of Crete*, 121, 183. The chroniclers Theophanes Continuatus from the Byzantine side and Yahua bn. Said and the kitab al-Uyun from the Arab side provide information on these events.

18 Tsougarakis, *Byzantine Crete*, 179–80. The *taktikon* of Escorial dated 971–975 or 979 mentions a *strategos* of Crete. Further reference to this officer comes from a seal of *strategos Kretes* Basil dated to the year 1000, and in the *Life* of St. John Xenos. See V. Laurent, "Le Statut de la Crète byzantine avant et après sa libération du joug arabe (961)," *Kretika Chronika* 15–16 (1961–62): 382–96.

19 Although Nikephoros Phokas did not intend the city of al-Khandaq as the capital of Byzantine Crete, the harbor of Chandax became an important center for the growth of the island in the second Byzantine period. Tsougarakis, *Byzantine Crete*, 271; and G. C. Miles, "Excavations at Ag. Petros, Herakleion 1967," in *Pepragmena tou G′ Diethnous Kretologikou Synedriou* (Athens, 1975), 3: 229. For an

attempt to reconstruct the topography of Byzantine Chandax see M. Georgopoulou, "The Topography of Chandax in the Second Byzantine Period," *Cretan Studies* 4 (1994): 65–110.

20 The exact date is not known, but the transfer from Gortyna to Chandax is confirmed by a document of 1118 that refers to the metropolitan church of Chandax; see N. Oikonomides, "Οἱ αὐθένται τῶν Κρητικῶν τό 1118 (The Masters of Crete in 1118)," in *Pepragmenat tou D′ Diethnous Kretologikou Synedriou* (Athens, 1981), 2: 308 (reprinted in N. Oikonomides, *Byzantium from the Ninth Century to the Fourth Crusade*, [London, 1992], xviii); Fr. Miklosich and J. Müller, *Acta et Diplomata Graeca Medii Aevi Sancta et Profana*, 6 (Vienna, 1890), 95–99; and further discussion in Georgopoulou, "Topography of Chandax," 78. A document of 1224 where the Greek bishop of Knossos calls himself "episcopo Connoxo de burgo civitatis Candide" (he was probably ousted by the new Latin archbishop) reconfirms this move; S. Xanthoudides, "Περί τῆς Μητροπόλεως Κρήτης καί τοῦ Μητροπολιτικοῦ ναοῦ τοῦ Ἁγίου Τίτου κατά τήν β' Βυζαντινήν περίοδον (On the metropolis of Crete and the cathedral of St. Titus during the second Byzantine period)," *Christianike Krete* 2 (1915): 318.

In the latest study on Byzantine Crete, Tsougarakis, *Byzantine Crete*, 236, argues that since Chandax was not intended as the capital by Nicephoros Phokas, the archbishopric was not moved from the old capital Gortys (where it had been since the fifth century) to Chandax in 961. Nevertheless, by 980 the title of the metropolitan had changed, possibly reflecting a change in the role that Gortys played in the ecclesiastical hierarchy of Crete: he was now called "the (one) of Crete" (*ὁ Κρήτης*) without specifying his see. According to the taktikon of Basil II (980) the island was divided into eleven bishoprics that were placed under the jurisdiction of the metropolitan of Crete: Gortys (presumably the metropolitan), Knossos, Arcadia, Cherronesos, Aulopotamos (possibly Mylopotamos), Agrion, Lampe, Kydonia, Hiera, Petra, Siteia, Kissamos. See G. Parthey, *Hieroclis Synecdemus et Notitiae Graecae episcopatum* (Berlin, 1866, Amsterdam anast., 1967), 198; and Xanthoudides, ibid., 336.

21 Leo the Deacon's vivid account of the siege of Chandax by Nicephoros Phokas describes the walls of the Muslim city in detail. See *Leo the Deacon* (Bonn, 1828), 11, lines 7–15. This wall rested on a foundation that was made of regularly cut ashlar blocks and was fortified with towers. The upper part of the wall was constructed with dirt and hair from goats and pigs and was wide enough for two chariots to run side by side. It was topped with crenellations and a rampart walk, and two deep, wide moats ran around the circuit.

22 N. Platon, "Καὶ πάλιν περὶ τῶν Βυζαντινῶν τειχῶν τοῦ Χάνδακος (Again on the Byzantine walls of Candia)," *Kretika Chronika* 4 (1950): 357, and Chrysoula Tzompanaki, *Χάνδακας. Η πόλη και τα τείχη* (Chandax. The city and the walls) (Herakleion, 1996), 111–86. In 1948 a 2.50-meter-long section of the southern city walls was uncovered. The interior was filled with rubble made up of uneven pieces of stone, mortar, and fragments of ceramic tiles, the types and date of which were not reported by the local archaeologists. The excavated walls were compared with those of Thessaloniki, which were fortified with square, low towers and were surmounted by crenellations, without the projecting border at the top, which is a Western feature.

The excavators maintain that the inner face of the wall (facing the city) used the foundations of the ninth-century Muslim fortifications. Traces of this wall are believed to have been found in the ashlar block, which was made of large cut blocks, and in parts of the walls that were built with semicut limestone. See "Χρονικά (Chronicles)," *Archaiologikon Deltion* 20 (1965): 573, and 21 (1966): 430.

23 The surviving section of the best-preserved tower extended 5.10 meters above the wall and was 6.50 meters wide, but not enough vestiges were uncovered to determine its original height. It could be reached from the interior of the city through a corridor; see Nikolaos Platon, "Νέα στοιχεῖα διά τήν μελέτην τῶν Βυζαντινῶν τειχῶν τοῦ Χάνδακος (New data on the Byzantine walls of Candia)," *Kretika Chronika* 6 (1952): 447–48, and Tzompanaki, *Chandax. The city and the walls*, 120–32. Some of these Byzantine towers were later used as storage space for ammunition.

24 See Tsirpanlis, *Catasticum*, 96–105, and Georgopoulou, "Topography of Chandax."

25 The city of Canea (modern Chania), the second important urban center on Venetian Crete, occupies the site of ancient Kydonia, a port city that served the large plain to the north of the White Mountains. Kydonia was raided by the Muslims in 673, but it must have bounced back economically as in the midtwelfth century it was renowned among Muslims as a center of excellent cheese production. The Muslim geographer al-Sarif-al-Adris described its cheese production; cf. Sefakas, *Concession by the Venetian Senate*, 55–68. Rethymnon occupies the site of ancient Rithymna, whose acropolis must have been located on the same hill where the Venetians established their fortified castle in the sixteenth century. Sitia probably occupied the site of ancient Etea, which served as the port of the ancient town of Praesos, and was a bishopric in the Byzantine period. It was the most important of the *castelli* in the eastern part of Crete but it never acquired the prominence of the other three cities of the island.

26 The text of the treaty between the commune of Genoa and Pescatore is published in the *Liber Jurium Reipublicae Genuensis*, n. 500, vol. 1, coll. 553–54 (*Historiae Patriae Monumenta*, vol. 7). The pertinent passage reads: "in qualibet ciuitate que fuerit in insula Crete dabimus comuni Ianue ecclesiam ruam balneum fondicum et furnum in ea parte ciuitatis, quam elegerit comune Ianue, uel eius nuncius; et in aliis quatuor locis ipsius insule quos elegerit comune Ianue uel nuncius eius; et per totam insulam Crete dabimus comuni Ianue curiam."

27 There are more indications that the state was revising its policy toward the settlement of Crete. For example, when in 1252 a new group of colonists was sent from Venice to populate the region of Canea, the doge decreed that the feudal lords should never own more than two *cavallerie* and that each family could possess a maximum of four fiefs in the same district. Clearly, the state responded to the increasing power of the feudal lords by restraining their acquisitions. See Sefakas, *Concession by the Venetian Senate*, 20.

28 Stephen Margaritis, *Crete and the Ionian Islands under the Venetians* (Athens, 1978), 52–53. The population of Candia according to the census of 1583 (Venice, Biblioteca Marciana, Ital. VII 1190 [8880], Pietro Castrofilaca, "Libro delle cose publiche del regno di Candia") consisted of 13,625 members of the middle class (Greeks, Armenians, and possibly some Italians) and 437 Greek priests, that is, 14,062 people. In addition there were 964 members of the Venetian nobility (164 nobles of the city and 800 fiefholders of the country) and 950 Jews, that is, a total of 15,976 people. According to these figures 84 percent of the population belonged to the middle class; maybe the majority of this group was Greek. The

nobility represented 5.7 percent of the total population and the Jews 5.6 percent. At the end of the sixteenth century Crete had a population of approximately 200,000 people. See also Maltezou, "Crete during the period of Venetian rule" 133–35.

29 The document was published by G. Cervellini, *Documento inedito veneto-cretese del Dugento* (Padova, 1906). It has been discussed by among others David Jacoby, "Byzantine Crete in the Navigation and Trade Networks of Venice and Genoa," in Laura Balletto, ed., *Oriente e Occidente tra Medioevo ed età moderna. Studi in onore di Geo Pistarino* (Genova, 1997), 519–20, who cautions the reader not to take its claims at face value, and Elisabeth Malamut, *Les Îles de l'empire byzantin VIIIe–XIIe siècles* (Paris, 1988), 125–26, who accepts these figures and extrapolates that the population of the whole island was between 60,000 and 100,000 people.

30 Sally McKee, "Uncommon Dominion," 24, and n. 46, and David Jacoby, "Social Evolution in Latin Greece," in *The History of the Crusades*, vol. 6 (Madison, Wisc., 1989), 195–196.

Thiriet's proposed numbers of Latins seem exaggerated. Freddy Thiriet, "Recherches sur le nombre des 'Latins'," 430–32, has estimated the number of settlers (including their families) who had reached the island by the end of the thirteenth century at ten thousand; two thousand to twenty-five hundred of them were pure Venetians. More than half of these people must have had residences in Candia. To arrive at this number Thiriet counted the total number of knights and sergeants who moved to Crete in the thirteenth century and multiplied this number by 6, assuming that the family of each feudatory counted five members. To that number he added the other Latins of non-Venetian descent and the clergy.

31 Gerola, *Monumenti veneti*, 3: 81.

32 Eduardo E. Lozano, *Community Design and the Culture of Cities. The Crossroad and the Wall* (Cambridge, 1990), 219. The walls personalize space so that you feel you are in a world of your own. See also Lozano's insightful discussion of the walls, gates, towers, and *campanili* as carriers of symbolic messages that permeate everyday life and discourse.

33 The word *civitas* was used in Italy to designate an episcopal city, although sometimes it referred to a fortified *castrum*. See Carlrichard Brühl, "Il 'Palazzo' nelle città italiane," in *La coscienza cittadina nei Communi italiani del Duecento* (Todi, 1972), 265.

34 The threat of the Ottoman Turks after the fall of Constantinople in 1453 triggered a major fortification campaign that lasted for several decades. After consultation with a military engineer, Enrico Franzosetto from Brescia, the Senate in Venice authorized the reinforcement of the old city walls and the fortification of the suburbs, which were only protected by a wall in a few places. The first steps to be taken in 1462 were the restoration of the existing walls and the excavation of the moats. Freddy Thiriet, *Regestes des délibérations du Sénat de Venise concernant la Romanie.* (Paris, 1961), 3: 212, no. 3020, and 242–43, no. 3160 (August 14, 1462); and Noiret, *Documents inédits*, 467–71.

35 Laurentius de Monacis, *Chronicon de rebus venetis ad U.C. ad annum MCCCLIV*, ed. Fl. Corner (Venice, 1758), book 9, 154–55. Antonio Calergi, "Commentari," 736, mentioned the same event in his chronicle. The text reads, "Il Duca (Tiepolo) vestitosi in habbito di donna segretamente con molti altri fedelli si calò dalle mura, et si salvò nella fortezza di Temene."

36 For the most detailed study of the sixteenth-century walls see I. Steriotou, *Τα βενετικά τείχη του Χάνδακα (τον 16ο και 17ο αι). Το ιστορικό της κατασκευής*

τους σύμφωνα με βενετικές αρχειακές πηγές (The Venetian walls of Candia in the sixteenth and seventeenth centuries. The history of their construction according to the Venetian archival sources) (Herakleion, 1998).

37 Platon, "New data," 439 and 442. The most apparent difference between Byzantine and Venetian fortifications is that the Venetians used somewhat smaller stones than the typical Byzantine fortifications, but this criterion is not enough to establish their date with certainty. As a result, except for a few cases, it is difficult to determine the origin of fortification structures on Venetian Crete. See also Gerola, *Monumenti veneti*, 1: 97.

38 Gerola, *Monumenti veneti*, 1: 114. A 1525 report of the *capitaneus* Tomaso Mocenigo gives information on the depth of the moat: it was 12 feet (4.17 meters) deep to the east, 31 feet (10.78 meters) deep to the west, and 64 feet (22.27 meters) deep to the south such that there was at least 6 feet of seawater all around the city.

39 ASV, DdC, b. 14, Bandi, f. 221r, no. 19 (March 19, 1349):

> Clamatum fuit publice per Johannem Marino gastaldionem quod omnes qui habent et tenent ad affictum tures comunis, teneant et debeant aptare, tenere e conservare ipsas tures in culmine; ita quod, in complemento affictationis sibi facte, restituant comuni in culmine; sub illa pena, qua alias fuit imposita illis que habent casale comunis ad affictum, que quidam pena est yperpera quingenta pro quolibet contrafaciente.

Despite these admonitions, in 1392 the terraces and staircases of the towers were in disrepair and their interior was full of garbage, making them ineffectual in times of war. So the state decided that only the towers that were not absolutely necessary for the defense of the city would be rented to individuals under the condition that they maintained them in a good condition. See Noiret, *Documents inédits*, 50–51.

40 Gerola, *Monumenti veneti*, 1: 115, and 3: 86–87. A restoration project was carried out in these quarters by Francesco Basilicata in 1625, and the plan that he executed offers valuable insights into the original appearance of this space.

41 Tzompanaki, *Chandax. The city and the walls*, 126–128.

42 *Relazione* of Gaspare Renier cited by Gerola, *Monumenti veneti*, 4: 91.

43 A public proclamation offers explicit information on the topography of the walls and the fortification towers in the area of the harbor: a large window opened in the wall of the mole beyond the small loggia/portico (*ultra loçetam*), which served as the residence of magister Victor Scanagata. Exactly across from this window stood a tower that abutted the arsenals and faced the *castello*. See ASV, DdC, b. 15, Bandi, f. 79r, no. 107 (July 10, 1361): "intra portum Candide ultra signa infrascripta, videlicet ultra foramen magnum quod est in muro molli ultra loçetam ubi habitat Magister Victor Scanagata, et ultra partem oppositam directe dicto foramini que est in turri versus castellum que turris confinat cum arsenatum."

44 Platon, "New data," 456, has shown that the military quarters were located in the vaulted spaces formed by the relieving arches of the fortification walls and some of them are still visible: the Venetians demolished the interior face of the city wall in order to expose the middle space with the arches.

45 This architectural drawing is preserved in the ASV, Photographic Archives, Provveditori da Terra e da Mar, f. 740, DS. 1. Unfortunately, the last portion of the plan, which depicted the western end of the warehouse, has not survived. The project took twenty-one years (1570–91) to be completed at a cost of fifty thousand hyperpera.

46 Gerola, *Monumenti veneti*, 3: 102.

47 This is stated in the *capitolare* of those responsible for the collection of the *comerclum*; cf. Ernst Gerland, *Das Archiv des Herzogs von Kandia im Koenigl. Staatsarchiv zu Venedig* (Strasbourg, 1899), 107. Although the surviving text dates from 1298–99, it is possible that this revenue had been used for the maintenance of the fortifications from the very beginning of the Venetian settlement on Crete.

48 ASV, Commemoriali, 1, f. 38v, no. 109, and Gerola, *Monumenti veneti*, 1: 106–7.

49 De Monacis, *Chronicon de rebus venetis*, book 10, 174: "nam Veneti contribuerant ducatos auri 30,000 pro refectione murorum Candide quos straverat motus terrae." In 1309 the Maggior Consiglio in Venice decreed that the construction of the city walls was completed, so the merchants need not pay the special tax anymore. See F. Thiriet, ed., *Délibérations des Assemblées vénitiennes concernant la Romanie*, 2 vols., Documents et Recherches 8 and 11, vol. 1 (1160–1363) (Paris, 1966), 120, no. 155.

50 Tsirpanlis, *Catastiacum*, no. 107, 196–7 (September 19, 1304): "Et predecessores domini patriarche, prelati et clerici hoc recognoscentes voluerunt, consenserunt et decreverunt, quod tenerentur ad dacium dicte porte, quod induxerunt, et constitutum fuit pro hedificatione et conservatione murorum civitatis Candide." From this document it seems that the church of Candia benefited – partly, at least – from the customs of the city.

51 Flaminio Corner, *Creta sacra seu de episcopis utriusque ritus graeci et latini in insula Cretae*, 2 vols. (Venice, 1755), 2: 5. The contributions of the clergy are documented in a letter that the Senate in Venice sent to pope Clement V. The document dates from 1309 but refers to the beginning of the Venetian rule on Crete. The relevant passage reads:

> Et quia hec provisio omnibus, etiam prelatis et clericis, utilis et necessaria visa fuit, ut in edificatione murorum civitatis eiusdem et eorum conservatione per laycos et clericos in hoc eo tempore sponte et liberaliter pro sua utilitate et necessitate succurreretur per certum datium de possessionibus prestandum, in ipso opere ponendum et consumandum, quod non recipitur nec consumitur nisi solum in ipsorum murorum edificatione et conservatione.

52 Démocratie Hemmerdinger-Iliadou, "La Crète sous la domination vénitienne et turque (1322–1684). Renseignements nouveaux ou peu connus d'après les pélerins et les voyageurs," *Studi veneziani* 9 (1967): 550: "navigamus Candiam civitatem muro fortissimo circumcintam, turribus atque aliis apparatibus decoratam."

53 Gerola, *Monumenti veneti*, 1: 108, and Marino Sanuto, *I Diarii (dall'autografo marciano It. VII, 228–286 [coll. 9215, 9273])*, R. Fulin et al., eds. (Venice, 1881), 6: 550.

54 F. Thiriet, *Duca di Candia. Ducali e lettere ricevute (1358–60/1401–5)* (Venice, 1978), 38–39, no. 43, and 103, no. 103; and Gerola, *Monumenti veneti*, 1: 107–108.

55 The same gate was also referred to as *porta maestra, porta grande*, and *portone*. In 1348 there is mention of an upper gate (*ad ianuam superiorem murorum civitatis*), which might refer to the main land gate of Candia. See ASV, DdC, b. 14, Bandi, f. 218v.

56 Although this gateway no longer survives, there are a few examples of emblems with the lion of St. Mark still standing in Herakleion. These are visible in the sixteenth-century gate of Jesù/Pantocrator and above the entrances to the sea fort.

57 ASV, DdC, b. 29, Memoriali 7, f. 20v (October 7, 1344).

58 ASV, DdC, b. 53, Miscellanea Processi e Carte Araldiche, fasc. 1. Copie di privilegii, documenti ecc. relativi alla famiglia Calergi, f. 6v (April 26, 1475) (Copy from the book "Missarum"): "et conveniente provisio per poter obstar alle machinationi dell'inimico, et oltra il far

condur delle vittuarie intro la terra, et reparar dentro per la debilità di muri, etiam sollicitar il lavorier del turion di San Francesco, et far le sarasinesche alla porta grande, et de fuora un revelin de terra, et altre cose necessarie."

59 Unfortunately, when Gerola visited Candia, only the east tower was still standing; traces of it were uncovered in 1952. Also, the documents that refer to this period are in a very bad state of preservation. In this instance I am reading closely the interpretation of the mutilated text by Gerola, *Monumenti veneti*, 1: 110–11, no. 5 and 7. Although the coat of arms of the duke was destroyed, the remaining escutcheons, i.e. that of the counselor Matteo Michiel, of the *capitan generale* Fantino Zorzi, and of the counselor Giovanni Moro, point to the period when all of them were in office, that is the years 1479–82.

60 ASV, DdC, b. 53, Miscellanea Processi e Carte Araldiche, fasc. 1. Copie di privilegii, documenti ecc. relativi alla famiglia Calergi, f. 6v (April 26, 1475).

61 Platon, "New data," 451–52, recorded the accidental finds of what looked like relieving arches in a nearby basement. I would like to thank Dr. Starida, the director of the excavations in the area, for allowing me to review the findings of the Archaeological Service in recent years. Unfortunately, nothing remained of the superstructure and in 1992 the Greek Archaeological Service decided to have the finds covered again.

62 Stergios Spanakis, "Κανονισμός τῆς φρουρᾶς τοῦ Βασιλείου τῆς Κρήτης (1588) (Regulation for the Guard of the Regno di Candia [1588])," *Kretika Chronika* 2 (1948): 80–81: "che li altri due capitani con le insegne debbino andare alla porta del Molo, dove capitano tutti li forestieri et l'altro alla Porta del Pandocratora, come porte più frequentate." The gate of the Pantocrator or Jesù was located in the new fortifications to the south of the city and is still standing.

63 In 1556 a proposal was brought forth to turn this gate into a monumental gateway covered by a vault (probably similar to the barrel vault arrangement of the land gate), and to reinforce it by a portcullis that would be closed at night. See Gerola, *Monumenti veneti*, 1: 115, n. 3: "Al porton del mollo bisognerebbe farli un volto sotto il quale la gente di giorno potesse andar dalla terra al porto a suo beneplacito, ma che la notte a suo piacer il castellano facesse calare tre sarasinesche, et separar la terra dal porto."

64 In 1580 Giovanni Mocenigo proposed the construction of eight arsenal vaults between the *scala degli Arsenali* and the *porta del molo;* see Gerola, *Monumenti veneti*, 4: 127. On the basis of the width of the last vaulted spaces that had been constructed in the 1550s (5.91 meters), the distance between the staircase and the gate of the arsenals must have been approximately 50 meters.

65 The coats of arms belonged to Venetian officials who had held office between November 1552 and July 1554. This period must coincide with the time when the works in the gate were accomplished. See Gerola, *Monumenti veneti*, 1: 115, n. 2, and 129.

66 G. Giomo, *I Misti del Senato della Repubblica Veneta, 1293–1331* (Armsterdam, 1970), 55 and 61; and Thiriet, *Délibérations des Assemblées*, 1: 79, no. 2. The available documentary evidence is limited, because the registers of the Senate for this period are lost.

67 The deliberation of the Senate in Venice has been published by Gerola, *Monumenti veneti*, 1/2: 414, n. 2. In 1341 the Maggior Consiglio of Candia appointed five *sapientes* to examine the needs of the city and to plan the fortification of Chanea. See P. Ratti-Vidulich, *Duca di Candia: Quaternus Consiliorum 1340–1350* (Venice, 1976), 8.

68 Spyridon Theotokes, *Θεσπίσματα τῆς Βενετικῆς Γερουσίας* (Deliberations of

the Venetian Senate), in *Μνημεῖα τῆς Ἑλληνικῆς Ἱστορίας* (Monuments of Greek History) 2/2 (Athens, 1937): 39, no. 32.

69 Gerola, *Monumenti veneti,* 1/2: 415, fig. 245. The walls were restored again in 1475 when the rectors were allowed to spend one thousand ducats, and numerous times during the early sixteenth century. A military plan showing the land walls preserved in the library of Torino, was published by Gerola.

70 It was clear, however, that once admitted within the city walls, the Jewish population had to reside in this quarter, which was separated from the rest of the city (i.e. its Christian inhabitants) by a wall.

71 Tafel and Thomas, *Urkunden,* 2: 471–72, no. 322, and Sefakas, *Concession by the Venetian Senate,* 15–17. A document of 1255 informs us that traffic had to go through a gate that was located to the west Gerola, *Monumenti veneti,* 1/1: 156, n. 3. These fortifications must have been put up hastily, however, since they did not hinder the Genoese from plundering the town in 1265; cf. F. C. Hodgson, *Venice in the 13th and 14th Centuries* A.D. 1204–1400 (London, 1910), 134.

72 The consensus of the archaeologists is that the fortifications were originally Byzantine with some later additions of the Venetians. See C. Davaras, *Guide to Cretan Antiquities* (Park Ridge, N.J., 1976), 49–50.

73 Tafel and Thomas, *Urkunden,* 2: 177. Nikos Papadakis, "Τό Μεσαιωνικόν τεῖχος τῆς Χαλκίδος (The medieval walls of Chalkis)," *Archeion Euvoikon Meleton* (1975): 293–306, has analyzed the archaeological material from salvage excavations in 1960s and 1970s. Ceramic sherds datable to the twelfth and early thirteenth centuries as well as coins of the late tenth and eleventh centuries and spoils from ancient Roman structures indicate that the Byzantine city walls that surrounded the city were (re)constructed during the Komnenian period, possibly as a way to repel the incursions of the Normans on the island in 1146. Nevertheless, the foundations of the walls themselves may be earlier, going back to the sixth century A.D.

74 Thiriet, *Délibérations des Assemblées,* 2: 217, no. 4550; 231, no. 1604.

75 Nicol, *Venice and Byzantium,* 188–227. In 1281 the Venetians signed a treaty at Orvieto with the pope and Charles of Anjou against Byzantium, but a rebellion against the Angevins made the treaty unnecessary.

76 Roberto Cessi, *Le Deliberazioni del Maggior Consiglio di Venezia* (Bologna, 1931), 3: 41 and 113.

77 Papadakis, "Medieval walls," 282–85.

78 Cessi, *Deliberazioni del Maggior Consiglio,* 3: 336.

79 C. N. Sathas, *Documents inédits relatifs à l'histoire de la Grèce au Moyen Age,* vol. 2 (Paris, 1880–82), 411.

80 Cessi, *Deliberazioni del Maggior Consiglio;* 3: 38 and 197.

81 The towers were used as private residences after the suburbs of the city were fortified. Gerola, *Monumenti veneti,* 1/1: 158–69. The earliest surviving plan of the city, a seventeenth-century view by A. Oddi (1601), depicts eleven or thirteen towers. In addition to Oddi's plan, the maps of Monanni, Basilicata, Mormori, and Coronelli are the best illustrations of the fortified city of Canea.

82 Remains of this tower with three coats of arms dating to 1477 were recorded by Gerola.

83 Alberto Rizzi, " *'In hoc signo vinces'*; i leoni di San Marco a Creta," in *Venezia e Creta,* 543–82, and Koder, *Negroponte,* 69–77.

84 Gerola, *Monumenti veneti,* 1/1: 169, nn. 2 and 5, and 1/2: 472. Another manuscript reports that one of the towers was damaged in the earthquake of 1303. Finally, a letter from Venice in 1450 allowed the

rector and the *capitaneus* to spend fifteen hundred hyperpera for the repair of the city walls; cf. ASV, DdC, b. 8, Missive e Responsive, fasc. 2 (ex. 2), f. 125v-126r, dated March 28, 1450.

85 Thiriet, *Déliberations des Assemblées,* 1: 166, no. 357. Between 1317 and 1320 Sitia is referred to in governmental records as a *castrum*, an indication that by that date it had already been fortified; Giomo, *Misti*, 61.

86 ASV, DdC, Missive e Risponsive, b. 8, fasc. 2, March 1450. The authorities granted five hundred hyperpera to the rector of Sitia for the repair of the fort and the towers. See also Gerola, *Monumenti veneti,* 1/1: 170–77, for a detailed account of the fortifications of Sitia in the sixteenth century.

87 Ennio Concina, *L'Arsenale della Repubblica di Venezia* (Milan, 1984), 84–85. The twelfth-century *vecchio arsenale* of Venice was enlarged in 1303 and 1325, and again in 1473. Further additions were made in the sixteenth century toward the area of the *fondamenta nuova.*

88 Thiriet, *Délibérations des Assemblées*, 1: 40; Scaffini, *Notizie*, 5, no. 81; and Theotokes, *Maggior Consiglio*, 2/1 (Athens, 1933), 14–15. The text, from the Avogaria di Comun, reads:

> Fuit capta pars quod mittatur precipiendo duche et consiliariis Crete sub debito sacramento, quod debeant fieri facere arsenatum Crete; ita quod navilium in eo possit stare sub cooperto et pro predictis faciendis fiat eis commissio de accipiendo mutuo yperpera MD et non possint ea expendere in alio aliquo modo et de intratis Crete recuperent et accipiant et expendant tantum in predicto negocio quod arsenatus bene compleatur.

89 ASV, DdC, b. 15, Bandi, f. 65r–v, no. 50, dated January 18, 1361:

> Clamatum fuit publice per suprascriptum gastaldionem quod nulla persona audeat accendere ignem in arsena nec de die nec de nocte sub pena yperperorum X pro qualibus persona et qualibet vice; de qua accusator, si fuerit, habebit dimidietatem et altera dimidietas deveniet in comune. Item si de cetero fiet aliquod danum in arsenatum tam de lignamen quam de aliis rebus comunis debebeant solvere comuni illud danum patroni illorum navigorum que tunc erunt ligata proper dictum arsenatum.

90 Thiriet, *Regestes des délibérations du Sénat*, vol. 1 (1329–99) (Paris, 1958), 100, no. 385. The text prescribed the new construction: "duos alios archus bene laboratos et ita fortes quod in eis possint salvari galee predicte sine danno nostri comunis." The caulkers of the city were employed to work in the arsenals until 1366; cf. Charalampos Gasparis, "Οἱ ἐπαγγελματίες τοῦ Χάνδακα κατὰ τόν 14ο αἰ. Σχέσεις μέ τόν καταναλωτή καὶ τό κράτος (The professionals of Candia during the 14th century. Relations with the consumer and the state)," *Σύμμεικτα* 8 (1989): 111. See also Ruth Gertwagen, "The Venetian Port of Candia, Crete (1299–1363). Construction and Maintenance," in I. Malkin and R. L. Hohlfelder, eds., *Mediterranean Cities. Historical Perspectives* (London, 1988), 153.

91 The nature of the works undertaken is not specified in the sources. See ASV, DdC, b. 30bis, Memoriali 29/2, f. 155r (1412); Memoriali 29/3, f. 268r–v (1413).

92 ASV, DdC, b. 2, Ducali e Lettere ricevute, fasc. 19, f. 3v, August–September 1443. The text reads "Significamus vobis quod die XXI Februari 1441 capta fuit pars tenoris infrascripti, videlicet cum murum arsenatus versus S. Daniele ruat et similiter culmi et colone culmorum et cohopertorum arsenatus noui ceperint ruere." There is no church of St. Daniel recorded in the area of the arsenals; maybe this refers to the nearby church of St. Pantaleon. For an analysis of this fire

see M. Manoussakas, "Νέα στοιχεῖα γιά τό Νικόλαο Σορβόλο, λιμενάρχη στό Χάνδακα, καί ἐμπειροτέχνη στήν ὑπηρεσία τῆς Βενετίας (New data on Nicolaus Svorolo, head of the port of Candia in the service of Venice)," *Kretika Chronika* 15–16 (1961–62): 140–55.

93 ASV, DdC, b. 32, Memoriali, fasc. 43, f. 12r–v, dated October 25, 1445. The document reads:

> quod pro durabilitate et concumsistentia laborerii ipse arsenatus deberet de novo laborari totus in volto formando et affirmando illum in crosiera et reducendo illum ex designatione facta in quinque squariis, sive partibus, longis passuum XXVIII. et largis pedum XXVI. pro quolibet, cum arsenatus primus habebat squaria vel divisiones sex poterant laborari galee et reliqua duo pedum XXIIII. unde consideratis his q(ua) merito consideranda erant prout casus et materia requirebant et facta extimatione de opere predictus dominus et eius consilium nolentes se impedire magnifico dominio Fantino Viario honorabili capitaneo Crete, deliberaverunt et difinierunt in concordio quod dictus arsenatus debeat laborari et percompleri in bona gratia ad modum predictum ultimate consultum.

On the shipbuilding activity see Noiret, *Documents inédits*, 433: "singulis duobus annis, videlicet tempore unius cuiusque regiminis, levari et perfici faciant unam galeam subtilem vel bastardam, sicut ipsi Regimini videbitur, prosequanturque ad laborandum, et fieri faciendum de ipsis galeis donec aliud sibi ordinaverimus."

94 Gerola, *Monumenti veneti,* 4: 124–31.

95 Sefakas, *Concession by the Venetian Senate,* 17, and Gerola, *Monumenti veneti*, 4: 137.

96 Giomo, *Misti*, 63. The text reads, "Facto arsenatu in Chanea detur dicto comuni lignum ut petitur."

97 The decision that dealt with both Canea and Retimo was taken in 1467 and the building was finished in 1526. See Gerola, *Monumenti veneti,* 4: 139–42. Four vaults were built in 1575, another four were erected by the *provveditore* Giacomo Foscarini in 1577–79, two more vaults were built in 1581, two more in 1584, and two more in 1585 by Alvise Grimani.

98 D. Jacoby, "Les Gens de mer dans la marine de guerre vénitienne de la mer Egée aux XIV et XV siècles," in Rosalba Ragosta, ed., *Genti del Mare Mediterraneo* 2 vols. (Naples, 1981), 1: 169–201, 189, and Alain Major, "L'Administration vénitienne à Négrepont," in *Coloniser au Moyen Age*, 256.

99 Gerola, *Monumenti veneti,* 4: 89, cites an embassy of the feudal lords in 1462, who maintained that "portus Candide est quasi anima et civitatis et insule." Similarly in the midfourteenth century the authorities in Venice had referred to the harbor as being necessary for the merchants and the citizens, but also for the very conservation of the city of Candia. See Theotokes, *Senate*, 2/2 (Athens, 1937), 24.

100 Gertwagen, "The Venetian Port of Candia," 147, and eadem, "L'Isola di Creta e i suoi porti (dalla fine del XII secolo alla fine del XV secolo)," in *Venezia e Creta*, 337–74. The first mention of works in the harbor of Rethymnon is attested in 1300, whereas Chania's port was started in 1318. Despite the relative importance that Chandax/Candia had within Crete, the port of Candia did not figure among the recommended harbors in a navigation instruction book that was compiled in the second half of the thirteenth century in Italy.

101 Museo Correr, Mss. P. D. 581 e/c 151: Porto di Candia. Notizie. See also the Relazione of Francesco Basilicata (1630) published by Spanakis, in *Monuments of Cretan History* 5 (1969): 81. In the eigh-

teenth century the size of the harbor seems to have diminished; it could host only twenty-five to thirty galleys. See O. Dapper, *Description exacte des îles de l'Archipel* (Amsterdam, 1703), 406.

102 Gertwagen, "The Venetian Port of Candia," 144, 146–47. The old breakwater had openings whose function was to let sand outside the harbor.

103 Thiriet, *Regestes des délibérations du Sénat*, 1: 130, no. 519; and Theotokes, *Senate*, 2/1, 164, no. 15. For instance, in 1373 the Venetian Senate ordered the reconditioning of the moats of Candia, but the document indicates that similar excavations of the moats happened periodically ("quod faciant cauari ipsas fossas per modum solitum"). The soil unearthed from the moat was to be deposited away from the port, in the area of the Katsambas river.

104 ASV, Senato Misti, Reg. 17, f. 46v, and Theotokes, *Senate*, 2/1: 120–22, 166–67, 172–73, 178, 203, 248–49. Venice sent metal, wood, and all the supplies that Francesco asked for the restoration of the port and the breakwater.

105 The chain is mentioned in 1363 (cf. Gertwagen, "The Venetian Port of Candia," 152) and again in 1420, when it needed to be repaired; cf. ASV, DdC, b. 30ter, Memoriali, f. 108v–109r.

106 Gertwagen, "The Venetian Port of Candia," 148.

107 Gertwagen, "L'Isola di Creta e i suoi porti," 358–62.

108 Paola Ratti-Vidulich, *Duca di Candia, Bandi (1313–1329)* (Venice, 1965), 130–31, dated July 11, 1323. Numerous proclamations of the city crier forbade the population to discard their old boats, iron, and wood into the harbor. See also ASV, DdC, b. 15, Bandi, f. 77v, dated June 7, 1361, and repeated in f. 125v, dated November 9, 1365. The text reads: "Clamatum fuit publice . . . quod de cetero nullus audeat ponere seu proicere savornam aliquam super molo portus, videlicet, in aliqua parte dicti moli, sub pena yperperorum .X. pro quolibet et qualibet vice et plus et minus ad voluntatem dominii."

109 Numerous decisions of the Maggior Consiglio and the Senate in Venice concern the port of Candia; cf. R. Cessi, *Le Deliberazioni del Consiglio, dei Rogati (Senato)*, 1 (Venice, 1960), 13, no. 55; 103, no. 4; and 179, no. 30; Giomo, *Misti*, 273; and Thiriet, *Délibérations des Assemblées*, 1: 81, no. 8, and 97, no. 67.

110 Ratti-Vidulich, *Bandi*, 23, no. 47, and 51, no. 144. The Dermata bay was located five hundred meters to the west of the main harbor and its name derived from the tanneries that were located near the shore.

111 ASV, DdC, b. 15, Bandi, f. 77v, dated June 7, 1361. Unfortunately the available documentary evidence does not indicate its precise position.

112 Thiriet, *Regestes des délibérations du Sénat*, 1: 202, no. 855.

113 The state gave orders to restore the port in 1302 and in 1312 the Maggior Consiglio in Venice decreed that five hundred hyperpera had to be spent on the port annually. See Thiriet, *Déliberations des Assemblées*, 1: 147, no. 271. Between 1317 and 1320 another two thousand hyperpera was sent from Venice for the same reason; see Giomo, *Misti*, 55, 60, 61. In 1322 the rector of Canea was authorized to spend one thousand hyperpera on the breakwater of the port; see Theotokes, *Senate*, 1/2 (Athens, 1936), 67, no. 7. For the port of Candia see Ruth Gertwagen, "Heraklion Harbour in the Venetian Imperial System of the Early Fourteenth century," in *1st International Symposium on Harbours, Port Cities and Coastal Topography. Cities on the Sea – Past and Present. Summaries* (London, 1986).

114 In 1387 the Senate in Venice ordered

the rector of Canea to have two large ships sunk at the entrance of the port in order to reduce its opening; ibid., 177, no. 732. In 1423 the authorities bought an old ship, which they would sink in the entrance of the harbor in order to decrease the opening of the port. See Thiriet, *Regestes des délibérations du Sénat,* 2 (1959): 205, no. 1890. However, in 1452 the port was again in terrible shape and the Senate decided to erect a new breakwater and to sink another galley in the harbor; ibid., 3: 179, no. 2904. Similar measures were taken in the fifteenth and sixteenth centuries.

115 Thiriet, *Déliberations des Assemblées* 1 (1966): 79, no. 2, and Giomo, *Misti,* 55; Theotokes, *Senate,* 2/2: 246; and Thiriet *Regestes des délibérations du Sénat,* 1: 173, no. 717.

116 Koder, *Negroponte,* 69–77.

117 Jan Morris, *The Venetian Empire. A Sea Voyage* (London, 1980), 57–58.

3: Venice, the Heir of Byzantium

1 F. Thiriet, *Regestes des délibérations du Sénat de Venise concernant la Romanie,* 3 (Paris and La Haye, 1961), 205–6, no. 2994.

2 Deborah Howard, *The Architectural History of Venice* (London, 1980), 26.

3 Richard Goy, *Venice. The City and Its Architecture* (London, 1997), 60–73.

4 See most recently Goy, *Venice. The City and Its Architecture,* 60–64. In addition to the standard surveys on Venetian architecture, we are fortunate to have a detailed representation of Venice in the view of the city drawn by Jacopo de Barbari in 1500; see Jürgen Schultz, "Jacopo Barbari's View of Venice. Map Making, City Views, and Moralized Geography before the Year 1500," *Art Bulletin* 60 (1978): 425–74.

5 Hermann Diruf, *Paläste Venedigs vor 1500. Baugeschichtliche Untersuchungen zur venezianischen Palästarchitektur im 15. Jahrhundert.* Beitrage zur Kunstwissenschaft Band 33 (Munich, 1990).

6 For instance a 1361 decree specified that the paved street (*saliçata*) that ran close to the *lobium* (loggia), a street used by the nobility for leisurely walks, had to be cleaned. See ASV, DdC, b. 15, Bandi, f. 73r, no. 78 (April 18, 1361):

> Clamatum fuit publice per Bartholomeum de Bonsilio gastaldionem ad hoc, ut saliçata que est prope lobium et calis contiguus dicte saliçate maneat continue mundi sicut expendit per nobilibus solitis platiçare et transire illac. Dominus Ducha (Marinus Grimani) et eius consilium mandant quod de cetero in predicta saliçata seu cali aliqua persona non audeat prohicere aliquam sordem, immundiciam, letamen aut quisquillias sub pena yperperorum .V. pro qualibet persona que contrafecerit et qualibet vice. Et committatur justiciariis quod studeant facere mundari saliçatam et calem predictas taliter quod continue maneant mundi.

By 1360 garbage collection had become a public service: four rubbish carts (two for the eastern part and two for the western part of the city) were assigned to collect the garbage of the city daily; see J. Jegerlehner, "Beiträge zur Verwaltungsgeschichte Kandias im XIV Jahrhundert," *Byzantinische Zeitschrift* 13 (1904): 459–61. Two different offices were in charge of these tasks: the *justiciarii* and the *domini de nocte* (something close to a police force). See also Angeliki Panopoulou, "*Circa mundiciam civitatis.* Μέτρα γιά τήν καθαριότητα τοῦ Χάνδακα ἀπό τόν 14° ὥς τόν 17° αἰῶνα (*Circa mundiciam civitatis.* Measures for the cleanliness of Candia from the 14th to the 17th centuries)," *Symmeikta 9* (1994). *Μνήμη Δ. Α. Ζακυθηνοῦ,* vol. 2, 183–212.

7 ASV, DdC, b. 15, Bandi, f. 79v, no. 109

(July 23, 1361) and f. 104v, no. 26 (April 10, 1363). The latter text reads

Clamatum fuit publice per Johannem Marino gastaldionem in lobio, ante porta Sancti Marci et in ruga, quod omnes habitatores de ruga magna magistra ab uno capite ruge usque ad aliud scopare debeant omni die veneris in man- ante suas portas et stratas, usque ad medietatem sive partis ruge, et quod aliquis non audeat proicere aliquam maliciam, immundiciam, quisquilias, splanaturas, lignaminum, corraminum et pellaminum et pannorum ab uno capite dicte ruge usque ad aliud. Et si viveneretur aliqua malicia proiecta ante portas alicuius persone ille ondet que proicerit illam vel salvat banum infrascriptum sub pena grossorum duodecim pro quolibet contrafaciente et qualibet vice, et accusator habeat tercium. Scientes quod omni die Sabati dominatio faciet inde accipi dictas scovadulias cum caro comunis.

8 C. N. Sathas, *Documents inédits relatifs à l'histoire de la Grèce au Moyen Age*, vol. 4 (Paris, 1883), 4, 18, and passim.

9 Theotokes, *Maggior Consiglio*, 1/2: 15 and 29. The text reads: "quod Ruga maistra de Candida, que est communis a Sancto Tito uersus mare debeat affictari, et etiam alia Ruga que est ab alio latere uersus eam et uersus mare . . . et qui eam uel eas acceperit teneatur facere fieri faciem de ante super Ruga de petra et calcina." The second street must have run beside the cathedral of St. Titus ending at the sea to the east of the ruga magistra. Gerola, *Monumenti veneti*, 3: 113, identified the secondary street with the one that ran from the piazza to the Judaica.

10 Theotokes, *Senate*, 2/1: 3. Unfortunately only the title of this deliberation is preserved.

11 Roberto Cessi, *Deliberazioni del Maggior Consiglio di Venezia*, 2nd ed. (Bologna, 1970), 3: 346. The duke and his counselors had the responsibility to decide which houses needed repair.

12 The subject of "vernacular" architecture has not been studied extensively. Hans Belting, "Introduction," in H. Belting, ed., *Il medio oriente e l'occidente nell'arte del XIII secolo* (Bologna, 1982), 1–10, explores the issue of the thirteenth-century artistic production as a Mediterranean koine under the influence of Venice and Byzantium.

13 Paola Pavanini, "Abitazioni popolari e borghesi nella Venezia cinquecentesca," *Studi veneziani* n.s. 5 (1981): 63–126.

14 Ruskin's typology was based on the types of arches used on the façades of Venetian buildings; cf. Paolo Maretto, *La Casa veneziana nella storia della città delle origni all'Ottocento* (Venice, 1986), 76–78. Two more structures, Ca' Businello and Ca' Barzizza, date from the same period.

15 W. Müller-Wiener, *Bildlexikon zur Topographie Istanbuls* (Tübingen, 1977), 244–47. The brick ornamentation of the Byzantine façade makes an impression different from that of the Venetian buildings.

16 Anastasios C. Orlandos, "Τά παλάτια καὶ τά σπίτια τοῦ Μυστρᾶ (The palaces and the houses of Mistra)," *Archeion ton Byzantinon Mnemeion tes Hellados* 3 (1937): 3–114, and idem, "Quelques notes complémentaires sur les maisons paléologuiennes de Mistra," in *Art et société à Byzance sous les Paléologues. Actes du colloque organisé par l'association internationale des études byzantines à Venise en Septembre 1968*, Bibliothèque de l'Institut Hellénique d'Études Byzantines et Post-Byzantines de Venise n. 4 (Venice, 1971), 75–82.

17 Maretto, *Casa veneziana*, 108–9 and 115. Some typical fourteenth-century houses in Venice are the palazzo Loredan-Gheltoff in rio di S. Gerolamo, the palazzo Magno-Bembo near the campo di Do Pozzi, the palazzo Viaro-Zane in campo di Santa Maria Mater Domini, the

late fourteenth-century house in rio della Pietà and the early fifteenth-century palazzo Zorzi in rio San Lorenzo. The traditional L-shaped layout was gradually transformed into a C-shaped design around the courtyard.

18 A useful survey and collection of this material can be found in Hemmerdinger-Iliadou, "Voyageurs" (1967 and 1973).

19 Schulz, "Jacopo Barbari's View of Venice," 426–27, fig. 1.

20 Dapper, *Description de l'Archipel* (1703), 407.

21 Giuseppe Giomo, *I "Misti" del Senato della Repubblica veneta, 1293–1331. Trascrizione dell'indice dei primi quattordici volumi perduti e Regesto di un frammento del primo volume* (Venice, 1887, repr. Amsterdam, 1970), 288–89, and Theotokes, *Senate*, 2/1: 20. Because of the fact that we only possess the title of this decree, we cannot determine the exact content of this decision.

22 The fortification of the city was finally triggered by the burning of the city by the Ottomans of Uluc Ali in 1571. For an excellent analysis of the fortifications of Retimo see Ioanna Steriotou, *Οἱ Βενετικές Ὀχυρώσεις τοῦ Ρεθύμνου (1540–1646)* (The Venetian fortifications of Rethymno [1540–1646]). (Thessaloniki, 1979), passim. For a description of the *Forezza* during the Ottoman period see George C. Miles, "Evliya Chelebi's Visit to Rethymnon," in *Pepragmena tou G′ Diethnous Kretologikou Synedriou* 3 (Athens, 1975), 220–24.

23 Sathas, *Documents inédits relatifs à l'histoire de la Grèce*, 4: 180.

24 Ibid., 4: 21, 111, 115, 137, 166.

25 The prominent Morosini fountain, which is still visible in the center of the square in modern Herakleion, was added in this area in 1626, following the construction of a large aqueduct that supplied the city with water.

26 E. Gerland, *Das Archiv des Herzogs von Kandia im Koenigl. Staatsarchiv zu Venedig* (Strasbourg, 1899), 120, and Maria Georgopoulou, "The Meaning of the Architecture and Urban Layout of Venetian Candia: Cultural Conflict and Interaction in the Late Middle Ages," Ph.D. Diss. (University of California Los Angeles, 1992), 155–58. There is a slight possibility that the older loggia was attached to the ducal palace. The current loggia is a sixteenth-century structure that was placed across the street from the earlier building and in this position disrupts the open space that would have been defined as piazza San Marco until the sixteenth century (Fig. 52). Most importantly the new loggia obstructed the view of the cathedral of St. Titus from the palace of the duke and the basilica of St. Mark. On the sixteenth-century building see Guglielmo Berchet, "La loggia veneziana di Candia," *Atti del Reale Istituto Veneto di Scienze, Lettere ed Arti* 61, pt. 2 (1901–2): 1–17, and Stergios Spanakis, " Ἡ Λόdjα τοῦ Ἡρακλείου (The loggia of Herakleion)," *Kretikai Selides* 3 (1938): 437–52 and 686–729.

27 ASV, Avogaria, Cerberus, reg. 19, c. 99r (May 9, 1293); and S. M. Theotokes, *Μνημεῖα τῆς Ἑλληνικῆς Ἱστορίας* (Monuments of Greek history), vol. 1, no. 2 (Athens, 1933), 31. The text reads: "Res incantande incantentur in plathea. Capta fuit pars quod addatur in capitularibus duche et consiliorum Crete quod omnes res comunis que debent incantari solum in plathea et non alibi."

28 ASV, DdC, b. 29bis 30, Memoriali 16/1, f. 28v–29r (February 1, 1369). A summary of the document has been published by Elisabeth Santschi, *Régestes des Arrêts Civils et des Mémoriaux (1363–1399) des Archives du Duc de Crète*, Bibliothèque de l'Institut Héllénique d'Études Byzantines et Post-byzantines de Venise 9 (Venice, 1976), 146–47, no. 385.

29 This information can be extracted from

archival documents regulating the market space in the piazza. In 1357 the *bandi* state that game should be sold in the piazza next to the pillory. See Ch. Gasparis, "Οἱ ἐπαγγελματίες τοῦ Χάνδακα κατά τόν 14ο αἰ. Σχέσεις μέ τόν καταναλωτή καί τό κράτος (The professionals of Candia during the 14th century. Relations with the consumer and the state), *Σύμμεικτα* 8 (1989): 100. Another pillory is attested in the suburbs of Candia in 1357 possibly to be used for a different kind of criminal; cf. A. Lombardo, ed., *Zaccaria de Fredo notaio in Candia (1352–57)* (Venice, 1968), 74, no. 103.

30 Theotokes, *Senate*, 2/1 (1936): 150, no. 46. The new rector was authorized to spend 100 hyperpera for the restoration of the *lobium*.

31 In 1535 the construction of the new *loggia* demanded the demolition of a shop that belonged to the monastery of Santa Maria della Misericordia. See a ducal letter to Duke Petro Buldu in ASV, DdC, b. 72, Estraordinario-Visite, Visite no. 4, f. 21r. The loggia is barely visible in the view of Corner on the left hand lower corner.

32 Gerola, *Monumenti veneti,* 3: 61–62.

33 Curuni-Donati, *Creta veneziana,* 262, nos. 1151–55.

34 Hippolyte Noiret, ed., *Documents inédits pour servir à l'histoire de la domination vénitienne en Crète de 1380 à 1485, tirés des archives de Venise* (Paris, 1892), 252, dated August 29, 1416. A decision of the Senate forbade the rectors to concede the area of the *platea* for the construction of buildings, because these buildings would abut the *castrum*.

35 Jordan Dimakopoulos, " Ἡ 'Lozza' τοῦ Ρεθέμνου. Ἕνα ἀξιόλογο ἔργο τῆς ἀρχιτεκτονικῆς τοῦ Michele Sanmicheli στή Κρήτη (The Loggia of Rethymnon. An important piece of the architecture of Michele Sanmicheli in Crete)," in *Pepragmena tou G΄ Diethnous Kretologikou synedriou* 2 (Athens, 1974), 64–83. The *loggia* is shown on a map of the city for the first time in 1559. See also the photographs published by Gerola, *Monumenti veneti*, 3: 63–68. On the basis of the rusticated masonry, J. Dimakopoulos proposed that the actual building belongs to the building campaign of Michele Sanmicheli in 1538–40 or to his nephew, Giangirolamo Sanmicheli (1542–49).

36 Jordan Dimakopoulos, "Μεγάλη βρύση, μιά βενετσιάνικη κρήνη τοῦ Ρέθυμνου (The Great Fountain, a Venetian fountain of Rethymnon)," *Kretika Chronika* 22 (1970): 322–43. The rector Rimondi also made another three fountains in the city, which do not survive. Basilicata's view of Retimo in 1627 clearly shows the piazza with the loggia, the fountain, and the clock tower. See Gerola, *Monumenti veneti,* 4: 111, fig. 68.

37 Following his election, the new duke was ordered to buy the clock in Venice and set it up in the area of the piazza for the use of the community. Thiriet, *Délibérations des Assemblées*, 2 (1364–1463) (Paris, 1971), 242, no. 1644, and Gerola, *Monumenti veneti*, 3: 72.

38 Gerola, *Monumenti veneti*, 3: 71–75, and J. Dimakopoulos, "Rethymniaka," in *Gerhard Mercator* (Athens, 1991), 53. Evliya Çelebi reported that the tower of the clock was used as a prison in Ottoman times. See Miles, "Evliya Chelebi's Visit to Rethymnon," 223.

39 Gasparis, "Professionals," 122, 124–25. We do not know the original number of the *ponderatores* in Candia, but assuming that their office was similar to that in Constantinople, in 1482 their number in Candia was increased from two to three (ASV, DdC, b. 32, Memoriali 47/1, f. 48v). The integrity of these public officers was key, of course. In 1362 a decree ordered the *ponderatores* to be more vigilant in weighing wholesale quantities of linen, cotton, candlewax, grain, and other commodities. The state scales had to be used only by those licensed to use them under a penalty of 50 percent tax on the

value of the commodity weighed. See ASV, DdC, B. 15, Bandi, f. 96r (August 7, 1352).

40 Ibid. 86–88. The *justiciarii* supervised the quality of the foodstuffs and the artisans and professionals and regulated the prices. They were also responsible for solving all disputes between the merchants and their clients and had the authority to impose fines of up to five hyperpera.

41 Ibid. 90–91. Bread was a highly regulated commodity since grain was a monopoly in Venice. A special office, the *officium panetterii*, set the rules for making bread and controlled its quality and price.

42 ASV, DdC, b. 14, Bandi, c. 26v (August 18, 1321); see also Paola Vidulich-Ratti, *Duca di Candia, Bandi (1313–1329)*, Fonti per la storia di Venezia, ser. I, Archivi Pubblici (Venice, 1965), 115, no. 306. This decree meant to regulate the production of weapons. See also Gasparis, "Professionals," 105–9.

43 ASV, DdC, b. 14, Bandi, f. 110v (October 1, 1336), and Gasparis, "Professionals," 102. No goldsmith was allowed to work during the day outside the area of the *platea* or have his workshop anywhere else but in the piazza. Similarly a 1315 decision of the Maggior Consiglio in Venice ordered all goldsmiths to work in the Rialto area.

44 Paola Ratti-Vidulich, *Duca di Candia: Quaternus Consiliorum 1340–1350* (Venice, 1976), 58, no. 104. In 1346 Bartholomeus de Benevento was appointed as the official horseshoer for the feudal lords for a period of six months; he was given a free shop in the piazza and an annual salary of 100 hyperpera.

45 ASV, DdC, b. 26, Sentenze, Reg. 2/2, f. 164r, no. 193 (September 21, 1370), and summary in Santschi, *Régestes des Arrêts*, 53, no. 226. In 1370 the barber Johannes Cumagioti rented a barber shop on the piazza; he was also allowed to keep his mill which was located to the east of the shop.

46 ASV, DdC, b. 29bis 30, Memoriali 22/5, f. 22r (June 7, 1391). A ducal act confirming the property that Nicoletus de Androcio inherited from his father, Alexis, included a two-story *speciaria* located on the piazza. The text reads, "assignaverunt sibi pro sua particula omnium dictorum bonorum inmobilium dicti quondam Alexii totam domum speciarie que est super Platea Candide infra et supra."

47 ASV, Notai di Candia, b. 233, f. 225v: notarius Andrea de Belloamore (March 16, 1319). The text reads: "quamdam partem de mia statione in platea posita, que habet ab exteriori parte sua versus plateam pedes IIII minus digites III, et ab interiori parte sua versus austrum et murum civitatis pedes III minus digites III; cum toto solario quod est in ea, et tantum pro curia ante eam quantum tibi pertinebit pro ea de iure." The unit of measurement in Venetian Crete was the Venetian *passus* (pace), which was equivalent to 1.74 meters. It was divided into five feet (pedes), which was further divided into fingers (*digites*). See Ennio Concina, *Pietre, parole, storia, Glossario della costruzione nelle fonti veneziani (Secoli XV–XVIII)* (Venice, 1988), 109–10.

48 ASV, DdC, b. 14, Bandi, f. 168r (September 8, 1343):

> Clamatum fuit publice per Georgium Cornario gastaldionem in lobio et in platea quod nulla persona audeat de cetero habere in platea aliquam arcellam per ponendo bladum vel legumen et quicumque habeat nunc aliquam arcellam huius modi debeat infra diem tercium eam inde collere sub pena yperperorum quinque per quolibet et qualibet vice; et quod committatur dominis de nocte, advocatoribus comunis, et justiciariis quod de predictis inquirant, et si quem contrafacientem repererint, condemnent eum de dicta pena de qua habeant tercium et si accusator fuit habeat similiter tercium et reliquum sit comunis.

The word *arcella* seems to refer to a bench with a cover made in the shape of an arch, a kind of movable kiosk. Later documentation suggests that the vendors were only allowed to rent from the state benches fixed onto the ground.

49 This is apparent in the case of melons. In 1350 the maximum price of each melon was fixed to two *soldi*. A year later the price of melons was reduced to one *soldum*, and it was stated that they should be exclusively sold in the piazza by the farmers who grew them. See Gasparis, "Professionals," 100.

50 Ibid., 99–100. Luckily the document (1360) specified the dimensions of benches that should be used by the vendors of vegetables: 1 pace by 3 feet (1.74 by 1.05 meters).

51 Ibid. Although there is no clear indication where these columns were located, one can surmise that the first group of benches had been arranged on the space closer to the ruga magistra, so the newer benches for fruit and vegetables were added on the other side, that is, the western side of the piazza. The maps and views of the city never indicate these columns in the area.

52 Ibid., 100.

53 The first indication of this is a document of 1269 noting that the counselors lived in the *castellum* of Candia. See Tafel and Thomas, *Urkunden*, 3: 110. The text reads, "Petrus Carazacaneno et Andreas Correr cucurrerunt pro consiliariis ad castellum, ubi stant."

54 Theotokes, *Monuments of Greek history*, vol. 2, no. 1 (Athens, 1936), 122.

55 This information is contained in the account of the duke Guido da Canal. See Gerola, *Monumenti veneti*, vol. 1, pt. 2: 131.

56 The *castellum* was enlarged and reinforced in the period 1523–40. This plan of the Rocca a Mare was executed in 1612 by the *provveditore* Francesco Basilicata. The two-story fort was surmounted by a large flat roof that accommodated cannons, ammunition, and barracks for the guard. See Stergios Spanakis, *Τό Ἡράκλειο στό πέρασμα τῶν αἰώνων* (Herakleion in the course of the centuries) (Herakleion, 1990), 124–25; and Gerola, *Monumenti veneti*, 1/2: 130–48. The architect who undertook the construction of the new fort was Antonio Saracini from Padua.

57 Gerola, *Monumenti veneti*, 1/2: 131. In 1523 the Senate decided to replace the old fort with a new structure, because

> per esser in cavo del muolo uno turion over forteza el qual haveva una muraglia grossa pie' 5 in 6 senza scarpa, fatta al tempo che non errano artellarie, et haveva il pian tanto alto da l'aqua che non se haria possù cum le artellarie offender una galia che venisse in porto quanto fusse dappresso, et havendo da la banda de levante modo de piantar artellarie circa passa 340 lontan, che cum poche canonade se haria buttà quella muraglia a terra.

58 Thiriet, *Délibérations des Assemblées*, vol. 1 (1160–1363) (Paris, 1966), 155. In 1314 a deliberation of the Senate in Venice stated that the female prisoners were detained in the *castellum*, which was not an adequate place for women.

59 De Monacis, *Chronicon de rebus venetis*, book 10, 177.

60 Gerola, *Monumenti veneti*, 1/2: 135. The northern plaque has an inscription with the date 1533 signaling the completion of the exterior walls.

61 A photograph that Gerola published in *Monumenti veneti*, 3: 8, fig. 16, shows that the ground floor of the ducal palace was pierced by slightly pointed arches. From the door and window that are included in the wall that blocked the arch we can deduce its approximate height to 2 to 2.50 meters.

62 This document from the Archives of the Kadi of Candia reports the possessions of Defterdar Ahmet Pasa in Crete and ex-

plicitly identifies the building as the *palazzo ducale.* An Italian translation is quoted by Gerola, *Monumenti veneti*, 3: 16. See also Xanthoudides, *Chandax-Herakleion* (Herakleion, 1964), 67, and S. Margarites, *Crete and Ionian Islands under the Venetians* (Athens, 1978), 33.

63 The document specifies that this structure was located near the staircase and may be identified with the public warehouse that occupied the old city walls to the west of the land gate after 1577. In the Greek transcription of the same document we read, "next to the staircase and in connection to the main building."

64 See the study of Stylianos Alexiou, "Τό δουκικόν ἀνάκτορον τοῦ Χάνδακος (The Ducal Palace of Candia)," *Kretika Chronika* 14 (1960): 102–6. Alexiou has gathered the visual representations of the ducal palace and tried to reconstruct its original appearance.

65 A similar tower was also erected at the corner of the ducal palace in Venice. See Alexiou, "Ducal Palace," 107. Behind this tower we can see the street that separated the ducal palace from the residence of the general.

66 Gerola, *Monumenti veneti*, 3: 12.

67 Sophia Antoniadis, *Il cronista Zancaruolo e gli avvenimenti cretesi del 1363* (Herakleion, 1963), 335. According to the chronicler Zancaruolo, the rebels of 1363 entered the palace by climbing on the roofs of the shops around it. Apparently, at least one side of the palace abutted private structures.

68 Alexiou, "Ducal Palace," 105. Alexiou thinks that the tripartite window belonged to this hall. Furthermore, he interprets the semicircular tympanum, or oculus, seen above the crenellations as a suggestion of a vaulted space beneath the tiles.

69 Corner, *Creta sacra*, 2: 409. From a letter of duke Hieronymus Donatus about the earthquake of 1508, we learn that the north side of the audience hall was destroyed along with the staircase. The document reads:

> Subinde discedimus in mediam aream Palatii, cuius jam Aula auditoria a Septemtrionali parti conciderat; et scalae ruinis, et fractis trabibus, et tabulis operiebantur. Sed nec tutus areae locus videbatur ob altitudinem aedificiorum, recepi me in altiorem partem fori non longe a Palatio, ubi casus murorum minus timeri posset, sub diversorio quodam ligneo, ubi Judaei treoneum coriarium exercent.

According to Marino Sanuto, *Diarii* (Venice, 1882), 7: 570, the earthquake destroyed the oldest part of the building. The text reads: "Il palazo del duca l'è im bona parte ruinata dal canto vechio, dove per ventura il non habitava; il resto è tutto resentito . . . il giorno [il duca] sta ne l'officio de l'avogaria, soto la parte bona del suo palazo." The combination of these two sources suggests that the oldest part of the building was the north. However, there is no mention in the documents of a major reconstruction of the palace.

70 In 1680 the traveler Bernard Randolph described the Sala di Consiglio (probably the major meeting room of the palace) in the ducal palace as being decorated with white marble and sculptural reliefs. See Hemmerdinger-Iliadou, "La Crète sous la domination" (1967): 612.

71 An inscription written in honor of Nicolò da Ponte, duke of Crete in 1621–22, was reportedly placed in the central courtyard of the palace, above the office of justice. See Gerola, *Monumenti veneti*, 3: 140, and Corner, *Creta sacra*, 2: 440. Also a seventeenth-century document referring to ceremonies taking place inside the courtroom of the ducal palace has been published by G. Gerola, "Una descrizione di Candia nel principio di seicento," *Atti della Accademia Roveretana degli Agiati* ser. 3, 14 (1908): 12–14.

72 Document cited by Gerola, *Monumenti*

veneti, 3: 15, n. 1, from ASV, Dispacci da Candia (May 2, 1536).

73 De Monacis, *Chronicon*, book 10, 181, in the account of the 1363 rebellion mentions a "sacellum Sancti Bernardi situm in palacium."

74 Gerola, *Monumenti veneti*, 3: 11. It is not clear from the sources how many people used the water of the cistern. In later times we know that there were other cisterns in various parts of the old city. Their remains are still preserved in the area close to the loggia and the church of St. Titus. The cistern of the ducal palace was repaired in 1419.

75 According to Venetian chronicles the ducal palace of Candia existed already during the revolt of the Hagiostefanites (1212–17). At the beginning of the rebellion (1213) the duke Giacomo Tiepolo was forced to take refuge in his palace, from which he eventually escaped dressed in women's clothes. See De Monacis, *Chronicon*, book 9, 154.

76 Hélène Ahrweiler, "L'Administration militaire de la Crète byzantine," *Byzantion* 31 (1961): 227, and Thiriet, *Romanie*, 125. Alain Ducellier, *La Façade maritime de l'Albanie au Moyen Age. Durazzo et Valona du XIe au XVe siècle*, Documents et recherches sur l'économie des pays byzantins, islamiques et slaves et leurs relations commerciales au Moyen Age 13 (Thessaloniki, 1981), 131, has also shown that in the cases in which the Venetian colonies did not correspond geographically to Byzantine administrative units, the new Venetian officials had titles that reflected their functions. However, in cases in which a Venetian colony was superimposed onto a Byzantine theme, like Crete, the colonists retained the titulature of the previous Byzantine administration, i.e. duke. This was probably done because the colonial subjects were already familiar with these titles.

77 Gerola, *Monumenti veneti*, 3: 27.

78 Ibid., 3: 29–31.

79 Tafel and Thomas, *Urkunden*, 2: 177.

80 An inscription uncovered near the piazza gives the year 1273 as the foundation date of a building that was made in honor of St. Mark. Koder, *Negroponte*, 91, has interpreted this inscription as referring to the construction of the palace of the *bailo*, which, according to the testimony of Rizzardo's chronicle relating the events of the Ottoman conquest of the city in 1470, stood in the piazza. For the chronicle of Rizzardo see M. Cicogna, *La presa di Negroponte fatta dai Turchi ai Veneziani nel 1470* (Venice, 1884), and a Greek translation by G. Gkikas, "Δύο βενετσιάνικα χρονικά γιά τὴν ἅλωση τῆς Χαλκίδας ἀπό τούς Τούρκους στά 1470 (Two chronicles for the capture of Chalkis by the Turks in 1470)," *Archeion Euvoikon Meleton* 6 (1959): 194–255.

81 Koder, *Negroponte*, 92–93. The ephor of Byzantine Antiquities has challenged Koder's identification of the residence of the *bailo* on this spot. See Demetris Triantafyllopoulos, "Τοπογραφικά προβλήματα τῆς Μεσαιωνικῆς Εὔβοιας (Topographical problems of medieval Euboea)," *Archeion Euvoikon Meleton* 15 (1974):254.

82 Chryssa Maltezou, "Byzantine Legends in Venetian Crete," in Ihor Sevcenko and Irmgard Hutter, eds., *Aetos: Studies in Honour of Cyril Mango Presented to Him on April 14, 1998* (Stuttgart and Leipzig, 1998), 237.

83 Josette Bapt, "Venise en Crète: Révoltes et soumissions," in *Coloniser au Moyen Age*, 359–60.

84 Tafel and Thomas, *Urkunden*, 2: 130: "damus et concedimus nostram *totam* insulam Cretensem vobis dilectis fidelibus nostris viris Venetis." The cadastral entries for the location of the fiefs suggest that by 1211 Venice had established its dominion only in the center and eastern part of the island; see Gasparis, "Land and Peasants," 31, n. 60. Most of the names of villages mentioned in the sources are in the *nomos* of Herakleion, with few villages in the

fringes of the territories of Lassithi and Rethymnon. In addition, whereas in the period before 1204 there were ten bishoprics on Crete, we know of only four functioning in the 1210s, Ario, Mylopotamo Chiron, and Calamon, all of which were located in the center of the island. See also Chryssa Maltezou, "*Concessio Crete* Παρατηρήσεις στά ἔγγραφα διανομῆς φεούδων στούς πρώτους Βενετούς ἀποίκους τῆς Κρήτης (*Concessio Crete* Observations on the documents distributing fiefs to the first Venetian colonists of Crete)," in *Λοιβή: εἰς μνήμην Ἀνδρέα Γ. Καλοκαιρινοῦ* (Herakleion, 1994), 109.

85 In 1222 sixty more *militie* were given to new feudal lords who were sent from Venice. Finally, in 1252 other colonists were sent to Crete to settle in the western part of the island, near Canea, where seventy-five more fiefs were designated to Venetian colonizers; see Tafel and Thomas, *Urkunden*, 2: 236, 470–80; and Santschi, *Feudum*, 37.

86 The cadastres are among the earliest documents to survive from Venetian Crete. There were originally six cadastres, one for every *sestiere*. Unfortunately, these documents have not survived in their totality. In the Venetian Archives only one tome survives intact, the *Catasticum del sestiere dei SS. Apostoli* (Duca di Candia, busta 18), and small fragments of the other *sestieri* (Duca di Candia, buste 19 and 20). Parts of the cadastres have been published by Gerland, *Archiv*, 76–81.

4: Patron Saints, Relics, and Martyria

1 A laconic record from the Procuratia de Supra (1544), published by Gerola, *Monumenti veneti*, 2: 40–41, tells of the takeover of the church: "Templum fuit Divi Titi . . . diuque greco ritu et schemate frequentatum; sed postquam dicioni venete tota insula subjecta est tandem latinum est factum."

2 We do not know the exact date of the construction of the Byzantine cathedral of Chandax, but the church must have been erected shortly after the reconquest of the city by Nikephorus Phokas, that is, in the tenth century.

3 *Biblioteca Sanctorum*, 12 (Rome, 1969), 505. Angelo Venier, a canon and archiepiscopal vicar of Candia, in his inventory of 1670, asserts that the cathedral of St. Titus had been built by Constantinopolitan artists. See M. S. Theochari, "Περί τήν χρονολόγησιν τῆς εἰκόνος Παναγίας Μεσοπαντιτίσσης (On the dating of the icon of the Virgin Mesopantitissa)," *Akademia Athenon, Praktika* 36 (1961): 279.

4 Tsirpanlis, *Catasticum*, no. 158, p. 237, and no. 161, p. 241. Except for a church dedicated to All Saints in the suburbs of Candia, no other church of the same name existed in the city. See G. Gerola, "Topografia delle chiese della città di Candia," *Bessarione* 22/1–4 (1918): 228, n. 1. The person who signed both documents, frater Philippus, was bishop of Ario and general vicar of the patriarch of Constantinople Nicolaus in Crete. He mentions the church of All Saints as his curia ("Datum in nostra curia in ecclesia Omnium Sanctorum"). This implies that in the early fourteenth century the main church of the Orthodox was still dedicated to All Saints.

5 Gerola, *Monumenti veneti* 2: 41, maintains that the church was rebuilt and reconsecrated in 1446. Actually the document reads, "consecratum fuit hoc altare in honorem." This point illustrates that at the time when the axial chapel was remodeled to house the tomb of Archbishop Fantinus Valaresso, only one altar was reconsecrated, not the whole church. For a recent synthesis of earlier accounts see Nike Kritsiotaki, " Ὁ ἱερός ναός τοῦ Ἁγίου Τίτου στό Χάνδακα (The holy church of St. Titus in Candia)," in *Pepragmena tou Z′ Diethnous*

Kretologikou Synedriou, Rethymnon 1995, vol. 2 pt. 1 (Rethymnon, 1997), 347–60.

6 J. Strzygowski, "Παλαιά Βυζαντινή βασιλική ἐν Χαλκίδι (Ancient Byzantine basilica in Chalkis)," *Deltion tes Historikes kai Ethonologikes Hetaireias tes Hellados* 2 (1887): 711–28. This may have been the Byzantine church of the Peribleptos where the Latin emperor Henry prayed in 1209.

7 Strzygowski, "Ancient Byzantine Basilica," 721. The church now has the following dimensions: forty meters long (the nave measures thirty-two meters) by twenty-two meters wide by twenty-one meters high. See also T. Theocharis, " Ἡ ξυλόστεγος βασιλική τῆς Ἁγίας Παρασκευῆς Χαλκίδος (The wooden roofed basilica of St. Paraskeve in Chalkis)," *Archeion Euvoikon Meleton* 8 (1960): 140–56. The basilica may have been shortened by at least one bay after the façade collapsed following the earthquake of 1853.

8 This sculpture could have also come from another Latin church in Negroponte, such as the Holy Apostles, St. John Chrysostom, St. Francis, or St. Clare. See N. I. Giannopoulos, "Χριστιανικαί ἀρχαιότητες Χαλκίδος. Ἡ Αγία Παρασκευή – Ἐκκλησίαι (Christian antiquities of Chalkis. Hagia Paraskeve – Churches)," *Deltion Historikes kai Ethnologikes Hetaireias tes Hellados* 9 (1926): 127–28.

9 Nikolaos Panagiotakes, " Ἀντιγραφεῖς καί κείμενα τοῦ κώδικα Marcianus grecus IX.17. Ἀνδρέας Σκλέντζας, (Copyists and texts of Codex Marcianus grecus IX.17. Andrea Sclentza)," *Ariadne* 2 (1984): 116, comments on lines 1–4 and 11–12. However, in 1467 there must have been at least eleven chapels inside the cathedral, because each of the eleven subcanons of the chapter was given the earnings of one chapel.

10 For instance, two chapels were erected (or endowed) after the third quarter of the fifteenth century. Franciscus Mudacio built a chapel dedicated to St. Francis just before 1463 and in 1473 Leonardus Mazamano decided to endow a chapel in front of his family tomb located in the cathedral; ASV, Procuratia de Supra, Chiesa, b. 102: 1669. Scritture chiesa cattedrale di Candia, f. 21r and 4r.

11 The will of the Venetian archbishop Fantinus Valaresso (1425/6–1443) specified that his tomb was to be set in the pavement of the church ("arca que nobis fieri veniat equalis cum pavimento"); ASV, Procuratia di Supra, Chiesa, b. 142: Diocesi di Candia, fasc. 5, f. 18r. Corner, *Creta sacra*, 2: 75, has recorded a now lost inscription at his tomb, cited also in Gerola, *Monumenti veneti*, 4: 307. On the reconsecration of the altar see ASV, Procuratia de Supra, b. 79, Processo 185, fasc. 1.

12 ASV, Procuratia de Supra, b. 79, Processo 185, fasc. 1. The reliquary is now lost, but following a 1627 transcription of the verses that decorated its sides, V. Laurent attributed its commission to Basileios Lekapenos, illegitimate son of the Byzantine emperor Romanos I (920–944). Unfortunately the inscription does not connect the reliquary with Crete and does not allow us to conclude whether it had been originally intended for the cathedral of Chandax. It is logical to assume that the relics were taken to Crete from Byzantium when Nikephoros Phokas took the island from the Muslims in the tenth century, in which case the reliquary may not have been made for this occasion. See E. Follieri, "L'ordine dei versi in alcuni epigrammi bizantini," *Byzantion* 34 (1964): 455–64. Follieri, on the basis of the correct sequence of the verses, identified the shape of the reliquary as a rectangular box similar to tenth-century Byzantine staurotheques.

13 A report in 1544 maintained that the blood of Christ had been taken to Crete from Constantinople. See ASV, Procuratia di Supra, Chiesa, b. 142, fasc. 5, f. 23r. In 1606 this valuable relic was shown to Jo-

hannes Habermacher, a traveler who visited the cathedral of St. Titus. See Hemmerdinger-Iliadou, "Voyageurs," (1967): 596.

14 The relic was covered with silver and had a gilded bronze crown. See ASV, Procuratia de Supra, b. 102, Scritture della Chiesa Cathedrale di Candia, f. 23r, also cited in R. Gallo, *Il tesoro di San Marco e la sua storia* (Venice, 1967), 125. The head of St. Barbara was given to the church of Santa Maria Formosa in Venice after the fall of Crete to the Ottomans; see G. Gerola, "Gli oggetti sacri di Candia salvati a Venezia," *Atti dell'Accademia degli Agiati di Rovereto* ser. 3, 9/3–4 (1903): 12.

15 All these relics, along with two boxes containing various others, were recorded in inventories of 1669 when they were transported from Crete to Venice. Gerola, "Gli oggetti sacri," 31. A devastating fire in 1544 damaged parts of the church but miraculously did not harm the precious relics of the cathedral; only the arm of St. Efrem was lost. See ASV, Procuratori di San Marco de Supra, Chiesa, b. 142, Diocesi di Candia, fasc. 5, f. 21v–23v. See also Gerola, *Monumenti veneti*, 2: 42 and Panagiotakes, "Copyists," 106.

16 This account records the damages that the cathedral suffered in the earthquake of 1508. It indicates that the building did not have a focal point toward the apse, suggesting that the church was a centralized building and not an elongated basilica. From ASV, Procuratia de Supra, 79, Processo 185, fasc. 1 cited in Gerola, *Monumenti veneti*, 2: 41. The document reads: "Erat id templum mira oedificii amplitudine atque altitudine spectandum, et prope innumeris columnis et varis ac raro marmore admirandum; sepulcris quoque in tropheis gentilibus virorum illustrium, et altaribus et sacellis preciosis its decoratum, ut huic urbi perpetuo ornamento futurum videretur."

17 ASV, Notai di Candia, b. 295, fasc. 1; not. Bentivegna Traversario (June 28, 1350). The passage reads, "hac conditione apposita et expressa quod dicta cuua laborari debeat ad tholum, eo modo, quo facta est cuua ecclesia (sic) Sancti Titi."

18 This is based on the observations of the traveler Evliya Çelebi; see Paulos Hidiroglou, *Das Religiöse Leben auf Kreta nach Ewliya Celebi*, Beihefte der Zeitschrift für Religions-und Geistesgeschichte 11 (Leiden, 1969), 28–29; and B. Demetriades, "Μνημεῖα τοῦ Ἡρακλείου κατά τόν Evliya Celebi (Monuments of Herakleion according to Evliya Çelebi)," *Ariadne* 6 (1993): 214–15.

19 Hidiroglou, *Religiöse Leben*, 75–76. According to the description of another traveler, Silidhar Findiqlili Mehmed Aga, the mosque had twelve arches/vaults, which rested on fourteen columns. In addition, twenty-seven columns carried a red cover. At their sides four cupolas were connected with two arches each. The mosque had seventeen windows. Three doors opened at the west, north, and south sides. In the interior there was a four-step staircase, possibly a reference to the minbar/pulpit. In front of the entrance door there were a monumental five-step staircase thirty yards wide and a forty-five-yard-long platform. On the four marble columns, on which the doorstep rested, there were arches with various figures, i.e. decorated archivolts. A flower garden with four fountains surrounded the mosque.

20 Evliya maintains that this vault (or dome) was newly made when he visited Crete; it was supported by six slender columns.

21 Demetriades, "Monuments of Herakleion," 215.

22 Harvard University, Houghton Library, MS. Riant 53, fos. 318r–v (February 25, 1662). The passage describes the ceremonial that took place inside the cathedral:

> entrando in istesso tempo in essa (la chiesa cattedrale) tanto Monsignor Illustrissimo Arcivescovo per la porta cha passa nel cortile et coridoio arciepiscopalle, quanto li sudetti Rapresentanti

per le altre porte di detta chiesa . . . Et doppo finita la funcione . . . viene acompagniato detto Monsignor Illustrissimo Arcivescovo dalli medessimi Eccellentissimi Rapresentanti vicino alla porta suddeta del cortille dall quale poi si licenciano.

23 Hidiroglou, *Religiöse Leben*, 75–76. The square bell tower/minaret was five stories high. The first floor had one arch, the second story had two arches, the third had a large arch framing two marble supports, the fourth had two square windows and a marble balustrade, and the fifth had a large arch with solid marble supports. The whole was topped with a dome and a male figure holding a cross that showed the direction of the wind.

24 The tombs of Bartholomeo Gradenigo (1233), Gulielmo Quirino (1399), Leonardo Trivisan (1412), Iohannes Lauredano (1422), Laurentius Bragadenus (1424), Benedetto Gritti (1475), and Marino Giustinian (1482) were set in the church. It is impossible to establish the appearance of these tombs as the church is no longer standing. It is quite likely, however, that the early tombs were rather inconspicuously placed in the pavement as we can still see them in the church of St. Mark nearby.

25 Tsirpanlis, *Catasticum*, 295. The document reads: "Dominationem vestram volumus etiam non latere, quod, postquam dacium illud dicte porte impossum fuit, reperimus, quod fuit annis duobus concessum archiepiscopo Cretensi pro hedificatione ecclesie Sancti Titi." Unfortunately, the surviving documents are not specific as to the extent of the rebuilding or restoration needed.

26 On the connection between Titus and Paul see Eusebius, *The History of the Church*, trans. G. A. Williamson (New York, 1965, repr. 1984), 109. The *Life* of St. Titus was allegedly written by Zenas the jurist, a disciple of Saint Paul. In fact, it was a legendary account composed in the period from the midsixth century to the end of the tenth century; see F. Halkin, "La Légende crétoise de Saint Tite," *Analecta Bollandiana* 79 (1961): 241–56.

27 J. P. Migne, *Patrologia Greca* XCVII, coll. 1141–69.

28 Halkin, "Légende," 244. With no direct information on the availability and popularity of Homer's poems in Byzantine Crete, we may assume that following the trend in the rest of the Byzantine empire the Homeric poems were easily accessible to educated people; see Robert Browning, "Homer in Byzantium," *Viator* 6 (1975): 15–33. The revival of interest in Homer in the twelfth century may have well been extended to Crete, which apparently had a higher level of literacy than other parts of Byzantium in 1200; see Nikolaos Oikonomides, "Ἡ ἐγγραματοσύνη τῶν Κρητικῶν γύρω στά 1200 (The literacy of the Cretans around 1200)," in *Pepragmena tou Z′ Kretologikou Synedriou. Rethymnon 1991*, pt. 2 (Rethymnon, 1995), 593–98. For an assessment of the study of Homer in Venetian Crete see Panagiotakes, "Italian Background," 291–93.

29 This tradition is contained in two versions edited by Halkin, "Légende," 241–56, who believes that the Cretans created this legend to enhance the scant biography and to glorify the name of the founder of their church. The text states vaguely that Titus performed miracles when he was traveling with Paul and then that his tomb had healing powers. See also Theochares Detorakes, *Οἱ ἅγιοι τῆς πρώτης Βυζαντινῆς περιόδου τῆς Κρήτης καὶ ἡ σχετική πρός αὐτοὺς φιλολογία* (The saints of the first Byzantine period in Crete and the relevant literature) (Athens, 1970), 19–45. The relevant text (Halkin, "Légende," 244–46) reads:

> The governor of Crete, who happened to be the uncle of Titus, having heard

about the salvific birth and baptism of our lord Christ and the miracles he performed in Jerusalem and other places, he decided, after deliberation with the head administrators of Crete, to send Titus with a few others to Jerusalem so that – they hear, tell and teach what they would see [there]. Titus went there and having seen and bowed in front of our lord Christ he saw all his wonderful deeds; he also saw the miraculous passion of the lord, and his entombment and resurrection and the holy ascension and the descent of the holy ghost to the apostles, and he believed. And he was among the hundred and twenty who believed to the lord because of the teachings of the greatest Peter, as it is written that "Cretans and Arabs" [will believe]. . . . And Saint Titus was ordained by the apostles and he was sent along with Paul to teach and ordain those that Paul had tested.

30 See *Kretika Chronika* 10: 219, fig. 14, and *Delton Christianikes kai Archaiologikes Hetaireias* 2 (1960–61): 9–51. A photograph of the wall painting in the church of St. Photeini has been published in K. Kalokyris, *The Byzantine Wall Paintings of Crete* (New York, 1973), 137, fig. 104.

31 Halkin, "Légende," 251.

32 Buondelmonti, *Descriptio Insule Candie*, 103, talks about St. Titus's body being buried in Gortyna, and Corner, *Creta sacra*, 2: 194, mentions the translation of the relics to Chandax before the arrival of the Venetians. R. Pashley, *Travels in Crete* (1837, Amsterdam anast., 1970), 175, recorded the medieval legends about the saint that circulated on Crete in his time; the body of the saint was never found after the capture of Gortys by the Muslims in the ninth century.

33 Tsougarakis, *Byzantine Crete*, 118; Antonio Di Vita, "Contributi all conoscenza di Gortina bizantina," in *Pepragmena tou E′ Diethnous Kretologikou Synedriou*, vol. 2: 140–41; and Dennis Sullivan, *The Life of Saint Nikon. Text, Translation, and Commentary* (Brookline, 1987), 21: 9. Although St. Nikon was in Crete after 961, the *Life* was written in the mideleventh century, when Gortyna may have still have been the metropolitan see.

34 The local character of St. Titus is emphasized by the fact that the cult of the saint was not very popular outside Candia. No other churches were dedicated to the saint on the island, except for the ruined early Christian cathedral in Gortyna. See *Biblioteca Sanctorum*, 12 (Rome, 1969), 505.

35 A. Xerouchakes, "Αἱ σύνοδοι τοῦ Γερόλαμο Λάντο Λατίνου Ἀρχιεπισκόπου ἐν Κρήτῃ (1467, 1474, 1486) (The Councils of Gerolamo Lando, Latin archbishop in Crete [1467, 1474, 1486])," *Theologia* 9 (1931): 28. In fact, the original letter of the pope in 1209 does not explicitly mention the church of St. Titus, but Crete in general; see Tafel and Thomas, *Urkunden*, 2: 87–88.

36 For an analysis of the Venetian view of sacred relics see A. Niero, "Reliquie e corpi di santi," in AA.VV. *Culto dei Santi a Venezia*, Biblioteca agiografica veneziana 2 (Venice, 1965).

37 George Clontzas was a Greek painter with Venetian clientele in Candia in the later sixteenth century. The icon is in the gallery of the Vatican library. See A. Muñoz, *I quadri bizantini della Pinacoteca Vaticana* (Rome, 1928), 12, no. 38, pl. 20, 1 and 2.

38 For a full discussion of the appropriation of the cult of Saint Titus in Venetian Crete see Maria Georgopoulou, "Late Medieval Crete and Venice. An Appropriation of Byzantine Heritage," *Art Bulletin* 77 (1995): 483–87.

39 For the text, dated 1248, see Tsirpanlis, *Catasticum*, 189: "Item habebat in consuetudine archiepiscopus, quod inuitabat annis singulis in festo Sancti Titi et procurabat ducam cum sua gente apud

metropolim." See also Maltezou, "Byzantine 'Consuetudines,' " 275.

40 Xerouchakes, "Councils of Gerolamo Lando," 28. The lauds to the doge started with the phrase "Illustrissimo et serenissimo Principe et domino," then "Sancte Marce! tu nos adjuva." For the duke the hymns said, "Illustrissimo et eccellentissimo domino," then "Sancte Tite! tu nos adjuva."

41 At least ten of the twenty-one solemn processions started or ended at the Latin cathedral, where Mass was celebrated and lauds were sung to the authorities. See Aspasia Papadaki, *Θρησκευτικές καί κοσμικές τελετές στή Βενετοκρατούμενη Κρήτη* (Religious and secular rituals on Venetian Crete)" (Rethymnon, 1995).

42 McKee, "The Revolt of St. Tito," 179 and 203.

43 E. Gerland, *Des Archiv des Herzogs von Kandia Koenigl. Staatsarchiv zu Venedig* (Strasbourg, 1899), 119–20, published a 1365 archival document referring to the festivities for the commemoration of the victory against the rebels (*De festivitate ad memoriam expugnationis urbis Candide quolibet anno celebranda*). The relevant section of the document reads: "magnificus dominus, dominus Petrus Mauroceno honorabilis duca Crete et egregii domini Nicolaus Ciurano et Ludovicus de Molino honorabiles consiliarii Crete, . . . ordinauerunt ad futuram memoriam, quod anno quolibet de mense Maii in X die fieri debeat una solemnissima processio eo modo, quo fit processio in die beati Uiti . . ." The feast of St. Vito (June 15) was instituted as a holiday in Venice in 1310 to commemorate the victory of doge Pietro Gradonigo over the revolt of Querini and Tiepolo; see Papadaki, *Religious and Secular Rituals*, 164, n. 9.

44 F. Corner, *Notizie storiche delle chiese e monasteri di Venezia* (Venice, 1758), 196. The relics were returned to Crete as late as 1966. See G. Olivotti, *Riportando il Capo di San Tito a Creta* (Venice, 1966).

45 Fra Noe, *Viaggio da Venezia al S. Sepolcro et al Monte Sinai* (Bassano, 1696), 16–17, traveled to the area before 1500; he reports: "Modone è città posta in Grecia et è assai bene munita, sopra il mare, nella provincia della Morea. Et ha arcivescovado et è nella chiesa parochiale, la quale è nominata San Giovanni, te viè il corpo di San Luca et il capo di Sant'Anastasio vescovo, e di qui partiti pervenissimo in Candia."

46 The Byzantine church located inside the old city had been taken over by the Angevin rulers of the island before the arrival of the Venetians in 1386. Eventually the Venetians built a new Latin cathedral in the suburbs, which was dedicated to St. Jacob (1633); cf. Aliki Nikeforou, *Δημόσιες τελετές στην Κέρκυρα κατά την περίοδο της Βενετικής κυριαρχίας 14ος–18ος αι.* (Public Ceremonies in Corfu during the period of Venetian rule 14th–18th centuries) (Athens, 1999), 79–81. Interestingly, in Corfu the Orthodox invented their own proper saint, St. Spyridon, whose relics arrived on the island in the fifteenth century and who delivered the town from the plague.

47 Raymond Matton, *Corfou* (Athens, 1960), 105.

48 A unique description of the interior of the church has survived in a detailed report of George Perpignano, bishop of Canea in 1620, at the Vatican library. Ubaldo Manucci, "Contributi documentarii per la storia della distruzione degli episcopati latini in Oriente nei secoli XVI e XVII," *Bessarione* year 17, vol. 30 (1914): 97–116. For an analysis of this report see Georgopoulou, "Meaning of the Architecture," 347–48.

49 Manucci, "Contributi documentarii," 102–4. The western gate was flanked by the sepulchral monuments of ca Dolfino

and ca Minoto, and a tomb of the Molin family was set above the arch of the western entrance. Very few remains of the Venetian church were preserved even when Gerola visited Crete: the northern side aisle with the bell tower, part of the ribbed vaulting of the sacristy resting on corbels, and a section of the semicircular apse and the choir; see Gerola, *Monumenti veneti*, 2: 100–5, fig. 65. Another photograph showing traces of the arches that supported the northern wall was published by Curuni and Donati, *Creta veneziana*, 251, no. 252.

50 Fedalto, *La Chiesa latina in Oriente*, 3 (Verona, 1978), 82.

51 Gerola, *Monumenti veneti*, 2: 105–7.

52 Flaminio Corner, *Creta sacra seu de episcopis utriusque ritus graeci et latini in insula Cretae*, 2 vols. (Venice, 1755), 2: 121–26, who recorded the bishops of Sitia, wrote about the church of St. Mark: "Ecclesia ejus S. Marci Evangelistae titulo decorata sex Canonicos praeter alios minoris officii clericos ad sacra omnia peragenta habebat, quorum quidem residentia ibi stetit, donec anno 1538."

53 Marco Petta, "Documenti di storia ecclesiastica," in *Pepragmena tou B′ Diethmous Kretologikou Synedriou* 3 (Athens, 1968), 216. An inventory of the possessions of the cathedral was made in 1637: its movable possessions were of inconsiderable value, except for a Byzantine icon of the Virgin and a painting depicting the Last Supper with the coats of arms of the Balbi family.

54 Gerola, *Monumenti veneti,* 2: 108. On February 10, 1645, the *provveditore generale* Andrea Corner wrote: "Quella chiesa cattedrale, che è di Vostra Serenità, ha dato inditio grande di venir a basso, et è stato necessario abbandonarla."

55 Historical Archives in Dubrovnik, Testamenta notariae, vol. 23, ff. 1–2 a tergo. The will was written on August 1, 1475. I would like to thank Professor Barisa Krekic for kindly sharing this information with me.

56 Tafel and Thomas, *Urkunden*, 2: 98–99. The text records the treaty between the doge and Geodfrey Villehardouin. The possessions of the towns and the bishoprics are also mentioned.

57 The importance accorded by the Venetian Republic to St. Mark and the saint's critical role in the construction of the "myth" of Venice have been the object of numerous studies. For an extensive bibliography see E. Muir, *Civic Ritual in Renaissance Venice* (Princeton, N.J., 1981).

58 Tafel and Thomas, *Urkunden*, 2: 132–33.

59 The *Provinciale Romanum* of 1228 reads, "Ecclesia Sancti Marci Cretensis debet annuatim ecclesie Romane pro censu I yperperum," cited in G. Fedalto, "La Chiesa latina a Creta dalla caduta di Costantinopoli (1204) alla riconquista Bizantina (1261)," *Kretika Chronika* 24 (1972): 152.

60 Gerola, *Monumenti veneti*, 2: 18.

61 The letter of Pope Gregory IX (Tafel and Thomas, *Urkunden*, 2: 349–51) reads, "vos (milites Cretenses) quandam Ecclesiam in fundo proprio ad honorem Dei et beati Marci Evangeliste in ciuitate, que dicitur Candida, sita in insula Cretensi, construere intendatis, et fundum ipsum Romane Ecclesie duxeritis offerendum."

62 Fedalto, "Chiesa latina a Creta," 163. Giorgio Fedalto has argued that the Venetian feudal lords of Crete addressed their letter to the pope, because either the archbishop's post in Candia was vacant or the archbishop was not present in Crete at the time. A third possibility that Fedalto has pointed out is that the people did not want to be subjected to the archbishop so they left the control of the church to the Apostolic Seat.

63 The basilica of San Marco in Venice was also managed by the *primicerius* in association with the Procuratia of St. Mark.

The *primicerius* was responsible for the spiritual care of the basilica, and the procurators managed the sanctuary and the treasury. See F. Corner, *Notizie storiche*, 198, and Guido Perocco, "History of the Treasury of San Marco," in *The Treasury of San Marco, Venice* (Milan, 1984), 65.

64 Gerland, *Archiv*, 67: "pro incambio unius petie terre vacue, que erat inter ecclesiam sancti Marci et murum civitatis et que erat de iure dicte Cretensis ecclesie, super qua laboratum fuit *campanile* dicte ecclesie sancti Marci et in parte remansit pro campo seu cimiterio dicte ecclesie . . . in MCCXXXXIII mense Februarii die XV intrante indicione II." In this document we are given the dimensions of the lot that the church gave up: 10 by 4 paces, that is 17.39 by 6.95 meters. It is possible that the lot for the "campanile" had comparable dimensions; most likely, however, it was smaller, because it was at a primary location that the church needed for the erection of the bell tower.

65 Although this is the first personification of the city that has survived, the artist must have been inspired by an earlier image in which the Venetian character of the city is symbolized by the ducal basilica.

66 S. Alexiou and K. Lassithiotakis, *Ἡ ἀποκατάστασις τοῦ ναοῦ τοῦ Ἁγίου Μάρκου τοῦ Χάνδακος* (The restoration of the church of St. Mark in Candia) (Herakleion, 1958). For a yearly account of the works see the reports in the *Kretika Chronika* from 1956 onward. The dimensions of the church are the following: the north wall is 33.95 meters long, the south wall 33.65 meters, the east wall 17.90 meters, and the west wall 17.60 meters. These dimensions are close to those recorded by the Ottomans in 1670, i.e. 32.50 by 17.40 meters (43 by 23 cubits), and suggest that the building has retained its medieval form; cf. Gerola, *Monumenti veneti*, 2: 21. The width of the north wall was 0.95 meter; that of the south wall was 1.05 meters.

Alexiou and Lassithiotakis decided to elevate the central nave and to pierce twenty-four clerestory windows. They also constructed a portico with five arches and repaved the interior. They kept four openings on the east side, and a small one in the tympanum; on the south side they preserved the central door and pierced a window in the tympanum; on the north wall five windows were preserved and a "Gothic" door was designed; on the south wall five windows were pierced facing the north wall windows. They also readjusted the level of the pavement and discovered the original column bases, which were shown to be reused from ancient structures of Crete.

67 Alexiou-Lassithiotakis, "Restoration," 13 and 19. In a report of the governor in 1552 we learn that the south and west sides of the church were stable, but the north wall leaned outward, pulling the columns and wooden supports. The sixteenth-century architect proposed to brace the four bays of the northern aisle by abutting four buttresses on the exterior wall. The document also mentions the four good "arches" of the church, a word that must refer to the bays defined by the nave arcade. Traces of two buttresses are visible in Gerola's plan of the church. Gerola, *Monumenti veneti*, 2: 25, fig. 4.

68 In 1370 the western window of the sacristy was walled in by the *primicerius*. See ASV, DdC, B. 29bis 30, Memoriali 16/2, fos. 21r-v (August 12, 1370). This damaged document informs us that the primicerius *** Geno was concerned about a garbage odor coming into the western side of the sacristy through the window ("in parte austri sacristie . . . immundicie que per fen[estram] sacristie intrabat fetor"). The name of the church is not legible, but the *primicerius* was responsible only for the church of St. Mark. He was allowed to build a stone wall ("murus de

petris et calce") in order to keep the odor away.

Indeed, in the plan drafted by Gerola there are traces of a wall perpendicular to the north wall of the church. This wall started at the first eastern bay and appears like a projection of the buttress, but might indicate the existence of the sacristy on that spot.

69 The document of 1552 mentioned the governor noted a certain "house of the Church" (*casa della chiesa*) adjacent to the south wall of St. Mark. See Gerola, *Monumenti veneti*, 2: 19.

70 Unfortunately, we possess no documentary information on the construction of the portico of St. Mark in Candia, a feature that was constructed de novo by the restorers in the 1950s. The sources inform us that the church of San Marco in Venice was adorned with a loggia as late as 1283. Clearly, for the Venetians the term *loggia* designated something other than a narthex, since the church of San Marco in Venice had a narthex from early on. In Venice the portico was erected in an area that previously had been occupied by three arches (*archivolti*) and a well at the beginning of the market; according to the prescriptions of the Maggior Consiglio it should measure approximately 10.50 meters. See Cessi, *Deliberazioni del Maggior Consiglio*, 3, 29, and 35.

71 A 1669 inventory of the church of St. Titus informs us that a painting (*quadro*) of the Virgin Mary was placed outside the church of St. Mark, in the loggia. See ASV, Procuratia de Supra, Chiesa, b. 102, 1669. Scritture Chiesa cathedrale di Candia, f. 40.

72 Almost all entries in the archival series *Bandi* explicitly mention that the city crier stood at the loggia of St. Mark, which apparently was the most visible place in town. See for example, Ratti-Vidulich, *Bandi*, 50. For the city crier in Venice see Alvise Zorzi, *Venice, the Golden Age, 697–1797* (New York, 1983), 265: he announced the decrees from the stump of a porphyry column, called the *Bando*, which was situated at the south corner of the church of San Marco.

73 Sanuto, *Diarii*, 7 (1882): 571. This information, found in a letter of ser Pietro Marzello, *capitaneo* of Crete, reads, "La torre de San Marco è tutta schantinata e aperta."

74 Ch. Maltezou, "Ἡ Κρήτη στή διάρκεια τῆς περιόδου τῆς Βενετοκρατίας (1211–1669) (Crete during the period of Venetian rule (1211–1669)," in N. Panagiotakes, ed., *Κρήτη. Ἱστορία καί πολιτισμός* (Crete, history and civilization) (Herakleion, 1988), 2: 141. The clock was transported from Venice and was installed for the needs of the commune.

75 Thiriet, *Assemblées*, 1: 126, no. 182 and 158. In 1309 the *primicerius* of the church, Niccolò Barozzi, asked the Regimen to address a plea to Venice for the release of the funds necessary for the restoration of the ducal chapel and his residence. In 1315 the duke was urged to begin the repairs immediately, and to take care of the residence of the *primicerius* at a second stage.

76 ASV, Senato Misti, Liber XVII, f. 46r (February 15, 1336); cited in Fedalto, *Chiesa latina*, 3: 44, no. 74.

77 Demus, *Church of San Marco*, 140.

78 Noiret, *Documents inédits*, 401, and Fedalto, *Chiesa latina*, 3: 234, no. 603. The term *paramenti* refers either to liturgical vestments or to church hangings. In this case it must refer to portable sacred objects used in processions.

79 For the churches of St. Mark in Beirut and Tyre see the treaties signed by the doge in Tafel and Thomas, *Urkunden*, 2: 126, 174, and the rich report of the *bailo* of Syria on the Venetian possessions in their Syrian colonies, 331–99.

80 See Koder, *Negroponte*, 91–93; also see chapter 3, n. 80.

81 Tasos Kalatheris, "Συμβολή στήν ἱστορία καί τοπογραφία τῆς μεσαιωνικῆς Χαλ-

κίδας (Contribution to the history and topography of medieval Chalkis)," *Euboia* 6 (1984) and Theodoros Skouras, *Χριστιανικά μνημεῖα τῆς Εὔβοιας* (Christian monuments of Euboea) (Chalkis, 1998), 193–94.

82 We have very little information on the churches of Modon. The documents published by Sathas contain three possible references to churches: la Madonna della spiagia (the church of the Virgin on the beach) and its annual fair; the bell of San Lio, which was probably a church too; and a vague reference to St. Mark; cf. Sathas, *Documents inédits relatifs à l'histoire de la Grèce*, 4: 7, 26, and 180.

83 Fedalto, *Chiesa latina,* 3: 82, no. 180.

84 Otto Demus, "A Renascence of Early Christian Art in Thirteenth-Century Venice," in *Late Classical and Medieval Studies in Honor of Albert Mathias Friend, Jr.*, ed. Kurt Weitzmann (Princeton, N.J., 1955), 348–61, has already demonstrated that the thirteenth-century artistic projects undertaken in Venice emulated the imperial Byzantine tradition, showing traces of an "imperialistic archaism."

85 Demus, *Church of San Marco*, 88–100.

5: The Blessings of the Friars

1 The crusades were implicitly equated with the struggle against heresy. See Franco Cardini, "Crusade and Presence of Jerusalem," in B. Z. Kedar, H. E. Mayer, and R. C. Smail, eds., *Outremer* (Jerusalem, 1982), 339. See also M. Luchaire, *Innocent III et la question de l'Orient* (Paris, 1907); J. Richard, *La Papauté et les missions d'Orient au Moyen Age (XIII–XV siècles)*, Collection de l'École française de Rome 33 (Rome, 1977); and K. M. Setton, *The Papacy and the Levant (1204–1571)*, vol. 1, *The Thirteenth and Fourteenth Centuries* (Philadelphia, 1976–78).

2 M. Roncaglia, *Les Frères Mineurs et l'église grecque orthodoxe au XIIIe siècle (1231–1274)* (Cairo, 1954); Emmet Randolph Daniel, *The Franciscan Concept of Mission in the High Middle Ages* (Lexington, 1975); and R. Loenertz O. P., "Les Missions dominicaines en Orient et la Société des frères Pérégrinants," *Archivum Fratrum Praedicatorum* 3 (1933): 48.

3 Jacques le Goff, "Ordres mendiants et urbanisation dans la France médiévale. Etat de l'enquête," *Annales Economies, Sociétés, Civilisations* 25 (1970): 931–32. Le Goff maintains that concerns of this kind were taken into account from the thirteenth century, when a series of measures were unified by pope Clement IV in the bull "Quia plerumque" of April 28, 1268. This bull set the distance between two Mendicant churches of different orders within a city to 300 cannes "mensurandum per aera," that is, around 500 meters. Later this distance was reduced to 140 cannes (250 meters), Ripoll, *Bullarium*, 495, no. 86.

4 According to an account of Antonius Hovaeus, a certain Count Gerardo was buried in this Franciscan church on Christmas Day of 1242. See P. Willibrordus Lampen, in *Archivum Historicum Franciscanum*, 22: 231.

5 This legend is mentioned in 1518 by the pilgrim Jacques le Saige, who also reported that a well miraculously appeared behind the Franciscan church of Candia. See Démocratie Hemmerdinger-Iliadou, "La Crète sous la domination vénitienne et turque (1322–1684)," *Studi veneziani* 9 (1967): 566–67, and G. Gerola, "I Francescani in Creta al tempo del dominio veneziano," *Collectanea Francescana* 2, no. 3–4 (1932): 305.

6 Fedalto, *Chiesa latina*, 3: 141, no. 350. The Venetian Senate ordered the Chapter of Crete to supply the monastery with the three hundred hyperpera that the friars had deposited for the construction of their church. The document reads: "Cum fratres minores Candide nobis (the Senate) suppli-

caverunt quod circha yperperorum trecenta, que restant de yperperis mille dimissis eisdem pro ecclesia depositata in camerlengaria Crete, dentur et assignentur pro dicta ecclesia, vadit pars, quod scribatur regimini Crete quod dicta yperpera trecenta dent dictis fratribus." It is not clear whether the phrase *pro fabrica ecclesie* means rebuilding or repair. The sum of 1,000 hyperpera suggests that the church needed major repairs or additions.

7 Two architectural drawings that were made in 1866 by Alexandrides portray the remains of the church after the earthquake. See *Homage to Crete 1884–1984* (Herakleion, 1984), figs. 32 and 33. Following 1669, the church of St. Francis had been converted into a royal mosque by the Ottomans (Hunkâr Cami). Only the sacristy and an octagonal building survived the demolition of 1867. In the Venetian period the sacristy was a square vaulted structure, but the Ottomans replaced its original vault with a flat roof. The large buttresses in the exterior of the sacristy defined spaces for pointed arch windows. The material from the monastery was used for the reconstruction of the Vizir Cami, which had also been damaged by the earthquake.

8 The report of the Latin archbishop Luca Stella in 1625 gives detailed information on the appearance of the Latin churches of Candia. See N. M. Panagiotakes, "Μαρτυρίες γιά τή μουσική στήν Κρήτη στή βενετοκρατία (Evidence for the music on Crete during Venetian rule)," *Thesaurismata* 20 (1990): 138, doc. no. 76, IV. In addition, an inventory recording the possessions of the monastery in 1417 located in Venice, Biblioteca Marciana, lat. IX, 186 (coll. 3400), offers invaluable information about the layout of the church (fos. 13r, 18r, and 24v.) For instance in f. 24v we learn that the altar of the St. Francis chapel was endowed by Franciscus Caravello in 1371. The only part of this important manuscript that has been published is a commentary on the books of the library by G. Hoffmann, "La biblioteca scientifica del monastero di San Francesco a Candia nel medio evo," *Orientalia Christiana Periodica* 8 (1942): 317–60.

9 The random nature of the available material does not allow a secure localization of these chapels. They were dedicated to St. George (mentioned in a notarial document of 1433), St. Michael (endowed by Marcus de Medio in 1391 as f. 14r of the aforementioned inventory reports), St. Nicholas (constructed at the tomb of the Venerio family in 1403), the Virgin Mary (mentioned in f. 21r of the inventory in the year 1411), and St. Mark (mentioned in f. 12r of the inventory in 1420). In addition, we learn of altars endowed by George Bolani that contained the tomb of the Geno family (mentioned in 1429), an altar of the Caravello family, and the chapel of Pope Alexander V, which was made in 1409. The sacristy was paid for by George Dono in 1432 (f. 14r). According to the report of Luca Stella and an inventory of 1669, there was also a chapel dedicated to St. Anthony of Padua, a major Franciscan saint. See M. Georgopoulou, "The Meaning of the Architecture," 197–98.

10 G. Meersseman, O. P., "L'architecture dominicaine au XIIIe siècle. Legislation et pratique," *Archivum Fratrum Praedicatorum* 16 (1946): 136–90; and Wolfgang Braunfels, *Monasteries of Western Europe: The Architecture of the Orders* (Princeton, N.J., 1973), 246.

11 G. Hoffmann, "Il Pensiero religioso nelle donazioni e nei testamenti dei Veneziani di Creta," *Civiltà Cattolica* 1 (1944): 221. Many dukes were buried in this Franciscan church, following the example of the doges in Venice: Francesco Morosini (1374), Egidio Morosini (1419), Giacomo Corner (1466), Andrea Marcello (1466), Bernardo Giustinian (1500), Giovanni Morosini (1503), Cosma Pasqualigo

(1505), Nicola Salamon (1580), and Marino da Pesaro (1625). See also Nikolaos Zoudianos, *Ἱστορία τῆς Κρήτης ἐπί Ἑνετοκρατίας* (History of Venetian Crete) (Athens, 1960), 1: 284–86.

12 For Pietro Casola see Hemmerdinger-Iliadou, "Voyageurs" (1973): 496. The paintings were mentioned by Alessandro Palatino of Reno in 1495; see Gerola, *Monumenti veneti,* 2: 113.

13 Inventory (as in n. 8), f. 13r.

14 Hemmerdinger-Iliadou, "La Crète sous la domination vénitienne et turque (1322–1684)," *Studi veneziani* 15 (1973): 496. In 1494 the pilgrim Pietro Casola reported that St. Francis was more beautiful than the cathedral of Candia.

15 The list of sacred vessels and relics that the pope sent to the monastery of St. Francis is given by Corner, *Creta sacra,* 2: 14. The rest of the gifts are mentioned in the unpublished chronicle of Andrea Corner, Historia Candiana, Biblioteca Marciana, Venice, Ital. VI 286 (coll. 5985), p. 24v. The pope "mando a fabricar in . . . la chiesa di San Francesco . . . con una capella grande con un arco grandissimo dove poste sono le sue armi . . . e sin da Roma mando anco la Porta grande d'essa chiesa di belissimo lavoro e di marmo finissimo." The chapel of Pope Alexander V was destroyed in 1852 by an Ethiopian kaymakim of the Turkish army, because he thought there was a treasure buried under it. See N. Staurakis, *Στατιστική τῆς Κρήτης* (Statistics of Crete) (Athens, 1890), 134–35, n. 1.

16 From the inventory (as in n. 8), f. 6v: "In primis unum quadrum magnum de argento cum smaltis ab una parte crucifixum et verginem et beatum iohannem launtibus et ab alia parte sanctos Antonium, Christofori et Andrea et intus est unum magnum pecium columpne Christi et hanc donauit conuentui dominus papa Allexander *[sic]* quintus."

17 This relic was placed in a reliquary commissioned by Marco Trevisan, minister of Romania; cf. inventory (as in n. 8), f. 6v: "Item brachium Sancti Simeonis apostoli totum copertum de puro argento cum manu etiam de argento totum de arger auratum pulcro opere quod brachium fecit fieri reverentus in Christo pater frater Marcus Triuisano de Veneciis, minister prouincie Romanie."

18 As we have seen in the previous chapter the relics of St. Stephen had adorned the high altar of the cathedral of St. Titus at least until 1446. We do not know why the precious reliquary of the protomartyr was seen in the church of St. Francis by two travelers: Alessandro Palatino del Reno (1495) and Pier Paolo Rucellai (1504). See Chapter 4, n. 12.

19 Inventory (as in n. 8), f. 6v: "Item reliquarium unum pro tunica sancti Francisci pulcrum cum pede de argento cum vitibus releuate et ponium et lapidibus vitreis legatis cum uno magno et pulcro cristallo et una capite superius quod donauit conuentui frater Franciscus Sanuto."

20 Corner, *Creta sacra,* 2: 412, publishes the letter of duke Hieronymus Donatus, which gives a detailed description. See also M. Sanuto, *I Diarii,* 7: 568. Further destruction occurred during the earthquake of 1596 when the cupola of one of the bell towers collapsed. Apparently the monastery had more than one bell tower in the sixteenth century.

21 This list of 1669 has been published by Gerola, "Francescani," 315.

22 Borsari, *Dominio veneziano a Creta,* 134. A list of Dominican convents composed by Bernard Gui in 1303 mentions six convents in the province of Greece, including St. Peter the Martyr in Candia and St. Nicholas in Canea; both were populated with friars from Lombardy. See R.-L. Loenertz, "Les Établissements Dominicains de Péra-Constantinople," *Échos d'Orient* 34 (1935): 335. On the history of the Dominican establishments dedi-

cated to St. Peter the Martyr see G. Meersseman, O. P., "Études sur les anciennes confréries dominicaines, II. Les confréries de Saint-Pierre Martyr," *Archivum Fratrum Praedicatorum* 21 (1951): 51–196.

23 ASV, DdC, b. 20, Frammento di Catastico Albo (S. Crucis), f. 18v. The entry in the feudal cadastre under the name of Thomas Fradello (c. 1224) is cancelled and in the margin another hand has marked that the house and the lot had been transferred to the friars.

24 ASV, DdC, b. 18, Catastico SS. Apostolorum, f. 307–308, and Borsari, *Dominio veneziano a Creta*, 79–80, n. 66, and 151–53. The street that ran between the monastery and the aforementioned piece of land was also given to the Dominicans.

25 ASV, DdC, b. 12, Deliberazioni del Maggior Consiglio, f. 97r, September 5, 1353, and f. 102r, dated October 5, 1357.

26 In 1972 the Greek Archaeological Service decided that the church should be restored to its sixteenth-century appearance (that is, after the remodeling that remedied the damages caused by the earthquake of 1508) and not to its original condition in the thirteenth century; cf. M. Borboudakis, "Χρονικά" (Chronicles), *Archaiologikon Deltion* 27 (1972): 668.

27 Richard Sundt, "*Mediocres domos et humiles habeant fratres nostri:* Dominican Legislation on Architecture and Architectural Decoration in the 13th Century," *Journal of the Society of Architectural Historians* 46 (1987): 398, 401. Compare the two-nave form of the church with the Dominican church of St. Sophia in Andravida, in the western Peloponnesos, which must have been built in the late 1220s; cf. Nancy K. Cooper, "The Frankish Church of Saint Sophia at Andravida, Greece," in Peter Lock and G. D. R. Sanders, eds., *The Archaeology of Medieval Greece*, Oxbow Monograph 59 (Oxford, 1996), 29–47; and Mary Lee Coulson, "The Dominican Church of Saint Sophia at Andravida," in the same volume, pp. 49–59, with earlier bibliography.

28 B. Kitsiki-Panagopoulos, *Cistercian and Mendicant Architecture in Greece* (Chicago, 1979), 88–90. The sanctuary was divided in two bays and measured 6.50 by 13 meters. The first bay was covered with a brick domical rib vault with heavy ribs of a round section. The second bay has been rebuilt and is now covered with a barrel vault. However, traces of the original rib vaulting are still visible at the four corners.

29 Ibid., 90, fig. 9, suggests that the remodeling of the church occurred after the 1508 earthquake, but there is no reason to reject the theory that is was done during the conversion of the church into a mosque by the Ottomans. Panagopoulos's reconstruction of the church proposes a transept not projecting farther than the side chapels.

30 Ibid., 90, argues that these were the original thirteenth-century windows. The difference in form must indicate two construction phases.

31 For Stella's report see N. Panagiotakes, *Ἡ Κρητικὴ περίοδος τῆς ζωῆς τοῦ Δομηνίκου Θεοτοκοπούλου* (The Cretan period of the life of Domenico Theotokopoulos) (Athens, 1987), 105–6. For the wills see ASV, Notai di Candia, b. 295, fasc. 6: not. Leonardus Cavisino (will of Petrus Grimaldo dated October 7, 1375); DdC, b. 30ter, Memoriali, fasc. 32, f. 63v (April 26, 1420); Notai di Candia, b. 295, fasc. 2: not. Giovanni Belli (May 7, 1376); Notai di Candia, b. 121, f. 66r-v and 170r-v: not. Cirillus Gradenigo (April 29 and July 26, 1495); in 1505 the painter Nicolaus Gripioti was commissioned to paint an icon of St. Christofal in the Bono chapel. See M. Constantoudaki-Kitromilidou, "Οἱ ζωγράφοι τοῦ Χάνδακος τό πρῶτον ἥμισυ τοῦ 16ου αἰ. μαρτυρούμενοι ἐκ τῶν

νοταριακῶν ἀρχείων (The Painters of Canadia in the first half the sixteenth century attested in notarial documents)," *Thesaurismata* 10 (1973): 364. In the seventeenth century (1634) this last chapel was adorned with a gilded altar dedicated to the patron saint of Lorenzo Bon. See Maria Kazanaki-Lappa, "Οἱ ζωγράφοι τοῦ Χάνδακα κατά τόν 17ο αἰώνα. Ἐκδόσεις ἀπό νοταριακά ἔγγραφα (The Painters of Candia in the 17th century. Editions from notarial documents)," *Thesaurismata* 18 (1981): 259–60.

32 Sundt, "*Mediocres domos*," 401 and 406.

33 Panagiotakes, "Evidence for the music," 138. Panagiotakes interprets another account of the music's attracting the faithful in the Dominican church as a possible reference to some kind of an orchestra or musical variety. An organ player was buried outside the western gate of the church in 1556 and the inscription that accompanied his tomb has been recorded by Gerola.

34 Kazanaki, "The painters of Candia in the 17th century," 259.

35 M. Constantoudaki, "Μαρτυρίες ζωγραφικῶν ἔργων *στό Χάνδακα σέ ἔγγραφα τοῦ 16ου καί 17ου αἰώνα* (Evidence on Paintings from Candia from documents of the sixteenth and seventeenth centuries)," *Thesaurismata* 12 (1975): 132. It is not clear what kind of evidence the notary drew on to arrive at such a date.

36 *Τό κάλλος τῆς μορφῆς. Μεταβυζαντινές εἰκόνες ΙΕ′–ΙΗ′ αἰώνων* (The beauty of the figure. Post-Byzantine icons of the 15th–18th centuries) (Athens, 1995), 191–92.

37 *From Byzantium to El Greco. Greek Frescoes and Icons* (Athens, 1987), 176–77, and Maria Vassilaki, "A Cretan Icon in the Ashmolean: The Embrace of Peter and Paul," *Jahrbuch der Österreichischen Byzantinistik* 40 (1990): 405–22.

38 Gerola, *Monumenti veneti*, 2: 125.

39 ASV, Notai di Candia, b. 295, fasc.4, f. 8r, not. Antonius Rodulfo (January 16, 1335), and b. 233, fasc. 1, f. 100v, not. Leonardus Quirino (November 29, 1326).

40 ASV, DdC, b. 26, Sentenze, Reg. 2/2, f. 164r, no. 192, dated September 13, 1370.

41 ASV, Notai di Candia, b. 295, fasc. 3, f. 9v, not. Albertino Maça, dated March 22, 1324. Mariçola, widow of Bonifacio Trivisano, requested to be buried in the monastery (*loco*) of the Preachers friars.

42 The lower stratum contained Byzantine ceramic from Constantinople dating to the eleventh and twelfth centuries. Two Byzantine coins of John II (1118–43) were also excavated; see M. Borboudakis, "Δοκιμαστική ἀνασκαφή Ἁγ. Πέτρου τῶν Ἑνετῶν Ἡρακλείου (Test excavations in St. Peter of the Venetians in Herakleion)," *Archaiologikon Deltion* 23/2 (1968): 427–29.

43 George C. Miles, "Excavations at Ag. Petros, Herakleion 1967," in *Pepragmena tou G′ Diethnous Kretologikou Synedriou* 3 (Athens, 1975): 225–30, esp. 228–29. The types of pottery that the excavators found were classified into five categories: (a) jugs with yellowish glaze; (b) jugs with transparent blue, green, yellow, or brown glaze; (c) examples of the so-called Perugian ware of 1520–30; (d) glazed sgraffito ware with flower motifs (blue, yellow, and green) dated to 1450–1500; (e) majolica plates, of the "Faenza" type of around 1530. See also Theodora Stillwell McKay, "A Group of Renaissance Pottery from Heraklion, Crete. Notes and Questions," in *The Archaeology of Medieval Greece*, 127–37.

44 A hoard of coins dating to the rule of Doge Francesco Foscari (1423–57) was unearthed in 1963 when the foundations of the hotel Xenia were laid near the monastery of St. Peter the Martyr. See S. Alexiou, "Χρονικά (Chronicles)," *Kretika Chronika* 17 (1963): 400. Forty-six coins were given to the Historical Museum of Crete.

45 Gerola, *Monumenti veneti*, 1: 116 and 2:

146–48. Fabri reported that the sea walls in front of St. Peter the Martyr were destroyed and mentioned the numerous windows and doors of the cells that opened to the sea. Furthermore, he was impressed by the fact that the friars could relax and study in these cells with the sound of the waves breaking so close to the walls of the monastery.

46 Ibid., 2: 127.

47 Nikolaos S. Staurinides, *Μεταφράσεις Τουρκικῶν ἱστορικῶν Ἐγγράφων ἀφορώντων εἰς τήν ἱστορίαν τῆς Κρήτης* (Translations of Turkish historical documents related to the history of Crete), 6 vols. (Herakleion, 1984–87), 1: 373–75. In a 1671 Turkish document regarding repairs made to the mosque, probably at the time of its conversion, "the walls of the courtyard were found to be in length and width 312 square tectonic cubits." Five doors were made, two stone pilasters were repaired, 130 glass windows were purchased, four doors of the gallery (*gynaikonites*) were mentioned, the bell towers (were there more than one?) were demolished, and a stone minaret was erected. The authorities also recorded a sundial above the entrance door. Was this a Venetian remain, or was it a new addition? Later (in 1708) more repairs took place in the mosque. From the documents we learn that the minaret had a staircase of 118 steps and that for the repair of the wooden roof of the mosque the material required consisted of 4,000 cacroni; 30,000 planks, 500 of which should be of walnut wood; 1,000 posts; 20 000 tiles; as well as 20 special posts to support the roof that were sent from Istanbul (16 cubits long by ½ cubit in width); ibid., 3: 360–61.

48 Three more dukes were buried in this Franciscan church: Pietro Emiliani (1345), Donato Truno (1385), and Priamo Truno (1500). See Gerola, *Monumenti veneti*, 2: 118, and Zoudianos, *History of Venetian Crete*, 284–85.

49 L. Wadding, *Annales Minorum, seu trium ordinum a S. Francisco institutorum*. 3rd ed., 32 vols (Florence, 1931–) 10: 213.

50 Panagiotakes, *The Cretan Period*, 106, and Staurinides, *Translations*, 2: 269. In 1685 two Armenians rebuilt one of the aisles of the mosque that had collapsed, for the sum of forty-five *grossi*.

51 Although the church suffered from the 1508 earthquake (see Corner, *Creta sacra*, 2: 412), the accounts of travelers throughout Venetian rule report that it was a huge structure and one of the most beautiful edifices of Candia. The impression of Cotovicus is cited by Gerola, *Monumenti veneti*, 2: 120.

52 Gerola, *Monumenti veneti*, 3: 148. Major renovations must have occurred in the conventual buildings in 1421. A notarial act of 1421 contains a contract for a 2-meter-wide stone staircase that was to be made outside the dormitory of the monastery. The stone-cutters also promised to cut a 1.75-meter-long block to serve as a lintel for the entrance door of the convent. See Chryssa Maltezou, "Métiers et salaires en Crète vénitienne (XVe siècle)," *Mélanges Freddy Thiriet*, in *Byzantinische Forschungen* 12 (1987): 327–28.

Also in 1431 the friars were granted a 5.21-meter-wide piece of land adjacent to the south wall of the monastery to repair the monastic cells that had been damaged by rain and old age. See ASV, DdC, b. 1, Ducali e Lettere Ricevute, fasc. 14, f. 69r, dated July 23, 1431.

53 In 1926 the building was transformed to a high school; a second story was created and doors and windows were opened. It survived until 1970 when the Greek authorities of the junta decided to demolish it in order to build a park at the spot. For the reaction of the Archaeological Service see Borboudakis, "Χρονικά (Chronicles)," *Archaiologikon Deltion* 28 (1973): 606–7. See also Kitsiki-Panagopoulos, *Cistercian Architecture*, 94. The dimensions of the nave were forty-four by sixteen

meters and those of the sanctuary seven by nine meters. The projecting apse was not recorded by Gerola at the beginning of the century, but it is clearly indicated in all the medieval plans of Candia.

54 Gerola, *Monumenti veneti*, 2: 121, noticed fragments of tombstones inside the minaret that were inscribed with the arms of the Cavalli family and the date 1521. It seems that the minaret was built with reused material from the interior of the church and probably from its cemetery as well.

55 Panagiotakes, "Evidence for the music," 112–19.

56 Gerola, *Monumenti veneti*, 4: 327. The inscription is now in the Historical Museum of Crete. See S. Alexiou, *Ὁδηγός Ἱστορικοῦ Μουσείου Κρήτης* (Guide to the Historical Museum of Crete) (Herakleion, 1953), 20–21, inscription no. 83. It reads: "Perill(ust)ri(s) d(ominus) Mapheus Malvezzo hanc aperuit janua(m) postqua(m) ere p(ro)prio chorum e medio eccl(esi)ae abstulit et illu(m) post altar(e) situavit mai(us), t(em)p(o)re prov(incia)latus fr(atr)is Vigilii Q(ueri)ni, a(nn) D(omini) 1616."

57 ASV, Notai di Candia, b. 295, fasc. 2, f. 17v: not. Bonacursius de Fregona, dated December 15, 1332.

58 ASV, Notai di Candia, b. 10, f. 10r: not. Angelus Bocantolo, dated March 30, 1348. The document reads, "pro laborerio ecclesie nove." It is hard to interpret the word *new* in this context. There is no other indication that the church was reconstructed. The most plausible explanation is that the document referred to a new chapel within the church.

59 ASV, Notai di Candia, b. 100, f. 36r: not. Johannes Gerardo, dated February 12, 1350. The document reads, "pro pictura ecclesie eiusdem monasterii." These paintings must have been whitewashed when the church was converted into a mosque.

60 We owe this description of the choir to the traveler Felix Fabri; cited by Gerola, *Monumenti veneti*, 2: 121.

61 This was decided by the Maggior Consilio di Candia on May 25, 1360. ASV, DdC, b. 12, Deliberazioni del Maior Consilio di Candia, f. 137v.

62 Gerola, *Monumenti veneti*, 2: 120, and Zoudianos, *History of Crete*, 1: 286.

63 The traveler Johannes Habermacher maintains that when he visited the cathedral of Candia in 1606 he was shown some of the Blood of Christ and an icon of the Virgin painted by St. Luke that had reached Crete from Rhodes in 1522. Apparently, Johannes confused the holy icons that he saw in Candia; the icon from Rhodes must have been the one in the Augustinian church of the Savior. See Hemmerdinger-Iliadou, "Voyageurs," 9: 597.

64 This lectern was decorated with an eagle; see Gerola, *Monumenti veneti*, 2: 120. For an enumeration of the altars see Panagiotakes, *The Cretan period*, 106–7.

65 Maria Constantoudaki, " Ἀνέκδοτα ἔγγραφα γιά τό ζωγράφο τοῦ 16ου αἰ. Ἰωάννη Γριπιώτη (Unpublished documents on the sixteenth-century painter Zuan Gripioti)," *Thesaurismata* 13 (1976): 292.

66 Gerola, *Monumenti veneti*, 3: 77.

67 The order was approved by Pope Alexander III in 1169 and promoted into a Mendicant order in 1591. Venice was one of the five provinces of the order. It was abolished in 1656. See *New Catholic Encyclopedia* (New York, 1967), 2: 790.

68 A. Lombardo, ed., *Zaccaria de Fredo notaio in Candia (1352–57)* (Venice, 1968), 80, no. 112. The guardian of the Scuola is mentioned in 1357.

69 Kitsiki-Panagopoulos, *Cistercian Architecture*, 95, and Gerola, "Francescani," 324. The dimensions of the main church are seventeen by thirteen meters. The apse measured four meters in length and five meters in width.

70 S. Papadaki, "Χρονικά (Chronicles)," *Ar-*

chaiologikon Deltion 16 (1960): 255, 17 (1961–62): 284, and 19 (1964): 458.

71 Borboudakis, "Test excavation at St. Peter," 427–28.

72 An inventory of the movable possessions of the monastery was drafted in 1390 when its administration was passed on to a new prior. See ASV, DdC, b. 11, Atti Antichi II, frammento 11(1), f. 45r, dated August 26, 1390.

73 ASV, DdC, b. 26, Sentenze, fasc. 7, f. 15v dated October 31, 1435. The document refers to a tomb belonging to ser Michael de Francisco. This tombal monument was the second tomb next to the door going to the cloister. See also Panagiotakes, *The Cretan period*, 105.

74 Toward the end of Venetian rule the monastery was turned over to the Dominicans; see Corner, *Creta sacra*, 2: 17–19.

75 The order received papal approval in 1249; cf. *The Catholic Encyclopedia*, 13: 736.

76 Gerola, *Monumenti veneti*, 3: 148.

77 Panagiotakes, *The Cretan period*, 107.

78 ASV, DdC, b. 32, Memoriali, fasc. 42, f. 25r, dated January 14, 1445, and ASV, DdC, b. 30ter, Memoriali 30, f. 46v, dated March 17, 1416.

79 ASV, DdC, b. 30bis, Memoriali 25/1, f. 36v-37r, dated February 21, 1400.

80 M. Chiaudano and A. Lombardo, eds., *Leonardo Marcello, notaio in Candia (1278–1281)* (Venice, 1960), 90, no. 251.

81 Luigi Pellegrini, "Insediamenti rurali e insediamenti urbani dei Francescani nell'Italia del secolo XIII," *Miscellanea Francescana* 75 (1975): 197–210, has suggested that the siting of Mendicant monasteries in empty parts of Italian cities or suburbs stimulated population growth in the areas around these establishments. It is reasonable to assume that a similar pattern of expansion can be applied outside the Italian territory as well. See also a similar approach for the relation of urbanization and the Mendicant churches in Le Goff, "Ordres mendiants et urbanisation," 924–46, and Braunfels, *Monasteries of Western Europe*, 137.

82 An atrium opened in front of the church in the early twentieth century; it probably dated from the Ottoman period when the church was transformed into a palace and was decorated with fountains and gardens as we learn from bishop George Mezo in 1660. See Petta, "Documenti di storia ecclesiastica," 215.

During the conversion of the church into a museum in 1962 the marble pavement, the door, and the window of the entrance were made anew; the walls were painted; and auxiliary spaces, i.e. laboratories and storerooms, were added. For the reports on these restorations see "Chronika," *Archaiologikon Deltion* 16 (1960): 271, and 17 (1961–62): 299.

83 Gerola, *Monumenti veneti,* 2: 130–34, and Beata Kitsiki-Panagopoulos, "Some Venetian Churches of Crete," *Arte veneta* 30 (1976): 20–25.

84 Gareth Morgan, "The Canea Earthquake of 1595," *Kretika Chronika* 9 (1955): 75–80. Morgan published the description of the earthquake by Onorio Belli. According to the vivid description of the tragic events the bell tower of St. Francis was seen swinging back and forth, almost touching the church of Santa Chiara (i.e. of the Clarisse), which was situated just across from St. Francis, as is also indicated in the plans of the city. The plan of Zorzi Corner (Fig. 110) refers to this church as Santa Chiara, the name of the founder of the order of the Clarisse.

85 Wadding, *Annales Minorum*, 9: 328. The convent was built by Constantia, widow of Petrus Zanei, and her daughter Maria.

86 Ubaldo Manucci, "Contributi documentarii per la storia della distruzione degli episcopati latini in Oriente nei secoli XVI e XVII," *Bessarione* year 17, vol. 30 (1914), 109. The monastery was suppressed for a while in 1474 because of the danger of the Turkish invasions, but in 1620 it counted once more among the

Latin establishments in the city; cf. John R.H. Moorman, *Medieval Franciscan Houses* (New York, 1983), 566, and Wadding, *Annales Minorum*, 14: 156.

87 Loenertz, "Les Établissements Dominicains de Péra-Constantinople," 335. The monastery in Canea was started in 1306 ("qui coepit anno MCCCVI").

88 Gerola, *Monumenti veneti*, 2: 135–40, and Manucci, "Contributi documentarii," 109. This oratory was decorated with scenes from the Passion and was endowed by the Scuola del Nome di Gesù.

89 Panagiotakes, "Evidence for the music," 135.

90 Manucci, "Contributi documentarii," 112–14. The rest of the conventual buildings were located to the south and comprised a kitchen, a pantry, a refectory, storage spaces, and other rooms whose function is not specified in the documents.

91 Gerola, *Monumenti veneti,* 2: 141. Curuni-Donati, *Creta veneziana,* 251, negative no. 261, has published Gerola's photograph of these remains.

92 Manucci, "Contributi documentarii," 109.

93 Gerola, "Francescani," 451.

94 Wadding, *Annales Minorum*, 10: 214. A plan of the city of Retimo drawn by G. Magagnatto in 1559 (Venice, Biblioteca Marciana, It. VI, 188) indicates the location of this church outside the walls of the city on a major road that led to the interior of the island.

95 Moorman, *Medieval Franciscan Houses,* 405. The Observants arrived in the city before 1424, but it not clear which one of the three monasteries belonged to them.

96 Gerola, *Monumenti veneti,* 2: 144–45.

97 ASV, Notai di Candia, b. 295, fasc. 2, not. Bonacursius de Fregona.

98 Gerola, *Monumenti veneti,* 2: 141–44.

99 Jordan Dimakopoulos, "A Mannerist Portal at Rethymnon after a Drawing by Sebastiano Serlio," *Archaiologika Analekta Athenon* 5, no. 1 (1972): 108–12. Dimakopoulos argues convincingly that this portal copies the design of a Corinthian triumphal arch from the fourth book of architecture of Sebastiano Serlio, p. 180.

100 Corner, *Creta sacra,* 2: 16 and 19. Nothing remains of Santa Lucia, but two localities in the city were known as *Santa Maria* and *Santa Caterina* at the beginning of the twentieth century so Gerola identified these places with the original location of the two churches.

101 Moorman, *Medieval Franciscan Houses*, 306–7.

102 Koder, *Negroponte*, 91.

103 Moorman, *Medieval Franciscan Houses*, 337 and 631.

104 Kitsiki-Panagopoulos, "Medieval Architecture in Greece. Western Monastic Orders in the Latin States Formed on Byzantine Territory," in *Actes du XVe Congrès International d'Études byzantines*, 2, pt. A (Athens, 1981), 281. It is not clear whether this establishment should be identified with a church dedicated to the Virgin recorded for the first time in a chronicle of 1205. Possibly the church that was recorded then was a Byzantine church that had nothing to do with the convent of the crusaders.

105 Koder, *Negroponte*, 94–95 and n. 163.

106 Deborah Howard, *The Architectural History of Venice* (London, 1980), 70.

107 For the impact of tall structures on people, see D. Conway, ed., *Human Response to Tall Buildings* (Stroudsburg, Pa., 1977). See also the following chapter.

108 Irene Bierman, "The Message of Urban Space: The Case of Crete," *Espaces et Sociétés* 47 (1985): 377–88. For my discussion of structures in the urban space I relied on the essay of Irene Bierman, who discerned between the different audiences that the Ottoman conquerors of Crete tried to impress with the mosques that they built in the cities.

6: The Greeks and the City

1 *Acta Ioannis XXII (1317–1334)*, ed. A. L. Tautu (Vatican City, 1952), n. 81.

2 Most of the port cities in the Eastern Mediterranean were inhabited by Venetians, Genoese, Catalans, French, Tatars, Jews, and Greeks. On these multiethnic societies see Angeliki Laiou, "Observations on the Results of the Fourth Crusade. Greeks and Latins in Port and Market," *Medievalia et Humanistica* 12 (1984): 48–49. Laiou observes that in contrast to the "political fragmentation of the Eastern Mediterranean," the trade system was "relatively unified" in terms of both contracts and commercial transactions.

3 A school where the children of the feudatories learned the Italian language is recorded in the second decade of the fourteenth century in Candia; see Chryssa Maltezou, "Ἡ Κρήτη στή διάρκεια τῆς περιόδου τῆς Βενετοκρατίας (1211–1669)" (Crete during the period of Venetian rule [1211–1669]), in N. Panagiotakes ed., *Κρήτη. Ἱστορία καί Πολιτισμός* (Crete. History and civilization) (Herakleion, 1988), 2: 53. For an overview of the Charalambos Gasparis, "Ἡ γλώσσα τῆς βενετικῆς γραφειοκρατίας. Ἡ ἀντιπαράθεση λατινικῆς καί ἑλληνικῆς γλώσσας στή Μεσαιωνική Κρήτη (13ος–15ος αἰ.) (The language of Venetian bureaucracy. The juxtaposition of Latin and Greek in Medieval Crete [13th–15th c.])," *Symmeikta* 9 (1994). *Μνήμη Δ. Α. Ζακυθηνοῦ*, vol. 2, pp. 141–56.

4 A ducal proclamation in 1333 was announced by the city crier in Greek outside the gate of Candia, where the majority of the population was Greek; see ASV, DC, b. 14, Bandi, f. 90v. Similarly, the statutes of Coron and Modon state explicitly that public announcements were made in both Latin and Greek in the castle and the marketplace. In one instance, however, in August 1341 the document specifies that the announcements would be made in Greek in the market ("al merchado in griego") and in Latin in the castle ("in castello in latin"); cf. Sathas, *Documents inédits relatifs à l'histoire de la Grèce*, 4: 7, and throughout pp. 1–186.

5 Alain Major, "L'Administration vénitienne à Négrepont," in *Coloniser au Moyen Age*, 254.

6 Tafel and Thomas, *Urkunden*, 2: 132. The doge ordered the colonists to leave the Orthodox churches and their ministers free. The document reads: "Ecclesias autem omnes suprascripte insulae debetis habere liberas et ministros earum; sed de possessionibus earum sic debet, sicut statuerit Dux qui erit ibi cum suo consilio."

7 This was not a phenomenon unique to Crete. As David Jacoby has rightly pointed out, "in all areas of the Eastern Mediterranean religious affiliation provided the basic criterion of social stratification." See D. Jacoby, "The Encounter of Two Societies. Western Conquerors and Byzantines in the Peloponnesos after the Fourth Crusade," *American Historical Review* 78 (1973): 889 and 903.

8 Benedict Anderson, *Imagined Communities. Reflections on the Origin and Spread of Nationalism*, 2nd ed. (London, 1991). On the notion of national identity in the medieval period and a critique of Anderson's dismissal of its existence, see Lesley Johnson, "Imagining Communities. Medieval and Modern," in L. Johnson et al. eds., *Concepts of National Identity in the Middle Ages* (Leeds, 1995), 1–21, esp. 4–5, and Anthony D. Smith, "National Identities. Modern and Medieval?" in ibid., 27.

9 McKee, "Uncommon Dominion," 200–8. What follows is based on McKee's understanding of the issue.

10 For instance, the Jewish community paid a collective tax to an official middleman, the *messeta* or *missetarius*. David Jacoby, "Venice, the Inquisition and the Jewish Communities of Crete in the Early 14th Century," *Studi veneziani* 12 (1970): 130.

11 The Venetian state owned the city of

Candia and its surroundings, as well as the territories that had previously belonged to the Byzantine emperor. See Tsirpanlis, *Catasticum*, 39.

12 R. Cessi, *Deliberazioni del Maggior Consiglio di Venezia*, 3 (Bologna, 1970), 311, and G. Scaffini, *Notizie intorno ai primi cento anni della dominazione veneta in Creta* (Alexandria, 1907), 59, no. 94.

13 Noiret, *Documents inédits*, 55–56.

14 Tafel and Thomas, *Urkunden*, 2: 131, and E. Santschi, *La Notion du "feudum" en Crète vénitienne (XIIIe–XVe siècles)* (Montreux, 1976), 30. The text reads: "Praeterea etiam in civitate Candida terras vel casas habere debetis convenientes, quas unicuique vestrum, sicut vos decet, Dux qui erit ibi cum suo consilio, asignare et dare debet secundum providentiam suam."

15 After the poet Stephanus Saclichi spent his father's possessions in gambling and prostitutes in the midfourteenth century, he had to retire at his estates in the countryside. The autobiographical poem that he composed describes the isolation that the previously wealthy feudatory felt in the countryside: he spent his days hunting, because there was no one to talk to. See A. F. Van Gemert, "Ὁ Στέφανος Σαχλίκης καὶ ἡ ἐποχή του (Stephanus Saclichi and his era)," *Thesaurismata* 17 (1980): 51.

16 Borsari, *Dominio Veneziano a Creta*, 32, n. 18. This document has been published by G. Cervellini, *Documento inedito Veneto-Cretese del Dugento* (Padova, 1906), 13–14, and Scaffini, *Notizie intorno ai primi cento anni*, 5–6.

17 Thiriet, *Délibérations des Assemblées*, 1: 145. The equivalent of one hundred *miliaria* is approximately forty-eight tons.

18 ASV, DdC, b. 18, Catastico SS. Apostolorum, f. 45, March 1235.

19 Gasparis, *The Land and the Peasants in Medieval Crete*, 33–37, observes that in the treaties signed by the Cretan rebels and the Venetian authorities in the thirteenth century, the Greek *archontes* managed to have the property that they possessed in the Byzantine period confirmed.

On the rebellions of the thirteenth century see Xanthoudides, *Venetian Rule on Crete*, 27–74, Borsari, *Dominio veneziano a Creta*, and Maltezon, "Crete in the period of Venetian rule," 115–35. The Hagiostefanites revolted first in 1211–13. They managed to conquer the castles of Sitia and Mirabello and the Republic asked the assistance of the governor of the Archipelago, Marco Sanudo, in confronting the rebels. Constantine Skordiles and Theodore Melissinos rebelled in 1219 and were the first Byzantine aristocrats to obtain landed possessions from the Republic. Following the 1222 Venetian colonization, the brothers Theodore and Michael Melissinos revolted in 1224. The Skordili and the Melissinoi were helped by the Byzantine emperor John III Vatatzes and rebeled between 1228 and 1236, with the inhabitants of Apano and Kato Syvritos joining them in 1234. A revolt incited by the Byzantine emperor Michael VIII Palaiologos and the Genoese broke out in 1262 but did not have any results because a major Greek *archon*, Alexios Calergis, opted to help the Venetians instead of the rebels. The Chortatzi family revolted in 1273–78.

20 As Maltezou, "Crete during the period of Venetian rule," 129–31, has pointed out, the surviving sources (i.e. the treaties signed by the Republic and the leaders of the revolts) do not tell the whole story about the reasons for these rebellions, which were not only economic, social, and political, but also religious, ethnic, and ideological. See also Borsari, *Dominio veneziano a Creta*, 30, and Nikos Svoronos, "Τό νόημα καί ἡ τυπολογία τῶν Κρητικῶν ἐπαναστάσεων τοῦ 13ου αἰ. (The Meaning and the typology of the Cretan revolts of the 13th century)," *Symmeikta* 8 (1989): 1–14.

21 The text of the treaty has been published

in Tafel and Thomas *Urkunden*, 2: 210–13. For an analysis of its significance see Borsari, *Dominio veneziano a Creta*, 36, 38.

22 For the text of the treaty see Tafel and Thomas, *Urkunden*, 2: 323–26; for a discussion of its terms see Borsari, *Dominio veneziano a Creta*, 43.

23 The relevant passage of the seventeenth-century chronicle of Antonio Trivan, "Racconto di cose varie," fos. 14v-15v, was published by Borsari, *Dominio veneziano a Creta*, 51, n. 72. I translate from the Italian:

"After the signing of the treaty with the Constantinopolitan archontopouloi, Signor Calergi, fearing for the loss of his life, left Candia and went to Venice accompanied by the duca Dandolo, where he stayed for a long time. Then he decided to come back to his country and returned to the kingdom [of Candia]. But because he did not feel secure residing in the city of the kingdom (i.e. Candia), where he feared for his life, he retired to his possessions in the country . . ." When his refuge was discovered by the other Greek lords "he came with all his family to reside in the metropolitan city of Candia, where he was welcome and honorably treated by all the people."

24 ASV, DdC, b. 18, Catastico SS. Apostolorum, f. 4 (November 6, 1258):

Sciendum quod Agathe relicta Marci Faletro divisit podere civitatis insimul cum Alexio Calergi; et hec est pars predicte Agathe que habet per longitudinem passus viginti sex et dimidium [46.11 m] ab utroque capite sicut extenditur recto tramite ab ambobus lateribus de oriente in occidente; que pars firmat in quadam calli que discurit inter predictam partem et domos communis versus levantem; ab alio capite versus occidentem firmat similiter in calli que discurit inter predictam Agatham et domos Angeli Trivisano; latere versus austrum firmat in calli que est inter palacium et predictum podere; aliud latere versus boream firmat in eodem Alexio Calergi.

I would like to thank Professor Laiou for suggesting to me that the name *Agathe* suggests a Greek origin for the wife of Marcus Faletro. Could we push the evidence further to propose that this Greek woman had family ties with the Calergis family?

25 ASV, DdC, b. 18, Catastico SS. Apostolorum, f. 1r. Marco Faletro had been given a piece of land that was located near the ducal palace (*iuxta domum domini duce*). The lot measured 11½ *passi* to the east (20.01 meters) by 22 *passi* to the north (38.28 meters) by 25 *passi* to the west (43.50 meters) by 26½ *passi* to the south (46.11 meters) where it bordered the ducal palace. The surface covered by this lot was approximately 1,340 square meters.

26 Ernst Gerland, *Das Archiv des Herzogs von Kandia in Koenigl. Staatsarchiv zu Venedig*, 121–33, and Stephanos Xanthoudides, "Συνθήκη μεταξύ τῆς Ἑνετικῆς δημοκρατίας καί Ἀλεξίου Καλλεργίου (Treaty between the Venetian Republic and Alexios Calergis)," *Athena* 14 (1902): 282–331. The appointment of the bishop was a one-time concession. He was appointed at the bishopric of Ario, the area where the extensive landholdings of Calergis were located.

27 The lands promised to Calergis in the treaty of 1299 had belonged to Nicolò Venier, and to the brothers Nicolò, Giovanni, and Lorenzo Barbadigo. In 1302 the Senate in Venice ordered the counselors of Candia to compensate these lords for the villages that the state took from them. See G. Giomo, *I "Misti" del Senato della Repubblica veneta 1293–1331* (Amsterdam, 1970), 290, 292.

28 The revolts did not stop completely in the fourteenth century, but they were not as extensive as in the previous century. See Stephanos Xathoudides, *Ἡ Ἑνετο-*

κρατία ἐν Κρὴτῃ καί οἱ κατά τῶν Ἑνετῶν ἀγῶνες τῶν Κρητῶν (Venetian rule in Crete and the fights of the Cretans against the Venetians)" (Athens, 1939), 74–81. The inhabitants of the Sfakia area revolted in 1319; the inhabitants of the village Margarites rebeled in 1330 against heavy taxation; and Leo Calergis and the Psaromilingoi revolted in 1341–48.

29 Maltezou, "Crete during the period of Venetian rule," 114.

30 Van Gemert, "Stephanus Saclichi," 37–38. The fragmentary records of the Senate mention that Stephanus, Zanachi, and the son of John Saclichi could have half a *militia* each.

31 Ibid., 36, 39–40. In 1206, 1268, and 1292 documents mention three members of the Saclichi family who were Greek priests. See also McKee, "The Revolt of St. Tito," 198–200.

32 Giomo, *"Misti" del Senato*, 304, no. 320. At the beginning of the fifteenth century a document forbidding the feudal lords to use their fiefs as collateral for loans from Jewish moneylenders explicitly mentions that this law also applied to the Calergis family and to all the other Greeks who owned fiefs. See Noiret, *Documents inédits*, 247.

33 Thiriet, *Regestes des délibérations du Sénat*, 1: 207, no. 880. This measure was taken to raise a considerable sum of capital, twenty thousand hyperpera.

34 Borsari, *Dominio veneziano a Creta*, 15 and 116. On the basis of a 1248–49 document in the *Catasticum ecclesiarum et monasteriorum*, f. 18v, Borsari has estimated the possessions of the Byzantine metropolitan of Crete at twenty-one villages, a nondetermined number of mills, vineyards in five villages, and olive tress in two villages.

For the property of the patriarch on Crete see also Zacharias N. Tsirpanlis, *Τό κληροδότημα τοῦ Καρδιναλίου Βησσαρίωνος γιά τούς φιλενωτικούς τῆς Βενετοκρατούμενης Κρήτης* (1439–17ος αἰ.) (The bequest of Cardinal Bessarion for the unionists of Venetian Crete [1439–17th c.]) (Thessaloniki, 1967), 51–66 and 176–236. The Latins maintained the patriarchal monasteries that were originally owned by the Byzantine patriarch of Constantinople. See Jean Longnon, "Le Patriarcat latin de Constantinople," *Journal des Savants* 126 (1941): 180.

35 Ernst Gerland, "Histoire de la noblesse crétoise, Part II," *Revue de l'Orient Chretien* 11 (1905–6): 59–60.

36 Fedalto, *Chiesa latina*, 1: 399. Although the final vote in the election of the archbishop of Candia was cast by the Latin patriarch of Constantinople, under whose jurisdiction the church of Crete was placed, Venice intervened in the selection of the higher Latin clergy (both the archbishop and the bishops of the island), attempting to persuade the Roman curia to appoint ecclesiastics who were on good terms with the Republic.

37 Freddy Thiriet, "Églises, fidèles et clergés en Crète vénitienne (de la conquête, 1204/1211 au XVe siècle)," in *Pepragmena tou D′ Diethnous Kretologikou Synedriou* 2 (Athens, 1981), 484–500; and N. B. Tomadakis, "La Politica religiosa di Venezia verso i cretesi ortodossi dal XIII al XV secolo," in *Venezia e il Levante fino al secolo XV*, 1, part 2 (Florence, 1973), 783–800.

38 C. Censi, "Senato veneto. 'Probae' ai benefici ecclesiastici," in C. Piana and C. Censi, *Promozione agli ordini sacri a Bologna e alle dignità ecclesiastiche nel Veneto nei secoli XIV–XV* (Florence, 1968), 313–454. See also Tsirpanlis, *Catasticum*, 85–86, and Stergios Spanakis, "Συμβολή στήν ἐκκλησιαστική ἱστορία τῆς Κρήτης στή Βενετοκρατία (Contribution to the ecclesiastical history of Venetian Crete)," *Kretika Chronika* 13 (1959): 243–88.

39 Tsirpanlis, *Catasticum*, 84.

40 N. B. Tomadakis, "Οἱ Ὀρθόδοξοι παππάδες ἐπί Ἑνετοκρατίας καί ἡ χειροτονία αὐτῶν (The Orthodox priests on Venetian Crete and their ordination)," *Kretika*

Chronika 13 (1959): 42, and Fedalto, *Chiesa latina*, 1: 393. In a case in which an archbishop usurped the rights of the state by referring to Crete as *nostra provincia* or *nostra Candide*, the Senate in Venice reacted very strongly, reminding Marco Justiniano that he should keep within the limits of his jurisdiction, as had his predecessors. See Fedalto, *Chiesa latina*, 3: 152.

41 Manousos Manoussakas, "Μέτρα τῆς Βενετίας ἔναντι τῆς ἐν Κρήτη ἐπιρροῆς τοῦ Πατριαχείου Κωνσταντινουπόλεως (Measures of Venice against the influence of the patriarchate of Constantinople on Crete)," *Epeteris Hetaireias Byzantinon Spoudon* 30 (1960–61): 85–144. Only one priest could be appointed in every village; ordination was allowed only when a post was vacant, and not before the age of twenty-five. See F. Thiriet, "La Situation religieuse en Crète au début du XVe siècle," *Byzantion* 36 (1966): 205; and M. Manoussakas, " Ἡ χειροτονία ἱερέων τῆς Κρήτης ἀπό τόν μητροπολίτη Κορίνθου (ἔγγραφα ις' αἰῶνα) (The ordination of Cretan priests by the metropolitan of Corinth [16th century documents]," *Christianike Archaiologike Hetaireia. Deltion* ser. 4, 4 (1964–65): 323.

42 Xanthoudides, *Venetian rule in Crete*, 161. The Orthodox priests (*papades*) were exempted from the *angarie*/corvées could not be drafted into the army; nor could they be used as *villani*, or *paroikoi*. Sally McKee has, however, recorded one instance when a Greek priest had to do an *angaria*.

43 M. Manoussakas, "Βενετικά ἔγγραφα ἀναφερόμενα εἰς τήν ἐκκλησιαστικήν ἱστορίαν τῆς Κρήτης τοῦ 14ου–16ου αἰῶνος (Πρωτοπαπάδες καί Πρωτοψάλται Χάνδακος) (Venetian documents on the church history of Crete in the 14th–16th c. [Protopapas and protopsaltes of Candia)," *Deltion tes Historikes kai Ethnologikes Hetaireias tes Hellados* 15 (1961): 151 n. 1. This institution was also known in the Venetian colonies of Corfu and Negroponte.

Although a religious figure, the *protopapas* was elected by the state authorities and not by the Latin archbishop, who tried unsuccessfully to change this practice in 1402. On specific documents concerning the election of the *protopapas* see Noiret, *Documents inédits*, 63, 136–37 and 148–49.

44 Tomadakis, "La politica religiosa di Venezia verso i cretesi ortodossi dal XIII al XV secolo," *Miscellanea byzantina-neohellenica* (Modena, 1973), 230.

45 Tsirpanlis, *Catasticum*, 34, and his article, "Νέα στοιχεῖα σχετικά μέ τήν ἐκκλησιαστική ἱστορία τῆς Βενετοκρατούμενης Κρήτης (13ος–17ος αἰ.) ἀπό ἀνέκδοτα βενετικά ἔγγραφα (New data on the ecclesiastical history of Venetian Crete [13th-17th c.] from unpublished Venetian documents)," *Hellenika* 20 (1967): 45–46 and 54.

46 Stylianos Pelekanides and Manolis Chatzidakis, *Kastoria* (Athens, 1985), passim.

47 This number represents all the Greek churches that are documented in one way or another in the surveyed archival documents in Venice. Unfortunately, there are no all-inclusive lists of the Greek Orthodox churches of Candia until the sixteenth century. A list of 1548 that contains the names of the Greek *papades* officiating in the city includes fifteen names of priests and at least twenty-three names of churches. It is possible, however, that some of the churches that were mentioned inside the city were actually located in the suburbs. For example, the church of St. Mary of the Angels is wrongly counted among the churches inside the city. See Harvard, Houghton Library, Ms. Riant 53, f. 8v, and Georgopoulou, "Meaning of the Architecture and the Urban Layout," 225–34.

48 This church should be probably identified with the dependency of the monastery of St. Catherine at Mount Sinai, mentioned

already in 1212. It is mentioned in the testament of Francesca Bon, wife of Matteo Gradenigo, in 1348. Francesca made a bequest of twenty hyperpera to the church for the commission of a religious painting (perhaps an icon). See Laiou, "Venetians and Byzantines," 42.

49 This must be the Byzantine church of Hagia Photeini. It is mentioned in the feudal cadastres of the thirteenth century (no. 29); cf. ASV, DdC, b. 18, Catastico SS. Apostolorum, f. 150 (May 1234). According to these cadastres the church of St. Lucy was located to the north of the possessions of Leonardus Urso and Johannes Fradello in 1234, thus being one of the earliest documented Greek churches inside the city. In 1331 one branch of the Saclichi family, Georgius and his wife, Maria, who was related to Hemanuel Ialina, erected a tomb therein; McKee, *Wills from Late Medieval Crete*, 2: 596–97. This family was among the noble Greek families of the city. The choice of this church as their resting place may indicate that they lived nearby. The church was surely an Orthodox foundation as in 1666 it issued a certificate of baptism performed by the *papa* Nicolò Perozalli; cf. ASV, Procuratia di San Marco de Supra, Chiesa, b. 142, fasc. 4, 61v-62r. It is unclear whether this church should be identified with the ruined church that St. Nikon restored in the late tenth century according to his *Life*; cf. Denis Sullivan, *Life of St. Nikon, text, translation, and commentary* (Brookline, Mass., 1987), 21: 20–29.

50 This church is mentioned in 1319, when it belonged to *papa* Hemanuel Papadocha. See ASV, Notai di Candia, b. 233, f. 211r, not. Angelo Donno.

51 Z. N. Tsirpanlis, " Ὁ Ἰωάννης Πλουσιαδηνός καί ἡ εκκλησία τοῦ Χριστοῦ Κεφαλᾶ (John Plousiadenos and the church of Christo Chefala)," *Thesaurismata* 3 (1964): 1–28. The church was located close to the residence of the capitaneus in the area between the church of St. Mark and that of St. Titus. The name of the church reflects its fourteenth-century owners: in December 1323 the deacon of Milopotamo conceded the church to Pothe Chefaladene (or Chefalacha) and her heirs. However, in 1445 the monastery of St. Sabas in Palestine claimed ownership of it.

52 It was located close to the Franciscan monastery of St. Francis (no. 10 on the map) and is first mentioned in a notarial document of 1330. See ASV, Notai di Candia, b. 295, fasc. 3, f. 12r, not. Albertinus Maça.

53 The church (no. 13 on the map) is mentioned in the 1330 will of Agnes, daughter of Alexios Calergi and wife of Chornarachi Cornario; McKee, *Wills from Late Medieval Crete*, 2: 542. It was situated near the house of the Cornario family.

54 In 1212 the doge Pietro Ziani confirmed the Byzantine possessions of the monastery of Sinai on Crete. See Tafel and Thomas, *Urkunden*, 2: 146–150, no. 233; and Emanuel G. Pantelakes, *Ἡ ἱερά μονή τοῦ Σινᾶ* (The Holy Monastery of Sinai) (Athens, 1939), 51, 56, and 61. On the papal bull of pope Honorius III see Fedalto, *Chiesa latina*, 1: 389, and G. Hoffmann, "Sinai und Rom," *Orientalia christiana*, 9/3, no. 37 (1972): 242–44.

55 In 1668 the *papa* Sava Negrini wanted to be buried in front of the entrance door of the church in the ten large slabs, next to the tomb of his father, Jeremiah. See Maria Kazanaki-Lappa, "Οἱ ζωγράφοι τοῦ Χάνδακα κατά τόν 17ο αἰώνα. Ἐκδόσεις ἀπό νοταριακά ἔγγραφα (The Painters of Candia in the 17th century, Editions from notarial documents)," *Thesaurismata* 18 (1981), 236.

56 Venice, Biblioteca Marciana, Antonio Trivan, "Racconto di varie cose," f. 16r. The text reads: "Morse il Calergi, al quale fu fatto un onorifico e distinto funerale, fu sepolto nella sua capella nel Monasterio di S. Caterina del Monte Sinai." Calergis

must have been a great benefactor of the monastery.

57 M. Vassilakis-Maurakakis, " Ὁ ζωγράφος Ἄγγελος Ἀκοτάντος. Τό ἔργο καί ἡ διαθήκη του (1436) (The painter Angelo Acotanto. His oeuvre and his will [1436])," *Thesaurismata* 18 (1981): 296. One of the donations to the Sinaites that stands out is that of a converted Jew, Andrea Bon, in 1410. See Noiret, *Documents inédits*, 201.

58 See ASV, Notai di Candia, b. 295, fasc. 1, f. 2v, not. Nicolò Mantuga for Maria (May 29, 1316), and fasc. 3, f. 7r, not. Albertino Maça for Challi (November 19, 1324).

59 Tsirpanlis, *Catasticum*, 220–21, no. 132.

60 Clear traces of the barrel vaulting of the nave with a few arches of St. Mary of the Angels survive inside a shop on Kalokairinou street, but according to Flaminio Corner, *Creta sacra*, 1: 229, the church was large and ornate in the seventeenth century.

61 Sparakis, "Contribution to the ecclesiastical history of Venetian Crete," 264, n. 59. The document describing the dimensions of the cemetery reads:

> versus septentrionem per suam latitudinem passus 5; incipiendo dicta latitudo ab angulis versus ponentem dicte ecclesie et eundo recto tramite per tramontanam et inde vadit versus austrum usque ad viam imperialem per suam latitudinem passus 6 et pedes 4½ et inde redit versus ponentem et venit per suam longitudinem passus 18 et pede uno.

In the *Catasticum* the dimensions were slightly different: 15 paces to the east, 3 paces to the north, and 1 pace to the south; Tsirpanlis, *Catasticum*, 220–21, no. 132. After the Ottoman conquest the cemetery measured 74 by 55 cubits. See Stavrinides, *Translations*, 1: 388. The entrance door of the church survived until 1973, but no photographs were available in the Archaeological Service.

62 Manoussakas, "Venetian documents on the church history of Crete," 166–73.

63 The wall painting was executed in two months (May 25 to the end of July) and the painter was paid fifty hyperpera. The contract for this commission was published by Mario Cattapan, "Nuovi elenchi e documenti dei pittori in Creta dal 1300 al 1500," *Thesaurismata* 9 (1972): 230. Cattapan's transcription reads *dhestera parisia*, which must be a faulty transliteration of the Greek "δευτέρα παρουσία" into Latin. The western wall of most Byzantine churches in Crete was decorated either with the Last Judgment or with the Dormition of the Virgin. For an overview of the painted decoration of the Byzantine churches of Crete see Manolis Borboudakis, " Ἡ βυζαντινή τέχνη ὥς τήν πρώϊμη βενετοκρατία (Byzantine art until the early Venetian rule)," in *Crete. History and civilization*, 2: 50.

64 The size of these structures was hardly ever larger than fifty square meters. See Tsirpanlis, *Catasticum*, 80–81.

65 Of course, other variables may have played a major role in the allocation of space, i.e. the wealth of the patron.

66 Here I follow the ideas put forth by Tsirpanlis, *Catasticum*, 56–57, regarding the expansion of the suburbs to the west and later to the south of the city.

67 Tzompanaki, *Chandax. The city and the walls*, 117.

68 ASV, DdC, b. 15, Bandi, f. 48r. Furthermore, people should attend religious services only in the church of their parish, unless they had moved to a different parish within the city.

69 A few prices attested in the midfourteenth century assert that the 200 hyperpera (2,400 *grossi*) was indeed a huge amount of money in 1360. In 1351 the authorities raised the daily salary of an unskilled workman to 6 *soldi* (plus or minus 2 grossi), that of a woodworker and his assistant to 4½ grossi plus vianda, that of a builder to 3½ grossi plus vianda, and

so on. Thus, the monthly salary of a workman was about 10 hyperpera. See Van Gemert, "Stephanus Saclichi," 61, and J. Jegerlehner, "Beiträge zur Verwaltungsgeschichte Kandias im XIV Jahrhundert," *Byzantinische Zeitschrift* 13 (1904): 473–74.

70 Similar concerns regulated the distance between Mendicant monasteries in the same city, as we have seen in Chapter 5.

71 Maria Vassilakis-Maurakakis, "The Church of Virgin Gouverniotissa at Potamies, Crete," Ph.D. Diss. (Courtauld Institute of Art, University of London, 1986), 41. Most of the churches date from the fourteenth and fifteenth centuries. In this section I rely on Mrs. Vassilakis-Maurakakis's conclusions and observations (pp. 66–70).

72 Ibid., 110.

73 Ibid., 64, ft. 42; Dimitrios Tsougarakis, "La Tradizione culturale bizantina nel primo periodo della dominazione veneziana a Creta. Alcune osservazioni in merito alla questione dell'identità culturale," in *Venezia e Creta*, 509–22; and Gerola, *Monumenti veneti*, 4: 513–78. Inscriptions commemorating Andronikos II Palaiologos are found in the church of St. John in Hagios Vasilios Pediados (1291), in St. Michael the Archangel in Doraki (1321), and in St. Paul at Pyrgiotissa near Hagios Ioannes in region of Herakleion (1303/4). Two more fourteenth-century inscriptions are found in the cave church of St. John at Koudoumas (1360) and the church of the Virgin Eleousa at Papagiannado (1363/64). Three other fifteenth-century churches display similar inscriptions: St. George at Exo Mouliana (1426/27), St. George at Embaros (1436/37), and St. Constantine at Avdou (1445). Another Greek donor inscription in the Historical Museum of Crete in Herakleion commemorates the Byzantine emperor John VIII Palaiologos (1425–48); see Alexiou, *Guide to the Historical Museum of Crete*, 20. Thiriet, *Romanie*, 118–19, has shown the specifically "national" character of Byzantine Christianity in its reverence of the Byzantine emperor, who was thought to be a living incarnation of the state and the church.

74 Vassilakis-Maurakakis, "Church of the Virgin Gouverniotissa," 70, and Klaus Gallas, Klaus Wessel, and Manolis Borboudakis, *Byzantinisches Kreta* (Munich, 1983), 124–25.

75 Stella Papadaki-Oakland, "Δυτικότροπες τοιχογραφίες τοῦ 14ου αἰώνα στήν Κρήτη. Ἡ ἄλλη ὄψη μιᾶς ἀμφίδρομης σχέσης (Fourteenth-century wall paintings of Western style in Crete. The other side of a two-way relation)," in *Euphrosynon. Aphieroma ston Manole Chatzedake* (Athens, 1992), 2: 491–516. Papadaki focuses on three churches in the southwestern part of the island – Christos at Temenia, St. Demetrios at Leivadas, and St. Photios at Hagioi Theodoroi near Sklavopoula – that seem to be painted by the same artist. She identifies a hybrid kind of art observable both in iconography and in style.

76 See S. Papadaki-Oakland, "Ἡ Κερά τῆς Κριτσᾶς. Παρατηρήσεις στή χρονολόγηση τῶν τοιχογραφιῶν της (The Kera of Kritsa. Observations on the dating of its frescoes)," *Archaiologikon Deltion* 22 (1967): 87–111.

77 K. Lassithiotakes, "Ὁ Ἅγιος Φραγκίσκος καί ἡ Κρήτη (St. Francis and Crete)," in *Pepragmena tou B′ Diethnous Kretologikou Synedriou* 2 (Athens, 1981), 146–54, and Manolis Borboudakis, "Ἡ τέχνη κατά τή Βενετοκρατία (The art during Venetian rule)," in *Crete. History and Civilization* 2: 233–88, esp. 259.

78 Jordan Dimakopoulos, "Ὁ Sebastiano Serlio καί τά μοναστήρια τῆς Κρήτης (Sebastiano Serlio and the monasteries of Crete)," *Deltion tes Christianikes kai Archaiologikes Hetaireias tes Hellados*, ser. 4, 6 (1972): 233–245.

79 This foundation is first mentioned in a document of 1356 (ASV, DdC, Atti An-

tichi b. 10bis, fasc. 6, f. 74r). The Vergici were a quite important family in Candia; a member of the family, Stamatis Vergici, is recorded in relation to slave trade in documents of 1381 and 1382. See Van Gemert, "Stephanus Saclichi," 70.

80 ASV DdC, Memoriali, b. 32bis, fasc. 49/9, f. 42v. The will of Constantine Sculudi has been published by C. N. Sathas, in Μεσαιωνική Βιβλιοθήκη (Medieval Library), 6 (Athens, 1894), 658–59. On pages 681–82 there is indeed mention of the church of the Savior called Sculudi. This church was located close to the Judaica (no. 39 on the map).

81 Tsirpanlis, *Catasticum*, 226–27, no. 141. The church had a cemetery covering an area of 33.20 square meters. It also possessed forty-five houses in the early fourteenth century.

82 Ibid., 232–33, no. 152. The church possessed some houses and a cemetery measuring 2½ paces to the south (4.34 meters) and 3 paces to the west (5.21 meters).

83 In 1548 there is mention of a church named San Zuane Christofilina; see Gerola, "Topografia." The title is much earlier, though: it is attested in an official document of 1355; cf. ASV, DdC, b. 10bis, Atti Antichi, fasc. 6, f. 17v. It is not clear how the name *Xafilino* was changed into *Christofilina*. The Greek letter chi must have been confused with the Latin abbreviation for *Christ*. By the seventeenth century the name of the church was recorded in full as Christofilina; even a Greek list of churches spells out the name *Christofilina* as a feminine epithet.

84 ASV, DdC, b. 30ter, Memoriali 31, f. 135r-v. The text reads:

> Per egregios dominos . . . consiliarios . . . concessum est de gratia Johanni Sotiriachi habitatori burgi Candide, quod possit construi facere in quoddam territorio suo confinante cum domo habitationis sue in contracta Sancti Salvatoris, unam ecclesiolam seu capellam sub titulo Sancti Nicolai; cum conditione hac, quod nullo modo habere possit enoriam, nec parochiam, nec diocesim, nec nocere alicui persone, sollummodo possit pro sua devotione facere ibi celebrari privatas missas.

85 ASV, DdC, b. 32, Memoriali, fasc. 42, f. 23r (January 7, 1445). The church is also mentioned in 1548, but the map of Werdmüller does not include it. It could be identified with his no. 58, 116 or 128 on the map.

86 For instance, travelers marveled at the devotion that the Greeks showed to the icon of the Madonna of St. Titus on the big feast days of the church or in times of need (see Chapter 8, n. 42).

87 Hemmerdinger-Iliadou, "Voyageurs," (1973): 475. The text reads: "etsont ces gens Grecs et y sont tous vestus de futaines, de jacquettes."

88 Hemmerdinger-Iliadou, "Voyageurs," (1973): 482–83.

89 Pietro Casola, *Canon Pietro Casola's Pilgrimage to Jerusalem in the Year 1494*, trans. M. Margaret Newett (Manchester, 1907), 203.

90 Eva Tea, "Saggio sulla storia religiosa di Candia dal 1590 al 1630," *Atti del Reale Istituto Veneto di Scienze, Lettere ed Arti* 72/2 (1912–13): 1377; Gerola, *Monumenti veneti*, 2: 10, and Corner, *Creta sacra*, 2: 30.

91 Hemmerdinger-Iliadou, "Voyageurs," (1967): 580. It is hard to dismiss this peculiar information on the grounds that Radzivil could not have known much about the difference between the Greek and Latin rites. One point is sure: that the language used in conjunction with this altar was Greek. It is also possible that a Greek priest performed Mass in the chapel. These "Greeks" could be part of the Unionist party, who kept their Greek liturgy but paid homage to the pope as well.

92 Corner, *Creta sacra*, 2: 31–33.

93 J. Baudot and P. Chaussin, "La Toussaint," in *Vies des saints et des bienheureux selon l'ordre du calendrier avec l'historique des*

fêtes, 11 (November), (Paris, 1954/1961), 16–22. See also Papadaki, *Religious and Secular Rituals in Crete*, 26.

94 ASV, DdC, b. 32, Memoriali, fasc. 44, f. 151r-v. The document reads:

Coram magnifico domino Antonio Diedo honorabile ducha Crete et eius consilio, ac magnifico Domino *** Bono honorabile capitanei Crete comparens nobilis vir ser Michael Gradonico quodam ser Petri *** dicens quod pro sua devotione et pro *** facto per eum promiserat per votum faciendi ecclesiam in capite moli portus Candide ad omnes suas expensas cum f*** *** et magnifici domini capitanei ***nomine Sancti Nicolai. Unde supplicat *** sibi dicta licentia de gratia *** ipsam ecclesiam in aliquo loco *** apto et abili ad hoc ***** non impediendo nec occupando aliquid in sinistrum agendorum comunis, sed potius sit cum commodo comunis et marinariorum conversantium in dicto molo. Ea propter considerata bona et laudabile devotione predicta et quod hoc sit pro cultu divino, ad honorem dei et pro reverentia Sancti Nicolai et hoc etiam cedit in bonum et commodum comunis et marinariorum conservantium in dicto molo pro custodia navigiorum; per magnificos dominos suprascriptos concessum est de gratia eidem ser Michaeli quod faciat ecclesiam predictam sicut petit. Quare debeat facere in solario a facie ponentis magazeni comunis existentis in testa moli predicti. Et sit in longitudinem passuum IIII. et *** *** **[lati]tudine per quantum extenditur facies illa porte magazeni non excedendo angulum eius. Et fiat hoc modo quod debeant fieri pilastra duo bona supra que deb[eant] fieri tres archi supra quibus sit firmatum pavimentum dicte ecclesie et sit illud pavimentum altum a terra secundum altitudinem porte de magazeni. Et altitudo ecclesie fiat per quantum erit conveniens et condecens. Et debeat fieri scalla petrina adherens [magazeni]s comunis per quam possit fieri introitum sive aditum et exitum dicte ecclesie; et fiat taliter dictum [labo]rerium quod ab infra ren*** lo a partibus sub pavimento per modum lobii. Ita quod **** possit se redure tempore pluvioso * cohoperto sicuri a pluvia pro suo commodo s[ine] impedimento.

Fl. Corner also mentions a public chapel dedicated to St. Nicholas close to the military warehouse at the mole; see Corner, *Creta sacra*, 2: 32: "S. Nicolai, sacellum publico armamentario navali coniuctum." Probably the *armamentarium navale* was the warehouse of the mole.

95 ASV, DdC, b. 32, Memoriali, fasc. 47/1, f. 28v.

96 ASV, DdC, b. 3, Ducali e Lettere Ricevute, fasc. 37. The church was included in a list of Greek Orthodox churches that was drafted in 1548; see Gerola, "Topografia," 246.

97 ASV, DdC, b. 32bis, Memoriali, fasc. 50/2, f. 46v (May 1, 1499). This information suggests the close connection of the Madonnina with the Latin church. N. Panagiotakes, *Ἡ Κρητικὴ περίοδος τῆς ζωῆς τοῦ Δομηνίκου Θεοτοκοπούλου* (The Cretan period of the life of Domenico Theotokopoulos) (Athens, 1987), 107.

98 Gerola, *Monumenti veneti*, 2: 158, and Staurinides, *Translations* 2 (1986): 401. The Ottomans restored the mosque in 1691: ten arches measuring 37 by 17 cubits (27.75 by 12.75 meters) and the roof were consolidated.

99 I would like to thank the ephor of Byzantine Antiquities, Manolis Borboudakis, for providing me with these photographs showing the archaeological remains before demolition.

100 McKee, *Wills from Late Medieval Crete*, 2: 530, no. 408.

101 G. Gerola and K. Lassithiotakis, *Τοπο-*

γραφικός κατάλογος τῶν τοιχογραφημένων ἐκκλησιῶν τῆς Κρήτης (Topographic catalogue of the wall-painted churches of Crete) (Herakleion, 1961), 72.

102 Tsirpanlis, *Catasticum*, no. 133, 221; and ASV, Notai di Candia, b. 295, fasc. 6, not. Leonardus Cavisino (December 23, 1373).

103 Peter Topping, "Armenian and Greek Refugees in Crete and the Aegean World (XIV–XV Centuries)," in *Pepragmena tou E′ Diethnous Kretologikou Synedriou* (Herakleion, 1985), 364–74. One of the two pertinent texts reads:

MCCCLXIII die octauo Junii

Capta Quod scribatur duche et consiliariis Crete super facto Arminorum partium maris maioris volentium venire cum suis familiis habitatum in insula Crete cum conditione quod et cetera. Quod jintellectis literis suis sumus contenti et placet nobis quod Aceptent uoluntatem et disposicionem dictorum Arminorum pro bono insule nostre tenendo modum in dando eis locum et tractando eos cum quam maiori comodo et bono poteruit pro nostro comuni non recedendo a mercato ullo modo Et quia uale esset si posset fieri inducere partem eorum ad ueniendum habitatum Mothonum pro bono dicti loci tantum nobis cari scribatur dictis duche et consiliariis quod in hoc faciant totum posse suum Et nichilominus non contentantibus illis non recedant atractatu et modo ueniendi in insula Crete ut est dictum.

104 Ibid., 366–67.

7: Segregation Within the Walls

1 Benjamin of Tudela, *The World of Benjamin of Tudela. A Medieval Mediterranean Travelogue*, ed. Sandra Benjamin (Madison, Wisc., 1995).

2 In Constantinople, the leader of the Jewish community was called *caput sinagoge*, the head of the synagogue. We can assume that the Venetians followed similar practices in most of their Levantine colonies. The Jewish community constituted a legal body governed by its own sets of ordinances. See David Jacoby, "Venice and Venetian Jews in the Eastern Mediterranean," in Gaetano Cozzi, ed., *Gli Ebrei a Venezia* (Milan, 1987), 41.

Specifically on Crete see David Jacoby, "Venice, the Inquisition and the Jewish Communities of Crete in the Early 14th Century," *Studi veneziani* 12 (1970): 127–28. The elders elected the head of the community, the *contestabile* (constable), and three *camerarii*. The *contestabile* is mentioned in documents for the first time in 1238. This title probably derives from the Greek κοντόσταυλος. Later, his title is also recorded as *commestabile*, or *condestabulo*. The three *camerarii* are first mentioned in 1433 (ASV, DdC, b. 31, Memoriali, fasc. 38, f. 202r): "secundum formam et continentiam dictorum ordinum debeant eligi et constitui unus commestabilis novus et III camerarii novi qui intrare debeant ad exercendum dictum officium quando illi qui sunt ad presens complerunt tempus suum."

3 Maria Georgopoulou, "Mapping Religious and Ethnic Identities in the Venetian Colonial Empire," *The Journal of Medieval and Early Modern Studies* 26/3 (1996): 480–87.

4 Zvi Ankori, "From Zudecha to Yahudi Mahallesi. The Jewish Quarter of Candia in the 17th Century," in *Salo Wittmayer Baron Jubilee* (Jerusalem, 1974), 1: 82. The first mention of the epithet *Judaica* (Jewish quarter) in Candia occurs in an entry in the inventory of a fief pertaining, or prior, to the government of Giovanni Michiel, duke of Crete in 1227–28. The Venetians also continued Byzantine practices in changing the Greek name, Ἰουδαϊκή to the Latin name *Judaica*, *Judeca*, or in the Vene-

tian vernacular *Zudecha*. See Jacoby, "Venice, the Inquisition and the Jewish Communities," 127.

5 Many Jews were in the tanning business; see Joshua Starr, *The Jews in the Byzantine Empire, 641–1204* (Athens, 1939), 1931. According to the account of the Jewish traveler Benjamin of Tudela, who visited Constantinople ca. 1165, many Jews were silk workers, merchants, and tanners.

6 The community statutes, the *Takkanoth Kandiya*, indicate a complex organization that could not have been achieved in the seventeen years that separate the beginning of Venetian rule and the first recording of the ordinances in 1228. E. S. Artom and M. D. Cassuto, eds., *Taqqanot Qandya we-Zikhronoteha* (Statuta Judaeorum Candiae eorumque memorabilia) (Jerusalem, 1943). Furthermore, the statutes explicitly mention the existence of four generations of Jews living in the city. The pre-Venetian origin of the Jewish quarter of Candia is also supported by the fact that Candia was the only city in Crete to host a Jewish quarter within the city walls. The new Jewish quarters that were established after the arrival of the Venetians in Canea and Retimo as well as in Negroponte were situated in the suburbs, outside the city walls.

7 See D. Jacoby, "Les Quartiers juifs de Constantinople à l'époque byzantine," *Byzantion* 37 (1967): 182 (reprinted in D. Jacoby, *Société et démographie à Byzance et en Romanie latine* [London, 1975]). For the Jewish quarter in Constantinople see also eidem, "The Jewish Community of Constantinople from the Komnenian to the Palaiologan Period," *Vizantijskij Vremennik* 55/2 (1998): 31–40.

8 Cecil Roth, *The History of the Jews of Italy*, (Philadelphia, 1946), 52.

9 In the thirteenth century there was a law forbidding the building of synagogues, but it was not strictly enforced; cf. S. Grayzel, *The Church and the Jews in the Thirteenth Century* (New York, 1966), 70–71. See also Robert Ian Moore, *The Formation of a Persecuting Society. Power and Deviance in Western Europe, 950–1250* (Oxford, 1987), 10, 36–39, and 42–45; and Jeremy Cohen, *The Friars and the Jews. The Evolution of Medieval Anti-Judaism* (Ithaca, N.Y., 1982), esp. 244–62, who attributes these changes to the teachings of the Mendicant friars. The Jewish populations were expelled from England in 1290, from France in the fourteenth century (1306–94), and from many areas of Germany in the fifteenth century; cf. Kenneth R. Stow, *The Jews. A Mediterranean Culture* (Fasano, 1994), 14.

10 Xanthoudides, "Treaty between the Venetian Republic and Alexios Calergis," 310. See also Salo Wittmayer Baron, *A Social and Religious History of the Jews*, 17 (New York, 1980), 68. No law prohibiting Jews from owning real estate in Byzantium seems to have existed.

11 For instance, the feudatory Johannes Cornario, son of Iacobus, possessed two empty lots situated inside the Jewish quarter next to the city walls (*in campo Iudaice*), which he rented to private individuals for twenty-nine years. See Carbone, *Pietro Pizolo*, 2: 50–51, no. 798, and 63, no. 824. Both documents are dated 1304. The first lot in the Judaica covered an area of twenty-seven square meters and was rented to Helinghiagho for 2 hyperpera per year. The other lot covered an area of forty-three square meters and the annual rent was 2 hyperpera. The rental agreement specified that on both lots the renters had to construct a house and could make use of the city wall (probably to abut their houses) for as long as they kept the lot.

12 Theotokes, *Senate*, 2/1 (1936), no. 35, 143. The document reads: "*extra confinia determinata*, inter que Iudei predicti secundum ordinem nostrum stare et habitare debent . . . que proprietates dictorum circauicinorum sunt eciam extra confinia dictorum Iudeorum, de gratia nostra ipsa

suas proprietates affictauerunt dictis Judeis et continue affictant" [emphasis mine]. Similar decrees had been promulgated for Negroponte (1304) and Canea (1325).

13 Nicol, *Byzantium and Venice*, 249, and Jacoby "Les Quartiers juifs," 205.

14 ASV, DdC, b. 29bis 30, Memoriali 22/6, f. 1r. The beginning of the document is missing:

> fecit in cali posito versus austru qui discurrit usque ad arcum de novo positum pro signo confinium Judaice. Et est sciendum quod domus que sunt in dicto cali ab alio latere versus austrum non possunt habitari nisi per Christianos; alie vero domus que sunt ab alio latere calis versus boream et habent in merohitum super dicto cali versus austrum remanent in Iudaica cum ista conditione: quod si Judei habitaverint in dictis domibus, non possint ullo modo habere merohitum super dicto cali, sed teneantur omnino murare portas et observare fenestras tam que respiciunt super dicto cali versus austrum quam a latere illo est versus levantem. Si vero Christiani habitabunt in dictis domibus possint habere introitum et exitum et fenestras super dicto cali ad libitum eorum, a dicto arcu novo facto pro signo dictorum confinium super quo arcu est effigies Sancti Marci cum aliquibus armis vadit recto tramite per lineam et ferit usque ad murum civitatis versus ponentem.

A summary of this passage has been published by E. Santschi, *Arrêts*, 280, no. 1275.

15 Benjamin Ravid, "The Legal Status of the Jews in Venice to 1509," *Proceedings of the Academy for Jewish Research* 54 (1987): 174, and R. Müller, "Les Prêteurs juifs de Venise au moyen age," *Annales* 30 (1975): 1277–1302.

16 Ravid, "Legal Status," 180–81. Apparently these restrictions were not strictly observed and the Senate had to reiterate the expulsion in 1402. Later (1408) the whole policy was modified to allow Jewish merchants (excluding moneylenders) to settle in the city for longer periods.

For the yellow badge see G. Kirsch, "The Yellow Badge in History," *Historia Judaica* 19 (1957): 103, 109. According to the Venetian decree Jews had to wear a yellow circle of the size of a four-denari loaf of bread. Ethnic differentiation by clothing was observed in the Crusader States in the Holy Land and was further promulgated in the Fourth Lateran Council of 1215.

17 J. Starr, "Jewish Life in Crete under the Rule of Venice," *American Academy for Jewish Research, Proceedings* 12 (1942): 77. The expulsion of the Jews from Venice may have caused the large wave of Jewish immigration that has been documented in this period, as well as the Spanish massacres of the 1390s; see Baron, *Social and Religious History of the Jews*, 17: 325.

18 Georgopoulou, "Mapping Religious and Ethnic Identities," 494, n. 58.

19 M. A. Shulvass, *The Jews in the World of the Renaissance*, trans. E. I. Kose (Leiden and Chicago, 1973), 118. The friars challenged the state licenses of Jewish moneylending businesses, known as *condotte*.

20 Jacoby, "Venice and Venetian Jews," 37. The measure of the badge was extended from Venice to Corfu, Negroponte, and Crete. In 1421 the counselors of Crete decided that Jewish men had to wear a badge bigger than the customary one and that the Jewish women of Candia had to wear a yellow veil around their head that had to be three fingers in width. The Jewish community managed to have this ordinance cancelled. See Thiriet, *Assemblées* 2 (1971): 145. The document reads, "portare debeant unum vellum gallum circa caput latitudine trium digitorum, ob quod dicte sue femine et mulieres non audeant exire domos." In 1430 the regulation of the badge was reinstated for the

Jews of the entire Venetian state, including Venetian ships. See Ravid, "Legal Status," 181, n. 23, and Kirsch, "Yellow Badge," 89–146.

21 C. N. Sathas, *Documents inédits relatifs à l'histoire de la Grèce au Moyen Age* (Paris, 1883), 4: 107–8.

22 Manousos Manoussakas, *Ἡ ἐν Κρήτῃ συνωμοσία τοῦ Σήφη Βλαστοῦ (1453–1454) καί ἡ νέα συνωμοτική κίνησις τοῦ 1460–1462* (The conspiracy of Siffi Vlasto in Crete [1453–1454] and the new conspiratory movement of 1460–1462) (Athens, 1960), 135–36.

23 Noiret, *Documents inédits*, 297–98, and discussed in D. Jacoby, "Les Juifs à Venise du XIVe au XVe siècle," in H. G. Beck et al., eds., *Venezia centro di mediazione tra Oriente e Occidente* (Florence, 1977), I: 163–216, 193. The decision reads:

> De cetero nullus Judeus vel Judea possit emere nec acquirere, in aliqua terra vel loco nostro, aliquam possessionem vel domum alicuius maneriei, vel sortis, vel aliquod aliud stabile, sub pena perdendi dictam possessionem, domum et aliud stabile. Reservato tamen ipsis Judeis omni eo quod sibi appareret promissum esse per nostra privilegia et scripturas, dumtaxat in Judaicis terrarum nostrarum maritimarum.

Apparently this decree was meant to reinforce a similar decision of 1334, which possibly had not been enforced.

24 J. A. Romanos, "Histoire de la communauté israélite de Corfou," *Revue des études juives* 23 (1891): 70.

25 For instance, ASV, Notai di Candia, b. 121, f. 32v, not. Cirillo Gradonigo, f. 42r: "In executione sententie . . . XLta consilio . . . per quam Iudei tenentur vendere omnas domos suas sitas in hac civitate." According to the decree of the *Quaranta*, Moises, son of Gephi sold his houses in the Judaica to Dominico Venerio.

26 ASV, DdC, b. 2, Ducali e Letter Ricevute, fasc. 25, quaternus 30 (October 24, 1464). This gate was enlarged for the convenience of the noblemen and the feudatories ("ut habiliorem per eam additum et transitum haberent").

27 Jacoby, "Les Quartiers juifs," 209. In a court case of 1424 we learn that Crusi and her husband, Joste Astru of Crete, were residents of the quarter of the Venetian Jews in Constantinople. On the freedom of the Candiote Jews to leave Crete to attend yeshivas see N. Porges, "Élie Capsali et sa chronique de Venise," *Revue des études juives* 78 (1924): 23. Elijah Capsali went to Padua in the early part of the sixteenth century, but his great uncle, Moses Capsali, had been the famous rabbi of Constantinople in the fifteenth century.

28 See Zvi Ankori, "Giacomo Foscarini and the Jews of Crete. A Reconsideration," *Michael. The Diaspora Research Institute Tel-Aviv University* 7 (1981): 101. This settlement was probably inhabited by poor Jewish immigrants and Karaites. For a concise overview of the Jewish quarter in the sixteenth century see Kostas Tsiknakes, "Ἡ ἑβραϊκή κοινότητα τοῦ Χάνδακα στά μέσα τοῦ 16ου αἰώνα (The Jewish community of Candia in the middle of the sixteenth century)," in *Anthe Chariton* (Venice, 1998): 729–52.

29 Belle D. Mazur, "Crete," in *The Universal Jewish Encyclopedia* (New York, 1939), 3: 410–12, has published two photographs of the synagogue's façade. For the destruction of the Jewish quarter of Herakleion see Judith Humphrey, "The Jews of Crete under German Occupation 1941–1944," *Bulletin of Judaeo-Greek Studies* 5 (1989): 18–26. For the synagogues in general see Zvi Ankori, "The Living and the Dead. The Story of Hebrew Inscriptions in Crete," *Proceedings of the American Academy of Jewish Research* 38–39 (1970–71): 19–20. In 1481 the Jewish traveler Meshullam da Volterra recorded four synagogues in Candia, all situated on the main street of the Judaica, near the waterfront. The eight different synagogue

names that can be drawn from the Jewish communal ordinances of the Venetian period must be alternative appellations for the same structures.

30 Jacoby, "Venice, the Inquisition and the Jewish Communities," 127. In the communal statutes of 1228 there is mention of one of the synagogues, implying that there were more than one (in Candia). The synagogue of the prophet Elijah was abandoned sometime after 1369, when regrets are voiced for its closure; see Ankori, "The Living and the Dead," 19, n. 25.

31 Artom and Cassuto, *Taqqanot*, 14, article 25, line 4. The people of three congregations/synagogues assembled in order to elect the seven elders of the community. Article 52 of the statutes (p. 52, line 46) mentions the three synagogal structures, each one of which contained a scroll where the communal statutes were inscribed.

32 In 1421 the unnamed synagogue belonged to Franciscus Trivisano, a converted Jew, but its ownership was contested by Sabatheus Casan, who maintained that his father had bought the synagogue for two hundred hyperpera in 1409 (ASV, DdC, b. 30ter, Memoriali 32, f. 151r–154r [February 27, 1421]. Franciscus argued that Sabatheus's claim was absurd because this ridiculously low price could barely cover the value of the foundations of the synagogue; in fact, the synagogue had a choir and columns costing more than eight hundred hyperpera. The authorities decided that Franciscus Trivisano was the legal owner, and they forbade the Jewish community from celebrating their rituals inside this synagogue under a severe penalty of five hundred hyperpera. Although we do not possess further evidence on this structure, it seems that this synagogue fell into disuse following 1421.

33 ASV, DdC, b. 31, Memoriali, fasc. 41, f. 23r (1439): the synagogue is described as being very old.

34 David Jacoby, "Quelques Aspects de la vie juive en Crète dans la première moitié du XVe siècle," in *Pepragmena tou G' Diethnous Kretologikou Synedrion* (Athens, 1974), 2 113–16, from *Takkanoth Kandiya* 14, 46, 52f. Starr, "Jewish Life in Crete," 98, records the synagogue name as *Soiletiko*. A document from the *incanti* (land auction sales) of Candia in 1345, in ASV, DdC, b. 25, Quaternus Cedularum Incantorum, fasc. 2, f. 6v, mentions another synagogue name: *de Stroviliaco* (in 1410 the term used is *Strouilatico*), which must be another version of *Siviliatiko*.

35 Jacoby, "Les Quartiers juifs," 213, has shown that Jews from Spain had reached the East as early as 1343. In that year the Jew Isaac Catelanus wrote his will in Constantinople. There is further evidence that Jews from Spain had come to Crete by the fourteenth century, see Benjamin Arbel, "The List of Able-Bodied Jews in the Cretan Town of Chaniá (Canea), 1536," in *Daniel Carpi Jubilee Volume. A Collection of Stories in the History of the Jewish People Presented to Daniel Carpi Upon His 70th Birthday by His Colleagues and Students* (Tel-Aviv, 1996), 28, with earlier bibliography.

36 ASV, DdC, b. 30bis, Memoriali Antichi, fasc. 29/1, f. 19v–20v (1411).

37 Every two years the head of the Jewish communities, i.e. the *comestabile*, and his assistants would elect three people, who, along with three other administrators elected by Cagus, would manage the synagogue. This committee of six was responsible for choosing the religious head of the synagogue; see ASV, DdC, b. 30ter, Memoriali 30, f. 11v–13r (October 21, 1415):

> Coram magnifico domino Petro Ciurano . . . comparuit Jaco dictus Bello Judeus, filius quondam Cagi Iudei, et produxit cartam completam et roboratam manu Zacharie de Fredo notarii in MCCCLXXIII mense Novembre die XXI, indicione XII [November 21,

1373] qua inter cetera continetur qualiter suprascriptus Cagi pater suus, qui habebat domus et possessionem cuiusdam sinagoge posite in Iudaica Candide, dicte Stroviliaticho et in ea facerat multas expensas. Cessit et renuntiavit comestabili et universitati Iudaice Candide ipsam sinagogam cum conditionibus quod, omnibus et singulis duabus annis in perpetuum comestabilis Iudaice Candide et camerarii, aut unus eorum, seu ille qui deputatus esset ad elimosinas ipsius sinagoge, eligere et deputare deberet tres personas sufficientes et idoneas ex una parte, et suprascriptus Cay, pater predicti Jaco dicti tam alios tres ex altera, ex quibus tribus personis per ipsum eligendis ipse possit esse unus, que sex persone *** eadem sinagogam Stroviliaticho et eligere et confirmare deberent unum bonum et idoneum ac sufficienten sacerdotem de eadem sinagoga.

38 Artom and Cassuto, *Taqqanoth*, 107, article 85, line 127.

39 Jacoby, "Quelques Aspects," 116. According to the text of Elea's testament, her wishes were the following: "Item volo et ordino quod domus tercii solarii domorum mearum magnarum positarum in Judaica civitatis Candide remaneant in sinagoga imperpetuum."

40 Even closer is the appellation *Beth ha-Knesseth ha-'Elyon* (Upper Synagogue), entered in a family record that was written in a Hebrew prayer book from Candia (now in Breslau) in the final period of Venetian domination (1653); see Ankori, "The Living and the Dead," 21, n. 26.

41 Starr, "Jewish Life in Crete," 98, and ASV, Notai di Candia, b. 121, f. 32v, not. Cirillo Gradonigo, f. 42r (1496).

42 Apparently members of the Jewish community were free to own property until 1423 (see earlier in this chapter, n. 23).

43 S. W. Baron, *The Jewish Community*, 2: 293. This ordinance is not unique to Candiote statutes, but in other cases the text prescribes that this refers only to a non-Jewish landlord, whereas the *Takkanoth Kandiya* does not.

44 Imhaus, "Les Maisons de la Commune," 132; and David Jacoby, "Venice and Venetian Jews in the Eastern Mediterranean," in *Gli Ebrei a Venezia*, 37, mentions one such case in 1432. On a particular court case of 1400 that justified the opinion of the defendant, Moises son of David, that he could build his house as high as he pleased, see Georgopoulou, "Mapping Religious and Ethnic Identities," 497.

45 Gerola, *Monumenti veneti*, 3: 203–4.

46 Carbone, ed., *Pietro Pizolo*, 1: 15–16, no. 19. According to Boerio, *Dizionario*, 767, the word *tressa* indicates a transverse section.

47 ASV, DdC, b. 11, Atti Antichi II, frammento 12 (April 6, 1403).

48 Gerola, *Monumenti veneti*, 2: 380, n. 4. The text reads, "nella più bella parte della città, sopra di mare, con case et stabili bellissimi." This traveler probably saw only the waterfront with the display of few elegant façades and did not realize the real conditions of the Judaica.

49 Zvi Ankori, "From Zudecha to Yahudi Mahallesi," 85 and 108.

50 Ibid., 126.

51 Ibid., 86–87.

52 ASV, DdC, b. 11, Atti Antichi, fragment 11/2, f. 69v (April 27, 1391). The document reads:

Per dominum ducham et eius consilium concorditer attenta supplicatione facta per Johannem Basilio, concessum fuit dicto Johanni de gratia speciali quod possit affictare Judeis quibus voluerit tres stationes ex illis stationibus *** suis, que sunt extra confines Iudaice, videlicet illas tres que sunt proximores [?] dictis confinibus Iudaice cum hac conditione: quod nullus Iudeus audeat habitare nec dormire de nocte in aliqua dictarum stationum sub pena yperperorum decem pro quolibet

Iudeo contrafaciente et qualibet vice. Et si dictus Johannes fuerit contentiens, perdat etiam ipse yperpera decem pro quolibet Iudeo contrafaciente et qualibet vice. Sed ipsi Iudei possint tenere ibi merces et alias res et vendere ea de die solummodo.

A similar act was recorded in 1406. DdC, b, 11, Atti Antichi II, fragment 14 (February 1, 1406/m.v. 1405). Special permission was accorded to Catherine, the widow of Philippus Pisani, to rent the houses that she owned close to the Judaica to Jews with the condition that these Jews would not spend the night there.

53 Zvi Ankori, "Jews in the History of Mediaeval Crete," in *Pepragmena tou B' Dietinous Kretologikou Synedriou* (Athens, 1968), 3: 330, has translated the text of the *Takkanoth Kandiya* from the edition of Artom and Cassuto, 28 and 67: "when on the border of the *Qahal* [the Jewish quarter] you hear the Brothers rattle for Vespers."

54 R. Cessi, *Deliberazioni del Maggior Consiglio*, 3 (Venice, 1950), 274. Jews have been attested on the island since 1268; see Jacoby, "Les Juifs à Venise," 168.

55 Koder, *Negroponte*, 86–88, and C. N. Sathas, *Documents inédits relatifs à l'histoire de la Grèce au Moyen Age* (Paris, 1880–82), 3: 279–80. The document dates to the fifteenth century but gives explicit information on the situation of the Jewish community in the midfourteenth century:

> [I]udei] cum antiquis temporibus habitarent extra civitatem Nigropontis ubi tunc derobabantur et capiebantur a Teucris venerunt habitatum postea ipsam civitatem uniscentes se cum christianis propter quod 1355 provisum fuit per consilium Rogatorum ut regimen Nigropontis statueret sibi locum posse habitare cum securitate qui esset separatus a christianis, quod regimen sibi assignavit certum locum in quo nunc est sua iudaica ubi sunt certe domus, que sunt in uno capite civitatis Nigropontis que sunt separate et divise a christianis.

56 Thiriet, *Regestes des délibérations du Sénat* 1 (1958): 346.

57 Nicholas Stavroulakis and Timothy J. DeVinney, *Jewish Sites and Synagogues of Greece* (Athens, 1992), 93.

58 I. Lévi, "Les Juifs de Candie de 1380 à 1485," *Revue des Études Juives* 26 (1893): 200–201

59 Sathas, *Documents inédits relatifs à l'histoire de la Grece*, 3: 279–80, no. 856 (see earlier in this chapter, n. 55); cf. Koder, *Negroponte*, 87–88, and Baron, *Social and Religious History of the Jews*, 17: 75.

60 Koder, *Negroponte*, 88, and Jacoby, "Venice and Venetian Jews," 38.

61 Demetris Triantafyllopoulos, "Τοπογραφικά προβλήματα τῆς Μεσαιωνικῆς Εὔβοιας (Topographical problems of medieval Euboea)," *Acheion Euvoikon Meleton* 15 (1974): 252.

62 Arbel, "The List of Able-Bodied Jews," 32–34.

63 Theotokes, *Senate* 2/1 (1936): 81, has published the Senate decree: "sit in libertate rectorum Chanee et eius consilii ponendi Judeos in aliquo loco burgi."

64 Baron, *Social and Religious History of the Jews*, 17: 68. See also Arbel, "The List of Able-Bodied Jews," 21–34.

65 Ankori, "The Living and the Dead," 33–37.

66 Arbel, "The List of Able-Bodied Jews," 31, and Stavroulakis and De Vinney, *Jewish Sites*, 96–98.

67 Thiriet, *Regestes des délibérations du Sénat*, 1: 29, no. 32, July 26, 1333.

68 Ankori, "The Living and the Dead," 16, n. 22.

69 Noiret, *Documents inédits*, 213, and I. Lévi, "Les Juifs de Candie de 1380 à 1485," *Revue des Études juives* 26 (1893): 198–208, 199.

70 D. Jacoby, "Un agent juif au service de la République de Venise. David Mauro-

gonato de Candie," *Thesaurismata* 9 (1972): 75.

71 Sathas, *Documents inédits relatifs à l'histoire de la Grèce*, 4: 64.

72 Joshua Starr, *Romania, the Jewries of the Levant after the Fourth Crusade* (Paris, 1949), 63, 71.

73 Ibid., 192, for the account of Pietro Casola, and Sathas, *Documents inédits relatifs à l'histoire de la Grèce*, 4: 33–34, 60, 65, 159–161. In 1437 and again in 1464 the Jews of Modon were required to lower the prices of their leather goods, especially shoes, to make them affordable to poor citizens.

74 Sathas, *Documents inédits relatifs à l'histoire de la Grèce*, 4: 61. There were also particular orders that prohibited the Jews from washing the hides on the beach near the church of the Virgin (1434); ibid., 153.

75 Romanos, "Histoire de la communauté israélite," 65–66, 69.

76 A. Agoropoulou-Birbili, *Ἡ Ἀρχιτεκτονική τῆς πόλεως τῆς Κερκύρας κατά τήν περίοδο τῆς Ἑνετοκρατίας* (The Architecture of the city of Kerkyra during the period of Venetian rule) (Athens, 1976), 28 and 113; K. Kairophylas, *Ἡ Ἑπτάνησος ὑπό τούς Βενετούς* (The Ionian islands under the Venetians) (Athens, 1942), 27; and Brian Dicks, *Corfu* (Newton, Mass., 1977), 74.

77 For example, an embassy of Corfiote Jews went to Venice in 1406 to ask protection against stoning. The Senate ruled that they should wear a yellow letter O sign on their outer garment to assure their protection by the state; cf. Romanos, "Histoire de la communauté israélite," 69–70. At the same time the Jewish community of Corfu was ordered to sell all landed possessions and animals except for those inside their quarter. In response the Senate instituted punishment of those who harassed Jews. These events should be seen in relation to the eviction of the Jews of Venice after the end of the war of Chioggia (see earlier in this chapter, n.16).

78 Romanos, "Histoire de la communauté israélite," 63–74.

79 Agoropoulou-Birbili, *The Architecture of the City of Kerkyra*, 116–17.

80 Stavroulakis and De Vinney, *Jewish Sites*, 65.

81 Porges, "Elie Capsali et sa chronique de Venise," *Revue des études juives* 77 (1923): 24–25, and 78 (1924): 28.

82 Manoussakas, *The Conspiracy of Siffi Vlasto*, 80–84.

83 It has been suggested that David tried to buy the respect of his coreligionists by trying to ameliorate the situation of the Jewish community; cf. Manoussakas, *The Conspiracy of Siffi Vlasto*, 84, 135–40.

84 Apparently this prohibition was very hard to enforce as it is repeated time and again. In 1576 the *provveditor* Giacomo Foscarini forbade the Jewish community to leave the ghetto from sunrise on Holy Thursday to Easter Sunday, as was also the custom in Venice. See Brian Pullan, *The Jews of Europe and the Inquisition of Venice, 1550–1670* (Oxford, 1983), 163. This ruling had to be enforced when feasts coincided (Easter and Passover), or when feasts contrasted (as in the case of the Jewish feast of Purim, which was celebrated with a masquerade and drinks in the midst of Christian Lent).

85 Sathas, *Documents inédits relatifs à l'histoire de la Grèce*, 4: 169. The document dates to 1445 and pertains to the Judaica of Modon. The castellan of Modon, Zacharia Valaresso, proclaimed that "quando el se trova alcun Zudio al passar del corpo del nostro Signor over de alcuna croxe over de alcuna inchona de chiexa lui se debia immediate partir non possando esser tegnudo d'alcun et se nol si partira et lui nol se inzenochiera in terra fin che la sia passade el sia lizito a cadaun tuorli le veste et capuzi da dosso le qual sia de chi le tuora al dicto muodo."

86 Walter Pakter, *Medieval Canon Law and the Jews*, Abhandlungen zur rechtswissenschaftlichen Grundlagenforschungen 68 (Edelbach, 1988), 27.

87 Porges, "Elie Capsali," (1924): 22.

88 Marco Petta, "Documenti di Storia Ecclesiastica relativi agli ultimi anni del dominio veneto a Creta conservati nell'Archivio della S. Congregazione di Propaganda Fide," in *Pepragmena tou B′ Dietnous Kretologikou Synedriou* (Athens, 1968), 3: 216–17, records a ceremony in 1659; Aliki Nikiforou-Testone, "Le metamorfosi dello spazio urbano nelle cerimonie pubbliche durante il periodo veneto, XIV–XIX sec.," in Ennio Concina and Aliki Nikiforou-Testone, eds., *Corfù. Storia, Spazio urbano e Architettura XIV–XIX sec.* (Corfu, 1994), 65; and Georgopoulou, "Mapping Religious and Ethnic Identities," 485. There is no documentary evidence available at this point to establish the date of origin of this ritual, but from the way the document is phrased it is clear that it was not a unique event.

89 For a general overview of the situation see Stylianos Alexiou, "Τό Κάστρο τῆς Κρήτης καί ἡ ζωή του στόν ΙΣΤ′ καί ΙΖ′ αἰώνα (The castle of Crete and its life in the 16th and 17th centuries)," *Kretika Chronika* 19 (1965): 146–78, and Peter Topping, "Co-Existence of Greeks and Latins in Frankish Morea and Venetian Crete," in *Acts of the 15th International Congress of Byzantine Studies* (Athens, 1976). On the role of Crete in international trade see Angeliki Laiou, "The Byzantine Economy in the Mediterranean Trade System, 13th–15th Centuries," *Dumbarton Oaks Papers* 34–35 (1980): 177–222. On the painters of Candia see Mario Cattapan, "Nuovi Documenti riguardanti pittori cretesi del 1300 al 1500," in *Pepragmena tou B′ Diethnous Kretologikou Synedriou*, 3 (Athens, 1968): 29–46, and eidem, "Nuovi Elenchi e documenti dei pittori in Creta dal 1300 al 1500," *Thesaurismata* 9 (1972): 202–35.

90 In 1356 the Senate in Venice specified that the annual contribution of the Jewish community had to reflect the number and wealth of the members of the community. See Thiriet, *Romanie*, 227–28.

91 Ibid., 407. In this case the state demanded twelve thousand ducats from the Jewish community to finance the Lombard war.

92 See Jacoby, "Un Agent juif," 68–96. From the numerous references to the moneylending activities of the Jewish community see among other things the fourteenth-century poem by Stephanus Saclichi, A. F. Van Gemert, "Ὁ Στέφανος Σαχλίκης καί ἡ ἐποχή του (Stephanus Saclichi and his era)," *Thesaurismata* 17 (1980): 42 and 84.

93 In contrast to the Venetians, who must have felt at home among the Greeks of Candia, many accounts of late medieval travelers display an open hostility toward the locals. See, for example, the grim picture that Francisco Suriano paints of the Cretans at the beginning of the sixteenth century:

> They are an accursed people worse traitors than the Albanians, vindictive murderers given to concubinage; homosexuals, enemies of churches, Mass, sermons, confession and communion, enemies of priests and friars and of every spiritual good: a people proud, pompous, vainglorious, vicious (bastards, perfidious, infamous) and finally worse, if you except baptism than the Moslems . . . The women are vain, waspish, wrinkled, grumbling and full of poison, but the men are most undisciplined.

Cited in Hemmerdinger-Iliadou, "Voyageurs" (1973): 510, from the translation of Th. Bellorini and Eug. Hoade, in *Studium Biblicum Franciscanum* 8 (1949).

94 This duty was regarded as a corvée (*an-*

garia). Certain Greeks were exempt from this corvée because they carried the icon of the Madonna of St. Titus in the weekly procession. In 1392 the Jews of Candia had been required to supply twelve men to guard the walls at the Judaica at night; see Starr, "Jewish Life in Crete," 77.

8: Ritualizing Colonial Practices

1 Sally Moore and Barbara Myerhoff, *Secular Ritual* (Amsterdam, 1977); Victor Turner, "Social Dramas and Stories about Them," in W.J.T. Mitchell, ed., *On Narrative* (Chicago, 1981); and Lina Padoan Urban, "Gli Spettacoli urbani e l'Utopia," in *Architettura e Utopia nella Venezia del Cinquecento* (Milan, 1980).

2 Sathas, *Documents inédits relatifs à l'histoire de la Grèce*, 4: 26.

3 Zacharias N. Tsirpanlis, "Νέα στοιχεῖα σχετικά μέ τήν ἐκκλησιαστική ἱστορία τῆς Βενετοκρατούμενης Κρήτης (13ος–17ος αἰ.) ἀπό ἀνέκδοτα βενετικά ἔγγραφα (New data on the ecclesiastical history of Venetian Crete (13th–17th c.) from unpublished Venetian documents)," *Hellenika* 20 (1967): 55.

4 Richard Trexler, *Public Ritual in Renaissance Florence* (Ithaca and London, 1991). Patricia Fortini Brown, *Venetian Narrative Painting in the Age of Carpaccio* (New Haven, Conn., and London, 1988), 167, argues that Venetian ceremonial was meant to mask social ambiguities and to present a carefully structured and stable society. Indeed, the fifteenth-century pilgrim Pietro Casola saw the Corpus Christi ceremony in Venice as a reflection of the "harmony of Venetian society." See Edward Muir, "Images of Power: Art and Pageantry in Renaissance Venice," *American Historical Review* 84 (1979): 40.

5 The most comprehensive studies of Venetian ceremonial are Edward Muir, *Civic Ritual in Renaissance Venice* (Princeton, N.J., 1981), and more recently Matteo Casini, *I Gesti del principe. La festa politica a Firenze e a Venezia in età rinascimentale* (Venice, 1996); on the fusion between sacred and lay ceremonials, and the emphasis on the performers of the ritual, see pp. 58ff. The sacred character of the Venetian Republic has also been examined by Silvio Tramontin, "San Marco," in *Culto dei santi a Venezia*, 62.

6 The *festo stelle* is recorded among other festivals in Crete in 1372, when the Senate in Venice ordered the authorities of Crete to limit the expenditure for public festivities to forty hyperpera per year. See G. Fedalto, *La Chiesa latina* 3 (1978), no. 258, 112.

7 Emmanuel M. Papadakes, *Μορφαί τοῦ Λαϊκοῦ Πολιτισμοῦ τῆς Κρήτης* (Forms of the folk culture of Crete) (Athens, 1976), 114; and A. Xerouchakes, "Αἱ σύνοδοι τοῦ Γερόλαμο Λάντο Λατίνου Ἀρχιεπισκόπου ἐυ Κρήτῃ (1467, 1474, 1486) (The Councils of Gerolamo Lando Latin archbishop of Crete [1467, 1474, 1486])," *Theologia* 9 (1931): 119.

8 Richard Trexler, *The Libro Cerimoniale of the Florentine Republic* (Geneva, 1978), 10; and Rab Hatfield, "The Compagnia de' Magi," *The Journal of the Warburg and Courtauld Institutes* 33 (1970): 107–61.

9 Tafel and Thomas, *Urkunden*, 2: 57–58, 94, 124, 132–33, 308.

10 Ernst H. Kantorowicz, *Laudes Regiae* (Berkeley/Los Angeles, 1946), 151. In the 1210 *promissio* of Manfredo, archbishop of Durazzo, Doge Petrus Ziani instructed the hierarch to perform such services for the doge five times a year: at Easter, Christmas, Epiphany, on the feast of Saint Mark, and on that of Saint Ysarius, the patron saint of the city; see Tafel and Thomas, *Urkunden*, 2: 124; Alain Ducellier, *La Façade maritime de*

l'Albanie au Moyen Age: Durazzo et Valona du XIe au XVe siècle* (Thessaloniki, c. 1981), 148; and G. Fedalto, "La Chiesa latina nel Levante veneziano," *Studi veneziani* 17–18 (1975–76): 53–54. The text reads, "Juravimus quoque, quod vobis et successoribus vestris laudes omni anno quinquies faciemus levari, in Pascha videlicet et Natali, in Epiphania et in festo beati Marci evangeliste et sancti Yssarii."

11 Tafel and Thomas, *Urkunden*, 2: 132–33. The feast of the Cretan church referred to is unquestionably that of Saint Titus.

12 Nikiforou, *Δημόσιες τελετές στην Κέρκυρα κατά την Περιόδο της Βενετικής κυριαρχίας 14ος–18ος αι.* (Public ceremonies in Corfu) at the time of Venetian rule (Athens, 1999), 79–81. By the end of the sixteenth century the Venetians instituted a mixed Greek and Latin liturgy in the cathedral of Corfu on the feast day of the saint, January 19. Most likely this refers to a much earlier practice as there was an Orthodox chapel within the cathedral from the time of the Angevins, who left Corfu in 1387.

13 Tafel and Thomas, *Urkunden*, 2: 308–9. The text reads, "Clerus autem in anno ter, scilicet in nativitate Domini in Pascha resurrectionis er in festo sancti Blasii, laudes cantabunt in maiori Ecclesia solempniter domino Duci, domino Patriarche, Archiepiscopo suo et Comiti omni anno." For the special devotion of the Ragusans to St. Blasius (Sveti Vlaho) since the tenth century see Barisa Krekic, *Dubrovnik in the 14th and 15th Centuries. A City between East and West* (Norman, 1972), 86–87. The relics of the saint are kept in the treasury of the cathedral.

14 Tafel and Thomas, *Urkunden*, 2: 124.

15 Ibid., 2: 125.

16 Francis W. Carter, *Dubrovnik (Ragusa). A Classic City-State* (London and New York, 1972), 90–91.

17 Tafel and Thomas, *Urkunden*, 2: 133. This part of the *Concessio insulae Cretensis* reads, "et si contigerit quod illuc veniremus nos vel successores nostri, recipietis nos cum clero, cruce precedente, et debetis nos secundo et tercio, si voluerimus, procurare."

18 Papadaki, *Religious and Secular Rituals*, 197–98.

19 The procession, which was instituted in 1365, was modeled after the procession performed on the feast day of St. Vitus. The text reads:

> in qua [processio] esse debeat totus clerus Candide et papates Greci referentes gratias altissimo creatori de beneficio supradicto, quam solemnius et magis deuote fieri poterit. . . . Ordinatum est etiam per suprascriptos dominum ducam et eius consilium, quod dies suprascripta X cuiuslibet mensis Maii succedentis sit solemnis et solemnissima debeat celebrari per quascumque personas sub pena ordinata de aliis festiuitatibus solemnibus.

See E. Gerland, *Das Archiv des Herzogs von Kandia in Koenigl-Staatsarchiv zu Venedig* (Strasbourg, 1899), 119–20.

20 On the legends of the constantinopolitan Hodegetria see Robin Cormack, *Painting the Soul. Icons, Death Masks, and Shrouds* (London, 1997), 58–63; Hans Belting, *Likeness and Presence. A History of the Image before the Era of Art* (Chicago, 1994), 73–77; and Mirjana Tatic-Djuric, "L'Icone de l'Odigitria et son culte au XVIe siècle," in *Byzantine East, Latin West. Art Historical Studies in Honor of Kurt Weitzmann* (Princeton, 1995), 557–568. Papadaki, *Religious and secular rituals in Venetian Crete* (Rethymnon, 1995), 185, relates two miracles that the icon performed in 1575 and in 1599. In both instances the icon cured a person who could not walk.

21 Venice, Biblioteca Marciana, Ital. Cl. VI 286 (coll. 5985), Chronicle of Andrea Cornaro, "Historia Candiana," book 7, f. 54, cited in Maria Theochari, "Περί τήν

χρονολόγησιν τῆς εἰκόνος Παναγίας Μεσοπαντιτίσσης (On the dating of the icon of the Madonna Mesopanditissa)," *Akademia Athenon, Praktika* 36 (1961): 274, n. 12. This follows a long tradition that attempts to authenticate and validate many sacred icons.

22 A testament of 1501 mentions the altar of the *Mesopanditissa* in the cathedral of St. Titus ("al altar de la nostra domina Mesopanditissa che est dentro la gexia de misser San Tito"). See ASV, Procuratia de Supra, Chiesa, b. 142, fasc. 5: Diocesi di Candia, f. 16r.

23 Venice, Marciana Library, Ms. Ital. Cl. VII 525 (coll. 7497), "Racconto di varie cose successe nel Regno di Candia dall'anno 1182, che si sono ribellati dalla devozione dell'impero Greco, sino all'anno 1669 che restò al potere dell'impero Ottomano, compilato dal Sig. Antonio Trivan," fos. 13r-13v. See also Theochari, "On the dating," 274, n. 13; and Georgopoulou, "Late Medieval Crete and Venice. An Appropriation of Byzantine Heritage," *Art Bulletin* 77 (1995): 487–89.

24 Theochari, "On the dating," 275, proposes a different etymology for the epithet *Mesopanditissa*. She suggests that in the Cretan dialect the adjective *μεσοπαντίτης* refers to "the one living in the interior areas" and the verb "μεσοπαντίζω" means "I arrive walking in the middle of a certain area." The suffix *-issa* is common in titles of the Virgin and it could refer to an attribute of the icon or its location within a church; cf. Vassilakis-Maurakakis, "Church of Virgin Gouverniotissa," 81–82. A corrupted form of the term appears in the will of Marchesina Popo, widow of Dominicus Popo, in 1348. The text reads: "Item dimitto yperperum unum pro uno faciolo fiendo in ecclesia Sancti Titi in Messopanditi"; cf. Sally McKee, ed., *Wills from Late Medieval Crete, 1312–1420* (Washington, D.C., 1997), 2: 89. Again here it seems that the term refers to a distinct location, perhaps in relation to the altar of the Virgin.

25 ASV, DdC, b. 29bis 30, Memoriali 15/3, fos. 38v-39r (July 10, 1368):

> illi qui deputati sunt ad levandum eius ymaginem, que quolibet die martis levatur, ad honorem dei genitricis et ad laudem dominationis et comunis Venetiarum non cogantur a modo indnt [?] per capitaneum burgi ut per alios officiales ad faciendum vaitam que fieri solet per habitatores dicti burgi sed sint ipsi exempti de ipsa vaita qui sunt numero per – . VIII. nomina eorum sint hec: Ser Dimitrius Seriga, Ser Georgius Quirino, Ser Elias Simbrago, Ser Nichiforus Paleologo, Ser Iohannes Brati, Ser Stamati Gisi, Ser Stamati Cumnino, Ser Michael Longovardo.

A summary is published by E. Santschi, *Arrêts*, 138, no. 298.

26 Papadaki, *Religious and Secular Rituals*, 186.

27 One of these icons, known as *Maria Romaia*, resided in the church of the Chalkoprateia; it joined the procession as well. On the procession in Constantinople see Nancy Patterson Sevcenko, "Servants of the Holy Icon," in *Byzantine East, Latin West. Art-Historical Studies in Honor of Kurt Weitzmann* (Princeton, N.J., 1995), 548–89, and Annemarie Weyl Carr, "Leo of Chalcedon and the Icons," in the same volume, 582.

28 Hemmerdinger-Iliadou, "Voyageurs" (1967): 597.

29 On the basis of Trivan's chronicle Theochari, "On the dating," 274, n. 13, argues that a weekly procession (every Tuesday) of the icon was instituted to commemorate the treaty, but there is no direct evidence that this was the reason for the procession. On the other hand, a report of the Latin archbishop Luigi Mocenigo in 1637 maintains that the procession was instituted after the last rebellion of the Greeks, i.e. 1363. See Marco Petta, "Documenti di Storia Ecclesiastica relativi agli

ultimi anni del dominio veneto a Creta conservati nell'Archivio della S. Congregazione di Propaganda Fide," in *Pepragmena tou B′ Diethnous Kretologikou Synedriou* 3 (Athens, 1968): 216.

30 R. L. Wolff, "Footnote to an Incident of the Latin Occupation of Constantinopl. The Church and the Icon of the Hodegetria," *Traditio* 6 (1948): 320. For the letter of Pope Innocent III condemning the acts of the Venetians see Tafel and Thomas, *Urkunden*, 2: 45–47:

> quandam iconam, in qua beatus Lucas evangelista imaginem beatae Virginis propriis manibus dicitur depinxisse, quam ob ipsius Virginis reverentiam tota Graecia veneratur. . . . Venetorum Potestas . . . ipsam iconam . . . postulavit . . . a preafato Imperatore [Henrici] fuisse promissam. . . .Ipsi [Veneti] vero . . . ostia sacrarii confregerunt, et asportantes exinde violenter iconam, eam in Ecclesia, quae Graece Pantocraton dicitur, collocarunt.

31 For a general account of these processions see Nancy Patterson Sevcenko, "Icons in the Liturgy," *Dumbarton Oaks Papers* 45 (1991): 45–57. On the specific cases see Sevcenko, "Servants of the Holy Icon," 549–50, and John Nesbitt and J. Wiita, "A Confraternity of the Comnenian Era," *Byzantinische Zeitschrift* 68 (1975): 360–84, who have published a twelfth-century document referring to a monthly procession of an icon in the city of Thebes centering around an icon of the Virgin from Naupaktos.

32 Xerouchakes, "Councils of Gerolamo Lando," 39.

33 The account of Angelo Venier (1670) was published by Theochari, "On the dating," 276. The original text is full of details about the parade of the icon: "si portava in diverse chiese greche a celebrar messe per voti di particolari, dando per ogni messa d'elemosina centimo uno che si spartiva tra essi et la Chiesa medesima et nel tornar a riponerla entrando per la porta della cathedrale cantavano ancora il laudo di Monsignore Arcivescovo." See also Papadaki, *Religious and Secular Rituals*, 179–87.

34 In 1368 the Orthodox canons of the church of St. Michael refused to follow the Western rite during the weekly public procession of the icon. See J. Gill, S. J., "Pope Urban V and the Greeks of Crete," *Orientalia Christiana Periodica* 39 (1973): 467–68, and Michel and Anne-Marie Hayez, eds., *Catholic Church, Pope Urbain V (1362–1370) Lettres Communes*, 7 (Rome, 1981), no. 22430, p. 383. Finally, in 1379 the Senate in Venice allowed both the Latin and Greek clergy to carry the Mesopanditissa in procession through the streets of Candia, probably making some unspecified concessions to the Orthodox priests. See M. Manoussakas, "Βενετικά ἔγγραφα ἀναφερόμενα εἰς τήν ἐκκλησιαστικήν ἱστορίαν τῆς Κρήτης τοῦ 14ου–16ου αἰῶνος (Πρωτοπαπᾶδες καί Πρωτοψάλται Χάνδακος) (Venetian documents on the church history of Crete in the 14th–16th c. [Protopapas and Protopsaltes of Candia])," *Deltion tes Historikes kai Ethnologikes Hetaireias tes Hellados* 15 (1961): 154–55, and Fedalto, *La Chiesa latina*, 3: 123–24.

35 Theochari, "On the dating," 276, published a Senate decision of 1515 that refers to the regular procession of the icon on Tuesdays. The document (Procuratia de Supra, b. 142, Processo 295, fasc. 1, f. 10r) reads:

> ordinemo, et firmiter statuimo che ogni marti et ogni altro giorno del'anno in questa città per la optima consuetudine, si farà procession alcuna. Tutti li papa et preti qualli di questa città siano obligati venire, come è debito suo, insieme con il suo protopapa ad honorar et compagnar quella; sotto pena per ogni volta a cadaun che mancasse di ipperperi 4, uno deli qual sia dello executor, et uno protopapa suo, et li duo siano del Ospidal dela Pietà,

reservando qualche causa di manifesta necesità, overo di qualche necesario suo negotio per il qual l'avesse licentia dal clarissimo Ducha, aliter non li vagli excusation alcuna nè si li possi sub debito sacramento rimetter over mondificar ditta pena.

In 1606 the penalty was raised to twelve hyperpera; see Papadaki, *Religious and Secular Rituals*, 179.

36 Ubaldo Manucci, "Contributi documentarii per la storia della distruzione degli episcopati latini in oriente nei secoli XVI e XVII," *Bessarione* year 17, vol. 30 (1914); 102. We know nothing more about the origin of the icon of Canea, nor do we have any evidence of its performing miracles.

37 ASV, Procuratia di Supra, Chiesa, b. 102: Scritture di Candia, f. 36r.

38 A seventeenth-century traveler, Wolfgang Stockman, reports that during the summer both Greeks and Latins took the icon in procession to the Augustinian monastery of San Salvatore to meet another icon of the Virgin. Then "a priest celebrates Mass and prays for rain. The icon is taken back to St. Titus and the miracle is done: it rains for half an hour." The way Stockman phrased his observations implies that he was so impressed by the efficacy of the rite that he thought this to have been an annual event. See Hemmerdinger-Iliadou, "Voyageurs" (1967): 597.

39 Ibid. Stockman, who arrived in Candia on August 8, mentions that the Greeks carried the icon in procession every Sunday to their cathedral and after the celebration of Mass took it back to St. Titus.

40 Georgopoulou, "Late Medieval Crete," 489, and Papadaki, *Religious and Secular Rituals*, 135–43. It seems that in Venice the solemn procession was instituted in 1407. See G. Gattinoni, *Il Campanile di San Marco* (Venice, 1910), 259. This custom must have been duplicated soon in Candia.

41 Chryssanthi Baltoyanni, "The Place of Domenicos Theotocopoulos in 16th-Century Cretan Painting, and the Icon of Christ from Patmos," in *El Greco of Crete*, 78–80, fig. 1, and P. Vokotopoulos, "Μιά ἄγνωστη εἰκόνα στό Σεράγεβο (An unknown icon in Serajevo)," *Deltion tes Christianikes Archaiologikes Hetaireias tes Hellados*, per. 4, 12 (1984): 9–31, fig. 2.

42 The manuscript Morosini-Grimani 96 (coll. 34) gives a very vivid, yet quite extravagant description of the adoration of the icon by the Greeks: "there was always a group of Orientals who repeated the scenes in the Temple of Jerusalem and who, during the big feast days, were not afraid to bring their beds to the altar of the Virgin Mary"; see Eva Tea, "Saggio sulla storia religiosa di Candia dal 1590 al 1630," *Atti del Reale Istituto Veneto di Scienze, Lettere ed Arti* 72/2 (1912–13): 1362.

43 Theochari, "On the dating," 277–79, published an inventory written in 1670 when the icon was moved to the church of Santa Maria della Salute in Venice. A similar inventory is published by G. Gerola, "Gli oggetti sacri di Candia salvati a Venezia," *Atti dell'Accademia degli Agiati in Rovereto* ser. 3, 9/3–4 (1903): 1–40.

44 For an account of the icon's arrival in Venice see *Il Tempio della Salute eretto per voto della Repubblica Veneta, 26–10-1630* (Venice, 1930); and Flaminio Corner, *Notizie storiche delle apparizioni e delle immagini più celebri di Maria Vergine Santissima nella città e dominio di Venezia* (Venice, 1761), 1–11.

45 Georgopoulou, "Late Medieval Candia," 490.

46 Venice, Museo Correr, Archivio Morosini-Grimani, b. 568/54, N3, "Solenità et Cerimonie che si costumano nella città di Candia." This manuscript was recently published by Papadaki, *Religious and Secular Rituals*, 197–208.

47 This was celebrated at the altar of St. Ius-

tina in the Augustinian church of San Salvatore.

48 Sathas, *Documents inédits relatifs à l'histoire de la Grèce*, 4: 169. Document dated to 1445.

49 Processions intended to commemorate earthquakes or to thank God for his miraculous intervention are attested to from the Byzantine period. Interesting depictions of such events can be found in the *Menologion of Basil II* at the Vatican (Vatican Lib. gr. 1613), a manuscript that was written and illustrated around the year 1000.

50 P. Casola, *Canon Pietro Casola's Pilgrimage (1494)* trans. M. N. Newett (Manchester, 1907), 199.

51 Papadaki, *Religious and Secular Rituals*, 124–28; text on p. 201.

52 Klaus Gallas, Klaus Wessel, and Manolis Borboudakis, *Byzantinisches Kreta* (München, 1983), 321–22, fig. 282.

53 Papadaki, *Religious and Secular Rituals*, 197–207. The commemoration of the battle of Lepanto was another occasion when the whole population was to be present in the festivities.

54 A bull that Pope Pius II issued for the protection and well-being of the twelve Uniate priests of Candia in 1463 is instructive as it shows explicitly the order to be followed in the litanies and processions. See H. D. Saffrey, "Pie II et les prêtres uniates en Crète au XVe siècle," *Thesaurismata* 16 (1979): 47:

> et quia, in processionibus et letaniis que in dicta insula fiunt, canonici ecclesie Cretensis predicte *presbyteros Grecos tam unitos quam scismaticos prefatos vocant eosque in ultimo loco collocant et non solum presbyteros latinos sed etiam omnes religiosos et etiam confraternitates secularium eis anteponunt*, in dictorum presbyterum Grecorum opprobrium et in causam ne alii uniantur videntes se esse ita deiectos, statuimus ut dicti presbyteri Greci uniti canonicos predictos et ceteros presbyteros seculares immediate succedant, presbyteri vero Greci adhuc in scismate permanentes pro confusione sua locum suum retineant ut uniti iniuriam patiantur et scismatici facilius ad unionem alliciantur [my emphasis].

55 Thiriet, *Déliberations du Sénat*, 3: 206, no. 2994, and full text in Noiret, *Documents inédits*, 449, dated June 12, 1455. In addition, the authorities of Crete asked the Venetian Senate for a list of all the feasts that should be observed according to the Venetian ecclesiastical calendar. The document reads:

> Quoniam, propter quandam consuetudinem positam per aliquos rectores preteritos, solemnitates plurimorum sanctorum in Candida observantur, in quibus non audetur operari, quia Regimen Crete constringit tam latinos quam grecos observare. Et sint plures quam hec que Venetiis observantur, Et ultra has greci etiam habent observare suas, et observando nostras, que plurime sunt, et suas similiter, hoc eis revertitur in maximum damnum. Ideo humiliter supplicatur pro ducali dominio, quod clementer dignetur providere quod Cretenses debeant observare solummodo dies festos que Venetiis observantur, et non amplius, et reliquos dies opperari possint; et quod ad nos de Venetiis mittentur dies festos sanctorum que solent Venetiis observari, ut ipsis eodem modo illas inde observari queant. Responsio . . . volumus et ordinamus quod, ultra festivitates ordinatas celebrari per Romanam Ecclesiam, nemo compelli possit per Regimen Crete vel aliorum locorum ad celebrationem alicuius festivitatis, nisi quantum pro devotione sua quilibet celebrari voluerit.

56 Vladimir Lamansky, *Secrets d'Etat de Venise. Documents, extraits, notices et études servant à éclaircir les rapports de la seigneurie avec les grecs à la fin du XV et au XVI siècle* (St.

Petersburg, 1884, repr. New York, 1968), 73, dated July 7, 1576.

57 Ibid., 123.

9: Colonialism and the Metropole

1 John Ruskin, *Stones of Venice* (London, 1867), 2: 66.

2 Gwendolyn Wright, "Tradition in the Service of Modernity. Architecture and Urbanism in French Colonial Policy, 1900–1930," *The Journal of Modern History* 59 (1987): 291–317.

3 Some of these issues are explored in Georgopoulou, "Late Medieval Crete," 491–96.

4 Deborah Howard, "Venise et la Dalmatie. San Michele in Isola," in Jean Guillaume, ed., *Les Débuts de la Renaissance* (Paris, in press).

5 The basilica of S. Marco was rebuilt in the latter part of the eleventh century. The new basilica was much larger than its predecessor, copied in form the church of the Holy Apostles in Constantinople, and was decorated – with mosaics and sculptural reliefs – according to Byzantine practices. See D. M. Nicol, *Byzantium and Venice: A Study in Diplomatic and Cultural Relations* (Cambridge and New York, 1988), 65; O. Demus, *The Mosaics of San Marco in Venice* (Chicago and London, 1984), 1: 2; and M. Muraro, "Varie Fasi di influenza bizantina a Venezia nel Trecento," *Thesaurismata* 9 (1972): 180–201.

6 On the intricacies of the exploitation of the Byzantine spoils, see M. Jacoff, *The Horses of San Marco and the Quadriga of the Lord* (Princeton, N.J., 1993) with extensive bibliography. On the significance of Byzantine objects taken to Venice, see also S. Bettini, "Venice, the Pala d'Oro and Constantinople," in D. Buckton, ed., *The Treasury of San Marco, Venice* (Milan, 1984), 35.

7 For a list of the sacred holdings in the S. Marco treasury see G. Perocco, "History of the Treasury of San Marco," in Buckton, *Treasury*, 65–68, with further bibliography. These relics reinforced the importance of the patron saint of Venice and the basilica of S. Marco. In this context see D. Pincus, "Christian Relics and the Body Politic. A Thirteenth-Century Relief Plaque in the Church of San Marco," in *Interpretazioni veneziane. Studi di Storia dell'Arte in onore di Michelangelo Muraro*, ed. David Rosand (Venice, 1984), 39–57. Pincus superbly interprets a group of sacred relics acquired in the thirteenth century as signs of political supremacy.

8 Jacoff, *Horses of San Marco*, 62–108.

9 E. Muir, "Images of Power. Art and Pageantry in Renaissance Venice," *American Historical Review* 84 (1979): 20; and V. Galliazzo, *I Cavalli di San Marco* (Treviso, 1981), 76–77. For specific descriptions of the new triumphant processions in the later thirteenth century, see Martin da Canal, *Les estoires de Venise. Cronaca veneziana in lingua francese dalle origini al 1275*, ed. A. Limentani, Civiltà Veneziana Fonti e Testi XII, 3rd ser. III (Florence, 1972), 247–63. On the origins of Venetian ceremonial in general, see G. Renier Michiel, *Origine delle feste veneziane*, 6 vols. (Milan, 1821–29).

10 See Tafel and Thomas, *Urkunden*, 2: 4; V. Lazzarini, "I Titoli dei dogi di Venezia," *Nuovo Archivio veneto*, n.s. 5 (1903): 271–311; and A. Pertusi, "Quedam regalia insignia," *Studi veneziani* 7 (1965): 3–123.

11 See D. Zakythinos, "La Conquête de Constantinople en 1204, Venise et le partage de l'Empire byzantin," in *Venezia dalla prima crociata alla conquista di Costantinopoli nel 1204* (Florence, 1966), 137–55; and see the Introduction, n. 6. The Venetians had been awarded the city of Adrianople and its adjacent area; the regions of Epirus; Acarnania; Aetolia; a

major part of the Peloponnesos; the islands of the Cyclades, Aegina; and Salamis; and the towns of Oreoi and Karystos on the island of Euboea.

12 Demus, *Mosaics*, 1: 205; and Nicol, *Byzantium and Venice*, 182–84.

13 H. Buchthal, *Historia Troiana. Studies in the History of Medieval Secular Illustration*, Studies of the Warburg Institute 32; 2nd ed. (Neudeln and Lichtenstein, 1978), 54–56, has argued convincingly that after 1204 Venice saw herself as the successor of the Christian late Roman empire. The constantinopolitan treasures turned the church of S. Marco into the major symbol of this idea of *renovatio imperii*, by making the basilica "look older than it was." See also M. Perry, "Saint Mark's Trophies. Legend, Superstition and Archaeology in Renaissance Venice," *Journal of the Warburg and Courtauld Institutes* 60 (1977): 27–49 (reprinted in Metropolitan Museum of Art, *The Horses of San Marco*, 104–10), with further bibliography.

14 G. Graziato, ed., *Le Promissioni del Doge di Venezia dalle origini alla fine del duecento*, Fonti per la Storia di Venezia, sez. 1, Archivi Pubblici (Venice, 1986), 7–22; and Gaetano Cozzi, "La Politica del diritto nella repubblica di Venezia," in *Stato, società e giustizia nella repubblica veneta, sec. XV–XVIII* (Rome, 1980), 32–33.

15 Thiriet, *Romanie*, 98–99.

16 On the earlier formation of the "myth" of Venice, see most recently T. S. Brown, "History as Myth. Medieval Perceptions of Venice's Roman and Byzantine Past," in R. Beaton and C. Roueché, eds., *The Making of Byzantine History. Studies Dedicated to Donald M. Nicol* (London, 1993), 145–57.

17 A. Maria Orselli, *L'Idea e il culto di santo patrono cittadino nella letteratura latina medievale* (Bologna, 1965), viii. For a broader understanding of the significance of the patron saint in the Middle Ages, see also H. C. Peyer, *Stadt und Stadtpatron im mittelalterlichen Italien. Wirtschaft, Gesellschaft, Staat*, Züricher Studien zur allgemeinem Geschichte 13 (Zurich, 1955).

18 See Chapter 4, n. 26. The earliest surviving manuscript (Paris, Bibl. Nat. grec 548) dates to the tenth century. See F. Halkin, "La Légende crétoise de Saint Tite," *Analecta Bollandiana* 79 (1961): 241.

19 The apostolic foundation of the church of Crete must have been the reason for the high position of the Cretan metropolitan in the ecclesiastical hierarchy of the Eastern church; see D. Tsougarakis, *Byzantine Crete. From the 5th Century to the Venetian Conquest* (Athens, 1988), 207.

20 This seal comes from the episcopacy of metropolitan Andrew. On the reverse are the cruciform monogram of Andrew and a circular inscription identifying Andrew as ΠΡΟΕΔΡΟΝ ΚΡΗΤΗϹ (that is, metropolitan of the island). Three more lead seals of a similar type exist. G. Zacos and A. Veglery, *Byzantine Lead Seals* 1, pt. 2 (Basel, 1972), 795–96, nos. 1293 a and b, 1294. The fourth is in the Historical Museum of Herakleion and was published by S. Xanthoudides, "Μολύβδιναι βοῦλλαι ἐκ Κρήτης," (Lead seals from Crete), *Epeteris Hetaireias Byzantinon Spoudon* 2 (1925): 42–49.

21 O. Demus, *The Mosaic Decoration of San Marco, Venice*, ed. H. L. Kessler (Chicago and London, 1988), 2; and Buchthal, *Historia Troiana*, 54.

22 Demus, *Mosaics*, 2: 199–201; Nicol, *Byzantium and Venice*, 24–26; and T. E. A. Dale, "Inventing a Sacred Past. Pictorial Narratives of St. Mark the Evangelist in Aquileia and Venice, ca. 1000–1300," *Dumbarton Oaks Papers* 48 (1994): 57–58. There is evidence for a cult of Saint Mark in Aquileia in the years 783–86; see *Bibliotheca Sanctorum*, 8 (Rome, 1967), col. 725.

23 This parallel can be extended to the similarities between the hagiographical

traditions regarding the two saints. All versions of the *Life* of St. Titus assert Paul's personal involvement in his investiture. Similarly, Saint Peter personally invested Saint Mark with the episcopal office before his departure for Aquileia; see S. Sinding-Larsen, *Christ in the Council Hall. Studies in the Religious Iconography of the Venetian Republic* (Spoleto, 1974), 182.

24 For an analysis of the Venetian view of sacred relics, see A. Niero, "Reliquie e corpi di santi," in S. Tramontin et al., *Culto dei santi a Venezia*, Biblioteca Agiografica Veneziana II (Venice, 1965), 181–208.

25 Demus, *Mosaics*, 2: 267, n. 12; Muir, "Images of Power," 21; Jacoff, *Horses of San Marco*, 44–45; and Dale, "Inventing a Sacred Past," 85–101. The legend of Saint Mark, which had been completed in the eleventh century, was revised by a group of Dominican friars, probably under the direction of the doge sometime between 1200 and 1260.

26 This vestibule was the seaward entrance of the basilica which was used as a ceremonial entrance on various occasions. See Demus, *Mosaics*, 1: 58, and 2: 185–94.

27 For a discussion of this legend as a primary component in the construction of the myth of Venice, see Sinding-Larsen, *Christ in the Council Hall*, 93. For the close relationship between Saint Mark and the doge (and the state), see also E. Muir, *Civic Ritual in Renaissance Venice* (Princeton, N.J., 1981), 78.

28 The *translatio* and reception of the saint's body were illustrated in the Pala d'Oro and in the vault of the south choir chapel dedicated to St. Clement. See Dale, "Inventing a Sacred Past," 66 and 70; and Demus, *Mosaics*, 1: 66–70.

29 Demus, *Mosaics*, 1: 69–70, and 2: 202–3. Demus has in fact tried to situate the mosaic above the Porta di S. Alipio historically by arguing that it depicts Doge Lorenzo Tiepolo (1268–75) and his family.

30 The second clause of this inscription now reads, UT VENETOS SEMPER SERVET AB HOSTE SUOS ("in order that he always protect his Venetians from the enemy"), but it was recorded differently in the seventeenth century; see J. Sansovino, *Venetia Città nobilissima et singolare descritta già in XIII libri. Et hora con molta diligenza corretta emendata e più d'un terzo di cose noue ampliata dal m.r.d. Giovanni Stringa* (Venice, 1604), 10; and Demus, *Mosaics*, 2: 201, 271. Relying on the usual accuracy of Stringa's accounts (Stringa was a canon of San Marco), Demus attributes the change in the inscription to a bad restoration in the eighteenth century.

31 *Bibliotheca Sanctorum*, 12 (Rome, 1969), col. 505. Outside Crete the saint appears on a wall painting in the church of St. Nicholas in the village of St. Nicholas near Monemvasia. See N. B. Drandakes, "Οἱ τοιχογραφίες τοῦ Ἁγίου Νικολάου στόν Ἅγιο Νικόλαο Μονεμβασίας (The wall paintings of St. Nicholas in the church of St. Nicholas in Monemvasia)," *Deltion Christianikes kai Archaiologikes Hetaireias*, ser. D, 9 (1977–79): 51–52, pl. 16a.

32 Giulio Cattin, *Musica e liturgia a San Marco. Testi e melodie per la liturgia delle ore dal XII al XVII secolo. Dal graduale tropato del duecento ai graduali cinquecenteschi*, 4 vols. (Venice, 1990), 1: 79 and 2: 415.

33 Claudio Bellinati, and Sergio Bettini, *L'Epistolario miniato di Giovanni da Gaibana*, 1 (Vicenza, 1968), fos. 4r and 6v, and vol. 2 (text), p. 96.

34 On Roman processions celebrating the various feast days of the Virgin, see H. Belting, "Icons and Roman Society in the Twelfth Century," in W. Tronzo, ed., *Italian Church Decoration of the Middle Ages and Early Renaissance. Functions, Forms and Regional Traditions* (Baltimore, 1989), 27–30, and Hans Belting, *Likeness and Presence. A History of the Image before the Era of Art* (Chicago, 1994), 63–73.

35 A. Niero, "Feste civiche religiose," in S.

Tramontin, ed., *Patriarcato di Venezia* (Padua, 1991), 325. The feast commemorated the recovering of some Venetian brides snatched by the citizens of Trieste in 943. This feast was originally centered around the church of S. Maria Formosa, presumably the oldest church dedicated to the Virgin in Venice. See G. Gattinoni, *Il Campanile di San Marco* (Venice, 1910), 221

36 Venice, Bibl. Marciana, Lat. III, 172 (2275) : Caeremoniale rituum sacrorum ecclesiae S. Marci Venetiarum; copy of the text of Bartolomeo Bonifacio. Other codices of Bonifacio's Rituum cerimoniale can be found in ASV, Consultore in Jure, Registri 555, and in the Museo Civico Correr, Cod. Cicogna, 2768; cf. James H. Moore, *Vespers at St. Mark's. Music of Alessandro Grandi, Giovanni Rovetta and Francesco Cavalli*, 2 vols. (Ann Arbor, Mich., 1981).

37 Bonifacio's Cerimoniale, f. 55v:

> Le processioni ordinarie sono queste videlicet: prima quella de Sancto Ysidoro alli XVI aprile / secunda quella del Corpo de Christo / Alla Salute per S. Antonio di Padua li 13 Zugno [added with another hand] / terza quella de San Vido alli XV Zugno / quarta quella della Apparition di San Marco alli XXV Zugno / quinta quella del Redentore la terza Domenica di Luglio / sesta quella di Sancta Marina all XVII Luglio / settima quella de Santa Giustina all 7 Ottobre / ottava quella de Santa Maria della Salute XXI Novembre.

38 For the most recent account and presentation of the cerimoniali of San Marco see Cattin, *Musica e liturgia a San Marco*, 1: 88–90, and J. H. Moore, "Bartolomeo Bonifacio's Rituum Ecclesiasticorum Ceremoniale. Continuity of Tradition in the Ceremonial of St. Mark's Venice," in M. Honegger-Ch. Meyer, ed., *La Musique et le rite sacré et profane. Actes du XIIIe congrès de la Société Internationale de Musicologie, Strasbourg 1982*, (Strasbourg, 1986), 2: 365–408.

39 Similar reasoning must govern another occasion described in the ceremonial of Bartolomeo Bonifacio (c. 14v):

> De tribus diebus Rogationum . . . cantato a cantoribus *Spiritus Sancte Deus miserere* (?) *nobis* litaniarum exeant ax sacrario quatuor intorticia [= torches or candles] in hastis, et crux inter quatuor ceres argenteos et intrent chorum, et facta ab omnibus reverentia coram altari portitores intorticiorum b[h?]astatorum procedant usque ad portam chori et ibi se addirment, remanente cruce cum cereis argentis ante altare in medio chori. Et decantato Sancte Marce letaniam procedatur et fiat processio. Via processionis sit ut in primis domenicis mensium, et in diebus mercurii.

40 Gattinoni, *Campanile*, 260–61.

41 Martin Schulz, "Die Nicopea in San Marco. Zur Geschichte und zum Typ einer Ikone," *Byzantinische Zeitschrift* 91 (1998): 475–501; Chryssa Maltezou, "Βενετία καί Βυζαντινή Παράδοση. Ἡ εἰκόνα τῆς Παναγίας Νικοποιοῦ (Venice and Byzantine tradition. The icon of the Virgin Nikopoios)," in *Symmeikta* 9 (1994) *Μνήμην Δ. Α. Ζακυθηνοῦ*, vol. 2: 7–20; and A. Rizzi, "Un'icona costantinopolitana del XII secolo a Venezia. La Madonna Nicopeia," *Thesaurismata* 17 (1980): 290–306. For earlier works referring to the miraculous icons in Venice, see Giovanni Tiepolo, *Trattato della Immagine della Gloriosa Vergine dipinta da S. Luca conservata già molti secoli nella Ducal Chiesa di S. Marco della città di Venezia* (Venice, 1618); Carlo Querini, *Relazione dell'Imagine Nicopea che si ritrova in Venezia nella Ducale di S. Marco* (Venice, 1645); F. Cornaro, *Venezia favorita da Maria. Relazione delle imagini miracolose di Maria conservate in Venezia* (Padua, 1758); Agostino Molin, *Dell'antticha immagine di Maria Santissima che si conserva nella basilica di San*

Marco in Venezia (Venice, 1821); and Giovanni Veludo, *Imagine della Madonna di S. Marco. Monumento bizantino illustrato da Giovanni Veludo* (Venice, 1887).

42 The icon is not reported among the sacred objects that survived the fire of 1231. See Rona Goffen, "Icon and Vision. Giovanni Bellini's Half-Length Madonnas," *Art Bulletin* 57 (1975): 508–9, and R. Gallo, *Il Tesoro di S. Marco e la sua storia* (Venice, 1967), 145.

43 The association of the icon with Saint Luke is first reported in the fifteenth century; see Goffen, "Icon and Vision," 508–9. R. Gallo suggests that the right hand of Christ has been retouched to make the sign of benediction according to the Latin rite; see Gallo, *Tesoro*, 145.

44 Molin, *Dell'antica immagine*, 2.

45 Belting, *Likeness and Presence*, 47–77.

46 The procession involving the Virgin Nikopoios is first reported in 1500 by Marino Sanuto but was probably instituted much earlier. See R. Fulin et al., eds., *I Diarii di Marino Sanuto (MCCCCXCVI–MDXXXIII) dall'autografo marciano ital. cl. VII codd. CDXIX–CDXXVII* (Venice, 1879–1903), III, col. 632; and Rona Goffen, *Piety and Patronage in Renaissance Venice. Bellini, Titian and the Franciscans* (New Haven and London, 1986), 142. The text of Sanudo reads, "Fo fato la procession atorno la piaza, e il patriarcha cantò la messa, e fo portà una nostra Dona atorno, si dice fata di man de San Luca."

47 Molin, *Dell'antica immagine*, 21.

48 ASV, Collegio Cerimoniale, vol. 2, f. 70r.

49 See D. Canal, *Brevi Cenni sopra la prodigiosa immagine di Maria vergine che si venera nella Basilica di San Marco in Venezia* (Venice, 1833); and *Litaniae secundum consuetudinem ducalis Ecclesiae Sancti Marci Venetiarum* (Venice, 1715).

50 Ibid., 285.

51 Goffen, *Piety and Patronage*, 139–42. All the ceremonies when the doge left the palace to follow Mass or another festivity are listed in an anonymous pamphlet preserved in the Library of the Museo Civico Correr in Venice, Op. P. D. 71, *Feste di palazo ne' quali sua serenità esce di quello con privilegio.* Per Giovanni Pietro Pinelli Stampator Ducale.

52 In 1589 and again in 1618 the icon was moved from the sacristy to the altar of St. Isidore – where it still stands today – for greater visibility. See J. H. Moore, "Venezia favorita da Maria. Music for the Madonna Nicopeia and Sancta Maria della Salute," *Journal of the American Musicological Society* 37 (1984): 304.

53 Sinding-Larsen, *Christ in the Council Hall*, 184, n. 1.

54 Moore, "Venezia favorita da Maria," 311, from Bartolomeo Bonifacio, *Rituum ecclesiasticorum ceremoniale* (1564).

55 According to Cattin, *Musica e liturgia a San Marco*, 1: 33, this act changed dramatically the nature of the ceremonial in San Marco in terms of quality. Unfortunately the codex of Moro has not been identified.

56 Susan Rankin, "From Liturgical Ceremony to Public Ritual. 'Quem Queritis' at St. Mark's, Venice," in Giulio Cattin, ed., *Da Bizanzio a San Marco. Musica e Liturgia* (Venice, 1997), 171–73. The chant does not exist in an isolated form in the Roman liturgy.

57 Although it is not clear when the myth of Venice's foundation was first elaborated, the day of the Annunciation was significant to the Venetians for several reasons: it was the day of the conception of Christ (thus, the beginning of the Christian era), it was connected with the founding of Rome, it was the beginning of spring, and it also marked the beginning of the Venetian calendar year. See Muir, *Civic Ceremonial*, 70–71; Dale, "Inventing a Sacred Past," 98; and Jacoff, *Horses of San Marco*, 52, n. 15. For the special devotion of the Venetians to the Virgin, see G. Musolino, "Culto Mariano," in Tramontin (see n. 26), 239–74; and Goffen, *Piety and Patronage*, 138–54.

58 Moore, "Venezia favorita da Maria," 322. For an account of the erection of the church by Longhena see Andrew Hopkins, "Plans and Planning for S. Maria della Salute, Venice," *Art Bulletin* 79 (1997): 440–65, esp. 443.

59 *Il Tempio della Salute eretto per voto della Repubblica Veneta, 26 Ottobre 1630* (Venice, 1930), 326.

60 Alberto Rizzi, "Le Icone bizantine e post-bizantine delle chiese veneziane," *Thesaurismata* 9 (1972): 255. There were four other Byzantine icons in the area: a paleologan Nikopoios in the treasury of San Marco; the Artokosta, which came from the cathedral of Mistra in the Morea in 1541 and is now in San Samuele; the Madonna della Pace in the Dominican monastery of SS. Giovanni e Paolo (this icon was that before which St. John of Damascus prayed; it was taken from Constantinople in 1349); and a fragment of a Hodegetria icon in the museum of Torcello.

61 Ennio Concina, "Venezia e l'icona," in *Venezia e Creta*, 530–38.

62 Cornaro, *Venezia favorita da Maria*, 30–31.

63 M. Cattapan, "Nuovi Documenti riguardanto pittori cretesi dal 1300 al 1500," in *Pepragmena tou B' Diethnous Kretologikou Synedriou* 3: 29, (Athens, 1968) and Sergio Bettini, *La Pittura di icone cretese-veneziana e i Madonneri* (Padua, 1933), 20–21.

64 Victor Lasareff, "Saggi sulla pittura veneziana dei secoli XIII–XIV. La maniera greca e il problema della scuola cretese," *Arte Veneta* 20 (1966): 43–46. See more recently the illuminating study of Anne Derbes, *Painting the Passion in Late Medieval Italy. Narrative Painting, Franciscan Ideologies, and the Levant* (Cambridge, New York, Melbourne, 1996), who argues for a rich and complex web of associations between the arts of Italy and the Levant/Byzantium in the thirteenth century.

65 More than 120 painters lived in Crete in the second half of the fifteenth century. See M. Muraro, "Varie fasi di influenza," *Thesaurismata* 9 (1972): 199–200.

66 Bettini, *La Pittura di icone cretese-veneziana*, 2–5.

67 Mario Cattapan, "Nuovi Elenchi e documenti dei pittori in Creta dal 1300 al 1500," *Thesaurismata* 9 (1972): 202–35.

68 Robin Cormack, *Painting the Soul. Icons, Death Masks, and Shrouds* (London, 1997), 215.

69 M. Muraro, "Varie fasi di influenza," *Thesaurismata* 9 (1972): 199–200.

70 See Lasareff, "Saggi sulla pittura veneziana," 48–49, for additional reasons that may have prompted people in Italy to acquire such objects.

71 Myrtali Acheimastou-Potamianou, *From Byzantium to El Greco. Greek Frescoes and Icons* (Athens, 1987), 179–80, pl. 46.

72 H. Belting, "Die Reaktion der Kunst des 13. Jahrhunderts auf den Import von Reliquien und Ikonen," in *Il Medio Oriente e l'Occidente nell'arte del XIII secolo* (Bologna, 1973), 42; and M. Chatzidakis, "La Peinture dei 'madonneri' ou 'vénéto-crétoise' et sa destination," in *Venezia centro di mediazione tra oriente e occidente (secoli XV–XVI)* (Florence, 1977), 2: 673–90. From a technical point of view the dark skin was a result of use of a dark green basis meant to create a corporeal illusion.

73 Cormack, *Painting the Soul*, 167–217.

74 Cattapan, "Nuovi Elenchi e documenti," 211–13.

75 Benjamin Ravid, "The Jewish Mercantile Settlement of 12th and 13th Century Venice. Reality or Conjecture?" *Association for the Jewish Studies Review* 2 (1977): 201–25, has shown that the two documents upon which this assumption was based were wrongly thought to have originated in Venice in this period. For a detailed account of Jewish presence in Venice see also B. Ravid, "The Legal Status of the Jews in Venice to 1509," *Proceedings of the American Association for Jewish Research* 54 (1987): 169–202.

76 Ravid, "Jewish Mercantile Settlement," 210.
77 Ariel Toaff, "Ghetto," in *Enciclopedia delle Scienze Sociali*, vol. 4 (Rome, 1994): 285, and S. W. Baron, *A Social and Religious History of the Jews* 9 (New York, 1965), 24–36.
78 For a concise treatment of the topic see Joshua Starr, *The Jews in the Byzantine Empire, 641–1204* (Athens, 1939), and *The Itinerary of Benjamin of Tudela. Travels in the Middle Ages;* intro. by Michael A. Signer, 1983, Marcus Nathan Adler, 1907, A. Asher, 1840 (Malibu, Calif.: 1983).
79 Starr, *The Jews of the Byzantine Empire*, 97.
80 Ibid., 23 and 144. The *Basilics* further stated that mixed marriages entailed the loss of power of litigation.
81 Ibid., 231.
82 Ibid., 24.
83 Starr, *Jews in the Byzantine Empire*, 43. Benjamin estimated that Thebes was populated by two thousand Jewish people, who worked in the silk industry.
84 D. Jacoby, "Les Quartiers juifs de Constantinople à l'épogue byzantine," *Byzantion* 37 (1967): 194. The Jewish quarter at Pera was raided by the crusaders and in 1261 the emperor Michael gave the area to the Genoese.
85 Ibid., 190.
86 Andrew Sharf, *Byzantine Jewry from Justinian to the Fourth Crusade* (New York, 1971), 16.
87 R. J. Moore, *The Formation of a Persecuting Society. Power and Deviance in Western Europe, 950–1250* (Oxford, 1987), 7. Moore studies the similar forms of persecution that were established for heretics, lepers, and Jews.
88 D. Jacoby, "Les Juifs à Venise du XIVe au XVe siècle," in *Venezia centro di mediazione*, 174.
89 D. Jacoby, "Venice and Venetian Jews in the Eastern Mediterranean," in G. Cozzi, ed., *Gli Ebrei a venezia, Secoli XIV–XVIII* (Milan, 1987), 34.
90 Jacoby, "Les Juifs à Venise," 179.
91 See also Jacoby, "Venice and Venetian Jews," 39.
92 Riccardo Calimani, *Ghetto of Venice* (New York, 1987), 9, and E. Ashtor, "Gli Inizi della comunità ebraica a Venezia," *Rassegna Mensile di Israel* 44 (1978): 689–90.
93 Noiret, *Documents inédits*, 297–98.
94 Ravid, "Legal Status of the Jews," 174–79.
95 R. Müller, "Les Prêteurs juifs de Venise au Moyen Age," *Annales* 30 (1975): 1291–94.
96 Jacoby, "Les Juifs à Venise," 167.
97 The yellow badge was inspired by the decisions of the Fourth Lateran Council of 1215. See Ravid, "Legal Status of the Jews," 180–81. This legislation was extended to women in 1443, as well as to pimps and prostitutes in 1416.
98 Ibid., 184.
99 Calimani, *Ghetto*, 29. As for the origin of the term *ghetto*, which appears for the first time in 1516, it is probably due to the existence of foundries in the area and derives from the Italian verb *gettare*, which means to pour or to cast; see B. Ravid, "The Religious, Economic and Social Background and Context of the Establishment of the Ghetti of Venice," in, *Gli Ebrei a Venezia*, 218.
100 Ennio Concina, *La Città degli Ebrei. Il ghetto di Venezia. Architettura e urbanistica* (Venice, 1991), and Brian Pullan, *Jews of Europe and the Inquisition of Venice, 1550–1670* (Oxford, 1983), 156.
101 Ravid, "Religious, Economic and Social Background," 219–25.
102 Jacoby, "Les Juifs à Venise," 210.
103 Pullan, *Jews of Europe and the Inquisition of Venice*, 153. In fact, since 1464 there were some provisions allowing the small Jewish community of Venice to worship in the houses that they rented as long as the congregation was not larger than ten people; see Ravid, "The Legal Status of the Jews," 188.

104 Pullan, *Jews of Europe and the Inquisition of Venice*, 22.

105 Ravid, "Religious, Economic and Social Background," 224.

106 The bell was specified as the *marangona*. See Calimani, *Ghetto*, 33, and Benjamin Ravid, "Curfew Time in the Ghetto of Venice," in Ellen E. Kittell and Thomas F. Madden, eds., *Medieval and Renaissance Venice* (Urbana, Ill., and Chicago, 1999), 241–42.

107 Under Doge Pietro Orseolo (991–1008) Venice had proudly proclaimed herself the "daughter of Byzantium." See G. Perocco, "Venice and the Treasury of San Marco," in Buckton, *Treasury*, 18.

108 Nicol, *Byzantium and Venice*, 178–79, and Sandra Origone, *Bisanzio e Genova* (Genova, 1992), 119–120. The treaty of Nymphaion, which Michael had signed with Genoa in 1261, awarded the Genoese estates in all major port cities of Byzantium including the Venetian colonies of Crete and Negroponte, which had to be reconquered from the Venetians.

109 Demus, *Mosaic Decoration*, 6. Work continued throughout the thirteenth century and even as late as 1308 mosaicists were employed for San Marco.

110 On the triumphant symbolism of the horses for Venice, see Perry, "Saint Mark's Trophies," 104–18; G. Perocco, "The Horses of San Marco in Venice," in *The Horses of San Marco, Venice*, 59; R. Padoan, "The Basilica, the Horses and Piazza San Marco," in *The Horses of San Marco, Venice*, 125; Galliazzo, *Cavalli*, 76–77; and U. Schulze, "Triumph und Apokalypse. Anfänge venezianischer Herrschafts- und Rechtsikonographie," *Marburger Jahrbuch für Kunstwissenschaft* 22 (1989): 186–87.

Conclusion: Crete and Venice

1 "For the enemies were beaten, taken, cut into pieces, chasen away, the citizens returned to freedom, the cities succumbed, Crete was once again under the earlier [Venetian] yoke, the victorious arms were laid down, the war ended without bloodshed, and glory and peace were attained in a treaty," from Petrarch, *Senilium Rerum Libri*, IV, 3, ed. Guido Martelloti (Torino, 1976), 54. These lines come from a letter of Petrarch to Pietro, rector of Bologna, where the author describes the festivities undertaken in Venice to celebrate the suppression of the rebellion of 1363 in Crete.

2 Letter of Marino Sanudo Torsello to Bertrand, cardinal bishop of Ostia and Velletri; passage translated in K. M. Setton, chap. IX, *The Cambridge Medieval History*, vol. 4, 2d ed., pt. 1 (Cambridge, 1966), 58, n. 2.

3 David Jacoby, "Cretan Cheese. A Neglected Aspect of Venetian Medieval Trade," in Ellen E. Kitten and Thomas F. Madden, eds., *Medieval and Renaissance Venice* (Urbana, Ill., and Chicago, 1999), 49–68.

4 Maria Georgopoulou, "Private Residences in Venetian Candia (Thirteenth to Fifteenth Centuries)," *Thesaurismata* 30 (in press).

5 Borsari, *Dominio veneziano a Creta nel XIII secolo* (Naples, 1963), 96–97. Unfortunately, family name is not always sufficient to indicate the ethnic background of an individual. In some instances, however, a case based on additional textual evidence, e.g. connection with an Orthodox or Catholic church, can be made.

6 Ibid., 99–101.

7 McKee, "Households in Fourteenth-Century Venetian Crete," *Speculum* 70 (1995): 27–67.

8 Mixed marriages between Latin fiefholders and Greeks were forbidden by law in the thirteenth century. The first concession in this regard was made in 1272; it was revoked in 1293. The need for the authorities to regulate the situation shows that intermarriages had occurred in the thirteenth century, as the Greek names of the wives of some feudal lords also attest. The inclu-

sion of a clause allowing mixed marriages in the 1299 treaty concluding the rebellion of Calergis indicates that this practice had been going on before the end of the century. See A. E. Laiou, "Venetians and Byzantines. Investigation of Forms of Contact in the Fourteenth Century," *Thesaurismata* 22 (1992): 33 and 36; and McKee, "Uncommon Dominion. The Latins and Greeks of Venetian Crete in the 14th Century," Ph.D. Diss., (University of Toronto, 1992), 113–14.

9 Sathas, *Documents inédits relatifs à l'histoire de la Grèce*, 4: 6–7.

10 Laiou, "Observations on the Results of the Fourth Crusade; Greeks and Latins in Port and Market," *Medievalia et Humanistica* 12 (1984): 54, discusses the 1331 will of the Venetian notary Stephano Bon, who was married to a Greek woman. This instance is not unique in Venetian Crete; nor it is reserved for people who had married a Greek woman. To cite just one famous example of a similar act of devotion to Latin and Orthodox churches, the testament of the Venetian nobleman Andrea Cornaro in the seventeenth century makes bequests to the major churches of Candia without distinguishing between their doctrinal differences; see John K. Mauromatis, " Ἑλληνικά ἔγγραφα (Δωρητήριο καί Διαθῆκες) τῆς μητέρας, τῆς κόρης καί τῆς ἐγγονῆς τοῦ Βιτσέντζου Ἰακ. Κορνάρου" (Greek documents – Donation and Testaments – of the mother, the daughter and the granddaughter of Vicenzo Jac. Cornaro)," *Thesaurismata* 16 (1979): 211.

11 On the persistence of Greek terms in agriculture and for the cultural significance of language see Dimitris Tsougarakis, "Cultural Assimilation through Language Infiltration. Some Early Examples from Venetian Crete," in Claudia Rapp et al., eds., *Bosphorus. Essays in Honor of Cyril Mango [Byzantinische Forschungen]* 21 (1995): 187–91.

12 The autobiographical poems of two Greek-speaking poets who grew up in Candia, Leonardo della Porta and Stephanus Saclichi, assert this fact; see Antonino Pertusi, "Leonzio Pilato a Creta prima del 1358–1359. Scuole e cultura a Creta durante il secolo XIV," *Kretika Chronika* 15–16/2 (1961–62): 370–80, and A. F. Van Gemert, "Ὁ Στέφανος Σαχλίκης καί ἡ ἐποχή του (Stephanus Saclichi and his era)," *Thesaurismata 17* (1980): 41. Greek was also taught by monks and Greek clergymen who were employed as tutors. A school was located in the center of town near the *ruga magistra*.

13 The text was published by Richard M. Dawkins, "Κρητική Ἀποκάλυψις τῆς Παναγίας (Cretan Apocalypse of the Virgin)," *Kretika Chronika* 2 (1948): 487–500. The popularity of this text is evident in its connections with some of the frescoes of the Last Judgment in churches of Crete.

14 Chryssa Maltezou, "Βενετική μόδα στήν Κρήτη. Τά φορέματα μιᾶς Καλλεργοπούλας (Venetian fashion in Crete. The clothes of a Calergis woman)," in *Byzantium. Tribute to Andreas N. Stratos*, vol. 1 (Athens, 1986), 140–47.

15 Sathas, *Documents inédits relatifs à l'histoire de la Grèce*, 4: 6

16 This information is contained in a letter that Pope Callixtus III sent to the inquisitor Simone de Candia in 1452. See G. Hofmann, "Papst Kalixt III. und die Frage der Kircheneinheit im Osten," *Miscellanea Giovanni Mercati* III (1946): 213.

17 "Bis saltem in anno publice in ecclesiis, cathedrali vel Sancti Marci, . . . legi fecere decretum prefati synodi; privatim vero in ecclesiis suis idem protopapas et reliqui catholici prima domenica singulis mensis . . . illud legant populo"; cf. G. Hofmann, "Wie stand es mit der Frage der Kirchenheit auf Kreta in XV Jahrhundert?" *Orientalia christiana periodica* 10 (1944): 96. On the disagreement of the Greek clergy of Crete with the decisions of the Synod

of Ferrara-Florence see N. Tomadakis, "Μιχαήλ Καλοφρενᾶς Κρής, Μητροφάνης Β′ και ἡ πρός τήν ἕνωσιν τῆς Φλωρεντίας ἀντίθεσις τῶν Κρητῶν (Michael Kalofrenas of Crete, Metrofanes II and their opposition to the Union of Florence)," *Epeteris Hetaireias Byzantinon Spoudon* 21 (1951): 110–44.

18 Zacharias N. Tsirpanlis, *Τό κληροδότημα τοῦ Καρδιναλίου Βησσαρίωνος γιά τούς φιλενωτικούς τῆς Βενετοκρατούμενης Κρήτης (1439–17ος αἰ.)* (The bequest of Cardinal Bessarion for the unionists of Venetian Crete [1439–17th c.]) (Thessaloniki, 1967), passim.

19 Maria Vassilakis-Maurakakis, "Western Influences on the 14th Century Art of Crete," *Jahrbuch der Österreichischen Byzantinis ik* 32/5 (1982): 307, fig. 2.

20 Van Gemert, "Stephanus Saclichi," 68. Although Saclichi does not seem to make any distinction between the Greek and Latin rites and there is a strong possibility that he himself was brought up according to the Catholic faith, the evidence from his poem points to the fact that the clergy in general was not very highly regarded among the population of the city. The evidence remains, however, that there was only one *papas* among the customers of the brothel, thus arguing for a stronger mistrust of the Latin clergy.

21 This famous revolt has spurred extensive studies. See most recently Sally McKee, "The Revolt of St. Tito in Fourteenth-Century Venetian Crete. A Reassessment," *Mediterranean Historical Review* (1994); J. Jegerlehner, "Der Aufstand der kandiotischen Ritterschaft gegen das Mutterland Venedig (1363–65)," *Byzantinische Zeitschrift* 12 (1903): 78–125; Agathangelos Xerouchakis, *Ἡ ἐν Κρήτῃ ἐπανάστασις τοῦ 1363–1366 καί τό διοικητικόν σύστημα τῆς Βενετίας ἀπέναντι τῶν κοινωνικῶν τάξεων καί τῆς Ἐκκλησίας κατά τήν μακράν περίοδον τῆς ἐν τῇ νήσῳ κυριαρχίας αὐτῆς* (1211–1669) (The Cretan rebellion of 1363–1366 and the administrative system of Venice in relation to the social classes and the church during the long period of Venetian domination [1211–1669]) (Alexandria, 1932); Sophia Antoniadis, "Ὁ χρονογράφος Zancaruolo καί ἡ ἐπανάσταση τοῦ 1363 (The chronicler Zancaruolo and the revolt of 1363)," *Kretika Chronika* 15–16/2 (1961–62): 353–62; eadem, *Il cronista Zancaruolo e gli avvenimenti cretesi del 1363* (Herakleion, 1963); S. Romanin, *Storia documentata di Venezia*, (Venice, 1855), 3: 217–27; and Xanthoudides, *Venetian rule on Crete*, 81–98.

22 Lorenzo de Monacis, *Chronicon de rebus venetis* (Venice, 1758), book 10, 184.

23 Chryssa Maltezou, "Byzantine Legends in Venetian Crete," in I. Sevcenko and I. Hutter, eds., *Aetos: Studies in Honour of Cyril Mango Presented to him on April 14, 1998* (Stuttgart and Leipzig, 1998), 233.

24 Steven B. Bowman, *The Jews of Byzantium 1204–1453* (University Ala., 1985), 341–343, and Avi Sharon in *Dialogos: Hellenic Studies Review* 6 (1999): 43–46.

25 Michel de Certeau, *The Practice of Everyday Life* (Berkeley, 1984), 37.

26 Eva Tea, "Saggio sulla storia religiosa di Candia dal 1590 al 1630," *Atti del Reale Istituto Veneto di Scienze, Lettere ed Arti* 72, no. 2 (1992–13): 1377.

27 Mauromatis, "Greek documents," 206–54, has published the testaments of three female members of an important Venetian family, the Cornaros. All three wills were written in Greek, indicating that at least the women of the family felt more comfortable with Greek than with Italian.

28 Marco Petta, "Documenti di storia ecclesiastica retativi agli ultimi anmi del dominio veneto a Creta conservati nell'Archivio della S. Congregazione di Propaganda Fide," in *Pepragmena tou B′ Diethnous Kretologikou Synedriou*, 3 (Athens, 1968), 213.

29 Mauromatis, "Greek documents," 208–9. All this reminds us of the realities of immigration today.

30 P. L. Vocotopoulos, "Τό λάβαρο τοῦ Φραγκίσκου Μοροζίνη (The Standard of Francesco Morosini)," *Thesaurismata* 18 (1981): 273–74.

31 On the Hagioi Deka see Theochares Detorakes, *Ἱστορία τῆς Κρήτης* (History of Crete) (Athens, 1986), 126.

32 This proud declaration of submission to the glory of Byzantium was proffered at the time of Doge Pietro Orseolo (991–1008). See G. Perocco, "Venice and the Treasury of San Marco," in D. Buckton, ed., *The Horses of San Marco, Venice* (Milan, 1984), 18.

SELECTED BIBLIOGRAPHY

Manuscript Sources

Archivio di Stato, Venice. Collegio Cerimoniale 1.

Compilazione Leggi. Busta 109: Candia.

Consultori in Jure, filza 403, pp. 63ff. (census of 1548); filza 482 (census of 1637).

Duca di Candia.

Notai di Candia.

Procuratia di Supra. Chiesa, busta 142: Diocesi di Candia.

Provveditori alle Fortezze. Busta 11, Rodolo IV; Busta 43, Rodolo II.

Trevisan, Nicolò. "Provveditori di Candia." Miscellanea codici N. 728. Mis. cose Venete, vol. I, N. 3.

Biblioteca Marciana, Venice. "Monumenta historica quae ad Cretam insulam se referunt o Monumenta historica Insulae Cretensis a Saec. XIII ad saec. XVI." Lat. X, 158 (3749).

"Relazione Ambascerie de feudati di Candia (1304–1619) [18th century]." Ital. VII, 1750 (8773).

Calergi, Antonio. "Commentarii delle cose fatte dentro e fuori del Regno di Candia, scritti da Antonio Callergi, gentilhuomo veneziano." Ital. VI, n. 155 (coll. 5801).

Castrofilaca, "Descrizione del regno di Candia [copy of 1583]." Ital VI, 156 (coll. 6005).

Corner, Andrea. "Historia Candiana." Ital. VI, 286 (5985). Also Ital. VI, 154, 177, 183, 286, 287.

Cornaro, Andrea. "Descrizione di Candia." Ital. VI 350 (5752).

Muazzo, G. A. "Cronica delle famiglie nobili venete che abitarono il regno di Candia." Ital. VII, 124 (coll. 7421), and Ital. Cl. VII, 196 (coll. 8578).

Muazzo, Antonio. "Chronika di Candia de 1204–1363 [16th century]." Ital VI, 339 (5992).

"Commissio Ducalis sub Duce Venetiarum Leonardo Lauredano data Paulo Antonio Miani Ducha Cretae designato. Codex est ornatus pictura affabre delineato [16th century]." Lat. X, 234 (3849).

"Chronicon Venetum ad 1360." Lat X, 36 (3326).

Gatto, Benetto. "Descrizione dell'isola di Candia." Ital. VII, 569 (coll. 7946).

"Descrizione del territorio di Canea & Descrizione dell'isola di Candia." Ital. VII, 363 (coll. 7873).

Trivan, Antonio. "Racconto di varie cose occorse nel Regno di Candia dall'anno 1182 sino al 1669 di Antonio Trivan notaro ducale in Venezia." Ital. VII, 525 (7497).

"Chronica Venetiarum [14th century]." Lat. X, 36 (coll. 3326).

"Descrizione dell'isola di Candia [17th century]." Ital. VI, 340 (5760).

Trevisan, Nicolò. "Cronaca veneta [ca. 1585]." Ital VII, 519 (8438).

"Candia Miscellanea [17th century]." Ital. VII, 1188 (9571).

Houghton Library, Harvard University. "Miscellanea di Candia (1523–1680)." Library of Count Riant, Ms. 53.

Museo Civico Correr, Venice. MS. Correr, B. 1210, Candia 2679 (cc. 39v-41v); Candia 2682 (c. 116r).

Archivio Morosini-Grimani, b. 568/54, N3. "Solenità et Cerimonie che si costumano nella città di Candia, 1595"; b. 568/5. Un libro in quarto senza cartoni delle cause che s'aspetta uno alla giudicatura di S. Duca . . . [17th century]."

Cod. Cicogna, no. 2525/43, "Guerra di Candia;" no. 2855/XXXIII, "Descrizione delle città di Candia, 16th century;" no. 3612, Avogaria di Comun, Memorie antiche di Candia; no. 3662. "Duchi di Candia. Elenco." (IV.253).

Miscellanea Correr, busta 1211, no. 2703; no. 2708. "Ordini fatte nel Regno di Candia dall'Illustrissimo et Eccellentissimo Signor Giacomo Foscarini Provveditor Generale et Inquisitor . . ."

Miscellanea P. D. no. 350.c (4). "Candia. Vendita di oggetti sacri di alcune chiese e Monasteri per sopperire alle spese per la guerra di Candia;" no. 581 e/c 151: Porto di Candia. Notizie; no. 581e/cc.173. "Cenni storici sulla organizzazione della "colonia" di Candia;" no. 601, c/1 659: "Candia. Chiesa;" no. 675: Part of the Calergi Archives.

Ms. Morosini 380. "Commissione Morosini."

MSS. Mocenigo: "Candia."

MSS. PD. C. 2759/VIII. "Chiesa Metropolita di Candia (copy of text of 1323, 26.VIII)" [typewritten copy from Mss. P.D. C.675/V(I)].

Op. P.D. 71. Anonymous pamphlet, "Feste di palazzo et giorni ne' quali sua serenità esce di quello [1656–1727]."

Querini-Stampalia Foundation, Venice. Baseglio, Girolamo. "Insulario di . . . detto Marafon padron di nave . . . anno Domini MDCXLV." Cl. III, B4, Cod. 14 (162), 1645.

"Portolano fatto dal meglior marinaro che naviga alli nostri tempi et refinato da Silvestro Querini adi primo Decembre MDCXII." Cl. III, B4, Cod. 7 (657), 17th century.

"Portulano nel quale si descrivono tutte le Città, Terre, Castelli, e Porti Marittimi di tutta l'Europa, con tutti li suoi Mari, e lori Fondo, Isole e Secche, e Mostrando parte dell'Africa e dell'Asia. In Cività Vecchia l'ANNO M.DC.LXVI." Cl. III, B2. cod. XVI (1305), 1666.

"Memorie e documenti storici riguardanti l'acquisto e il possesso di Candia." Ms., cl. IV. cod. 190 (817), fos. 1–30.

Published Primary Sources

Artom, E. S., and H.M.D. Cassuto, eds. *Statuta Judaeorum Candiae eorumque memorabilia (Takkanot Candia)* (In Hebrew). Jerusalem, 1943.

Barbaro, Ermolao. *Legislazione Veneta. I Capitolari di Candia*. Venice, 1940.

Buondelmonti, Cristoforo. *Florentini Librum Insularum Archipelagi*, ed. De Sinner. Leipzig and Berlin.

Descriptio Insule Crete et liber insularum, Cap. XI: Creta, édition critique par Marie-Anne Van Spitael. Herakleion, 1981.

Canal, Martin da. "La Chronique des Veneciens, des origines à 1275." *Archivio Storico Italiano* 8 (1972): 231–766.

"Les estoires de Venise: Cronaca veneziana in lingua francese dalle origini al 1275," ed. Alberto Limentani. *Civiltà Veneziana Fonti e Testi*, 3rd ser., 12. Florence 1972, 247–63.

Carbone, S., ed. *Pietro Pizolo notaio in Candia*, 2 vols. Venice, 1978.

Çelebi, Evliya. *Seyahatnamet*, bk. 7, 383; bk. 8, 300. Istanbul, 1928.

Cervellini, Gianbattista. *Documento inedito Veneto-Cretese del Dugento*. Padova, 1906.

Cessi, Roberto, ed. *Gli statuti veneziani di Jacopo Tiepolo del 1242 e le loro glosse*. Memorie del Reale Istituto Veneto di Scienze, Lettere ed Arti, vol. 30, no. 2. Venice, 1938.

Cessi, Roberto, ed. *Deliberazioni del Maggior Consiglio di Venezia*. 3 vols. R. Accademia dei Lincei, Atti delle Assemblee Costituzionali Italiane del Medio Evo al 1831, Serie terza. Parlamenti e Consigli Maggiori dei Comuni Italiani, sezione prima. Bologna, anast. repr. 1970–71.

Cessi, Roberto, and P. Sambin, ed. *Le deliberazioni del Consiglio dei Rogati (Senato), serie "Mixtorum", libri I–XIV*. Venice, 1960.

Cessi, Roberto, and Mario Brunetti, eds. *Le deliberazioni del Consiglio dei Rogati (Senato) serie "Mixtorum," Libri XV–XVI (1332–35)*. Venice, 1961.

Corner Flaminio. *Creta sacra seu de episcopis utriusque ritus graeci et latini in insula Cretae*, 2 vols. Venice, 1755.

Ecclesiae Venetae et Torcellanae antiquis monumentis illustratae, 18 vols. Venice, 1749.

Coronelli, Vincenzo. *Città, fortezze, isole e porti principali d'Europa*. Venice, 1689.

Isolario. Vol. 1. Venice, 1696.

Regno di Candia e Cipro. Venice, [1700].

Città Fortezze, Porti ed altri luoghi del Regno et Isola di Candia. Venice, 1706.

Dandolo, Fantinus (bishop of Padova and archbishop of Candia), *Hec est tabula huius libri et intitulatur Compendiu catholica fidei, etc. Incipit Compendium reverendissimi in christo patris et d. Domini Fantini Dandulo Archiepiscopo Cretesis pro catholice fidei istructione breve ac utile clericis et maxime presbiters pro animarum sallute circa eorum subditos etc.* by Mathias van der Goes. Antwerpen, 1485.

Danduli Andreae Chronicon, ed. Ettore Pastorello, in L. A. Muratori, ed., *Rerum Italicarum Scriptores* 12, cols. 1–524. Milan, 1728, repr. Bologna, 1941–49.

Diaconos, Theodosios. *Theodosii Diaconii de Creta Capta*, ed. Criscuolo. Leipzig, 1979.

Documenti ad res venetas et Levantis illustrantia, ed. la R. Deputazione di storia patria.

Douais, C. *Acta capitulorum provincialium O.F.P.* 1re province de Provence, Province romaine, Province d'Espagne. Toulouse, 1894.

Falkener, E. "La descrizione dell'isola di Candia. A Manuscript of the 16th century." In *The Museum of Classical Antiquities*. London, 1852–53, 263–308.

Gasparis, Charalambos, *Franciscus de Cruce. Νοτάριος στόν Χάνδακα, 1338–1339. Franciscus de Cruce. Notaio in Candia, 1338–1339.* Istituto Ellenico di Studi Bizantini e Postbizantini di Venezia, Graecolatinitas Nostra Fonti 1. Venice, 1999.

Gerland, Ernst. *Das Archiv des Herzogs von Kandia im Koenigl. Staatsarchiv zu Venedig*. Strasbourg, 1899.

Giomo, Giuseppe. *I "Misti" del Senato della Repubblica veneta, 1293–1331. Trascrizione dell'indice dei primi quattordici volumi perduti e Regesto di un frammento del primo volume* Venice, 1887, repr. Amsterdam, 1970.

Homann, Johann Baptist, 1663–1724. *Insula Creta hodie Candia* . . . Nürnberg, n.d.

Hopf, Karl. *Veneto-Byzantinische Analekten*. Vienna, 1859, repr. Amsterdam, 1964.

Hopf, Karl. ed. *Chroniques gréco-romanes inédites ou peu connues*. Berlin, 1893.

Lamansky, Vladimir. *Secrets d'Etat de Venise. Documents, extraits, notices et études servant à éclaircir les rapports de la seigneurie avec les grecs à la fin du XV et au XVI siècle*. St. Petersburg, 1884, repr. New York, 1968.

Lombardo, Antonino, ed. *Documenti della colonia veneziana di Creta*. Vol. 1. *Imbreviature di Pietro Scardon (1271)*. Turin, 1942.

Lombardo, Antonino, ed. *Le deliberazioni del Consiglio dei XL della Repubblica di Venezia*. 2 vols. Venice, 1957–67.

Lombardo, Antonino, ed. *Zaccaria de Fredo notaio in Candia (1352–1357)*. Venice, 1958.

Lombardo, Antonino, and M. Chiaudano, eds. *Leonardo Marcello, notaio in Candia (1278–1281)*. Venice, 1960.

Lombardo, Antonino, ed. *Nicola de Boateriis notaio in Famagosta e Venezia (1355–1356)*. Venice, 1973.

McKee, Sally, ed. *Wills from Late Medieval Crete*. 3 vols. Washington, D.C., 1997.

Marcello, Domenico. *Relazione di Domenico Marcello ritornato di consigliere di Candia delle cose di quel regno, 1574*, ed. Lorenzo Fracasso. Venice, 1858.

Meursius, Joannes, filius. *Maiestas Veneta, sive de serenissima Venetorum Reip. cum in Creta, tum in Cipro, titulo regio, bono iure vindicato, contra Anonymum dissertatio*. Lugduni Batavorum, 1640.

Creta, Cyprus, Rhodus. Amsterdam, 1675.

Miklosich, Franz, Ritter von and I. Müller eds. *Acta et diplomata graeca medii aevii sacra et profana*. 6 vols. Vienna, 1890.

Monacis, Lorenzo dei. *Chronikon de rebus venetis usque ad annum 1354*, ed. Fl. Corner. Venice, 1758.

Monticolo, Giovanni, and Enrico Besta, eds. *I Capitolari delle Arti Veneziane sottoposte alla Giustizia a poi alla Giustizia Vecchia, dalle origini al MCCCXXX*, 3 vols. Rome, 1896–1914.

Morosini, Andrea, "Degl'Istorici delle cose veneziane. Historiarum Venetarum." In *Collezione Istorie delle cose veneziane*. Vol. 6, book 12. Venice, 1719, 166–67.

Morozzo della Rocca, R., and A. Lombardo, eds. *Documenti del commercio veneziano nei secoli X–XIII*. Turin, 1940.

Morozzo della Rocca, R., ed, *Benvenuto di Brixano, notaio in Candia, 1301–1302*. Venice, 1950.

Morozzo della Rocca, R., ed. *Lettere di mercanti a Pignol Zucchello (1336–1350)*. Venice, 1957.

Nani Mocenigo, F. *Capitolare dei Signori di Notte*. Venice, 1877.

Noiret, Hippolyte. *Documents inédits pour servir à l'histoire de la domination vénitienne en Crète de 1380 à 1485, tirés des archives de Venise*. Paris, 1892.

One in the service of the Republique. *A Description of Candia in Its Ancient and Modern State*. London, 1670.

Piacenza, F. *L'Egeo redivivo ossia chorografia dell'Arcipelago di Candia e di Cipri*. Modena, 1688.

Predelli, R., ed. *I Libri commemoriali della Repubblica di Venezia, Regesti*, 8 vols. Venice, 1876–1914.

Querini, L. *Relazione dell'isola di Creta scritta da L. Querini nell'anno 1595 con note di Gaetano Casoni*. Florence, 1897.

Randolph, B. *The Present State of the Islands in the Archipelago Sea of Constantinople and Gulph of Smyrna with Other Islands of Candia and Rhodes*. Oxford, 1687.

Santschi, Elisabeth, ed. *Régestes des Arrêts Civils et des Mémoriaux (1363–1399) des Archives du Duc de Crète*. Bibliothèque de l'Institut Héllénique d'Études Byzantines et Post-byzantines de Venise 9. Venice, 1976.

Sanuto, Marino. *I Diarii (dall'autografo marciano IT. VII, 228–286 (coll. 9215, 9273)*. R. Fulin et al., eds. Venice, 1879–1902.

Sathas, Constantinos N. *Μεσαιωνική Βιβλιοθήκη* (Medieval library). 6 vols. Venice, 1872–94.

Documents inédits pour l'histoire de la Grèce au Moyen Age. 9 vols. Paris, 1880–90.

Scaffini, G. *Notizie intorno ai primi cento anni della dominazione veneta in Creta*. Alexandria, 1907.

Spanakis, Stergios, ed. *Μνημεῖα Κρητικῆς Ἱστορίας* (Monuments of Cretan history), 6 vols. Herakleion, 1970–76.

Stahl, Alan M., ed. *The Documents of Angelo de Cartura and Donato Fontanella: Venetian Notaries in Fourteenth-Century Crete* Washington, D.C., 2000.

Staurinides, Nikolaos S. *Μεταφράσεις Τουρκικῶν Ἱστορικῶν Ἐγγράφων ἀφορώντων εἰς τήν ἱστορίαν τῆς*

Κρήτης (Translations of Turkish historical documents related to the history of Crete), 6 vols. Herakleion, 1984–87.

Tafel, G. L. F. and G. M. Thomas. *Urkunden zur älteren Handels und Staatengeschichte der Republik Venedig mit besonderen Beziehungen auf Byzanz und die Levante.* Fontes Rerum austriacum 2. 3 vols. Vienna, 1856–57.

Theotokes, Spyridon M, ed. *Μνημεῖα τῆς Ἑλληνικῆς Ἱστορίας* (Monuments of Greek history). 2 vols. Athens, 1933–37.

"Τά καπιτουλάρια τῆς βενετοκρατουμένης Κρήτης 1298–1500 (The Capitolari of Venetian Crete 1298–1500)." *Epeteris Hetaireias Kretikon Spoudon* 4 (1941): 114–75.

Thiriet, Freddy, ed. *Regestes des délibérations du Sénat de Venise concernant la Romanie.* 3 vols. Documents et Recherches 1, 2, and 4. Paris, 1958–61.

ed. *Délibérations des Assemblées vénitiennes concernant la Romanie.* 2 vols. Documents et Recherches 8 and 11. Paris 1966–71.

ed. *Duca di Candia. Ducali e lettere ricevute (1358–60/1401–5).* Venice, 1978.

Thomas, L. F. *Die ältesten Verordungen der Venezianer für ausvärtige angelegenherten.* Munich, 1873.

Thomas, G. M. "Commission des Dogen Andreas Dandolo für die Insel Creta von Jahre 1350." *Abhandlungen der Bayerische Akademie der Wissenschaften*, J. Cl. XIV, Band I, Abt. n. 180. Munich, 1877.

ed *Diplomatarium veneto-levantinum*, 2 vols. Venice, 1880–99.

Val, P. du. *Descriptio de l'Isle de Candie.* Paris, 1657.

Vidulich-Ratti, Paola, ed. *Duca di Candia, Bandi (1313–1329).* Fonti per la storia di Venezia, ser. 1, Archivi Pubblici. Venice, 1965.

ed. *Duca di Candia. Quaternus Consiliorum 1340–1350.* Venice, 1976.

Villehardouin, Geoffroi de. *La Conquête de Constantinople*, ed. E. Faral, I. Paris, 1938.

Secondary Sources

Agoropoulou-Birbili, A. *Ἡ Ἀρχιτεκτονική τῆς πόλεως τῆς Κερκύρας κατά τήν περίοδο τῆς Ἑνετοκρατίας* (The Architecture of the city of Kerkyra during the period of Venetian rule). Athens, 1976.

Alexiou, Stylianos. *Ὁδηγός Ἱστορικοῦ Μουσείου Κρήτης* (Guide to the Historical Museum of Crete). Herakleion, 1953.

"Τό δουκικόν ἀνάκτορον τοῦ Χάνδακος" (The ducal palace of Candia). *Kretika Chronika* 14 (1960): 102–6.

"Τό Κάστρο τῆς Κρήτης καί ἡ ζωή του στόν ΙΣΤ' καί ΙΖ' αἰώνα (The Kastron of Crete and life therein in the 16th and 17th centuries)." *Kretika Chronika* 19 (1965): 146–78.

Alexiou, Stylianos, and Kostas Lassithiotakis. *Ἡ ἀποκατάστασις τοῦ ναοῦ τοῦ Ἁγίου Μάρκου τοῦ Χάνδακος* (The Restoration of the Church of St. Mark in Candia). Herakleion, 1958.

Ankori, Zvi. "Jews and the Jewish Community in the History of Medieval Crete." In *Pepragmena tou B' Diethnous Kretologikou Synedriou.* Vol. 3. Athens, 1968, 312–67.

"The Living and the Dead. The Story of Hebrew Inscriptions in Crete." *Proceedings of the American Academy of Jewish Research* 38–39 (1970–71): 1–100.

"From Zudecha to Yahudi Mahallesi. The Jewish Quarter of Candia in the Seventeenth Century." In *Salo Wittmayer Baron Jubilee Volume.* Vol. 1. Jerusalem, 1974, 63–127.

Antoniadis, Sophia. "Ὁ χρονογράφος Zancaruolo καί ἡ ἐπανάσταση τοῦ 1363 (The Chronicler Zancaruolo and the revolt of 1363)." *Kretika Chronika* 15–16/2 (1961–62): 353–62.

Il cronista Zancaruolo e gli avvenimenti cretesi del 1363. Herakleion, 1963.

Arbel, Benjamin. "The List of Able-Bodied Jews in the Cretan Town of Chaniá (Canea), 1536." In *Daniel Carpi Jubilee Vol-*

ume. A Collection of Studies in the History of the Jewish People Presented to Daniel Carpi upon his 70th Birthday by His Colleagues and Students. Tel-Aviv, 1996, 21–34.

"Colonie d'oltremare." In A. Tenenti and U. Tucci, eds. *Il Rinascimento Società ed economia.* Vol. 5, *Storia di Venezia delle origini alla caduta della Serenissima.* Rome, 1996, 947–85.

Arslan, Edoardo. *Gothic Architecture in Venice,* trans. Anne Engel. London, 1972.

Arslan, W. *Venezia gotica. L'architettura civile.* 2nd ed. Milan, 1986.

Ashtor, Eliyahu. "The Venetian Supremacy in Levantine Trade. Monopoly or Pre-Colonialism?" *Journal of European Economic History* 3, no. 1 (1974): 5–53.

Balard, Michel. *La Romanie Génoise (XIIe–début du XVe siècle),* 2 vols. Rome and Genova, 1978.

Balard, Michel, and Alain Ducellier, eds. *Coloniser au Moyen Age.* Paris, 1995.

Bandia, Katerina. " Ἡ βενετοκρητική συνθήκη τοῦ 1265. Διπλωματική ἔκδοση τοῦ κειμένου (The Veneto-Cretan treaty of 1265. Diplomatic edition of the text)." *Kretike Hestia* ser. D, 2 (1988): 102–35.

Berchet, Guglielmo. "Relazione della missione del Reale Istituto Veneto per la ricerca e lo studio dei monumenti veneziani nell'isola di Creta." *Atti del Reale Istituto Veneto di Scienze, Lettere ed Arti* 60 (1900): 63–69, 181–91.

Boerio, Giuseppe. *Dizionario del dialetto veneziano.* Venice, 1856, repr. Turin, 1967.

Bon, Antoine, *La Morée Franque. Recherches historiques, topographiques et archéologiques sur la principauté d'Achaie (1205–1430). Texte.* Bibliothèques des écoles françaises d'Athènes et de Rome vol. 213. Paris, 1969.

"Monuments vénitiens en Grèce centrale et dans le Peloponnèse jusqu'au 15e siècle." In A. Pertusi, ed., *Venezia e il Levante fino al secolo 15,* Vol. 2. Florence, 1974, 41–68.

Borboudakis, Manolis. "Δοκιμαστική ἀνασκαφή Ἁγ. Πέτρου τῶν Ἑνετῶν Ἡρακλείου (Test excavations in St. Peter of the Venetians in Herakleion)." *Archaiologikon Deltion* 23 (1968): 427–29.

" Ἡ βυζαντινή τέχνη ὥς τήν πρώϊμη βενετοκρατία (Byzantine art until the early Venetian rule)." In Nikolaos Panagiotakes, ed., *Κρήτη. Ἱστορία καί πολιτισμός* (Crete. History and Civilization). Vol. 2. Herakleion, 1988, 9–104.

ed. *Icons of Cretan Art. From Candia to Moscow to St. Petersburg.* Exhibition Catalogue, Herakleion, 1993.

Borgis, R. "Creta nel Duecento. Dai Commentari di A. Callergi cronista veneziano del sec. XVI." *Quaderni Medievali* 28 (1989): 37–68.

Borsari, Silvano. *Il Dominio veneziano a Creta nel XIII secolo.* Naples, 1963.

Studi sulle colonie veneziane in Romania nel XIII secolo. Naples, 1966.

Boschini, Marco. *La carta del navigar pitoresco.* 1613–78.

Bouras, Charalambos. "Βενετική Ἀρχιτεκτονική στήν Ἑλλάδα (Venetian architecture in Greece)." *Architektonika Themata* 4 (1970): 78–83.

Brown, Patricia Fortini. *Venice and Antiquity. The Venetian Sense of the Past.* New Haven, Conn., 1996.

Bury, J. B. "The Lombards and Venetians in Euboea." *Journal of Hellenic Studies* 7 (1886): 309–52; 8 (1887): 194–213; 9 (1888): 91–117.

Carile, Antonio. "Partitio terrarum imperii Romaniae." *Studi veneziani* 7 (1965): 125–305.

Certeau, Michel de. *The Practice of Everyday Life.* Berkeley, 1984.

Cessi, Roberto. *Le colonie italiane medievali in Oriente.* Vol. 1. *La Conquista.* Venice, 1942.

Politica ed economia di Venezia nel trecento. Saggi. Rome, 1952.

Storia della Repubblica di Venezia. 2nd ed. Milano and Messina, 1968.

Chaireti, Maria. "Τά παλαιότερα Κατάστιχα

τοῦ Ἀρχείου τοῦ Δούκα τῆς Κρήτης ὡς ἱστορικαί πηγαί (The Oldest Registers of the Archives of the Duca of Crete as historical sources). *Kretika Chronika* 21 (1969): 499–514.

Chambers, D. S. *The Imperial Age of Venice 1380–1580.* London, 1970.

Chatzidakis, M. "Essai sur une école dite 'Italogrecque' précédée d'une note sur les rapports de l'art vénitien avec l'art crétois jusqu'à 1500." In A. Pertusi, ed., *Venezia e il Levante fino al secolo XV.* Vol. 2. Florence, 1973, 69–125.

Chidiroglou, Paulos. *Das Religiöse Leben auf Kreta nach Evliya Celebi.* Beihefte der Zeitschrift für Religions-und Geistesgeschichte Vol. 11. Leiden, 1969.

" Ἱστορικά τινα τοῦ Να'ιμή διά τά Μουσουλμανικά τεμένη τῶν Χανίων (Some Historical Information by Na'ima on the Muslim mosques of Chanea)." *Kretika Chronika* 21 (1969): 243–54.

Chojnacki, Stanley. "Crime, Punishment and the Trecento Venetian State." In Lauro Martinez, ed., *Violence and Civil Disorder in Italian Cities, 1200–1500.* Berkeley, 1972, 184–228.

Clutton, Elisabeth, and A. Kenny. *Crete.* The Islands Series. North Pomfret, Vt., 1976.

Concina, Ennio. *Structure urbaine et fonction des bâtiments du XIV au XIX siècle: une recherche à Venise.* New York, 1981.

La macchina territoriale. La progettazione della difesa nel Cinquecento veneto. Rome and Bari, 1983.

L'Arsenale della Repubblica di Venezia. Tecniche e istituzioni dal medioevo all'età moderna. Milan, 1984.

Pietre, parole, storia. Glossario della costruzione nelle fonti veneziane (secoli XV–XVIII). Venice, 1988.

Concina, Ernio, U. Camarino, and D. Calabi. *La città degli ebrei. Il ghetto di Venezia: architettura e urbanistica.* Venice, 1991.

Constantoudaki-Kitromilides, Maria. "Οἱ Κρητικοί ζωγράφοι καί τό κοινό τους. Ἡ ἀντιμετώπιση τῆς τέχνης τους στή βενετοκρατία (The Cretan painters and their audience. The reception of their art during the Venetian rule)." *Kretika Chronika* 26 (1986): 246–61.

Cooperman, Bernard, and Roberta Curiel. *The Venetian Ghetto.* New York, 1990.

Cormack, Robin. *Painting the Soul. Icons, Death Masks, and Shrouds.* London, 1997.

Cosentini, S. "Aspetti e problemi del feudo veneto-cretese (secc. XIII–XIV)." *Quaderni della Rivista di Studi Bizantini e Slavi* 3 (1987): 27–30.

Cozzi, Gaetano, ed. *Gli Ebrei a Venezia. Secoli XIV–XVIII.* Atti del Convegno internazionale organizzato dall'Istituto di storia della società e dello stato veneziano della Fondazione Giorgio Cini. Venezia, Isola di San Giorgio Maggiore, 5–10 giugno, 1983. Milan, 1987.

Cozzi, Gaetano, and M. Knapton. *La Repubblica di Venezia nell'età moderna. Dalla guerra di Chioggia al 1517.* Turin, 1986.

Curuni, Spiridione Alessandro, and Lucilla Donati. *Creta Bizantina,* Università degli studi di Roma – "La Sapienza." Quaderni di Architettura e restauro nell'Area Mediterranea 1. Rome, 1987.

Creta Veneziana. L'Istituto Veneto e la Missione Cretese di Giuseppe Gerola. Collezione fotografica, 1900–1902. Venice, 1988.

Dellwing, Herbert. *Studien zur Baukunst der Bettelorden im Veneto. Die Gotik der monumentalen Gewölbebasiliken.* Munich and Berlin, 1970.

Demos Herakliou (Δῆμος Ηρακλείου). *Τεῦχος τιμητικόν Στεφάνου Ξανθουδίδου* (Volume honoring Stefanos Xanthoudides). Herakleion, 1969.

Demus, Otto. "Oriente e Occidente nell'arte veneta del Duecento." In *La civiltà veneziana nel secolo di Marco Polo.* Storia della Civiltà veneziana 1. Florence, 1955, 109–26

The Church of San Marco in Venice: History, Architecture, Sculpture. Dumbarton Oaks Studies 6. Washington, D.C., 1960.

De Vos, George, and Lola Romanucci-Ross.

"Ethnicity. Vessel of Meaning and Emblem of Contrast." In George de Vos and Lola Romanucci-Ross, eds., *Ethnic Identity: Cultural Continuities and Change.* Palo Alto, Calif., 1975, 363–90.

Dimakopoulos, Jordan. "Μεγάλη Βρύση. Μιά Βενετσιάνικη κρήνη τοῦ Ρέθυμνου (The Great Fountain. A Venetian fountain in Rethymnon)." *Kretika Chronika* 22 (1970): 322–43.

"Ἡ Lozza τοῦ Ρεθέμνου. Ἕνα ἀξιόλογο ἔργο τῆς ἀρχιτεκτονικῆς τοῦ Michele Sanmicheli στή Κρήτη (The Loggia of Rethymno: An important piece of architecture of Michele Sanmicheli in Crete)." In *Pepragmena tou G' Diethnous Kretologikou Synedriou.* Vol. 2. Athens, 1974. 64–83.

"Le fortificazioni e le porte di Candia." *Castellum* 16 (1973): 89–107.

"Ἡ πύλη τοῦ Ἰησοῦ τῶν Βενετσιάνικων ὀχυρώσεων τοῦ Χάνδακα (The Gate of Jesus in the Venetian fortifications of Candia)." *Frouriaka Chronika* 1 (1973): 175–212.

"Ἡ ἐκκλησία τοῦ Ἁγίου Ρόκκου στά Χανιά (The Church of San Rocco at Chania)." In Ἐκκλησίες στήν Ἑλλάδα μετά τήν Ἅλωση (Churches in Greece after the fall of Constantinople). Athens, 1979, 257–67.

Τά σπίτια τοῦ Ρεθέμνου. Συμβολή στη μελέτη τῆς Ἀναγεννησιακῆς ἀρχιτεκτονικῆς τῆς Κρήτης τοῦ 16ου και 17ου αἰώνα. (The houses of Rethymno. Contribution to the study of the Renaissance architecture of Crete in the 16th and 17th centuries). Rethymno, 1977.

Ἡ *κατοικία στήν Κρήτη κατά τήν τελευταία περίοδο τῆς Βενετοκρατίας* (The Residences in Crete during the last period of Venetian rule). Athens, 1997.

Enlart, Charles. "Quelques monuments d'architecture gothique en Grèce." *Revue de l'Art Chrétien*, 4th ser., 8 (1897): 309–14.

Fasoli, Gina. "Nascita di un mito." In *Studi storici in onore di Gioacchino Volpe*, Vol. 1. Florence, 1958, 445–79.

"Liturgia e cerimoniale ducale." In *Venezia e il Levante fino al secolo XV* 1, pt. 1. Florence, 1973, 261–95.

Fatourou-Hesychaki, K. "Ἡ Κρητική Ἀναγέννηση καί τά Ἰταλικά πρότυπα τῆς ἀρχιτεκτονικῆς της (The Cretan Renaissance and its Italian architectural prototypes)." *Ariadne* 1 (1982): 103–38.

Fedalto, Giorgio. "La Chiesa latina nel levante veneziano." *Studi veneziani* 17–18 (1975–76): 43–93.

"La Chiesa latina a Creta." *Kretika Chronika* 24 (1972): 145–76.

La Chiesa latina in Oriente, 3 vols. Verona, 1973/1981.

Fotheringham, J. K. *Marco Sanudo, Conqueror of the Archipelago.* Oxford, 1915.

Franchetti Pardo, Vittorio. *Storia dell'Urbanistica. Dal trecento al quattrocento.* Roma and Bari, 1982.

Franco, Fausto. "Per il 'corpus' e il restauro integrale dei monumenti veneti in Levante." *Atti dell'Istituto Veneto* 101 (1941–42): 235–42.

Franzoi, Umberto, Terisio Pignatti, and Wolfgang Wolters. *Il Palazzo Ducale di Venezia.* Treviso, 1990.

Fugagnollo, Ugo. *Bisanzio e l'Oriente a Venezia.* Trieste, 1974.

Fumo, Enrico. "Castelli e Fortezze veneziani a Creta." *Rivista militare Italiana* 13 (1904).

Furlan, Italo et al., eds. *Venezia e Bisanzio.* Exhibition Catalogue, Venice, Palazzo Ducale 8 June–30 September 1974. Milano, 1974.

Gallas, Klaus. "Mittel- und spätbyzantinische Sakralarchitektur der Insel Kreta. Versuch einer Typologie der kretischen Kirchen des 10.–17. Jh." Dissertation der technischen Universität Berlin, 1983.

Gallas, Klaus, Klaus Wessel, and Manolis Borboudakis. *Byzantinisches Kreta.* Munich, 1983.

Gallina, Mario. *Una società coloniale del Tre-*

certo. *Creta fra Venezia e Bisanzio*. Venice, 1989.

Gasparis, Charalambos. "Συναλλαγές μέ ἀντικείμενο κατοικίες στήν περιοχή τοῦ Χάνδακα τό ΙΓ' καί ΙΔ' αἰ. (Exchanges of houses in the area of Candia in the 13th and 14th centuries)." *Thesaurismata* 19 (1982): 102–20.

Ἡ γῆ καί οἱ ἀγρότες στή Μεσαιωνική Κρήτη 13ος–14ος αἰ. (The Land and the peasants in medieval Crete, 13th–14th Centuries). National Hellenic Research Foundation Monographs 4. Athens, 1997.

"Οἱ ἐπαγγελματίες τοῦ Χάνδακα κατά τόν 14ο αἰ. Σχέσεις μέ τόν καταναλωτή καί τό κράτος (The Professionals of Candia during the 14th century. Relations with the consumer and the state)." *Symmeikta* 8 (1989): 83–133.

Georgopoulou, Maria. "The Meaning of the Architecture and Urban Layout of Venetian Candia: Cultural Conflict and Interaction in the Late Middle Ages." Ph.D. Dissertation, UCLA, 1992.

"The Topography of Chandax, Capital of Crete in the Second Byzantine Period (961–1204)." *Cretan Studies* 4 (1994): 91–136.

"Late Medieval Crete and Venice: An Appropriation of Byzantine Heritage." *Art Bulletin* 77 (1995): 479–96.

"Mapping Religious and Ethnic Identities in the Venetian Colonial Empire." *Journal of Medieval and Early Modern Studies* 26 (1996): 467–96.

"Private Residences in Venetian Candia (thirteenth to fifteenth centuries)." *Thesaurismata* 30 (in press).

Gerland, Ernst. "Histoire de la noblesse crétoise." *Revue de l'Orient Latin* 10 (1903–4): 172–247; 11 (1905–6): 7–144.

Gerola, Giuseppe. "La Dominazione genovese in Creta." *Atti dell'Accademia degli Agiati di Rovereto*, 3d ser., 8, no. 2 (1902): 134–75.

"Gli Oggetti sacri di Candia salvati a Venezia." *Atti dell'Accademia degli Agiati di Rovereto*, 3d ser., 9, no. 3–4 (1903): 1–40.

I monumenti veneti nell'isola di Creta, 4 vols. in 5 parts. Venice, 1905–32.

"Una Descrizione di Candia nel principio di seicento." *Atti della I. R. Accademia degli Agiati di Rovereto*, 3d ser., 14 (1908): 1–15.

"I monumenti medioevali nelle Tredici Sporadi." *Annuario della R. Scuola Archeologica di Atene e delle Missioni Italiane in Oriente* 1 (1914): 169–356; 2 (1916): 1–101.

"Topografia delle chiese della città di Candia." *Bessarione* 22, no. 1 (1918): 99–119; no. 4 (1918): 239–81.

"I Francescani in Creta al tempo del dominio veneziano." *Collectanea Francescana* 2, no. 3 (1932): 301–25; no. 4 (1932): 445–61.

"Elenco topografico delle chiese affreschate di Creta." *Atti del Reale Istituto Veneto di Scienze, Lettere ed Arti*, 94, pt. 2 (1934–35): 139–216.

Gerola, G., and Kostas Lassithiotakis. *Τοπογραφικός κατάλογος τῶν τοιχογραφημένων ἐκκλησιῶν τῆς Κρήτης* (Topographic catalogue of the wall-painted churches of Crete). Herakleion, 1961.

Gertwagen, Ruth. "Heraklion Harbour in the Venetian Imperial System of the Early Fourteenth Century." In *1st International Symposium on Harbours, Port Cities and Coastal Topography. Cities on the Sea – Past and Present, Summaries*. London, 1986.

"The Venetian Port of Candia, Crete (1299–1363). Construction and Maintenance." In I. Malkin and R. L. Hohlfelder, eds., *Mediterranean Cities. Historical Perspectives*. London 1988, 141–58.

"L'Isola di Creta e i suoi porti (dalla fine del XII secolo alla fine del XV secolo). In Gherardo Ortalli, ed., *Venezia e Creta*, 337–74.

Giannopoulos, N. I. "Χριστιανικαί Ἀρχαιότητες Χαλκίδος. Ἡ Ἁγία Παρασκευή – Ἐκκλησίαι (Christian antiquities in Chalkis. St. Paraskeve – churches)." *Deltion tes Historikes kai Ethnologikes Hetaireias tes Hellados* 9 (1926): 117–29.

Gill, J. "Pope Urban V (1362–1370) and the Greeks of Crete." *Orientalia Christiana Periodica* 39 (1973): 461–468.

Goffen, Rona. *Piety and Patronage in Renaissance Venice.* London and New Haven, 1986.

Golubovich, G. "Le Province dell'Ordine Minoritico nei Secoli XIII e XIV in Europa e nell'Oriente Francescano." In *Biblioteca bio-bibliografica della Terra Santa e dell'Oriente francescano* 2 (1913): 214–260.

Gouma-Peterson, Thalia. "Crete, Venice, the 'Madonneri' and a Creto-Venetian Icon in the Allen Art Museum." *Allen Memorial Art Museum Bulletin* 25, 2 (Winter 1968).

Goy, Richard. *Venice. The City and Its Architecture.* London, 1997.

Grabar, André. "Byzance et Venise." In *Venezia e l'Europa.* Venice, 1955. 52–86

Graf Zu Dohna, H. "Kreta unter dem Banner von S. Marco." *Nord und Süd* 97/290 (Breslau, 1901).

Greene, Molly. *A Shared World. Christians and Muslims in the Early Modern Mediterranean* Princeton, N.J., 2000.

Guidoni, Enrico. *Storia dell'Urbanistica. Il Duecento.* Roma, Bari, 1989.

Hadjinikolaou, Nicos, ed. *El Greco of Crete. Proceedings of the International Symposium Held on the Occasion of the 450th Anniversary of the Artist's Birth. Iraklion, Crete, 1–5 September 1990.* Herakleion, 1995.

Hatjipanou, P. V. "Ἡ Εὔβοια κατά τήν Φραγκοκρατίαν (Euboia during Frankish rule)." *Archeion Euvoikon Meleton* 1 (1935): 22–36.

Hazlitt, William C. *The Venetian Republic. Its Rise, Its Growth and Its Fall, 421–1797.* Vol. 1. New York, 1915.

Hemmerdinger-Iliadou, Démocratie. "La Créte sous la domination vénitienne et turque (1322–1684). Renseignements nouveaux ou peu connus d'aprés les pélérins et les voyageurs." *Studi veneziani* 9 (1967): 535–623; 15 (1973): 451–584.

"Deux Descriptions inédites de la Crète de la fin du XVIIIe siècle d'après le dossier Mar. B7 440 des Archives Nationales de Paris." *Leimonarion* 73–74 (Athens, 1973), 799–810.

Heyd, W. *Le Colonie commerciali degli Italiani in Oriente,* 2 vols. Venice, 1868.

Histoire du commerce du Levant au Moyen Age, 2 vols. Leipzig, 1923.

Hodgson, F. C. *Venice in the Thirteenth and Fourteenth Centuries. A.D. 1204–1400.* London, 1910.

Hoffmann, G. "Il Pensiero religioso nelle donazioni e nei testamenti dei Veneziani di Creta." *Civiltà Cattolica* 95, 1 (1944): 220–26.

Howard, Deborah. *The Architectural History of Venice.* London, 1980.

Venice and the East. The Impact of the Islamic World on Venetian Architecture 1100–1500. New Haven and London, 2000.

Huse, Norbert, and Wolfgang Walters. *The Art of Renaissance Venice, Architecture, Sculpture and Painting, 1460–1590.* Chicago, 1990.

Imhaus, Brunehilde. "Les Maisons de la Commune dans le district de Candie au XIVe siècle." *Thesaurismata* 10 (1973): 124–37.

Jacoby, David. *La Féodalité en Grèce mediévale. Les "Assises de Romanie." Sources, application et diffusion.* Paris and La Haye, 1971.

"Venice, the Inquisition and the Jewish Communities of Crete in the Early 14th Century." *Studi veneziani* 12 (1970): 127–44. Reprinted in Jacoby, D., *Recherches sur la Méditerranée orientale du XIIe au XVe siècle. Peuples, sociétés, économies.* London, 1979.

"Venice and Venetian Jews in the Eastern Mediterranean." In Gaetano Cozzi, ed., *Gli Ebrei a Venezia.* Milan, 1987, 29–58.

Studies on the Crusader States and on Venetian Expansion. Northampton, England, 1989.

"Byzantine Crete in the Navigation and Trade Networks of Venice and Genoa." In Laura Balletto, ed., *Oriente e Occidente tra Medioevo ed età moderna. Studi in onore di Geo Pistarino.* Genoa, 1997, 517–40.

"Creta e Venezia nel contesto economico del Mediterraneo orientale sino alla metà del Quattrocento." In Ortalli, Gherardo, ed. *Venezia e Creta,* 73–106.

Jacoby, D., Benjamin Arbel, and Bernard Hamilton, eds. *Latins and Greeks in the Eastern Mediterranean after 1204.* London and Totowa, N.J., 1989.

Jegerlehner, J. "Der Aufstand der kandiotischen Ritterschaft gegen das Mutterland Venedig (1363–65)." *Byzantinische Zeitschrift* 12 (1903): 78–125.

"Beiträge zur Verwaltungsgeschichte Kandias im XIV Jahrhundert." *Byzantinische Zeitschrift* 13 (1904): 435–79.

Jorga, N. "Rapports italo-orientaux dans l'art du Moyen-Age." In *Mélanges Charles Diehl.* Paris, 1930. 59–69.

"Documents concernant les Grecs et les affaires d'Orient tirés des registres de notaires de Crète." *Revue Historique du Sud-Est Européen* 14, no. 4–6 (1937): 89–115.

"Enchères des fiefs et vignobles de la République vénitienne en Crète au XIVe siècle." *Epeteris Hetaireias Vyzantinon Spoudon* 51 (1974): 195–210.

Kalokyris, K. D. *The Byzantine Wall Paintings of Crete.* New York, 1973.

Keckemet, Dusko. *Lo sviluppo urbano del porto di Spalato.* Zagreb, 1981.

Kitsiki-Panagopoulos, Beata. "Some Venetian Churches of Crete." *Arte veneta* 30 (1976): 20–29.

Cistercian and Mendicant Monasteries in Medieval Greece. Chicago and London, 1979.

"Medieval Architecture in Greece. Western Monastic Orders in the Latin States Formed on Byzantine Territory." In *Actes du XVe Congrès International d'Études byzantines.* Vol. 2, pt. A. Athens, 1981, 273–88.

Koder, Johannes. *Negroponte. Untersuchungen zur Topographie und Siedlungsgeschichte der Insel Euboia während der Zeit der Venezianerherrschaft.* Österreichische Akademie der Wissenschaften. Philosophish-Historiche Klasse. Denkschriften 112 Band. Vienna, 1973.

Laiou, Angeliki. "The Byzantine Economy in the Mediterranean Trade System, Thirteenth–Fifteenth Centuries." *Dumbarton Oaks Papers* 34–35 (1980): 177–222.

"Observations on the Results of the Fourth Crusade; Greeks and Latins in Port and Market." *Medievalia et Humanistica* 12 (1984): 47–60.

"Venetians and Byzantines. Investigation of Forms of Contact in the Fourteenth Century." *Thesaurismata* 22 (1992): 29–43.

Laiou-Thomadakis, Angeliki. "Quelques Observations sur l'économie et la société de la Crète vénitienne (ca. 1270–ca. 1305)." In *Bizanzio e l'Italia. Raccolta di studi in memoria di Agostino Pertusi.* Milan, 1982, 177–98.

Lane, Frederick C. *Venice. A Maritime Republic.* Baltimore and London, 1973.

Lasareff, Victor. "Saggi sulla pittura veneziana dei secoli XIII–XIV. La maniera greca e il problema della scuola cretese." *Arte Veneta* 19 (1965): 17–31; 20 (1966): 43–61.

Lassithiotakis, K. "Πόλεις τῆς Κρήτης," *Eos,* 3d ser., 7, no. 76–84 (Athens, 1964): 81–102.

Lauritzen, Peter, and Alexander Zieleke. *Palaces of Venice.* London, 1992.

Leicht, Pier Silverio. "Le colonie veneziane." *Rivista Storica del Diritto Italiano* 25 (1952): 35–60.

"Documenti di Candia veneziana del secolo XIV." *Rivista Storica del Diritto Italiano* 25 (1952): 173–83.

Lévi, I. "Les Juifs de Candie de 1380 à 1485."

Revue des Études Juives 26 (1893): 198–208.

Lévi-Provençal, E. "Une Description arabe inédite de la Crète." In *Studi orientalistici in onore di Giorgio Levi della Vida*. Vol. 2 Rome, 1956, 49–57.

Loenertz, R., O. P. "Fr. Simon de Crète, inquisieur en Grèce et sa mission en Crète." *Archivum Fratrum Praedicatorum* 6 (1936): 372–78.

"Documents pour servir à l'histoire de la province dominicaine de Grèce." *Archivum Fratrum Praedicatorum* 14 (1944): 78–81.

Lucchetta, G. "L'Oriente Mediterraneo nella cultura veneta." In AA. VV. *Storia della cultura veneta*, G. Arnaldi and M. Pastore Stocchi, 3, pt. 2. Vicenza, 1980.

Luce, S. B. "Modon – a Venetian Station in Medieval Greece." In *Classical and Medieval Studies in Honor of E. K. Rand*. New York, 1938, 195–208.

Mallett, M. E., and J. R. Hale. *The Military Organization of a Renaissance State. Venice c. 1400 to 1617*. Cambridge, 1984.

Maltezou, Ch. " Ἡ Κρήτη στή διάρκεια τῆς περιόδου τῆς Βενετοκρατίας (1211–1669) (Crete during the Venetian domination (1211–1669)." In N. Panagiotakes, ed. Κρήτης. Ἱστορία καί πολιτισμός (Crete. History and civilization). Vol. 2. Herakleion, 1988, 105–61.

"Byzantine 'Consuetudines' in Venetian Crete." *Dumbarton Oaks Papers* 49 (1995): 269–80.

"Byzantine Legends in Venetian Crete." In Ihor Sevcenko and Irmgard Hutter, eds., *Aetos. Studies in Honour of Cyril Mango Presented to Him on April 14, 1998*, Stuttgart and Leipzig, 1998, 233–42.

ed. *Πλούσιοι καί φτωχοί στήν κοινωνία τῆς Ἑλληνολατινικῆς Ἀνατολῆς/ Ricchi e poveri nella società dell'Oriente Grecolatino*. Biblioteca dell'Istituto Ellenico di Studi Bizantini e Postbizantini di Venezia no 19. Venice, 1998.

Mancini, E. "Le Fortificazioni veneziane di Candia e la loro distruzione." *Illustrazione Italiana* 30/14 (April 5, 1903): 268–71.

"The Historical and Social Context." In David Holton, ed., *Literature and Society in Renaissance Crete*. Cambridge and New York, 1991, 17–47.

Maretto, Paolo. *La casa veneziana nella storia della città dalle origini all'Ottocento*. Venice, 1986.

Margaritis, Stephen. *Crete and Ionian Islands under the Venetians*. Athens, 1978.

Mc Andrew, John. *Venetian Architecture of the Early Renaissance*. Cambridge, Mass., and London, 1980.

McKee, Sally. "Uncommon Dominion. The Latins and Greeks of Venetian Crete in the 14th Century." Ph.D. Diss., University of Toronto, 1992.

Uncommon Dominion. Venetian Crete and the Myth of Ethnic Purity. Philadelphia, 2000.

- "Households in Fourteenth-Century Venetian Crete." *Speculum* 70 (1995): 27–67.

"The Revolt of St. Tito in Fourteenth-Century Venetian Crete. A Reassessment." *Mediterranean Historical Review* 9 (1994): 173–204.

Mertzios, D. " Ἡ συνθήκη Ἑνετῶν – Καλλέργη καί οἱ συνοδεύοντες αὐτήν κατάλογοι (The Treaty between the Venetians and Kallergis and the lists that accompany it)." *Kretika Chronika* 3 (1949): 262–92.

Ἡ Μεσαιωνική πόλη Χανίων. (The Medieval City of Chanea) [no pl.], 1977.

Michiel, Giustina Renier. *Le Origine delle feste veneziane*. 6 vols, 2d ed. Milan, 1829.

Miller, William. *The Latins in the Levant (1204–1566)*. London, 1908.

"Crete under the Venetians 1204–1669." In *Essays on the Latin Orient*. Cambridge, 1921, repr. Amsterdam, 1964, 177–98.

Molmenti, Pompeo. "I Monumenti di Candia e Cipro." *Tribuna*, February 15, 1901.

La Storia di Venezia nella vita privata dalle origini alla caduta della Repubblica. 3 vols. Turin, 1880, repr. Trieste, 1973.

Moutsopoulos, Nikolaos C. "Οἱ Φράγκικες ἐκκλησίες στήν Ἑλλάδα (The Frankish churches in Greece)." *Technika Chronika* 1 (1960): 13–33.

"Châteaux-Forts vénitiens en Grèce." *L'architettura militare veneta del Cinquecento*. Centro Internazionale di Studi di Architettura "Andrea Palladio" di Vicenza. Milan, 1988, 135–45.

Mouvements de population et problèmes de colonisation en Romanie Greco-Latine du X au XIII siècle, Third Byzantine Symposium. Strasbourg, 1979.

Muir, Edward. "Images of Power. Art and Pageantry in Renaissance Venice." *American Historical Review* 84 (1979): 16–52.

Civic Ritual in Renaissance Venice. Princeton, N.J., 1981.

Müller, Reinhold C. "The Procurators of San Marco in the 13th and 14th Century. A Study of the Office as a Financial and Trust Institution." *Studi veneziani* 13 (1971): 105–220.

Muraro, Michelangelo. "Varie fasi di influenza bizantina a Venezia nel Trecento." *Thesaurismata* 9 (1972): 180–201.

"L'isola di Creta e l'arte bizantine a Venezia." In *Scritti di storia dell'arte in onore di U. Procacci*. Vol. 1. Milan, 1977, 69–72.

"Creta fra Bisanzio e Venezia." In *Pepragmena tou D' Diethnous Kretologikou Synedriou, Herakleion, 1976*. Vol. 2. Athens, 1981, 292–97.

Muratori, Saverio. *Studi per una operante storia urbana di Venezia*, 2 vols. Palladio, 1–2. Rome, 1959.

Muschino, Giovanni. "Culto Mariano." In *Culto dei Santi in Venezia*, 239–74.

Nicol, Donald M. *Byzantium and Venice. A Study in Diplomatic and Cultural Relations*. Cambridge, 1988.

Niero, A. "Correnti spirituali nei secoli XIII e XIV." *Componenti storico-artistiche e culturali a Venezia nei secoli XIII e XIV*. Ateneo Veneto. Venice, 1981.

Nikeforou, Aliki. *Δημόσιες τελετές στήν Κέρκυρα κατά την περίοδο της Βενετικής κυριαρχίας 14ος–18ος αι*. (Public Ceremonies in Corfu at the time of Venetian rule, 14th–18th centuries). Athens, 1999.

Orlandos, Anastasios K. "Προστομιαῖον τοῦ Μουσείου Ἡρακλείου (A Well in the Herakleion Museum)." *Archaiologikon Deltion* 9 (1925): 188–91.

"Νεώτεραι ἔρευναι ἐν ἉγίῳΤίτῳ τῆς Γορτυνίας (New researches at St. Titus of Gortys)." *Epeteris Hetaireias Vyzantinon Spoudon* 3 (1926): 301–28.

Ortalli, Gherardo, ed. *Venezia e Creta. Atti del Convegno Internazionale di Study. Iraklion-Chania, 30 settembre–5 ottobre 1997*. Istituto Veneto di Scienze, Lettere ed Arti. Venice, 1998.

Paliouras, A. *Ὁ ζωγράφος Γεώργιος Κλόντζας (1540–ci. 1608) καί αἱ μικρογραφίαι τοῦ κώδικος αὐτοῦ* (The Painter George Clontzas (c. 1540–1608) and the miniatures of his codex). Athens, 1977.

Panagiotakes, Nikolaos, ed. *Κρήτη. Ἱστορία καί Πολιτισμός* (Crete. History and civilization), 2 vols. Herakleion, 1987–88.

Ἰταλικές Ἀκαδημίες καί θέατρο. Οἱ Stravaganti τοῦ Χάνδακα (Italian Academies and theater. The Stravaganti of Candia)." *Theatro* 27–28 (1966): 39–53.

Panagiotakes, Nikolaos. *Ἡ κρητική περίοδος τῆς ζωῆς τοῦ Δομηνίκου Θεοτοκοπούλου* (The Cretan period of the life of Domenico Theotokopoulos). Athens, 1987.

"Μαρτυρίες γιά τή μουσική στήν Κρήτη στή βενετοκρατία (Evidence for the music in Crete during Venetian rule)." *Thesaurismata* 20 (1990): 7–169.

"The Italian Background of Early Cretan Literature." *Dumbarton Oaks Papers* 49 (1995): 281–323.

Papadaki, Aspasia. *Θρησκευτικές καί κοσ-*

μικές τελετές στή Βενετοκρατούμενη Κρήτη (Religious and Civic Ceremonies in Venetian Crete). Nea Christianike Krete Parartema no. 1. Rethymnon, 1995.

Papas, C. *L'Urbanisme et l'architecture populaire dans les Cyclades*. Paris, 1957.

Pashley, Robert. *Travels in Crete*, 2 vols. London 1837, repr. Amsterdam 1970.

Pavanini, Paola. "Abitazioni popolari e borghesi nella Venezia cinquecentesca." *Studi veneziani*, n.s., 5 (1981): 63–126.

Pertusi, Agostino, ed. *Venezia e l'Oriente fra tardo Medioevo e Rinascimento*. Civiltà Europea e Civiltà Veneziana, Aspetti e Problemi 4. Venice, 1966.

ed. *Venezia e il Levante fino al secolo XV. Atti del I Convegno internazionale di storia della civiltà veneziana (Venezia 1–5 Giugno, 1968)*, 2 vols. Florence, 1971–74.

Peruccio, Daniele. "Une société coloniale du XIVe siècle. Les 'bourgeois' de Candie." *Bulletin de la Faculté des Lettres de Strasbourg* 45 (1967): 420–28.

Petta, Marco. "La Chiesa latina di Creta negli ultimi anni del dominio veneto." *Bollettino della Badia Greca di Grottaferrata* 22 (1968): 3–56.

"Documenti di Storia Ecclesiastica relativi agli ultimi anni del dominio veneto a Creta conservati nell'Archivio della S. Congregazione di Propaganda Fide." In *Pepragmena tou B' Diethnous Kretologikou Synedriou*. Vol. 3. Athens, 1968, 212–23.

Platon, Nikolaos. "Συμβολή εἰς τό τοπωνυμικόν, τήν τοπογραφίαν καί τήν ἱστορίαν τῶν πόλεων καί φρουρίων τῆς Κρήτης (Contribution to the toponymics, topography and history of the cities and of the castles of Crete)." *Kretika Chronika* 1 (1947): 239–48.

"Καί πάλιν περί τῶν Βυζαντινῶν τειχῶν τοῦ Χάνδακος (Again on the Byzantine Walls of Candia)." *Kretika Chronika* 4 (1950): 353–60.

"Νέα στοιχεῖα διά τήν μελέτην τῶν Βυζαντινῶν τειχῶν τοῦ Χάνδακος. (New Data on the Byzantine walls of Candia)." *Kretika Chronika* 6 (1952): 439–59.

Porfyriou, Heleni. "La Cartografia veneziana dell'isola di Creta." In Ortalli, Gherardo, ed., *Venezia e Creta*, 375–414.

Practikides, Zacharias. *Χωρογραφία τῆς Κρήτης συνταχθεῖσα τῷ 1818* (Chorography of Crete compiled in 1818). Herakleion, 1983.

Prodi, Paolo. "The Structure and Organization of the Church in Renaissance Venice. Suggestions for Research." In J. R. Hale, ed., *Renaissance Venice*. London, 1973, 409–30.

Psilakis, B. *Ἱστορία τῆς Κρήτης* (History of Crete). Athens, 1899.

Pullan, Brian. *Rich and Poor in Renaissance Venice*. Oxford, 1971.

Ratti, Antonio. "Le Carte geografiche di Candia nel Museo Correr." *Bolletino dei Musei Civici Veneziani* 1, no. 4 (1979): 86–101.

"I Cartografi di Creta nati o residenti nell'isola." In *Pepragmena tou E' Diethnous Kretologikou Synedriou*. Vol. 2. Herakleion, 1985, 330–37.

Reinich Sullam, Giovannina. *Il Ghetto di Venezia. Le sinagoghe e il museo*. Rome, 1985.

Renier Michiel, Giustina. *Origine delle feste veneziane*, 5 vols. Milan, 1821.

Rizzi, Alberto. "Le Icone bizantine e postbizantine delle chiese veneziane." *Thesaurismata* 9 (1972): 250–91.

Romanin, S. *Storia documentata di Venezia*, 10 vols. Venice, 1855.

Samona, G., et al. *Piazza San Marco. L'architettura, la storia, le funzioni*. Venice, 1982.

Santifaller, L. *Beitrage zur Geschichte des lateinischen Patriarchats von Konstantinopel (1204–1261) und der venezianischen Urkunde*. Weimar, 1938.

Santschi, Elisabeth. "Contrats de travail et d'apprentissage en Crète vénitienne au XIVe siècle d'après quelques notaires." *Revue Suisse d'Histoire* 19 (1969): 34–74.

"Procès criminels en Crète vénitienne

(1354–1389)." *Thesaurismata* 7 (1970): 82–96.

"Aspects de la justice en Crète vénitienne d'après les Memoriali du XIVe siècle." *Kretika Chronika* 24 (1972): 294–324.

"Contribution l'étude de la communauté juive en Crète vénitienne au XIVe siècle, d'après les sources administratives et judiciaires." *Studi Veneziani* 15 (1973): 177–211.

La notion du 'feudum' en Crète vénitienne (XIIIe–XVe siècles). Montreux, 1976.

Sanudo, M. *De Origine, situ et magistratibus urbis Venetae ovvero La Città di Venetia (1493–1530)*, ed. A. Caracciolo Aricò. Milan, 1980.

Sefakas, G. A. *Παραχώρησις ἀπό τῆς Ἑνετικῆς Συγκλήτου τοῦ διαμερίσματος τῶν Χανίων ὡς φεούγου εἰς Ἐνετούς εὐγενεῖς ἐν ἔτει 1252* (The Concession by the Venetian Senate of the department of Chanea as a feudum to Venetian nobles in the year 1252). Athens, 1940.

Setton, K. M. *The Papacy and the Levant (1204–1571)*. Vol. 1. *The Thirteenth and Fourteenth Centuries;* Vol. 2. *Fifteenth Century*. Philadelphia, 1976–78.

Simopoulos, Kyriakos. *Ξένοι ταξιδιῶτες στήν Ἑλλάδα*, 2 vols. (Foreign Travelers in Greece). Athens, 1973.

Smith, A. C. *The Architecture of Chios*, ed. P. P. Argenti. London, 1962.

Sorde, Simon, Lesley Johnson, and Alan V. Murray, eds. *Concepts of National Identity in the Middle Ages*. Leeds Texts and Monographs. New Series 14. Leeds, 1995.

Spanakis, Stergios. "Συμβολή στήν ἐκκλησιαστική ἱστορία τῆς Κρήτης στή Βενετοκρατία (Contribution to the history of Venetian Crete)." *Kretika Chronika* 13 (1959): 243–88.

Ἡ θρησκευτικο-εκκλησιαστική κατάσταση στήν Κρήτη τόν XVI αἰώνα (The religious-ecclesiastical situation on Crete in the 16th century). *Kretika Chronika* 21 (1969) 134–52.

Ἡ Ὕδρευση τοῦ Ἡρακλείου 828–1939 (The Watering of Herakleion). Herakleion, 1981.

Τό Ἡράκλειο στό πέρασμα τῶν αἰώνων (Herakleion in the course of the centuries). Herakleion, 1990.

Spratt, T.A.B. *Travels and Researches in Crete*. London, 1865.

Spuler, Bertold. "Les Chrétiens orientaux et leurs relations avec les vénitiens en général pendant la domination latine dans le Levant." In *Venezia e il Levante fino al secolo XV*. 679–686. Vol. 1, pt. 2. Florence, 1971.

Stahl, Alan M. *The Venetian Tornesello. A Medieval Colonial Coinage*. American Numismatic Society, Numismatic Notes and Monographs 163. New York, 1985.

Starr, Joshua. *The Jews in the Byzantine Empire, 641–1204*. Athens, 1939.

"Jewish Life in Crete under the Rule of Venice." *Proceedings of the American Academy for Jewish Research* 12 (1942): 59–114.

Romania, the Jewries of the Levant after the Fourth Crusade. Paris, 1949.

Staurakis, N. *Στατιστική τοῦ πληθυσμοῦ τῆς Κρήτης μετά διαφόρων γεωγραφικῶν, ἱστορικῶν, ἀρχαιολογικῶν, ἐκκλησιαστικῶν κτλ εἰδήσεων περί τῆς νήσου* (Statistics of the population of Crete with various geographical, historical, archaeological, ecclesiastical, etc. notices on the island). Athens, 1890.

Steriotou, Ioanna. *Οἱ Βενετικές Ὀχυρώσεις τοῦ Ρεθύμνου (1540–1646)* (The Venetian Fortifications of Rethymnon [1540–1646]). Thessaloniki, 1979.

"Le Mura di Candia nel quadro delle fortificazioni veneziane di Creta." *Castellum* 24 (1984): 87–98.

"Città portuali dell'isola di Creta alla fine del Medioevo." In Poleggi, E., ed., *Città portuali del Mediterraneo. Storia e archeologia*. Genoa, 1989, 42.

"Βενετοί καί δημόσια ἔργα στόν ἑλληνικό χῶρο (Venetians and public works in the area of Greece)." In *Ὄψεις τῆς Ἱστορίας τοῦ Βενετοκρατούμενου Ἑλληνισμοῦ*

Ἀρχειακά τεκμήρια (Views of the History of Venetian-ruled Hellenism. Archival Evidence). Athens, 1993.

"Ὁ Χάνδακας πρίν ἀπό τή μεγάλη πολιορκία σέ σχέδιο τοῦ Μανέα Κλόντζα (Candia before the great siege in a sketch of Maneas Clontzas)." *Thesaurismata* 26 (1996): 225–40.

Τά βενετικά τείχη τοῦ Χάνδακα (τόν 16ο και 17ο αἰ. Τό ἱστορικό τῆς κατασκευῆς τους σύμφωνα μέ βενετικές ἀρχειακές πηγές (The Venetian walls of Candia in the sixteenth and seventeenth centuries. The history of their construction according to the Venetian archival sources). Herakleion, 1998.

Tamassia Mazzarotto, Bianca. *Le Feste veneziane: I giochi popolari, le cerimonie religiose e di governo*. Florence, 1961.

Tassini, G. *Feste, Spettacoli, Divertimenti e Piaceri degli Antichi Veneziani*. Venice, 1891, repr. Venice, 1961.

Tea, Eva. "Saggio sulla storia religiosa di Candia dal 1590 al 1630." *Atti del R. Istituto Veneto di Scienze, Lettere ed Arti* 72, pt. 2 (1912–1913): 1359–1433.

Theochari, Maria S. "Περί τήν χρονολόγησιν τῆς εἰκόνος Παναδίας Μεσοπαντιτίσσης (On the dating of the icon of the Virgin Mesopantitissa)." *Akademia Athenon, Praktika* 36 (1961): 272–80.

Theophaneides, B. D. "Ενετικά καί Τούρκικα μνημεῖα δυτικῆς Κρήτης (Venetian and Turkish monuments of Western Crete)." *Epeteris Hetaireias Kretikon Spoudon* 4 (1941): 96–106.

Theotokes, Spyridon M. *Εἰσαγωγή εἰς τήν ἔρευναν τῶν μνημείων τῆς ἱστορίας τοῦ Ἑλληνισμοῦ καί ιδίᾳ τῆς Κρήτης ἐν τῷ κρατικῷ ἀρχείῳ τοῦ Βενετικοῦ Κράτους* (Introduction to the research of the monuments of the history of Hellenism and especially of Crete in the State Archives of the Venetian State). Corfu, 1926.

"Αἱ συνέπειαι τῆς συνθήκης τοῦ 1299, μεταξύ Βενετίας καί Ἀ. Καλλέργη (The Consequences of the Treaty of 1299, between Venice and A. Kallergis)." *Akademia Athenon, Praktika* 5 (1930): 455–60.

"Κατάλογος χειρογράφων τῆς Ἐθνικῆς Βιβλιοθήκης τοῦ Ἁγ. Μάρκου ἐν Βενετίᾳ (Lists of the manuscripts in the Library of San Marco in Venice)." *Hellenika* 4 (1931): 399–423.

Thiriet, Freddy. "Les Chroniques vénitiennes de la Marcienne et leur importance pour l'histoire de la Romanie Greco-vénitienne." *Mélanges d'archéologie et d'Histoire publiées par l'École Française de Rome* (1954): 241–92.

"Sui dissidi sorti tra il Comune di Venezia e i suoi feudatori di Creta nel trecento." *Archivio Storico Italiano* 114, no.4 (1957): 699–712.

La Romanie vénitienne au Moyen Age. Le développement et l'exploitation du domaine colonial vénitien (XII–XV siècles). Paris, 1959. 2d ed., 1975.

"La Situation religieuse en Crète au début du XVe siècle." *Byzantion* 36 (1966): 201–12.

"La Condition paysanne et les problèmes de l'exploitation rurale en Romanie greco-vénitienne." *Studi veneziani* 9 (1967): 36–37.

"La Symbiose dans les États latins formés sur les territoires de la Romanie byzantine (1221–1261). Phénomènes religieux." In *Rapports et Co-rapports. XV Congrès International d'Études Byzantines*. Athens, 1976.

Études sur la Romanie greco-vénitienne, X–XV siècles. London, 1977.

"Églises, fidèles et clergés en Crète vénitienne (de la conquête, 1204/1211 au XVe siècle)." In *Pepragmena tou D' Diethnous Kretologikou Synedriou*. Vol. 2. Athens, 1981, 484–500.

Tiberi, Claudio. "Monumenti veneziani a Creta." In *Venezia e il Levante fino al secolo XV*. Vol. 2. Florence, 1974, 67–107.

Tiepolo, Maria-Francesca. "Note sul riordino degli archivi del Duca e dei Notai di

Candia nell'archivio di Stato di Venezia." *Thesaurismata* 10 (1973): 88–100.

Tomadakis, Nikolaos B. "La Politica religiosa di Venezia verso i cretesi ortodossi dal XIII al XV secolo." In *Venezia e il Levante fino al secolo XV*, Vol. 1, pt. 2. Florence, 1973, 783–800.

Topping, Peter. "Co-Existence of Greeks and Latins in Frankish Morea and Venetian Crete." In *Acts of the 15th International Congress of Byzantine Studies*. Athens, 1976.

Studies on Latin Greece A.D. 1205–1715. London, 1977.

Tramontin, Silvio. "Influsso orientale nel culto dei Santi a Venezia." In *Venezia e il Levante fino al secolo XV*. Vol. 1, pt. 2. Florence, 1973, 801–20.

et al. *Culto dei Santi a Venezia*. Venice, 1965.

Trexler, R. *Public Life in Renaissance Florence*. Ithaca and London, 1980.

ed. *Persons in Groups. Social Behavior as Identity Formation in Medieval and Renaissance Europe*. Binghamton, 1985.

Trincanato, E. "Venezia nella storia urbana." *Urbanistica INU* 52 (1968): 7–69.

Tsirpanlis, Zacharias N. " Ἀπό τήν φιλορθόδοξη πολιτική τῆς Βενετίας στήν Ἑλληνική Ἀνατολή (From the pro-Orthodox policy of Venice in the Greek East)." *Epeteris Hetaireias Vyzantinon Spoudon* 39–40 (1972–73): 295–311.

"*Κατάστιχο Εκκλησιῶν καί Μοναστηρίων τοῦ κοινοῦ" (1248–1548). Συμβολή στή μελέτη τῶν σχέσεων Πολιτείας καί Ἐκκλησίας στή Βενετοκρατούμενη Κρήτη* ("Catasticum of the churches and the monasteries of the Commune" [1248–1548]. Contribution to the study of the relations between church and state in Venetian Crete). Ioannina, 1985.

Tsougarakis, Dimitris. *Byzantine Crete. From the 5th Century to the Venetian Conquest*. Historical Monographs 5. Athens, 1988.

Tzompanake, Chrysoula. *Χάνδακας. Ἡ πόλη καί τά τείχη* (Chandax. The city and the walls). Hetaireia Kretikon Historikon Meleton. Herakleion, 1996.

Van Gemert, A. F. " Ὁ Στέφανος Σαχλίκης καί ἡ ἐποχή του (Stephanus Saclichi and his era)." *Thesaurismata* 17 (1980): 36–130.

Vasileiades, Demetrios B. *Εἰσαγωγή στήν Αἰγαιοπελαγίτικη λαϊκή ἀρχιτεκτονική* (Introduction to the folk architecture of the Aegean). Athens, 1955.

Τό Κρητικό σπίτι. Ἀυτό τό καταφύγιο κι αὐτό τό ὁρμητήριο (The Cretan house. This refuge). Athens, 1976.

Vassilakis-Maurakakis, Maria. " Ὁ Ἄγγελος Ἀκοτάντος. Τό ἔργο του καί ἡ διαθήκη του (1436) (Angelos Akotantos. His work and his will [1436])." *Thesaurismata* 18 (1981): 47–80.

"The Church of the Virgin Gouverniotissa at Potamies, Crete." Doctoral Thesis, Courtauld Institute of Art, University of London, 1986.

Venezia centro di mediazione tra Oriente e Occidente, secoli XV–XVI. Aspetti e problemi. Florence, 1977.

Verlinden, Charles. *The Beginnings of Modern Colonization*. Ithaca, 1970.

Wace-Dawkins. "The Towns and Houses of the Archipelago." *Burlington Magazine* 26, no. 141 (1914): 99.

Wolff, R. L. "The Latin Empire of Constantinople and the Franciscans." *Traditio* 2 (1944): 221ff.

"The Organization of the Latin Patriarchate of Constantinople, 1204–1261. Social and Administrative Consequences of the Latin Conquest." *Traditio* 6 (1948): 44–60.

"Romania. The Latin Empire of Constantinople." *Symposium* 23 (1948): 1–34.

Wyrobisz, A. "L'Attività edilizia a Venezia nel XIV e XV secolo." *Studi veneziani* 7 (1965): 307–43.

Xanthoudides, Stephanos. "Συνθήκη μεταξύ τῆς Ἑνετικῆς δημοκρατίας καί Ἀλεξίου Καλλεργίου (Treaty between the Venetian Republic and Alexios Kallergis)." *Athena* 14 (1902): 282–331.

"Ἐπαρχίαι καί πόλεις τῆς Κρήτης (Regions and cities of Crete)." *Epeteris Hetaireias Vyzantinon Spoudon* 3 (1926): 34–66.

Ἡ Ἑνετοκρατία ἐν Κρήτῃ καί οἱ κατά τῶν Ἑνετῶν ἀδῶες τῶν Κρητῶν (Venetian rule in Crete and the battles of the Cretans against the Venetians). Athens, 1939.

Χάνδαξ–Ἡράκλειον. Ἱστορικά σημειώματα (Chandax-Herakleion. Historical notes). Herakleion, 1927.

Ἱστορικά σημειώματα. Ὁ ναός τοῦ Ἁλίου Τίτου. Ὁ Ἀπόστολος Τίτος (Historical Notes. The church of St. Titus. The Apostle Titus). Herakleion, 1925, 2d ed., ed. Theodore Tzedakis, Herakleion, 1974.

Μελετήματα (Studies). Herakleion, 1980.

Xerouchakis, Agathaggelos. *Ἡ ἐν Κρήτῃ ἐπανάστασις τοῦ 1363–1366 καί τό διοικητικόν σύστημα τῆς Βενετίας ἀπέναντι τῶν κοινωνικῶν τάξεων καί τῆς Ἐκκλησίας κατά τήν μακράν περίοδον τῆς ἐν τῇ νήσῳ κυριαρχίας αὐτῆς (1211–1669).* (The Cretan rebellion of 1363–1366 and the administrative system of Venice in relation to the social classes and the church during the long period of Venetian domination [1211–1669]). Alexandria, 1932.

Βενετοκρατούμενη Ἀνατολή Κρήτη καί Ἑπτάνησος (Venetian Orient, Crete and Ionian Islands). Athens, 1934.

Youmbakis, G. *Fortezza. The History of the Venetian Fortress at Rethymnon,* trans. F. J. Featman. Rethymnon, 1970.

Zevas, Dionysis A. "Βενετσιάνικα κάστρα στήν Ἑλλάδα (Venetian fortresses in Greece)." *Frouriaka Chronika* 1 (1973): 109–25.

Zoudianos, Nikolaos. *Ἱστορία τῆς Κρήτης ἐπί Ἑνετοκρατίας* (History of Venetian Crete). Athens, 1960.

INDEX